BOURGEOIS DIGNITY

DEIRDRE N. McCLOSKEY

Bourgeois Dignity

WHY ECONOMICS CAN'T
EXPLAIN THE MODERN WORLD

THE UNIVERSITY OF CHICAGO PRESS ·ʒ· CHICAGO AND LONDON

DEIRDRE N. MCCLOSKEY is Distinguished Professor of Economics, History, English, and Communication at the University of Illinois at Chicago.

The University of Chicago Press, Chicago 60637
The University of Chicago Press, Ltd., London
© 2010 by The University of Chicago
All rights reserved. Published 2010
Printed in the United States of America
20 19 18 17 16 15 14 13 12 11 10   1 2 3 4 5

ISBN-13: 978-0-226-55665-9 (cloth)
ISBN-10: 0-226-55665-4 (cloth)

Library of Congress Cataloging-in-Publication Data

McCloskey, Deirdre N.
  Bourgeois dignity : why economics can't explain the modern world /
Deirdre N. McCloskey.
      p.   cm.
  Includes bibliographical references and index.
  ISBN-13: 978-0-226-55665-9 (cloth : alk. paper)
  ISBN-10: 0-226-55665-4 (cloth : alk. paper)   1. Economic history.   2. Economics—
Philosophy.   3. Europe—Economic conditions.   4. Middle class.   I. Title.
  HC51.M395 2010
  330—dc22   2010018367

Alexander Gerschenkron

1904–1978

Model and mentor

Pars enim scientia est, scire quid nesco

CONTENTS

A big change in the common opinion about markets and innovation, I claim, caused the Industrial Revolution, and then the modern world. The change occurred during the seventeenth and eighteenth centuries in north-western Europe. More or less suddenly the Dutch and British and then the Americans and the French began talking about the middle class, high or low—the "bourgeoisie"—as though it were dignified and free. The result was modern economic growth.

That is, ideas, or "rhetoric," enriched us. The cause, in other words, was language, that most human of our accomplishments.[1] The cause was not in the first instance an economic/material change—not the rise of this or that class, or the flourishing of this or that trade, or the exploitation of this or that group. To put the claim another way, our enrichment was not a matter of Prudence Only, which after all is a virtue possessed by rats and grass, too. A change in rhetoric *about* prudence, and about the other and peculiarly human virtues, exercised in a commercial society, started the material and spiritual progress. Since then the bourgeois rhetoric has been alleviating poverty worldwide, and enlarging the spiritual scope of human life. The outcome has falsified the old prediction from the left that markets and innovation would make the working class miserable, or from the right that the material gains from industrialization would be offset by moral corruption.

In other words, I argue that depending exclusively on materialism to explain the modern world, whether right-wing economics or left-wing historical materialism, is mistaken. The two books to follow will make the positive case for a rhetorical, or ideological, cause of our greatly enlarged human scope. Here the case is negative. The usual and materialist economic histories do not seem to work. Bourgeois dignity and liberty might.

Such a theme is old-fashioned, as old as eighteenth-century political theory. Or it is new-fashioned, as new as twenty-first-century studies of discourse. Either way, it challenges the usual notions about "capitalism." Most people harbor beliefs about the origins of the modern economy that historical and economic science have shown to be mistaken. People believe, for example, that imperialism explains European riches. Or they believe that markets and greed arrived recently. Or they believe that "capitalism" required a new class or a new self-consciousness about one's class (as against a new rhetoric about what an old class did). Or they believe that economic events must be explained "ultimately," and every single time, by material interests. Or they believe that it was trade unions and government protections that have elevated the working class. None of these is correct, as I hope to persuade you. The correct explanation is ideas.

I've tried to write a book engaging the educated reader. But the argument has to use the findings of economic and historical specialists, and to get down into some of the details of their arguments. I tell the story of modern economic growth, summarizing what we have thought we knew from 1776 to the present about the nature and causes of the wealth of nations—how we got refrigerators and college degrees and secret ballots. The book tests the traditional stories against the actually-happened, setting aside the stories that in light of the recent findings of scientific history don't seem to work very well. A surprisingly large number of the stories don't. Not Marx and his classes. Not Max Weber and his Protestants. Not Fernand Braudel and his Mafia-style capitalists. Not Douglass North and his institutions. Not the mathematical theories of endogenous growth and its capital accumulation. Not the left-wing's theory of working-class struggle, or the right-wing's theory of spiritual decline.

Yet the conclusion is in the end positive. As the political scientist John Mueller put it, capitalism—or as I prefer to call it, "innovation"—is like Ralph's Grocery in Garrison Keillor's self-effacing little Minnesota town of Lake Wobegon: "pretty good."[2] Something that's pretty good, after all, is pretty good. Not perfect, not a utopia, but probably worth keeping in view of the worse alternatives so easily fallen into. Innovation backed by liberal economic ideas has made billions of poor people pretty well off, without hurting other people.[3] By now the pretty good innovation has helped quite a few people even in China and India. Let's keep it.

The Big Economic Story of our times has not been the Great Recession of 2007–2009, unpleasant though it was. And the important moral is *not* the one that was drawn in the journals of opinion during 2009—about how very rotten the Great Recession shows economics to be, and especially an economics of free markets. Failure to predict recessions is not what is wrong with economics, whether free-market economics or not. Such prediction is anyway impossible: if economists were so smart as to be able to predict recessions they would be rich. They're not. No science can predict its own future, which is what predicting business cycles entails. Economists are among the molecules their theory of cycles is supposed to predict. No can do—not in a society in which the molecules are watching and arbitraging.[4]

The important flaw in economics, I argue here, is not its mathematical and necessarily mistaken theory of future business cycles, but its materialist and unnecessarily mistaken theory of past growth. The Big Economic Story of our own times is that the Chinese in 1978 and then the Indians in 1991 adopted liberal ideas in the economy, and came to attribute a dignity and a liberty to the bourgeoisie formerly denied. And then China and India exploded in economic growth. The important moral, therefore, is that in achieving a pretty good life for the mass of humankind, and a chance at a fully human existence, ideas have mattered more than the usual material causes. As the economic historian Joel Mokyr put it recently in the opening sentence of one of his luminous books, "Economic change in all periods depends, more than most economists think, on what people believe."[5] The Big Story of the past two hundred years is the innovation after 1700 or 1800 around the North Sea, and recently in once poor places like Taiwan or Ireland, and most noticeably now in the world's biggest tyranny and the world's biggest democracy. It has given many formerly poor and ignorant people the scope to flourish. And contrary to the usual declarations of the economists since Adam Smith or Karl Marx, the Biggest Economic Story was not caused by trade or investment or exploitation. It was caused by ideas.

Innovation backed by ideology, then, promises in time to give pretty good lives to us all. Left and right tend to dismiss the other's ideology as "faith." The usage devalues faith, a noble virtue required for physics as much as for philosophy, and not at all irrational. But maybe both sides are correct. A socialist maintains her faith in governmental planning despite the evidence that it doesn't work to the benefit of the poor. A conservative maintains his faith that what's good for the military-industrial complex is good for the country despite the evidence that it impoverishes and coarsens the people.

I claim that a true liberalism, what Adam Smith called "the obvious and simple system of natural liberty," contrary to both the socialist and conservative ideologue, has the historical evidence on its side. Despite the elements of regulation and corporatism defacing it (and the welfare programs improving it), it has worked pretty well for the poor and for the people for two centuries. I reckon we should keep it —though tending better to its ethics.

In *The Bourgeois Virtues: Ethics for an Age of Commerce* (2006; which started tending to the ethics) I thanked some of the many people who have pushed my thoughts along. I give here additional thanks for this second volume in a projected series of six. The participants in the Economic History Workshop at Northwestern University heard a version of the first few chapters of the present book in March 2008, and gave me much good advice. The brown-bag workshop in my Department of History at the University of Illinois at Chicago has heard an outline of the argument three times. The Project on Rhetoric of Inquiry (Poroi) at the University of Iowa has heard it once, in the fall of 2008. Parts of chapter 11 on productivity change in Britain derive ultimately from my contributions to *The Economic History of Britain*, edited by Roderick Floud and myself, in the first edition of 1981 and the second of 1994. I thank Roderick for his encouragement at the time, and lament our present distance. Parts of chapters 14 on thrift appeared in Josh Yates, ed., *Thrift and American Culture* (Columbia University Press, 2009), and in *Revue de Philosophie Économique* (2007). Parts of 26 and 27 on imperialism appeared in the *South African Journal of Economic History* in 2006; much of chapters 30, 31, and 32 on eugenic materialism appeared in the *European Review of Economic History* (2008b) and the *Newsletter of the Cliometrics Society* (2008c). Early and scrappy versions of the entire argument appeared in the *American Scholar* (1994a) and the *Journal of Economic History* (1998). A seminar early on at the Institute for Historical Research in London, hosted by Negley Harte, was especially inspiriting, as were, late in the revisions, speeches during 2009 to Rhodes College in Memphis, the University of Mississippi at Oxford, the Population Center at the Booth School of Business of the University of Chicago, the Mont Pelerin Society in Stockholm; and in Washington, D.C., to American University, the World Bank, the Mercatus Center of George Mason University, and the Society of Government Economists.

I thank Beth Marston for her exceptional research assistance in the summer of 2008, with books and especially with computers, and Susan Mac-

Donald for her stellar work on my website (deirdremccloskey.org, at which you and I can discuss the project). Perhaps, too, having mentioned computers and the Internet, this is the place to thank the sober and unselfish Project Gutenberg, the bourgeois but (we pray) nonmonopolizing Google, Inc., and the disreputably democratic, quirkily anarchic, and therefore sometimes mistaken, but nonetheless very helpful Wikipedia. "The electronic word" (as the rhetorician Richard Lanham puts it) is transforming scholarship just as it is transforming much of life.[6] It is a case of creative construction and destruction. I cannot thank the Internet itself, because it is a spontaneous order arising from innovative and bourgeois people, and has no nameable entrepreneur or politician or bureaucrat to thank (well, not quite: Bernardo Batiz-Lazo of the University of Leicester is nameable, and is to be thanked for his forum at nep-his@lists.repcc.org). Yet come to think of it, the electronic words fashioned inside the virtual halls of Gutenberg, Google, and Wiki, and the conversation stimulated by Bernardo's site, also depend largely on spontaneous orders and bourgeois creativity—which is the point of the book.

I thank the Stellenbosch Institute for Advanced Study, and especially Bernard Lategan, Stanislav du Plessis, and Hendrik Geyer for arranging a calm period in South Africa in May 2008 to work on the manuscript. I give the same thanks to the School of Business, Economics and Law, and the groups in Economic History and in the ethics of banking, in particular Rolf Wolff, Sten Jönsson, Rick Wicks, Christer Lundt, and Barbara Cziarnawska, for a very fruitful month at the University of Gothenburg in the final days of the writing. My colleagues in our Chicago Area Seminar in the History of Economic Thought, John Berdell, Stephen Engermann, Samuel Fleischacker, Mark Guglielmo, and Joseph Persky, gave me last-minute advice. Anthony Waterman of St. John's College of the University of Manitoba, a long-distance friend, read the manuscript with care and saved me from numerous errors. So, too, was Margaret Jacob of UCLA a friend, reading my draft with a critical historian's eye for the University of Chicago Press, as was Tyler Cowen of George Mason University, with a critical economist's eye. The College of Liberal Arts of the University of Illinois at Chicago under deans Stanley Fish and Dwight McBride has been helpful. My thanks therefore go to them, and to the taxpayers of Illinois and the tuition-paying students of UIC who made their help possible. When Antoine Lavoisier, the theorist of oxygen and nitrogen, a nobleman (you can check it on Wikipedia), was to be arrested in the Terror, he is said to have protested that he was a scientist. According to the story the officer was unmoved: "The Republic has no need of scientists." Our republic, fortunately, has seen the need. And I thank my students, whether tuition-paying or not, in various courses on the subject during the 1990s and 2000s, at UIC and at the University of Iowa and Erasmus University of Rotterdam and the University of the Free State in South Africa. Teaching and writing suit each other. The Continental research institute with no teaching, though it sounds at first like a scholar's paradise, seems a poor plan.

I thank especially the participants in a small conference about an embarrassingly confused amalgam of this second volume of the Bourgeois Era and of the third and fourth soon to appear (*The Bourgeois Revaluation*, volume 3; and *Bourgeois Rhetoric*, volume 4), which took place in January 2008 at the Mercatus Center at George Mason University. The participants were Paul Dragos Aligica, Gregory Clark, Henry Clark, Jan de Vries, Pamela Edwards, Jack Goldstone, Thomas Haskell, Leonard Liggio, Allan Megill, John Nye, Alan Ryan, Virgil Storr, Scott Taylor, and Werner Troesken, with redoubled thanks to the organizers Claire Morgan and Rob Herritt. It was inspiriting to have so many fine scholars, a number of them old friends, encouraging me and correcting me and instructing me. Think where a woman's glory most begins and ends/ And say her glory was: she had such friends.

1

THE MODERN WORLD WAS AN ECONOMIC
TIDE, BUT DID NOT HAVE ECONOMIC CAUSES

Two centuries ago the world's economy stood at the present level of Bangladesh. In those good old days of 1800, furthermore, the average young person in Norway or Japan would have had on past form less rational hope than a young Bangladeshi nowadays of seeing in her lifetime the end of her nation's poverty—or at least the beginning of the end. In 1800 the average human consumed and expected her children and grandchildren and great-grandchildren to go on consuming a mere $3 a day, give or take a dollar or two.[1] The figure is expressed in modern-day, American prices, corrected for the cost of living. It is appalling.

By contrast, if you live nowadays in a thoroughly bourgeois country such as Japan or France you probably spend about $100 a day. One hundred dollars as against three: such is the magnitude of modern economic growth. The only people much better off than $3 or so up to 1800 were lords or bishops or some few of the merchants. It had been this way for all of history, and for that matter all of prehistory. With her $3 a day the average denizen of the earth got a few pound of potatoes, a little milk, an occasional scrap of meat. A wool shawl. A year or two of elementary education, if lucky and if she lived in a society with literacy. She had a 50–50 chance at birth of dying before she was thirty years old. Perhaps she was a cheerful sort, and was "happy" with illiteracy, disease, superstition, periodic starvation, and lack of prospects. After all, she had her family and faith and community, which interfered with every choice she made. But at any rate she was desperately poor, and narrowly limited in human scope.

Two centuries later the world supports more than six-and-half times more souls. Yet contrary to a pessimistic "Malthusian" belief that population growth would be the big problem, the average person nowadays earns and consumes almost ten times more goods and services than in 1800. Despite the disturbing pauses during the three dozen or so recessions that have roiled the world's economy since 1800, nearly every trough of a business cycle has been followed in a few years by a new all-time peak in the welfare of the poor of the earth, and the cases of very long recoveries were those from the two world wars, now distant.[2] Starvation worldwide is therefore at an all-time low, and falling. Literacy and life expectancy are at all-time highs, and rising. Liberty is spreading. Slavery is retreating, as is a patriarchy enslaving of women.

In the now much richer countries, such as Norway, the average person earns fully forty-five times more than in 1800, a startling $137 a day, or $120 a day for the average person in the United States, or $90 in Japan.[3] The environment—the concern of a well-to-do and educated bourgeoisie—is in such rich places improving. Even the merely improving places, like China, which is still very poor at $13 a day but much better off than in 1978, have started to care about the future of the earth.[4] Economic history has looked like an ice-hockey stick lying on the ground. It had a long, long horizontal handle at $3 a day extending through the two-hundred-thousand-year history of *Homo sapiens* to 1800, with little bumps upward on the handle in ancient Rome and the early medieval Arab world and high medieval Europe, with regressions to $3 afterward—then a wholly unexpected blade, leaping up in the last two out of the two thousand centuries, to $30 a day and in many places well beyond.[5]

True, some whole countries, and many people even in rapidly growing places like China or especially India, remain terribly poor. Out of the 6.7 billion people on the planet the terribly poor constitute a "bottom billion," thankfully shrinking, but for the present suffering the appalling $3 a day that had been the human lot since the African savannah. Some hundreds of millions live on a bare dollar, sleeping on mats on the streets of Mumbai.[6] Some 27 million are literal slaves, such as the Dinkas in Sudan. And many girls and women worldwide, as in much of Afghanistan, are held in slavish ignorance. Yet the share of the terribly poor and the terribly unfree in world population is now falling faster than at any time in history. World population has in fact been decelerating since the 1970s, and in a few generations will actually start falling.[7] Look around you at modern family sizes.

In fifty years, if things go as they have since 1800, the terribly poor will have become adequately nourished. Slaves and women will be largely free. The environment will be improving. And the ordinary person worldwide will have become bourgeois. In 1800 there were good reasons to be pessimistic—though many people in that bright dawn were in fact optimists. Nowadays, although an age of widely circulating tales of impending catastrophe, there are many more reasons to be optimistic about our future.

In a good deal of the world the optimistic outcome has already happened. Marxists have long been vexed by the complacently bourgeois character of the American working class. The economic historian Werner Sombart asked in 1906, "Why is there no socialism in the United States?" and answered that "all socialist utopias come to grief on roast beef and apple pie."[8] It turned out that the prosperous Americans were merely showing the way for the British and the French and the Japanese. We seem to be on track to merge not into a universal class of the proletariat but into a nearly universal class of the innovative bourgeoisie. (I use the French word *bourgeoisie* in its wide sense, as the hiring or owning or professional or educated class [*bourgeois*, without the *-ie* on the end, "boor-zhwa," is the adjective, and is also the male person of the class, singular and plural], usually in towns, the "middle class." I do not use it in its frequent Marxist sense as *la haute bourgeoisie*, the class of captains of industry alone.) Your physical therapist, now earning $35 an hour, or $280 a day, working for AthletiCo, who went to university and then to graduate work and now to continuing education, does not regard himself as a wage slave.[9] He works four days a week, and his wife, also a physical therapist, three. He and she can at any moment become a little company in private practice. The relations of production no longer tell much about the mentality or the prospects of hired labor. You work for a wage. Do you feel immiserized? Reflect, oh dear bourgeois-by-education reader, on the real and demeaning poverty of your own ancestors in 1800, and offer thanks to the Bourgeois Era and to the Age of Innovation.

In 2007 the economist Paul Collier observed that for decades "the development challenge has [been thought of as] a rich world of one billion people facing a poor world of five billion people. . . . By 2015, however, it will be apparent that this way of conceptualizing development has become outdated. Most of the [formerly poor] five billion, about 80 percent [or four billion], live in counties that are indeed developing, often at amazing speed."[10] Collier is right, and the sums in 2015 will be more like six billion rich or richifying people facing a bottom billion of persistently poor.[11] Witness richifying China and India nowadays—places still poor by the standard of Hong Kong or Belgium, but growing in real income per head at amazing, unprecedented speeds, twice or three times faster than other countries—7 to 10 percent per year. Their growth rates are faster than the rates at which the United States or Japan ever grew, and imply a quadrupling of human scope every twenty or fourteen years, in a short generation. In two such generations their real incomes per head will have risen by a factor of sixteen, to the $48 a day the United States enjoyed in the 1940s. The fact provides some scientific ideas about what to do for the bottom billion or so.

Yet Collier also says that "since 1980 world poverty has been falling *for the first time in history*." That last is mistaken (though perhaps he means the absolute numbers of poor people instead of their share, in which case maybe he is right). As a *share* of all the world's population the world's poverty has been falling not for two decades but for two centuries. A higher and higher share have become since 1800 those $30- or $48- or $137- or $280-a-day folk, in the top four to six billion. Witness again Norway and Japan, once abysmally poor. The history provides some scientific ideas about how we got here and where we are going.

The last two centuries worldwide favored the ordinary person, especially a person who lived in a bourgeois country. Consider a third cousin once removed of mine, thirty-five-year old Eva Stuland, in Dimelsvik on the Hardanger Fjord of western Norway. In 1800 our mutual ancestors had been $3-poor. Compare Bangladesh. Yet by now, ten generations further on, the honest, educated, and oil-blessed Norwegians have the second-highest average income in the world. Expressed in American prices of 2006 it is fully $50,000 a year for every man, woman, and child, that $137 a day. (Tiny Luxembourg ranks first out of 209 countries at $60,000 a head; closed-citizenship Kuwait ranks third at $48,000; and the big U.S.A. lumbers along at merely fourth, $44,000—nonetheless a stunning increase over the U.S.A. in 1900 or 1950, and most stunningly for the American poor.)[12] Fru Stuland consumes with her $137 a day a good deal of Belgian chocolate and a summer home in the mountains and a nice little Audi (her husband Olaf has the BMW). Her daily *earnings* are of course much higher than $137—compare the AthletiCo therapist—because the average consumption per Norwegian includes allotments for Eva's young children and for her parents and her grandmother on pensions. She and the rest of the Norwegians work fewer hours per year than the citizens of other rich countries, and many fewer hours than the workaholics in Japan or the U.S.A. At birth Eva could have expected to live to age eighty-five. Her own two children will probably live even longer, and certainly will be even better off financially than she is, unless they decide on careers in fine arts or charitable works—in which case the satisfactions from such sacred careers amount to income.[13] Norway contributes more per capita to international governmental charities than any other country. Eva supports nonviolent and democratic institutions. She graduated from the University of Bergen, studying mathematics. She works as an actuary in an insurance company, getting six weeks of paid vacation a year in Sicily or Florida. Her husband (who is by no means her lord and master) worked as a diver on the oil rigs for a few years, but now is deskbound at Statoil's regional office. As a girl at school Eva read many of the works of Ibsen in Norwegian, and a couple even of Shakespeare in simplified English. She's been pleased to attend performances of both at the National Theatre in Oslo over the mountains. Her home resonates with recordings of the music of Edvard Grieg, who in fact was a not-so-distant relative on her mother's side.[14]

Why did it happen? How did average income in the world move from $3 to $30 a day? How did the Norwegians move from being poor and sick and marginally free and largely ignorant to being rich and healthy and entirely free and largely educated?

The main point of this book is that the hockey-blade leaps, such as Norway's from $3 to $137 per head, with its cultural and political accompaniments, did *not* happen mainly because of the usual economics. That is, they did not happen because of European trade or Dutch investments or British imperialism or the exploitation of sailors on Norwegian ships. Economics did matter in shaping the pattern. It usually does. Exactly who benefited and exactly what was produced, and exactly when and where, was indeed a matter of economics—a matter of incomes and property and incentives and relative prices. If a historian doesn't grasp the economics he will not understand the pattern of modern history. The pattern was shaped by the trade in cotton and the investments in seaports, by the supply of steam engines and the demand for elementary education, by the cost of wrought iron and the benefit of railways, by the plantation exploitation of slaves and the market participation of women. Economics of a material sort can surely explain why Americans burned wood and charcoal many decades longer than did the forest-poor and coal-rich people of inner northwestern Europe. It can explain why education was a bad investment for a British parlor maid in 1840, or why the United States rather than Egypt supplied most of the raw cotton to Manchester, England, or to Manchester, New Hampshire, or why indeed the cotton growers of the present-day African Sahel are damaged by protection for American cotton. Economics can explain why a comparative advantage in making cloth out of cotton shifted from India to England and then back to India.

Economics, though, can't explain the rise in the whole world's (absolute) advantage from $3 to $30 a day, not to speak of $137 a day. That is the main scientific point of the book. Economics can't explain the blade of the hockey stick. It can't explain the onset or the continuation, in the magnitude as against the details of the pattern, of the uniquely modern—the widespread coming of automobiles, elections, computers, tolerance, antibiotics, frozen pizza, central heating, and higher education for the masses, such as for you and me and Eva. If an economist doesn't grasp the history she will not understand this most important of modern historical events. An economics of a bourgeois or Marxist sort does not account for the unprecedented size and egalitarian spread of the benefits from growth, only the details of its pattern. Material, economic forces, I claim, were not the original and sustaining causes of the modern rise, 1800 to the present. Economics does most usefully explain how the rising tide expressed itself in microgeographical detail, channeled into this or that inlet, mixing with the river just so far upstream, lapping the dock to such-and-such a height. But the tide itself had other causes.

∞

What then? I argue here, and in complementary ways in the two volumes to follow, that innovation (not investment or exploitation) caused the Industrial Revolution. Many historians and economists would agree, so there's not much that is surprising in that part of the argument. But I also argue—as fewer historians and very few economists would—that talk and ethics and ideas caused the innovation. Ethical (and unethical) talk runs the world. One-quarter of national income is earned from sweet talk in markets and management.[15] Perhaps economics and its many good friends should acknowledge the fact. When they don't they get into trouble, as when they inspire banks to ignore professional talk and fiduciary ethics, and to rely exclusively on silent and monetary incentives such as executive compensation. The economists and their eager students choose Prudence Only, to the exclusion of the other virtues that characterize humans—justice and temperance and love and courage and hope and faith—and the corresponding sins of omission or commission. The theorists of prudence forbid ethical language, even in the word-drenched scene of banking. Such a reduction to Prudence Only works reasonably well in some parts of the economy. You'll do well to choose Prudence Only, and silent incentives, when trying to understand covered interest arbitrage in the foreign exchange markets. But it doesn't explain the most surprising development of all.

In particular, three centuries ago in places like Holland and England the talk and thought about the middle class began to alter. Ordinary conversation about innovation and markets became more approving. The high theorists were emboldened to rethink their prejudice against the bourgeoisie, a prejudice by then millennia old. (Sadly, the talk and prejudice and theory along such lines didn't alter right away in China or India or Africa or the Ottoman lands. By now it has, despite resistance from European progressives and non-European traditionalists.) The North Sea talk at length radically altered the local economy and politics and rhetoric. In northwestern Europe around 1700 the general opinion shifted in favor of the bourgeoisie, and especially in favor of its marketing and innovating. The shift was sudden as such things go. In the eighteenth and nineteenth centuries a great shift occurred in what Alexis de Tocqueville called "habits of the mind"—or more exactly, habits of the lip. People stopped sneering at market innovativeness and other bourgeois virtues exercised far from the traditional places of honor in the Basilica of St. Peter or the Palace of Versailles or the gory ground of the First Battle of Breitenfeld.

To speak for a moment to my economist colleagues, some of us have saved our models in the face of a dawning realization of how radical the development was in the eighteenth and especially in the nineteenth and twentieth centuries by speaking of "nonlinearities" or "economies of scale" or "multiple equilibria." Though such tricks are fun to think about, they don't work scientifically. Some other economists, now led by an astonishing group of economic historians with a serious focus on growth theory and growth theorists with a serious focus on history, argue instead that Europe, and especially Britain, was preparing for the blade of the hockey stick for centuries. The new history has a theme similar to an old history attributing Europe's excellence to its ancient civilization, Christian and humanist, from

Israel and Greece, and the Germanic tribes in the forests. The trouble is, as the best among the economists admit with puzzlement, that India and the Arab lands and Iran and China and especially Japan were equally excellent and ready. Many such rich areas long before had the low interest rates and good property laws praised by the economists—China in the seventeenth century, Northern Italy in the fifteenth century, the Arab world in the tenth century, Rome in the first century. But for millennia no blade of the hockey stick ensued.[16] When ideology changed, it did.

∞

I am claiming that the economy around the North Sea grew far, far beyond expectations in the eighteenth and especially in the nineteenth and most especially in the twentieth century *not* because of mechanically economic factors such as the scale of foreign trade or the level of saving or the amassing of human capital. Such developments were nice, but derivative. The North Sea economy, and then the Atlantic economy, and then the world economy grew because of changing forms of speech about markets and enterprise and invention. Technically speaking (I continue saying to my economist colleagues), the new conversation caused the dimensions of the Edgeworth box to explode. Pareto-optimal reallocation by exchange within a fixed box, or reallocation by aggression along the contract curve, or the modest expansion of the box achievable by investment, was not what happened—though it is these three which economists want most to talk about, because they understand them so well. On the contrary, the production possibility curve, the dimensions of the Edgeworth box, leapt out, radically, and from the point of view of conventional economics, inexplicably.[17]

The argument in truth should not shock a thoughtful economist. All economists have realized since the 1870s that economics is something that happens between people's ears. The economists learned so from the various forms of neoclassical economics Mengerian or Marshallian, or from institutionalism or from modern Marxism. Valuations, opinions, talk on the street, imagination, expectations, hope are what drive an economy. In other words, you don't have to be a materialist, denying the force of ideas, just because you are an economist. Rather to the contrary. One of the leading contributors to the new growth theory, Robert Lucas, declared that "for income growth to occur in a society, a large fraction of people must experience changes in the possible lives they imagine for themselves and their children. . . . In other words . . . economic development requires 'a million mutinies.'"[18] Lucas's formulation is more psychological than the sociological and rhetorical one proposed here. But in any case, to believe that habits of the lip changed in the seventeenth and especially the eighteenth century, for various good and interesting reasons—some in turn material, some autonomously rhetorical—does not deny conventional economics a place. It merely takes speech seriously within the economy and the society. It initiates a humanistic science of the economy, "humanomics" as the economist Barton Smith calls it. Speech, not material changes in foreign trade or domestic investment, caused proximally the nonlinearities, or (expressed in more conventional theorizing) the leaping out of the production possibility curve, the imaginings of possible lives. We know this empirically in part because trade and investment were ancient routines, but the new dignity and liberty for ordinary people were unique to the age. What was unique was a new climate of persuasion, out there in the shops and streets and coffeehouses populated by the bourgeoisie. As I shall try to persuade you, oh materialist economist.

LIBERAL IDEAS CAUSED THE INNOVATION

The change in talk and thought about the bourgeoisie (to turn back to the rest of you) was probably of greater importance for explaining the modern world than the clerical Reformation in Germany after 1517, or the aristocratic Renaissance during and long after the Tuscan Trecento. Yet both of these influenced the talk, as did probably more powerfully a third great R-shift of early modern times, the successful Revolts and Revolutions across more than two centuries which shook Holland and Britain and America and Poland and finally France and all its Napoleonic conquests. The focus here, though, is on a fourth great and (for a while) uniquely European R-shift—the "Bourgeois Revaluation," achieved peacefully during the seventeenth and eighteenth centuries in Holland and Britain. You can imagine the enrichment part of the modern world without the Renaissance, the Reformation, or even the Revolutions—however much they contributed indirectly to how we live now. But you can't imagine the enrichment part without the Revaluation. An old class of town dwellers, formerly despised by the clergy and the aristocracy and the peasantry, began to acquire a more dignified standing, in the way people thought and talked about it, in European rhetoric about middle-class activities. And along with a new dignity the bourgeoisie began to acquire a new liberty. Both were rhetorical events.

Among the seven principal virtues, faith is the virtue of backward looking, of having an identity.[1] Keep the faith. Dignity encourages faith. You are dignified in standing, in being who you most truly are, and have been. A Chicagoan. A scholar. A woman. Hope by contrast is the virtue of forward looking, of having a project. Liberty encourages hope. You are free within the terrible limits of scarcity to venture. To change who you are. To start a business making adjustable wrenches. To become a professor of Assyriology. I claim here that the modern world was made by a new, faithful dignity accorded to the bourgeois—in assuming his proper place—and by a new, hopeful liberty—in venturing forth. To assume one's place and to venture, the dignity and the liberty, were new in their rhetorics.

And both were necessary. My libertarian friends want liberty alone to suffice, but it seems to me that it has not. Changing laws is not enough (though it is a good start—and rotten laws can surely stop growth cold). True, from 1600 on the new dignity and the new liberty normally reinforced each other, and such a reinforcement is one possible source of the economist's "non-linearities." Dignity and liberty are admittedly hard to disentangle.[2] But dignity is a sociological factor, liberty an economic one. Dignity concerns the opinion that others have of the shopkeeper. Liberty concerns the laws that constrain him. The society and the economy interact. Yet contrary to a materialist reduction, they are not the same. Laws can change without a change in opinion. Consider prohibition of alcohol and then of drugs over the past ninety years. And opinion can change without a change in laws. Consider the decades-long drift toward independence among the English North American colonists.

It matters that dignity and liberty work together. Liberty without dignity, such as the lack of dignity that the wandering merchant faced outside his home city in medieval Europe or China or South Asia or Africa, makes for activity without faithful self-esteem, the eager but lowly and self-despising niggling of the marketplace. Willa Cather wrote in 1931 of "nervous little hopper men, trying to get on," by contrast with her admired bourgeois successes of the early Midwest, R. E. Dillon and J. H. Trueman, true indeed.[3] If thus lacking in dignity, the little hopper bourgeoisie is under assault from politics and society and literature, which makes for bad economic politics, as in Habsburg and then Bourbon and then Fascist Spain, and $3 a day. A leading example in European history is that of the Jews, liberated legally during the eighteenth and nineteenth centuries but not accorded dignity—with the dismal result of Russian pogroms and Viennese anti-Semitic politics and the Final Solution.

Likewise, dignity without liberty makes for status without hope, merely another version of the hierarchy of olden times, as in the overregulated guild towns of Venice or Lübeck in their maturity. It happened repeatedly

early and late that a vigorous, innovating bourgeoisie settled at last for local political power, and ceased innovating, as did (until they awoke during
the nineteenth century) the Swiss "patriciate," or the Dutch "regents." The
merchant aristocracy of Venice was closed in 1297, and yet the Venetians by
unusual patriotism and focus were able to hold the golden East in fee for
centuries after. The more usual case is that an oligarchy arises, then closes,
and then promptly goes to sleep. Sleeping while collecting rents is so much
more pleasant than striving. If the bourgeoisie were thus admitted into the
elite, but at the price of disabling itself from alert and outward-looking innovation, the modern world would look a good deal like the *ancien régime*
of Northern Italy or the Hansa, at $1 to $5 a day.

All this changed on a large scale, first in Holland, in the Bourgeois Revaluation from the seventeenth through the nineteenth century. People needed
to be persuaded to accept the outcome of innovation. It was a complicated
cultural task, the creation of what the great economist Joseph Schumpeter,
looking back with nostalgia from 1942 on Europe just before the First World
War, called a "business-respecting civilization." But it did happen, and for
the first time and uniquely in northwestern Europe, by a series of happy preconditions and accidents. Revaluations of the honorable transcendent, no
longer confined to heroism or saintliness or courtly grace, changed society
and politics. It became honorable—"Honorable!" the aristocrat snorts—to
invent a machine for making screws or to venture in trade to Cathay. By
contrast, what Tocqueville called "habits of the heart" did not change much.
The initiating change was not psychological (as for example Max Weber
claimed in 1905, and Robert Lucas in 2002), nor economic (as Karl Marx
and Friedrich Engels claimed in 1848, and Douglass North in 1990), but sociological and historical and political. That is, around 1600 on a big scale in
pioneering Holland, and then around 1700 on a bigger scale, and permanently, in innovating Britain, some of the elite began to revalue the town
and its vulgar and corrosive creativity.

John Lilburne, one of the gentry-origin, merchant-radicals of London (he
was born in the royal place at Greenwich), a Leveller of the English Revolution after 1642, saw it in 1653 as a law of God and England that "no man . . .
may be put to answer for anything but wherein he materially violates the
person, goods, or good name of another."[4] Leave us alone, milord, unless we
steal. By the 1660s the Dutch cloth merchant Pieter de la Court was declaring that "a power of using their natural rights and properties for their own

safety ['the pursuit of happiness' soon became the usual phrase] . . . will be to the commonalty . . . an earthly paradise: for the liberty of a man's own mind, especially about matters wherein all his welfare consists, is to such a one as acceptable as an empire or kingdom."[5] No aristocratic empires or kingdoms, please; we're bourgeois, and merely want the liberty to get on with the workaday task of pursuing happiness. In 1690 an English merchant to the Ottomans, Dudley North (himself from an aristocratic family), wrote in an even more modern and economistic and bourgeois way that "there can be no trade unprofitable to the public, for if any prove so, men leave it off; and wherever the traders thrive, the public, of which they are a part, thrives also."[6] Therefore, *laissez faire* (make what you want, free of regulation), as the early eighteenth-century French theorists of bourgeois life such as Pierre de Boisguilbert began to say, and later *laissez passer* (trade what you want).[7]

Such promarket opinions have never become universal. Though his audience included a big proportion of the merchants and apprentices of businesslike London, Shakespeare's only plays touching on the bourgeoisie are *The Merchant of Venice* and *The Merry Wives of Windsor*. In *The Merchant* the bourgeois Antonio is silly in his love for aristocratic Bassanio, and the other major bourgeois figure is Shylock. All the other works of the Bard sing of honorable aristocrats or comical peasants or sweet shepherds (priests are notably rare). His honored characters, speaking in blank verse rather than comical prose (*The Merry Wives* is almost all in bourgeois/commoner prose), reflected the sociology of dignity in his times, and the hierarchical conventions of the Elizabethan theater. The elite took a century or more after the age of Shakespeare to begin speaking of commercial creativity as OK, acceptable, not-to-be-sneered-at, as in all the many works of Daniel Defoe, and then the essays and plays of Addison and Steele, and then the "bourgeois tragedies" on the stages of England and France and Germany, and then above all in the modern European novel. Two centuries after Shakespeare the heroes even in Jane Austen's novels, though noncommercial gentry, think in terms of sense *and* sensibility, prudence *and* love. And dear Jane herself speaks enthusiastically in her letters about her bourgeois business of authorship, and relishes her royalties. Yet anticommercial snobbery even in Britain did not entirely end, ever. You see it in Emma Woodhouse's ill-begotten advice to Harriet Smith in *Emma* (1815) not to marry the merely bourgeois farmer Robert Martin. One of Jane's brothers became for a while an *haut bourgeois* banker—though two others ended up as aristocratic admirals in the Royal Navy. Aristocratic or Christian virtues never entirely left the imagination of the West, or of the East. They sometimes were mischievous, as in Japanese militarism or American fundamentalism; yet sometimes they were a glorious completion of bourgeois ethics.

The liberty half of the Revaluation was equally, and more famously, slow in coming. The domination of British politics by an illiberal and antibourgeois and indeed antidemocratic Establishment did not entirely end, ever—consult for instance the British TV comedy of the 1980s, *Yes, Minister*. As the historian Margaret Jacob argued long ago, and as the historian Jonathan Israel has confirmed lately in the history of ideas, the free-market and free-voting "radical Enlightenment" of people like the Levellers, de la Court, Spinoza, Mandeville, Rousseau, Paine, Benjamin Rush, Mary Wollstonecraft, and some of the well-named Freemasons was undercut by the more conservative Enlightenment of Locke, Newton, Voltaire, Adam Smith, John Adams, and others of the Freemasons, in the utter liberty of trade that the radicals sometimes favored, among other matters—though note that both sides of the Enlightenment contained admirers of the bourgeoisie.[8] (And of course the reactionary powers for centuries fought both Enlightenments with galley and with rope. In France during the term of the laws 1686–1759 prohibiting the importation or making of printed calicoes—this to protect wool and linen manufacturers, and so a bourgeois party of the old and mercantilist sort—the Swedish economist and historian Eli Heckscher reported that the measures "cost the lives of some 16,000 people, partly through executions and partly through armed affrays, without reckoning the unknown but certainly much larger number . . . sent to the galleys. . . . On one occasion in Valence, seventy-seven were sentenced to be hanged, fifty-eight were to be broken on the wheel, 631 were sent to the galleys.")[9]

In many places in Northwestern Europe, however, the new and liberal bourgeois values, and the Revaluation, triumphed, with startling economic results. The historian of technology Christine MacLeod dates the final apotheosis of the inventor in Britain to the early nineteenth century. Certainly the shift in rhetoric beginning in seventeenth-century Holland needed to be tended, as ideologies do. MacLeod tells for example of the campaign before 1834 to erect in Westminster Abbey—there among the kings and priests and poets—a big statue of the inventor of the separate-condenser steam engine, James Watt (1736–1819; the statue was later shifted to St. Paul's): "Not to perpetuate," the inscription reads, "a name which must endure while the peaceful arts flourish, but to show that mankind have learned to honor those who best deserve their gratitude . . . [such as James Watt,] who enlarged the resources of his country, increased the power of man, and rose to an eminent place among the most illustrious followers of science and the real benefactors of the world." A contemporary asked in vexation "what this vast figure represents, what class of interests before unknown [well, hardly 'unknown'], what revolution in the whole framework of modern society."[10] He was behind the curve. MacLeod notes that the *Times* as early as April 22, 1826, had declared that inventors were "the elect of the human race."[11] She detects during the 1830s "a marked alteration in the attitudes of judges and juries towards patentees. . . . The balance of success in litigation shifted towards prosecutors of infringements, as patentees began to be regarded less as grasping monopolists [of Elizabethan date, for example], and more as national benefactors," sixty years after Adam Smith had fully articulated the case.[12] The real benefactors of the world came to be seen as commercial innovators and followers of "science" (which by the way was still being used then in the old sense: Watt was an instrument maker, not a physical "scientist" in the definition later prevalent in English, as was for example his friend the chemist and physicist Joseph Black, who initiated the science of thermodynamics).

Such dignity for innovation and liberty for enterprise are sometimes still opposed, which along with a bad climate and a bad start is why some countries remain poor. True, if supporters of subsidies to American cotton growers were capable of shame, eastern Burkina Faso and the rest of the Sahel would do better. Ethical failures in the global North, such as the rhetoric of zero-sum "protection" and "competitiveness," contribute to keeping such places poor. Yet even with a bad climate and a bad start and an unethical policy in the North of protecting its own rich farmers and trade unions, and helping them to compete by suppressing competition, such places do not have to remain poor. That's the difference on past form between bottom-billion Bangladesh now and Norway or Japan in 1800, whose poverty then seemed hopeless, an old rugged cross to be taken up without complaint (you'll get pie in the sky when you die). When a stable though tyrannical country like China or a turbulent though law-governed country like India started to revalue markets and innovation, and to give a partial liberty to commerce, the food and housing and education for the average person commenced exploding. In a few generations China and India, I repeat, if

they don't revert to anti-innovation, will have a standard of living beginning to approach Eva's. Already they have entered Collier's Top Four to Six
Billion. Imagine the artistic and intellectual flowering when 37 percent of
the world's population is well-off enough to pick up a brush or pen or flute
or computer. An internal ethical change is doing it, and it began in northwestern Europe a little before and after 1700.

It wasn't "capitalism" that was new in 1700. Markets and nonagricultural
property and a town-living middle class in charge of them are very old. The
market economy, contrary to what you might have heard, has existed since
the caves. The anthropologist Jack Goody declares that "trade was essential to the growth of human life from the earliest times, including the institution of the market and the rise of some specialized individuals (later
merchants)."[13] The invention of full language, by some accounts occurring
somewhere between 70,000 and 50,000 BCE in Mother Africa, shows up
archaeologically for example in a big and sudden increase in the distance
traveled by stone for tools, such as flint or obsidian, scores of miles in trade
instead of the former few. So it went, for millennia. The invention of agriculture required a walled town to guard the crop harvested, in Jericho in
Israel and Catalhöyük in Turkey, after 8000 BCE. For millennia the towns
proliferated, with their markets and their bourgeoisies and their enterprises.
In the third millennium BCE the urban merchants from the Indus Valley
in what is now Pakistan exported grain and cotton cloth to the towns of
Sumer in southern Iraq. Credit and its premise of monetary accumulation is
ancient.[14] Stamped or cast metal coinage was invented around the eighth or
seventh century BCE simultaneously in China, India, and what is now Turkey. But long before, and in many places long after, people had used monetary equivalents such as bars of copper or iron, coils of silver, or cattle, or
cowry shells, or cacao beans, or the pieces of cloth used as money at Prague
in 965 CE.[15] The big market of Tlatelolco, next door to Tenochtitlan in what
is now Mexico City, serviced daily in 1519 CE tens of thousands of customers, paying with cacao beans. "Back at least as far as the third millennium
B.C.E.," writes the economic historian George Grantham, "farmers on some
islands in the Aegean Sea were producing olive oil and wine in amounts
greatly exceeding domestic consumption requirements."[16] Their balance of
trade would have been squared with money substitutes like wheat from the
mainland, or later with copper bars or tin.

The conventional history of "commercialization" and especially "monetization," and their opposites "self-sufficiency" and "communal property rights," with an allegedly sharp distinction between rural *Gemeinschaft* (inherited, emotional community) and urban *Gesellschaft* (created, cold society), and a recent "rise of rationality" and a lamentable dominance of *Gesellschaft*, are for the most part myths, created by German scholars in the nineteenth century under the influence of a Eurocentric Romanticism of race, and in reaction to the universalist claims of the French and Scottish Enlightenments. But on the contrary (and in agreement with the French and the Scots), from the earliest times peasants and townsfolk, farm and factory, were motivated by the same set of human virtues and vices. Ferdinand Tönnies, who developed the vocabulary of *Gemein-* and *Gesellschaft*, declared in 1887 that "one could . . . hardly speak of commercial *Gemeinschaft*." Yes one can, and for business to function well it must be an emotional community. "The *Gemeinschaft* of property between husband and wife cannot be called *Gesellschaft* of property."[17] Oh yes, it can, and had better be if wives are to have independent identity.

There is no change in human nature from olden to modern times, and the attribution of a novel "rationality" to a society capable of world wars and modern sports seems at least strange. In particular the townsfolk worldwide appear to have had pretty much the same psychological makeup as the modern bourgeoisie, as we can infer for example from the curses directed at them early in the first millennium BCE by the Hebrew prophets (Amos 8:4–7, Hosea 12:7–8, among many cases). There was no rise in the "rationality" of the bourgeois in, say, the sixteenth century. The businesspeople wanted profit then as now, as do all humans—and as do all forms of life. Grass is rational. The townsfolk wanting profit believed that the very best way to attain it was by arranging for monopolies enforced by corrupt judges and kings and mayors, who then as now were very willing to participate: the wool and linen manufacturers of France, for example, persuaded the state to send importers of cotton cloth to the galleys or the breaking wheels. But the bourgeois were willing to innovate if compelled by competition and enabled by cooperation, and honored to boot. They only awaited the sociological and political Revaluation in northwestern Europe, and the closing of protectionist avenues for local enrichment and the elevation of inventors to fame, to begin innovating on an immense scale, creating a unique and enriching Bourgeois Era.

Nor of course was innovation entirely novel in 1700. Women and men had always been creative in weaving cloth or knapping arrowheads. An Upper Paleolithic burst of creativity in making tools and ornaments and musical instruments gives another sign of the coming of fully modern language, as does the use of oceangoing boats to get proto-New-Guineans and proto-Australians across the Wallace Line shortly before 40,000 BCE.[18] Around 4000 BCE the Indo-Europeans of Ukraine, whose remote ancestors had turned left on leaving Africa, appear to have domesticated the horse; and they went on to conquer or repopulate or inspire Europe, Iran, and much of South Asia. Around 3500 BCE the Taiwanese natives, originally from China, and ultimately like all of us out of Africa, appear to have invented the outrigger canoe; and they went on to populate the Pacific.

Until 1800 of our era, however, such innovations had allowed expansion of humans merely in numbers and ecological range, or the replacement of one culture by another, without improvement of the human lot. Until two centuries ago, for Malthusian reasons, the better clothing and better boats had done nothing to change the $3-a-day life—nothing at all, from Zulu farmer to Eskimo hunter. If things got better for a certain group of people, the people had more children, and so things got worse, by what economists call "diminishing returns to labor, given land." Even the "European marriage pattern," in which many people did not marry at all, or married late, having lower completed family sizes, made things only a little better, and could not break through $3 a day. True, as the anthropologist Marshall Sahlins argued long ago, and persuasively, the "stone-age economics" of hunter-gatherers allowed working many fewer hours than agriculturists did.[19] (But the late economic historian Stanley Lebergott sharply contradicted Sahlins's implied anti-industrial story: "Americans could choose equal simplicity [as the Bushman's life], and live on 300 nuts a day, half a pound of raw meat, and some vegetables. But they would need to work only 2 hours a week to do so [a fraction even of Sahlins's low estimate of the time budget], given superior U.S. production methods."[20]) Shifting to the laborious cultivation of fields of grain, requiring storehouse and guards, turned out to support cities and temples and then literacy. It was a tradeoff, a sparsely populated hunting/grazing ground of illiterates traded off for a densely populated city with a rich elite and a few readers and many fewer writers (and the seeds, long dormant, of the modern industrial world).[21] Yet the point here is that neither choice, neither the Amazonians nor the Sumerians, improved the scope of the average person until the industrial world. For most people up to 1800, whether average nomads or average Romans, a typical life was poor, narrow, illiterate, sick, and brief.

What was different after 1800, and with unstoppable force after 1900, was a novel and immense and sustained, almost lunatic, regime of innovation, finally breaking the Malthusian curse. As people enriched, they eventually started having fewer rather than more children, quite against Malthusian expectations—though even with large families, such as in bourgeois England, the enrichment would have taken place, so unprecedentedly powerful was it. The innovation of steam engine or corporate form or airplane or Wal-Mart for the first time made ordinary people richer, then vastly richer, than had the ancient routine of hunter-gatherer or nomadic herder or settled farmer or imperial subject, and encouraged the moderns to have smaller and more educated families. The riches interacted with the society and the polity in a blessed liberalism. Mario Vargas Llosa, the novelist and liberal, argued that one should read the Spanish public intellectual of the 1920s, José Ortega y Gasset, "to rediscover that—contrary to what those people bent on reducing liberalism to an economic recipe for free markets, low tariffs, controlled government spending and the privatization of business, suppose— liberalism is, above all, an attitude toward life and society based on tolerance and coexistence, on respect for the rich history and unique experiences of different cultures, and on a firm defense of liberty. . . . Economic freedom is a key element of the liberal doctrine, but certainly not the only one."[22] Think again on the poverty and illiberality of your ancestors, and rejoice.

3

AND A NEW RHETORIC PROTECTED THE IDEAS

As the economist and rabbi Israel Kirzner has argued, innovation depends on alertness.[1] A big or small entrepreneur, encouraged by dignity and enabled by liberty, alertly notices an opportunity, and takes it. To have good effects in social terms, of course, the alertness cannot be of the monopolizing sort that the ancient and modern bourgeoisie has so persistently sought, or of which the Tammany Hall politician George Washington Plunkitt spoke in 1905: "There's an honest graft, and I'm an example of how it works. I might sum up the whole thing by sayin': 'I seen my opportunities and I took em.'"[2] Such "opportunities" to extract bribes out of a government-enforced monopoly will at best shuffle the community's income from the taxpayer to Plunkitt. More likely the shuffling will reduce the size of the pie. And modern protectionism, which the French journalist and liberal theorist Frédéric Bastiat spoofed in 1845 in his petition of the candle makers against the light of the sun, certainly does reduce the size of the pie, by keeping people in less productive jobs—such as making candles that could be extinguished if the day's light were allowed in. What we produce is what we consume. Protection, retaining people in the wrong jobs making candles for light that could be provided free by the sun, means less for the average person to consume.[3]

Bastiat's funniest example of what is wrong with ancient urban monopolies or modern protectionism is the "negative railroad." A railroad was proposed in the early 1840s from Paris to Madrid. The city of Bordeaux, at a third of the distance, demanded that the railroad break there, on the argument that the break would "create jobs" for porters and hotels and cabs. (The cities of Paris, London, and Chicago have long had such arrangements, extracted by politics and monopoly. Passenger trains do not skirt principal cities. They go into them and end. During the railway age in the United States we said, "Change in Chicago.") Bastiat noted that according to such "job-creating" logic *every* town along the route should see its opportunity and take it. "Change in Ablon-sur-Seine, Evry, Ballancourt-sur-Essonne, La Ferté-Alais." Every few kilometers, at every country village, the railroad on the way to Madrid would end at a Gare du Nord to be resumed at a Gare du Sud, after job-creating expenditure for freight and travelers en route. All the national income of France and Spain would come to be "generated" by the Paris-to-Madrid railroad, at the cost of all other forms of production and consumption. Jobs would be "created." The protected production, forced by politics, would replace better uses of labor and capital. It would be a *negative* railroad, a triumph of protectionism and industrial planning achieved through what economists would later call "rent seeking" by the politicians of Bordeaux or Ablon-sur-Seine.[4]

By contrast, the society is in fact made better off if the opportunity is an actual improvement in how things are provided—rather than a rent-seeking opportunity for legalized theft such as blocking the sun's light entering houses, or building a negative railroad. Innovation is positive sum. Move the marketplace to a truly more convenient location. Produce Greek olive oil at a low cost to sell high. Invent the container ship. Discover $E = mc^2$. Devise the personal computer.

Yet such alert activities, especially in towns, had always been scorned by the elite. After all, the elite of Brahmins and warriors lived by the dignified collection of rents or taxes imposed on the lower classes—the proletarian *Shudra* and the bourgeois *Vaishya*. The Shudra lived by physical work, by which they were polluted. And a middleman from the Vaishya, who improved life for all by purchasing a bolt of cloth or an idea for an invention at a low price and selling it at a higher price to people who valued it still more, seemed to the world's elite before the Revaluation to be a mere lying trickster. In 44 BCE Cicero declared that "commerce, if on a small scale, is to be regarded as vulgar; but if large and rich . . . it is not so very discreditable . . . if the merchant, . . . contented with his profits, . . . betakes himself from the port itself to an estate in the country."[5] A merchant, said Cicero, lived by making the worse product seem the better, which was shameful (though an orator like himself, who earned the price of his tenement houses in central Rome and his country estate by making the worse legal case seem the better, was of course one of nature's noblemen). In 1516 the blast by Thomas More—or, rather, by his character Raphael Hythloday ("peddler of nonsense": in most seasons Sir Thomas was canny in making his own position a little bit ambiguous)—can stand for the abuse directed for millennia at the vulgar traders and innovators of the towns: "They think up . . . all ways and means . . . of keeping what they have heaped up through underhanded deals, and then of taking advantage of the poor by buying their labor and toil as cheaply as possible. . . . These depraved creatures, in their insatiable greed, . . . are still very far from the happiness of the Utopian commonwealth. [Where] once the use of money was abolished, and together with it all greed for it, what a mass of troubles was cut away!"[6] The Earl of Leicester, sent by Elizabeth in the 1580s to meddle in the politics of the already bourgeois Dutch, did not trouble to conceal his contempt for the "Sovereign Lords Miller and Cheeseman" with whom he had to deal.[7] And even the commercial Dutch had a proverb, *Een laugen is koopmans welvaart,* "A lie is a merchant's prosperity."

After about 1700 in Britain, however, as earlier in Holland, the vulgarities of the economy and of money and of dealing, with their unsettling creativity, came gradually to be talked about as noncorrupting. They began to be seen in theory as worthy of a certain respect, as not being hopelessly vulgar or sinful or underhanded or lower-caste. In a word, they became dignified, in part because they were recognized as good for the nation, not a useless scam. The very idea of virtue and dignity in (of all places) the economy—even in small-scale commerce, in buying grain low to sell high, or making cheese— had been proposed tentatively by a few professors in Italy and Spain and France. In the middle of the thirteenth century Thomas Aquinas had written in the style of his ancient and antibourgeois authorities, especially of Origen and St. Augustine and the desert fathers, and of Aristotle the teacher of aristocrats, that "trading, considered in itself, has a certain debasement attaching thereto, in so far as, by its very nature, it does not imply a virtuous or necessary end."[8] Yet Thomas and the other urban monks of his time wrestled against the inherited style, contradicting the world-denying ideology of stoic and stylite by emphasizing that working is like God's creativity. (*Laborare est orare,* to work is to pray, the Benedictines had long said: the liberal Freemasons of the Bourgeois Revaluation adopted it as their motto). Even, Aquinas suggested, trading is worthy: "Nevertheless the gain which is the end of trading, though not implying, by its nature, anything virtuous or necessary, does not, in itself, connote anything sinful or contrary to virtue: wherefore nothing prevents gain from being directed to some necessary or even virtuous end, and thus trading becomes lawful. Thus, for instance, a man may intend the moderate gain which he seeks to acquire by trading for the upkeep of his household"—the "upkeep," for example, of an establishment of fifteen rooms and twenty servants in a tower castle in Prato.

No one in charge in Prato or Florence or Barcelona after 1200 actually thought that buying low and selling high was immoral—they left such primitive notions to the folk of the interior North (the *coastal* northerners already had their own vigorous traditions of commerce). Yet eventually in the North Sea lands, during the seventeenth and especially during the eighteenth century, many of the clerisy of artists and intellectuals, and even a few churchmen and aristocrats, whether coastal or interior, came to tolerate and in a small way to admire the bourgeoisie, in the way their coastal ancestors had admired, or feared, or joined, the merchant-vikings. Thus the Bourgeois Revaluation.

Toward 1800 many northwestern Europeans, and toward 1900 other Europeans, and then toward 2000 many ordinary people elsewhere, came to accept the outcome of the market with more or less good grace. As Christine MacLeod puts it, by the standard of the "aristocratic cultural hegemony" of earlier times "the inventor was an improbable hero," buying ideas low and selling them high. Yet certainly in Britain by the middle of the nineteenth century the inventor had become just that, an acknowledged benefactor of the world.[9] The Dutch and the Americans, then the British, and then many other people for the first time on a big scale, such as the Swedes late in the nineteenth century, looked with favor on the market economy, and even on the creative destruction coming from its profitably alert innovations. Later the American westerns from *The Virginian* (novel 1902; films 1929, 1946) to *Shane* (novel 1949; film 1953) praised honest and nonviolent business.[10] In 1913 Willa Cather, without the antibourgeois sarcasm which her fellow members of the American clerisy were beginning to develop, has her heroine, Swedish-American Alexandra Bergson, exclaim, "There's Fuller [the real estate man] again! I wish that man would take me for a [business] partner. He's feathering his nest! If only poor people [such as Alexandra's unenterprising brothers] could learn a little from rich people!"[11] Japanese salarymen became heroes of novels. Against resistance from many in the clerisy of avant-garde intellectuals and artists, the world began to revalue the bourgeois towns. In 2005 the English philosopher and writer from Switzerland, Alain de Botton, spoke of his boring and bourgeois hometown, Zurich, whose "distinctive lesson to the world lies in its ability to remind us of how truly imaginative and humane it can be to ask of a city that it be nothing other than boring and bourgeois." He quoted Montaigne, writing in the last decades of the sixteenth century:

> Storming a breech, conducting an embassy, ruling a nation are glittering deeds. [But] rebuking, laughing, buying, selling, loving, hating, and living together gently and justly with your household—and with yourself . . . —is something more difficult. Whatever people may say, such secluded lives sustain in that way duties which are at least as hard and tense as those of other lives.[12]

The Bourgeois Revaluation was not simply a "rise of the middle class," if by that is meant a coming of an enlarged bourgeoisie to political power. Outside the scattered republics of Northern Italy, the Hansa, the Netherlands, Switzerland, and Geneva, and the British colonies in North America, such a step was long delayed. The middle class, as the historian Jack Hexter pointed out long ago, is always "rising"—and yet only lately even in bourgeois England has it found room at the top.[13] It hadn't found it, really, even in the nineteenth century, and certainly hadn't in the aristocratic sixteenth and seventeenth centuries. Aristocrats ran Britain until very late—Winston Churchill, for instance, was born in Blenheim Palace, and showed it.[14] Until recently a plummy BBC or Oxbridge accent was compulsory among the English to advance to political power, and was helpful even to many politicians of the Celtic Fringe. And a wealthy merchant's son from Bristol attending Eton and Christ Church acquired anyway his aristocratic airs, and a commission in a fashionable regiment.

The key economic event of early modern times is instead a Revaluation of bourgeois behavior, an increased if sometimes embarrassed acceptance by others and by themselves of the bourgeois' virtues—the rebuking, laughing, buying, selling so far from glittering deeds. As the historian Joyce Appleby put it in 1978, speaking of the late seventeenth century and after, the middle class in England "coalesced with, rather than displaced, the existing ruling class. . . . Social change . . . requires not a new class but a modern class, however formed."[15] Or rather, I would say, it requires a change in attitude toward an existing class. In Holland first, and then in the English-speaking lands and then elsewhere, attitudes changed.

The market and the bourgeoisie in the Revaluing countries repaid the compliment with a stunning enrichment of nearly all, and the piling up (the ruling class noted with approval) of materials of war. The bourgeoisie enacted for the first time at a large scale a social drama in which it enjoyed dignity and liberty, yet was forced out into the cold of innovation by withdrawal of mercantilist protection. (The bourgeoisie did not, by the way, need self-consciousness to play such a role—the belief that a social class must be self-conscious to constitute a social class has long been a red herring drawn across the historian's trail.) The bourgeoisie, through its innovation and its competition for customers, made itself rich, and also—promoting an end which was no part of its intention—increased the welfare of the poor in Britain and then elsewhere, at first by 100 percent and at length by 900 percent, then 1,500 percent, then beyond, up to that $100 or so a day. It's happening now even in Ghana and in Egypt.

In the event, by the new probourgeois, egalitarian talk (or "self-dependence," as John Stuart Mill called it), a positive-sum game was freed to some extent from zero-sum politics. The idea of progress through bourgeois dignity and liberty took hold of the social imaginary of the West. Napoleon's armies saw it as their first duty after a conquest to abolish the monopolizing guilds. In 1857 the Danish Sound tolls for getting into and out of the Baltic, which for centuries had been collected from Hamlet's Helsingør ("Elsinore," said Shakespeare), were eliminated by international treaty (with substantial monetary compensation to Denmark from the countries thus liberated). By the middle of the nineteenth century both Britain and France were free-trading nations.[16] And all were on their way to bourgeois enrichment.

∞

I am claiming, in other words, that the historically unique economic growth on the order of a factor of ten or sixteen or higher, and its political and spiritual correlates, depended on ideas more than on economics. The idea of a dignified and free bourgeoisie led to the ideas of the steam engine and mass marketing and democracy. "During its rule of scarce one hundred years," wrote Marx and Engels in *The Communist Manifesto* of 1848, "the bourgeoisie has created more massive and colossal productive forces than have all preceding generations."[17] True, and in the next hundred years it created many more, with a consequent betterment of the formerly impoverished, quite contrary to what Marx and Engels expected in 1848, and contrary to what the well-meaning people of the left down to the present, such as the

American filmmaker Michael Moore, keep saying. And it raised the human spirit, contrary to what Thomas Carlyle expected in 1829, and contrary to what the well-meaning people of the right down to the present, such as the American journalist Pat Buchanan, keep saying. A young American critic of Carlyle's moral pessimism, Timothy Walker, a host to Tocqueville in Cincinnati during his American tour, noted in 1831 that we are not speaking of Athenian aristocrats supported by the labor of women and slaves, but Democratic Humanity in the mass. "Our doctrine is that men must be released from the bondage of perpetual bodily toil before they can make great spiritual attainments."[18] And so the Americans did, compliments of their bourgeois people such as Walker.

But ideas, not mere trade or investment or exploitation, did the creating and the releasing. The leading ideas were two: that the liberty to hope was a good idea and that a faithful economic life should give dignity and even honor to ordinary people, to My Sovereign Lord Cheeseman as much as to Your Grace the Duke of Leicester. The very concept of justice shifted, away from the justice of giving His Grace his due and toward the justice of honoring contracts. The vocabulary (dating from the Latin inspired by Aristotle) was an old "distributive" justice as against a new "commutative" justice, the old justice of status as against the new justice of contract. (The modern left has returned to distributive justice, another of many instances of the modern left resembling in doctrine the old, preliberal right.) Aquinas had said, as if in preparation for the "democratic" shift (though seventeenth-century Holland, not to speak of eighteenth-century England, was hardly democratic): "In distributive justice a person receives all the more of the common goods, according as he holds a more prominent position in the community. This prominence in an aristocratic community is gauged according to virtue, in an oligarchy according to wealth, in a democracy according to liberty, and in various ways according to various forms of community."[19] John Locke replaced such justice by a commutative justice that honored everyone, and not merely the privileged by inheritance, under which the duke was expected to pay his tailoring bills, and property was justified by labor. Adam Smith likewise introduced a democratic redefinition of the old notion of distributive justice, which had favored an elite, by one according honored status to everyone, including the poor.[20] The disruptive outcome of such a bizarre egalitarianism, many Europeans came to believe, should be encouraged.

To use the word Marx taught us, the modern world arose out of an entirely new "ideology." Or, equivalently, it arose out of an entirely new social "rhetoric"—an older term meaning about the same thing. For example, the word "honest" in Shakespeare's time, as you can see in dictionaries of Shakespearean English or by searching the texts of the plays, was understood mainly as "noble" (that is, honorable in an aristocratic way, achieved in battle or at court: "Honest, honest Iago"). Its rhetoric changed radically in the eighteenth century, coming to mean mainly "dignified as an ordinary person" and "truth-telling" (that is, reliable in a bourgeois way, for making deals). In the eight works of Jane Austen written from 1793 to 1816 (including *The Watsons*, 1804, unfinished, and her early and unpublished *Lady Susan*, but not including her last, unfinished *Sanditon*), "honest" occurs thirty-one times.[21] In six of these thirty-one occasions it means "upright," dominantly in the old phrase an "honest man." Never is it used in Shakespeare's old sense "of high social rank, heroic in battle, aristocratic." Another third of the time it means "genuine," as in "a real, honest, old-fashioned boarding-school" (*Emma*), very far indeed from "honest" as "aristocratic." In its dominant modern sense it occurs again a third of the time in the meaning "sincere," and in four out of the thirty-one total occurrences in the restricted sense of "truth-telling." The 1934 *Webster's New International Dictionary* labels as archaic "honest" in sense 1, "held in honor," with the example of "honest" (chaste), as in the old phrase an "honest woman" (applied repeatedly to Desdemona in *Othello*). It labels as obsolete "honesty" in sense 1a, "honor." "Honest" in the now-dominant sense 2 means, the dictionary declares, fair, upright, truthful "as, an honest judge or *merchant*, [or an honest] statement" (italics supplied). No talk of aristocrats and honorable war. What is astonishing, and revealing of the Bourgeois Revaluation, is that an identical shift of meaning from an aristocratic to a bourgeois meaning of "honesty" took place at the same time during the Revaluation in other Germanic and Romance languages of commerce, such as in Dutch *eerlich* and Italian *onesto*.[22]

"The great chain of being"(*scala naturae*: the staircase of nature, though a staircase no one was meant to ascend: "chain" is better), dominated the Elizabethan world picture as it had since Plato. It was the endlessly refreshed hierarchy of dignities, which had ruled since the first large-scale agricultural societies in Iraq and Egypt and north China or for that matter Hawaii.[23] Yet in the seventeenth century in northwestern Europe it began to break down, and by the nineteenth century the great chain was viewed by many as reactionary—though for all that still having practical force. Probably because of the successful revolts from above and below 1568 to 1689, Holland and England and Scotland experienced a shrinkage in what sociologists call "social distance" (to use the terminology of the sociologist Georg Simmel, its originator, and of the Americans Robert Park and Emory Bogardus, its first systematic users, early in the twentieth century).[24] The eighteenth-century French progressives had theorized the shrinkage, in Voltaire and Rousseau and the other bogeymen of the reactionary powers—powers decidedly opposed to the shrinkage of social distance. To apply a modern analogy, northwestern European society by 1800 was lurching away from, say, old South Asian or Korean levels of deference, and starting toward new American or Israeli levels. They did not, to put it mildly, get all the way. Yet around the North Sea the barons and bishops reluctantly moved over a little for townspeople, and at length even for plowmen. Ordinary northwestern Europeans acquired a dignity and liberty, first in Holland and then elsewhere, that the proud man's contumely had long been devoted to suppressing.

In a striking remark in 1908 Simmel brought into focus the old image of the bourgeois man: "In the whole history of economic activity the stranger makes his appearance everywhere as a trader, and the trader makes his as a stranger."[25] An instance from the fourteenth century is Boccaccio's tale of Saladin disguised as a merchant (*in forma di mercatante*). Around 1600, though, a new rhetoric of nonstrangeness arose in Holland, and later in England, and still later in other places down to the present. In the revolutionary year of 1795 the poet and plowman Robert Burns declared that "The pith o' sense, an' pride o' worth,/ Are higher rank than a' that. . . . / A man's a man for a' that." In fictional 1820 in a fictional and reactionary Kingdom of Parma, Stendhal's character the Conte Mosca della Rovere notes with characteristic insight that "it is doubtful whether the *mania of reverence* [for us aristocrats] will last out our time."[26] In Europe, the times, they were a-changin'.

For their part the northwest European townspeople lost their grip on cozy medieval monopolies. They got in exchange a new dignity as innovators, and a smaller social distance from the revered elite. (Nonetheless in fictional Parma in 1820 the bourgeois were still disdained by the aristocracy and gentry, and in 1839 when he wrote the novel still by Stendhal himself.)[27] The bourgeois became at last the new heroes of the first thoroughly bourgeois-respecting societies on a big scale, first Holland, then Britain, and then yet more so, with anticipations, the United States. Walt Whitman wrote in 1855 that what was astonishing about American citizens (the word "citizen," of course, would have left out at the time women, blacks, Indians, immigrants, and many of the poor native white men) was "the air they have of persons who never knew how it felt to stand in the presence of superiors."[28]

The new dignity for trading and innovating in ordinary life had, it goes without saying, causes itself. Some of the causes were economic and material, surely. Yet some, equally surely, were rhetorical and ideal. For example: the immense payoff from positive-sum politics in Holland could inspire direct imitation in England, as it has in present-day India. Matter then could be said to have moved other matter, interests to have spawned new interests. The elite interest in funding for ships and armies certainly did move policy and attitudes: look at Peter the Great's attempts to modernize Russia for purposes of national glory (and not to make his people better off). But you could just as well call it an ideal cause—after India had stagnated during the License Raj of the four decades after Independence it was the irritating *idea* of the enemy China growing fast after 1978 that at last stimulated a rhetorical Revaluation, especially after 1991. Likewise, during the seventeenth century the success of commercial Holland stuck in the craw of English people, the way the recent success of innovative Hong Kong and Taiwan stuck in the craw of mainland Chinese people, and inspired them to imitate.[29] The chain-like causation of successive Bourgeois Revaluations is similar to the causation of nationalism in reaction to conquering nationalisms, English to French, or English to Indian. That, too, you could call either material or ideal.

But Marx erred in claiming (as he and Engels ordinarily did claim) that ideological or rhetorical change *always* reflects the material economy of interests. It was no material, merely prudential, interest that drove Hitler's or Stalin's or Mao's regime to murder tens of millions merely of its own people, or Pol Pot's to murder a third of the Cambodian population.[30] It was ideology, during the century of warring ideologies. Doubtless the ideas themselves had some partial dependence on interests. But not always. People do not become conservatives or liberals, fascists or communists, always because of self-interest. Their willingness to die for such causes shows their commitment, as the economist and philosopher Amartya Sen would say, or it shows their ethical complexity for good or evil, as I would say.[31]

In the crucial early case from 1600 to 1800 in northwestern Europe the words and ideas led the way. Wrote Joel Mokyr in 1990: "Economists have traditionally been leery of *mentalités* as a factor in long-term economic development. In the [then] budding literature on the economic rise of the West, such factors have been ignored or curtly dismissed," as in works down to 1986 by John R. Hicks, Douglass North, Robert Paul Thomas, Eric Jones, Nathan Rosenberg, and L. E. Birdzell.[32] Economists, and even some of these, have grown wiser since then. European revolutions, reformations, renaissances, and especially revaluations made townspeople bold and raised them in the estimation of their fellows. As the economist Deepak Lal put it recently, "Capitalism as an economic system [I would call it 'innovation'] came about when the merchant and the entrepreneur finally were given social acceptance ['dignity'] and protection from the predation of the state ['liberty']."[33] As Lal's colleague in history at UCLA, Joyce Appleby, put it recently, "The riddle of capitalism's ascendancy isn't just economic but political and moral as well: How did entrepreneurs get out of the straitjacket of custom ['liberty'] and acquire the force ['liberty'] and respect ['dignity'] that enabled them to transform, rather than conform to [more 'liberty' and a new standard for 'dignity'], the dictates of their society?"[34] The North Sea lands arrived at the "bourgeois dignity" of my title, with the liberty to venture. The material economy followed.

4

MANY OTHER PLAUSIBLE STORIES
DON'T WORK VERY WELL

Quite a few of my social-scientific and even many of my humanistic colleagues will be strongly inclined to disagree, and not merely about my praise for the bourgeoisie. They have the idea, held with passionate idealism, that ideas about ideas are unscientific. For about a century, 1890 to 1980, the ideas of positivism and behaviorism and economism ran the social-scientific show, and many of the older showpeople still adhere to the script we learned together so idealistically as graduate students.[1] Economists and historians who believe themselves to be quite exempt from any philosophical influences are usually the slaves of some defunct philosopher of science a few years back—commonly a shakily logical positivist nearly a hundred years back.

Their faith is admirable. Yet in denying (before the scientific conversation begins) the relevance of words and rhetoric and identity and creativity, in favor of numbers and interest and matter and Prudence Only, they are standing against a good deal of the historical evidence, not to speak of science studies in the half century since Thomas Kuhn. The opponents of ideas as causal are what the modern Marxists call with a sneer "vulgar" Marxists—wanting passionately to be seen as tough-minded behaviorists, positivists, materialists, quantitative, "evidence based," every single time, regardless of the common sense or the historical evidence. Their methodology, they are quite sure, yields the only scientific truth. It is their identity, which is why they become upset and abusive when some unScientific fool claims that something was caused by ideas. They even feel (I seem to recall) that it is masculine to deny ideas. The trouble is that such a methodological preconception is often historically wrong. The American constitution, for example, as the historian Bernard Bailyn argues, was a creative event in the realm of ideas—and its economic origins are easily exaggerated.[2] "The Atlantic democratic revolutions of the later eighteenth century," writes Jonathan Israel, "stemmed chiefly from a general shift in perceptions, ideas, and attitudes," a "revolution of the mind."[3] The abolition of slavery, a policy once advocated merely by a handful of radical churchmen (and the Baron de Montesquieu), played in the 1820s and 1830s a role in British politics, and later of course a much bigger role in American politics. It had less to do with the North's material interests than with cheap printing interacting with evangelical Christianity. As Lincoln famously said on being introduced to the author of *Uncle Tom's Cabin* (1852), "So this is the little lady who wrote the book that made the big war." Books can indeed make wars—Erskine Childers's spy novel, *The Riddle of the Sands: A Record of Secret Service* (1903), was no minor influence on the Anglo-German naval rivalry. Socialist ideas and at length socialist reality spread after the disappointed revolutions of 1848 in congresses and party meetings and manifestos. Various nationalisms had spread across Europe in reaction to Napoleon's conquests, but then were matured in poetry and songs of risings and in the screeds of exiles resident in London. Talk, talk, talk. Ideas matter.

To explain the new dignity of the middle class in northwestern Europe, and to explain the success it brought to the modern world, the social scientists need to moderate their fervent ideology of materialism—though of course without denying material forces. They need to collect the facts on ideas and rhetoric and social distance—though still collecting facts on the price of iron and the size of bribes to congressmen, too. It is not a rule of scientific method that an economic subject, such as revolutionary economic growth, must entail a narrowly economic explanation. Marshall Sahlins put it this way:

> It is not that the material forces and constraints are left out of account, or that they have no real effects on [the] cultural order. It is that the nature of the effects cannot be read from the nature of the forces, for the material effects depend on their cultural encompassment. . . . The practical interest of men in production is symbolically constituted. . . . Nothing in the way of their capacity to satisfy a material (biological) requirement can explain why . . . dogs [in the West] are inedible but the hindquarters of the steer are supremely satisfying of the need to eat.[4]

In his recent history of the American business school and its role in legitimizing and then corrupting professional managers, the sociologist Rakesh

Khurana declared that "I take it that ideational interests can be important factors in a professionalization project, and that statements of them must sometimes be taken at face value, . . . along with social roles and private (material or power) interests."[5] Likewise the sociologist of religion Rodney Stark, without by any means neglecting material forces, urges us to take sometimes at face value, or at any rate *some* value, the actual content of religious doctrine.[6] Sometimes people mean what they say, or at least they say by accident their meaning. Words are facts for a social science, too.

The present book supports such a balancing step indirectly, by looking at a representative sample of apparently promising materialist and antirhetorical explanations of the Industrial Revolution and the modern world—explanations such as investment or exploitation or geography or foreign trade or imperialism or genetics or property rights. It finds them to be surprisingly weak. It concludes therefore (I admit the inferential gap) that the remaining explanations, such as ideas and rhetoric, must be strong. (The two books to follow will offer more positive evidence for the change in rhetoric.)

The critical method of "remainders" or "residues" was recommended in his *System of Logic* (1843) as one of four methods of induction by J. S. Mill, that admirably learned and open-minded scholar. "Subducting from a given phenomenon," wrote Mill in his high-flown but lucid style, "all the parts which, by virtue of preceding inductions, can be assigned to known causes, the remainder will be the effect of the antecedents which have been overlooked, or of which the effect was as yet an unknown quantity."[7] In simple language, take out what you can measure, and what's left is the impact of what you can't. If the economic and material causes usually proposed as explanations for the Industrial Revolution turn out to be weak, then the large remainder might well be the effect of a remaining antecedent—a rhetorical change, perhaps. If the new/old investment and trade can't do it, maybe the new ways of talking and thinking can. The crucial remaining antecedent, I claim, was a rhetorical change around 1700 concerning markets and innovations and the bourgeoisie, a rhetoric spreading after 1800. It was merely a change in talking and thinking about dignity and liberty. But it was historically unique and economically powerful. It raised the tide (though on the time scale of all human history, by the way, the tide was more like a tsunami; the implied suddenness of the Japanese word better fits the case).

The materialist accounts are many, from the "original accumulation" favored by early Marxist historians to the "new institutionalism" favored by late Samuelsonian economists.[8] The criticism made here does not hurl into the eighth circle of Hell every possible version of the theories suggested up to now; nor does it damn their advocates, many of whom are my personal friends and admired colleagues, whether Marxist or Samuelsonian. Their arguments may well be true that posit a surplus value staying with capitalists for a long time, or that explain with reallocations some increases of efficiency here or there of 2 or 3 percent of national income. The scientific evidence, however, seems to be strong that the economistic, Prudence Only theories, whether taken individually or together, can't explain the startling rise of real incomes from 1700 to the present, thousands of percents. Rhetoric perhaps can.

The negative case made here, summarizing fifty years of research by economic and historical scientists, is:

Foreign trade was too small and too anciently common to explain the rising tide after 1700 in northwestern Europe. Capital accumulation was not crucial, since it is pretty easily supplied. Literacy, for example, is a form of investment in human capital, but responds to demand. Coal can be and was moved. Despite what you may think, European empires did not enrich the imperial countries, and anyway the chronology is wrong, and anyway imperialism was commonplace in earlier times. Likewise, the institutions of property rights were established many centuries before industrialization, in China more even than in Europe. The European marriage pattern was not only European. Greed didn't increase in the West. In bourgeois countries during the Industrial Revolution the Catholics did just as well as the Protestants, at least when in similar circumstances, as they were in Amsterdam. The Muslims and the Hindus and the Buddhists, or for that matter the Confucians and most of the animists, could think as rationally about profit and loss as did the Christians. Populations had grown, even explosively, in earlier times and other places. The Black Death hit all of Eurasia. Genetic variation and evolution work too slowly and irrelevantly to explain European success. Until the eighteenth century many parts of the Far and Near and Southern East were as rich, and appeared to be as ready for innovation, as parts of the West—except at length in the crucial matters of the dignity and liberty of the bourgeoisie. Until the seventeenth century the Chinese and the Arabs practiced a science more sophisticated than the European one. The science of the Scientific Revolution was in any case mostly about prisms and planets, and before the twentieth century even its other branches did not much help in worldly pursuits. True, European science was in its non-normal, revolutionary episodes an important parallel in the realm of ideas to the acceptance of creative destruction. But the new dignity and liberty for innovators was a rhetorical event outside of science, and it influenced science itself by elevating bourgeois stick-to-itiveness (such as Charles Darwin's) over aristocratic gestures (such as Lord Bacon's).

In 1500 only one of the ten largest cities in the world, Paris, was in Europe. In 1800 still only Paris, London, and Naples ranked so.[9] After a century of shocking divergence, however, only one city outside Europe or the United States was in the top ten (namely, Tokyo, and this after Japanese industrialization had taken hold).[10] Yet in our own times, it is estimated that by 2015 only two cities with only partial European origin, Mexico City and São Paulo, will be in the top ten. Jack Goody calls it "alternation," and economists call it "convergence." "No one wishes to deny Europe (or America) its recent advantage," writes Goody, "only to dispute the reasons given which all too often relate to imaginary long-term superiority. . . . The advantages . . . are of much more recent and specific origin."[11] The wheel turns. In short, the Europeans were not economically special until about 1700. They showed most plainly their special ingenuity only briefly in the two centuries after 1800 (as they had by then been showing for some centuries their special brutality). By the early twenty-first century they had reverted to not being special at all, even in brutality. The episode of their innovative specialness, and the rising tide, came from a change in their economic rhetoric. It made the difference.

∞

"Teach the conflicts," says my colleague in English at the University of Illinois at Chicago, a past president of the Modern Language Association, Gerald Graff. With Cathy Birkenstein he has brought the idea to fruition in a rhetoric for students called *They Say/I Say: The Moves That Matter in Academic Writing* (2005).[12] Their brilliant little handbook notes that a student—or a scientist—can't see what's distinctive even in her own position if she can't summarize reasonably fairly what *others* think. I test here reasonably fairly the numerous (sadly mistaken) alternatives to the (correct) theory that a change in rhetoric caused the Industrial Revolution and the modern world. To use the piece of argumentative rhetoric in Graff and Birkenstein's title, "My honored if misled friends in economics, history, and economic history say that the modern world came from trade or exploitation or legal change. *They say* that. *I say*, no, it didn't. It came from a change in the rhetoric about the common economic life, which led to the Franklin stove and the Bessemer process and peaceful transitions of political power and all our joy."

Such a methodical rejection-of-alternatives, I admit, is a little irritating—one tires of being told what did *not* happen. And there is always the embarrassing danger which Montaigne noted: "Our reasons and arguments in controversial matters can ordinarily be turned against ourselves; and we run ourselves through with our own weapons."[13] Yet such hazardous naysaying is after all the conventional ideal in the philosophy of science—if commonly overlooked in practice (the practice is more usually what sociologists of science call the Empiricist Monologue, that is, My Wonderful Theory And *Only* My Wonderful Theory). A recent rejection-of-alternatives article in *Science*, for example, describes the "solar model problem," namely, the problem that elements heavier than hydrogen and helium in the sun are more common than is implied by models of convection. The author politely rejects four "straightforward" hypotheses "receiving some initial support." "Perhaps the only proposal left still standing," he concludes, "is internal gravity waves."[14] Similarly, in 1965 Arno Penzias and Robert Wilson discovered the background radiation of 3 degrees kelvin from the Big Bang by ruling out alternative explanations for the static noise in their new microwave detector pointed at the night sky, including for example the activities of certain local pigeons. Ideally we "encompass" other people's theories in our own and show triumphantly that our theory explains the facts while theirs do not. The pigeons didn't do it. Surely, therefore, the Big Bang must have.

In the ancient world, Plato's dialogues used the same method of rejecting alternatives and teaching the conflicts, as in *Republic*, book 1 (for example, Steph. 335), with Socrates as the encompasser. Talmudic Judaism used another. St. Thomas Aquinas used still another, influenced to some degree it appears by Maimonides, as well as by a budding university tradition of disputation after Peter Abelard, intensifying the centuries-old spirit of Christian theological dispute after Irenaeus and Origen. In early modern science the classic case was Galileo's *Dialogo* of 1632, where the sun-as-center "Simplicio" had rings—or orbits—run around him by the Copernican master. (Galileo may not have endeared himself to the Inquisition by naming the anti-Copernican "Simplicio," supposedly in honor of a sixth-century Neoplatonist named Simplicius [classical Latin "of one nature," from *sim-*

plex; in modern Italian, *simplice*, "straightforward"; but in medieval Latin "naïve."])

In medicine the classic case was the demonstration in 1855 by John Snow (1813–1858), following on his earlier inquiry in 1849, that cholera was caused, as he put it, by people being "supplied with water containing the sewage of London."[15] He examined various named alternatives to the water-borne theory, such as miasma or person-to-person contagion. He gradually accumulated evidence that the alternative theories were untenable—devising for example clever maps of London based on house-to-house surveys during the 1854 epidemic. In particular he concluded that "if the cholera had no other means of communication than those [claimed in the older theories] which we have been considering, it would be constrained to confine itself chiefly to the crowded dwellings of the poor, and would be continually liable to die out accidentally in a place, for want of the opportunity to reach fresh victims; but there is often a way open for it to extend itself more widely, and to reach the well-to-do classes of the community; I allude to the mixture of the cholera evacuations with the water used for drinking and culinary purposes." Likewise here: The idea of dignified merchants and free manufacturers can spread more widely and quickly than trade or empire or investment or an asserted British racial superiority, and can explain more easily how others came finally to master the trick. The United States, Belgium, France, Germany, Italy, Korea, Taiwan, Hong Kong, Spain, Thailand, Botswana, China, India, and their imitators grew because they did.

In modern economics the classic use of remainders was the productivity calculations made in the 1950s by John Kendrick, Moses Abramovitz, and Robert Solow (anticipated in 1933 by the economic historian G. T. Jones).[16] Using "marginal productivity theory," the economists took out the impact on output per head of sheer capital accumulation, piling brick on brick. Take out what you can measure directly, and what's left is what you can't—namely, the not-directly-measurable impact of innovation. The present book takes out what one can measure directly in the materialist and economistic explanations of the sharp rise of incomes after 1800, and finds their measure to be small. What's still left standing is—let us pray—the not-directly-measurable innovation released by the rhetorical change.

I assemble here a catholic sample of the scientific and philosophic work bearing on the hypothesis. I myself have done since the 1960s some research on economic history, especially British, and since the 1980s I've done some philosophical and literary-critical writing as well. But most of the evidence and reasoning I use here was discovered or invented by others. The book is an essay, not a monograph. Specialists will spot the old pieces of news.

We economic historians, for example, have known since the 1960s that capital accumulation can't explain the Industrial Revolution or its follow-on, the blade of the hockey stick. The news hasn't gotten around much to our academic colleagues. It is resisted even by a few sadly misled economic historians. Our economist colleagues in growth theory and economic development resist it fiercely. They want very much to go on believing that the quantity of output depends not on ideas independent of material causes but mainly on the labor applied and most especially on the masses of physical and human capital present, $Q = F(L, K)$—so lovely is the equation, so tough and masculine and endlessly mathematizable. And a left-leaning Department of French would simply be stunned to hear that innovation does *not* depend on accumulated capital ripped from the proletariat. The scientific finding, though, is elderly, and secure.

Likewise the literary critics know that the bourgeoisie read, and wrote, the European realist novel, from *Robinson Crusoe* to *Rabbit Is Rich*, celebrating and attacking the bourgeois virtues, though the critics differ on exactly how.[17] The related notion that novels and plays therefore teach a good deal about the history of bourgeois ideology and innovation, which will strike the average economist as scandalously unscientific, will provoke yawns in the Department of English. Yet that scientific finding, too, is elderly and secure.

(I use throughout the word "science," by the way, in the wide sense of "serious and systematic inquiry," which is what it means in every language except the English of the past 150 years: thus in Dutch *wetenschap*, as in *kunstwetenschap* ["art science," an English impossibility], in German *Wissenschaft* as in *die Geisteswissenschaften* [the humanities, literally a very spooky sounding "spirit sciences"], or in French *science* as in *les sciences humaines* [serious and systematic inquiries concerning the human condition, such as studies of literature or philosophy or anthropology, literally "the human sciences," another impossible contradiction in modern English], or plain "science" in English before 1850 or so. Thus Alexander Pope in 1711: "While from the bounded level of our mind / Short views we take, nor see the lengths behind: / But more advanced, behold with strange surprise / New distant scenes of endless *science* rise!"[18] He did not mean physics and chemistry. John Stuart Mill used the science word in its older sense in all his works.[19] Confining the word to "physical and biological science," sense 5b in the *Oxford English Dictionary*—which was an accident of English academic politics in the mid-nineteenth century—has tempted recent speakers of English to labor at the pointless task of demarcating one kind of serious and systematic inquiry from another.)

Likewise, no one in a department of philosophy, whether or not they agree with it, will be startled by "virtue ethics," explained in *The Bourgeois Virtues* (2006) and used here from time to time to talk about the ethical change in the Bourgeois Revaluation. (For example, I used it a while ago to speak of the virtues of hope and faith redirected by the Revaluation.) She might be more comfortable with Kantian and utilitarian arguments—in philosophical lingo, "deontological" and "consequentialist" ethics—which arose in the eighteenth century and which have since then dominated academic philosophy. The academic hegemony of utilitarianism 1789 to the present, for example, reappears in vulgar form in the business school's supposition that adding up "stakeholders" is the only ethical argument, or in the economics department's supposition that $U = U(X,Y)$ is the only way to think about human choice. But the philosopher will at least have heard of the more ancient theory, and of its recent and feminist revival. No surprise.

What is surprising in the book, and therefore less scientifically secure, is the claim that in the eighteenth century the ideal and the material connected, and powered the modern world. Even that hypothesis, however, has ancestors.

5

THE CORRECT STORY PRAISES "CAPITALISM"

The book is the second of a half dozen planned, three written including this second one, the first published in 2006, intended as a full-scale defense of our modern form of innovation—universally if misleadingly called "capitalism." The books are meant for skeptical people like you who think markets and innovations need such a defense. The implied readers of the books are at present rarities—a scientist who takes the humanities seriously, admitting that novels and philosophies are data, too; a humanist who enjoys calculation, admiring even economistic arguments; or a common reader who delights in listening patiently to evidence and reasoning that overturn most of his own left- or right-wing folklore about what happened in the economy 1600 to the present.[1]

Together the books make one big argument. The argument is: Markets and innovation, which are ancient but recently have grown dignified and free, are consistent with an ethical life. An ethical and rhetorical change in favor of such formerly dishonorable activities of the bourgeoisie—innovating a fulling mill for woolens or innovating a bank for paying florins in England easily—happened after 1300 in isolated parts of the European south (Florence, Venice, Barcelona), as in many other scattered locales in the world, and in many other eras, and after 1400 or so in other towns of the south (such as Lisbon) and the Hansa towns of the north, and after 1600 in larger chunks of the north (Holland), and after 1700 in England, Scotland, and British North America, and after 1800 in southern Belgium, the Rhineland, northern France, and then the world. Such words or conversations or rhetoric mattered to the economy, and still do. The words enabled after 1800 a big fall in poverty and a big rise in spirit.

Yet in the late nineteenth century the artists and the intellectuals—the "clerisy," as Samuel Taylor Coleridge and I call it—turned against liberal innovation. The treason of the clerisy led in the twentieth century to the pathologies of nationalism and socialism and national socialism, and in the twenty-first century to the pieties of radical environmentalism, and to the dismal pessimism of the union left and the traditional right. The clerisy provided the "scientific" justifications for such attitudes, as in scientific materialism or scientific imperialism or scientific racism or scientific Malthusianism or, lately, scientific neoeugenics. The scientific schemes reasserted an elite control over newly liberated poor people. Consider Mao's *Little Red Book*, say, or Hitler's *Mein Kampf*, which extracted from the scientific dreams of left or right a plan for an ant-colony society governed by the Party. Or consider the more polite versions of elite control, such as the great statistician Karl A. Pearson in 1900 approving of scientific racism in support of imperialism: "It is a false view of human solidarity, which regrets that a capable and stalwart tribe of white men should advocate replacing a dark-skinned tribe which can . . . [not] contribute its quota to the common stock of human knowledge."[2] In 1925 he wrote against Eastern European Jewish migration to Britain, on the grounds that "this alien Jewish population is somewhat inferior physically and mentally to the native population," for example in "cleanliness of clothing."[3] Or consider the great American jurist Oliver Wendell Holmes, Jr., sneering in 1895 in social Darwinist style that "from societies for the prevention of cruelty to animals up to socialism, we express . . . how hard it is to be wounded in the battle of life, how terrible, how unjust it is that any one should fail."[4] In 1927 he approved of compulsory sterilization on grounds of scientific utilitarianism and eugenics: "It is better for all the world, if instead of waiting to execute degenerate offspring for crime, or to let them starve for their imbecility, society can prevent those who are manifestly unfit from continuing their kind. The principle that sustains compulsory vaccination is broad enough to cover cutting the Fallopian tubes. Three generations of imbeciles are enough."[5] Sadly, such stuff wasn't "junk science" or "pseudoscience," easily demarcated by methodological rule from the real stuff. It was regular, front-line, widely accepted science, such as now the environmentalism without economic content published regularly in *Science*. Science is a wonder, but it is not always the same as wisdom. And a little learning is a dangerous thing.

The clerisy's anti-innovation and antimarket and antiliberty rhetoric in the years since 1848, though repeated down to yesterday, misapprehends the scientific history. The clerisy says that every spillover in the environment justifies world-governmental control. Scientific economics suggest that it does not. Some spillovers are best treated at the local level, or by making not less private property, but more. The clerisy says that lack of elite control of human breeding will cause the race to degenerate. Scientific genetics suggests that it does not. Human abilities flourish from diversity, as they will in a while in Africa. The clerisy says that innovation impoverishes people. Scientific economics suggests that it does not, as it has not in Hong Kong. It enriches most of them. The clerisy says that state planning or nationalist mobilization is better than voluntary commercial peace. Scientific history suggests not, as it did not in the USSR. Socialism and nationalism have regularly disrupted the prosperity provided by bourgeois commerce. The clerisy says that the modern urban world is alienated. Scientific sociology replies on the contrary that bourgeois life in France strengthened numerous if weak ties, and freed people from village tyrannies, as it did in modern Spain or Greece. The clerisy says that the market and its economic liberties are politically dangerous. Political science suggests that on the contrary they give ordinary people dignity and make them mild and tolerant, as they have in the Netherlands and Sweden, at any rate by the standards of alternative arrangements.

The present book is the second, I say, in a set of six called The Bourgeois Era. The Bourgeois Era offers an "apology" for the modern world—in the Greek sense of a defense at a trial, and in the theological sense, too, of a preachment to you-all, my best-beloved infidels or ultraorthodox or middle-of-the-road. My beloved friends on the political left have joined with my also beloved, but also misled, friends on the political right in asserting that capitalism, as Marx put it in 1867, is "solely the restless stirring for gain. This absolute desire for enrichment, this passionate hunt for value."[6] Many on the left have been outraged by what they take to be the bad material results of the history—though misapprehended, because the desire for enrichment is after all universal, and the material results of its modern bourgeois fulfillment have in fact been startlingly good for the world's poor, not bad. Many on the right have on the contrary been pleased by the same misapprehended history. They join their opponents on the left in believing that Marx was right to define the modern world as the restless stirring for gain. Such greed, they affirm with a smirk, is "good" for three-car garages and time-shares in Barbados. Get used to it.

And on both political wings many of a less ruthless character are dismayed by the spiritual vulgarity they detect in a novel greed. They look into the future darkly. Such pessimism typifies some on the left (though accompanied by a longer-term apocalyptic optimism), who see in every business downturn the final crisis of global capitalism. Another sort of pessimism typifies some on the right (accompanied by no such longer-term optimism), who see in every new cultural fashion a corruption arising from the rule of the vulgar.

Admittedly, myopic pessimism, from the right or left, sells. The late Allan Bloom's right-wing pessimism, *The Closing of the American Mind* (1987), sold half a million copies merely in hardback. Shortly afterward, at a little conference we both attended, Allan was the assigned commentator on an essay of mine entitled "If You're So Smart, Why Aren't You Rich?" He started with a little joke: "I should note that I now *am* rich." Paul Ehrlich's *The Population Bomb* (1968) sold three million copies total, and little or none of what it confidently predicted came to pass. I bought a copy of Ravi Bahtra's *The Great Depression of 1990* (another event which didn't happen, though in 1987 that book, too, sold well) at a prepulping sale in 1992 for $1.57. I show it to my students as an exhibit against economic pessimism.

So I admit that my optimistic view of the modern world and especially of its long-term prospects is less profound than the Chicken Little predictions of my good friends on the right and on the left. Still, when set beside the conviction that the End is Near, the optimistic, anti–Chicken Little view I retail here has at least the merit of being scientifically correct.

The first volume, *The Bourgeois Virtues: Ethics for an Age of Commerce* (2006), asked whether a bourgeois life can be ethical. It replied that it is, and was, and could be, and should be. The present volume, as I've said, makes the case for an ethico-rhetorical Industrial Revolution by criticizing on economic and historical grounds the materialist explanations. I'm not happy to be so critical of a materialist economics that I have loved and learned and taught since 1961. An economist like me loves the routine of trade or of accumulation or property, which are things she understands pretty well, and can even calculate. Allow me to show you on the blackboard the proofs that protectionism is bad and that investment is good. And look here: I can show with a little math that a lack of private property leads to a tragedy of the commons. Beautiful stuff.[7]

By contrast, ideas and rhetoric stand at present outside her economic science. Even the best economists fail to notice that humans are talking animals and that the human animals put more of meaning into their talk than

"I bid $2.71828."[8] In explaining the most important economic event since the invention of agriculture, or perhaps since the invention of language, the facts seem to demand a rejection of the materialist and antirhetorical ideology I so long advocated. A materialist economic science appears, in other words, to need a good deal of amending.

The opposite of "materialist" is not exactly "idealist," if by that is understood a Hegelian notion of an Absolute Sprit or the like. The scientific alternative to a dogmatically materialist, positivist, behaviorist ideology would still admit that the mode of production matters, sometimes. But it would note that talk matters, too. Consider the parallel terms in a nonphilosopher's philosophizing, "objective" and "subjective." As any philosopher after the critics of Descartes can tell you, neither objective nor subjective can be had (recent philosophers have put the point in a more sophisticated way, but it still approximately holds). If the "objective" is "what is really there in God's eyes," what Kant called the "noumena," we humans here below will never quite see it, short of the Second Coming. Is the universe made from strings? Does the communion wafer change in essence to Christ's body? Is it possible for the Cubs to win the World Series? And if the "subjective" is what is in my mind, you can never really know it (notice the rhetorical force of the word "really" in such statements). Do you really experience the color red the same way I do? Neither of us will ever know. Do all the brain scans you want: you can't feel exactly like me.

What we *can* know is neither objective nor subjective, but (to coin a word) "conjective," what we know together in our talk.[9] Spell it out: conjective, *together* thrown. The chief discovery of the humanities in the twentieth century was that a human science must be about the conjective, the palpable phenomena to examine. No science can be about the hopelessly unattainable objective or subjective. As Niels Bohr put it, even physics is about what we humans can say. The conjunctivist admits of course that a clam sits in the sea, perhaps even in God's eyes, but she points out that what constitutes a "fruit of the sea" for eating purposes is always a matter of agreement among humans. That doesn't make "clam" a figment, but it does make it conjective. As Sahlins put it in 1976, rejecting the "procrustean opposition of 'idealism' and 'materialism' by which the discussion customarily proceeds," a human "must live in a material world, [a] circumstance he shares with all organisms, but . . . he does so according to a meaningful scheme of [human] devising, . . . according to a definite symbolic scheme which is never the only one possible."[10] He says elsewhere that "nature as it exists in itself is only the raw material provided by the hand of God, waiting to be given meaningful [note the word] shape and content by the mind of man. It is as the block of marble to the finished statue."[11]

It all strikes me now as obviously so. But when Sahlins first said it (he following many others from Protagoras to Dewey and James, to Wittgenstein, with his contemporaries Geertz and Rorty) I rejected it out of hand.

I am not, believe me, an idealist by predilection. I'm a disappointed materialist. I was in the early 1970s a stubbornly ignorant positivist, as most economists are, but came gradually to realize that the conjective is what we can know. You should become a conjectivist, too.

A third volume, soon to appear, *The Bourgeois Revaluation: How Innovation Became Virtuous, 1600–1848*, shows in detail how attitudes toward bourgeois life changed. A fourth, tentatively called *Bourgeois Rhetoric: Interest and Conversation during the Industrial Revolution*, develops an amended economic science acknowledging that humans do speak their meanings, and shows how their speaking changed to make possible the bourgeois dignities and liberties and revaluations and rising boats.[12] It cashes in the claim by the economist and philosopher Frank Knight in 1935 that "economics is a branch of aesthetics and ethics to a larger degree than of mechanics."[13] A fifth volume, *Bourgeois Enemies: The Treason of the Clerisy, 1848 to the Present*, will explore how after the failed revolutions of 1848 we European artists and intellectuals became in our rhetoric so very scornful of the bourgeoisie, and how the gradual encroachment of such ideas motivated the disasters of the twentieth century—and how they can motivate fresh disasters if we neglect to contradict the left- or right-wing theories. And the last, *Bourgeois Times: Defending the Defensible*, will look into present-day anti-innovation and antimarket rhetoric, such as the alleged sins of globalization, the despoilment of the environment, the evil of commercial free speech known as advertising, the alleged dependence of innovation on an alleged reserve army of the unemployed.

The books lean on each other. If your worries about the ethical foundations of innovation and markets are not sufficiently met here, they perhaps are more fully met in *The Bourgeois Virtues*. If you feel that not enough attention is paid here to unemployment or global warming, more will be paid in *Bourgeois Times*. If you wonder how the present book can claim that words matter so much, consider *The Bourgeois Revaluation* and *Bourgeois Rhetoric*.

If you feel that the story here does not explain why such a successful bourgeois life came to be despised in deeply progressive and deeply conservative circles, some of your questions will be answered in *Bourgeois Enemies*.

The apology does seem to take six volumes. I apologize. A philosopher recently wrote, to explain why he crammed his opus on "warranted [Christian] belief" into three stout books rather than allowing himself four, that "a trilogy is perhaps unduly self-indulgent, but a tetralogy is unforgivable."[14] Here you have in prospect, God help you, a sestet, and this is merely volume 2.[15] But bourgeois life and innovation since 1848 have had a voluminously bad press, worse even than warranted Christian belief. The prosecution in the past two centuries has written out the indictment of the developing free and bourgeois and business-respecting civilization in many thousands of eloquent volumes, from the hands of Robert Southey and Schiller and Carlyle and Dickens (the critics of innovation, I repeat, were not all of the left), of Alexander Herzen, Baudelaire, Marx, Engels, Mikhail Bukharin, Ruskin, William Morris, Nietzsche, Prince Kropotkin (my hero at age fourteen, when I fell in love with socialist anarchism down at the local Carnegie-financed library), Tolstoy, Shaw, Ida Tarbell, Upton Sinclair, Rosa Luxemburg, Emma Goldman (another admired figure, when I later as a young economist reaffirmed antistatist convictions), D. H. Lawrence, Bertrand Russell, Lenin, Trotsky (companion of a brief adolescent flirtation with communism), John Reed (ditto), Veblen, Ortega y Gasset, Sinclair Lewis, T. S. Eliot, Virginia Woolf, Mussolini, Giovanni Gentile, Hitler, Heidegger, Wittgenstein, F. R. Leavis, Karl Polanyi, Walter Benjamin, Sartre, Simone de Beauvoir, Simone Weil, Dorothy Day, Woody Guthrie (whose songs and singing made me for a while in college a Joan Baez socialist—the leftish critics of bourgeois dignity and liberty have all the best tunes), Pete and Peggy Seeger (ditto), Ewan MacColl (so too), Lewis Mumford, Hannah Arendt, Herbert Marcuse, Maurice Merleau-Ponty, J. K. Galbraith, Louis Althusser, Allan Bloom, Fredric Jameson, Saul Bellow, Howard Zinn, Noam Chomsky, Eric Hobsbawm, E. H. Carr, E. P. Thompson, Ernest Mandel, Immanuel Wallerstein, Paul Ehrlich, Stuart Hall, C. L. R. James, George Steiner, Jacques Lacan, Stanley Hauerwas, Terry Eagleton, Alain Badiou, Slavoj Žižek, Charles Sellers, Barbara Ehrenreich, Naomi Klein, Nancy Folbre (a personal friend), Jamie Galbraith (ditto), and Jack Amariglio (double ditto). Few people have defended commerce from this magnificent flood of eloquence from the pens of left progressives and right conservatives—jeremiads against markets and innovation which stretch from the Hebrew prophets through Plato and the

Analects of Confucius down to the present—except on the economist's Prudence Only grounds that after all a great deal of money is made there. In offering merely six volumes in defense, after such grand prolixity in the prosecution, I admire my restraint. As Henry Fielding wrote toward the end of *Tom Jones*, a "prodigious" book, "When thou hast perused the many great events which this book will produce, thou wilt think the number of pages contained in it scarce sufficient to tell the story."[16]

The Bourgeois Era, in other words, tries to initiate a defense of our bourgeois lives that goes beyond economic balance sheets, without ignoring them. It offers the outlines of an ethical rhetoric for our globalized souls, an idealism of ordinary life such as Henrik Ibsen and Willa Cather were formulating. It recoups the virtues for the lives, neither heroic nor saintly, that most of us in fact live. If you were raised on the left or the left-middle and were taught to believe that innovation and the bourgeois life were born in sin, and that they impoverish and corrupt the world, as in globalization and financial meltdowns, perhaps one or two of the books can plant a seed of doubt. And likewise, perhaps, the books can plant the self-critical seed if you were raised on the right or the right-middle and were taught to believe that (admittedly) capitalism is "solely the restless stirring for gain, this absolute desire for enrichment," yet a materially efficacious desire for enrichment— but that the economists and calculators have corrupted our holiness and demeaned our nobility, as in rock music and feminism and deconstruction since the 1960s, and the glory of Europe is extinguished forever.[17]

What the philosopher Charles Taylor said about "authenticity" my books say about "innovation": "The picture I am offering is rather that of an ideal that has degraded but that is very worthwhile in itself, and indeed, I would like to say, unrepudiable by moderns. . . . What we need is a work of retrieval, through which this ideal can help us restore our practice."[18] Innovation backed by probourgeois rhetoric made people well-to-do, and made possible the modern pursuit of authenticity. The sestet of the Bourgeois Era can perhaps persuade you, whether progressive or conservative or standing in between, that your belief that innovation is especially greedy, and the bourgeoisie sadly ignoble and unspiritual, might—just might—be mistaken. And as a work of retrieval perhaps it will persuade you that to continue attacking a virtuous life in commerce, or for that matter to continue defending a greedy life in commerce, corrupts our souls, and poisons our politics.

6

MODERN GROWTH WAS A FACTOR

OF AT LEAST SIXTEEN

The heart of the matter is sixteen. Real income per head nowadays exceeds that around 1700 or 1800 in, say, Britain and in other countries that have experienced modern economic growth by such a large factor as sixteen, at least.[1] You, oh average participant in the British economy, go through at least sixteen times more food and clothing and housing and education in a day than an ancestor of yours did two or three centuries ago. Not sixteen percent more, but sixteen *multiplied* by the old standard of living. You in the American or the South Korean economy, compared to the wretchedness of former Smiths in 1653 or Kims in 1953, have done even better. And if such novelties as jet travel and vitamin pills and instant messaging are accounted at their proper value, the factor of material improvement climbs even higher than sixteen—to eighteen, or thirty, or far beyond. No previous episode of enrichment for the average person approaches it, not the China of the Song Dynasty or the Egypt of the New Kingdom, not the glory of Greece or the grandeur of Rome.

No competent economist, regardless of her politics, denies the Great Fact. The economist Stephen Marglin, for example, emphasizes community, which he believes was undermined by the Fact and its accompanying rhetoric of Prudence Only. As a convinced socialist he believes that power and striving had more to do with the Fact than a free-market economist believes.[2] Yet both a neo-Marxist economist and a free-market economist accept the great magnitude of the enrichment as a Fact. Likewise the economic historian Gregory Clark emphasizes a Darwinian struggle for eminence, which he believes explains the Fact. As a recently convinced eugenicist he thinks that people are fated to be who they were born to be, which a true liberal finds ethically alarming, and anyway scientifically dubious.[3] Yet both a eugenic economist and a true liberal economist accept that the Fact broke the Malthusian curse.

Many noneconomists or nonhistorians, though, whether in their politics left or right, are suspicious of innovation and hostile to markets, and remain unaware of the magnitude involved. They know *something* happened, of course—and that a vulgarly bourgeois apologist will claim "progress," probably disputable and in any case deeply damaging to the poor, or to a graceful life. But the noneconomists and the nonhistorians left and right and middle have little idea of how very, very enriching the Fact has been for ordinary poor people, and how enabling of graceful lives of authenticity. They worry that in the Neoliberal Order (as the economic historian Angus Maddison calls it), 1973 to the present, growth rates in the parts of the world that have rejected or regulated bourgeois dignity and liberty have fallen, sometimes to below zero. They do not realize that even including the places with the bad luck to reject liberalism the world's growth rate recently has been far above the rates 1913–1950, a little above 1870–1913, and gigantically above anything seen before 1870.[4] If you ask the regular readers of the *Nation* or of the *National Review* how much more material ease the average American had gained by the time of President Clinton as compared with President Monroe they will come up with a figure such as . . . go ahead: make a guess . . . perhaps, 200 percent or even 400 percent, maybe 800 percent—not, as is the case, *1,700* percent, a factor of nearly eighteen, which is a lower bound on the American history. It is to be compared with the 1,500 percent in Britain. Both were astounding.

The lack of precision in the estimates is worth the attention of specialists. But it is not important for the purpose here. The British or American or Japanese or South Korean increase could have been eight or ten or thirty-five times its level in 1700, rather than sixteen or eighteen, and leave the heart of the matter undisturbed. People had always produced and consumed about $3 a day. By now they consume $30 a day if they are average denizens of the world, and $137 if Norwegians. The scientific fact established over the past fifty years by the labors of economists and economic historians is that modern economic growth has been astounding, unprecedented, unexpected, the greatest surprise in economic history. It fulfilled and overfulfilled the egalitarian vision of Levellers and radical *philosophes* and Tom Paine.

For the first time the economy performed for the People instead of mainly for the Privileged.

"*Real* national income per head" purports to measure what is earned by the average person in the nation as a whole, taking out merely monetary inflation. It measures the stuff per person we have—the pounds of bread or the number of haircuts, back and sides—not the mere dollars or yen. That's why economists call it "real," a word they favor. Thomas More disdained the grotesque consumerism of his early sixteenth-century England in which "four or five woolen cloaks and the same number of silk shirts are not enough for one [very well-off] person, and if he is a bit fastidious not even ten will do."[5] Nowadays the merely average person in England has the equivalent of twenty or thirty, and the fastidious boast hundreds. I once helped a friend in New Jersey sort through and rehang the T-shirts her family had accumulated. We got to three hundred that afternoon and stopped counting. By contrast, your great-great-great-great grandmother had a dress for church and a dress for everyday and maybe a coat, or at least a shawl, and maybe some shoes, or at least some clogs. In summer and in warm climes she went barefoot, and got hookworm.

If your ancestors lived in Finland the factor of real material improvement is more like twenty-nine, the average Finn in 1700 being only 60 percent better off in material terms than the average African at the time. If you are African American you are forty or fifty times better off than the Africans in your lineage in 1800. Since 1800 the average Norwegian has become also forty-five times better off. In 1700 the Netherlands was the most bourgeois and therefore the richest country in the world, 70 percent better off per capita than the soon-to-be United Kingdom. So if your ancestors lived in the Netherlands, the modern improvement is only a factor of roughly ten. It is measured, however, as all these figures are, in the cautious way that does not take account of the high qualities of modern pills and housing and message-sending. The actual Dutch factor must be a lot higher—look at the average Jan Steen household in seventeenth-century paintings and compare it with the riches of Haarlem or Hilversum nowadays. In Japan the factor since 1700 is fully thirty-five.[6] Latin America, though its "lagging" is much lamented, still provides its poor with vastly more food and education than in 1800. In South Korea the cautiously measured factor since 1953, when income per head (despite access to some modern technology: motor trucks, electric lights) was about what it had been in Europe 450 years before, is almost eighteen. The South Korean revolution was crammed into four decades instead of, as in the first Dutch and British cases, stretched out over three centuries.

Like the realization in astronomy during the 1920s that most of the "nebulae" (Latin "mists, confusions, errors") detected by telescopes were in fact other galaxies unspeakably far from ours, the Great Fact of economic growth, discovered by historians and economists in the 1950s and elaborated since then, changes everything.

∞

And in truth the amount by which average welfare multiplied under actually existing innovation exceeds by far the official and cautious statistics. Stuff unimaginable in 1700 or 1820 crowds our lives, from anesthesia to air conditioning. The new stuff makes the factors of sixteen or eighteen or even thirty into gross understatements. The economist Steven Payson reckoned in 1994, using Sears, Roebuck catalogues, that the ability of goods to provide human satisfaction sharply increased during the years he studied, from 1928 to 1993. He compared the prices of "representative goods" in successive years, the "goods" being defined in terms of human abilities to make use of them and in terms of the physical laws constraining their development. The improvement in human abilities to visualize a scene in a Panasonic PV-22 camcorder with 8× zoom in 1993 over a Brownie camera in 1928 is constrained by the laws of optics and of the human eye and of the human imagination. Price differences in the catalogues can measure the value consumers put on such goods. Quite ordinary goods improved sharply over the period—Payson finds a quality improvement of 2.7 percent per year in men's shoes, 2.1 percent in sofas and love seats, 2.8 percent in gas ranges—implying more than a doubling of quality every thirty years or so. But goods that experienced paradigm shifts improved vastly more: an astounding 7.46 percent per year for the human cooling devices—electric fans in 1928 as against air conditioners in 1993—cumulating to a factor of eighty-eight times better service (with the largest change from 1953 to 1958, during the transition to air conditioning), and an even more astounding 9.25 percent per year for the visualizing devices, Brownie as against Panasonic, concentrated in 1969 and 1973.[7] The official way in which 1928 prices are made equivalent to 1993 prices of goods does not begin to capture such improvements as Payson detected.

William Nordhaus, a very useful economist at Yale, starts his 1997 paper on the economic history of lighting with the conventionally measured factor of eighteen in American real income per head since 1800, or a factor of thirteen if one is talking about real wages rather than real total income per head.[8] The economist Lawrence Officer has recently shown that real earnings in American manufacturing, allowing for all forms of compensation (such as old age insurance and health care), rose in fact much further over the period, some thirty-seven times.[9] Nordhaus notes, however, what is known to all us professional economists (you amateurs will have to rely on common sense)—that the price indexes that are employed to take out the effects of inflation rise too steeply, because the stuff being priced gets better and gives more services for each supposedly inflation-corrected dollar. Air conditioning instead of fans à la Payson. Three-car garages in the standard house instead of one-car garages. Electric lights instead of candles. Anesthesia instead of a pint of whiskey and a bit for your teeth.

Such unmeasured improvement in quality has happened recently, to take a politically sensitive example, from 1970 to 1992, when the United States and many other countries saw a stagnation of real wages officially measured—the official money wage divided by the official consumer price index. You will hear critics on the left saying that the ordinary person in the United States did not gain anything from 1970 to 1992, and is still struggling. They want to believe, always, that the Final Crisis of Capitalism is upon us. The leftward critics are not entirely wrong in their worry about the period before the Clinton boom. The conventional measure of prices from 1970 to 1992, though, didn't adequately reflect the rising space per dollar of housing and the cheapening visualizing of cameras and the rarely puncturing automobile tires. Most economists reckon that on account of quality improvements the inflation rate conventionally measured was overstated in the period by about 1 percent a year (and continues to be overstated by about the same extent).[10] When allowing for the better quality of goods and services, therefore, the period of nominal stagnation in real wages witnessed (at 1 percent per year and no other improvement) a rise of about a third in the properly corrected real wage, which is what matters.[11]

The gain per head of merely 1 percent a year is not wonderful economic growth. The American average since 1820 has been in real terms per head more like 2 percent.[12] Something bad did happen to the rate of innovation in the American economy from 1970 to 1992. And therefore the real wages of ordinary folk did not rise at the rate they had for example from 1945 to 1970.

The event certainly bears examining, and lamenting. The economist Benjamin Friedman has shown how politics deteriorates as rates of growth decline toward zero.[13] One percent is perilously close to zero, and sure enough the politics of the United States and other advanced countries such as Britain became correspondingly nasty in the period. Yet neither was the growth among ordinary people literally zero, as my friends on the left so confidently and indignantly claim. Capitalism wasn't in crisis from 1970 to 1992. During and after those years it raised the standard of living of poor people worldwide at the fastest rate in history (and after the dot-com boom of the 1990s, according to the economist Robert Gordon, the American economy itself stopped rewarding the very rich disproportionately). The real welfare of workers in the United States 1970–1992 did not in fact stagnate—as you can see in the statistics of housing space per person or automobiles per person or restaurant meals per person. It modestly rose, from continuing innovation, such as automatic hammers for housing construction and fast-food chains widening the reach of their noxious but cheap fare. Anyone who lived through the period knows that it did, though the official and uncorrected statistics can overcome her common sense. From 1968 to 1993 Payson's five Sears catalogue providers of satisfaction from walking, sitting, cooking, cooling, and visualizing sharply improved in quality.[14] Too little of the improvement is captured in the conventional consumer price index.

And the very poor got much better off materially, even in the recent period of growing inequality. The historian, demographer, and Nobel economist Robert Fogel's point in a 2002 book is that the United States has a much smaller problem by now with the *physical* condition of the poor—this in contrast to 1900—than with what he calls their "spiritual" condition.[15] Many Americans were physically miserable in 1900, but poor people now are not suffering mainly from physical deprivation—they are suffering instead from Drug War deprivation of their neighborhoods, or teachers'-union deprivation of their schools, or hip-hop deprivation of their children's ideals, or anti-black and anti-immigrant deprivation of their opportunities. Michael Cox and Richard Alm made some controversial assertions in a book of 1999 about the class mobility of the American poor. But their statistics on what the poor consume are not controversial. They conclude that "poor households of the 1990s in many cases compared favorably with an average family in owning the trappings of middle class life. For example, almost half the poor households in 1994 had air conditioners, compared to less than a third of the country as a whole in 1971."[16] That's right, as anyone knows who lived during the 1970s and knew poor people, or was herself poor. During the American 1940s, which some of us also lived through, really poor people didn't have running water or electricity, and no civilian (until after the war) had access to penicillin. The merely average poor person lived in half the space that a poor person lives in now, and didn't have a car. In 1938 Americans had a car for every 4.4 people, which left out the really poor; in 1960 Americans had a car for every 2.4 people; in 2003 for every 1.3 of a person. Even many very poor Americans in 2003 drove cars—even on occasion in 1938. When the Soviet authorities during the 1940s exhibited the 1940 movie of *The Grapes of Wrath* as evidence of how miserable the poor were in capitalist America, it backfired. What amazed the Soviet audiences was that the Joad family fled starvation *by car*.

∞

The longer-term point is that correctly measuring the prices of things greatly increases the estimate of modern economic growth, 1800 to the present. Is a house a house is a house? Not if the number of people per house falls: in 1910 nearly a quarter of American houses had bedrooms in which more than three people slept; in 1989 only 1 percent did. Older people know that when they were kids it was routine for siblings to share rooms; now it is routine for Junior to have his own room. In 1890 only a quarter of urban houses had running water; in 1989 virtually all did.[17] Cox and Alm observe that a three-minute long-distance call across the U.S.A. in 1915 cost ninety hours of common labor.[18] In 1999 it cost a minute and a half. No wonder your great granny is always saying "This call must be costing you a fortune." It once did. In 1900, Cox and Alm note, a pair of scissors cost the modern per-labor-hour equivalent of $67, which is why in the old days a middle-class mother had the one pair, carefully guarded, and used it to make clothing, and only on special rainy days would she let Sis use it to cut up last year's Montgomery Ward catalogue for paper dolls. Fogel calculates that in 1875 in the United States the average family spent 74 percent of its income on food, clothing, and shelter. In 1995 it spent 13 percent.[19]

Nordhaus makes the point about the fall in the real cost of goods and services by studying over centuries the cost of one item, lighting.[20] Lighting is easy to measure, in lumen hours per dollar of expenditure, say, or more to the point in lumen hours per hour of human work to get the dollars.

Conventional price indexes of lighting can be tracked year by year with the money price of, say, tallow candles or the fancier wax candles, and this works fine for a while in the early nineteenth century, when candles were in fact the main source of indoor lighting. Yet over as long a period as 1800 to 1992 it would be crazy to take the price of wax candles, used nowadays of course only for ceremonial purposes, as "the price" of lighting. No, the service of lighting, Nordhaus observes, became much cheaper in the nineteenth century, with the provision of gaslights to towns, and the invention of broad wicks for oil lamps, and the marketing of whale oil for house lighting; and then it became a lot cheaper again with kerosene and coal oil, and then a whole lot cheaper with electric lighting, which itself has continued to cheapen down to the fluorescent replacements for incandescent bulbs we are now beginning to use. Cheap LED lighting cannot be far behind. It is increasingly used for traffic lights. In other words, we can easily follow the price of each such form of lighting in its own era, but not well across eras. "Better to eat dry bread by the splendor of gas," wrote the clergyman and wit Sydney Smith in 1820, "than to dine on wild beef by the light of candles."[21] The problem is worse for many products less measurable than lighting. What's the early nineteenth-century price of antidepressants? Movies on TV? The Internet? How much would you pay in 1850 to get from Chicago to London in seven and a half hours?

We can, though, follow the candlepower per hour generated by lighting of various sorts in actual use and compare it to the labor hours required to buy it. Nordhaus confirms what you might expect if you've watched a lot of British historical movies on TV: that the growth in effective lighting has been very, very large, in the tens of thousands of lumen hours per hour of labor. On South Dearborn Street in Chicago stands the seventeen-story Monadnock Building, lovingly restored to its historical ambiance down to every visible detail. (The northern half of the Monadnock, finished in 1891, was the last Chicago skyscraper to depend on thick, load-bearing masonry; the southern half, started in 1891, was among the first to depend on structural steel.) One of the restored details is the lighting in halls and elevators, with tiny incandescent lights reproducing the feeble glow of 1891. If you doubt that lighting has been revolutionized, visit the Monadnock Building.

Nordhaus reckons, to be crudely quantitative about it, that around 9000 BCE it took fifty hours of labor to gather enough bundled kindling or whatever to achieve a thousand lumen hours of lighting (think of our ancestors deep in the Altamira caves drawing aurochs and horses and the stick-figured humans hunting them). In 1800 with candles it took five hours (think of John Adams scribbling by luxurious wax candlelight long letters to Talleyrand to prevent war with France). In 1900, thanks to kerosene and the new electric lights in town, feeble though they were, it took only 0.22 hours, a revolution, allowing long hours of reading after sunset. ("The house was quiet and the world was calm. / The reader became the book; and summer night / Was like the conscious being of the book.") In 1992, thanks to the radical cheapening of electricity-based lighting, it took a mere 0.00012 hours, a re-revolution. The outcome was a cheapening in eleven millennia by a factor of 417,000, and in the last two centuries alone by 41,700 (note the over-neat homology in the figures: Nordhaus is not claiming to measure very accurately; it is orders of magnitude he seeks). And the rate of fall in the past two centuries, of course, was immensely accelerated compared with the mere factor of ten between the age of olive oil lamps in Roman times and the age of European candles in Georgian times (such as Benjamin Franklin as a boy helped his father make)—showing the stunning enrichment from very recent European technology. (And it shows, too, the Chinese exception as to the level of technology, if not its modern rate of change. In the fourth century BCE some of the Chinese were using *natural gas* for lighting, and later they carried the gas about in bags.)[22]

Look around your house or street this evening and assess the lighting you get and how many candles would be its equivalent—if you could cram in the candles, as in the Great Hall scenes of Harry Potter movies, or Scandinavian parties at Christmas, or the Sistine Chapel, whose ceiling painting was damaged by centuries of candle smoke. If you fancy that it would be oh-so-romantic to live back in such ill-lit days, then the economic and social historians suggest gently that you think again. In the days of candles the average adult slept ten hours a night in winter rather than the eight she now sleeps. The miserable cold of an evening was literally not worth the candle, and dark prevailed late on a summer night, when the house was quiet and the world was calm.

Nordhaus extends the argument, more speculatively but plausibly, to other inventions such as airplanes, insulin, radar, telephones, and the rest, and in a rough guess to all sectors of the economy. (The great student of national income, Angus Maddison, scorned the calculations under a sneering heading: "Hallucinogenic History: Nordhaus and [Bradford] DeLong." But in the passage Maddison stayed uncharacteristically at the level of indignation, and gave no reasons.)[23] What an hour of work could buy of lighting and all sorts of things, Nordhaus reckons, has dramatically risen since 1800 if you take into account the rise in the quality of such goods as "lighting" and "housing" and "transportation" and "medical care" and the rest.

Take medical care. The doctor and essayist Lewis Thomas, dean of Yale's and New York University's medical schools, "the father of modern immunology," reckoned that until the 1920s going to a doctor lowered your odds of survival. Most medical care was done at home, and a middle-class home in the 1920s in well-to-do countries was always supplied with a big one-volume medical encyclopedia about how to care at home for scarlet fever and how to deliver babies. Mothers were nurses. The biggest improvement didn't come until the late 1940s, with penicillin for civilian use. Andrew Carnegie despite his wealth could not buy a cure for the pneumonia that killed his mother, and the great sociologist Max Weber died at the height of his powers in 1920 of pneumonia, too—a disease I myself have had twice, and was cured of the last time in three days.[24] Or take psychiatry. Until the coming of psychotropic drugs, invented during the 1950s and in common clinical use by the 1970s, the psychiatrists had nothing to do for depression (and at one point, to their shame, for homosexuality) but to talk gently to you, and then in desperation apply electroshock.

Nordhaus concludes that from 1800 to 1992 in the American economy the real wage—the money wage divided by the prices of things, but properly corrected for their improving thingness—grew not by that conventionally and crudely measured factor of thirteen, but anywhere from a low estimate of a factor of forty to a high of a factor of 190. One hundred and ninety. Good Lord. Call it as a rough and ready average a factor of one hundred. That's one hundred times greater ability to buy with an hour of work. Two orders of magnitude.

If you run your eyes around your room now and try to push back in imagination to the life of your great-great-great-great-grandmother, you will find pretty reasonable a factor of one hundred in per capita capacity-to-buy-the-services-of-stuff. You are reading now by a light many times brighter than the candlesticks your ancestor could bring to bear, and candles were anyway to be used sparingly, and only at dark of the moon, in order to get to the outhouse in Council Bluffs or to the end of a row in Salford without tripping and killing yourself. You, by contrast, have such light available in a score of places inside and outside your house.[25]

If you want to write to your lover it will be on a laptop with the calculating power of a building full of older "computers" (until the 1940s the word meant "women employed to add up long columns of figures"), on which you can type effortlessly, and then e-mail the note to the other side of the world in a split second (instead of the gradually lengthening days or weeks required by the Postal Service). Or when scribbling a shopping list you can use a ballpoint pen, which eases handwriting by a factor of perhaps six over quill and ink. You do not write much more quickly, but you spend no time at all the way your ancestor did sharpening quills or dipping ink—and the ink froze in the winter, because, remember, she had no central heating, and had to write with gloves with those little holes at the tips of the fingers. And in any case the ballpoint with which you now write, and the paper on which you write, cost a trivial amount of your time to buy, compared to earlier hours of work per fountain pen or paper sheet. When ballpoints were first introduced after World War II they were expensive like fountain pens, requiring many hours of your work to buy. Now you have forty or fifty of them jammed in various coffee mugs around your house—by actual count I have about a hundred (but after all, my work is scribbling). The clerk in the store often forgets to take back his pen when you sign a credit-card slip. And come to mention it, the credit facilities you enjoy are many times more efficient than the means of payment in 1800. The book you bought with the credit card costs a fraction of what a book did in 1800 in terms of human labor. The paper is cheap, the printing electronic, the binding done by machine. Some bookstores now have automatic machines with any of *two million* out-of-print titles which can be made into a physical book on the spot in twenty minutes. And Google is working to supply you with access to twelve million titles in the ether. A poor but devoted scholar sitting in Bogotá will have instant, searchable command of the whole of the University of Michigan library. For this and thousands of other similar reasons, your real income is vastly higher than that of your ancestors—and so you can have many more books than even Thomas Jefferson did, if you are a bookish sort, purchasing with ease from Sandmeyer's Bookstore or the Seminary Co-op in Chicago or Powell's Books in Portland or Amazon.com, or from Google. That is your widened scope. And on and on.

You can see the factor of one hundred from the other, producing side of the economy in the frantic development of new and improved products for consumers. American grocery stores try out something like ten thousand new products every year. A friend of mine in advertising had the Pringle's Newfangled Potato Chips account back in the 1970s when they still tasted like cardboard. New, new, new. The economic historian Maxine Berg has argued persuasively for "incorporating product innovation [that is, new and improved stuff] into the analysis of the industrial revolution."[26] She cites an American economic historian, the late Kenneth Sokoloff, arguing that new products drove a good deal of industrial innovation in the United States early in the nineteenth century, giving demand a role in innovation.[27] Neglecting product as against process innovation is what Gordon and Payson and Nordhaus are complaining about: it results in a gigantic understatement of the rising scope of modern economies, because a light bulb (if you have electric service in your house, that is) is a much better consumer product for achieving lighting than a candle, as an air conditioner is better for achieving cooling than a 1928 electric fan. Against the focus on process innovation usual in studies of the Industrial Revolution, Berg finds in British patents in the eighteenth century an astonishing proliferation of carved or molded glass, retractable toast racks, japanning (with a polite bow to the reverse engineering of Eastern inventions), tin plate buttons, and 115 patents for stamping, pressing, and embossing metals.[28]

Not that process innovations are to be set aside. The point is that process innovation is itself entangled with product innovation. Berg notes that "producers of small tools as well as complex lathes and engines" that made for faster production of a given product "were often the same individuals producing ornamental stamped brassware, medallions and mechanical toys."[29] Products for consumers led to producers' goods for factories. And the correct measurement of producers' goods has the same problem of better and better quality that the measurement of consumers' goods has. Using, like Payson, the Sears, Roebuck catalogues as historical sources, and with the econometrics of hedonic price indices, Robert Gordon, who pioneered these methods in the 1970s, found that the rate of rise of the prices of producers' goods (lathes, motors, and so forth) have like consumer goods been substantially overstated by not including their improving quality.[30] In short, we're *much* better off now compared to 1800, even than the exploding conventional measures of national product suggest.

7

INCREASING SCOPE, NOT POT-OF-PLEASURE
"HAPPINESS," IS WHAT MATTERED

To be sure, the new and better and more abundant stuff—which remember covers nonstuff stuff like haircuts and education and entertainment—does not include all of human fulfillment and does not measure even what it claims to measure perfectly well. The forests primeval and the hosts of golden daffodils have shrunk (though on the other hand ordinary people with more leisure and more means of travel can reach the remaining spots more cheaply in hours of labor spent, to visit, say, the South Rim of the Grand Canyon in early July, or in late January if they want the experience without crowds). And the extra utility coming from each addition to the gigantic new pile of stuff, as the economists say, diminishes. You may own eighteen times more chairs than your ancestors in 1700, but you don't enjoy eighteen times more chair-sitting pleasures. In other words, this radical, hundred-fold increase is an increase in possibilities, strictly defined, and is not measured on the same scale of happiness viewed as cat-like pleasures of the day, or even as the deeper goal of human fulfillment. In discussing Nordhaus's results, the equally useful economists Timothy Bresnahan and that same Robert Gordon note that the utility from the last unit of increase of lighting, from ninety-nine- to one-hundred-fold (which after all is only 1 percent), is surely a great deal less than that from the first few, from two- to three- to four-fold.[1] The one hundredth ballpoint is less pleasure-producing than the second or third. "Diminishing returns," or more exactly in this case diminishing "marginal utility," is one of the pieces of economic jargon that have slipped into the common tongue, like "GDP" or "the balance of payments." You are pretty much right in your idea of what it means.

Doubtless, if she were lucky enough in 1800 to miss smallpox and mal-nourishment, the Scottish nut-brown maiden, "Her eye so mildly beaming / Her look so frank and free," matched in happiness (viewed in pot-of-pleasure terms) the average person on the streets of Glasgow nowadays. At any rate, that is what recent research on "happiness" claims, and somewhat plausibly.[2] The economist, historian, and demographer Richard Easterlin, who introduced happiness studies into economics, concluded recently that "how people feel they ought to live . . . rises commensurately with income. The result is that while income growth makes it possible for people better to attain their aspirations, they are not happier because their aspirations, too, have risen."[3] A poor Glasgow maiden with an IQ of 140 in 1800 could aspire to no better position than head cook in an aristocratic house, and was very glad of that—her equally intelligent mother had aspired to head milkmaid. The new cook was "happy."

Easterlin argues, against the "freedom-from-want" claims of scholars like Abraham Maslow and Ronald Inglehart (believing that the hierarchy of needs can in fact be satisfied), that "economic growth is a carrier of a material culture of its own that ensures that humankind is forever ensnared in the pursuit of more and more economic goods."[4] The "happiness" literature, you can see, is predisposed to find modern levels of consumption vulgar and corrupting, a pointless arms race. The field has become one of the scientific legs of the century-old campaign by the American clerisy against the "consumerism" to which the nonclerisy are so wretchedly enslaved, as described in the writings of the economist Robert Frank or the sociologist Juliet Schor or the economist Tibor Scitovsky or indeed the sociological economist of a century ago, the great Thorstein Veblen.[5]

Admittedly, we are "ensnared," even "enslaved." Social science since Veblen, however, has discovered a reply: *any* level of income is a "carrier of a material culture," $3 a day as much as $137 a day. The anthropologists and psychologists and even an occasional economist point out that any meal-taking or shelter-building or tale-telling "ensnares" its people, the Bushmen of the Kalahari no less than the Floor Traders of Wall Street.[6] The economic historian Stanley Lebergott asked "What society is committed to mere physical survival?" and quoted Whitehead: "Men are children of the Universe with . . . irrational hopes. . . . A tree sticks to its business of mere survival; and so does an oyster."[7] Not us. Sahlins puts it this way: "Men do not merely 'survive.' They survive in a definite way," the way of the tribe.[8]

"Consumerism," such as the extracaloric value of a meal of grubs and rabbit meat shared over the campfire by beloved fellow tribespeople, characterizes all human cultures—which rather undermines the scientific or political usefulness of the term.

Easterlin urges us to resist consumerism and become "masters of growth."[9] One wants to be wary of such urgings that "we" do something, since the "we" is so easily corrupted, for instance by rabid nationalism, or by the mere snobbery of the clerisy. Easterlin would agree. But surely in an ethical sense he is right. "We" need to persuade each other to take advantage of modern freedom from want for something other than watching television and eating more Fritos and strutting about in a world of status-confirming consumption. We are ensnared, admittedly, as our ancestors were. Vanity of vanities, all is vanity, saith the Preacher, and vexation of spirit. In modern conditions of wide material scope, however, we would hope that the ensnaring would be worthy of the best versions of our humanness, ensnared by Mozart or by the celebration of the mass or by day five of a test match for the Ashes at Lord's on a perfect London day in early June. Yet that advice, to be nobly ensnared, has been a staple of world literature since the invention of writing. Ignoble enslavement in cockfights and excessive personal ornamentation has nothing much to do with the Great (and Liberating) Fact of modern growth—except that thanks to the Fact a vastly larger percentage of humanity can indulge in vaster vulgarities, yet because of education is open to the advice to avoid them. It should be sweetly persuasive advice, not a taxed, or a compelled, or even a nudged one, though of course determined by the clerisy's own justly admired standards.

Which raises another, humanistic criticism of the recent literature by economists on "happiness." The literature pays no attention to reflections on happiness that are nonquantitative or nonmathematical. ("Quantitative" and "mathematical," by the way, are not the same thing; often in the recent literature the two have no scientific connection, though hauled out separately to give an air of verisimilitude to an otherwise bald and unconvincing tale). In his recent book, *Happiness: A Revolution in Economics* (2008), the brilliant insider critic of economics, Bruno Frey, another friendly acquaintance of mine with whom I usually agree (like Richard Easterlin and Robert Frank), devotes just one sentence to discussing "happiness" before so-called "measurement" appears: "For centuries, happiness has been a central theme of philosophy."[10] That's it. Oh, dear, dear Bruno. He does not mention that happiness has been a central theme, too, of poetry and stories and biography and religion. The lone footnote attached to the lone sentence cites six items on "how philosophers have dealt with the topic of happiness"—six out of the approximately 670 items in the book's long bibliography. In the next sentence Frey turns firmly away from such rubbish, and toward "the empirical study of happiness"—as though Sophocles' *Antigone* or Plato's *Republic* gave no insight into happiness worthy of the word "empirical" (from the Greek "experience"), at any rate by comparison with asking random Greeks on the streets of Athens whether they are "happy" on a three-point noninterval scale.

The result is that "happiness," setting aside such silly ruminations on a full human life as the Bhagavad Gita or the Hebrew Bible, or the lives and works of Buddha or Aristotle or Rumi or Shakespeare or for that matter Adam Smith, is reduced to self-reported declarations—added up by scores 1 to 3 ("not very happy" = 1, "pretty happy" = 2, "very happy" = 3). An interviewer surprises you on the street, puts a microphone in your face, and demands to know, "Which is it, 1, 2, or 3?" Even the technical problems with such calculations are formidable. For one thing, a noninterval scale is being treated as an interval scale, as though a unit of 1.0 between 2 and 3 were God's own view of the difference between "pretty" and "very." It would be like measuring temperature by asking people to rate things as "pretty hot" = 2, "very hot" = 3, and expecting to build a science of thermodynamics on the "measurements" thus generated. For another, the literature regularly depends on misuse of the bankrupt notion of "statistical significance." Virtually every paper using the surveys takes "statistical significance" to be the same thing as scientific significance.[11] For still another, the measurement and the mathematical theory, as I've noted, live on different planes.

And the so-called "empirical" results thus achieved are often scientifically unbelievable on their face. Frey for example reports on results from 1994–1996 in the United States that claim the bottom decile of income earners to be "happy" to the extent of 1.94 on the 3-point scale, as against 2.36 for the top decile. One is gratified that the result is based on a massive, carefully done survey by the National Opinion Research Center. That's great. It can be compared and averaged and regressed, at any rate if one is willing to ignore the philosophical and technical problems. Yet does anyone actually believe that an American earning $2,596 a year in 1996 prices (which is the figure) and living in crime-ridden public housing was only 18 percent less happy in a seriously relevant sense than someone earning $61,836 and living in an apartment building with a doorman? (If you do not believe it, then you are not justified in regressing such a number on other variables.)

I realize that many of my respected colleagues in economics are willing to go along with such a fiction. I wish I could:

> "I can't believe *that!*" said Alice.
>
> "Can't you?" the Queen said in a pitying tone. "Try again: draw a long breath, and shut your eyes."
>
> Alice laughed. "There's no use trying," she said "one *can't* believe impossible things."
>
> "I daresay you haven't had much practice," said the Queen. "When I was your age, I always did it for half-an-hour a day. Why, sometimes I've believed as many as six impossible things before breakfast."

One of the proponents of happiness studies, the eminent British economist Richard Layard, is fond of noting that "happiness has not risen since the 1950s in the U.S. or Britain or (over a shorter period) in western Germany."[12] Such an unbelievable allegation merely casts doubt on the relevance of "happiness" so measured. No one who lived in the United States or Britain in the 1950s (I leave judgments on West Germany in the 1970s to others) could believe, before or after breakfast, that the age of *Catcher in the Rye* or *The Loneliness of the Long-Distance Runner* was more fulfilling than recent life.

Even in their own dubiously "measured" terms, further, such facts have been plausibly disputed, for example by Inglehart and associates in 2008 on the basis of large, multicountry data sets. "Happiness [even measured in the unbelievable way, and therefore regressable] rose in forty-five of the fifty-two countries for which substantial time-series data were available. Regression analyses [even using the bankrupt notion of statistical significance] suggest that the extent to which a society allows free choice has a major impact on happiness."[13] And even in the allegedly depressive United States, Britain, and West Germany, the "change in percentage of those saying they are very happy from earliest to latest survey for all countries with a substantial time series" was very large—if, again, "large" in such numbers is meaningful in God's eyes.

The main problem, though, as I said, is that the insights of poets and tale-tellers and historians and philosophers from the beginning into what human happiness actually is have simply been bypassed. "Happiness" viewed as self-reported mood is surely not the purpose of a fully human life. If you were given a drug like Aldous Huxley's imagined soma, you would report a happiness of 3 to the researcher every time. Something is screwy. Ask yourself: if you could experience a wonderful life in half an hour hitched up to a super-duper machine (as the philosopher Robert Nozick put it), but then died, would you take the offer? Not unless you were about to die anyway. You have a life and an identity of your own, which you cherish, regardless of "happiness." The point is made by numerous modern philosophers—Mark Chekola (2007), for example, as earlier by Nozick and David Schmidtz— and by other philosophers and theologians and poets back to Confucius, Lord Krishna, and before.[14] If we economists are not going to get any deeper than the dubious pot-of-pleasure theory of happiness, perhaps we ought to stick with what we can in fact know scientifically—namely, national income properly measured, as "potential" or what I call "scope" or what Amartya Sen and Martha Nussbaum call "capabilities"—the ability to read, for example, or the potential to become the founder of a new business, or a cultivated talent as an artist.

Modern economic growth gives the scope to do much more, whether or not the opportunity has been fully seized by everybody. It is pointless to urge a Higher Life on people dying on the streets of Kolkata. That was Mother Teresa's project, and one can reasonably doubt its ethical value (if not in its own terms its theology). Sen and Nussbaum wisely turn away from pot-of-pleasure "happiness" and focus on the measurement of capabilities, which surely are much larger in Norway today than in India in 1800, or now.[15] The ancestors of the very clever professors, whether advocating or disputing pot-of-pleasure measures of happiness—Easterlin, Frank, Schor, Veblen, Frey, Layard, Chekola, Nozick, Schmidtz, McCloskey, Nussbaum, Sen—were illiterate peasants or impoverished shoemakers (well . . . perhaps not Sen's). Unless they were among the tiny group of privileged rajahs or bishops, or the still tinier group who achieved through spiritual exercises a state of nirvana or blessedness without the ephemeral things of this earth, they were not close to the "happiness" in any fully human sense that a rising percentage of the world's people now enjoy.

You can take a pessimistic line and claim with many critics of innovation that a "materialistic and individualistic culture," as Easterlin puts it, is created by economic growth. The evidence seems weak. As the historian Lisa Jardine has inferred from the paintings and other worldly goods admired in Europe 1400 to 1600, the "bravura consumerism" of the times was an expression of the Renaissance, and of "the fierce pride in mercantilism [by which she seems to mean "merchant-ness," not its more usual meaning of protectionist economic policies] and the acquisitiveness which fueled its enterprises . . . , a celebration of the urge to own, the curiosity to possess the treasures of other cultures."[16] Note, however, that on Jardine's evidence, materialism and individualism are not recent. They are not confined to Europe in the industrial era.

"Industrialization," writes the historian Peter Stearns in a drearily conventional way, "has brought a steady increase in materialism. . . . Consumerism, always associated with industrialization as cause and effect, focuses personal goals on the acquisition of goods, from Main Street to Moscow."[17] One wonders whether Professor Stearns has considered the world around him, in which people routinely devote themselves to lives of scholarship, or to accepting Christ as their personal savior, and whose children have become artists taking up lofts in every embourgeoisfying neighborhood in the country; or whether he has heard of the Renaissance. Consumption itself is a matter of talk, and modern lives give more materials to talk with. "The object," Sahlins observes, "stands as a human concept outside itself, as man speaking to man through the medium of things." In a rich world it is "capable of serving, even better than the differences in animal species [in the totemism of tribal humans], as the medium of a vast and dynamic scheme of thought."[18] For all the chatter in the journals of opinion about the wretched materialism of modern life, studies in the psychology of goods find that poor people in poor countries put more, not less, value on the possessions they do have than people who possess more. Such findings seem plausible, even on economic grounds: diminishing returns make your seventeenth Windsor chair less fascinating. One recent survey by social psychologists notes that "cultural critics frequently assert that people living in Western nations hold a stronger belief than those in less developed nations (or past societies) that happiness comes from increased affluence and material possessions, yet evidence in the literature [of that same questionable subjective well-being, alas] suggests otherwise."[19]

Stearns's conventional wisdom again: "Other [noncapitalist] cultural activities, including art, the humanities, religion, and the people who specialize in them, tend to lose ground." No they don't. In rich countries the museums and concert halls nowadays are full. The times of flowerings of high culture have uniformly been times of lively commerce, from ancient Greece through Song China and Renaissance Italy down to the Dutch Golden Age or the flowering of American high culture after World War II, with the additional stimulus then from revolutionized higher education. Among the thirty democratic countries of the Organization for Economic Cooperation and Development today some 27 percent of the adult population twenty-five to sixty-four years old have completed tertiary education, ranging from Turkey's 10 percent up to Canada's 47 percent.[20] The university graduates of Europe therefore probably now exceed its total population in 1800. Such booming cultural activity makes for many lives beyond materialism. The economist of culture Tyler Cowen points out that modern life has produced more artists alive today than all artists in previous ages combined.[21] During the 1960s more professors were hired in American postsecondary institutions than in the entire history of American education. The expansion of higher education yielded, for example, a big audience in the United States and Britain for serious literary fiction.[22]

Terry Eagleton, a brilliant, useful, and left-wing literary critic of serious literary fiction, makes the conventional claim that the bourgeoisie is to be blamed for the "monstrously egoistic civilization they have created"—as though he had not encountered Chaucer and his Pardoner, or Shakespeare and his Iago, representatives of monstrously egoistic civilizations of church and castle.[23] To yearn for a simpler time when getting and spending was not so much with us is mostly a version of the pastoral, repeated in every world literature in every age, pretty much independent of the sociological evidence. Theocritus and after him Horace lamented the passing of a golden age of nymphs and shepherds. In 1767 Adam Ferguson, as Eagleton notes, lamented the "detached and solitary" people of Scotland, whose "bands of affection are broken." Wordsworth and Goethe a third of a century later, then Disraeli and Carlyle and Dickens another half a century later, lamented it as well. We are always already lamenting becoming urban and selfish and alienated. The years when our parents were children are seen as blessed times of familial and social solidarity, the clerisy's version of a Norman Rockwell world, whether in the 1920s or the Golden Age of Cronos.

But it's not so. If seen through scientific history rather than through Hellenistic pastoralism or German Romanticism, the *Gemeinschaft* of olden times proves to be defective. The murder rate in villages in thirteenth-century England was higher than high murder-rate police districts now.[24] Medieval English peasants were in fact mobile geographically, "fragmenting" their lives.[25] The imagined extended family of "traditional" life never existed in England.[26] The Russian *mir* was not egalitarian, and its ancientness was a figment of the German Romantic imagination.[27] The sweetness of the old-fashioned American family, treated nostalgically for example in the old TV program *I Remember Mama*, has been greatly exaggerated, and was in fact more like that in the movie *There Will Be Blood*.[28] Vietnamese peasants in the 1960s did not live in tranquil, closed corporate communities.[29] Love, in short, is arguably thicker on the ground in the modern, Western, capitalist world. Or at any rate it is not obviously thinner on the ground than in the actual world of olden and allegedly more solidarity-drenched times. The feminist economist Nancy Folbre remarks that "we cannot base our critique of impersonal market-based society on some romantic version of a past society as one big happy family. In that family, Big Daddy was usually in control."[30]

The sociologist Robert Bellah and his coauthors of *The Habits of the Heart* (1985, 1996) reiterate the tale of lost solidarity. It is one of their main themes. "Modernity," they say without offering evidence—why seek evidence for so obvious a truth?—"has had . . . destructive consequences for social ecology . . . , [which] is damaged . . . by the destruction of the subtle ties that bind human beings to one another, leaving them frightened and alone."[31] They worry that "the first language of America," individualism, "may have grown cancerous."[32] They give aesthetic and moral meaning to their everyday lives as social scientists by detecting through traditional forms of scrutiny of their neighbors a "weakening of the traditional forms of life that gave aesthetic and moral meaning to everyday living."[33] Everyone believes it. Everyone does, that is, except the historians who have examined the comparative evidence.

In any event the modern Glaswegian descendent of the nut-brown maiden, in whom the old intelligence shines, has gigantically greater scope, whether or not she has been persuaded to take full human advantage of it. She has hugely greater opportunities—scope, capabilities, potential, real personal income—for what Wilhelm von Humboldt called in 1792 that *Bildung*, that "self-culture," "self-development," life plans, second-order preferences, which is success in life. She can do one hundred times more of many things, leading a fuller life—fuller in work, travel, education, ease of housekeeping, ease of listening to "The Nut-Brown Maiden" in English and Gaelic on the Internet. A well-fed cat sitting in the sun is "happy" in the pot-of-pleasure sense of happiness studies. What the modern world offers to men and women and children (as against cats and other machines for pleasure) is not merely such "happiness" but a uniquely enlarged scope to be fully realized human beings. True, one can turn away from *Bildung*, and watch reality TV all day. Nonetheless, billions are enabled to do more. And they can have nowadays, too, in proper moderation, more cat-like, materialistic, economist-pleasing "happiness" if they wish. Bring on the Baskin-Robbins ice cream.

8

AND THE POOR WON

Nor during the Age of Innovation have the poor gotten poorer, as people are always saying. On the contrary, the poor have been the chief beneficiaries of modern capitalism. It is an irrefutable historical finding, obscured by the logical truth that the profits from innovation go in the first act mostly to the bourgeois rich. But in the second act, and in massively documented historical fact, other bourgeois rush forward at the smell of profit. Prices fall relative to wages, which is to say that goods and services expand per person—they have again and again and again—and the poor get better off in real terms. Such a crucial, long-term dissipation of profit is not mere logic, or some unsupported neoliberal article of faith. It has happened repeatedly since 1800, the Bourgeois Deal: "Let me get very rich by buying innovations low and selling them high (and do please refrain from stealing from me, or interfering), and I'll make *you* pretty rich, too." That's what happened in economic history. That's why you earn and spend so much more than $3 a day.

So sophisticated a writer as Eagleton leaves his readers in 2009 with a socialist *cri du coeur* against a "political system which is incapable either of feeding humanity or yielding it sufficient justice."[1] It is historically and economically mistaken. The system has delivered in bulk the feeding ($30 a day vs. $3 a day, West Germany in 1989 versus East Germany, Norway now versus Norway in 1800) and the justice (democracy, anticolonialism, a free press, the end of lynching, equality for women, independence for the Republic of Ireland). In every half century if not in every single decade the within-country equality of distribution has improved, and never over a generation has it much worsened. When the rich have gotten richer, as after 1978 in the United States, the poor have *not* gotten poorer—merely richer at a smaller pace than your local portfolio manager. Eagleton's ancestors and mine in mad Ireland were dirt-poor. In terms of real comfort they stood cap in hand far below their Anglo-Irish masters. Look at us now. In 2002 the Irish Republic's GDP per capita in purchasing-power-parity dollars was third in the world, just ahead of the U.S.A.'s, where many of the once-Irish then lived.[2] Neoliberal Ireland ranked in 2005 first among 111 countries in the *Economist*'s quality-of-life index, two ranks above Norway and twelve above the United States.[3]

Look again at your own ancestors compared with your present condition. You are much better off, and have much more scope to pursue *Bildung*. Admittedly you don't own a seventy-five-foot yacht. Too bad. Being an adult person of sense, however, who reads books and thinks for herself, you know that such pleasures of the rich and famous exceed yours only by a little in actual human value—there's the scientific truth in happiness studies, the truth that a pot-of-pleasure happiness has sharply diminishing marginal utility. "Gie fools their silks, and knaves their wine; / A man's a man for a' that." As the historical anthropologist Alan Macfarlane puts it, "There has been a massive leveling. . . . There has recently [in the late twentieth century] been a tendency for the gap between rich and poor to open up again. At a wider view, however, there is no longer a vast gap between the 1–5 percent who have 1000 times the income of the average. . . . There is a more gradual gradient of wealth."[4] And if not of wealth, then surely of real comfort.

I considered the statistical claim that the American poor have done badly in the late twentieth century. In relative terms the claim is true and lamentable, as I said, a result of an education-hungry economy facing a stagnation in already-rich countries in the percentage of college-educated people (education leapt up in such places during the expansion of the 1960s, but then leveled off), and a globalization that brings $30 a day to the very poor of the earth but with the side effect to some degree of slowing the growth of wages in rich countries.[5] A similar rise in the British and American premium on skill is said to explain somewhat growing inequality in the early nineteenth century.[6] Then it fell back. The division of the pie has for such reasons fluctuated some. Yet the income distribution is remarkably stable over centuries. Gini coefficients and Pareto parameters, as the economists put it, don't change very much. To take the recent rise of inequality in advanced countries, especially in the United States, as the beginning of a permanent trend and the fulfillment of Marx's prediction of immiserization is to ignore the long-run fact (and, as I said, the short-run fact, too) that real incomes of poor people have increased even in the past few decades even in advanced countries, and have exploded in countries adopting dignity and liberty for the bourgeoisie: India, China, Ireland. Recent assaults on neoliberalism by, for example, the brilliant Marxist geographer and anthropologist David Harvey (2007) start their story in 1970. To start much earlier, in 1800, say, or 1900, would transform the story into a success for technological change making poor people well off. (In a recent piece Harvey focuses, as left and right tend to do, on the destructive side of creation: "Rapid technological change . . . throws people out of work," as though in the next act real wages did not rise [as they have] or other jobs get invented [as they were] or real consumption for the poor rise [as Harvey admits it did].)[7]

Economic historians agree that the poor have benefited the most from modern economic growth. Your ancestors, mine. In no economy is the pie divided out perfectly equally, then or now, here or there. It is true of any actually existing system. If you think full-bore communism was in practice egalitarian, think again. Lebergott reckoned that in 1985 the Soviet elite family (the top 1.6 percent) consumed at least 3.8 times what the average Soviet family did; so too did the top 1.5 percent of the U.S. income distribution then—and the Chinese top party members eight times more.[8] In logic, of course, someone always occupies the bottom 10 percent of the income distribution, except at Lake Wobegon. It would be true even if the average world income were Norway's $137 instead of its actual $30 per day. Since 1800, however, the whole distribution has moved up. In statistics and in substance the very poorest have benefited the most. Robert Fogel, a careful student of such matters, notes that "the average real income of the bottom fifth of the [American] population has multiplied by some twentyfold since 1890, several times more than the gain realized by the rest of the population."[9] The bottom 10 percent have moved from undernutrition to overnutrition, and from crowded slum housing to uncrowded slum housing, and from broken-down buses to broken-down automobiles. An improvement means more to you and me, the descendents of groveling peasants, Monty Python–style, than does the gain to Her Ladyship in the big house from increasing her stock of diamond necklaces from one to sixteen (as blameworthy as such profligacy is). Famine has lessened worldwide—this contrary to the alarms from environmentalists such as the paleontologist Niles Eldridge, who predicted confidently in 1995 that "the have-nots will . . . increasingly succumb to famine."[10] No, they won't, and don't, and recently haven't. As the economic historian Cormac Ó Gráda wrote in 2009, "Famines are less frequent today than in the past and, given the right conditions, less likely in the future." He notes that "even in Africa, the most vulnerable of the seven continents, the famines of the past decade or so have been, by historical standards, 'small' famines."[11]

The economist Branko Milanovic has recently noted, as many have, that most person-by-person inequality nowadays comes not from unusual extractions by the elite of each country but from variations across countries in per capita income.[12] When income distribution has worsened between countries, such as between Hong Kong and the People's Republic of China from 1948 to 1978, or between West and East Germany from 1949 to 1990, or South and North Korea from 1953 to the present, or Little Havana in Florida and Big Havana in Cuba 1959 to the present, or Turkey and Iraq 1950 to the present, or Botswana and Zimbabwe from 2000 to the present, it has often been because the stagnating countries rejected openness and innovation, often in spectacularly perverse style.[13] Their masters dishonored the bourgeoisie and did not give it the liberty to innovate. They jailed millionaires and enslaved women and planned the economy with a corrupt or power-hungry or merely stupid purpose. Many on the European left still admire Kwame Nkrumah (1909–1972), as a socialist idealist. Yet his idealism 1955–1966 ruined the poor of Ghana. One of the richest economies of Africa became in a decade one of the poorest. The rulers of failed economies such as Sicily in Mafia-dominated days or a segregated Southern United States, when not motivated by growth-killing ideologies of left or right, accomplished the same result by simply terrorizing and stealing, as now in Nigeria (or as in some parts of Europe before the bourgeois age, and in some parts still). Under such rulers the economic pie does not get larger, and so the grossly misgoverned countries fall behind the pretty-good pie-enlarging countries, for all their imperfections, such as West Germany or Turkey.

Even somewhat sluggishly growing countries—Brazil comes to mind—have been able to make up in part for their low rates of income growth (at least by the stunning standards of the rapidly growing and selectively free-market places like Korea or Singapore or, wonder of wonders, Vietnam) by improving death and illness rates. Such improvement, of course, is an imported fruit of modern and bourgeois economic growth. But in truth Brazil under president Luiz Inácio Lula da Silva, he of rational populism, has grown pretty smartly, with a better political foundation for sustaining the growth, perhaps, than Russia and China among the four "BRICs" (India being the I). A place like the often Communist-governed Kerala state in southwest India still expresses in hard form the hostility to bourgeois innovation that characterized all of India in the four sad decades after independence. Yet Kerala makes up for low growth of income with the lowest rates of illiteracy and the highest life expectancies in South Asia—compliments of medical and other discoveries by bourgeois innovators elsewhere, admittedly, but also compliments of a Keralese history of excellence in education and honesty in government. Compare the city of Bologna in Italy, which for a long time was governed well by communists. (Kerala, however, is also known as the Indian capital of the brain drain, since its policies are irrationally hostile to enterprising people. They leave.)

The economic history of innovation therefore fulfils the so-called difference principle of the philosopher John Rawls, most famously the author of *A Theory of Justice* (1971). The principle is that a change is ethically justified when it helps the very poorest. Markets and the bourgeoisie and innovation did. (Rawls, by the way, is properly read in his wider *oeuvres* as nonsocialist, maybe even a little promarket.)[14] No one of sense views multiple mansions for millionaires as the payoff of modern economic growth chiefly to be admired. Neither did Rawls. Neither did the actually existing Age of Innovation, not over the long run, in the second and third acts of a liberal economy.

The overcautiously measured factor of sixteen or eighteen, or its correctly measured and much higher equivalent, has solved many of the problems of poverty. You can see the solutions in bits of the larger story. The descendants of the poor people in Alabama whom Walker Evans photographed in 1936 for his book with James Agee, *Let Us Now Praise Famous Men*, are today perhaps ten or twenty times materially better off (in the cautious metric) than their famous ancestors. They graduate from college, often, and always drive a car. Some of them teach English at Duke. The surviving children of the migrants from Great Plains agriculture whom John Steinbeck wrote about in 1939 in *The Grapes of Wrath* are easily eight or even sixteen times better off than their parents were then. They have substantial houses in El Cerrito and buy their coffee at Peet's. Some of them teach economics at Berkeley. All the more revolutionary, therefore, has been the change since 1700 in the scope for the average resident of Britain, or since 1820 for the average resident of the United States, or since 1868 for the average resident of Japan, or since 1978 for the average resident of China. All these people started out unspeakably poor, living on $1–$5 a day. The economy around them innovated, and their children and grandchildren became well-to-do bourgeois (though the Chinese have a couple of generations to go), even if still employees.

∞

"Capitalism developed," we say. We say it especially about what came later as a result of the rhetorical Revaluation. Europe and its offshoots became more and more "capitalistic," right down to intercontinental jet travel and the subprime mortgage crisis. Europeans prefer to call their system a "social market economy," yet they admire innovators, and for the most part do not trammel the innovations (the long struggle over Sunday-closing laws in Germany and France and the Netherlands illustrates the temptation to trammel). The Chinese insist on calling what they do when they buy low and sell high "communism." Mainland Chinese graduate students visiting American universities have as a result no grasp of the central ideological struggle of the twentieth century. Americans by contrast have more readily accepted the word once used to sneer at markets and innovation and private property, "capitalism," and the American graduate students have a firmer grasp of the history.

Yet the word "capitalism"—a coin which like "ideology" was struck around 1800 and whose value in our scientific rhetoric is due mainly to Marx's appropriation of it—points in the wrong direction, to money and saving and accumulation.[15] It brings to mind Scrooge McDuck in the Donald Duck comic books, with his piles of money. Or in a slightly more sophisticated version it brings to mind Charles Montgomery Burns in *The Simpsons*, with his piles of factories. What's wrong with such images? This: the world did not change by piling up money or capital. It changed by getting smarter about steam engines and wiser about accepting the outcome of innovation.

Nonetheless the economists since the eighteenth century have favored the notion of piled-up capital as the maker of modernity, because it emphasizes cost, about which they are expert, and because it is easy to describe statistically and mathematically. Since the late nineteenth century the master mathematical expression claiming that piles of capital acquired at great cost, K, together with existing labor, L, cause our enrichment measured in "Quantity" of goods and services—namely, $Q = F(K, L)$—has thrilled the bourgeois economists, and has satisfied their Augustinian-Calvinist theology.[16] The Marxist economists, too, have gone on talking about capital accumulation and the absorption of surplus value, with more Augustinian-Calvinist theology. The economists, though, are off the mark, and so are the cartoonists of Scrooge and Burns. The routine repetition of investment, neatly arranged by capital accumulation in buildings and roads and machines and even educations, doesn't swing ("Two chords and a backbeat," the jazz musicians snicker).[17] Innovation does. If it ain't got that swing, it don't mean a thing. Piling up is not the heart of economic growth. Innovation is. Let's retire the fraught and misleading C-word.

We'll do better to call what was born in Europe in early modern times, enriching the world during the nineteenth and twentieth centuries beyond all expectations, by some word without the misleading connotations of "capitalism." "Progress" is too vague and too loaded politically. If you like neologisms you can call it "innovism." But the best of a weak field seems to be simply "innovation." The economic historian Nick von Tunzelmann notes that "technological change became cumulative. . . . The breakthroughs . . . led to a succession of further advances. . . . Earlier changes involved a period of disequilibrium [when, say, the undershot waterwheel had been introduced] followed by a return to some kind of equilibrium as the . . . change was absorbed. . . . Instead, [in the two centuries since 1800] a systemic change took hold in which entrepreneurs had to suppose that any improvement . . . might soon be eclipsed."[18] Bill Gates fends off claims that Microsoft is a monopoly by noting that at the very moment he is speaking some bright entrepreneurs in a garage might be devising the innovation that will overturn Microsoft—the way Steve Jobs and he, a couple of college dropouts, overturned Big Blue. The new rhetoric which in time made the modern world has also been called "the triumph of entrepreneurship" or "the honoring of commercial and mechanical innovation" or "continuously emergent novelty" or "the invention of invention" or "creative destruction" of an old product by a new (or sometimes, as Tunzelmann argued, "creative accumulation" of new qualities in an old product, or an entirely new product) or "good capitalism" (as Baumol, Litan, and Schramm [2007] describe American entrepreneurial capitalism) or, in a phrase that Wynton Marsalis and Geoffrey Ward improvised recently to describe the social significance of jazz, an "explosion of consensual creativity."[19] Using an expression like "The Age of Innovation" as a synonym for the misleading "Modern Capitalism" will point in the right direction. As the economist Allyn Young put it in 1928, it was "an age when men had turned their faces in a new direction and when economic progress was not only consciously sought but seemed in some way to grow out of the nature of things."[20]

The enrichment of any nation that has allowed innovation and the bourgeois virtues to do their work—that is, the enrichment by historical standards of the average person, and the truly poor person in Rawlsian style as much as the captain of industry—argues in favor of innovation and the bourgeois virtues. It supplies so to speak a practical justification for the bourgeois sin of being neither a soldier nor a saint. You might reply, and truly, that money isn't everything. As Samuel Johnson replied, though, "When I was running about this town a very poor fellow, I was a great arguer for the advantages of poverty; but I was, at the same time, very sorry to be poor."[21] No one who bought a lottery ticket has yet turned down a check for her winnings. Or you may ask the inhabitants of India (average per capita income in 1998 in 1990 U.S. purchasing power dollars $1,746) or China ($3,117 then) whether they would have liked a U.S. income, at that time $27,331, a lottery of birth. The figures are only a little less tilted to the American side now. Or you can note the direction of permanent migration then, and more so now—West Africans waiting in Libya to make a perilous crossing to Italy, or Mexicans braving the deserts of the American Southwest to engage north of the border in the appalling crime of working hard for Anglos at low wages. As a Hispanic comedian said early in the 2008–2009 recession, "You will know that things are *really* bad in the U.S. when the Mexicans *stop coming*." In the 1930s they did stop coming, and many fewer came in 2009 than in 2007.

9

CREATIVE DESTRUCTION CAN BE JUSTIFIED THEREFORE ON UTILITARIAN GROUNDS

The claim that the poor have been the chief beneficiaries of bourgeois dignity and liberty can be given a philosophical justification. I would rather use "virtue ethics" and speak of the better people that the modern world has raised up. It would be easy to show, from the fall of public whippings to the blossoming of modern music. But let me concede for a moment to my hard-headed and utilitarian colleagues, by philosophizing a bit on their grounds.

Some of the enrichment by innovation was win-win, a "creative accumulation," in Tunzelmann's phrase. Think of the hula hoop or the skateboard, new products with no close substitutes to be damaged by the novelty. Yet most novelties do damage some people—from "creative *destruction*," in the phrase of Werner Sombart's (1863–1941) made famous by Joseph Schumpeter (1883–1950). Win-*lose*, in other words, is commonplace. Think of the new fold-up-and-carry canvas lawn chairs, which once sold for $40 and now for $6, which have bankrupted companies making the older aluminum chairs. They in turn had bankrupted the old wooden folding deck chairs, which in turn had bankrupted the still older Adirondack nonfolding wooden chairs. Chicago prospers mightily, and windily proclaims its might, and so St. Louis comparatively does not. Steam engines put waterwheels out of business, slowly. Buggy whips lose their appeal. WalMart cheapens goods to the poor by underselling inefficient local monopolies in retailing.

If the Bourgeois Deal did not have its crucial second act, in which *you*, the poor, are made better off, then a system of profit making would have no ethical justification. If profits simply piled up in the hands of the bourgeoisie, no one would praise innovation, whether it was creative accumulation or creative destruction. But in fact, because of entry at the smell of profit dissipating the rewards to inventing the light bulb or innovating the auto assembly line, the share of profit in national income is rather small and has not risen over the history of innovation. And the absolute size of the pie to be shared out between the high-hat profit makers and the deserving poor has grown enormously, because of creative destruction or creation encouraged by profit and by a new bourgeois liberty and dignity.[1]

Creative destruction happens not only in the economy. Innovating in the production of sugar or the organization of corporations creates some losers as well as many winners—but so do artistic or intellectual innovations. Charlie Parker and Dizzy Gillespie put out of business many a jazzman of the Age of Swing, as swing had put out of business Dixieland, and Dixieland had put out of business ragtime. The customers who loved Parker and his bebop were among the winners. Those who loved the earlier jazz, such as the English poet Philip Larkin, were the losers. Coco Chanel bankrupted many a dressmaker of the older sort, though freeing many women by inventing the little black dress and also a version of the bourgeois man's suit, for dignity in the men's business.[2] Albert Einstein made obsolete the many physicists who believed that the universe in the large was Euclidian and Newtonian. And shortly afterward Niels Bohr and Werner Heisenberg and their quantum mechanics made Einstein's mature thinking obsolete in the small. It is not true that free trade in goods or art or ideas helps every single person.[3]

Yet the fact of destruction somewhere does not by itself make free trade in goods or art or ideas a bad idea. The accounting has in fact overwhelmingly been win-win-win-win-win-lose. Add up the wins. Or at any rate so enlightened Europeans and the new bourgeois liberals claimed, contrary to the zero-sum notions that had governed the world up to then, in which every win to Europe was supposed to have arisen from a comparable loss to the rest. It lives on, I repeat, in recent talk about "competitiveness." "Win minus lose equals zero. Profit is evil." No, said the enlightened liberals like Mill, not usually—not if the social accounting is win-win-win-win-win-lose.

∞

The calculation of win-win-win-win-win-lose is known in philosophy as "act" (or direct) utilitarianism, one early exposition being Mill's. The balance of social gain to some innovation is claimed to be positive if you take winners with losers and add them up (somehow). In business schools one speaks of "stakeholders," and stops the ethical analysis at the accounting of gain and loss.

Mill developed, though, a more sophisticated idea, too: "rule" or indirect utilitarianism.[4] Start by admitting that each act of buying or innovating may have losers. Indeed, unless the item bought has no alternative buyer or employment, or unless the innovation or the new idea puts no one out of work, it must. If I buy a Picasso I am literally taking it away from *someone*. The price the someone faces for substitutes for *The Old Guitarist* must rise. If the someone has no ethical commitment to the outcome of voluntary markets and has a veto on my purchase, he will surely exercise it. Similarly with innovations. A society in which literally everyone has to agree to such a change in how property rights are allocated between him and me (such as the reallocation of *The Old Guitarist*) may have the merit of a splendid equality, but it will not be progressive technologically—or artistically or intellectually or spiritually. Markets will be turned into politics, as though my consumption of peanuts were the business of every other person in the peanut market, or for that matter in the electorate. Spillovers—for example, your son's lethal peanut allergy—do make a purchase of peanuts into a collective good consumed by a club or a polis, yet still something that needs to be dealt with in a context otherwise of private property. Robert Frank argues persuasively that the context of consumption, in which we all unconsciously decide what is a respectable standard of furnishing for our houses, constitute a spillover that might warrant a consumption tax—think of the bankrupting competitions in Pakistan to give the most expensive wedding in the neighborhood; or think of the gradually rising standard of what constitutes an adequate wardrobe.[5] But he does not recommend socializing all our consumption decisions.

And certainly mere personal envy should not in a liberal society be considered a spillover to be dealt with. The danger in bringing one-man-one-vote democracy into the economy is that it can indulge envy and kill the expansion of the pie. A better version of democracy is that of the Age of Innovation, that of dollar votes, in which people are forced to consider the opportunity cost of their choices, and are not allowed to exercise costless political votes to allocate costly goods in their favor. That Harry merely envies your consumption of peanuts, or is outraged that you buy them at a low price at WalMart, should not be allowed to stop you from buying another bag. In the Russian fable the peasant Ivan is told by God that he can have anything he wants, but on the irritating condition that his neighbor Boris will get twice as much. Ivan is stumped, since like many Russians in olden times he is governed chiefly by envy. "Aha," he says at last to God. "I have it. Give me a gift—the gift of having *one* of my eyes plucked out." The comparable fable in Czech tells of God and St. Peter wandering the countryside in disguise looking for lodging and being refused, until at last a poor but hospitable peasant couple take them in. God reveals himself, and tells them that for their good deed they can have anything they want. The husband and wife briefly consult together. The husband begins, "We have only miserable chickens, but our neighbor has a goat that yields milk every day. . . . " God anticipates: "You mean that you want a goat, too?" "No. We want you to kill the neighbor's goat." No progress.

What Mill and Henry Sidgwick (1838–1900) and Peter Singer (1946–) and other sophisticated utilitarians urged in developing a Rule (or "preference") version is that to assure progress we make our ethical and political decisions not at the level of acts but at the level of rule-making *about* acts. We can thereby avoid the win-lose logic of allocation, and avoid, too, other and more dramatic paradoxes in act utilitarianism.[6] The economist James Buchanan has long claimed that such a leap to a constitution-making level "serves to facilitate agreement."[7] Harry may not on the market day agree that you and not he should get the bag of peanuts, but perhaps at a constitutional convention he can more readily agree that interference in your or my peanut purchasing is unjust. The Hobbesian-Kantian-Millian-Buchanian-Rawlsian ploy undergirds what Buchanan calls "constitutional political economy." "If politics is conceptualized as a two-stage or two-level process (the constitutional [or rule] and the post-constitutional [or act])," he writes," the agreement criterion . . . [has] more acceptable implications."[8] It was what Buchanan and Gordon Tullock were about when they posited in *The Calculus of Consent* (1962) a veil of uncertainty concerning which side of the market or the vote you will end up on, behind which you make constitutional rules. It is also what their friend John Rawls was about in his later *A Theory of Justice* (1971) when he imagined a prenatal veil of ignorance behind which you decide whether our society will have slavery or not.

If the argument is true, though, there is a still higher level (and by Buchanan's logic it should be still "more acceptable"), the level of ethics—such as an ethic of not indulging envy, or an ethic of caring about constitutional arrangements exhibiting justice, or an ethic of accepting the outcomes of voluntary markets. We will not make good constitutions, much less engage in good acts, unless we are first ethical, in a full way involving the seven principal virtues. Hobbes, Buchanan, Rawls, and the others want to slip past the ethical requirements for their systems by appealing to claims that the player's "interest will be more effectively served" (as Buchanan puts it) by agreeing to rule utilitarianism. They can't, I think, slip past with such a Prudence Only argument. Constitutional political economy, as Marxists and conservatives agree, needs a foundation of ethics.[9]

Yet Buchanan is right, even if incomplete. On historical grounds I am claiming that a crucial change happened around 1800 at the ethical level—making possible for example the burst of actual constitution-making in North America, Poland, and France during the late eighteenth century. The society came to abide by the market's equilibrium (agreeing to let Boris prosper), or to abide by more or less democratic government, or to abide by the amiable political fiction that all people (except my slaves, Jefferson would add), are created equal. The outcome was good for the least among us.

∞

To the practical economist, nonetheless, a lower-level, act utilitarianism has its charms. She points out that if the price of lumber is higher in England than in Sweden, then shipping Swedish lumber from Norrland to London creates value, by the amount of the price difference less the transaction costs. An innovation in manufacturing lumber or in organizing the trade can be seen as the same sort of alert arbitrage, buying low an idea for lumber ships or steel saws or wholesale marketing, and then selling it high. Again the gain in value is the price difference. The differential less the transaction costs makes "profit" in the economist's sense, that is, a reward to having a new idea—a new allocation of timber, a new diesel engine, a new financial asset. Sven Svenson the Swedish lumber king is made better off, as is Jones the lumber merchant in London—and his employees and customers. True, if Sweden exports its lumber, some people are hurt. The London price of lumber originating in Wiltshire (which is of course a substitute for Swedish lumber) goes down, and the fall in price will measure the loss to Jack Wrightman, the owner of a big stand of timber in Wiltshire. The Swedish price is pushed up by the English demand, damaging Swedish consumers. And Jon Jonson back in Sweden, the competing lumber duke, is certainly made worse off by King Svenson's success. He is envious of it, too, even apart from the resulting loss of his income, and would veto it if he could. Kill the neighbor's goat.

The economic logic, however, is that the act of taking advantage of a price difference, or a profit opportunity, moving stuff from low-valued uses to high-valued uses, creates a net and national gain in value-in-use. It appears as an uptick in national income. One should of course worry about the distribution of income, but the historical evidence is that the gain gets spread in the long run even to the very poorest, by competition among businesses. After all, poor people in rich economies are in fact vastly better off—they would not be, I repeat, if wicked capitalists had managed to keep all the profit from innovation forever, stopping the economy in the first act. Remember the American poor of the 1930s, and how they and their children prospered. The price differential is not, as a muddy populism claims, "merely profit," as though profits were earned outside the society, and as though they were earned by stealing and not by alertness to new ways of doing things, and as though the profits never subsequently declined in the face of competing entry into the profitable trades. People benefiting from the original low-valued use are hurt, true. But more people (weighted by purchasing power) are helped—because the price they pay falls. Other suppliers of lumber or any substitute for lumber are hurt. The people helped are the many demanders of any complement, such as houses made with wood.

It looks complicated. On a blackboard, however, the economist can show you that under rather easy-to-believe assumptions the net gain to national income from allowing free trade in lumber is always positive. It would take me about half an hour, if you have the patience, to show you the diagrammatic proof. If you are good at math I could show you in five minutes. As Bastiat said early in the history of laissez-faire arguments, "what I save by paying nothing to the sun [for indoor illumination in the day time], I use for buying clothing, furniture, and [even] candles."[10] It is all quite simple, the economist says—unless, she will concede with a certain unease, "second-best" considerations or "nonconvexities" intervene, or unless you do not approve ethically of weighting people by purchasing power.[11]

Blackboard proofs and their uneasy assumptions of first-best and amoral income distribution aside, though, the historical facts speak loudly enough. Clearly, *some* people are hurt by economic change, every time, just as some are hurt by intellectual change or fashion change or climate change. New ideas hurt people earning their incomes from old ideas. As Mokyr puts it,

Economists tend to believe that most of [the] costs are at most temporary phenomena. Yet technological progress is hardly ever . . . an improvement for everyone affected: there are losers in the process, and while gainers could compensate them [thus says the economist, pointing to the blackboard], it is only rarely that they do. The stronger the aversion to the disruption of the existing economic order, the less likely is it that an economy would provide a climate favorable to technological progress.[12]

Yet equally clearly, the gain since 1800 from economic change has massively outweighed in monetary and ethical terms the loss to English woodmen disemployed by Swedish timber, or American blacksmiths disemployed by automobiles, or Indian bullock-drivers disemployed by motor trucks. The Win-Win-Win-Win-Wins far outnumber the lone Lose. To put it back into the terms of rule utilitarianism and constitutional political economy, what sort of society would you rather be born into: one that forbad every innovation that resulted in any loss whatever to anyone, and rested therefore at $3 a day, and held that the sun "rose" and that painting must always be representational, or one that allowed innovation, perhaps with a social safety net like Norway's, and resulted in $137 a day, and allowed Copernicus and Picasso to make old ideas obsolete?

That's why it is scientifically important to grasp the great magnitude of modern economic growth. When the value created is merely the modest efficiency gains noted in the nineteenth century by the classical British economists, one might reasonably stand in doubt, and fall back into the protectionist measures favored by both conservatives and progressives. (Though the blackboard, I say, still provides the true liberal with a proof of gain from free trade, however uneasy the proof; and a more robust proof is to note that keeping people in their old jobs forever, which is what protectionism does, would plainly be a mistake; and a still more robust one is to note that if protection against free trade is good for the country, why not for the region, or the city, or the neighborhood, or your house?) But when the value created is a factor of ten and more—a movement from $3 to $30, not to speak of $3 to $137, a radical up-scaling (I say again to my economist colleagues) of the Edgeworth box—it becomes much harder to argue that the loss to the substitutes (other suppliers of lumber, say) does in historical fact overwhelm the gain (to buyers of wood, say, or people who live in wooden houses). Or, to speak again in terms of constitutional political economy from behind the veil of uncertainty, it becomes much harder to argue that one would prefer (from behind the veil, that is, uncertain as to your own ultimate position in society) to enforce rules leading to the ignorant $3-a-day society rather than to the wise $137-a-day one. "The conflict between winners and losers from new technologies," writes the economist Peter Howitt, summarizing the historical work by Mokyr, "is a recurrent theme in economic history, and the difficulty of mediating the conflict affects society's willingness to foster and tolerate economic growth."[13] Bourgeois dignity and liberty.

10

BRITISH ECONOMISTS DID NOT RECOGNIZE THE TIDE

The thing to be explained, then, is the gigantic material enrichment of the modern world, an enrichment permitting lives of greater spiritual and intellectual scope for the poorest among us. In Britain since the eighteenth century it was (conservatively measured) a factor of sixteen. Some of the world's people have not been able to take full advantage of innovation and of the bourgeois virtues. Even so the real and cautiously measured income per head in the world has increased since 1800 by a factor of ten—this in the teeth of a rise in population of a factor of over six and a half. Why?

Britain was first, and therefore Britain is a good place to go hunting for answers. The economy was viewed as a thing separate from the polity early in Britain (and earlier still in Holland, and later in France, and much later in Germany), which is one bit of evidence that a bourgeois rhetoric was forming. Britain led in the study of economics—assisted by Spanish professors, Dutch merchants, French physicians, and Italian penologists—from the English political arithmeticians of the seventeenth century down through David Hume, Adam Smith, T. R. Malthus, David Ricardo, John Stuart Mill, and the British masters of the subject in the early twentieth century. Economics was for a long time a British and even disproportionately a Scottish subject. Only after the Second World War did it become, like many other fields of the intellect, dominantly American.

Oddly, the British economists around 1776 or 1817 or 1871 did not recognize the factor of sixteen as it was beginning to happen. Even now their heirs in America sometimes forget it. The theories of the economists took useful account of little changes—a 5 percent rise of income when cotton factories grew, or a 10 percent fall when Napoleon ruled the Continent. They did not notice, however, that the change to be explained, 1780–1860, was not 5 or 10 percent but 100 percent, and was on its way to that unprecedented 1,500 percent conservatively measured relative to what it was in the eighteenth century. Only recently, beginning in the 1950s, has the inquiry into the nature and causes of the wealth of nations begun to recognize the oversight.

In the late 1940s Joseph Schumpeter was already scornful of the classical economists for their failure to see what was happening. T. R. Malthus (1766–1834) and David Ricardo (1772–1823) "lived at the threshold of the most spectacular economic development ever witnessed. . . . [yet] saw nothing but cramped economies, struggling with ever-decreasing success for their daily bread."[1] Their student Mill (1806–1873) even in 1871 "had no idea of what the capitalist engine was going to achieve."

The enrichment was noticeable to some even in 1830. Macaulay the historian wrote then:

> If any person had told the Parliament which met in perplexity and terror after the crash in 1720 that in 1830 the wealth of England would surpass all their wildest dreams, . . . that London would be twice as large . . . and that nevertheless the rate of mortality would have diminished to one-half, . . . that men would be in the habit of sailing without wind and would be beginning to ride without horses, our ancestors would have given as much credit . . . as they gave to *Gulliver's Travels*. Yet the prediction would have been true.[2]

In his *Essay on the Principle of Population* (1798) the Anglican priest and economist Malthus had predicted the opposite. His point is still popular among radical environmentalists, who view natural resources per human as the problem, or perhaps just humans, and dream of the Garden without Adam and Eve, and watch with delight the TV show *Life after People*. The radical environmentalists do not realize that gradually after 1800 natural resources became no longer the main scarcity. Nowadays (it is wisely said) there are no natural resources, only human resourcefulness. Yet Malthus told a great truth about *earlier* history. In medieval England, for example, during the two centuries before 1348 a rising population *had* become poorer, and in Elizabethan England the impoverishment happened again, for the same reason of rising population facing a given stock of land, diminishing returns. When land was still the chief resource in the economy, and economic resourcefulness was not the way to achieve honor, more English people meant less land per head and therefore less grain per head. In late

Georgian and early Victorian England, however, a rising population became, through now-honored ingenuity, a good deal richer. Land fell dramatically in its power to constrain humans.

The fact was contrary to every prediction of the classical economists, and fits poorly with the analysis of many of their successors down to the present.[3] Most economists scorned the notion of free lunches, and still scorn it. I have long instructed undergraduates in acknowledging the tragic fact. In the sweat of thy face shalt thou eat bread. One can shuffle labor and the like from one use to another, and gain efficiency, but never, the economists declared, gain easy gold at the hand of fey or elf. And therefore the economists, unlike the historian Macaulay or the mathematician and engineer Charles Babbage, saw nothing in prospect around 1830 but misery for the working man and riches for the landowners. Like modern environmentalists the classical economists depended on blackboard propositions ("ultimately, all resources are limited"), not the evidence before their eyes. And later the neoclassical economists, and then still later the Samuelsonians among them, worked feverishly to deny the evidence (as I did early in my career) by recalculating the free lunch as capital accumulation.

In 1845 Mill summarized the matter with his customary lucidity and justice. Until the Reverend Malthus wrote, the condition of the working class was considered by most a hopeless case—"a provision of nature," as Mill expressed it, "and as some said, an ordinance of God; a part of human destiny, susceptible merely of partial alleviation in individual cases, from public or private charity."[4] Malthus, at any rate in the second edition in 1803 of *An Essay on the Principle of Population*, showed that poverty was a consequence of population growth but that he had given reason for hope, not despair. (As an Anglican priest he perhaps worried about his earlier bald statement of the Principle of Population in 1798, because *acedia*, despair, a lack of Christian hope, is the second greatest sin against the Holy Spirit.) A given technology could support the poor in a little better style, if they could only be made prudent and conscientious in having children—which a middle-way Anglicanism, for example, could preach in good conscience. Beyond Malthus's promise of modest improvement through sexual restraint Mill noted two additional forms of optimism, less plausible he thought (the thought seemed reasonable in 1845, before the late nineteenth-century explosion in real wages). "The only persons by whom any other opinion [than the age-old pessimism about the poor doomed to earn a dollar or two or three a day—maybe five if they would but adopt sexual restraint] seemed to be entertained, were those who prophesied advancements in physical knowledge and mechanical art, sufficient to alter the fundamental conditions of man's existence on earth; or who professed the doctrine, that poverty is a factitious thing, produced by the tyranny and rapacity of governments and of the rich." From Mill's other writings one can infer that he took little hope from the "prophesied advancements in physical knowledge." In that prediction he proved spectacularly wrong. Nor did he believe that revolutionary redistribution would work. In that he proved unhappily right.

The economists, in other words, did not notice that something entirely new was happening from 1760 or 1780 to 1860. As the demographer Anthony Wrigley put it a while ago, "The classical economists were not merely unconscious of changes going on about them that many now term an industrial revolution: they were in effect committed to a view of the nature of economic development that ruled it out as a possibility."[5] At the moment (in, say, 1848) that John Stuart Mill came to understand an economy in equilibrium, the economy grew away from the equilibrium. And by the time he died, in 1873, the growing away was accelerating worldwide: during 1820 to 1870 Angus Maddison reckons world per capita real income grew at 0.53 percent per year, but during what he calls the "Liberal Order" of 1870 to 1913 it grew at 1.3 percent per year.[6] It was as though an engineer had satisfied herself of the statics that kept a jumbo jet from collapsing as it sat humming on the tarmac, but then failed to notice when the whole thing took off into flight.

The economists then believed, as many of them do down to the present, that they possessed a complete theory of the social laws of motion. They overlooked applied innovation. That is, they overlooked the creativity of the conversation in a modern economy, its emergent character. The economist Basil Moore has expressed the point in a brilliant critique of economics by saying truly that since the first Industrial Revolution the world economy has become nonlinearly dynamic.[7] The economist Friedrich Hayek (1899–1992) had expressed a similar point, that economies are unpredictable because they are the outcome of human conversation.[8] The future of the mathematical conversation, for example, is unpredictable, because if it were predictable we would now know the mathematics that is supposed to be in the future. It wouldn't be future. The same is true of vast swathes of human activity, from fashion to engineering.[9] The Hollywood proverb is "nobody knows anything." In other words, artistic success is not mechanically predictable. (*Box-office* success, on the other hand, can be predicted pretty well—blow up enough cars and you'll get the fourteen-year-old boys into the seats; once such a formula is known, however, the producer's success will be judged by how regularly she exceeds it.)[10] The static economics which Moore and Hayek criticize worked just fine before the Revaluation. And for the short and medium run it still illuminates many routine parts of the economy. Don't throw it away, because the routine is, naturally, pretty common. But the economy after the late eighteenth century, viewed over the long run, became increasingly nonroutine, startled by steam engines, electrified by generators, confused by computers, and above all revivified by Revaluations.

In 1767 Josiah Wedgwood (he of fine china in imitation of the Chinese) was writing that "a revolution was at hand," at any rate in the making of pottery.[11] Beyond pots and beyond Britain, Rousseau and later Condorcet were declaring that humans are indefinitely perfectible. In 1783 Samuel Johnson declared, "The age is running mad after innovation; all the business of the world is to be done in a new way; men are to be hanged in a new way," and himself took an interest in new ways of brewing.[12] The guillotine was perfected in France early in the Revolution as a new way of giving all classes the great benefit of execution by ax. In 1787 the dissenting preacher, political radical, and insurance actuary Richard Price was still more broadly optimistic (the very words "optimism" and "pessimism," by the way, were eighteenth-century philosophical coinages):

> It is the nature of improvement to increase itself. . . . Nor are there, in this case, any limits beyond which knowledge and improvement cannot be carried. . . . Discoveries may, for aught we know, be made in future time which, like the discoveries of the mechanical arts and the mathematical sciences in past time, may exalt the powers of men and improve their state to a degree which will make future generations as much superior to the present as the present are to the past.[13]

The chemist Humphrey Davy in 1802 was also optimistic: "We may look for . . . a bright day of which we already are beyond the dawn."[14] By 1814 the merchant and calculator Patrick Colquhoun was admiring "the improvement of the steam engines, but above all the facilities afforded to the great branches of the woolen and cotton manufactories by ingenious machinery, invigorated by capital and skill, and beyond all calculation."[15]

And by 1830 a historian like Macaulay, as I have noted, respectful of the economics of his day but with a long view, could see the event better than could most of his economist friends. He wrote: "If we were to prophesy that in the year 1930 a population of fifty million, better fed, clad, and lodged than the English of our time, will cover these islands, that Sussex and Huntingdonshire will be wealthier than the wealthiest parts of the West Riding of Yorkshire now are, . . . that machines constructed on principles yet undiscovered will be in every house, . . . many people would think us insane."[16] Later in the nineteenth century and especially in the socialist days of the mid-twentieth century it was usual to deprecate such optimism, and to characterize Macaulay in particular as hopelessly "Whiggish" and bourgeois and progress-minded and pro-innovation. He certainly was all that, a bourgeois to the core. Whiggish and bourgeois and progress-minded and vulgarly proinnovation though he was, he was in his prediction exactly right, even as to British population in 1930. (If one includes the recently separated Republic of Ireland, he was off by less than 2 percent.)

The pessimists of Macaulay's times, both economists such as Mill and antieconomists such as John Ruskin, were mistaken. True, they were at the time, as pessimists always are, fashionable—Schumpeter remarks in this connection that "pessimistic views about a thing always seem to the public mind to be more 'profound' than optimistic ones."[17] You look less of a fool if you predict disaster and it doesn't happen than if you predict progress and it doesn't happen—witness the career of the biological doomster Paul Ehrlich, which flourishes despite errors of prediction that would ruin the credibility of a scientist in most other fields, even in economics. Or maybe the popularity of pessimism arises from a feeling that the gods or the devils will be angry if you predict progress. Better understate. Such is said to be the origin of pessimistic routines of conversation among Yiddish speakers—even before the Holocaust made their pessimism look prescient.[18]

People from Francis Bacon to Macaulay were the foolish optimists of the Enlightenment. They thought of unlimited progress, not merely the respectable yet modest gains from trade. During the 1830s and 1840s the optimists (as Schumpeter did call them), Henry Carey in the United States and Friedrich List in Germany, with mathematicians like Babbage in England, "saw vast potentialities looming in the near future."[19] Optimistic fools they were (and Carey and List were foolish protectionists as well). Yet they were correct about the magnitude of the rising tide. Their opponents the classical economists were in their pessimism quite wrong. It could make one suspicious of fashionable pessimism nowadays.

The classical economists from Adam Smith to Marx were writing before the upsurge in real wages for British and French and American working people in the second half of the nineteenth century, and long before the explosion of world income in the twentieth century. They imagined a moderate rise of income per head, perhaps at the most by a factor of two or three, such as might conceivably be achieved by Scotland's Highlands becoming similar to capital-rich Holland (Smith's view) or by manufacturers in Manchester appropriating savings for reinvestment by exploiting their poor workers (Marx's view) or by the savings generated from globalization being invested in European factories (John Stuart Mill's view). (To speak again to my economist colleagues, they all contemplated moving down the marginal product of capital—not its shocking, factor-of-sixteen lurch to the right.) But the classical economists, to repeat, were mistaken, and so are my economist colleagues when they think in classical terms.

Probably the slow start (slow at any rate by later standards) explains why industrial change was largely invisible to economists and some others assigned to watch it—though it was not invisible to many possessed of common sense and eyes to see. Macaulay wrote in 1830, "A single breaker may recede; but the tide is evidently coming in."[20] The tide indeed: the economics, as I said, explains the shape of the tide's fingers invading the land, but not the force of the hand itself. The early Victorian poet Arthur Hugh Clough did *not* praise innovation—although he was the son of a cotton manufacturer, he hated the whole thing, as did most Romantics—and he would be irritated to see his verse used to capture what happened economically down to, say, 1860:

> For while the tired waves, vainly breaking,
> Seem here no painful inch to gain,
> Far back, through creeks and inlets making,
> Comes silent, flooding in, the main.

11

BUT THE FIGURES TELL

Nicholas Crafts and C. Knick Harley, arguing for a very gradual onset of the Industrial Revolution, and a narrow industrial range for its innovations until the late nineteenth century, dispute the pattern that many other students of the matter claim to see.[1] The Two Nicks, as we affectionately call them, see the big changes as occurring after 1820 and especially after 1848.[2] And the Nicks give more weight to science than economic historians like Maxine Berg and Pat Hudson and Peter Temin and Richard Sullivan and I would, who think that for a long time innovation came mainly from workshops, not from laboratories, and came in great volume in the form of new products that the conservative measures of national income capture poorly, rather than from new scientific processes, which the conservative measures capture better. Big industries like brewing were revolutionized in the eighteenth century, as the economic historian Peter Mathias has shown, but do not, as he points out, figure much in the conventional historiography, focused on cotton and iron.[3]

We optimists, in other words, would claim that one can detect widespread productivity change in the eighteenth century, measurable for example by input and output prices in dozens of industries, and in patent applications for entirely new products (though we would admit that the work on primary sources required to be quite sure of the calculation has not been done widely enough), or by testimony up and down the country in novels and plays and letters about improved roads and agriculture and humming industrial districts making beer and cutlery and toys and watches (though we would admit that the work on these primary sources, too, has not been done widely enough). And therefore we would see a quickening of growth some decades earlier.[4] We optimists believe that there are good reasons to think that the slow-growth Industrial Revolution of the Two Nicks contradicts pretty solidly documented progress in a wide range of British industries in the classic period 1760–1860. Even so Romantic and conservative and pessimistic an observer as Samuel Taylor Coleridge in the pessimistic year of 1817 could write—while setting it beside the loss from the business cycle so evident in that year—"I am not ignorant that the power and circumstantial prosperity of the nation has been increasing during the [past sixty years], with an accelerated force unprecedented in any country, the population of which bears the same proportion to its productive soil; and partly, perhaps, even in consequence of this system. By facilitating the means of enterprise, it must have called into activity a multitude of enterprising individuals and a variety of talent that would otherwise have lain dormant."[5] The Nicks argue that productivity outside a few progressive sectors was nil—which contradicts the industrial studies. The aggregate statistics of the Two Nicks, therefore, must be too low, because they imply an implausibly small (namely, nil) productivity growth in glass, chemicals, shoemaking, brass, toys, instruments, and the like calculated as what's left over.

Let us live easy, though: these are small differences of emphasis. We all, optimists and comparative pessimists alike, agree that something extremely strange, and enriching, and world-changing, took place in parts of Britain somewhere around 1820, give or take forty years. For most if not all scientific purposes the range 1780 to 1860 for a radical change is accurate enough, and especially in view of the astounding enrichments that followed. Surely by 1860 (say) a much larger nation was much richer per head, and much more likely to sustain innovation, as never before in history. Britain was beginning the factor of sixteen—and the factor of one hundred comprehensively measured.

Using for Britain proper the conservative Crafts and Harley figures (and very roughly factoring in some sluggishness for Ireland, then a big part of the United Kingdom), before national income is more accurately measured in Charles Feinstein's estimates from 1855 on, Angus Maddison gives a series of U.K. per capita income in "1990 international Geary-Khamis dollars" (table 1).

When did it start? The question matters if asked at the level of centuries rather than decades. If it started in the early Middle Ages the sort of explana-

Table 1. Conservatively measured, the improvement in the U.K. occurred sometime around 1800, then accelerated

	REAL ANNUAL GDP PER HEAD IN 1990 DOLLARS	ANNUAL GROWTH RATE FROM PREVIOUS DATE	POPULATION (MILLIONS)
1600	$ 974	—	6.2
1700	1,250	0.25	8.6
1820	1,706	0.26	21.2
1850	2,330	1.0	27.2
1870	3,190	1.5	31.4
1913	4,927	1.0	45.6
2001	20,127	1.6	59.7

Source: Maddison 2006, pp. 437, 439, 443 for real GDP per head; pp. 413, 415, 419 for population. Growth rates are compound annually.

tions one would offer would be different than if it didn't really get going until 1860. Various emblematic dates have been proposed—January 1, 1760, when the furnaces at Carron Ironworks, Stirlingshire, were lit; the five months in 1769 during which Watt took out a patent on the separate condenser in his steam engine and Arkwright took out a patent on the water frame for spinning cotton; or the famous day and year March 9, 1776, when Adam Smith's *The Nature and Causes of the Wealth of Nations* provided a rhetoric for the age. But some think centuries earlier. It sometimes seems that every economic historian has a favorite date, and a story to correspond. Eleanora Carus-Wilson spoke of "an Industrial Revolution of the thirteenth century." She found that the fulling mill (that is, a machine for thickening wool cloth) was "due to scientific discoveries and changes in technique," especially the control of water power, and "was destined to alter the face of medieval England," crushing the urban centers formerly leading in making cloth.[6] Looking at the matter from 1907 the American historian Henry Adams could see a "movement from unity into multiplicity, between 1200 and 1900, . . . unbroken in sequence, and rapid in acceleration."[7] The economic historians Eric Jones and Angus Maddison and the economist Deepak Lal have taken a similar long view of European exceptionalism.[8] In 1888 Walt Whitman opined that "the ferment and germination even of the United States today . . . [dated] back to the Elizabethan age," and expressed in his poetic prose the continuity of history: "Indeed, when we pursue it, what growth or advent is there that does not date back, back, until lost—perhaps its most tantaliz-ing clues lost—in the receding horizons of the past?"[9] Yet the most widely agreed period of the beginning of It, whatever exactly It was that led to the factor of sixteen, is still the late eighteenth century. Such suddenness and recentness fits the history better. Maddison, who thinks that Europe started in 1820 quite far ahead of the rest, nonetheless emphasizes that the growth of incomes per head in Europe up to then were modest, and afterward, very fast. That is all the chronology needed for the point here.

If the onset of modern economic growth fed on itself, then its start could be a trivial accident, and indeed back, back, until lost. Mokyr identifies this pitfall in storytelling: rummaging among the possible acorns from which the great oak of the Industrial Revolution grew "is a bit like studying the history of Jewish dissenters between 50 BCE and 50 CE. What we are look-ing at is the inception of something which was at first insignificant and even bizarre," though "destined to change the life of every man and woman in the West."[10] Yet one might wonder—the point will be made many times here in various different ways—why then it did not happen before. "Sensitive dependence on initial conditions" is the technical term for some "nonlin-ear" models—a piece of so-called "chaos theory." But under such circum-stances a history becomes untellable, the most tantalizing clues lost.[11] It may be so—the world may be in fact nonlinear dynamic, as Basil Moore argues. In such a case, though, we will need to give up our project of telling of its origins, because the true causes will consist of horseshoe nails lost and but-terfly effects too small to be detected. The reasons are the same as those that make it impossible to forecast distant weather: "Current forecasts are use-ful for about five days," writes a leading student of such matters, "but it is theoretically impossible to extend the window more than two weeks into the future."[12] It is "theoretically" impossible because the fluid mechanics, the radiative transfer, the photochemistry, the air-sea interactions, and so forth "are violently non-linear and strongly coupled." The flap of the wings of a butterfly in Mongolia, said Edward Lorenz, the inventor of such thinking, can three weeks later cause a hurricane in Cuba.

Anyway industrialization when it got going happened at a stately pace. Britain was no factory in the mid-nineteenth century. In 1851 the number of British people employed in textiles, then at the frontier of innovation, was much smaller than in agriculture and a little smaller than in "domestic and personal service," neither of which was much altered by new technologies—

though agriculture was just beginning to be so altered.[13] The economic historian John Clapham made the point in 1926, observing that in 1831 "the representative Englishman . . . was not yet . . . either a man tied to the wheels of iron of the new industrialism, or even a wage earner in a business of considerable size."[14] "As late as 1851, he noted, half the household lived in "rural" districts, and only some of these contained factories or coal pits. "At what point" in the nineteenth century, he concluded, "the typical worker may be pictured as engaged on tasks which would have made earlier generations gape is a matter for discussion. It may be suggested here that this point will be found some rather long way down the century."[15] The massive number of household servants makes the point, but even in British manufacturing it was true that gape-worthy activities were not all that common until late in the nineteenth century. As Maxine Berg and Patricia Hudson have noted, some technologically stagnant sectors (building, say, or the making of clothing before the sewing machine, or indeed all services) saw large expansion and bigger employment, while some technologically progressive sectors saw little or none (paper making, until the stamp taxes were repealed). Some industries working in large-scale units did little to change their techniques (naval shipyards early in the period). Some in tiny firms were brilliant innovators (the metal trades, from Britain's big lead in using coal to boil metals and glass, and in metal-bashing).[16] Immense mills in the famous sectors were not the whole of the factor of two down to the middle of the nineteenth century, and nothing like all of the later factor of sixteen. Steam power in Britain increased by a factor of fully ten from 1870 to 1907 ("some rather long way down the century"), long *after* the dark, satanic mills first enter British consciousness.[17]

Productivity change 1780–1860 was famously fast in textiles. It's still happening, down to the present. Cotton cloth, a luxury in 1700, had become by the middle of the nineteenth century the commonest, cheapest cloth. It therefore found new uses. In a small way the same thing has happened since 1982 in the making of "sandwashed" silk. And so for every fabric. Synthetic fibers like the first one, rayon, or the next big one, nylon, were once rather expensive. Now you have a closet full of clothing made of all sorts of now cheap fibers derived from oil. And a big closet: houses built in the nineteenth century have little or no closets, because you depended then on armoires in which to store your tiny stock of clothes.

One can best see productivity change in the prices of the things produced.

Prices permit a simple (if underused) way of measuring productivity change before modern statistics on aggregates like "the capital stock" and other fancies. A piece of cotton cloth that was sold in the 1780s for seventy or eighty shillings (two months' wages for a workingman) was by the 1850s selling for around five shillings (a few days' wages), on its way by now to a few minutes' wages. A small part of the decline in the price of finished cotton cloth was attributable to declines in the prices of raw cotton itself—say, after the introduction of the cotton gin (improved in 1793 on the basis of numerous earlier machines), and especially the four-fold increase in yields of cotton coming from breeding experiments in the American South, and the resulting expansion of cotton acreage in America.[18] Yet the price of other inputs into cotton rose. By 1860, for example, money wages of cotton workers had risen markedly over what they were in 1780. Why then did the price of manufactured cloth fall? It fell because organization and machinery were massively improved in cotton textiles, 1780 to 1860—and just as massively afterward.

The case is typical in showing more about the variation around average performance than one might at first think knowable. The calculation shows for example that productivity change slowed in cotton during the very early nineteenth century—because power weaving, which came late, was apparently less important than power carding of the raw wool and power spinning of the wool into yarn. And it exhibits one of the main findings of economic historians, that invention is not the same thing as innovation.[19] The heroic age of invention in cotton textiles—the sheer devising of the first version of macroinventions—ended by the late 1780s, by which time Hargreaves, Arkwright, Kay, Crompton, and Cartwright had all had their great days. Yet their inventions saw steady improvement later. The pattern is typical, invention being only the first step. The same is true, for example, of railways, which improved in scores of small ways right into the twentieth century, such as by diesel engines, with large declines in real costs. A fifty-car train was impossible without late innovations in hydraulic brakes and automatic switching. And still later the hundred-car train that in 1920 required by the "full crew laws" six men based in a caboose (on the Milwaukee Road with my grandfather as conductor in charge) came to run with two men, without caboose. The real cost of cotton textiles had halved by the end of the eighteenth century. Yet it was to halve twice more by 1860. And then again and again.

No sector was as progressive in the classic period of the Industrial Revolution as cotton textiles. In iron the productivity grew a half to a third as fast, which makes the point that productivity is not the same as production. The production of iron increased enormously in Britain 1780 to 1860 — by a factor of fifty-six, in fact, or at 5.5 percent per year.[20] ("Small growth rates," as you might be inclined to think that 5.5 is, make for big factors of increase if allowed to run on: 5.5 percent is explosive industrial growth by historical standards, a doubling every $72/5.5 = 13.2$ years; thus South Korean real income per head since 1953.) The expanding British industry crowded out the iron imported from Sweden and proceeded to make Britain the world's forge. The point, though, is that it did so mainly by applying a somewhat improved technology (called puddling) to a much wider field, not by the spectacular and continuous falls in cost that cotton witnessed. The calculation goes thus: The cost of inputs to iron (mainly coal) changed little from 1780 to 1860. During the same span the price of the output (wrought iron) fell from £20 a ton to £8 a ton, a Good Thing, surely. The fall in real costs, again, is a measure of productivity change. So productivity in wrought iron making increased by a factor of about 2.5, an admirable change. Yet over the same years the productivity in cotton textiles, we have seen, increased by a factor of 7.7.

Other textiles imitated the innovations in cotton, significantly cheapening their products, though usually less rapidly than the master industry of the age: as against cotton's 2.6 percent productivity change per year, worsteds (wool cloth spun into a thin yarn and woven flat, with no nap to the cloth) experienced 1.8 percent and woolens 0.9 percent.[21] Coastal and foreign shipping, though, did experience explosive rates of productivity change similar to those in cotton textiles (some 2.3 percent per year as compared with 2.6 in cotton). The figure depends on Douglass North's estimates for transatlantic shipping during the period, rising to 3.3 percent per year 1814–1860.[22] Again the "low" percentage is in fact large in its cumulative effects: freight rates and passenger fares fell like a stone, from an index of around 200 after the Napoleonic Wars to 40 in the 1850s. Canals and railways experienced productivity change of about 1.3 percent.[23] Transportation was therefore among the more notably progressive parts of the economy.

Yet many other sectors, like iron as we have seen, experienced slower productivity change until late in the nineteenth century. The productivity change in agriculture was once believed to be slower still during the

Industrial Revolution, dragging down the economy-wide average. The Two Nicks, supported by the researches of the ingenious Gregory Clark and other agricultural historians, believe on the contrary that it did pretty well, some 0.7 percent per year in productivity change.[24] Anyway, taking one year with another, 1780–1860, agriculture was still nearly a third of national income, and so it mattered a good deal, and its productivity change was anyway slower than such leaders as cottons and worsted and canals and railways. Productivity change varied radically, as it has continued to do, one sector taking the lead in driving up the national productivity while another settles into a routine of fixed technique, computers taking over the lead from chemicals and electricity. Agriculture itself, for example, came to have quite rapid productivity change in the age of the reaper and the steam tractor in the nineteenth century. And selective breeding of animals and plants was probably even more important—still more so in the age of genetic engineering in the twentieth century.[25] From 1780 to 1860, though, textiles and transport were the leaders. Bravo for the brave British.

12

BRITAIN'S (AND EUROPE'S) LEAD
WAS AN EPISODE

Yet one must take care. In the face of such wonderful activities in the eighteenth century and early nineteenth centuries, it is customary for Europeans, and especially British Europeans, to puff with pride, and start talking about how anciently exceptional the Europeans, and especially the British, and even most especially the English, have been. Alan Macfarlane has long argued, and persuasively, that English individualism was ancient, showing up for example in marriage patterns among the Anglo-Saxons, at any rate when they got to England, and in the noncollectivist notions of property in Germanic law before they had.[1] Yet the Chinese, after all, have their own exceptionality, which could plausibly have contributed to early industrialization. The people who managed to organize such astounding projects of collective engineering as the Great Wall and the Grand Canal and admiral Zheng He's expeditions to Africa, and who for centuries had the largest cities in the world, are not obviously incapacitated for economic growth. The same could be said of the Egyptians, the Romans, the Abbasids, the Ottomans, the Incas, or for that matter the Mississippian mound builders. In the event, however, the northwest Europeans and especially the British started modern economic growth, and so they tend to congratulate themselves, and view themselves as the naturally Top Nations. The rhetoric of nationalism, not to speak of racism, rather easily slips in. It provides a nice, self-justifying warmth if you are European, and most especially if you are a British European.

Until the nineteenth century, however, as sociologists and historians and economists such as Jack Goldstone, Kenneth Pomeranz, and Robert Allen at first argued, the rich areas of, say, China were comparable in income to those of Europe, such as Britain.[2] The assertion did not go without challenge — for example from Broadberry and Bishnupriya (2005), who plausibly counterasserted that the rich areas of China looked more like the *poor* areas of Europe well before 1800. And recently Allen and his colleagues have confirmed such a pattern.[3] (Hans-Joachim Voth and Nico Voigtländer [2008], building on the counterassertion, argue for a "first divergence," that is, higher real wages in northwestern Europe than in the Yangtze Valley before 1800. Their argument is remarkable: the Black Death enticed people into towns, where they died [the Chinese cities were healthier], thus relieving Malthusian pressure and allowing real wages to rise.) Whatever one thinks of the starting point for the "second divergence," though, no one disagrees that China was ahead in, say, 1500, and fell dramatically behind by the late nineteenth century (the era of the second and more important divergence). That's the main point: European technological superiority was *not* medieval or ancient.

The group who in the past couple of decades have made the China-admiring discovery are called the "California School" (because many of its teachers are in California).[4] After graduate work, so to speak, with Jack Goody and Joseph Needham, the school has taught us the error in many of the claims of deep-set European exceptionalism — such as the European marriage pattern, or the inventiveness of Europeans in water- and windmills and the like, or Europe's alleged long lead in riches, or in Marx's analysis the shift from oriental despotism through feudalism to the triumph of the bourgeoisie (Marx is the grand-daddy of Eurocentrism).[5] "Some of the errors," Jack Goldstone charitably suggests, "come simply from comparing a fairly detailed and learned understanding of change in Europe with a rather vague and over-simplified understanding of change in Asia."[6] Thus Marx, again, or the historian David Landes (1924–).

Joseph Needham (1900–1995) and his sinologist colleagues inspiring the California School have shown in the past fifty years that the Chinese were in fact astoundingly inventive for millennia before the West caught the bug. (One awaits a similar demonstration for the South Asians: begin with cotton cloth and scientific grammar.[7] Or the Arabs: begin with universities and astronomy and horticulture.[8]) The West did not realize how much it owed to the Chinese, or in what ways it was anticipated, commonly by many hundreds of years, such as the blast furnace (which was thought to be Swedish) or thin castings of iron (thought to be Dutch). The Chinese had mapped their realm with gridded precision hundreds of years before European cartographers were still inclined to fill empty places on maps with the equivalent of the proverbial "here be dragons." Remarkably, until Needham's scholarship the Chinese themselves, in the face of Western hubris, had forgotten their pioneering.

Robert Temple wrote in 1986 an engaging popular exposition of Needham's twenty-four stout volumes.[9] Temple gives in the third, 2007 edition a table of 110 inventions anticipated by the Chinese, and often used on a large scale. (Simon Winchester's popular biography of Needham has a fuller list of about 275, including such miracles as a wheelbarrow *with sails* from the sixth century CE, and soil science or ecology from the fifth century BCE).[10] We all know about paper, invented and in common use in China in the second century BCE (even for clothing; though not used for writing until the first century CE; so writing on one's sleeve is also Chinese). It was not manufactured in the West until the thirteenth century CE, a lag of 1,500 years. Or consider cardboard, invented two centuries before Europe caught on. Or the compass, invented and in common use in China in the fourth century BCE (though not used for navigation at sea until the late first millennium CE), not adopted in the West until the twelfth century CE, a lag again of 1,500 years.[11] About the gun the Westerners were more urgently curious, and the lag was only fifty years after its invention in China in 1180 CE, though the Song armies stayed ahead of the West for a long time, shooting cannonballs and bombs at Mongols (who quickly learned to shoot back). An economist would know of paper money, too, with a lag of 850 years until the desperate New Englanders thought to use it, too. (When Benjamin Franklin returned to Boston after some years prospering in Philadelphia he exhibited his coin, as he put it, as a "raree show" for the paper-using Bostonians.) An agricultural historian might have known that the iron-share, curved-moldboard plow, invented by the Chinese 500 years BCE, came from China to Holland in the seventeenth century, and thence to England. Few could have known before Needham, however, that the Chinese invented the seed drill 1,800 years before its use in the West, the crank handle 1,100 years before, deep-drilling for natural gas 1,900 years, the wheelbarrow 1,300 years, a place for zero in a decimal system 1,400 years, and knowledge of the circulation of the blood by 1,800 years before Harvey.

Needham's work established the now-accepted truth that European technology was inferior to Chinese (or Japanese or Indian or Arab or Persian or Ottoman) until about 1500, and in many ways was inferior still in 1700 (by which date Europeans still had not reverse-engineered or mechanized such ancient Eastern crafts as thin-wall porcelain, japanning lacquers, or the making and printing of fine cotton cloth). Needham and collaborators and followers have shown that the claim by the historians Lynn White and David Landes for unusual European innovativeness stretching back to the tenth century appears to be mistaken. The windmill, for example, was Arabic. True, the Europeans in the Middle Ages invented all by themselves the fulling mill, and perfected the mechanical clock (given special emphasis by White, but invented according to Needham in the eighth century CE in China, and not reinvented until 1310 by the Europeans, having heard of the Chinese machine), and invented eyeglasses, and dubiously independently, if you insist on Eurocentrism worthy of the old Soviet regime, invented the blast furnace in Sweden—though long after the Chinese, and using, funnily enough, exactly the design of furnace pioneered in China in the century before.[12] Good for the Europeans. By now, however, most students of technology affirm that the Europeans had to learn from the Chinese or others, starting in the late first millennium, the stirrup, horse collar, printing, metal moveable type (invented by Koreans in the twelfth century), multiple-masted fore-and-aft rigging, and literally scores of other inventions large and small. China ruled. The sinologist Peter Perdue explains that the expenses of overland transport on the Silk Road required precisely "a mysterious fabric whose production technology China monopolized for two thousand years," namely, silk, finally stolen by the wily Italians, along with noodles.[13] In the early seventeenth century, Needham writes, "Francis Bacon had selected three inventions, paper and printing, gunpowder, and the magnetic compass, which had done more, he thought, than any religious conviction, or any astrological influence, or any conqueror's achievement, to transform completely the modern world. . . . All of them were Chinese."[14] Until 1600 or so, considering also the Eastern lead then in art and music and literature and philosophy, and considering too the beginning about then of the brutal Western empires, the situation calls to mind Gandhi's witticism on being asked what he thought of Western civilization: "I think it would be a good idea."

Yet Joseph Needham's work shows something else, too, which he emphasized and puzzled over and which is also relevant to the story here. From the seventeenth century on, in a rising wave of creativity the Europeans stole, copied, adopted, improved, extended, reverse-engineered, and above all applied what they had learned from the Chinese, and from anybody else they chanced to encounter on their fanatical and profitable peregrinations— coffee from the Ethiopians via the Ottomans, for example, or potatoes and tomatoes and tobacco from the Native Americans, the use of blank space in painting from the East Asians. Lady Mary Wortley Montagu (1689–1762) brought the Ottoman method of inoculation for smallpox back to England, using it with success on her own children.[15] Down to 1800, in other words, one can argue as Goldstone does that the Europeans were merely "catching up with the advanced civilizations of Asia, which already produced high-quality cotton, porcelain, and cast iron in vast quantities."[16] During their catching up, though, the Europeans were coming to admire bourgeois virtues, such as the hopeful and courageous project of innovation . . . and innovation and innovation and innovation, even in painting.

By contrast in the few centuries before 1800 the Chinese (and the Koreans and the Japanese and the Ottomans and the Mughals and the Aztecs and the Incans) became for various reasons (Goldstone argues) fatally satisfied with their own arts and panoplies. European scribes attempted to retard the spread of printing there. But in the long run they failed. Meanwhile the Koreans, who had invented metal moveable type centuries before, acquired an alphabet, which would have made moveable type as valuable there as in Europe—but were blocked in its application by the educated elite fearful that high-prestige Chinese writing in characters would be downgraded. For the Ottomans, as Metin Cosgel, Thomas Miceli, and Jared Rubin have noted, there was a nearly three-century delay after Gutenberg in allowing books to be printed in Arabic script. Yet the Ottomans adopted gunpowder technology with lightning speed.[17] The hostility of the Qing regime at Beijing to innovation might be explained by sheer Confucian conservatism. But sheer Islamic conservatism evidently cannot explain the print-versus-gun case at Istanbul and environs. Cosgel, Miceli, and Rubin show that gunpowder, when monopolized, most gratifyingly strengthened the state. But the printing press was seen as a potential threat to the monopoly of religious authority—and religious authorities provided the nonviolent half of the state's support, by offering loyalty to its legitimacy. The recent history of Iran has illustrated again the tight connection in Islam between religious authority and state legitimacy, a connection broken in Europe by the sixteenth century, earliest in Italy: contrast Heinrich IV, the Holy Roman Emperor, standing in the snow for three days in Canossa in 1077 to get the approval of Pope Gregory VII, with the Venetians' chronic defiance of papal edicts, and four-and-a-half centuries after Canossa, in 1527, Gustav Vasa of Sweden plundering the pope's monasteries and Henry VIII of England imitating him in 1536.

Needham had argued that the "relentless experimentation" that overcame Europe around 1700 was "like the merchant's standard of value." Precisely. Merchants in Europe—not state bureaucrats, whatever their religious motivation—came to rule, at any rate in matters of port improvements and glass making and trade to the Indian Ocean, if not politically. In speaking to Western visitors Chairman Mao is supposed to have summarized the conventional Chinese regret about the three inventions that Bacon stressed: "Our fathers were indeed wise. They invented printing, but not newspapers. They invented gunpowder, but used it only for fireworks. Finally, they invented the compass, but took care not to use it to discover America." His formulation (if indeed he said it) contains more than a little Orientalism, and the details are not exactly true (for example the sneer about fireworks). But there's something in it.

Why the difference between China and Europe in the rate of technological change during and after the eighteenth century, admitting the Eastern superiority in original level? One conventional argument is that the (often) unified Chinese state was bad for the bourgeoisie and their disruptive projects of innovation, at any rate by the eighteenth century. The sinologist Owen Lattimore expressed the conventional explanation in 1940: "Europe changed in a way that led to a money economy and industrialism, while China changed in a way that created a centralized imperial bureaucracy, of which the personnel was recruited generation by generation from the landed gentry, whose combination of landed interest and administrative interest kept innovation well in check and prevented industrial development almost entirely. In Europe a varying landscape encouraged a number of different kinds of extensive farming and mixed farming. Even under feudalism there was a considerable need for trade."[18] Since then doubt has accumulated that Lattimore was correct. It is certainly not correct to believe that Europeans were advanced in the development of a "money economy." The Europeans had it from the earliest times, but the Chinese had it, too, and they had in addition paper money as I noted centuries before the Europeans did, and wide trade. The "need for trade" was felt by the Chinese as much as by the

Europeans—the Grand Canal, after all, was a matter of trade, as was the shipment of silks and porcelain westward. K. Chao wrote in 1964 against the notion that it was a lack of capitalist institutions that held back the Chinese: "During nearly two thousand years [in China] a person could sell his labor on the free market. . . . A person could obtain land by purchase, . . . renting it out or working it himself. Those who had capital could invest it in a variety of ways."[19]

But again there's something in the notion that centralized control began to stall innovation, and more in it as the early modern world unfolds. Admittedly the Chinese invention of an educated bureaucracy beginning with the First Emperor (unifying China with fire and sword by 221 BCE) was hardly unique. It was preceded by imperial administrations in the ancient Near East, and reinvented by the Europeans as the imperial institutions of Alexander's and Caesar's descendents in the Mediterranean, and then re-re-reinvented by the European nation state in the sixteenth and especially the seventeenth century CE and later (the Prussians were to call their version of it the *Beamptenstaat*: the bureaucracy state). The point in each case was to subordinate everyone to the emperor/king by robbing a senatorial class or a feudal aristocracy of its separate power—and of course to continue withholding power from hoi polloi. Centralization on the scale of the whole of Europe had precursors in the bureaucracy of the church, copied from that of the Roman Empire.

Yet later and secular versions of the Europe-wide project could not be sustained, despite the earnest efforts to that end of Charlemagne, Philip II, Louis XIV, Napoleon, Hitler, and Stalin, at any rate until the peaceful conquests in our own times by the treaties of Rome and Maastricht. The Chinese version, by contrast, was thorough and continuous—"a civil service unimaginable in extent and degree of organization to the petty kingdoms of Europe," as Needham put it.[20] (Chinese economic history can therefore be investigated with a wealth of statistics unimaginable in Europe until its own modern bureaucratic and statistical era after 1800, which so impressed Weber.)[21] The Chinese bureaucracy, Needham argues, "in its early stages strongly helped science to grow," albeit sometimes for such purposes as accurately casting the horoscopes of the emperor's fourth son. In its later stages, however, when the Europeans were learning to use such Chinese inventions as the belt drive, the suspension bridge, the spinning wheel, decimal fractions, the canal pound-lock, and sea mines, and indeed the examination bureaucracy itself, the Chinese bureaucracy under the Qing emperors, writes Needham, "forcibly inhibit[ed] further growth, and in particularly prevented a break-through which has occurred in Europe." The Hungarian-French sinologist Étienne Balázs found deeper historical roots. Writing of "China as a permanently bureaucratic society," he claimed that the sprouts of capitalism were crushed by the Confucian mandarins.[22] The historical sociologist Michael Lessnoff summarizes the supposed results of neo-Confucianism under the Qing: "The Chinese state, which earlier [say, from the First Emperor through the Song] frequently sponsored technological innovation and economic enterprise, became the disseminator and enforcer of an anti-technological, antiscientific and anti-mercantile culture."[23] European-style centralized states have done similar work in the twentieth century, forcibly if often democratically inhibiting growth by preventing voluntary exchanges and demeaning bourgeoisies in a protectionist New Zealand or a populist Argentina or an authoritarian North Korea. And on the contrary China in 1978 began to grow when the center relaxed its control of local experiments in capitalism.

What Lessnoff calls "the second Weber thesis" (the first and more famous being the mistaken one that Calvinism accounts for modern economic growth) is that "compared with their Islamic, Chinese, and Indian counterparts, European cities, not only in antiquity but in the Middle Ages, enjoyed much greater independence."[24] According to Weber, Lessnoff points out, "the concept and reality of *citizenship* were unique to the West. . . . The cities of China and Islam were amalgamations of clan and tribal groups, not unified communities." It might be true, and is amplified in fact by Balázs.[25] The city-states of early Greece find answer in the free cities like Lübeck of the Holy Roman Empire (at any rate by the time in the European Middle Ages that it had become neither holy nor Roman nor an empire). We must, though, be wary of falling into the habit that Goldstone noted—of starting with our detailed knowledge of our own urbanizing West and contrasting it with a mythological picture of a Mysterious Orient. At its center, for example, the Roman Empire looked like the Eastern sultanate vivid in the Western imagination, Nero burning the city of Rome for seven days on a whim. Yet its bureaucracy and even its army were always small, for the same reasons that Chinese armies in the interior (as against the frontier) and the corresponding taxes to pay them were small. The Roman cities governed themselves within the empire.

The dignity of cities in the West surely presages the Revaluation of the seventeenth and eighteenth centuries. It may have been new, and certainly the new honor for city dwellers was new in England. Many Englishmen were taught by the astounding successes of the Dutch city states to turn away from the projects of honorable display characteristic of a rural and aristocratic society. Joyce Appleby observed that "envy and wonder stimulated a great deal of economic thinking in England during the middle decades of the seventeenth century. . . . The sustained demonstration of . . . Dutch commercial prowess acted more forcefully upon the English imagination than any other economic development."[26] Not all the English abandoned aristocratic values. Many continued to charge nobly for the guns, or to stake their wealth on the turn of a card. By the eighteenth century, however, many of them, especially the bourgeois among them and a surprisingly large number of embourgeoisified noblemen and gentry, were launched on careers of generating "a wave of gadgets" (to use the unconsciously brilliant phrase of an English schoolboy on an exam paper in economic history long ago) which has not ceased sweeping over us.[27]

An original accumulation (you might say) of habits of free publication and vigorous discussion created, as Mokyr argues in *The Gifts of Athena* (2002), "a world in which 'useful' knowledge was indeed *used* with an aggressiveness and a single-mindedness that no other society had experienced before. . . . It was the unique Western way."[28] Well, perhaps not unique until the explosion of the nineteenth century—China in the second century BCE looks pretty good at such using, as did fifth-century BCE Greece, or first-century CE Rome. And not so incidentally the criterion of "usefulness" is not intrinsic in the invention itself, but is economically determined by consumer valuations.[29] Horoscopes about the coming battle will seem more "useful" in some systems of value than inventing another siege engine or, of all pointless things, a steam engine. But anyway the West kept going, and going, while other cultural areas were pausing, to all our gain.

We do not yet know for sure why the making and using of new knowledge kept going in northwestern Europe, though many historians suspect that Europe's political fragmentation, "the ancient clotted continent," was the ticket to the modern world.[30] It led to incessant war (excepting occasional successes in utopian schemes of peacemaking such as the Treaty of Venice [1454]), but also comparative liberty for enterprise. Columbus, for example, was able to shop around his dubious proposal. Erik Ringmar observes that "from the seventeenth century onward European societies seemed to re-place one another as leaders. . . . In the long run reactionary societies lost out. The Central Kingdom had no such competitive dynamic, since there was no other society worthy of notice to which to lose out.[31] Japan achieved artificially, by prohibiting foreigners to set foot on its soil from 1637 to 1868, what China achieved by conquest of a gigantic, uniformly administered land—the very opposite of Europe's fragmentation. Centuries later the at-tempts by the British Parliament to restrict the export of machinery and machinists were undermined by smuggling and by liberty of movement in a Western Europe without passports.

Yet against such an argument, the German lands, thoroughly fragmented up to 1871, were not until the nineteenth century places of much innovation in machinery (though very much so by the eighteenth century in music and philosophy). And India was at many times fragmented, with hundreds of ra-jas and languages, without a great deal of innovation coming out of it. What is now Indonesia, too. And again, second-century BCE China was unusu-ally centralized but unusually inventive, too. Goldstone concludes sensibly that being a part of a fragmented Europe sometimes helped and sometimes hurt.[32] Little Portugal, the very soul of entrepreneurial exploration in the fifteenth and sixteenth centuries, emerged in 1640 from its temporary union with Spain without recapturing the spirit of "we must sail," and became one of the least literate and least entrepreneurial of Western European nations. After the age of Henry the Navigator the Portuguese stopped asking ques-tions and stopped allowing free answers. "Those immeasurable qualities of curiosity and dissent that are the leaven of thought," writes David Landes, were simply dropped. An English diplomat in 1670 declared of Portugal that "the people are so little curious that no man knows more than what is merely necessary for him."[33]

Literacy especially—serviced enthusiastically from the relatively if not absolutely free presses of northern Protestantism—made for a lively econ-omy. By 1900, when illiteracy in Britain was down to 3 percent (though one wonders at the practical import of such a low figure; in Prussia at the time it was reported as zero), in Portugal it was 78 percent.[34] Perhaps the fragmen-tation of Europe worked instead by way of a free press bought by literate people (remember Mao's formula), acquainting more people with the new idea of applying new ideas. Such an argument would at least date the un-usual creativity of European conversations properly, beginning small in the late fifteenth century and becoming cacophonous by the eighteenth century.

On August 18, 1520, the press of Melchior Lotther at Wittenberg issued four thousand copies of, as Luther put it, a "broadside to [the Emperor] Charles and the nobility of Germany against the tyranny and baseness of the Roman curia," *To the Christian Nobility of the German Nation*, and the next week the press was preparing over four thousand more of a longer version.[35] Between 1517 and 1520 about *three hundred thousand* copies of Luther's work, including *To the Christian Nobility*, were printed and sold.[36] Perhaps had the Emperor Charles V or Pope Leo X been able to exercise the sort of control over the presses of Germany that Suleiman the Magnificent of the Ottomans or the Qianlong Emperor of China could, the outcome would have been different.

The improved rhetoric permitted by a free press, though, was slow in coming. Private letters throughout Europe until modern times were routinely subject to opening and reading by the secret police—the police developed elaborate ways of faking the original seals. Until the late seventeenth century, indeed, writing of any sort was doubtfully free even in England. In 1579 Queen Elizabeth, outraged by a pamphlet written by the Puritan John Stubbs attacking her negotiations for marriage into the (Catholic) French royal family, had his right hand struck off by a cleaver, hammered home with a croquet mallet—after which he removed his hat with his left hand and shouted "God save the Queen!" Yet Cyndia Clegg has argued about this and other Elizabethan cases that the censorship was clumsily unsystematic, and as Milton argued in "Areopagita" that it was anyway an innovation.[37] Control of what people read did not much attract the attention of the authorities before the printing press, and especially before works appeared in the vulgar tongues (Galileo might have gotten away with his curious views of the heavens had he not written them out in his persuasive Italian). In the Stubbs case, for example, the law evoked was an arguably obsolete one referring to the former Queen Mary's husband, not a claim to a routine right to censor all publications.[38] Stubbs and his publisher and his printer were prosecuted for libel, not treason (had it been treason the punishment would not have been mere maiming but a slow death worthy of a Mel Gibson movie; Elizabeth in fact disingenuously claimed to be seeking a charge of treason in order to impress her French allies against the Spanish). Grave matters of national survival, Clegg notes, hung on the long dalliance of Elizabeth with the heir to the French throne. The time was, after all, before the defeat of the Armada.

Censorship in China was much more routine and thorough, such as in the eighteenth century executing a man and enslaving his family for printing the character for the emperor's name. Later censorships in Europe, such as the Index of Forbidden Books, though repeatedly attempted down to recent British prosecutions under the Official Secrets Act for publishing books about the activities of MI6, were undermined by publication in other jurisdictions in fragmented Europe, first Venice and then Basel and Holland, and by smuggling. Remember the *Chatterley* ban, or *The Tropic of Cancer.*

13

AND FOLLOWERS COULD LEAP OVER STAGES

At any event the results of the compounding of ancient Chinese (and Arab and Ottoman and Incan and African) inventions with the modern burst of European creativity lie around you now—computers, electric lights, electric machinery, precision tooling, plastic printers, oil-based fabrics, telephones, pressed wood, plywood, plasterboard, plate glass, steel framing, reinforced concrete, automobiles, machine-woven carpets, central heating and cooling, all invented in the nineteenth and twentieth centuries in a Europe that practiced innovation with a lunatic enthusiasm, and had no emperor to gainsay the practice.

Therefore the stage theories dating from the eighteenth century, which used an analogy with the growth of trees, are mistaken. Smith, Marx, the German Historical School, Modernization Theory, and the American economic historian Rostow were all off the mark.[1] Countries do not resemble trees in growing strictly on their own, from the leaf, the blossom, or the bole. In historical fact, no stages of acorn, sapling, young tree, old oak must be grown through. The younger "trees" can skip stages by borrowing leaves or whole branches directly from the older trees—just as the West borrowed from China, and as now China is borrowing at a manic pace from the West.

And likewise, for the same reasons, the tree-like and stage-dependent metaphor that characterizes modern "growth theory" in technical economics is misleading. The great economic historian Alexander Gerschenkron (1904–1978) emphasized the pressure of an anxious backwardness on how a "stage" would take place in, say, Russia as against England. And the great economic historian Sidney Pollard (1925–1998) added to this "the differential of contemporaneousness," which is to say the varying regional or international contexts in which a "stage" lives, such as England in a world of technological backwardness, or China today in the midst of Asian Tigers.[2] Countries do not grow by themselves, like trees. They are shaded by others, or can borrow growth.

Furthermore the stage theories depend on accumulated capital, and therefore predict a sluggishness in growth that tracks the history poorly. The ur-model of growth theory, Solow's, was found shortly after its invention in the 1950s to take a century after a disturbance to get within 90 percent of its steady state, which should have alerted the capital-favoring growth theorists that their models have something wrong with them.[3] As we know better now than an economist could have in 1957, catching up under bourgeois dignity and liberty takes decades, not centuries. Look at Singapore, or Sicily. At the Milan meetings of the International Economic History Association in September 1994 I asked a Uruguayan economic historian much infected by the new growth theory how long he thought it would take his country to catch up to the North. "Two centuries," he replied, sadly. A theory, it seems, can drive even a superb scholar insane. Such academic insanity is contradicted by the historical evidence, from Germany in the nineteenth century to Taiwan in the twentieth—that a country honoring and liberating its bourgeoisie can achieve modern standards of living for even its very poor in a couple of generations. Three at most.

The other popular and unhistorical metaphor is of a footrace, in which, naturally, countries that start later must take longer to catch up. Thus Gustav Schmoller of the German Historical School, justifying mercantilist regulations to protect the silk industry in Prussia, wrote in 1884:

> Berlin in 1780–1806 stood *almost on a level* with all the other places where the silk industry was carried on. It was mainly through the silk industry that Berlin became an important factory town, and the town whose inhabitants were distinguished by the best taste in Germany. Of course people in Berlin could not yet produce quite so cheaply as the manufactures of Lyons *which were three centuries older*; in many of the finer wares they *were behind* Krefeld, Switzerland and Holland; but they *had caught up with* Hamburg and Saxony.[4]

But earlier and later starts on the footrace do not matter in a world in which people can listen to each other, and learn. They can cut across the racetrack, or take a taxi to the head of the marathon.

For the same reason the recent theories popular in schools of business of "competitiveness" are not persuasive. Michael E. Porter's book in 1990, *The Competitive Advantage of Nations*, was ignored by economists, but created a stir among business-school academics. It spoke in baseball terms of competitiveness as depending on success in four corners of a "diamond" originating from a "home base." The long distances in the great free-trade area of the United States, for example, gave it a competitive advantage in the making of very large engines for motor trucks. Howard Davies and Paul Ellis, though, put their finger on the central confusion underlying Porter's book—it confuses "'competitiveness' construed as productivity and 'competitiveness' construed as the market share held by a sub-set of industries."[5] Being productive, producing a great deal with few inputs, is certainly a good idea. No one would dispute that. It is called Getting Rich By Being Smart. But getting a large market share has little to do with getting rich, or being smart. Bangladesh has a high share of the world's jute market. Norway has a low share of the world's agricultural machinery market. Market share is determined not by what economists since David Ricardo have called *absolute advantage*—how productive you are per hour of labor compared with your "competitors," say—but by *comparative* advantage—how productive you are in raising jute compared with other uses of *your* time making, say, combine harvesters. If, considering your opportunity cost in harvesters when you make a ton of jute, you are the right country to assign to jute making, that is best for you and for the world. It's like assigning tasks in a household. Mom may have an absolute advantage in both sweeping and cooking, but if she has a *comparative* advantage in cooking, then little Johnny should be assigned to the broom if the family is going to make the most of its labor. Rich or poor (that is, having a high or a low absolute advantage in making goods and services), every country always has some *comparative* advantage. There is work for everyone in a household or on a team. That India has a comparative advantage in outsourced computer advice, and a large market share, does not mean that India is richer than the United States (which itself has in fact an *absolute* advantage in computer advice) or that India has "beaten" the United States. Comparative advantage says that the United States has better uses for its graduate engineers than the way engineers are used in India—fielding hysterical calls, for example, from elderly lady professors of economics and history in Chicago about the wretched Microsoft Vista product she has been condemned to use.

The historian David Landes in his splendid, learned, Eurocentric book of 1998, *The Wealth and Poverty of Nations*, attacks throughout the economist's notion of comparative advantage. But of course he doesn't understand it. Not a bit. He disdains such knowledge. Such obduracy is bound to annoy an economist. For God's sake, David, she exclaims, you can get comparative advantage straight, once and for all, by reading and reflecting on the chapter about it in any first-year economics text, and never again misapply it (as Landes does in about half of the numerous instances in which he mentions it). Paul Krugman is quoted by Landes as saying that Listian, Porterish, nationalist economics is "based on a failure to understand even the simplest economic facts and concepts." I have to agree with Krugman here (as I do only about 85 percent of the time—the 15 percent remainder usually being crucial). Retorts Landes angrily to Krugman's jibe: "Peremptory and dismissive."[6] (David should talk. In peremptory and dismissive responses to serious arguments with which he disagrees, he has a comparative advantage). On another page of the ten or so in which he mangles comparative advantage, he attacks (p.172) an obvious argument I have long made that "unfavorable" balances of trade are *good* for the country having them, such as America's with Japan in the 1970s: get Toyotas, give green pieces of paper. Great deal! How much patience are Krugman and I supposed to have with people who will not crack a freshman economics book yet insist on talking about economics, and wax indignant instead of making coherent arguments? When Landes says for example that "comparative advantage is not fixed, and it can move for and against," he is combining a truism with nonsense.[7] Comparative advantage can change, but trade is always advantageous. There's no "against" in specializing for trade.

But the best that human frailty is likely to achieve in confusing absolute and comparative advantage came from someone who presumably *had* studied freshman economics with some care. Lester C. Thurow, an economist and at the time the dean of the business school at MIT, wrote in 1985 *The Zero-Sum Solution: Building a World-Class American Economy*. The book treats income as being extracted like success in a footrace or in American football yardage from non-Americans, especially from Asian non-Americans (it was 1985, note, and the anti-Japanese panic was at its height). "To play a competitive game is not to be a winner," Thurow declares. "Free-market battles can be lost as well as won."[8]

Thurow is off the mark. There's no "against," no "battle lost," in specializing for trade. If the "competitive" game is free exchange and innovation, then almost everyone who plays the game wins, if not as a producer, then as a consumer.[9] Modern economic growth has *not* been "zero-sum," a point on which as I have said most economic historians of whatever politics agree. In the trade-and-imitate game, the people in different countries exchange goods and services. If you insist on looking at exchange and innovation as games, then they are games in which everybody wins, like square dancing. The game theorists call them positive-sum. The "beaten" countries in the supposedly "competitive" game (such as at length even Britain itself) end up richer than some of the "winners"—in 2006 real national incomes per head in Britain and Japan and Germany were nearly identical, despite a century of claims that first Germany and then Japan were "beating" old Britain.[10]

True, looked at from the factory floor in Detroit, a market with competing suppliers in Japan or Korea—or for that matter in California or Tennessee—*is* zero-sum, which gives Thurow's assertions an air of plain common sense. (Though the same argument applies to competition from other Americans; you would think the fact would give pause: why not "protect" General Motors from Ford, to "create jobs"?) You could once hear versions of the xenophobic common sense of "competiveness" from Lou Dobbs nightly on CNN (Dobbs majored in economics at Harvard College, but didn't understand; to be quite fair, though, I majored in economics, too, a couple of years earlier—and I also didn't understand, until returning to the same point in graduate school and then teaching it and then writing books about it: drink deep, or taste not the Pierian spring; or at least don't close your mind on first hearing the argument). The negative-sum game metaphor looks at only one side of the economy, the producing side. Mercantilists of all ages have done so. As Adam Smith said, though, "Consumption is the sole end and purpose of all production [and therefore it is the end and purpose of all exports]; and the interest of the producer ought to be attended to only so far as it may be necessary for promoting that of the consumer."[11] We do not live to work, or to export. We work, or export, to live. One has to include in the accounting the Japanese consumers made worse off by Japan's mercantilism in the late twentieth century, or the American consumers made better off by America's move to free trade. It's a matter, again, of Toyotas for green pieces of paper.

The metaphor of the zero-sum footrace in the theories of Defoe or List or Schmoller or Landes or Thurow or Porter or Dobbs or your local politician gets some of its appeal from a wider tragedy in which it plays, namely, the tragedy that eventually the rest of the world caught on to what northwestern Europe and its offshoots had stumbled into during the eighteenth and nineteenth centuries. Britain was first, and what happened in Britain has therefore been of considerable interest. A Britain tragically surpassed in the footrace of nations tells a story easy to lament. Landes, for example, has long interpreted modern history as a footrace between Britain and the rest, in for example his long classic essay of 1965, reprinted and extended as a book in 1969, whose essence was a conference paper of 1954, *The Unbound Prometheus: Technological Change and Industrial Development in Western Europe from 1750 to the Present.* His antieconomic metaphor of "leadership" in a race pervades his rhetoric, as in his chapter headings— "Closing the Gap," "Short Breath and Second Wind." He asks in the middle third of the book, "Why did industrial *leadership* pass in the closing decades of the nineteenth century from Britain to Germany?"[12] He answers that the British racers in the lead slacked off, and were beaten. "Thus the Britain of the late nineteenth century basked complacently in the sunset of economic hegemony. . . . Now it was the turn of the third generation, the children of affluence ['affluence'? British real national income per head in 1880 was about $3,500 in 1990 prices, equal in real terms to that of Sri Lanka in 2001], tired of the tedium of trade and flushed with the bucolic aspirations of the country gentleman. . . . They worked at play and played at work."[13]

The evidence for such Victorian economic failure is slight. And in truth it would be strange if a Britain "beating" the world in the 1850s suddenly by the 1870s could do little right. The facts show that nothing so strange occurred.[14] Similar facts undermine the current fable in which the United States is cast in the role of the leader suddenly unable to finish the race—though mysteriously still producing the fourth-highest real, purchasing-power-corrected national income per capita in the world, after tiny Kuwait, Luxembourg, and Norway, and a third greater than the "competitors" who "beat" it, such as Germany or Japan, and nine times the real income per capita of China, said to be coming to "dominance." Superior technologies in one place get adopted sooner or later in another. It is not easy, and the delay can be decades. But on a longer timescale it happened massively 1800 to the present. In the long run it doesn't matter that Davy, Swan, Edison, Latimer, Whitney, and Coolidge coinvented the incandescent light bulb in England and the

United States. It didn't stay there. It burned brightly, and pretty promptly, in Naples and Beijing.

Yet what is more important here is that the entire, popular business of thinking of ranks and league tables and races and football yardage in which nations are "beaten" or "decline" or "lose" tells the story the wrong way. The prize for merely second place, or tenth place, was not poverty, or even loss of political hegemony.[15] "Beaten" Britain is still the eighth-largest economy in the world, the second-largest source of direct foreign investment, and a permanent member of the United Nations Security Council; and London is the second-largest financial center in the world. Before the British, the leading case of "failure" was the United Provinces of the Netherlands in the eighteenth and early nineteenth centuries. With what result? Disaster? Poverty? No. True, the Netherlands has ended small and militarily weak, a tiny linguistic island in a corner of Europe. Yet by any historical or international standard it has become fabulously wealthy (at $38,000 per year per head in 2006, only a little below the world-"beating" U.S.A., and higher than Britain, which in the nineteenth century allegedly beat it), and indeed it is still among the most influential investors in the world. Relative "decline" is no decline at all. As his children grow up, a father does not lament that his share in the poundage of the house declines. And at the bottom of the league tables, after all, a relatively primitive Russia in modern times literally beat Napoleon, and then for an encore, though still primitive relative to Western Europe, literally beat Hitler.

The footrace metaphor mixes up political dominance with economic prosperity. The fevered essays in most issues of *Foreign Affairs* that predict the "rise" of China, say, or the "decline" of the United States freely mix the two. The rise and decline of nations, to borrow the book title by the late economist Mancur Olson (1981), or the rise and fall of the great powers, to borrow the title by the historian Paul Kennedy (1987), suggests that coming in first matters vitally, in the macho style of Teddy Roosevelt's "strenuous life." It doesn't.

Kennedy is the most explicit, but the related assumption that *military* strength explains why Westerners have a lot of cargo pops up all over.[16] Even from wise heads, it is mistaken. The brilliant physiologist, ornithologist, geographer, and world historian Jared Diamond, for example, wrote in 1997 that "technological and political differences as of A.D. 1500 were the immediate cause of the modern world's inequalities."[17] Why? Because "empires with steel weapons were able to conquer." But does military conquest make the conqueror rich? True, it makes him richer than his victims dead from smallpox and steel swords. It does nothing, however, to explain the gigantic enrichment 1800 to the present of the West and the North, and now the East and the South. Being Top Nation militarily is *caused* by being rich (though remember Russia in 1812 and 1942, and now China at a mere $13 a day, and much less during the Korean War). It does not on the whole cause the riches. Killing aborigines or bossing around impoverished traditional peasants is not the way to get plate glass, political freedom, sewerage systems, long retirement, stereo sets, magnesium ladders, the forty-hour week, and the higher education for serious spiritual growth.

∞

As the inventive panoply multiplies it becomes easier and easier to take advantage of it, and to adapt the panoply to one's own purposes, good or bad. The metaphors of a growing tree or a football game or a footrace should give way to one of an exchange of ideas—though a mere "exchange" of ideas, even though correct in stressing the mutual advantage, is itself not quite apt. Tunzelmann has wisely remarked that technology "cannot be reduced to information, such as often found in economist's treatments. . . . [It] has to be learned . . . through processes only partially understood."[18] The processes are what the chemist and philosopher Michael Polanyi (the economic historian Karl Polanyi's smarter brother) called "tacit knowledge."[19] Tunzelmann gives Polanyi's example of learning to ride a bicycle: "No amount of printed instruction on how to ride will enable most people to hop on a bicycle for the first time and confidently pedal off." Another economic historian, the late John R. Harris, showed in detail that transfers of furnaces technology for making iron and glass between so similar nations as Britain and France 1710 to 1800 depended on tacit knowledge difficult to convey.[20] It is a point that the sociologist of science Harry Collins has made about experiments. The tacit practices of one laboratory are difficult to reproduce, especially at the pioneering margin of cultivation of science where things are necessarily difficult.[21] Likewise for industrial tricks. And therefore the merely economic metaphor of a smooth "exchange of ideas" does not tell the whole story.

Anyway, England in the eighteenth century could not possibly have experienced the present-day Chinese growth rate of real income per head of 10 percent per year, even in its greatest booms. The Chinese depend on ideas developed earlier and slowly in the West, after the Asian Exchange of blast furnace and cotton, such as modern earthmoving equipment and computers. The doubling of income per head in a mere seven years that the Chinese rate implies could not happen before very recent times, with gigantic piles of already-invented ideas such as the power loom or the light bulb or the printed circuit waiting to be borrowed, if one will but let people use them for the profit due a person with a newly borrowed idea, and cease from sneering at and stealing from and executing those who earn the profits. The historian of technology David Edgerton speaks of "the shock of the old," in which people—even very poor people in the *favelas* of Brazil—keep finding new uses for old technologies, such as sheets of corrugated iron.[22] Invent as you will iron or paper or printing slowly over many centuries; it is not enough for the breakthrough. What's needed, wrote Madame Chen Zhili, state councilor of China for education, science, technology, and culture, in a touching preface to Temple's popularization of Needham in 2007, is "innovation [which] is the spirit of a nation and the endless momentum for a nation's prosperity."[23] The innovation in China did not depend on China reaching the correct stage of growth, but on Madame Chen Zhili and her colleagues in the Central Committee finally allowing local mayors and businesspeople to try out experiments in non-communist economics, such as not outlawing manufacturers or not re-educating land speculators. Neighboring Burma and North Korea show what happens if on the contrary you carry on with militarist or socialist policies, and China can show it again if it retreats from innovation in favor of the old Maoists or the new crony capitalists.

China and India, in other words, can take off the shelf the inventions laboriously developed by the Watts and the Edisons of the past three centuries—and by the Chinese and Indian inventors of earlier centuries, together with the Incan potato breeders and the brass casters of Benin, all of whose inventions had been taken up eagerly by the curious Westerners. Indians invented fine cotton cloth, which then became the staple of Manchester, but latterly in its fully mechanized form became again the staple of Mumbai. The Chinese invented mass-produced pig iron, which then became the staple of Swedish Uppland and English Cleveland and American Gary, but latterly with some additional chemical engineering the staple of the Kamaishi Works in Japan and now the Anshan works in China. And so Sweden in the late nineteenth century and then Japan in the early and middle twentieth century and China in the early twenty-first century caught up astonishingly quickly.[24]

A poor country that adopts thoroughgoing innovation, therefore, can get within hailing distance of the West, as I said, in about two generations. That does not mean that catch-up is inevitable. A country such as Venezuela that insists on driving away its entrepreneurs, or a country like Sweden 1960– 1990 that pursues social-democratic equality in education to the neglect of quality or efficiency, can kill economic growth for a while. Like Tolstoy's unhappy families, the countries with bad economic policies are unhappy each in its own way.

Good policies are boringly similar: rule of law, property rights, and above all dignity and liberty for the bourgeoisie. The happy countries end up looking similar, because each has automobiles, computers, higher education. Good policy allows taking technology off the shelf, and achieving a pretty good life for ordinary folk in two or three generations. It has happened repeatedly, as when the United States adopted British manufacturing, or Germany the same. Consider such recent miracles of leaping over putatively inevitable stages as Taiwan or Hong Kong or Singapore. Perhaps we should stop being gobsmacked every time it happens. The historical sociologist Erik Ringmar speaks of institutions encouraging "reflection [having ideas], entrepreneurship [implementing them], and pluralism [allowing them to flourish without interference]," applying such notions to the success of Europe, and then of East Asia.[25] Give people liberty to work and to invent and to invest, and treat them with dignity, and you get fast catching up. Goldstone puts it this way: "What Japan's success does demonstrate is something that has been shown in Korea and Taiwan as well—that a unified people under firm government direction [but a firmness that does not include counterproductive corruption or grossly misled planning] determined to import and implement Western industrial technology can do so in about four decades. This is about the time it has taken to transform South Korea from an African level of agricultural poverty to one of the world's leading industrial economies; similarly for Taiwan. Both have risen to this level from minimal beginnings after the Korean War of the 1950s and the Chinese Civil Wars of the 1940s."[26]

Richard Easterlin would agree with the speed implied by the metaphor of "taking technology off the shelf." He wrote in 2003 that "since the early 1950s, the material living level of the average person in today's less-developed countries . . . , which collectively account for four-fifths of the world's population, has multiplied by threefold," much faster than presently rich countries grew in the nineteenth century.[27] It has led to Paul Collier's Top Four to Six Billions. Similarly rapid has been the rise in life expectancy and the fall in fertility and the rise of literacy: on all counts, notes Easterlin, it is "a much more rapid rate of advance . . . than took place in the developed countries in the past."

In other words, what does not need much scientific inquiry is how the Indians and Chinese, having been denied innovation for decades by imperial edict and warlord pillaging and socialist central plan and lack of widespread education (the last is Easterlin's argument), can get rich quickly by gaining peaceful access to well-stocked shelves of inventions, from the steam engine to the forward contract to the business meeting.[28] Routine economics predicts that, after decades of disastrous economic luck, the misallocations and spurned opportunities will be so great that considerable fortunes can be made pretty easily, and the average income of poor people can be raised pretty easily, too. Economists say, "People will pick up $500 bills on the sidewalk," earning enormously high percentage returns on their investments in stooping—unless, indeed, you jail people who specialize in picking up the bills, as once in Albania and still in Cuba. If Brazil and South Africa can be persuaded to adopt the liberal economic principles that are presently enriching China and India (and that had enriched Britain and Italy more slowly and therefore less obviously), there is no reason why in forty years the grandchildren of presently poor Brazilians and South Africans cannot enjoy something pretty close to Western European standards of living. That's not ideological prejudice, some neocon fantasy in support of American imperial power. It's a soberly obvious historico-experimental fact, which has already curbed American power. On the other hand, if Brazil and South Africa persist in unhelpful economic policies (such as South Africa's labor laws based on German models), they can retain a gigantic, unemployed underclass and an inferior position relative to the United States, just as long as they find that attractive.

So the spread of economic growth is no deep puzzle. It is worth scientific inquiry, of course, but has the character of normal science, and the events it studies have the character of normal investment. Again and again the fashionable fatalism that regards this or that case as "hopeless" (in the 1960s we thought China and India were), and the subtle racism that thinks it impossible that *they* will ever be as rich and famous as *we* are, has been proven wrong. Allow people to take technologies off the shelves, or up off the sidewalks, and adapt them to Indonesian or Mauritian or Irish circumstances for personal glory or profit, and the local bourgeoisie will do well for the nation, too. It is the Bourgeois Deal. Much ink has been spilt on the issue of "convergence." Pessimists like Luis Bértola point to alarming failures of whole regions like Latin America to keep pace with Europe or the United States or, lately, East Asia.[29] But we optimists note that in any case a country like Mexico has gained immensely from the Bourgeois Deal compared with its position in 1800. Bértola's figures, based on Maddison's, show that Mexico went from $693 a head per year in 1820 (expressed in 1990 American dollars) to $7,137 in 2003, more than a factor of ten, and not allowing for better products. True, in his tables the "West" achieved this level in the 1960s. But is a forty-year lag, considering the continuing ride up the blade of the hockey stick that Mexico is sharing with others, a cause for deep despair? From 1950 to 2001 in Maddison's own tables the forty-seven Latin American countries (including the Caribbean) more than doubled their real incomes per head. Likewise, political scientists looking at Italy, such as Edward Banfield or Robert Putnam, have long argued that ancient cultural and institutional failures have kept Sicily and the rest of the South from coming level with the industrial North. What the institutional pessimists overlook is that meanwhile Southern Italy, like Mexico, has risen out of medieval standards of living. Catania is not Milan. But the Catanians have automobiles and marble-floored houses and vacations in Norway. After such successes, there is no reason to believe that Mexico and Sicily will always be poor, or always lag. Japan didn't. Spain didn't.

The bigger scientific puzzle is how the shelves, or the sidewalks, got so very well stocked in the first place. The central puzzle, in other words, is not so much why there was in Britain after 1760 a burst of what Joel Mokyr calls "macroinventions" (steam, textile machinery) but why the burst did not fizzle out later, as earlier times of innovation had—such as during the "industrial revolution of the thirteenth century." "The 'classical' Industrial Revolution in the eighteenth century," Mokyr notes, "was not an altogether novel phenomenon."[30] Not altogether. You can see efflorescences, as Goldstone calls them, in ancient China and in seventeenth-century Holland. But the continuation certainly *was* novel.

14

THE TIDE DIDN'T HAPPEN BECAUSE
OF THRIFT

How, then? How and why did the first Industrial Revolution happen, with its astonishing follow-on in the nineteenth and twentieth centuries? In this book we specialize in widely believed explanations that don't work very well. One widely believed explanation is thrift.

The word "thrift" in English is still used as late as John Bunyan to mean simply "wealth" or "profit," deriving from the verb "thrive" like "gift" from "give" and "drift" from "drive" (the derivation was still vibrant in 1785 to a scholarly poet like William Cowper, who laments the working poor in The Task (17, bk. 4),"With all this thrift they thrive not"). But sense 3 in the *Oxford English Dictionary* is our modern one, dating significantly from the sixteenth century: "So I will if none of my sons be thrifty" (1526); "food is never found to be so pleasant . . . as when . . . thrift has pinched afore" (1553).

The modern "thrift," sense 3, can be viewed as a mix of the cardinal virtues of temperance and of prudence in things economic. Temperance is the cardinal virtue of self-command in the face of temptation. Lead me not into temptation. Prudence, by contrast, is the cardinal virtue of practical wisdom. Give us this day (a way to make prudently and laboriously for ourselves) our daily bread. It is reason, know-how, rationality, efficiency, getting allocation right, savoir faire. Prudence without temperance does not in fact do the task it knows it should thriftily do, and knows how to do. Temperance without prudence, on the other hand, does not know in practice what to do: *ne savoir pas faire*. A prudent housewife in the "Ladder to Thrift," as the English agricultural rhymester Thomas Tusser put it in 1580, "makes provision skillfully."[1] Without being full of skill, that is, prudent, she does not know how to be thrifty in saving tallow for candles or laying up salt mutton for Eastertide.

Prudent temperance has in a sense no history, because it happens by necessity in every human society. The Hebrew Bible, for example, speaks of thrift, though not very often, usually associating it with diligence: "The sluggard will not plough in the autumn by reason of the cold; therefore shall he beg in [the] harvest, and have nothing"; "Seest thou a man diligent in his business? He shall stand before kings" (Proverbs 20:4; 22:29). Jesus of Nazareth and his tradition used parables of thrift to point to another world, though again the parables of thrift are balanced by parables of entrepreneurship such as the parable of the talents, or of liberality, such as changing water into wine to keep the party going.[2] "Eat and drink," advises the Koran, "but do not be wasteful, for God does not like the prodigals" (7:31). In the Koran, as in the Jewish and Christians books, thrift is not a major theme.

Of course other faiths than the Abrahamic also admire on occasion a prudent thrift. The Four Noble Truths of Buddhism, to be sure, recommend that life's sorrow can be dissolved by the ending of desire, in which case advice to be thrifty would be lacking in point. Be "thrifty" with your modest daily bread in your monk's cell? Buddhism is similar in this respect to Greek and Roman stoicism, which advocated devaluing the world's lot, an inspiration early and late for Christian saints of thriftiness. Yet Buddhism allows for prudent busy-ness, too. The "Admonition to Singâla" is in the Buddhist canon "the longest single passage . . . devoted to lay morality."[3] Buddha promises the businessman that he will "make money like a bee" if he is wise and moral:

> Such a man makes his pile
> As an anthill, gradually.

And then it counsels an astounding abstemiousness, far beyond that contemplated even in Max Weber's worldly asceticism:

> He should divide
> His money in four parts;
> On one part he should live,
> With two expand his trade,
> And the fourth he should save
> Against a rainy day.

The rate of savings recommended is fully 75 percent—though with no allowance for charity, which made the Buddhist commentators on the text uneasy.

In England the thirteenth-century writers of advice books to Norman-English landowners start with a little bit on thrift and then go on to the prudent details of managing an agricultural estate. The third paragraph of *The Husbandry* by Walter of Henley, after a bow in the second paragraph to the sufferings of Our Lord Jesus, prays "that according to what your lands be worth yearly . . . you order your life, and no higher at all."[4] And then in the same vein for five more paragraphs. The anonymous *Seneschaucy*, written like Walter in Norman French in the late thirteenth century, instructs the lord's chief steward "to see that there is no extravagance . . . on any manor. . . . and to reduce all unnecessary expenditure . . . which shows no profit. . . . About this it is said: foolish spending brings no gain."[5] The passage deprecates "the practices without prudence or reason" (*lez maners saunz pru e reyson*). So much for a *rise* three or four centuries later of prudence, reason, accounting, rationality, Calvinist asceticism, and thrift. From the camps of the !Kung to the lofts of Chicago, humans need to live within their incomes, being by their own lights "thrifty."

The prehistory of thrift, in other words, extends back to the Garden of Eden. It is laid down for example in our genes. A protoman who could not store fat on his thighs and stomach thriftily in feast times would suffer in famine and leave fewer children. And therefore his descendent in a prosperous modern society needs irritatingly to watch his weight. Prudent temperance does not require a stoic or monkish or Singâla abstemiousness. A ploughman burning 3,000 calories a day had better get them somehow. One should be thrifty in eating, says Tusser, but not to the point of denying our prudent human solidarity:

> Each day to be feasted—what husbandry worse!
> Each day for to feast is as ill for the purse.
> Yet measurely feasting with neighbors among
> Shall make thee beloved, and live the more long.[6]

And so too actual luxury, the opposite of thrift. "Depend on it, sir," said Samuel Johnson in 1778, "every state of society is as luxurious as it can be. Men always take the best they can get," in lace or food or education.[7] Marx noted cannily that "when a certain stage of development has been reached [notice the stage-theoretic vocabulary that Marx borrowed from eighteenth-century pioneers], a conventional degree of prodigality, which is also an exhibition of wealth, and consequently a source of credit, becomes a business necessity. . . . Luxury enters into capital's expenses of representation."[8] It sounds plausible enough. Otherwise it would be hard to explain the high quality of lace on the collars of black-clad Dutch merchants in paintings of the seventeenth century, or indeed the Dutch market for the paintings in their hundreds of thousands that reflected back in oily richness the merchants and their world.

The average English and American English person from the sixteenth through the eighteenth century, then, surely practiced thrift. Yet this did not distinguish her from the average English or American English person before or after, or for that matter from the average person anywhere on earth since the Fall. "'My other piece of advice, Copperfield,' said Mr. Micawber, 'you know. Annual income twenty pounds, annual expenditure nineteen nineteen and six, result happiness. Annual income twenty pounds, annual expenditure twenty pounds ought and six, result misery.' . . . To make his example the more impressive, Mr. Micawber drank a glass of punch with an air of great enjoyment and satisfaction, and whistled the College Hornpipe. I did not fail to assure him that I would store these precepts in my mind, though indeed I had no need to do so, for, at the time, they affected me visibly."[9]

Thrift in the sense of spending exactly what one earns is indeed forced by accounting. Not having manna from heaven or an outside Santa Claus, the human world must get along on what it gets. If we do not at least hunt or gather, we do not eat. The world's income from the effort must equal to the last sixpence the world's expenditure, "expenditure" understood to include investment goods. So too Mr. Micawber. If he spends more than he earns he must depend on something turning up, such as a loan or a gift or an inheritance. He draws down his credit. In the meantime his transfers from his diminishing balance sheet—what he owns and owes—pays to the last sixpence for his glass of punch and his house rent.

Thrift in the sense of spending less than one earns and thereby accumulating investments as a capital sum is again a matter of accounting. You must allocate everything you earn somehow, to bread and punch or to bonds and house building or to sheer waste and your mattress. If you can resist consuming soft drinks and other immediate consumption goods, "abstaining from consumption" in the economist's useful way of putting it, you necessarily save. That is, you add to your bank account or to your mattress or to your capital in education or in battleships. Of course you can allocate foolishly or well, to bombs or to college educations, to glasses of punch or to a savings account.

There is nothing modern about such accounting. It comes with life and the first law of thermodynamics, in the Kalahari or in Kansas City. In particular, because of the peculiarly unproductive character of their agriculture, the preindustrial European world needed urgently to abstain from consumption, "consumption" understood as immediate expenditures that are not investments in some future. Yields of rye or barley or wheat per unit of seed planted in medieval and early modern agriculture in northern Europe were extremely low: only three or four—they are fifty or so now for wheat, and eight hundred for the maize introduced after Columbus. (In monsoon Asia the flooding rains allow the cultivation of rice, which has always had a high yield-seed ratio, with the additional benefit that the annual and sometimes biannual flooding would fertilize and weed the fields, without plowing. Rice was introduced by the Muslims into Spain and Sicily, and it spread by the fourteenth century into, for example, the Po Valley in Northern Italy.)[10]

The low yields of wheat, barley, and oats forced northern Europeans in the good old days, if they did not want to starve next year, to refrain from a great deal of consumption this year. No matter how much your stomach growled with hunger as you did it, one quarter to one third of the grain crop had to go back into the field as seed in the fall or the spring, its fruit to be harvested the next September. It had better. In an economy in which the grain crop was perhaps half of total income, the seed portion alone of medieval saving implied an aggregate saving rate of upward of one half times one quarter, that is, 12 percent. The rate of saving in modern industrial economies is seldom above 10 or 20 percent. No wonder there was little savings available for trying out innovations—and the less so because the crops were variable. Medieval life was precarious (with yield-seed ratios or 3 or 4, it is no wonder) and innovation correspondingly dangerous.[11]

The trade in grain was restricted to the parts of Europe served by rivers and seas, since overland cartage was enormously expensive when roads were mere tracks through the mud—and even coastal water transport was at first expensive as a share of the price. The price of wheat in Valencia, Spain, in 1450 was 6.7 times the price in Lwów, Poland (by 1750 it had fallen to a few percentage points of difference).[12] Therefore local grain storage for local consumption was also high by modern standards. Nowadays if the grain crop does poorly in America the market easily supplies the deficiency from the other side of the world. No need to store seven year's plenty. In the late Middle Ages some grain did flow from the Midlands to London or from Burgundy to Paris. Yet it began to flow from as far away as Poland to Western Europe in large amounts only gradually during the sixteenth and seventeenth centuries, by the efforts of innovative Dutch merchants and shipbuilders. Only in the nineteenth century did it come from so distant a clime as Ukraine or, later, North and South America, or finally Australia. Until the eighteenth century therefore the grain crops in the narrow markets tended to fail together. The potato famine of the 1840s was the last big replay in Europe of a sort of undiversified catastrophe commonplace there in the 1540s, and more so in the 1340s. Grain storage, in other words, amounted to another desperate form of saving, crowding out more modern forms of investment.[13] In such circumstances you stored grain in gigantic percentages of current income, or next year you died. In West Germanic languages such as Dutch, German, and Old English, the word cognate with "starve" (for example, modern Dutch *sterven*, modern German *sterben*, Old English *steorfan*) is the main word for "die."

Such desperate scarcities were broken in the New World of the British Americans, who ate better than their Old World cousins within a generation of the first settlements. It was not a remarkable achievement, considering that the American rivers were full of fish and the woods full of game, and that their cousins back in England were then passing through the worst times for the workingman since the early fourteenth century.[14] Plentiful land in Massachusetts or Pennsylvania, at any rate on the literal frontier, made it unnecessary to save so much in grain, which anyway was high-yield maize. The forced thrift was freed for other investments.

Yet notice: although the North American English (and the French, Dutch, Swedes, and Germans there) became as early as the late seventeenth century pretty well off by the wretched European standards, and therefore freed from using up their savings protecting next year's grain crop, what became British North America and then Canada and the United States was by no means the home of the Industrial Revolution. It was too small in population, too far away from a mass of consumers, too tempted by a comparative advantage in agriculture and forestry products, or for that matter too restricted by French or British mercantilism. The northeast of the United States, like southern Belgium and northern France, was to become a close follower, of course, in the 1790s and 1800s. The rapid American adoption of manufacturing surprised many people, such as John Adams. He told Franklin in 1780 that "America will not make manufactures enough for her own consumption these thousand years."[15] "Yankee ingenuity" is not a myth, as the quick industrialization of New England was to show. The North American colonies did indeed contain many ingenious inventors willing to get their hands dirty. Even the North American slave areas were not inventive deserts by any means: look at Jefferson's ingenuity, and the improvement of cotton varieties.

But the leaders of industrialization, from the 1760s, were northwest England and lowland Scotland. These were lands of grindingly *necessary* thrift. Yields of agriculture were still low—the real "agricultural revolution" came finally in the nineteenth century (not as used to be thought in the eighteenth) with guano, selective breeding, steel plows, cheap water transport, reaping machines, commodity exchanges, and clay-pipe drainage. In short, the homeland of the Industrial Revolution was not a place of excess savings waiting to be redirected to factories.

The point is that there is no aggregate increase in thrifty savings to explain the modern world. Thrifty saving is not peculiar to the Age of Innovation. Thrift or prudence did not increase in the childhood of modernity. Actual saving stood high before modern times, and did not change much at the time of modern innovation. It changed only *after* the innovation had given us new opportunities to invest. We were routinely thrifty long before we were mainly urban, and long, long before we came to celebrate bourgeois dignity and bourgeois liberty and the creative destruction which they wrought.

Looking at thrift in a cheerful way, the starting point used to be said to be (according to Max Weber in 1905, for example) a rise of thriftiness among Dutch or especially English Puritans. Marx characterized such classical economic tales, from which Weber took his inspiration, as praise for "that queer saint, that knight of the woeful countenance, the capitalist 'abstainer.'"[16] We can join Marx for a moment in disbelieving the optimistic tale—noting again, and contrary to Marx's own pessimistic version of the same tale, that abstention is universal. Saving rates in Catholic Italy or for that matter Confucian Buddhist Taoist China were not much lower, if lower at all, than in

Calvinist Massachusetts or Lutheran Germany. According to recent calculations by economic historians, in fact, British investment in physical capital as a share of national income (not allowing for seed investment) was strikingly *below* the European norm—only 4 percent in 1700, as against a norm of 11 percent, 6 percent as against 12 percent in 1760, and 8 percent against over 12 percent in 1800.[17] Britain's investment, though rising before and then during the Industrial Revolution, showed less, not more, abstemiousness than in the less advanced countries around it.

The evidence suggests, in other words, that saving depends on investment, not the other way round. If you want to do well, you should innovate, with a modest stake borrowed from your brother, and then set aside out of your profit from having a good idea (if indeed it is good) the additional savings to reinvest in your expanding business. Your savings rate will rise, but as a result of your innovation, not as a precondition of it. When in the nineteenth century the rest of Europe started to follow Britain into industrialization, its savings rates rose, too. Yet the rest of Europe's markedly higher rates during the eighteenth century did not cause it then to awaken from its medieval slumbers. Saving was not the constraint. As the great medieval economic historian M. M. Postan put it, the constraint was not "the poor potential for saving," but the "extremely limited" character in pre-nineteenth-century Europe of "opportunities for productive investment."[18] Innovation was it.

15

CAPITAL FUNDAMENTALISM IS WRONG

Innovation, not the sheer piling of productive investments, dominates economic growth. The late Charles Feinstein, who pioneered the estimation of the national accounts of Britain back into the mid-nineteenth century and before, disagreed. He argued that "in the earlier stages of economic development, increases in the stock of physical capital accounted for a large part of the rise in output per man hour; workers were able to produce more because they had more capital to work with."[1] Yet such capital-induced rises in output per man hour were limited. Doubling the number of horses that a plowman works with does indeed raise wheat output per man hour a little—though much less than a doubling (it will raise it by 100 percent [from the doubling of the horses] multiplied by the share of horses in the cost of producing wheat, perhaps 5 percent).[2] Multiplying the traditional equipment in scythes and open drains and barns *without innovating* does not come close to yielding a factor of sixteen, and does a poor job explaining even the factor down to 1860 of two. Innovating in clay-pipe underdrainage and plant breeding and forward markets and mechanical reapers and experimental stations and diesel tractors and railcar delivery systems and hybrid corn and farm cooperatives and chemical herbicides does the job better.

Feinstein knew all this, of course. He was a great and learned economic historian. He observed that "more recently [than 'the earlier stages of economic development'] . . . advances in the quality of equipment have become progressively more important." He could not surrender, however, what the economist William Easterly (2001) has called "capital fundamentalism." Innovation "must be embodied in physical equipment," Feinstein declared, thus retaining investment in the leading role. (His assertion is true for reaping machines and diesel tractors; but for organizational innovations such as selective breeding it is largely false.) The embodiment "made investment and saving . . . crucial to economic growth." The truth of the assertion comes from the mere accounting—no investment, of course, no reaping machine. But it is false in an economic sense. Attributing the Age of Innovation to the piling up of capital is like attributing Shakespeare to the English language or to the Roman alphabet. Yes, the Bard needed the language and even the alphabet. Granted. Yet is "crucial" the right concept of causation to use?

The supply of saving to one region such as Lancashire or one country such as Britain—even economically bulky Britain around 1840—came at a fixed rate of interest, 4 or 6 percent. What made for the demand for saving was the usefulness of a loan to build a barn or a machine, a usefulness which economists call the "marginal product of capital." Piling brick on brick, however, or even machine on machine, led to rapidly diminishing returns. Think of a ditchdigger oversupplied with shovels, or a 100-acre farm with six tractors and only one worker. In 1848, and through to the last edition in 1871, Mill declared, quite correctly, that "the richest and most prosperous countries would very soon attain the stationary state, if not further improvements were made in the productive arts."[3] During the 1930s and early 1940s the prospect of diminishing returns deeply alarmed economists such as the British economist John Maynard Keynes and the American follower of Keynes at Minnesota and Harvard, Alvin Hansen.[4] They believed that the technology of electricity and the automobile were exhausted, and that sharply diminishing returns to capital were at hand, especially in view of declining birthrates. People would save more than could be profitably invested, the "stagnationists" believed, and the advanced economies would fall into chronic unemployment. In line with the usual if doubtful claim that spending on the war had temporarily saved the nonbombed part of the world's economy, they believed that 1946 would see a renewal of the Great Depression.

But it didn't. Stagnationism proved false.[5] Instead, world income per head grew faster from 1950 to 1974 than at any time in history, and the liberal countries boomed. That is, innovation prevented the return to capital from declining. Improved washing machines and better machine tools and innovative construction techniques and a thousand other fruits of resourcefulness made people richer, and incidentally kept investment profitable. In terms an economist will understand, the demand curve for capital moved steadily rightward, and has been doing so since the eighteenth century. The steadily rising opportunity for profitable investment is one of the self-correcting mechanisms that ends recessions (and the waves of excessive optimism about such opportunities are what causes the recessions in the first place). During the slump the innovations and other opportunities for profit pile up on the shelf of Good Ideas until the temptation to make a fortune by using them becomes irresistible.[6] The business cycle begins in the late eighteenth century, just when innovation becomes important. Earlier ups and downs in the economy were dominated by wars and harvests, not by cycles of optimism and pessimism about innovation. The historian Julian Hoppit, who has looked into these matters, quotes Coleridge asserting in 1817 that "the spirit of commerce will occasion great fluctuations, some falling while others rise," some dozen or so years peak to peak.[7] Coleridge's "spiritual" analysis is sound. Fractional reserve banking had existed long before in places like Florence, and was therefore not strikingly new in the eighteenth century in Britain. Considering that capital accumulation had always existed, and banking since the ancient Greeks, too, the novelty of the cycle in the late eighteenth century suggests just what Tunzelmann and I are claiming: that innovation is the central peculiarity of capitalism.

Tunzelmann argues indeed that in some cases technological change works mainly through increasing the capital employed, not only by raising productivities.[8] (To continue with an audience of economists for a moment, the area under the marginal product of capital is of course national income as a whole [up to a constant of integration, to be precise]. You can devise models in which saving out of the rising national income finances innovation, which raises income, which raises innovation, in a virtuous spiral. But then you have to explain why such a mechanism applies only to the past two or three centuries. You are back to having to explain the Age of Innovation by something unique to the Age of Innovation, pushing out the marginal product of capital. It can't be mainly endogenous.)[9] British and then European and then human resourcefulness that was rare before 1700 and increasingly common afterward made us rich. Like Shakespeare's alphabet, the saving and investment required to express the innovations were rather easily supplied.

The ease shows in Feinstein's own splendid table of investment as a share of gross national incomes of a dozen countries, 1770–1969.[10] The claim is

that investment was "crucial" for innovation. From 1770 to 1839 Britain was
the most innovative economy on earth, and later it was no slacker, arriving at last among the richest countries. And yet savings/investment rates in
Britain were lower than in most of other countries in Feinstein's table, as I
noted, and by the late nineteenth century about half of the British savings
were invested abroad. Britain's savings rate averaged from 1770 to 1839 about
7.5 percent, and not until the 1960s did it briefly exceed 15 or 16 percent.
The early 7.5 percent figure was exceeded by every one of the other eleven
countries, taken over the two or three decades in which their figures begin
to be available—decades which usually correspond to their entry into industrialization. It is Feinstein who introduces here the talk of "stages," and
so there cannot be a complaint that France in the 1820s and 1830s is not to
be compared with Britain earlier: the comparison is at the same "stage."
And putting stage thinking aside, in any given decade across the table the
British rates are commonly lower than in the other countries. If investment
and saving were crucial to economic growth, then Britain with its low rates
of investment would not have been the leader in industrialization. Rates of
investment and saving rose as a *result* of innovation. They did not cause it.

What was indeed "crucial" was the innovation itself, the steam engines
and the steel ships, the hybrid corn and the agricultural cooperatives. What
was crucial was working smarter, not harder, as the South African economist Stan du Plessis puts it.[11] Du Plessis is summarizing what all economists
and economic historians have known since the 1960s—that sheer accumulation of frozen labor in capital is not what let us break out of the ancient
pattern in which we expected to earn the same income as our parents and
grandparents and great-grandparents. Yet in 2003 Feinstein (also by the way
a South African) was still resisting the finding, part of which he himself had
established. He quoted with approval an opinion of the economist Arthur
Lewis in 1954, when capital fundamentalism was forming, and in advance
of the scientific work showing it to be misleading, that "the central problem
. . . is to understand . . . [how] a community which was previously saving
and investing 4 or 5 percent of its national income or less converts itself
into an economy where voluntary saving is running at about 12 or 15 percent."[12] I have noted that in a northern European agricultural economy with
low yield-seed ratios, the figure for saving has to be much higher than 4 or
5 percent. Perhaps Lewis meant by "voluntary saving" the saving above
"involuntary"—net of depreciation, say, and net of the storing of seed. In

that case, though, the innovations that made physical depreciation lower or that made unnecessary massive "involuntary" saving for seed are what explain the modern world, not piling brick on brick. And anyway the Lewis-Feinstein argument would have led to modern economic growth in, say, ancient Greece or China, in which savings rates could easily be driven up to 12 or 15 percent—merely force the slaves in the silver mines of Laurion, or the workers before they were entombed in the Great Wall, to eat less.

Capital fundamentalism, in short, has been rejected scientifically, despite echoes in the minds of economists, who want it to be true. Capital is a fine thing to have. Yet when the prospect for innovation is large, the capital to exploit the innovation is easily gotten by loan. Capital is not the constraint, not in the long run. The capital to make an innovation can be extracted from or given by others in the society, if the institutions of coercion or credit are not clogged. They typically have not been, from the earliest times—but the context of ideas has been. Smarter work did the modernizing. Innovation puts smartly into practice the idea of a light bulb or of limited liability or of assembly-line hamburgers. The word "capitalism," with its hidden assumption that piling up frozen labor does the trick, du Plessis notes, was applied in the nineteenth century to the system of property rights coordinated by prices before we grasped that the innovation suddenly flowing from such an ancient system is what chiefly mattered, and that what chiefly mattered in causing the innovation, unclogging the channels of ideas, was an entirely new honor and freedom for the bourgeoisie.

Schumpeter, the leading modern exponent of innovation as the key, defined capitalism variously at various times. His definition in *Business Cycles* (1939) was "that form of private property economy in which innovations are carried out by borrowed money."[13] In other words, "We shall date capitalism as far back as the element of credit creation," by which he meant fractional reserve banking—in effect any sort of money storage in which the storer is not legally or practically liable to keep all the money on hand all the time. He noted that such institutions existed in the medieval Mediterranean before they existed in northern Europe, and so he would have been unsurprised to find business cycles there—though it is suggestive, as I have said, that they are not to be found anywhere until the Age of Innovation, and then only in places touched by it. (Schumpeter, by the way, did not realize that Asia had banks hundreds of years before.) He claimed in his *History of Economic Analysis* that "by the end of the fifteenth century most of the phenomena we are in the habit of associating with that vague word Capitalism had put in their appearance."[14] And yet it would be three more centuries before modernity emerged, economically speaking. Finance and saving and investment cannot have been crucial, or else Florence or Augsburg (or Athens or Beijing or Istanbul) would have innovated us into the modern world.

Capitalism on Schumpeter's 1939 definition forms part of a private enterprise economy, but there can be private enterprise and innovation without credit—and therefore it appears without "capitalism." Note, however, that what is at stake in Schumpeter's argument is the use to which the thrift is put, not its total amount. Schumpeter affirmed that finance was used for *innovation*. Yet even Schumpeter, the innovator of innovation in the analysis of the economy, allows himself to be tempted by the word "capitalism" into overemphasizing finance. It was not thrifty finance that changed everything, as he himself elsewhere declares. What changed everything, said Schumpeter, was using commercial trust for *innovation*, such as Newcomen's tinkering with atmospheric engines, Rothschild's massive arbitrage, Edison's first generator in Manhattan, Alfred P. Sloan's years at General Motors.

The history of thrift was revolutionized around 1960, in other words, when economists and economic historians realized with a jolt that thriftiness and savings could not explain the Industrial Revolution. The economists such as Abramowitz, Kendrick, and Solow discovered that only a smallish fraction of recent economic growth can be explained by routine thrift and miserly accumulation (and even that fraction depended, I say again, largely upon innovations pushing out the productivity of capital accumulation). At the same time the economic historians were bringing the news that in Britain the rise in savings was too modest to explain much at all. Simon Kuznets and later many other economists, such as the same Charles Feinstein, provided the rigorous accounting of the fact—though as economic students of capital accumulation, I have noted, they could never quite overcome their initial hypothesis that Capital Did the Trick. The aggregate statistical news was anticipated in the 1950s and 1960s by numerous economic historians of Britain such as François Crouzet and Philip Cottrell and Sidney Pollard, in detailed studies of the financing of industry. Peter Mathias summarized their case in 1973: "Considerable revaluation has recently occurred in assessing the role of capital."[15] That is no overstatement.

The historical trouble, I repeat, is that savings and urbanization and state power to expropriate and the other physical-capital accumulations that are supposed to explain modern economic growth have existed on a large scale since the Sumerians. As Jack Goody notes, "There was nothing intrinsic about the east that inhibited mercantile—that is, capitalist—activity."[16] Yet modern economic growth, that wholly unprecedented factor of multiplication in the high teens (or low hundreds if the improved quality of goods is measured properly), is a phenomenon of the past two centuries alone. Something happened in the eighteenth century that prepared for a temporary but shocking great divergence of the European economies from those of the rest of the world.

The classical and flawed view, overturned by the economic historians of the 1950s and 1960s, is that thrift implies saving which implies capital accumulation which implies modern economic growth. It lingered in a few works such as Rostow's *The Stages of Economic Growth* (1960), and most unhappily in Easterly's capital fundamentalism of foreign aid, 1950 to the present. The belief was that if we give Ghana over several decades large amounts of savings, leading to massive capital investments in artificial lakes and Swiss bank accounts, and give Communist China not a cent, Ghana will prosper and Communist China will languish.[17] Of course. Inevitably. The mathematics on the blackboard says so.

16

A RISE OF GREED OR OF A PROTESTANT ETHIC DIDN'T HAPPEN

Nor does modern innovation have anything unusually "greedy" about it. The great French anthropologist Marcel Mauss expressed in 1925 the by then conventional but mistaken wisdom that "it is our Western societies which have recently made man an economic animal. . . . Homo oeconomicus is not behind us, but lies ahead. . . . For a very long time man was something different. . . . Happily we are still somewhat removed from this constant, icy, utilitarian calculation."[1] Mauss was wrong in imagining that modern people are especially calculating, although it is true that they are more respectful of calculation, sometimes foolishly so. He was wrong to think that there is an advanced form of consumption that is icily utilitarian, since all consumption is of use because people feel it is, whether baked goods or Bach, not because of some cold essence (which is something we have learned subsequently from anthropologists such as Mary Douglas). But he was most wrong to think that earlier people were less economic, less oriented toward prudence—a virtue which when not accompanied by other virtues we call the vice of "greed"—and that by contrast the modern, allegedly utilitarian consumer is especially greedy. Coleridge and Carlyle and Emerson and Dickens, and behind them Schiller and the German Romantics, had attacked utilitarianism in similar terms a century before Mauss. They accepted the self-glorifying claim of the Utilitarians themselves that the prudence that the Utilitarians so admired was a new virtue, to be set against the irrationalities of the Gothic era. Yet what was actually new in the nineteenth century was the *theory* of prudence, a new admiration for prudence, not its practice.

Max Weber in 1905, when the German Romantic notion that medieval society was more sweet and less greedy and more egalitarian than the Age of Innovation was just starting to crumble in the face of historical research, thundered against such an idea that greed is "in the least identical with capitalism, and still less with its spirit." "It should be taught in the kindergarten of cultural history that this naïve idea of capitalism must be given up once and for all." In his posthumous *General Economic History* (1923) he wrote, "The notion that our rationalistic and capitalistic age is characterized by a stronger economic interest than other periods is childish."[2] The infamous hunger for gold, "the impulse to acquisition, pursuit of gain, of money, of the greatest possible amount of money, has in itself nothing to do with innovation. This [greedy] impulse exists and has existed among waiters, physicians, coachmen, artists, prostitutes, dishonest officials, soldiers, nobles, crusaders, gamblers, and beggars. One may say that is has been common to all sorts and conditions of men at all times and in all countries of the earth, wherever the objective possibility of it is or has been given."[3]

Marx, in characterizing capitalism in 1867 as "solely the restless stirring for gain," said he was quoting the bourgeois economist J. R. McCulloch's *Principles of Political Economy* (edition of 1830): "This inextinguishable passion for gain, the *auri sacra fames* ['for gold the infamous hunger'], will always lead capitalists."[4] But, replied Weber, it leads everyone else, too. *Auri sacra fames* is from *The Aeneid* (19 BCE), book, line 57, not from the Department of Economics or *Advertising Age*. People have indulged in the sin of greed, a Prudence Only pursuit of food or money or fame or power, since Eve saw that the tree was to be desired, and took the fruit thereof. Soviet Communism massively encouraged the sin of greed, as its survivors testify. Medieval peasants accumulated no less "greedily" than do American corporate executives, if on a rather smaller scale. Hume declared in 1742, "Nor is a porter less greedy of money, which he spends on bacon and brandy, than a courtier, who purchases champagne and ortolans [little songbirds rated a delicacy]. Riches are valuable at all times, and to all men."[5] Of course.

Many readers of the magnificent historical chapters 25–31 of *Capital* will find all this hard to believe. Marx's eloquence persuades them that someone writing in 1867, very early in the professionalization of history, nonetheless got the essence of the history right. Another of his great riffs, chapter 15, "Machinery and Modern Industry" (150 pages in the Modern Library edition of the English translation), trumpeted the truth that he was witnessing an age of innovation. He subordinated the tune, however, to his historical harmonizing, the growth of surplus value. The history that Marx thought he perceived went with his erroneous logic that capitalism—drawing on an anticommercial theme as old as commerce—just *is* the same thing as greed. Greed is the engine that powers his sequence of M → C → M′. It says: Money starting through some original greedy theft or thriftiness as an amount M gets invested in Capital (commodities used for profit), which is intrinsically exploitative (and so amplifies the original theft or thrift), generating surplus value greedily—though structurally—appropriated by the capitalist to arrive at a new, higher amount of money, MĐ. "We have seen how money is changed into capital; how through capital [a] surplus-value is made, and from surplus value more capital." And then again and again and again, in the inaccurate English translation of Marx's German, "endlessly."[6]

The classical and Marxist idea that capital begets capital, "endlessly," is hard to shake. Thus Immanuel Wallerstein in 1983 spoke of "the endless accumulation of capital, a level of waste that may begin to border on the irreparable."[7] It has recently revived a little among economists, in the form of the new growth theory, which gives M → C → M′ a mathematically spiffed-up form. Both Marxist and bourgeois economists overlook the entry at the smell of profit, which shifts surplus value from the capitalist to whom it first accrues to the working-class consumer of now cheaper bread and roses. It's not in their models, so they suppose it's not in the world.

The "endless"/"never-ending" word, by the way—which was echoed during the Dark Ages in rural and monkish economic theory and still resonates in all our notions of "capitalism"—originated twenty-two centuries before Marx in the Greek aristocratic disdain for commerce. People of business (declared aristocratic Plato and aristocrat-admiring Aristotle) are motivated by *apeiros* (unlimited) greed. Thus Aristotle in the *Politics*. The "no limit" in Aristotle is about buying low and selling high, which is supposed not to exhibit the diminishing returns that, say, agriculture does.[8] In the thirteenth century St. Thomas Aquinas, referring to Aristotle with a little less than his customary enthusiasm for the Philosopher, retails the usual complaint against retailing, which depends on "the greed for gain, which knows no limit and tends to infinity."[9] As the political scientist John Danford observes, "The belief that there is something objectionable about [arbitrage] has persisted for more than two thousand years. . . . The enduring legacy . . . was . . . the view that . . . commerce or the acquisition of wealth is not merely low; it is unnatural, a perversion of nature, and unworthy of a decent human being."[10]

For all Marx's brilliance—anyone who does not think he was the greatest social scientist of the nineteenth century has not read enough Marx, or is blinded by ideology or by the appalling effects of Marxian writings on the politics of the twentieth century—he got the history wrong. Whatever the value of his theories as a way of asking historical questions, you cannot rely on Marx for any important historical fact: not on the English enclosure movement, not on the fate of the factory workers, not on the results of machine production, not on the false consciousness of the working class. The great Marxist historian Eric Hobsbawm, for example, a proud member of the Communist Party of Great Britain until its dissolution in 1991, admits that the historical science of Marx and Engels was on many points "thin."[11] No serious Marxist historian writing in English, such as Hobsbawm or Christopher Hill or E. P. Thompson, has relied for historical facts on Marx.

It is not some special Marxian fault. The same is true of the other practitioners of merely philosophical history before the facts started at last arriving in bulk after the full professionalization of history, during the twentieth century. Locke, Hume, Rousseau, Smith, Hegel, Macaulay, Tönnies, Durkheim, and even, a late instance, Max Weber on many points, and still later Karl Polanyi (and, less excusably, the many recent followers of Polanyi, who should have been reading the scientific history written since 1944 that has overturned most of Polanyi's historical notions), got the historical facts more or less wrong, and tended to get them wrong in the same way.[12] For your understanding of the past you would be foolish to depend mainly on Polanyi or Weber or even my beloved and liberal Macaulay, or even my worshiped and liberal Adam Smith. But people do. And so the theory of capitalism that educated people to this day carry around in their heads springs from the antibourgeois rhetoric of Polanyi, Marx, St. Benedict, Aristotle. It is economically mistaken. And the point here is that it is historically mistaken as well.

∞

Max Weber's *Protestant Ethic and the Spirit of Capitalism* of 1905 has inspired an enormous literature. What seems to have charmed people about it is that it combines an idealist focus on "spirit" with a materialist and Marxist focus on accumulation. The result of Weber's intellectual diversification has been that defenders of Weber keep springing up, despite repeated findings that his connecting of late Calvinism to the Great Fact (a hypothesis which he himself appears to have dropped after 1905) doesn't work very well. The economist J. Bradford DeLong, for example, wrote in 1989 a characteristically brilliant defense of the Weberian hypothesis against the libertarian notion that liberty suffices, and therefore that countries will converge to the best standard if you just let people get on with it. Prominent among his cases in 1989 showing that Catholicism kills enterprise were Ireland, Spain, and Portugal. By contrast, "the seven countries with predominantly Protestant religious establishments all have higher 1979 per capita income levels than the other seven countries."[13] Unfortunately for Weberians and for DeLong, *since* 1979, or 1989, Ireland, Spain, and Portugal have been economic miracles of liberal economic policy. Ireland is the most thoroughly liberal example, with very low corporate taxes, and therefore it went from being one of the poorest countries in Europe in 1979 to having in 2002 the second highest per capita real income in the world. And the Irish Catholics still go to church, in much greater numbers than the nominally Protestant British or Swedes.

The myth of *Kapitalismus* says that thrift among the bourgeoisie consisted precisely in the absence of a purpose other than accumulation for its own sake, solely the restless stirring for gain. Declared the man himself in 1867, capitalism entails "accumulation for accumulation's sake, production for production's sake." "Accumulate, accumulate! This is Moses and the prophets!"[14] Thus the left-wing economist, my misled but princely acquaintance the late Robert Heilbroner (1919–2005): "Capitalism has been an expansive system from its earliest days, a system whose driving force has been the effort to accumulate ever larger amounts of capital itself."[15] Thus Weber, too, in 1905: "The *summum bonum* of this ethic [is] the earning of more and more money. . . . Acquisition . . . [is] the ultimate purpose of life."[16] Weber here, contrary to his thundering quoted above, retails Marx, money-to-capital-to-money. True, skill at acquisition is supposed in *The Protestant Ethic* to be an "expression of virtue and proficiency in a calling." But innovation was in historical fact not skill at accumulation. Imagination was not restless stirring for gain. Socially profitable originality was not duty in a calling. What made us rich was a new rhetoric that was favorable to unbounded innovation, imagination, alertness, persuasion, originality, with individual rewards often paid in a coin of honor or thankfulness—not individual accumulation restlessly stirring, or mere duty to a calling, which are ancient and routine and uncreative. Though often Good Things.

This is not to say that the Reformation, and even specifically Calvinism, had no effect on the rise of innovation. But the effect was probably less through the doctrine of predestination than through the way some Protestant churches were governed. The core idea of Reformed and Anabaptist churches was to recover Christianity as they believed it was practiced in the first and second centuries, before the development of a state-sponsored hierarchy of bishops. A Catholic (and Lutheran and Anglican) notion that a hierarchy was needful was to be displaced by a notion that God would provide guidance to the priesthood of all believers. The extreme case was the Society of Friends (known to their enemies as Quakers) which in its very name embodied the congregational, or indeed an individual, notion of church governance. The absence of church hierarchy among the more radical Protestants (not I repeat among the Lutherans or Anglicans) perhaps led to the idea that hierarchy is unnecessary for a polity and an economy, too. Early moderns were alarmingly willing to impose their religious ideas on others, as the mutual slaughter of the Wars of Religion shows, and such willingness reached all social strata. It would be no great surprise if individual or congregational governance of a church, as against the hierarchies of bishop-led confessions, taught people to venture in business—many became shepherds who had been sheep. But note the difference from Weber's hypothesis of a psychological change emerging from the doctrine of predestination. Joyce Appleby, who should know better, writes down the conventional tale in a recent book: "Protestant preachers produced great personal anxiety by emphasizing everyone's tenuous grip on salvation" (as though Savonarola or the Dessert Fathers did not preach the same, with opposite economic results).[17] She continues her recital of Weber: "This promoted an interest in Providence in which believers scrutinized [economic] events for clues to divine intentions, . . . [which] turned prosperity into evidence of God's favor." Yet such a connection between Calvinist orthodoxy and business psychology has been repeatedly demolished since Weber wrote (I repeat: he himself dropped the hypothesis after 1905). Quakers entertained no such anxiety-provoking doctrine, but were famously successful in business, at any rate after the orthodox Calvinists stopped hanging them on Boston Common.

17

"ENDLESS" ACCUMULATION DOES NOT TYPIFY THE MODERN WORLD

At the level of individuals there has never been any evidence for the psycho-historical change that is supposed to characterize modern forms of greedy thrift. People were greedy and thrifty long before, as I said, and as Weber in his more lucid moments said, too. The chief evidence for a change in the *Geist* of thriftiness that Weber himself gave in *The Protestant Ethic and the Spirit of Capitalism* is a humorless reading of Benjamin Franklin's two-page *Advice to a Young Tradesman* (1748). "One need not have been Caesar," Weber noted elsewhere, "in order to understand Caesar."[1] But Weber did not understand Franklin. He missed for example the deflating sting in the last lines of *Advice*: "He that gets all he can honestly, and saves all he gets . . . will certainly become *rich*, if that Being who governs the world, to whom all should look for a blessing on their honest endeavors, doth not, in His wise providence, otherwise determine." So nothing happens "certainly," young tradesman, even if you bizarrely save *all* you get (as Franklin assuredly did not). And Weber missed in "He that murders a crown, destroys all that it might have produced, even scores of pounds" the parodic echo of the previous year's "Speech of Miss Polly Baker." Avid Franklin readers, of whom there were many, would have noted the echo. Prosecuted for giving birth to her fifth illegitimate child, Polly as ventriloquized by Franklin chides "the great and growing number of bachelors in the country, many of whom, . . . have never sincerely and honorably courted a woman in their lives; and by their manner of living leave unproduced (which I think is little better than murder) hundreds of their posterity to the thousandth generation. Is not theirs a greater offence against the public good, than mine?" The Yale historian and editor of the massive Franklin Papers, Claude-Anne Lopez, once remarked in a television interview that Franklin will lack an adequate biography until someone with a sense of humor attempts it.

Weber read Franklin's *Autobiography*, and like many others, such as Werner Sombart, he took as the man's essence the notorious printed account book of virtues that a young printer in Philadelphia used to discipline himself (George Washington was doing the same thing a few years later, in a somewhat less bourgeois form of 110 rules of civility and good behavior devised by a sixteenth-century Jesuit and reprinted in English in the seventeenth century ["Sleep not while others speak"]; it was an outward and visible discipline natural for an upwardly mobile American distant from the *politesse* of the metropolis; in fact such handbooks proliferated in the parts of Europe that allowed the hierarchies to be ascended). Declared Weber, "The real Alpha and Omega of Franklin's ethic . . . in all his works without exception" is that expression of proficiency in a calling. No it isn't. Like many other readers of Franklin, especially non-American readers—most famously D. H. Lawrence in his *Studies in Classic American Literature* (1923)—Weber missed the joke. Lawrence called Franklin "the sharp little man. . . . The pattern American, this dry, moral, utilitarian little democrat," and other Europeans have viewed him with similarly humorless and uncomprehending scorn.[2] Weber's nephew wrote a book in 1936 explaining why Uncle Max got Franklin so wrong: "Nations are curiously incapable of understanding each other's sense of humor. . . . [Weber] carefully constructed an elaborate theory of Franklin's ascetic economic ethos as one of the essential foundations of modern capitalism, . . . which is repeated uncritically from all kinds of pulpits . . . with learned mien and a pronounced shyness to consult the sources."[3]

The wigless, "ascetic" image of the frontiersman that Franklin projected for political purposes in France (he was imitating his fellow Pennsylvanians, the Quakers) was contradicted even there by his actual behavior in good-humored dalliances with the wives of French aristocrats. And he was nothing like single-mindedly devoted to his calling as a printer and businessman, even when before age forty-two he was practicing it. Young and old, Franklin was multiminded. Weber failed to recognize Franklin's actual behavior as a loving and passionate friend and patriot, a deeply curious man very willing to wander from his calling to measure the temperature of the Gulf Stream, or devise magic squares on the basis of number theory, though getting the current job completed on time; or his amused ironies about his young self. Amused self-ironies were a *franklinische*, and later an American, specialty. The most well-known of the amused self-ironies in Franklin's *Autobiography* is his comment about a late addition to his checklist of virtues, Humility: "I cannot boast of much success in acquiring the *reality* of this virtue; but I had a good deal with regard to the *appearance* of it." It is hard to miss the nudge in the ribs. In their eagerness to pillory the bourgeoisie, though, some people have missed the joke.

Franklin's writing, when not deadly serious (after all, he helped draft the Declaration of Independence, which could have gotten him hanged, and the Treaty of Paris), is jammed with such clowning around. In 1741 *Poor Richard's Almanac* predicted only sunshine, every day of the year. "To oblige thee more," Poor Richard explained to his dear reader, "I have omitted all the bad weather." The parody shouts itself. Yet many readers of Franklin don't get it—most influentially they didn't get his self-parodying compilation of Poor Richard's proverbs, *The Way to Wealth*. It was published in 1758, when Franklin was precisely *not* pursuing wealth as a printer, or anything else of proficient and profitable calling, but representing the Pennsylvania Assembly in London, at his considerable personal expense, having entirely abandoned the "duty of the individual to increase his capital" that Weber nonetheless saw in him. The historian Jill Lepore notes that *The Way to Wealth* is "among the most famous pieces of American writing ever, and one of the most willfully misunderstood." Its thrifty recommendation of "no gains without pains" and other supposedly bourgeois formulas "has been taken for Benjamin Franklin's—and even America's—creed."[4]

Yet only a humorless reading would find in it a sharp little capitalist, a pattern American, declaring for Prudence Only, a creed of greed. Mark Van Doren tried in 1938 to get people to read Franklin rightly, complaining for example that the "dry, prim people. . . . praise [Franklin's] thrift. Yet he himself admitted that he could never learn frugality, and he practiced it no longer than his poverty forced him to." Quoting Van Doren, Lepore lists Franklin's massive purchases in 1758 sent back to his wife in Philadelphia. Franklin attached a proud spender's notation that "there is something from all the china works in England."[5] The misreaders, Van Doren had continued, "praise his prudence [by which Van Doren means merely cautiousness, not the wider and ancient notion of practical wisdom used here, which Franklin surely had in abundance]. But at seventy he became a leader of a revolution."

Lepore points out that most of Poor Richard's proverbs in the almanacs themselves were not in fact about Prudence Only. Franklin selected the money-making ones for *The Way to Wealth* because in 1758 his mission in London was to try to persuade the British government to remove some small taxes on their fellow countrymen in the colonies. To his fellow colonists, in line with his optimism at the time that with temperance on both sides the Empire could hold together, he was noting in the voice of Father Abraham that "the taxes are indeed very heavy . . . but we have many others, and much more grievous to some of us. We are taxed twice as much by *idleness*, three times as much by *pride*, and four times as much by *folly*." The figure of argument was ancient, and nothing like American or utilitarian. Seneca wrote: "Show me a man who isn't a slave. One is a slave to sex, another to money, another to ambition. . . . There's no state of slavery more disgraceful than one that's self-imposed."[6] And "Franklin might have chosen to compile instead," Lepore notes, "the dozens of Poor Richard's proverbs advising *against* the accumulation of wealth. *The poor have little, beggars none; / The rich too much, enough not one.*"[7]

Lepore agrees with all careful students of Franklin that, as the man himself put it, he "would rather have it said, *He lived usefully*, than, *He died rich*." Ben was no saint. He owned slaves just as long as it was politically expedient, and talked out of both sides of his mouth in damning or defending the practice. He disowned his beloved son William for the sin of Toryism, a sin which a third of the American population practiced. He was a tough guy, no roly-poly figure of fun. But he was not a monster of calculation, either. Greedy thrift in the Marxian tale, by contrast, has the sole telos of dying rich. Charles Dickens, brought up to the law in London, who himself was an entrepreneur in theater and publishing but could not understand other profitable trades, gave us Scrooge, and his Disney descendant Scrooge McDuck—accumulate, accumulate. Max Weber, at least in 1905, modified the pointlessness of the impulse to accumulate, accumulate by claiming that "this philosophy of avarice" (allegedly Franklin's, remember) depends on a transcendent "*duty* of the individual toward the increase of his capital," yielding a "worldly asceticism."[8] Yet Franklin had lost most other traces of his ancestors' Calvinism, whether spiritual or worldly (by contrast with his abstemious young friend and enemy John Adams, for example). And he abandoned at age forty-two "endless" accumulation and devoted the other half of his long life to science and public purposes, and world-relishing consumption.[9] If, as Weber argued, the religious element drops out and accumulation takes over, one would like to know why accumulation did *not* take over, in Franklin after age forty-two, or in Carnegie in old age, or in Gates in middle age. The same could be said, and has been by Joel Mokyr, about the rigorous Calvinists of seventeenth-century Holland—the same ones who spent their incomes on merchant palaces along the Singel, and on luscious oil paintings officially warning of the vanity of mere matter by showing a polished silver tray with a half-peeled lemon and a beaker full of the warm south. So much for "worldly asceticism" or "ever larger amounts of capital itself" or a "duty toward the increase of capital" or "accumulate, accumulate."

Many fine scholars have taken in with their mothers' milk a belief that modern life is unusually devoted to gain, and that thrift is therefore something recent, dirty, greedy, and bourgeois, though lamentably profitable— not because the bourgeoisie got new ideas for trade and production but because of exploitation in $M \rightarrow C \rightarrow M'$. "The unlimited (*apeiros*) hope for gain in the market," writes the otherwise admirable political theorist Joan Tronto, "would teach people an unworkable premise for moral conduct, since the very nature of morality seems to dictate that desires must be limited by the need to coexist with others."[10] Yet running a business, unlike professing at a university, would teach anyone that gain is limited. Dealing in a market, unlike sitting in seat G7 in the Reading Room of the British Museum during the 1850s and 1860s composing burning phrases against the market, would teach anyone that desires must be limited by the need to coexist with others. The tuition provided by a market-and-innovation society in scarcity, other-regarding, and liberal values is an ethical school. As the historian Thomas Haskell put it in 1985, "Contrary to romantic folklore, the marketplace is not a Hobbesian war of all against all. Many holds are barred. Success ordinarily requires not only pugnacity and shrewdness but also restraint," that is, the virtue of temperance.[11]

Even so fine a historian as the anthropologist Alan Macfarlane believes the Aristotelian/Marxist/Weberian lore: "The ethic of endless [there it is again: *apeiros*] accumulation," he writes, "as an end and not a means, is the central peculiarity of capitalism."[12] If it were, the miser would be a strictly modern figure, and not proverbial in every literature in the world. Around 1665 the poet Abraham Cowley (a royalist version of Milton) wrote of avarice that "there is no vice that has been so pelted with good sentences, and especially by the poets, who have . . . moved, as we say, every stone to fling at it," and gave an example from his own pen:

What would content you? who can tell?
Ye fear so much to lose what ye have got
As if ye lik'd it well,
Ye strive for more as if ye lik'd it not.

He translates Horace to the same effect, and quotes a line he attributes to Ovid: *Desunt luxuriae multa avaritiae omnia* ("Many things are wanting to Luxury, [but] everything to Avarice"; compare Franklin's formulation, "The rich too much, enough not one").[13] As Cowley implies, however, you can go anywhere in literature or preaching or law from Mesopotamia to the moderns and find similar sentiments about the avaricious miser—who is supposed in modern theorizing to arise suddenly around 1750 out of Calvinist ancestry in the form of the sharp little man, this dry, moral, utilitarian little democrat. In China the poet Tang Bo Ju-yi (772–846 CE) complains of the salt-tax monopolist (the Chinese state sold and resold to the bourgeoisie the right to buy and sell salt) that "The salt merchant's wife / has silk and gold aplenty, / but she does not work at farming [in Confucianism the only honorable source of gain for the nonelite], / . . . Her gleaming wrists have gotten plump, / Her silver bracelets tight." Or Liu Zong-yuan (773–819 CE), in a parable comparing the miser to a pack beetle: "Those in our own times who lust to lay hold of things, will never back away when they chance on possessions by which to enrich their household [just like the beetle, carrying on his back whatever useful thing he encounters, twice his weight]. They don't understand that it encumbers them, and fear only that they won't accumulate enough."[14] Accumulate, accumulate.

"In this consists the difference between the character of a miser," wrote Adam Smith in 1759, "and that of a [thrifty] person of exact economy and assiduity. The one is anxious about small matters for their own sake; the other attends to them only in consequence of the scheme of life which he has laid down for himself."[15] He might as well have been describing Ben Franklin before he was wealthy, or Smith's friend Mr. William Crauford, a merchant of Glasgow, whom he did describe in 1758: "Who to that exact frugality, that downright probity and plainness of manners so suitable to his profession, joined a love of learning, . . . an openness of hand and a generosity of heart . . . candid and penetrating, circumspect and sincere."[16] Accumulate, accumulate, or plumping one's wrists, or laying hold of everything like a pack beetle, is not a "scheme of life" in the sense of a balance of virtues that Smith had in mind.

At the level of the society as a whole there *is* "unlimited" accumulation, at least if rats and fire and war and revolution do not intervene. Corporations are streams of such accumulation, having legally infinite lives—though in truth many little corporations die every year, and a few big ones, too (thus recently in a rush Lehman Brothers, Washington Mutual, WorldCom, and General Motors).[17] The individual economic molecules who make up the river of innovation may not always want to accumulate, accumulate beyond age forty-two, but the river as a whole, it is said, keeps rolling along. True, and to our good. The books and machines and improved acreage and splendid buildings and so forth inherited from an accumulating past are good for us now. Praise be to the ancestors.

There is no historical case, however, for accumulate, accumulate being peculiar to modern times. Midas and Crassus and Seneca accumulated. The presence of old buildings is not historically recent, suddenly accumulated in the Age of Innovation. Very long-lived institutions like families or churches or royal lineages existed before 1700, and were themselves, too, sites of accumulation. Thus the city of Teotihuacan northeast of Mexico City, built around 100 CE, came to be reused after its abandonment around 700 CE as a place sacred to the gods. Thus the long-lived improved acreage in Europe could spread up the hillsides under the pressure of population before the Black Death, as expensively constructed paddy fields did in East Asia. Thus the long-lived medieval cathedrals, and eastern temple complexes, were raised over centuries. Thus the long-lived Oxford colleges were built, and endowed with long-lived real estate, itself the accumulated investment in long-lived drains and stone fences and brick barns. Thus the canals of China and the roads of Peru. Thus, indeed, some companies: the oldest mining company in the world, first mentioned in 1288, is Stora Kopparberg ("Great Copper Mountain"), in the Dalarna district of Sweden; and the Monte dei Paschi di Siena, founded in 1472, still practices banking.

18

NOR WAS THE CAUSE ORIGINAL ACCUMULATION OR A SIN OF EXPROPRIATION

Yet naturally, if you think up a waterpower-driven spinning machine, as both the Chinese and the British did, to bring the thought to fruition you need some thrifty savings, somehow accumulated by someone. But another of the discoveries of the 1960s by economic historians was that the savings demanded by England's heroic age of mechanization were quite modest, nothing like the eventually massive offspring of the "original accumulation of capital" that Marxist theory posits. Early cotton factories were not capital-intensive. Even in the 1830s, as François Crouzet noted, the percentage of all capital in the cotton textile industry "sunk into fixed assets . . . was indeed small (25 percent, 20 percent, or less) even in the most 'capital intensive' firms."[1] The source of the industrial investment required was short-term loans from merchants for inventories and longer-term loans from relatives—not savings ripped in great chunks from other parts of the economy. Such chunk-ripping "capitalism" awaited the Railway Age.

The original or primitive accumulation was according to Marx the seed corn, so to speak, or, better, the starter in the sourdough, in the growth of capital. We're back to thrift or savings, not by historical fact but by blackboard logic. "The whole movement," Marx reasoned, "seems to turn on a vicious circle, out of which we can only get by supposing a primitive accumulation, . . . an accumulation not the result of the capitalist mode of production, but its starting point."[2] The reasoning sounds plausible, and appeals, like Malthusian predictions of limits, to a mathematics. But it didn't happen. As Alexander Gerschenkron put it in 1957, with characteristic sarcasm, the primitive or original starting point is "an accumulation of capital continuing over long historical periods—over several centuries—until one day the tocsin of the Industrial Revolution was to summon it to the battle-fields of factory construction."[3]

Marx's notion in *Capital* was that an original accumulation was a sine qua non, and had nothing to do with "that queer saint . . . of the woeful countenance, the capitalist 'abstainer.'" There was no saintliness involved. The original accumulation was necessary (Marx averred) because masses of savings were necessary, and "conquest, enslavement, robbery, murder, briefly, force, play the greater part."[4] He instanced enclosure in England during the sixteenth century (which has been overturned by historical find-ings that such enclosure was economically minor) and in the eighteenth (which has been overturned by findings that the labor driven off the land by enclosure was a tiny source of the industrial proletariat, and enclosure happened then mainly in the south and east where in fact little of the new sort of industrialization was going on, and where agricultural employment in newly enclosed villages in fact increased).[5] He gave a large part then to regulation of wages in creating a proletariat for the first time in the sixteenth century (which has been overturned by findings that nearly half the labor force in England as early as the thirteenth century already worked for wages; and that attempts to control the labor market did not work).[6] And then to the slave trade: "Liverpool waxed fat on the slave-trade. This was its method of primitive accumulation" (which has been overturned by findings that the alleged profits were no massive fund).[7] Later writers have proposed as the source of the original accumulation the exploitation by the core of the pe-riphery (Poland, the New World).[8] Or the influx of gold and silver from the New World—strange as it is then that imperial Iberia did not industrialize. Or the exploitation of workers themselves during the Industrial Revolution, out of sequence. Or other loot from imperialisms old and new, too small as a percentage of European income to matter much, and also too late. Or, fol-lowing on Marx and Engels's assertion in the *Manifesto*, even seventeenth-century piracy, tiny impositions on the flow of Spanish treasure by Sep-hardim venturing from Jamaica and runaway slaves from Hispaniola.[9]

None of these, it has been found since scientific history became a large-scale enterprise in the twentieth century, makes very much historical sense. If they happened at all, they are too small to explain what is to be explained. Such historical findings are in truth not very surprising. After all, conquest, enslavement, robbery, murder—briefly, force—has characterized the sad annals of humankind since Cain and Abel. Why did not earlier and even more thorough expropriations cause an industrial revolution and a factor of sixteen or twenty or one hundred in a widened scope for the average European, or non-European? Something besides thrifty self-discipline or violent expropriation must have been at work in northwestern Europe and its offshoots in the eighteenth century and later. Self-discipline and expropriation have been too common in human history to explain a revolution gathering force in Europe around 1800.

As a practical matter a pile of physical capital financed from, say, the Dutchman Piet Heyn's capture of a Spanish treasure fleet in 1628 would by the year 1800 melt away to nothing. It does not accumulate. It depreciates. And as Gerschenkron noted, "Why should a long period of capital accumulation *precede* the period of rapid industrialization? Why is not the capital as it is being accumulated also invested in industrial ventures?"[10] Why not indeed. In the story of original accumulation the clever capitalists are supposed to let their capital lie idle profitlessly for centuries until the "tocsin" sounds.

People seem to be mixing up financial wealth and real wealth. Financial wealth in a bank account is merely a paper claim to the society's real wealth by this person against that person, Piet Heyn against Joost van den Vondel. The society's real wealth itself, on the other hand, is a house or ship or education. From the point of view of the society as a whole, the real wealth, not paper claims or gold coins, is what's needed for real investment. The paper claims are merely ways of keeping track of who owns the returns to the capital. They are not the real physical or educational capital itself. You can't build a factory with pound notes, or dig a canal with stock certificates. You need bricks and wheelbarrows, and people healthy and skilled to wield them. Mere financing or ownership can hardly be the crux, or else the Catholic Church in 1300, with its dominate command of tokens of European wealth, would have created an industrial society. Or the Philips II, III, and IV of Spain—who after all were the principal beneficiaries of the treasure fleets the English and Dutch and French privateers and pirates preyed upon—would have financed industrial revolutions in Bilbao and Barcelona, instead of obstructing them.

Any original accumulation supposed to be useful to any real industrialization must be available in real things. Yet as the Koran says, "What you possess [in real, physical things] will pass, but what is with God will abide"

(16:96). "These lovely [earthly] things," wrote Augustine, "go their way and are no more. . . . In them is no repose, because they do not abide."[11] Jesus said, "Do not lay up for yourselves treasures on earth, where moth and rust destroy and where thieves break in and steal; but lay up for yourselves treasures in heaven." A treasured house built in 1628 out of Piet's paper claims got by devising a new way of robbing Spain would be tumbled down by 1800, unless its various owners had continued to invest in it. A real educated person of 1628 would not abide, a real machine would be obsolete, a real book would be eaten by worms. The force of depreciation makes an original accumulation spontaneously disappear.

This is not to say, note well again, that conquest, enslavement, robbery, and murder play no part in European history. A Panglossian assumption that contract, not violence, explains, say, the relation between lord and peasant defaces the recent work on "new" institutionalism, such as that of Douglass North.[12] Yet, *pace* Marx, modern economic growth did not and does not and cannot depend on the scraps to be gained by stealing from poor people. It is not a good business plan. It never has been, or else industrialization would have happened when Pharaoh stole labor from the Hebrew slaves (though, by the way, recent evidence suggests that the workers making pyramids were hired labor with good working conditions—more very early "capitalism"). Stealing from poor people, when you think about it, could hardly explain enrichment by a factor of sixteen, not to speak of one hundred. Would you do so well by robbing the homeless people in your neighborhood, or by breaking into the home of the average factory worker? Would grabbing stuff from the poor of the world enrich the average person in the world, including most surprisingly the poor victims themselves, by a factor of ten since 1800? Does it strike you as plausible that British national income depended on stealing from an impoverished India? If so, you will need to explain why real income per head in Britain went *up* sharply in the decade after Britain "lost" India, and so too for all the imperial powers after 1945: France, Holland, Belgium, and at length even rapacious, Fascist Portugal.

Modern economic growth has not depended on saving, and therefore has not depended on stealing to get the saving, or any other form of original accumulation, even the peaceful practice of the knights of the woeful countenance abstaining from consumption. Turgot and Smith and Mill and Marx and Weber and the new growth theorists among the economists, all of whom emphasize capital accumulation, get the story quite wrong. That the oldsters got it so wrong is unsurprising, considering the stately pace at which the economies they were looking at were improving, at least by contrast with the frenetic pace after 1848 and especially after 1948, and most especially worldwide after 1978. (The new growth theorists of the 1980s and after have less excuse; they should have learned by now that modern economic growth is bizarre, and therefore not about routine accumulation.) The early economists had a notion of modest modernization to the level of, say, the prosperous Netherlands in 1776, easily achievable by peace and routine investment—not a transformation to a level of suburban America in 2010, achievable only by a rate of innovation each year such as had never, ever happened before. "All the authors [who] followed the Turgot-Smith line," wrote Schumpeter as the frenzy was becoming apparent, "[were] at fault in believing that thrift was the all-important [causal] factor."[13] Most savings for innovation, Schumpeter had noted twenty years earlier, "does not come from thrift in the strict sense, that is from abstaining from consumption . . . but [from] funds which are themselves the result of successful innovation" (in the language of accounting, "retained earnings").[14] The money for the few massive and capital-intensive innovations such as railways, he argued, comes from banks using "money creation." (The mysterious phrase "money creation" means simply the loans beyond the gold or dollars in their vaults that venturing bankers can make, on the hopeful supposition that not everyone will want gold or dollars back at the same time. In a word, it is credit.)

Schumpeter, though, did not fully appreciate that even in the twentieth century of wide markets and big laboratories a company can expand without massive loans, rather in the way that the first innovations of the Industrial Revolution relied on retained earnings, trade credit, and modest loans from cousins and scriveners and solicitors. It is still true in many sectors: Ingvar Kamprad built up the Swedish furniture giant, IKEA, without loans or public offerings. The big public offerings that were required from 1840 to 1940, and most particularly after World War I, by capital-intensive industries such as railways, steel, chemicals, automobiles, electricity generation, and oil exploration and refining were unique, and made the modern stock markets. Sidney Pollard wrote in 1981 that "the whole of European technology, including that of the pioneering countries, changed over time to become more capital intensive."[15] Economics as a science grew up in the Age of Capital (as Eric Hobsbawm called it). Naturally the economists such as Mill or Marx or Marshall or Keynes became obsessed with physical accumulation.

"Capitalist production," Marx declared, "presupposes the pre-existence of considerable masses of capital."[16] No it doesn't. A modest stream of withheld profits (whether accounting profits or the economist's notion of profits as a reward to a new idea) will pay for repairing the machines and acquiring new ones, especially the uncomplicated machines of 1760, and now again the complicated but capital-cheap machines of the computer age. In 1760 the most complicated European "machine" in existence was a first-rate ship of the line, itself continuously under repair. Nowadays it is your friendly computer geek.

∞

So far as the origin of innovation is concerned, the "masses" of capital could be in 1760 modest in magnitude—again the starter in sourdough bread—and could come from small change anywhere, not from some great original sin of primitive accumulation. The conviction that innovation was born in sin, though, has proven hard to shake. It gets its staying power from guilt meeting zero sum. We are rich. Surely (by zero-sum logic) we got so by stealing. As the Master himself put it, "Primitive accumulation plays in Political Economy about the same part as original sin in theology."[17] Most intellectuals, who do not grasp the productivity of conversation in innovation and cooperation in markets, and the resulting productivity of creative destruction and therefore the derivative role of accumulation, take such illogic as a known fact. The historian Louis Dupré pauses in his recent survey of the French Enlightenment to gesture toward the quite different Enlightenment going on in Scotland at the time. He commends Adam Smith for "a genuine concern for the fate of the workers," but then asserts as though we all know it to be true that "an unrestricted market economy could not but render their lot very harsh, especially during the early period of industrial innovation when accumulation of capital was largely to be earned at their expense."[18] Not surprisingly, Dupré offers no evidence for such an obvious truth. It is part of our intellectual upbringing—not something requiring evidence—that accumulation is the key to growth and that accumulation depends on the sacrifice of workers (who apparently did not have a "harsh" lot before the early period of industrial innovation).

Thus Sellar and Yeatman in their spoof of English history, *1066 and All That: A Memorable History of England* (1931), describe "the Industrial Revelation" as the most memorable of the discoveries made around 1800, namely, "the discovery (made by all the rich men in England at once) that women and children could work for 25 hours a day in factories without many of them dying or becoming excessively deformed."[19] Most educated people believe such a history is approximately correct, and credit for example Charles Dickens as an accurate reporter on the industrial result. For all his literary merits, Dickens seldom ventured north of London, knew little of industrialization, and spoke instead of poverty of a traditional sort in London itself, which he viewed from a perch in the bourgeoisie. His most industrial book, *Hard Times* (1854), for all its charm, grossly misrepresents workers, trade unionists, entrepreneurs, even circus performers. The claim that immiserization is inevitable, a God-arranged sacrifice anticipating the Second Coming, religious or socialist, has no empirical base. It arises from Malthus in 1798, reaffirmed by *The Communist Manifesto* in 1848—and more deeply from a Christian embarrassment of riches.[20] The great economist and Marxist Joan Robinson noted the contradiction between volumes 1 and 3 of *Capital* on this score: "The attempts of the fundamentalists of Marxism to believe in the growing misery of the workers and the falling rate of profit at the same time have caused a lot of confusion."[21] So it has.

Sacrificing the workers was not how the accumulation that did happen was achieved. Workers in industrial areas of Britain were, to be sure, wretchedly poor. Yet so, to a greater degree, were Dickens's preindustrial poor of London. And so was every ordinary person in the world in the times before the greater day of the bourgeoisie and invention and innovation—all our ancestors lived on that wretched $3 a day, and it took many decades after industrialization began for steam and steel and stock exchanges to have much of an effect on average wages. True, children worked in cotton mills and lead mines:

> My father was a miner and lived down in the town.
> 'Twas hard work and poverty that always kept him down.
> He aimed for me to go to school, but the brass he couldna' pay,
> And so I went to the washing rake for four pence a day.[22]

Yet children had always worked, and late-nineteenth-century industrialization reduced rather than increased their number picking coal or retying broken yarn. Factory work was seen by the children themselves as better than farmwork.[23] Early on, the wages rose a little in the industrial areas of England or Scotland or Belgium, despite a rising population overall and the weight of the Napoleonic struggle. The coal miners and cotton mill workers and even the lead miners were notably better off than their country cousins, which is partly why they left the farms of Ireland and the Highlands of Scotland in the first place. In short, as many have noted since Friedrich Hayek and Max Hartwell and Thomas Ashton first spoke in the 1950s against the Fabian socialist version of British history, innovation was not born in a sin of expropriation.[24]

19

NOR WAS IT ACCUMULATION OF HUMAN CAPITAL, UNTIL LATELY

It is not adequately acknowledged by Hobsbawm and other historical materialists, long lamenting the dominion of capital that 1840–1940 became an age increasingly of human capital. (Yet the teachers of the doctrine of physical capital as dominant are commonly employed in the enlarging industry made possible by the Age of Innovation, the very one that supplies the human capital). The result of the coming of human capital was the opposite of expropriation: the workers became the capitalists. The Age of (Physical) Capital is drawing to a close, replaced by an Age of (Human) Capital. Capital is dead; long live capital. By now in rich countries the returns to human capital account for a much higher share of national income than do the returns to the land and especially to the machinery whose mode of accumulation so exercised the very first generation of economic historians—Marx, Arnold Toynbee (uncle of the historian of universal history), and their followers.

Without the Revaluation of bourgeois innovation, however, human capital would have piled up merely another item in the Age of Capital. It would give no persuasive explanation of the early parts of the enrichment, or of the decisive and creative part of its follow-on. The Age of (Human) Capital depended on massive innovation to maintain the value of the capital accumulated. The economic historian David Mitch, the doyen of educational historians of Britain, has shown that education of the masses played a small role in the early years of the Industrial Revolution. "England, during its Industrial Revolution 1780 to 1840," he writes, "experienced a notable acceleration in economic growth [Mitch is of the optimist school] yet displayed little evidence of improvement in the educational attainments of its workforce."[1]

Granted, a wholly illiterate country could hardly have taken advantage of the steam engine in the way the British did. And the economic historians Becker, Hornung, and Woessmann (2009) have argued persuasively that Prussian counties with higher educational attainments in 1816 were better able to adopt innovations in industries *other* than textiles. Mitch makes a similar point about pioneering Britain with a hilarious counterfactual (intentional hilarity is not all that common in economic history) in which he imagines switching the populations of Britain with that of the Eskimo far north.[2]

By contrast, Richard Easterlin has answered the question "Why isn't the whole world developed?" by pointing to "the extent of [a] population's formal schooling." The difference between the two writers can be explained by the periods that they are studying. Human capital, I repeat, has lately become indubitably important, though dependent as all forms of capital are in innovation to keep it from declining in marginal value—modern management techniques for CEOs, engineering for engineers, medicine for doctors. Yet around 1840, in Mitch's period, it's hard to make the case that it was important for coal miners or cotton mill workers. A miner at the coal face was highly skilled, but most other workers in and around the pits were not, and anyway the hewer's skill had nothing to do with book learning. Easterlin points out that the spread of technology is "personal," in just the sense that the chemist and philosopher Michael Polanyi used the word in his book *Personal Knowledge* (1958). Easterlin quotes the economist Kenneth Arrow: " It seems to be personal contact that is most relevant in leading to . . . adoption" of a technique.[3] Technical knowledge is largely tacit, non-write-downable, and requires people quick on the uptake. Quickness of uptake—most relevant to recent years in which the technology to be taken up is so ample—can be encouraged by literacy in the modern world. The Koreans, education-mad since 1953, provide an example.

Yet quickness of uptake can also be *discouraged* by learning to read, producing a rote-learning bureaucracy hostile to innovation. In that case the accumulation of human capital can be a bad idea, negative capital. If the sociology and politics are hostile to innovation, as for example they were in late imperial China, education can be bad for economic growth. Mokyr makes a similar point, observing that in the absence of high social prestige for innovators, "during most of history, children who received an education were kept away from practical matters."[4] The result, he argues, is that innovations by low-status slaves, workers, and women seldom got spread by literacy. And if teaching many more people to read was good for the economy, as it surely has been late in the Age of Innovation, it must be explained why Attic Greek potters in the sixth century BCE signing their painted vases (*Sophilos megraphsen*, "Sophilos drew me," around 570 BC) did not come to use water power to run their pottery wheels and thence to ride in railway cars to Delphi behind a puffing locomotive. And if not in 570 BCE, then why not later in the long history of the unusually literate Greeks? Easterlin in fact agrees, noting that high educational attainment in Spain at its height was offset by the rigid (and antibourgeois) control by the post-Reformation Church.[5]

Education can make people spiritually free (thus a "liberal" education, from Latin *liber*, free) without making them rich. The historian George Huppert has told of the invention of more widespread education in Europe from the sixteenth century on.[6] But the "grammar" schools prepared young men for careers in the clerisy, such as Huppert's hero the naturalist Pierre Belon (1517–1564), or Pierre Ramus (1515–1572), the Huguenot reformer and destroyer of the medieval rhetorical tradition. (The mushrooming academies, teaching bourgeois ways of making and doing things to lads intending careers in commerce, however, had a more practical curriculum than the grammar schools.) In France especially, Huppert argues, education down to the level of village schools for peasants became a passion in the sixteenth century, and a worry for the church: "Even in the smallest towns of the kingdom," a priest complained, "merchants and even peasants find ways of getting their children to abandon trade and farming in favor of the professions," creating a new and secular clerisy and breaking the great chain of being.[7]

Yet education without the new bourgeois rhetoric is merely a desirable human ornament, not the way to human riches. It makes for a clerisy that may in fact be hostile to bourgeois values, and very willing to be of professional service to the antieconomic projects of the emperor or the lord bishop. "For two centuries," wrote Mill in 1845, "the Scottish peasant, compared with the same class in other situations, has been a reflecting, an observing, and therefore naturally a self-governing, a moral, and a successful human being—because he has been a reading and a discussing one; and this he owes, above all other causes, to the parish schools. What during the same period have the English peasantry been?"[8] Yet the superior education, right up to the notable superiority in the eighteenth century of Scottish and

German and Dutch universities over English and French universities, did not make Scottish or German economic growth superior to English and French (though the Dutch, with their dignified and liberated and educated bourgeoisie, had done all right in the seventeenth century). Education proved to be of little use without the liberal political rhetoric, as in Holland and then in England and Scotland, that made economic and intellectual innovation dignified and free.

The economic historian Lars Sandberg in a famous essay spoke of Sweden as "the impoverished sophisticate."[9] In 1800 the Swedes, though among the poorest group in Europe, read at least the Good Book, because Luther had demanded it, and indeed Sweden boasted a very old university in Uppsala. In the late nineteenth and especially in the twentieth century, Sandberg argued, Sweden finally could take advantage of its literacy. There is no doubt that education does matter mightily now to Sweden's position as one of the richest countries in the world. Without a liberalized attitude toward innovation, however, such sophisticates would have worked at keeping their country impoverished. The educated Chinese elite did. The educated Spanish elite did.

Consider the South African Boers. After the heroism, and race war, of the Great Trek of the 1830s, the Afrikaners settled into economic stagnation. Yet supposedly they had a responsibility, as fiercely convinced Calvinists, to become educated enough to read the Bible. Many in fact did not. Olive Schreiner wrote a novel about Afrikaner farm life in the 1860s. Her character the Afrikaner Tant' [Aunt] Sannie declares, "Didn't the minister tell me when I was confirmed not to read any book except my Bible and hymnbook, that the Devil was in all the rest?"[10] There was some doubt that Tant' Sannie could read much even of the two books recommended by the dominee. The reforms of Afrikaner education after 1900 were accompanied by a self-conscious attempt to persuade the Dutch- and German- and French-descended South Africans to adopt pro-innovation attitudes they had formerly disdained (as characteristic of the unholy English or Jews).[11]

The truth remains that education by itself does not yield much. Cubans nowadays go to school, as they did also before the Revolution, if now strictly limited in what they are permitted to read (a bookstore in Havana has the usual books on technical subjects like engineering; but in history or the social sciences it stocks nothing beyond the Marxist-Leninist orthodoxy). Yet the Cubans at some points (Fidel repeatedly changed the laws) could not start a restaurant or take their farm produce to markets (Raul has somewhat relented), and so they remain to this day cripplingly poor, disabled from exercising bourgeois virtues—in sharp contrast to their cousins in Miami. Cuba's income per head by 2001, despite all its alleged investment in human capital, was still about what it had been in 1958, while all around it since the Cuban Revolution income per head had almost doubled.[12] In 2009 the country was malnourished. The cousins in Miami, by contrast, whether much educated or not, were doing a lot better, because they lived in a bourgeois society. And they could read what they wanted.

You will say if you are on the left, "But Cubans as you admit are educated, and well cared for in their hospitals," at least until the collapse of 2009 (preceded by the collapse of 1991, and that one preceded by numerous other collapses). Yet so were they before 1958 well educated and well cared for, by the standards of the day. That's why Cuba was in 1958 such a promising country, though ruled by a different gang of thugs from the present one. Yet after 1959 the Cubans fled from the workers' paradise, just as the skilled are fleeing today from Venezuela, Bolivia, Ecuador, and Nicaragua, to places where economic opportunities are better than at home. A democratic social scientist should be inclined to put weight on how people vote, with their feet, or their boats.

The sociologists Victor Nee and Richard Swedberg, further, note that in recent decades China, which had ruined its educational system in the Great Leap Forward, has grown vigorously.[13] Russia led the world in education during the Communist period (compare Cuba in medicine), and in some ways still does (the country with the highest percentage of university graduates is still Russia, by a good margin). Yet it is notably lacking in the toleration for bourgeois innovation that China has surprisingly evolved, and has not grown except when oil prices are high. Thus: specialize in table tennis and sending professors to re-education camps, like the Chinese, and prosper. Win chess matches and lead the world in certain fields of mathematics, like the Russians, and stagnate. It appears that education does not suffice. Bourgeois dignity and liberty does, and ends by financing the accumulation of human capital for a massively wider human scope.

∞

What did not happen in any case, in short, was a big rise in European thrift, whether from the knights of woeful countenance or from exploitation.

Nothing much changed from 1348 to 1700 or from 1700 to 1848 in the actual circumstances of thriftiness. And the modest changes did not matter much. Individual Dutch and English-speaking people who initiated the modern world did often practice personal thrift—or often did not; as they still do, or do not. Look at your improvident cousin with $20,000 of credit-card debt, or on the other side your miserly neighbor. And changes in *aggregate* rates of saving drove nothing of consequence. No unusual Weberian ethic of high thriftiness or a Marxian antiethic of forceful expropriation started economic growth. East Anglian Puritans learned from their Dutch neighbors and coreligionists how to be thrifty in order to be godly—to work hard in order, as John Winthrop put it, "to entertain each other in brotherly affection."[14] That's lovely, but it's not what caused industrialization. You can see that it didn't from the delay of modern (as against early-modern) industrialization even in the Protestant and prosperous parts of the Low Countries, or for that matter in thrifty East Anglia, or in the lack of divergence in thrift between seventeenth-century French Calvinists and Catholics in Montpellier.[15]

The habits of thriftiness and luxury and profit, and the routines of exploitation, are humanly ordinary, and largely unchanging. A surprising support for such a point comes from a follower of Karl Polanyi: "There are always and everywhere potential surpluses available. What counts is the institutional means for bringing them to life . . . for calling forth the special effort, setting aside the extra amount, dividing the surplus."[16] As the theologian and social observer Michael Novak puts it, "Weber stressed asceticism and grind; the heart of the system is actually creativity."[17] That's what was new. Modern economic growth depends on applied innovation in crafting gadgets (organizational and intellectual gadgets such as law partnerships and the calculus as much as physical ones), what the philosopher Whitehead called the invention of the method of invention. The invention of invention appears in turn to depend on bourgeois dignity and liberty—at any rate when the ingenious gadgets were first invented, not merely borrowed, as later the USSR and the People's Republic of China were able to do (though sluggishly when under central planning). "We doubt not," wrote a pamphleteer against machine-breaking in 1675, "but innovation will find encouragement in England."[18] And so it did.

There are many tales told about the prehistory of thrift. The central tales are Marxist or Weberian or now growth-theory-ish. They are mistaken. Accumulation has not been the heart of modern economic growth, or of the change from the medieval to the early-modern economy, or from the early-modern to the fully modern economy. It has been a necessary medium, but rather easily supplied, like Shakespeare's alphabet. The substance has been innovation. If you personally wish to grow a little rich, by all means be thrifty, and thereby accumulate for retirement. But a much better bet is to have a good idea and be the first to invest in it. And if you wish your society to be rich you should urge an acceptance of creative destruction and an honoring of wealth if obtained honestly by innovation. You should not urge thrift, not much. (Nor especially should you recommend sheer wealth acquired by stealing, such as the program of making a "middle class" in certain African countries by enriching the state bureaucrats in the main cities at the expense of farmers.)[19] You should work for your society to be free, and thereby open to new ideas, and thereby educable and ingenious. You should try to persuade people to admire properly balanced bourgeois virtues, without worshiping them. Your society will thereby become very, very rich. American society nowadays is notably unthrifty. The fact is much lamented by modern puritans, left and right. Yet because the United States accepts innovation and because it honors Warren Buffett it will continue to be rich, in frozen pizzas and in artistic creativity and in scope for the average person.

"Thrift" has been much praised in American civic theology. "Work hard, follow the rules," say the American politicians: "Anyone can achieve the American Dream." No, sadly, they cannot, if the Dream is of riches. Accidents happen; the Being who governs the world doth sometimes, in His wise providence, determine that accumulation comes to naught; and great riches come mainly from great and creative alertness. Like many other of the sacred words, such as "democracy" or "equality" or "opportunity" or "progress," the rhetoric of thrift and hard work and following the rules turns out to be more weighty than its material force. It's time for the old tale of thriftiness to be retired, and an accurate history of innovation to take its place.

20

TRANSPORT OR OTHER DOMESTIC RESHUFFLINGS DIDN'T CAUSE IT

The economic historians have not so far discovered any single material factor essential to British industrialization. A long time ago Gerschenkron argued that the notion of essential prerequisites for economic growth, single or multiple, is one that needs skeptical handling.[1] Gerschenkron's economic metaphor, that one thing can "substitute" for another, applies to Britain itself as much as to the other countries (from later research there is some doubt, actually, concerning the other countries). Economists believe with good reason that there is more than one way to skin a cat. If foreign trade or entrepreneurship or saving had been lacking, the economist's argument goes, other impulses to growth could have taken their place (with a loss, but usually a modest one), if the opportunity for profit from a new allocation were there. A vigorous domestic trade or a single-minded government or a forced saving from the taxation of agriculture could take the place of the British ideal of the merchant left alone by government to reinvest his profits in a cotton factory.

Transportation, for example, is often cast in the hero's role. The static tale is most easily criticized. Canals carrying coal and wheat to the docks at a lower price than cartage, better public roads bringing coaching times down to a mere day from London to York, and then the railway steaming into every market town were all of course Good Things. Yet their effect on national income can be shown to be small.

The way it can be shown is a technique much used by economists, which will be worked hard here. Think of a sector such as transportation as having a certain weight in national income and a certain percentage increase per year in productivity. If you multiply the two you have calculated the national gain from the increase in productivity per year. The technique depends on the economist's metaphor of the economy as a "production function," a sort of sausage machine of inputs yielding outputs—the $Q = F(K, L)$ mentioned earlier. The robustness of the calculation is a consequence of what is known informally among economists as Harberger's Law (after A. C. Harberger, a Nobel-worthy economist at Chicago and then UCLA, famous for such calculations).[2] That is, if one calculates a gain amounting to some fraction from a sector that amounts to (again) a fraction of the national economy, one is in effect multiplying a fraction by a fraction. Suppose G percent of gain comes from a sector with a share of s percent of national income, which is its weight for calculating the national gain (a gain in making hats is less important than one in transportation). It follows from highly advanced mathematics (don't try this at home) that the resulting fraction, G times s, is smaller than either of its terms, since both are fractions less than 1.0. If you have three or four such terms you arrive at even smaller percentages. For most sectors and most events—here is the crucial point that will make the technique do work for the larger story—the outcome is a small fraction when set beside the 1,500 percentage points of growth to be explained in Britain 1780 to the present, or even beside the 100 percentage points of growth to be explained 1780 to 1860.

Transportation is never more than 10 percent of national income—in Britain it was something like 6 percent 1780-1860. Britain was well supplied with good harbors for its massive coastwise transportation, and in the lowlands of England the rivers flowed gently like sweet Afton when large enough for traffic at all. Mother Nature had given Britain a low cost of transportation by water, even when the waterways were unimproved by lighthouses, river dredging, and stone-built harbors. The further lowering of the cost by introducing canals and railways would yield an improvement of, say, 50 percent (a figure easily justified by looking at freight rates and price differentials). The 50 percent fall in transport cost, though, applies only to the portion of traffic not carried on unimproved water—say likewise 50 percent. By Harberger's Law, then, 50 percent of 50 percent of 6 percent will save a mere 1.5 percent of national income. One would welcome a tiny share of 1.5 percent of national income as one's personal income; and even spread among the population it is not to be scorned. But it is not by itself the stuff of "revolution," and it is three orders of magnitude less than 1,500 percent.

Yet did not transportation above all have "dynamic" effects? It seems not, though historians and economists have quarreled over the matter and it would be premature to claim that the case is entirely settled.[3] The most powerful case against the importance of dynamic effects was mounted by Robert Fogel on a long evening in Toronto against the speculations to the contrary by the economic historian Paul David.[4] David had harshly criticized on "dynamic" grounds Fogel's calculation of "social saving" (which it can be shown is the same as a change in national income) given in Fogel's book of 1964, *Railroads and American Economic Growth*. Fogel, in a fifty-four-page rebuttal (which he read in its entirety that evening after dinner), calculated the possible dynamic effects and found them to be small.[5]

In framing the calculation of dynamic effects of transportation a few points need to be kept in mind. For one thing, the attribution of dynamism sometimes turns out to be erroneous double counting of the static effect. Historians will sometimes observe with an air of showing the large effects of transport that the canals or the railways caused transport costs to fall *and* increased the value of coal mines or made possible larger factories— "dynamic" effects (the word is protean). But the coal lands and factories were made more valuable simply because the cost of transporting their outputs was lower. The higher rents or the larger markets are alternative means of measuring what is the same thing, the fall in the cost of transporting coal or pottery or beer.[6] To add them together would be to count the same effect twice.

For another, some of the dynamic effects would themselves depend on the size of the static, 1.5 percent effect. For example, one "dynamic" effect is that the new income is saved, to be reinvested, pushing incomes up still further, by the much-honored logic of "accumulate, accumulate." The trouble is that the additional income in the first round is very small. A 1.5 percent first round leads to a much smaller second, and a still smaller third round.

And if the additional saving would lead to a *bigger* second and then a still bigger third round, and so forth, there's something strange about the model—perhaps "economies of scale" have been thrown into the model at just the right time to make it explosive, as in modern growth theory. In that case anything, simply anything, could have started off the dynamo, and could have done so at any time from ancient Tyre or Xianyang to the present. Explosive models that give no reason for becoming explosive exactly in 1700 or 1800 CE have not explained the sharpest upturn of real incomes per head in history. They have merely renamed the upturn "economies of scale."

The new growth theory in economics revives in this way an idea of Alfred Marshall in 1919 and of Allyn Young in 1928 that bigger is better, if you have smart neighbors, especially in its economies-of-scale and especially in its economies-of-neighborhood form initiated by among others Paul Krugman and David Romer and Charles Sabel (the latter two, I am pleased to note, were my students as undergraduates; I wish Krugman had been one, too). For example, people gathered in cities sometimes do a little better (and sometimes a little worse). Measurement of the betterment shows it to be small, on the order of perhaps 10 percent in a city. That's enough to explain why Chicago beat out Milwaukee or St. Louis, and so explains the geography of production and consumption. A good thing to know. Interesting. Let me show you the mathematical model. The 10 percent, however, does not go very far in explaining an enrichment of 100 percent or 1,500 percent. The theories, in other words, are a trifle exiguous. And they tend to tautology. Though humility is not Krugman's principal virtue, he does charmingly admit that his version of the "new economic geography" has such a handicap. He quotes against himself a "sarcastic physicist" as remarking, "So what you're saying is that firms agglomerate [in cities; or in economic growth] because of agglomeration effects?"[7]

And there's a deeper problem with transport dynamics. Such truly dynamic effects as externalities leading to agglomeration effects may arise from expensive as much as from cheap transportation. Forcing more industry into London in the early nineteenth century—imagine for example humming cotton mills down at Kew in lilac time—might have achieved economies of scale in 1776 or 1815 which were in the event dissipated by the country locations chosen under the regime of low transport costs (and, to be serious about the history, country locations chosen because they were free from the constraints of regulations in the literal City of London or its westward extensions). In fact, precisely because of greater London's advantages in transport costs to its numerous consumers at home and abroad, before the eighteenth century it *was* the manufacturing center of England, containing fully 10 percent of the English population in the mid-seventeenth century. Once you introduce the possibility of economies of scale, in other words, the balance of swings and roundabouts has to be calculated, not merely asserted. After all, what economists call a "nonconvexity" is precisely the anti-invisible-hand point of industrial policy and infant-industry protection and path dependence and other alleged deviations from the competitive approximation. If you believe in nonconvexities, I say to the state-trusting economists, you can't just blithely assume that they work the way you want them to work. It is in the nature of nonconvexities that they may *not* so work. That is, they aren't provable on a blackboard in even their direction of effect. Manufacturers did relocate to Manchester and Birmingham at the call of a little cheaper labor and a little cheaper transport. So? Which way does it lean?

∞

Sector by sector the older heroes have fallen before the research of the economists and historians. Marx put great emphasis for instance on the enclosure of open fields, that is, the dissolution of the medieval agricultural community and its translation into compact, individualistic farms. He claimed that enclosure enriched the investing classes and drove workers into the hands of industrialists. Most educated people believe the tale as gospel truth, and are quite sure that a lot of industrial investment came from the profits from enclosures, and that the workforce for industrialization was "pushed off the land." Sellar and Yeatman capture the bits we can remember: "There was an Agricultural Revelation which was caused by the invention of turnips and the discovery that Trespassers could be Prosecuted. This was a Good Thing, too, because previously the Land has all been rather common, and it was called the Enclosure movement and was the origin of Keeping off the Grass, . . . [culminating] in the vast Royal Enclosure at Ascot."[8]

By now, though, several generations of agricultural historians have argued (contrary to the Fabian theme first articulated in 1911, which followed Marx) that eighteenth-century enclosures were in many ways equitable and did not drive people out of the villages.[9] True, Parliament became in the eighteenth century an executive committee of the landed classes, which made the overturning of the old forms of agriculture easier than it had been under earlier and royal supervision. Oliver Goldsmith lamenting the allegedly deserted village wrote in 1770 that "those fenceless fields the sons of wealth divide, / And even the bare-worn common is denied." Yet contrary to the pastoralism of the poem—which as usual reflects aristocratic traditions in poetry back to Horace and Theocritus more than evidence from the English countryside—the commons was usually purchased rather than stolen from the goose. One can point with sympathy to the damaging of numerous poor holders of traditional rights without also believing what appears to be false—that industrialization depended in any important way on the taking of rights from cottagers to gather firewood on the commons. Industrialization, after all, occurred first in regions to the north and west, mainly enclosed long before, such as Lancashire or Warwickshire, and especially (as Eric Jones pointed out) in areas bad for agriculture, not in the fertile East Midlands or East Anglia or the South—the places where the parliamentary acts of the eighteenth century did transform many villages, though none "deserted." In such freshly enclosed areas, I repeat, the local populations *increased* after enclosure.

The result of enclosure was a bit more efficient agriculture. Perhaps the efficiency is why enclosure increased employment, because it raised a little the quantity demanded for now more productive workers. But was enclosure therefore, to take the optimistic view, the hero of the new industrial age? By no means. Nothing much would have changed had English agriculture, like agricultures on the Continent, resisted enclosure until a century after industrialization.[10] The productivity changes were small, perhaps a 10 percent advantage of an enclosed village over an open-field village, and the profits were small in national terms, though constituting a large increase over the previous rents (about doubling, which explains why they happened: indeed, that's the most reliable method of calculating the productivity change).[11] Agriculture was a large fraction of national income (shrunk perhaps to a third by 1800), but the share of land to be enclosed was only half the land of England (the rest was those "regions mainly enclosed long before").[12] Harberger's Law asserts itself again: ($\frac{1}{3}$) ($\frac{1}{2}$) (10 percent) $= 1.7$ percent of national income to be gained from the enclosure of open fields. Improved road surfaces around and through the enclosing villages might have been more important than the rearranging of scattered plots on which most historical attention has been lavished (straightening and resurfacing of roads accompanied enclosure, but the effect is seldom stressed).

Nor was Adam Smith correct that the wealth of the nation depended on the division of labor. True, the economy did specialize. Ann Kussmaul's pioneering work on rural specialization showed it happening in England from the sixteenth century onward.[13] Maxine Berg and Patricia Hudson have emphasized that modern factories need not have been large. Yet the factories nonetheless were closely divided in their labor, since they supplied their neighboring factories.[14] Most enterprises were tiny. They accomplished the division of labor through the market, as Smith averred. It has long been known that metal working in Birmingham and the Black Country, for example, or in Sheffield, was broken down into hundreds of tiny firms, anticipating by two centuries the "Japanese" techniques of just-in-time inventory and detailed subcontracting. A division of labor certainly did happen, widely.

That is to say, the proper dividing of labor, like the proper marshaling of transport and enclosure, made the economy more efficient. Britons got closer to their production possibility curve, as the economists put it. Gains were to be had, which suggests why they were seized (compare agglomeration effects explaining specialization of, say, Chicago in meatpacking). French engineers at the time were amazed by the division of labor in Britain. The division of labor, however, was much noted also in China at the time—though it did not in China result in an industrial revolution. And a new technique of specialization, like an advantage from agglomeration in Chicago or like the enclosure of open fields, can be profitable to adopt yet lead to only a small effect on productivity nationally. For example the modest, if by no means unimportant, productivity changes from the puddling and rolling of iron amounted 1780 to 1860 to about 0.9 percent per year in the industry, which itself was not gigantic.[15] The national gains, weighting the 0.9 percent by the small size of the iron industry even in iron-mad Britain, were modest in the absence of dynamic effects, because the static gains from more complete specialization are limited by Harberger's Law.

Consider the following extreme thought experiment. Specialization in the absence of technological change can be viewed as the undoing of bad locations for production. Some of the heavy clay soil of the Midlands was put down to grazing, for example, which suited it better than wheat. Or the labor of the Highlands was ripped off the land, to find better employment—higher wages, if less Gaelic spoken—in Glasgow or Nova Scotia or North Carolina. The size of the reallocation effect can be calculated, à la Harberger. Suppose a quarter of the labor of the country was misallocated. And suppose the misallocation was bad enough to leave, say, a 50 percent wage gap between the old sector and the new. This would be a large misallocation, indicating a large-scale irrationality of laborers in not moving to better jobs—or, more likely, a large-scale blockage laid down by bosses or a government controlled by bosses. The wage gap created by South African apartheid was even greater than 50 percent. But it seems unlikely that British wage gaps were as large as can be created by a sophisticated and powerful modern state intent on discrimination.

Now imagine the labor moves to its proper industry, closing the gap. As the gap in wages closes, the gain gradually shrinks, finally to zero. So the gain from closing it is so to speak a triangle (called in economics in fact a Harberger Triangle), whose area is half the rectangle of the wage gap multiplied by the amount of labor involved. So again: ($\frac{1}{2}$) ($\frac{1}{4}$) (50 percent) = 6.25 percent of labor's share of national income, which was at the time about half, leaving a 3 percent gain to the whole. The gain, as usual, is worth having. Yet it is not itself the stuff of revolutions. The division of labor doesn't by itself seem to do the trick.

To believe such a calculation you have to believe in the approximate truth of what the economists call "marginal productivity theory." That is, in line with bourgeois and largely British economics after 1870 (with Continental contributions from people like Walras and Wicksell and Menger, and Americans like Clark) you have to believe that businesspeople hire labor and capital and land because they think they'll turn a profit (whether routine profit as a reward to ownership or "supernormal" profit as a reward to a new idea). If you doubt it, perhaps I can quickly persuade you (I am not optimistic) by noting that the few dozen recessions that modernizing economies have experienced since 1800 were likewise misallocations—25 percent of labor unemployed in the U.S.A. and Germany in 1933 as the worst case, with corresponding massive idling of capital. But income in such episodes did not fall by the 90 percent implied by the hypothesis of great sensitivity to misallocations. It fell pretty much in line with the proposition that a worker or a machine is employed up to the point where it just earns its wage or rental: in the American and German case by 1933 by about a third. If marginal productivity theory and the invisible hand were false, misallocations during recessions would have had much larger consequences.[16]

The economic historian Jeffrey Williamson would in some ways disagree. In 1990 he argued that in the early nineteenth century in Britain "imperfect capital markets starved industry for funds, driving a wedge between rates of return in industry and agriculture. Since the industrial capital stock was, therefore, too small, industrial jobs were fewer than they would have been had capital markets been perfect."[17] That is, he claims there was an economically relevant gap between high returns to capital and labor in cotton mills and coal mines against low returns in agriculture. He uses a four-sector general equilibrium model of the sort he has pioneered in economic history and economic development to argue that factually speaking the capital-market gap and the labor-market gap amounted by 1850 (say) to a 7 percent lower real GDP than would have obtained in a perfected world.[18] Perhaps. One can quarrel with details of his model. And 7 percent is not the stuff of revolutions. Further, Williamson himself—who is always generously comprehensive in his bibliography—notes that many people (such as Crouzet and, with much less authority, McCloskey, who unlike Crouzet has not done primary research into the matter) do not believe the imperfections existed in the first place. Long ago the economist George Stigler wrote a devastating essay against the conversation-ending rhetoric of "imperfections in the capital market."[19] A historian ignores Stigler to his peril.[20]

And Williamson makes the crucial point against his own argument (I told you he is intellectually honest): "The view that wage and rate of return gaps represent disequilibrium and factor market disequilibrium may also be challenged."[21] Yes, it may. The question is whether an observed gap is economically relevant. A higher rate of return to the owner of a wool mill as against a sheep farm may have come from a greater degree of risk in making cloth than in raising wool. A higher wage in the industrializing North than in the agricultural South of England may have come from costs of moving, including cultural tastes, and the disamenities of smoky Preston, which is a point that Williamson himself demonstrates is factually relevant to the period. He writes, "Some portion of the higher earnings of urban residents may be simply compensation for the disamenities of urban life and work."[22] If so, the gaps represent reasonable adjustments to available opportunities, not sluggish stupidity. A southern agricultural laborer ordered peremptorily to go north to Preston would incur costs of travel, retraining, homesickness, nastiness (to his southern mind) of northern life, tearing of social bonds—all of which would overweigh the future returns from a higher money income. If at liberty, and nobody's fool, he would disobey the order. The capital and labor markets would then be, the economists would say, "in equilibrium," despite the observed wage gap. Free lunches from reallocation would not be sitting around uneaten, because they would not in fact be free of relevant cost.

Gaps between industrial and agricultural wages have persisted in every country in the world for decades, even centuries. For example, they persisted for the whole of the nineteenth century, as Williamson notes, in the fabled land of mobility and liberty and being nobody's fool but your own, the United States. Such persistent gaps on the order of 50 or 100 percent, most economists would suspect, cannot be viewed simply as stupidly ignored free lunches. A mill owner could think of twenty different ways to pick up the lunch if it were merely a matter of stupidity. Bring a cartload of southern workers to Preston. Move the mill to Sussex. And the laborers have every incentive to pick it up and themselves eat the free lunch. Yet some economists have felt comfortable in assuming stupidity, and then calculating the gain from reallocating labor across the wage gap, decade by decade, as though it were a free lunch sitting on the kitchen table for a hundred years, to be slowly, persistently dined on. In honor of a great economist scientist who made it fashionable, the calculation might be called the Kuznets Fallacy. The fallacy is to believe without historical inquiry that every price divergence represents a neglected opportunity for arbitrage, buying low to sell high, without costs of transaction. It doesn't seem so.

21

NOR GEOGRAPHY, NOR NATURAL RESOURCES

Geography is still another popular explanation that does not seem to work very well. The title page of my copy of Jared Diamond's *Guns, Germs, and Steel: The Fates of Human Societies* (1997) contains an excited notation from when I first read it, in August 2000: "The best book I've read in years." It's still true, and I read a lot of books. I started the book with a certain professional indignation—"Wait a minute, I'm the economic historian here. Who's this guy?" But he won me over in twenty pages. Diamond argues persuasively that the east-west axis of Eurasia from Spain to Japan made for shared domestications of plants and animals—wheat, rice, horses, chickens—which the north-south places like sub-Saharan Africa or the isolated places like Australasia or the north-south *and* isolated places like the Americas could not enjoy. His is a powerful argument for why "advanced" societies tended strongly to be Eurasian, from Rome to China (he does also emphasize that in Africa and in Polynesia and the Americas the advance was coming along, slowly—though in the sixteenth through nineteenth centuries it was shorted out by European conquests).

Diamond reports the question of his New Guinean friend Yali, and says that he takes it as his guide: "Why is it that you *white people* developed so much cargo?"[1] Good question. The abundance possessed by the non–New Guinean folk stunned Yali and his countrymen into cargo cults attempting during and after World War II to bring back the big airplanes of the Japanese and Allied conquerors. Diamond's geographical argument, however, breaks down when the focus narrows geographically, as it must narrow to really answer Yali's question: why did the cornucopia of cargo pour out of *north-*

western Europe (and out of its offspring Australia, south of New Guinea, and out of its northward imitator of Europe, Japan, perhaps "white" from a New Guinean point of view)? The correct answer, which Diamond does not give, is that the northwest European "white people" had an industrial revolution and the other people—whether Eurasian or African or Meso-american—did not, until after the northwest Europeans had led the way. Italians, Iraqis, Indians, Chinese, and other beneficiaries of the 4,000-year head start in civilization coming out of the Fertile Crescent did not get to the cornucopia first. The Dutch and British did, closely followed by the French and Germans and Americans. Why? Diamond's brilliant explanation of why China and Turkey both had domesticated chickens and domesticated wheat tells why you would not have expected an industrial revolution among the Incas or the Zulus—at any rate not in 1491 CE or 1815 CE. Yet his explanation sheds no light at all on why Holland and then Britain fashioned the first modern economies out of the widely shared heritage of Eurasia, and therefore developed so much cargo.

Diamond gets sidetracked—as people tend to do—into the very different question of why European people were so good at *violent conquest* after 1492. He gives for example an account of Pizarro's capture of the Inca emperor in 1533 in a long chapter 3, "Collision at Cajamarca," concluding that "the title of this book will serve as a shorthand for [the] proximate factors," namely guns, germs [smallpox especially], [sword and armor] steel, horses, ships, empires, and writing.[2] Such factors, and a mad confidence born from the myth of the Christian knight, certainly do explain Pizarro's exploits. The bold exploits, however, have nothing to do with diesel engines and electric lights and cargo planes, which constitute the "cargo" that Yali was asking about. After a while, for example, the conquered people had themselves, by the very fact of conquest, access to the Eurasian crops and animals and iron so laboriously accumulated. The 8,000-year-old divergence thereby became irrelevant to Yali's inquiry. What now mattered was the divergence after 1700 CE and especially after 1800 CE of northwestern Europe from the Chinese or the Ottoman or the Mughal or the Spanish or the other advanced Eurasian empires.

Indeed, the particular selection of Diamond's title—guns, germs, and steel—were irrelevant to the Industrial Revolution in the narrow sense. Before the late nineteenth century, steel in its exact chemical definition (iron with less than 2 percent carbon, and with no significant impurities) was very expensive, and was therefore used only for edge weapons and armor for the aristocracy, the better to slaughter German peasants and Incan soldiers and (with the most honor-acquiring enthusiasm) other European aristocrats. You can argue correctly that boring of cannon by John Wilkinson led the way (because Watt the instrument maker realized its use) to precision boring of steam cylinders, but until the late nineteenth century the metal bored was not low-carbon "steel": it was bronze available all over Eurasia and Africa, or cast iron produced in bulk, a technique invented by the Chinese or the Bantu Africans, take your pick. The Asians bored their cannons, too (and indeed steel made in modest bulk was an Indian invention, around 300 BCE). Muskets and pistols had little to do with industrialization (interchangeable parts could have come from any mass-produced mechanical device—clocks, for example). Precision scientific instruments and clock making depended very little on military production and much more on peaceful products made out of cast and wrought iron (wrought iron is iron with small amounts of carbon, like steel, but also with impurities in the form of embedded slag) and out of tiny steel machine parts such as springs. And anyway the cotton textile machinery of Britain was first made largely out of wood, and only later out of iron, and only late in the nineteenth century did it come to made out of the newly cheapened steel. Germs deriving from Eurasian domestic animals (among others, smallpox from cow pox) killed 95 percent of native Australians and Americans (depopulating for example an Amazonia that before the Europeans sustained many millions of people, in an agriculture that until recently was thought impossible with the poor, leached soils of the rain forest). Yet the Native American holocausts during and after the sixteenth century contribute nothing to understanding why northwestern European people in the nineteenth and twentieth developed so much cargo. To repeat, killing people, whether on purpose with steel or by accident with disease, does not usually make you rich.

Diamond concludes the Pizarro chapter by announcing that the rest of the book will discuss "no longer the questions of proximate causation that this chapter has been discussing," but "why all those immediate advantages came to lie more with Europe than the New World."[3] He's back to touting the advantages of Eurasia. Something, however, has gone wrong with the line of argument. True, the conquests can be explained by the immediate European advantages (most of it—and even some of the diseases—recently borrowed from the East). Yet conquest is not the same thing as enrichment by a factor of sixteen. In 1800 most Europeans and many even in Holland and England still earned the ancient $3 a day. Yali's question about cargo in the late twentieth century has been lost in answers to questions about violence in the sixteenth century. You can see it in the outcome of an incident Diamond relates. Pizarro extracted from the Incan emperor a ransom of gold filling a room about fourteen feet on all sides (after taking delivery, he of course murdered the emperor anyway: Pizarro was neither an honorable merchant nor a gentleman). It was a down payment on the river of gold and silver that poured into Spain for hundreds of years. Yet by 1800 Spain was among the poorest countries in Europe, well into the $3-a-day category, and stayed behind northwestern Europe until its miraculous transformation through bourgeois dignity and liberty much later. Though once far famed for violent conquest, Spain had not learned even by 1900, except in the Basque or Catalan regions, how to industrialize, and even by 1975 it had not learned how to postindustrialize. Diamond's focus on the reasons for conquest after 1492 has diverted him from the reasons for the revolution after 1700 in the making of cargo. He doesn't answer the question he poses.

∞

Jeffrey Sachs and his coauthors cannot be charged with not answering the question they pose: do "tropical ecozones and landlocked countries face obstacles to development not faced by temperate-zone and coastal economies?" Yes, they do: "The tropical regions are nearly uniformly poor, while temperate regions have a wide income range with a small proportion (7 percent) of the temperate-zone populations at [annual] income levels below $2000 [or $4.48 a day], compared with 42 percent of the tropical-zone population."[4] Sachs, though, is not asking how northwestern Europe stole a march after 1700 on other temperate-zone populations such as the Chinese or the Ottomans. His tropical focus is persuasively argued, and he is not claiming that the tropics are geographically doomed—merely that they need tropical-specific research, such as cheap vaccines for malaria, and good governance. After all, Singapore, only 120 miles north of the equator, has a per capita income only a few cents per day lower than that of the United States.

The temperate-tropical division, in other words, like Diamond's axes of continents, cannot explain what needs explanation historically: why English people got so much cargo, and why by contrast temperate-zone Chinese people in 1700 CE or temperate-zone Roman people in 100 CE did not. After all, northwestern Europe initiated the modern world when still debilitated by cholera and smallpox and tuberculosis and especially by a malaria similar to the one so devastating to modern Africa, under the name of "ague" (from which for example Oliver Cromwell died), called among the industrious Italians *mala aria*, "bad air."[5] Malaria reached its global peak, including much of Europe, in the nineteenth century, just when Europe was industrializing. Something other than disease patterns was involved in the Industrial Revolution.

That's not to say that improved mortality and morbidity arising from better diets and from public health measures in advance of the germ theory of disease had nothing to do with the Great Fact.[6] Healthy people can work harder, and smarter. Longer life makes investment in human capital rational (just as the thirteenth-century invention of eyeglasses, as David Landes notes, gave detail craftsmen a much longer effective life over which to amortize the costs of training).[7] A Europe wracked with water-borne diseases, not to speak of the White Plague of tuberculosis ("consumption") which rose and fell in a puzzling pattern centered on the nineteenth century, had a handicap in doing its job. And yet Europe did it, and got healthy mainly as a result of the Great Fact. Health was not its cause.

Mellinger, Sachs, and Gallup also argue persuasively that in recent times access to cheap oceangoing transport is crucial. Yet their present-day map of "land within 100 km of an ice-free coast or sea-navigable river," defined as the nine-meter draft of modern oceangoers, shows north China and Egypt as instances.[8] And in 1700, with shallower drafts of smaller ships, and none of the postindustrial improvements in Europe and the United States of rivers and harbors (the St. Lawrence Seaway; the numerous European ship canals as in the Netherlands and Germany), the map would look even less favorable to Europe and the United States, and relatively more favorable to places like China, Japan, and the Ottoman Empire—which nonetheless did not stage an industrial revolution.

Sachs and his coauthors, of course, are not attempting to explain the Industrial Revolution geographically. They would probably agree (Montesquieu and Henry Buckle to the contrary) that geography does not explain Europe's head start. After all, the supposedly vigorous northern air featured (by Europeans) in geographical theories also weakened European people through lung infection, such as the chronic bronchitis that plagues England to this day. And as I said, the bad air too once carried a mosquito that infected Europeans with deadly and debilitating ague.

∞

A subspecies of the geographical argument is "resources." Economists call natural resources "the original and indestructible properties of the soil," in Ricardo's phrase, or simply "land." Though most don't, some economic historians continue to put weight on Britain's unusual gift from nature. The gifts of nature are what noneconomist journalists call "resources" when they wonder why Congo and Russia with so much gold, diamonds, copper, chromium, cassiterite, and coltan are not as rich as France and Japan with none. The journalists and diplomats talk about oil, say, as being essential—which they believe implies that conquering the oil land is a good idea, invading (say) Sumatra in 1941 or Iraq in 1915. Such fractured economic logic exhibits the political problem with supposing that land makes for growth. It supports a species of diplomatic folly about "resources" which the economists have tried and tried without success to dislodge. The result of the folly has been such political catastrophes as the Japanese-American disputes about oil in the 1930s and early 1940s, or German theories of *Lebensraum*, or in 2003 the invasion of Iraq, again.

The scientific problem, and the reason that most economists think the resource theory is foolish, is that since 1800 land has fallen steadily in importance. The share of land in national income, including the value of oil land, has shrunk in a modern economy so much that the gifts of nature have ended up economically speaking trivial—at 2 or 3 percent of national income. Shades of Harberger. We saw the unimportance even of the much-discussed oil land during the run-up of oil prices in 2008. Prices at the pump that noneconomists believed would herald the end of Western civilization had in the event modest economic effects. People feel instinctively that oil is "basic," because it enters into so many products. To this the economist replies that all products are basic, which is to say that all products enter directly or indirectly into the production of others. The economy is a circular flow. "Basic" is therefore pretty much meaningless. Pencils and flower pots and bed frames are as "basic" as oil is.The shred of meaningfulness the word retains is the ball-bearing theory of strategic bombing—bomb the ball-bearing factories, you see, and the German war machine will have to stop. The theory is especially popular among American military strategists, who like the idea of saving the lives of American boys by putting them into capital-intensive flying machines with bombs instead of infantry battalions with rifles. Yet in fact the Germans (and the North Vietnamese and others on whom the theory has been tried) went elsewhere, such as underground, or in the Soviet case, with Germans themselves as the economic experimenters, east of the Urals. Nothing is essential, say the economists. There is more than one way to skin a cat, and more than one way to make a ball bearing. Strategic bombing, even excusing its dubious ethics of burning little children to death in order to get at the ball-bearing factories, doesn't work, as was discovered in post–World War II investigations by Allied economists. There are substitutes for everything—not perfect, but good enough that the choke-point ideas arising from a fixed-coefficient model ("Germany *needs* ball bearings, made in easily-bombed Cologne") don't work, and the bombing causes far less than a 100 percent loss of the industry bombed. (The argument, and the finding that it was empirically relevant, by the way, is another triumph for the marginal productivity theory of distribution.)

In one version, the resource theory of growth resembles the accumulation theory of growth. You get some profit from land or fish or oil or coal, it is said, and then reinvest it, and get rich. (By the way, Ricardo emphasized the *indestructible* character of [say] land close to London, and pointed out that mere extraction of fertility or coal [or later oil] is not a use of land defined as indestructible but is rather the use of capital defined as a stock to be used up. A stand of trees is a stock of capital, to be used up slowly or quickly depending on the rate of interest, not an "original and indestructible character" of the soil, or location, location, location.) The resource theory has the same flaw as the accumulation theory—that it cannot explain the gigantic enrichment of the average modern person.

Belief in the resource theory, for example, distorted South African economic policy for decades. It finally dawned on white South Africans that merely having a stock of gold and diamonds in the ground does not make for a modern economy—and that most particularly it does not do so if innovations depending on high human capital do not get used because you are intent for political reasons on keeping blacks and coloreds uneducated. Hong Kong and Singapore and Japan, with little in the way of natural resources, and Denmark with nothing but land for cows, leapt into the modern world, while most of the South African population did not. The Icelanders, to pick a very different case, worship fish as the source of their wealth.

Yet it was Icelandic education intersecting with the demands of a modern world, not the wide ocean, that made the place rich, and will allow it to recover pretty quickly from its unhappy experiment with U.S. mortgage-backed securities and the buying of Mercedes autos on credit. As the economic historian Eric Jones puts it, about a country supposedly rich in "resources," "The more meaningful assets of the United States were [not its resource endowments but] markets and institutions capable of vigorously exploiting its endowment."[9]

NOT EVEN COAL

Yet four impressive scholars recently have insisted on coal: Anthony Wrigley (1962, 1988), Kenneth Pomeranz (2000), Robert Allen (2006, et al., 2009), and John Harris (1998). The historical demographer Wrigley has long claimed that the substitution of mineral fuel for wood and animal power made the Industrial Revolution. In one sense he is obviously correct, since wood could not have easily fueled the steam engines and blast furnaces of England—though observe that well into the nineteenth century the United States used wood to power steamboats on the Mississippi and used charcoal to refine iron in Pennsylvania. Yet coal deposits do in fact correlate with early industrialization. The coal-bearing swath of Europe from Midlothian to the Ruhr started early on industrial growth. English coal was important from an early date in heating London's homes, blackening the Black Country, eventually running Manchester's steam engines—though Manchester, New Hampshire's cotton mills kept using falling water. It is hard to imagine big electricity-generating stations running on logs. Eventually hydroelectric and especially atomic power did something in replacing coal, and we all hope that wind and solar and geothermal power will prevail. But dirty old King Coal still matters a lot.

Yet the sheer availability of coal does not seem, at least on static grounds, to be important enough for the factor of sixteen, or even a doubling 1780–1860. As Eric Jones observed, a capability of exploiting an endowment may matter more. Obviously coal determined *where* industry was, but one must not confuse location with overall extent and national gain.[1] Economically speaking, a coal theory, or any other one-step geographical theory, has an appointment with Harberger. The share in national income of land was much higher in the eighteenth century than now (perhaps 20 percent then as against 2 or 3 percent now), but the share of coal land within all land was small.[2] The calculations would be worth doing, but they probably would turn out like the others. Gregory Clark and David Jacks have recently argued that substitutes for coal meant that an upper bound on the loss from a coal-less Britain would have been a mere 2 percent of national income—when what is to be explained is a 100 percent increase down to the mid-nineteenth century and much larger increases afterward.[3] Think of ball bearings and Allied bombs.

Especially, coal could be moved, and was—it went to Amsterdam and London, moving about Europe and the world like Swedish iron and lumber, or French salt, or Irish cattle. The presence of coal somewhere reachable at low cost may have been important for the steam stage of industrialization, say 1800–1950. And before the railway a transport route by sea would have been very important. The point, however, is that the coal didn't need to be on the spot. As Goldstone notes, if the coal fields had been located in Normandy, then the London fireplaces and the Cornish pumping engines would have imported their coal from France, and we would have no sage talk about the necessity of British coal inside the legal confines of Britain. Yet Normandy would not necessarily have industrialized, if lacking the requisite dignity and liberty of the bourgeoisie (whose standing there, at any rate in the minds of the Parisian clerisy around 1856, may be inferred from *Madame Bovary*). The place where steam engines were most used was Cornwall, with no coal—but gigantic amounts of it across the Bristol Channel in South Wales. Norrland in Sweden exported lumber and paper pulp, but did not make the house frames or the paper.

The recent advocates for coal are right, however, to emphasize that any argument about industrialization needs to be made comparatively. The Chinese in the seventeenth century had long been using coal on a big scale to get, for example, the high temperatures to fire ceramics, exporting the result westward.[4] Kenneth Pomeranz argues for the importance of the accident that in Europe, especially in Britain, cheap coal sat close to populations. China's coal was far away from the Yangtze Valley—the valley being until the nineteenth century a place which was in other ways, he argued (though later proven mistaken), comparable to Britain in wealth, at the high end of the $3 \pm $2 a day of our ancestors. The valley was where the demanders of coal and in particular the skilled craftsmen were. China very early used coal (and natural gas, of all things), but its coal was inland, with no cheap water routes like London's "sea coal" from Newcastle, used in English lime kilns and glassmaking from the thirteenth century on, and by around 1600 increasingly for house fuel (the local price of firewood had sharply risen).

Yet one might object that a more vigorous protoinnovation ("vigorously exploiting its endowment") would have *moved* the industry to, say, Manchuria (not entirely unnaturally, perhaps, under the rule of Manchus after 1644), or at any rate to some other coal-bearing lands of the gradually widening Central Kingdom, exporting the finished products instead of the raw coal. After all, eventually China did just that, as on a smaller geographical scale the British did in the (newly) industrial northwest and northeast, or the Germans in Silesia, or on a larger scale the Europeans in exporting finished products to the world. You do not have to move coal—even before the railway made moving it cheap. You can move people or move finished goods or both.

Coal as merely a new source of heating, in short, does not work very well for explaining our riches. Robert Allen, who would disagree, has emphasized that coal was relatively cheap in England compared with labor, as against its high relative price on much of the Continent. By the end of the eighteenth century, certainly in London, and even the once-poor North, English people enjoyed higher real wages than most of the Continent, except the Netherlands: "Craftsmen in London or Amsterdam earned six times what was required to purchase the subsistence basket [of goods], while their counterparts in Germany or Italy only 50% more than that standard."[5] His argument is that cheap coal relative to scarce labor led to innovation. That is, he attributes the scale of British innovation to the pattern of factor scarcities. Labor was scarce relative to coal fuel in Britain, *and so* innovations would be labor-saving. *And so* Britain would have a large volume of innovations.

Neither "and so" makes much economic sense. The economic historian H. J. Habakkuk in 1962 put forward the same argument about the United States during the nineteenth century: labor was scarce relative to capital, *and so* America innovated by saving labor. Allen himself accurately summarizes one crushing point against such an argument, following critics such as Peter Temin and other economic historians reacting to Habakkuk: "One problem is that businesses are only concerned about costs *in toto*—and not about labor costs or energy costs in particular—so all cost reductions are equally welcome."[6] Well put. As another leading student of technology, Tunzelmann, remarks, "In truth, it is extremely difficult to make a logical theoretical argument for the seemingly self-evident proposition that scarce labor should induce labor-saving bias in technology."[7] A shilling got from saving not labor but coal (coal saving was in fact the obsession of early users of steam engines, as Margaret Jacob has shown from their writings) is the same shilling that one got from saving labor (which Jacob notes was seldom mentioned by the engineers she has studied).[8] If one would prefer an inconclusive theoretical argument over a conclusive empirical finding such as Jacob's (at the University of Chicago after its better day of true empiricism they say, "That's all right in practice, but what about in theory?"), one could refer to the economist Daron Acemoglu's argument about the set-up costs of research: precisely because coal was abundant in Britain the engineers sought innovations that justified the set-up costs of looking into ways of saving it, not labor.[9] Later, in the nineteenth century, as Allen and I discovered some time ago, British iron- and steelmaking made advances mainly by saving coal, as in for example Neilson's recycling of hot gases from the blast furnace to cut coke usage by two-thirds, or the hard driving later in the century with similar results.[10] By that time Britain had even higher wages, and the real price of coal had not much changed. What happened, one may ask, to the alleged labor-saving bias between the late eighteenth and the late nineteenth centuries?

If wages relative to coal prices were all that mattered, Jacob has also noted, Belgium and the extreme south of the high-wage Netherlands, both of which had coal, and in any case could import it very cheaply from Northumberland across the North Sea, would have been the Birminghams and Manchesters of the late eighteenth century. And to look at the point from the opposite side, why did not industry on the *low*-wage parts of the Continent away from the Netherlands therefore explode with *coal*-saving innovations? As Mokyr puts it, "Economies that had not coal would constantly be under pressure to develop more fuel-efficient techniques, or engines that used alternative sources of energy," instancing windmills in Asia or water mills in Rome (both of which, he notes, were *not* greatly improved subsequently, or used to power an industrial revolution).[11] You can see the underlying illogic: *something* is always relatively scarce, "and so" innovation in saving the scarce input will be high. "And so" every age and place has an incentive to innovate in great volume. The logic has somehow gone astray.

Cheap coal can indeed explain the location of power-hungry industries in Lancashire vs. Wiltshire, or Birmingham vs. Bordeaux (though, by the way, Allen does not sufficiently acknowledge the importance of water power). If one is willing to glide by the point that a shilling is a shilling, as Allen does so glide, after tipping his hat to the critics of Habbakuk, then the high ratio of wages to coal might be supposed, illogically, to affect the composition of innovations. The matter to be explained in the Industrial Revolution, though, is not the composition of innovation, but its magnitude. Patrick O'Brien and Caglar Keyder recognized the point long ago, arguing that France took "another path" than Britain did to the twentieth century. One could ask therefore why in eighteenth-century Italy or indeed China there was not a labor-*using* path to the modern world. That British innovations were biased (as the economists put it) toward labor saving, if they were (though in iron making, as I said, they definitely were not, and about the whole economy the econometric studies agree that Britain was not), says nothing at all about how many innovations in total the British would make. If spaghetti is cheap relative to rice in Italy compared with Japan you can expect Italians to eat relatively more spaghetti than rice. Yet such an expectation does not say anything about how much food in total the two countries will consume, one sort of food aggregated with another. In explaining modern innovation the aggregate is what matters, not the pattern.

It is easy to get confused about the economics here. China did use labor-intensive methods of all kinds. Doing so, however, is merely using old technology (not innovating new technology, that is, getting really new ideas) in a way determined by the abundance of labor relative to, say, land. In such matters, Allen properly affirms, relative prices matter. Yet using people to hoe the fields by hand instead of using capital-intensive methods such as great iron plows is not an advance of the sort that made us rich compared to our great-great-great-great-great grandparents. It is not an "advance" at all, in fact, but a choice of different routines from existing plans of business, different paths on the same map. Allen cites Rainer Fremdling, who has persuasively shown that the nonuse of coke for iron on the Continent before the 1850s—it had been in use in Britain for a century by then—was not an entrepreneurial failure (as Landes for example had argued) but a matter of relative prices.[12] Peter Temin had argued earlier, likewise, that the use of charcoal for blast furnaces in the United States in the same era was another case in point: wood for charcoal was cheap relative to coal there.[13] And I had done the same sort of research on British iron makers about a claimed "failure" to use now *Continental* techniques of by-product coking later in the century, or a "failure" to have in other ways the same pattern of use of ideas as the Americans or Germans (David Landes again made the claim I was criticizing; Landes does tend to scold for sloth and incompetence whomever was not using whatever he asserts without quantitative inquiry was the best technique; it is a corollary of his race-to-the-swiftest, *élan-vital* theory of world history and his overuse of second-guessing).[14]

Splendid though such quantitative researches in historical economics are, however, they are not the same as explaining the innovativeness of British vs. Continental economies in the eighteenth and early nineteenth centuries, or the innovativeness of Europe generally 1700 to 1900. To explain the size as against the composition of innovativeness you need factors like a lead in the practical side of the Enlightenment (Jacob, Goldstone, Mokyr, Israel) or in entrepreneurial *élan vital* (Landes; though note how poorly the hypothesis does in the late nineteenth century) or—to come to the One True Explanation—in the extent to which a rhetoric of dignified and liberated business had been adopted (McCloskey). One needs, to put it again in economic jargon, an explanation of absolute, not comparative, advantage.

Relative prices of the sort economists usually concern themselves with, in other words, have a highly doubtful connection with the amount of innovativeness in total. As Allen argues, the scale of Britain's mining of coal and lead and tin explains "why steam engine research was carried out in England."[15] That sounds reasonable. Margaret Jacob for example would probably agree. For the same reasons, as Alan Olmstead and Paul Rhode have recently argued, biological innovation in crops and livestock took place in the United States during the nineteenth century—this against still another version of the scarce-labor hypothesis (which claims that mechanization was the key to American agricultural improvement).[16] Economies of scale in a leading industry, though, is not a theory of the amount of innovation of all sorts, in banking and insurance and cotton and wool and glassmaking and printing. The total amount of innovation is what is to be explained. You can, again, lose on the swings what you gain on the roundabouts: America's attention to innovation in agriculture, natural though it was, left less attention to be devoted to innovation in chemicals.

The historian John Harris argued for coal in a way that makes more sense than the static arguments favored by the economists. He wrote that in Britain in the seventeenth century and before, "the move to general use of a cheaper mineral fuel . . . nearly always necessitated important technical change in order to accommodate the use of the equipment of the relevant industry," such as glass making or salt making. "The long success with this change of fuel . . . over a couple of centuries was a major reason for a willingness to try new methods in other industrial fields and to be prized away from traditional practices."[17] Yes: the accident of easy coal and expensive forests could lead to a tinkering mentality (say) about applications of heat. (Though again the Chinese were in such matters many centuries ahead.) In this case, however, the Coal Effect works through habits of the mind, not (as the economist would wish) directly through relative prices. I stand with the admirable Tocqueville: "Looking at the turn given to the human spirit in England by political life; seeing the Englishman . . . inspired by the sense that he can do anything . . . I am in no hurry to inquire whether nature has scooped out ports for him, or given him coal or iron."[18]

∞

How far have we gotten?

The claim is that the economist's static model does not explain the factor of sixteen. The static model and its quasidynamic extensions can tell what did *not* cause the Industrial Revolution and its sequel, correctives to popular fable and sharpeners of serious hypotheses. It is useful science. Yet the kind of growth contemplated in the classical models, embedded nowadays deep within economics as a system of thought, was not the kind of growth that overtook Britain in the late eighteenth century and then was gloriously continued in the nineteenth century and then in the wide world.

One might reply that many small effects, static and dynamic, could add up to the doubling of income per head to be explained: trade, coal, education, canals, peace, investment, reallocation. The late Charles Feinstein suggested this to me at a conference bringing the "new" economic history to Britain in the 1980s. I honor the broad-minded impulse to avoid unicausal explanations. But on the other hand the purpose of a science is to uncover causes. If one cause such as gravity explains most of a phenomenon, such as the acceleration of a falling stone, then there can't be a complaint that "unicausal explanations are always wrong in [physics or] history." Sometimes they are right, or right enough for scientific purposes. Sometimes air resistance doesn't matter very much, and then Galileo's merely unicausal rule does the job: $a = g = 32$ ft./sec./sec.

And another trouble—the historical trouble emphasized before—is that many of the suggested effects, whether in the first or the second century of modern economic growth, were available for the taking in earlier centuries. The mystery inside the enigma of modern economic growth is why it is so very modern. If canals, say, are to explain some major part of the growth of income, it must be explained why a technology available since the beginnings of settled society, and used with increasing sophistication in many of them from the third millennium BCE on, was suddenly so very useful as to cause an epochal rise in productivity around 1800 CE. The Chinese invented the pound lock in 984 CE (it got to Europe in 1373) and in 1327 CE completed the Grand Canal of 1,100 miles (the Canal du Midi from the Atlantic to the Mediterranean, the pride of French rationalist engineering, was completed only in 1681 CE and was a mere 149 miles). China had constructed elaborate systems of lockless transport canals many centuries earlier, as of course did ancient Mesopotamia and the Indus Valley civilization.[19] The Iranians dug long tunnels through mountains to water their plains, as did the people of Teotihuacan. The Romans led water for scores of miles on arches and through tunnels. What, then, is so special about the Bridgewater Canal (1776) bringing coal to Manchester?

In any case, adding up the material causes proposed for the Industrial Revolution doesn't seem to work, either. One trouble is that adding up a dozen effects shown to be individually on the order of 1 or 2 percent still does not come close to the 100 percent rise of income per head in the first century of the Industrial Revolution. (I repeat: the capital accumulation supposed to "explain" the rise would not have happened if the innovation had not happened; marginal products would have been promptly driven down to zero.) And the deeper trouble is that the doubling is not enough, since in short order the result of modern economic growth was not a factor of two or even three but a factor of sixteen—not 100 percent but 1,500 percent—and greatly larger if the better quality of goods and services like lighting and health care and education could be properly accounted for. And the still deeper problem is that what needs to be explained is why the multiple causes converged in the late eighteenth century. To this question I have an answer. The historians who hypothesize a happy conjuncture of otherwise routine economic forces do not.

The classical model from Smith to Mill was one of reaching existing standards of efficiency and equipment. Allocate things until the supply price equals the demand price, and capture the efficiency gains. Nice. It is a pure

theory of the virtue of prudence, that is, economics in the style of Jeremy
Bentham (1748–1832) and Paul Samuelson (1915–2009). As an account of
modern economic growth the model looked quite plausible until the late
nineteenth century. To attach it to a place: the model was one of reaching
Holland's riches in 1700. And indeed as late as 1870 the Western European
countries had merely accomplished such a catching up with Holland, so far
as average income per head was concerned. (They had by then prepared
the technical and organizational grounds for a growth gigantically beyond
old Holland, and Holland itself was beginning to industrialize seriously, but
that is another and later matter). According to Maddison's figures, per capita
income in the Netherlands was $2,110 in 1700 ($5.70 a day expressed in 1990
dollars), which was about what had been achieved in most Western European countries by 1870—for example, France at $1,876 and a collection of
the twelve richest European countries at $2,086.[20] No wonder the classical
economists imagined limits close to what they could see plainly in Holland,
and had no idea that the $5.40 a day (in 1990 prices) that the average Western
European earned in 1870—again, a little less than what the average Dutch
person had earned 170 years earlier—was to increase by the end of the twentieth century to an astounding $50 a day, and higher.

Holland was to the eighteenth century what Britain was to the late eighteenth and the nineteenth, and America was to the twentieth, a standard
for the wealth of nations. "The province of Holland," wrote Adam Smith
in 1776, speaking in precise terms about the western province of the United
Provinces, whose main port was Amsterdam, "in proportion to the extent of
its territory and the number of its people, is a richer country than England.
The government there borrows at two percent, and private people of good
credit at three. The wages of labor are said to be higher in Holland than in
England, and the Dutch . . . trade upon lower profit than any people in Europe."[21] Smith's emphasis on routine profit at the margin is characteristic of
the classical school. The classical economists thought of economic growth
as a set of prudent investments which would, of course, decline in profit as
the limit was reached. (The anxieties of stagnationism in the 1940s among
economists such as Keynes and Alvin Hansen, as I've noted, were similar.
They reckoned that opportunities had been exhausted, and that after the war
the Great Depression would resume. On the political left, Baran and Sweezy
[1966] kept up the stagnationist argument for some decades after its time.)

Smith spoke a few pages later of "a country which had acquired that full complement of riches which the nature of its soil and climate, and its situation with respect to other countries allowed it to acquire."[22] He opined that China "neglects or despises foreign commerce," and "the owners of large capitals [there] enjoy a good deal of security, [but] the poor or the owners of small capitals . . . are liable, under the pretense of justice, to be pillaged and plundered at any time by the inferior mandarins."[23] In consequence the rate of interest in China, he claimed, was 12 rather than 2 percent. Not all the undertakings profitable in a better ordered country were in fact undertaken, says Smith, which explains why China was poor. Smith and his followers sought to explain why China and Russia were poorer than Britain and Holland, not why Britain and then Holland were to become in the century or two after Smith so very much more rich (Smith, incidentally, was off in his facts about China, as most Europeans were: not all the Chinese were in fact poor, and China engaged in foreign trade on a large scale, and even the "inferior mandarins" gestured toward Confucian standards). The revolution of spinning machines and locomotive machines and sewing machines and reaping machines and insurance companies and commodity exchanges and universities that was about to overtake northwest Europe was not what Smith had in mind. He had in mind that every country, backward China and Russia, say, and the Highlands of his native Scotland, might soon achieve what the thrifty and orderly Dutch had achieved. He did not have in mind the factor of sixteen that was about to occur even in the places in 1776 with a "full complement of riches."

In the event, a vastly fuller complement of riches came from bourgeois dignity and liberty inspiriting innovation in machines, both physical and social. The supply and demand curves whizzed out, making the classical and modern economists' obsession with moving from nonequilibrium to equilibrium along fixed curves look beside the point. The cool and calculative virtues of prudence and temperance and justice were not the virtues most called for—hope and courage were, with supports in love and faith. Smith wrote a book about temperance and a book about prudence and planned to write one about justice. Temperance, prudence, and justice: he especially admired these three cool and public virtues, admitting love and courage only on the side, and trying to exclude entirely the incense-smelling virtues of faith and hope.[24] And yet hope and courage dominate innovation. Smith, of course, did mention innovation, in his discussion of the division of labor: "Men are much more likely to discover easier and readier methods of attaining any object, when the whole attention of their minds is directed towards the single object."[25] And he was eloquent on the need for sound governmental institutions, such as public schools and sensible commercial policies. What is striking in his and subsequent discussions, however, is how much weight was placed on mere prudent (and just and temperate) reallocations. Yet the reallocations, the reshufflings, the moving even of coal—mere efficiencies—we have found, were too small to explain what is to be explained.

23

FOREIGN TRADE WAS NOT THE CAUSE,
THOUGH WORLD PRICES WERE A CONTEXT

Any trade, whether foreign or domestic, reshuffles. It doesn't discover (except in the wide and wise sense that assigning goods to their highest-valued user does discover their best use, and is therefore a good idea, even if not transformative). After all, trade is merely the moving of stuff from one place to another. Voluntary trade is prudent, temperate, commutatively just—and even at moderate markups it is profitable, too. Therefore it happens. Yet shuffling stuff about for a modest productivity gain, even if a large gain in the margin of profit, is not the same thing as revolutionizing the means of production. Shuffling resources about is not the way to get the cautiously estimated factor of sixteen.

Anyway, as the economic historian John Chartres argues, Britain had "well before 1750 . . . an unusual flexibility in the employment of its factor endowments."[1] It had none of the internal tariffs that harried French businesspeople well into the nineteenth century, and few of the obstacles to the employment of women in industry that stifled enterprise in China or the Arab world, and none of the class barriers to mobility among industries that shackled India (and especially did so after European theories of cultural stages took hold under the British Raj). So in Britain there were few enough £100 notes lying on the ground ready to be picked up. Expanding the woolen industry and shrinking the growing of wheat might achieve for the nation, if the reshufflers were lucky or skilled, a national gain of 10 percent. But not 1,500 percent. To put the findings another way, we have learned since 1970 many nots: that industrialization in Britain was not a matter of internal reallocation of the labor force, nor of transport innovation, nor of investment

in factories, nor even of foreign trade—all of which are matters of reshuffling the employment of labor, land, and capital. The making of the modern
world was not a matter of a merely reshuffling prudence and temperance.

Consider foreign trade. An old tradition beginning with Arnold Toynbee in 1884 and carried into the 1960s by the American economic historian Walt Rostow and by the British economic historians Phyllis Deane and
W. A. Cole, and still popular among most general historians and some economic historians, puts emphasis on Britain's foreign and colonial trade as
an "engine of growth." Deane and Cole quite properly observe that the
"sheer weight in total economic activity" of foreign trade was highest in the
late nineteenth and early twentieth centuries, not in the eighteenth or early
nineteenth. They nonetheless conclude that during the classic period of the
Industrial Revolution the foreign markets were "probably crucial in initiating the process of industrialization."[2]

What the research since 1970 has discovered, though, is that the existence of the rest of the world mattered for the British economy, but not in
the way suggested by the metaphor of an engine of growth, or crucialness.[3]
True, there is a correlation, which was what inspired the metaphor in the
first place. The correlation was expressed in 2006 by Allen, who declared
briskly that "econometric analysis shows that the greater volume of trade
[per capita in the Netherlands and Britain] explains why their wages were
maintained (or increased) even as their populations grew."[4] "Econometric
analysis" sounds impressive, but let me tell you that it commonly depends
(as here) on a misuse of something called a *t* test. And anyway it means
merely *post hoc ergo propter hoc*—trade was high, and then wages were, too.
Post hoc is a suggestive form of reasoning, but by itself is often misleading.
Ante hoc ergo non propter hoc, "before this therefore *not* because of this,"
delivers every time: the dignity of the North Sea bourgeois rose before they
achieved an industrial revolution, and so it is not (as Marx averred) their
success that explains all their dignity. But *post hoc*, which is the only insight
the proud econometrician can offer, does not deliver every time. That is
why, as the econometricians have sadly had to admit, no serious economic
issue since the Second World War has been settled by econometrics.

The great historian of the slave trade Joseph Inikori believes that "technological change was trade driven," but his arguments are correlations based
on an elderly model of industrialization by import substitution (the same
model of "dependency" that inspired Latin America in the 1960s and 1970s
to adopt economically disastrous policies of protectionism).[5] He claims that

technological change happened chiefly in the "socially and agriculturally backward northern counties" of England, a claim that would surprise James Watt, a Scot settled in Birmingham in the West Midlands, not to speak of his fellow instrument makers in London.

And if trade causes technological change, why not in the great trading empires of the past? Something was peculiar about northwestern Europe. It was not trade. Inikori believes that his study "provides sufficient proof that the Industrial Revolution in England was a product of overseas trade—the first case of export-led industrialization in history."[6] But *why* the first? Exports grew, sometimes explosively, in many other times and places—the Silk Road, for example, when political unity was established in central Asia. Why not trade-powered industrialization, from Sumer on? Inikori and many others have emphasized the thrusting Atlantic trade of the eighteenth century. But trade had thrust earlier and elsewhere. They have not explained why other trades did not have similar effects, or why in the eighteenth century foreign trade would suddenly provoke innovation that the same sort of thrust of trade did not provoke in Europe in the sixteenth. Foreign trade is not the special episode that could explain the Industrial Revolution.

Consider France. French foreign trade in the eighteenth century grew *faster* than British. If foreign trade were the engine, then one would have expected the Industrial Revolution to have been mainly French. It was not. The economic historian John Nye argues that the effective constraint on French progress was not its foreign trade but its domestic trade. Britain in such a view was from early times a nation of free trade *internally*, unlike France. Nye argues persuasively and surprisingly that Britain in fact was *internationally* less a free-trade country than France—but that Britain was more free-trading internally. France, and Spain (and of course those geographical expressions "Italy" and "Germany"), had high internal tariffs until the nineteenth century. France was and is famously centralized in some aspects of governance, but for many centuries England had been more effectively centralized in fiscal and contract law. France, in other words, was centralized in the wrong way, with *intendants* from Paris and officials in the provinces interfering with the dignity and liberty of innovators at every turn. The French state imposed quality standards on textiles, and gave subsidies to enterprises it approved of, licensed some companies and refused licenses to others, and anyway charged tariffs on movements of goods even into Paris (see the third act of *La Bohème*).

Nonetheless France had a pretty large domestic market. Guillaume

Daudin concluded that in the eighteenth century "for all types of high value-to-weight goods, some French supply centers reached 25 million people or more. For all types of textile groups, some French supply centers reached 20 million people or more. Even taking into account differences in real, nominal and disposable income per capita, these supply centers had access to domestic markets that were at least as large as the whole of Britain. Differences in the size of foreign markets were too small to reverse that result."[7] A market of 20 or 25 million souls is not small, even nowadays, and in 1801 it was 40 percent larger than the entire population of the United Kingdom. The size of the internal British market, in other words, does not seem to explain Britain's lead. In short, eighteenth-century foreign and domestic trade in Britain, and their alleged economies of scale, do not seem to be special.

∞

Many historians have noted that the very reason that Columbus sailed the ocean blue was to get access to what was already a great playground of foreign trade by Arabs, Chinese, Japanese, Indians, Indonesians, and Africans, namely, the Indian Ocean and its sources of supply extending from Africa to Japan. "The Indian Ocean," notes Jack Goody, "was crisscrossed by trade routes at least from the third millennium BCE (with Mesopotamia)."[8] In the tenth century CE the Zhizo people, on what is now the border of South Africa with Zimbabwe, along the Limpopo River three hundred miles from the eastern coast of Africa, acquired *Indonesian* products, exchanging their gold for glass beads brought directly five thousand miles across the Indian Ocean on the equatorial trade winds. The successor culture there of "K2," with its capital in the thirteenth century at Mapungubwe, traded its gold for *Chinese* porcelain, which had traveled 7,000 miles.[9] By 1500, Goldstone notes in summarizing recent work (some of it the pioneering work by that same Atlantic-trade-favoring Robert Allen), "Asia generally had greater agricultural productivity and more refined craftsmanship than Europe [because even the clever Italians looked feeble beside the Indians and Chinese] and offered a wide variety of products, such as silk and cotton fabrics [because European linens and woolens were not good for everyday use in the Gangetic plain in summer; by contrast every well-to-do European lusted after the gauzy and colored fabrics of the East, and the Italian and then other European borrowers of Chinese technology could not make enough of it until well into the Industrial Revolution], porcelain, coffee, tea, and spices that

Europeans desired."[10] The ancient Romans had the same problem of a silver drain to the East, so desirable were the oriental products. The navigational miss in 1492 by the Admiral of the Ocean Seas in his search for the East Indies nonetheless in time gave the miserably poor Europeans, with what the historical sociologist Erik Ringmar calls their "slack-jawed admiration for East Asia," something useful for getting into the Indian Ocean trade: Incan gold and Mexican and Peruvian silver.[11] As the Marxist historian Andre Gunder Frank put it, Europe "used its American money to buy itself a ticket on the Asian train."[12] And in the meantime the Portuguese had rounded the Cape of Good Hope.

Yet attributing the Industrial Revolution to the European trade with the Indian Ocean is a dubious project. The question arises, for example, why the lag in causation was 250 years, from 1500 to 1750. And if trade is such a very enriching, and then industrializing, activity, why did not the Indian Ocean traders and manufacturers themselves have their own industrial revolution, centuries before the backward Europeans—or at the worst with the same mysterious 250-year lag as required by the hypothesis that European trade with the East was an engine of growth? After all, the Orientals were closer to the action that the Europeans so craved to get into. It cannot be an advantage (the economist would observe) to be *further* from the storied East and its Industrial-Revolution-making trade, can it? Amsterdam and Glasgow and Boston were about as far away as one could get. Europe's small share of the vast inside-Asia trade was strictly limited by how much gold and silver the Europeans could offer, because until well after the Industrial Revolution was under way the Asians had little use for the notably crude European manufactures.[13] Goldstone explains the ending by the Chinese in 1433 of very long, government-sponsored voyages of discovery not in terms of a "turn inward" (which is false: Chinese ships and merchants continued long *commercial* voyages) but "for the same reason the United States stopped sending men to the Moon after 1972—there was nothing there to justify the costs of voyages, in the Chinese case with hundreds of ships and tens of thousands of men. The further China sailed, the poorer and more barren the lands that they found. Goods of value came mainly from India and the Middle East, and they had already been pouring into China by established land and sea routes for hundreds of years."[14] Why then did not the Asian vastness of trade act as an engine of growth, quite independent of the Europeans? And if being marginal to the trade but enjoying a tenuous connection is somehow an advantage, why not industrialization at Mapungubwe or at Edo?

∞

Trade is no engine. Yet what is true is that the British economy cannot be understood in isolation, certainly not in the eighteenth century, and in many ways not before. It has become increasingly clear from the work of Jeffrey Williamson and Larry Neal among others, for example, that Britain functioned in an international market for investment funds.[15] That is, the trade in bonds was of Europe, not of each country in Europe. More exactly the fact has been rediscovered—it was a commonplace of economic discussion by observers such as the stockbroker and economist Ricardo in the 1810s, though it became obscured in economics by the barriers to trade erected during the Great European Civil War of the twentieth century, especially during the 1930s and 1940s. By 1780 the capital market of Europe, centering in Amsterdam and London and Paris, was sophisticated and integrated. Savings flowed with ease from French pocketbooks to Scottish projects.

True, the biggest sums were governmental debt to pay for Europe's incessant wars. The amounts raised for the projects of peace, such as canals in England in the 1780s, were often last in line, not least because governments enforced usury limits which cut funds off abruptly during an inflation (money interest rates would be pushed up by the inflation). The old finding of Pollard and others survives: industrial growth was financed locally, out of retained earnings, out of commercial credit for inventories, and out of investors marshaled by the local solicitor.[16] The interest rate still mattered (even though the international capital market was not used to fund industrialization until the mid-nineteenth century, and then mainly for railways), as is plain for example in the sharp rises and falls of enclosure in the countryside with each fall and rise in the rate of interest, or in the booms and busts in canal building, like housing construction nowadays. People were sharply aware that the opportunity cost of investing in straightening and surfacing local roads or in a steam mill to forge nails was an always less troublesome investment in government bonds. But the interest rate on consolidated British government stock, in turn, was determined by what was happening in wider capital markets than the local solicitor's office, and as much by Amsterdamers as by Londoners.

The same had also long been true of the market in grain and many other goods. Ricardo assumed so in his models of trade around 1817, as though the fact were given, simple, obvious, trivial, not worthy of comment. The disruptions of war and blockade from time to time masked the convergence. Regulations such as the Corn Laws, or imperial schemes to subsidize West Indian landowners with powerful friends in government, could sometimes stop it from working. Europe by the eighteenth century, though, had a unified market in, say, wheat. Fernand Braudel and Frank Spooner showed long ago in their astonishing charts of prices that the percentage by which the European minimum was exceeded by the maximum price of wheat fell from 570 percent in 1440 to a mere 88 percent in 1760, and much less for actual trading pairs.[17] Similar work recently by Studer, Zanden, Shiue, and Keller showed that Chinese and Japanese correlations of prices fell with distances between grain markets to about the same degree as in Europe by 1800 (the correlations fell in India and Southeast Asia much faster, indicating a less integrated market than in China or Europe).[18] Centuries earlier the price of gold and silver had become international, though the apparently bottomless hunger of the East for precious metals kept the divergence in value from disappearing completely.[19] The economic historians Kevin O'Rourke and Jeffrey Williamson have shown that in the fancier items of east-west trade the divergence was not pronounced enough to explain the rise in the volume of their trade.[20]

And by 1800 and certainly by 1850 wheat, iron, cloth, wood, coal, skins, and many other of the less fancy materials useful to life were beginning to cost roughly the same in St. Petersburg as in London, and to a lesser extent in New York and even in Bombay, by an economically relevant standard of "roughly." The only relevant standard for "one market" is similarity of prices. The standard of what is "similar" must be economic and historically comparative, not an arbitrary standard of a *t* test of "significance" in correlation.[21] (Braudel and Spooner grasped this, as do O'Rourke and Williamson.[22] Unhappily a good deal of the recent historical work on price convergence has substituted arbitrary standards of "cointegration" for economic thought.)[23] European and then world prices continued to converge in the nineteenth century, a benefit of the rapid growth of productivity in shipping and railways and in other costs of transaction, such as insurance and information and port charges.

The convergence is important because it says that an economic history imagining the British or even the Chinese economy in isolation is the wrong way to look at it. If the economy of the whole of Europe from Poland to Venice is determining the price of food, for example, or the economy of the whole world the price of ceramics, it is not a wise principle in writing the economic history to treat the British or Chinese markets for food or manufactures as though each could determine its own prices by its own curves of supply and demand. Local determination of prices, of course, could happen behind completely protective tariffs. Until the 1840s, admittedly, the British imposed prohibitive tariffs on quite a few goods. But even with a good deal of protection, a general equilibrium would indirectly tie British prices to the world's prices. The exception would be such cases as the rigorous Tokugawa exclusions—though even in that case the Japanese continued to trade with China. In most cases the assumption of a closed economy, such as was made during the little controversy in the 1960s over agriculture's role in English industrialization, will stop making sense.[24] The supply and demand for grain in Europe (or indeed with less force the supply and demand in the wider world) was setting the prices, such as those faced by British farmers in 1780. The supply and demand merely in the British portion of Europe could set merely the *amounts* of wheat and wood brought into Britain, net. The intrusion of the world's market became so strong that the domestic, closed-economy story no longer makes any sense, though it has been told and retold by historians and economists fascinated by the availability in the eighteenth century of statistics of production and prices. The mistaken, domestic story is like blaming the current administration in Washington for the price of oil—which is determined by the world's supply and demand, not by the White House.

In the seventeenth and eighteenth centuries one can tell a domestic story of agricultural improvement in England—the application, say, of Belgian and Dutch farming methods (though recent work has shown that they were not applied enough to constitute then an "Agricultural Revolution").[25] Yet one can't reasonably tell a domestic story of the *price* of wheat or cattle or much else except hay or certain kinds of labor, because the markets of Europe as a whole set the prices of wheat and cattle. (Hay down to the present is a local product, because it is of course heavy relative to its per volume price. Hay was cheaper in, say, 1914 in the United States than in England, with consequences for the costs of local wagon transport dependent on hay-fed horses. A large share of the shipping space from the United States to France during the Great War was devoted to hay to feed a cavalry in readiness for a breakthrough.)[26] Likewise one can tell an English story in the eighteenth century of how much was saved. Yet you can't reasonably tell an English story of what interest rate it was saved at, nor how much was available for English investment, in view of foreign savers and investors expressing their opinions in the capital markets of Paris and Amsterdam.

Joseph Inikori has argued that high transport costs before the Railway Age made regions such as Britain's industrial North, or the less progressive South (which as he points out began in 1600 as much more "developed" than the North), into export enclaves. "Research by historical geographers," he claims, "shows . . . industrialization that was highly regional."[27] The "more developed" part of the story is true. By the early nineteenth century the southerners in England were casting envious eyes north at bustling Liverpool and Manchester and Halifax. According to Inikori the historical geographers claim that inside the "regional economies . . . there was keen competition but between them there was very little . . . because of the structure of internal transportation costs. . . . Hence, over time regional concentration of the leading industries was determined by success or failure in the promotion of overseas sales."

Inikori is again correct to stress that the foreign context for European economies was important—though the goods traded in the eighteenth century were minor elements of the economy (if not of little girls), such as sugar and spice and everything nice. Yet by the time that cotton goods and especially such heavy items relative to value as iron became important in foreign trade, the Railway Age had arrived, and talk of enclaves stopped making sense. Considering the mobility of capital and labor, it probably had stopped making sense by 1750 or 1800. Inikori believes that "inter-regional migration was a minor source" of new labor for the mills, which again is correct if he means that southern agricultural workers did not turn up for work in Wigan (but literally wrong: Irish-born were one out of every 4.5 people in Liverpool in 1851, and one out of every 6 in Manchester.)[28] The weakness in Inikori's argument that is most relevant here, though, lies in the phrase "very little" (competition between enclaves). Inikori and the historical geographers offer no relevant comparative standard of "very little." They commit in a qualitative way the same error as do the more mathematically muscular t-testers of cointegration. They have no standard to judge "little," and so miss the gigantic secular improvement in European (and regional) economic integration, 1500–1840.

Pollard argued persuasively that for many questions what is needed is a European approach, or at least a north–western European regional approach.[29] The new global history suggests that an even broader canvas would be appropriate for many questions. For economic purposes beyond explaining the market in hay and houses, Pollard argued, the region studied should be *larger* than the nation, not smaller. He wrote in 1973 that "the study of industrialization in any given European country will remain incomplete unless it incorporates a European dimension: any model of a closed economy would lack some of its basic and essential characteristics."[30] The political analogue is that it would be strange to write a history of political developments in Britain or Italy or Ireland 1789 to 1815 without mentioning the French Revolution. Politics became international—not merely because French armies conquered most of Europe but because French political ideas became part of political thinking, whether in sympathy or in reaction. Likewise in economic matters. The world economy from the eighteenth century (and to a large degree before) provided Britain with its framework of relative economic values, wheat against iron, interest rates against wages.

The point is crucial for understanding why the classical economists were so far off in their predictions. British landlords (they predicted in the early nineteenth century) would engorge the national product, because land was the limiting factor of production. Yet the limits on land seen by the classical economists proved unimportant, because by cheapening transport in the nineteenth century the northwestern Europeans gained an immense hinterland, from Chicago and Melbourne to Cape Town and Odessa.[31] Britain was tied to the world like Gulliver to the ground, by a hundred tiny threads, because of the improvement of ocean shipping (iron and then steel hulls; steam ships and then superheated steam ships, two thirds of them built on the Clyde; wide stone quays and then concrete quays, and then steam gantries and then diesel gantries for offloading cargo). Grain production in Ukraine and in the American Midwest could by the 1850s begin to feed the cities of an industrial Britain. And the price of wheat in Britain was constrained even earlier. One cannot calculate elasticities of demand and supply on the assumption that the price was set at home—not in the seventeenth century, and certainly not in the nineteenth. As Jeffrey Williamson has argued recently, any purely economic impacts on the British economy had to work through changes in relative prices. And relative prices, as he also observed, were increasingly an international affair.[32]

24

AND THE LOGIC OF TRADE-AS-AN-ENGINE
IS DUBIOUS

Trade, then, was important as a context for British growth (and Chinese growth and many other growths, too). Pollard noted on the basis of statistics by Paul Bairoch that the proportion of the population outside of agriculture that Britain had in 1790 was not reached by the Continent of Europe until the middle of the twentieth century. "British industrialization was played out against a backward world, the British economy specializing . . . in the world economy [in a way] which was no longer open to the later comers. . . . The different circumstances in relation to their surroundings, in which industrialization took place first in Britain, then among the early followers, and then among the later ones, profoundly affected their actual history."[1] He cites the protectionist panic caused by the "flood" of British exports to the Continent during 1815–1817, which left "a scar on the psyche of [Continental] Europe which took nearly two generations to heal."[2] Meanwhile, Prussia became protectionist.

Yet trade was not an engine of growth. Trade explains some of the patterns of production, but not the size of production. To recur to an earlier metaphor, it accounts for how far the sea reaches up the estuary at high tide but does not explain the tide itself. Mokyr makes the clearest case.[3] The underlying argument is that domestic demand could have taken the place of foreign demand (Mokyr earlier had shown likewise that the shuffling of domestic demand was no more promising).[4] To be sure, Britons could not have worn the amount of cotton textiles produced by Lancashire at its most productive. Cotton dhotis designed for the working people of Kolkata would not have become fashionable at Marks and Sparks on the High Street of Salisbury or Aberdeen. In that case, however, the Lancastrians would have done something else with the labor and capital and resources and ingenuity employed in cotton textiles. As Hume put it in the 1740s, "If strangers will not take any particular commodity of ours, we must cease to labor in it." Of course. Yet, he continued (in another of his anticipations of modern economics), "the same hands will turn themselves towards some refinement in other commodities, which may be wanted at home."[5] Or rather, *will* be wanted at home, since that is how the alternative employment will be guided, as though by an invisible hand. Supply, when so guided by prices, creates its own demand through the expenditure of the income earned, and the prices adjust to clear the market. Or so they usually have. A world in which markets did not approximately clear would be one with massive, 1930s-style unemployment all the time. The exporting of cotton cloth is not sheer gain. The gain is acquired at the cost of something else that Britain could have done, such as building more houses in Cheshire or making more wool cloth in Yorkshire.

Consider the opportunity costs of producing American medical equipment for exports. Pittsburg doesn't produce such things out of thin air. To make the magnetic resonance machine sold to, say, Finland, the Pittsburghers divert labor, capital, natural resources from other potential employments, local or elsewhere, such as the employment of making more education at the University of Pittsburg, or moving to Philadelphia and making more candy. Exports are not the same thing as new income. They are new markets for exportables—which is to say new ways of getting importable things—not new income. They are a way of acquiring Nokia cell phones by showering the Finns with American machinery, telecommunications equipment and parts, aircraft and aircraft parts, computers, peripherals and software, electronic components, chemicals, medical equipment, agricultural products, bonds, and engraved pieces of paper (costing 4 cents each to make) marked "dollars."

Manufacturing the cell phones in America for Americans ("Buy American") is a rather worse deal for Americans. But it is no catastrophe. American national income would not deflate to zero like a balloon if we did not trade with Nokia. (Motorola will be glad to explain that point to you.) Given innovation (which gives the most), the source of wealth is specialization and trade within a country, regardless of whether the country then sells snowmobiles to the Eskimos or TV sets to Nebraskans. Domestic efficiency is what gets us out to the production possibility curve, as economists put it (and innovation pushes the curve out). Your nation, or town, or even in the extreme your own household, does not *have* to trade with outsiders to live. Each of us could be an innovative and alert Crusoe on his island and survive without exporting or importing. The point is obvious for big, innovative countries like France or the United States, which can do much better than "survive" without foreign trade. The people of the United States or France can achieve very high incomes by attending to innovation, and by trading merely with other American or French people within their borders, if persuaded by protectionists to do so (as in earlier eras both nations were so persuaded, and still are for parts of agriculture).

In other words, the primitive conviction most noneconomists have that foreign trade is the only source of wealth, that money must somehow come from outside to puff up the economy and make us rich, is mistaken. You see the mistake in the claim that subsidizing a new sports stadium will "bring dollars into the community." The extra dollars are profitable only for a local owner of land. They have no effect on the rewards to mobile labor and capital, which move in at a fixed reward determined in the wider economy. Public opinion gets fooled into voting for the stadium, because it hears of "multiplier effects." The phrase sounds like technical economics, but only a deeply misled economist thinks that multiplier effects work in anything but conditions of mass unemployment.[6] You can see the power of the conviction that a foreign, outside trade is the only source of wealth in the role of fish exports in the political economy of Iceland, or of exports generally in that of Japan and now China. The conviction is imprudent and unjust, good for a few exporters and bad for everyone else. "Export or die" (or its Latin American translation, "import-substitute or die") is foolish. It has undermined wise domestic policies for growth in poor countries such as elementary education and open markets and the enforcement of sensible property laws. Imports and the exports to get them are a shift of attention, not consciousness itself. Trade as an essential engine: it seems not.

Yet the trade, of course, benefits the traders on both sides, to some degree, or else it wouldn't have happened. But again—here's the nub of the issue— the benefit can be shown in static terms to be small. One of the chief findings of the "new" economic history, with its conspicuous use of economic rhetoric, is that static gains, as I have said, are very often small. Robert Fogel's startling calculation in 1964 of the social savings from American railways in 1890 is the leading case.[7] It was replicated by Hawke in 1970 for Britain with broadly similar results (though higher on account of denser passenger traffic). In countries (unlike Britain or the United States) that did *not* have easily navigable rivers, such as Mexico (Coatsworth 1979) and Italy (Fenoaltea 1971–1972), the impact of railways turned out to be greater. Yet it was never enough to account for any but a small portion of modern economic growth. Fogel's finding, with Harberger's, was part of the gradual realization by economists in the 1960s that their beloved supply-and-demand framework did not explain the Great Fact. However essential one may be inclined to think railways were, or how crucial foreign trade to British prosperity, or how necessary the cotton mill to industrial change, the calculations lead to small figures, far below the factor of sixteen, or even a doubling.

For trade, how so? Think of British foreign trade around 1841 as an industry. It made consumable imports of wheat and lumber by making and then selling to foreigners the exports of iron and cotton textiles. From an economist's point of view that is all foreign trade is—a machine for making imported sausage for consumption out of sacrificed inputs of domestic labor, land, and capital. In 1841 the mighty United Kingdom exported some 13 percent of its national product. The terms of trade is the "productivity" of the industry that "makes" wheat out of the cotton textiles sacrificed (that is, the textiles exported for the use of foreigners). The terms of trade tell how many bushels of wheat the British got for each yard of textiles. From 1698 to 1803 the range up and down of the three-year moving averages of the gross barter terms of trade was a ratio of 1.96, highest divided by lowest; Imlah's net barter terms later range over a ratio of 2.32, highest divided by lowest.[8] So over century-long spans like these, the variation of the terms on which Britain traded was about 100 percent. Only 13 percent of any change in income, then, can be explained by foreign trade, speaking in static terms and assuming full employment (which is the only reasonable assumption to make from peak to peak of the business cycle): $100 \times 0.13 = 13$ percent. Apparently we have another popular cause that doesn't work very well, quantitatively speaking. Remember: it is 1,500 percent we are intent on accounting for.

One might be tempted to see growth of sheer output sent abroad as itself an engine of growth. As has long been realized, however, to do so assumes that massive portions of the economy were idle (in contrast to the full-employment assumption that I just made). And no historical evidence has been marshaled to make plausible an assumption of massive unemployment with its multiplier effects over the long run—no evidence, for example, that real wages peak-to-peak were unresponsive to changes in the relative scarcity of labor. The issue again is the truth or falsehood of the theory of marginal productivity. The economist Theodore Schultz decades ago confronted the assumption of idle hands in India ("underemployment, surplus labor") by noting that during the 1919 influenza epidemic there, which killed an appalling 5 percent of the Indian population, agricultural output did not stay constant—as it should have if the marginal productivity of additional labor in the countryside were in fact zero.[9] It fell, a little less than 5 percent. If surplus labor does not apply to India in 1919, then surely it does not apply to Britain in 1719.

The so-called "vent-for-surplus" model boldly supposes, on the contrary, that any sales abroad put formerly idle, zero-product people to work. (Yet why don't sales at *home* have the same "job-creating" effect? In which case, why would *foreign* trade be a special matter?) Exports to French colonies in the eighteenth century, for example, are said to have put to work previously idle French workers. (I repeat: why did not domestic demand for carriages and servants have the same effect?) In the 1780s, however, the share of colonial exports in French manufacturing was only 2.5 percent.[10] Prados de la Escosura argued for the parallel case of the Spanish Empire. The loss of even that enormous empire to the activities of Hidalgo y Costilla and Simón Bolívar and others resulted in little if any loss to the metropolis.[11] Again: trade doesn't seem to work.

Trade, then, cannot be an engine of growth—not in the simple way envisioned by noneconomists, at least, and anyway not on the scale necessary to explain much of the 1,500 percent growth per capita in Britain from 1700 to 2000. The deepest economic reasoning is that the borders of countries cannot be important, or at any rate not important enough to make flows of exchange over a border into an engine producing results on the scale of modern economic growth. Trade, after all, is trade, and it shouldn't much matter whether you trade with someone down the street or with someone on the other side of the world. There's nothing magic about goods crossing borders, as the Swedish economist Bertil Ohlin noted long ago. (Swedish and Canadian economists, by the way, accustomed to living beside the great bears of Germany and the United States, tend to get this economic point right: one could instance Knut Wicksell or Eli Heckscher, Robert Mundell or Harry Johnson.) Your own, personal trade with the rest of the world is most of your consumption: you don't make much for yourself. But that is so merely because you are little relative to the wide world. Big countries like India or the United States tend to have lower shares of exports in national product than do little countries like Taiwan or the Netherlands. Thus among twenty major economies in 1992 a population 1 percent larger was associated with a ratio of exports to national product 1 percent lower.[12] Unsurprisingly.

If a border was closed and is now opened there is a gain, the modest Harbergerian one of increased specialization. The most extreme cases in modern times are the substantial gains of income arising from the opening of Japan in the 1860s or the opening of Eastern Europe in the 1990s.[13] The sheer tearing down of borders, however, does not normally have the power to enrich us gigantically. For example it did not do so even for the striking cases of Japan and Eastern Europe. It took many decades of adopting innovation for Japan to begin to reach European incomes; and Eastern Europe, two decades after escaping from the protectionist grip of the Warsaw Pact, still lags, but with prospects. The (South) Korean case is often offered as trade-led, and there is merit in the argument.[14] But Korea's move to freer trade after 1961 enriched the country in a modern context in which innovations could be massively transferred from outside (though, by the way, even the industrious Koreans have yet to achieve more than 40 percent of American income per head). Without the previous innovations, more trade merely specializes—which is a good thing, but not revolutionizing. By contrast Mokyr's "macro inventions" in the making of cloth and surgeries and computers certainly do have the power to enrich us gigantically, trade or not. Even the violent separation of East and West Germany had left on the table, to be seized on unification, "only" a factor of, say, two or three. Not sixteen. Even an idiotically centrally planned economy in 1988 had access to the main sources of modern riches—electricity (intermittently), reinforced concrete (with too much sand), machine-made raincoats (in a lovely Kelly green, only).

If borders were such an engine of growth, the economist points out, then one could draw an international border in England from Dover to Wroxeter, calling "foreign" all trade across the Watling Street border thus created, into and out of the ancient Danelaw, and thereby make trade *within* England into an engine of growth. Or you could call left-handed English people "foreigners," and achieve the same result. The accounting reductio shows that there cannot be something special about *foreign* trade. If a demand by consumers that relocates production from one side of the English Channel to the other, or from one side of Watling Street to the other, or from left-handed people to right-handed, is enriching on anything but a modest Harbergerian scale, then one has an economic perpetual motion machine, by the mere words of the accounting. Words aren't *that* powerful.

And historically, yet again, the problem is that if such a machine worked for Britain in the eighteenth century and for Europe generally in the nineteenth century, why didn't it work elsewhere and in earlier times? That is the central *historical* reason that something peculiar to the eighteenth century must explain the peculiarity of the eighteenth century and its denouement. Trade is ancient, as old at least as language. When people start talking in the full way we now call language, around it seems 70,000–50,000 BCE (some students of the matter say much earlier, but with less evidence), they start trading, and we find the detritus of the trade in their graves and trash dumps. Much later, in the Bronze Age (or stone in Mesoamerica), great trading empires with enriched metropolises were commonplace. The tin to alloy with copper to get durable bronze was shipped by Phoenicians and then Greeks to the Mediterranean from faraway Cornwall. "The light-hearted [Greek] master of the waves / [sailed] to where the Atlantic raves / outside the Western Straits, /. . . . and on the beach undid his corded bales." Big cities and big trade have characterized many places from Mexico City to Hangchow. The Indian Ocean, to repeat, was a trading lake for a millennium before the Europeans got to it. The Northern Italian cities were traders, certainly, and they had even the European cultural traits that some historians believe made European success so inevitable from the Middle Ages on. But why then didn't the Florentines create an industrial revolution? "They did," one might reply. No they didn't, not on the scale of *the* Industrial Revolution, and especially its outcome. The same objection can be raised to modern growth theory among economists, which in parlor-trick fashion inserts economies of scale into the story just when they are needed to reproduce in the mathematics the rumblings of productivity in the eighteenth century, and the innovation gone mad of the late nineteenth.

∞

The theorist of foreign trade Ronald Findlay and the economic historian Kevin O'Rourke collaborated in 2007 in a magnificent history of world trade since 1000 CE.[15] There is much to admire in the book, in particular its cosmopolitan sweep. Findlay and O'Rourke are nothing like Eurocentric, and think big.

When they come to the Industrial Revolution, though, their arguments become somewhat less persuasive. After a good deal of complaining about the historical economics that they themselves are practicing, Findlay and O'Rourke come to the nub of their argument. "International trade," they claim, "was a key reason why the British Industrial Revolution was different" in not petering out, as had previous efflorescences (Goldstone's very appropriate word for the numerous lurches forward in technology that the world had previously seen, but without permanent effect on the welfare of the average human).[16] "For a small European country like Britain"—note that "small" is a somewhat strange characterization of one of the most populous countries in Europe—"overseas markets were vital if its Industrial Revolution was to be sustained."[17]

And then Findlay and O'Rourke make a crucial connection to Britain's military adventures: "In a mercantilist world in which nations systematically excluded their enemies from protected markets [a claim which makes it hard to understand the very large volume of British-Continental trade, which also took place in a mercantilist world] British military success over the French and other European rivals was an important ingredient in explaining her subsequent rise of economic prominence."[18] Trade was important, they claim, and imperialism supported trade. Thus the title of their book, *Power and Plenty*, and its theme, dating to the economist Jacob Viner in modern times, but ancient anyway: that aggression is good for you. Thus too Mephisto in *Faust*, part 2: "War, trade, and piracy together are / a trinity not to be severed."[19]

In correspondence with me O'Rourke has amiably disputed such a bald formulation of the theme. Yet in an essay with Leandro Prados de la Escosura and Guillaume Daudin published after his book with Findlay he writes: "Trade profited merchants, but also yielded revenues to the state; while the state needed revenues to secure trading opportunities for its merchants, by force if necessary."[20] "Force" surely means "aggression," and in the essay it is repeatedly cashed in this way, in a football-and-war rhetoric of "preeminence," "dominant position," "struggle for power and plenty." In all of O'Rourke's work the gains from trade are said to be dependent on violence against "competitors," as in a zero-sum footrace. One would not learn from such passages in Findlay and O'Rourke or in O'Rourke, Prados de la Esco-

sura, and Daudin that trade is mutually beneficial, a matter mainly of cooperation, not competition.

True, people *thought* that mercantilist aggression was good for them.
"Trade and empire," O'Rourke and his 2008 coauthors continue, "were thus
inextricably linked in the minds of European statesmen [about which the
historian asks: because it is true in the world, or because they were misled?],
. . . which explains the incessant mercantilist warfare of the time."[21] It is the
rhetoric of business-school deans and big-thinking journalists. But it is not
sound, then or now, whatever people believe.

An instructive example of the unsound connection of aggression to economic success is the military historian Correlli Barnett's brilliant old book of
1972, *The Collapse of British Power*, an influence for example on the Thatcher
administration in Britain. As in many of the pages of Findlay and O'Rourke,
you can learn a lot from Barnett. But he, too, mixes rank in the league table
of power with economic success, and assumes as Findlay and O'Rourke do
that what people thought at the time was an important connection among
trade, empire, military might, and domestic prosperity was in fact the case.
Thus Barnett:

> In the eighteenth century the English ruling classes—squirearchy, merchants, ar-
> istocracy—were men hard of mind and hard of will. Aggressive and acquisitive,
> they saw foreign policy in terms of concrete interest: markets, national resources,
> colonial real estate, naval bases, profits. . . . They saw national power as the es-
> sential foundation of national independence; commercial wealth as a means to
> power; and war as among the means to all three. They accepted it as natural
> and inevitable that nations should be engaged in a ceaseless struggle for survival,
> prosperity and predominance.[22]

That's right. That's what they thought. But they were wrong. And Barnett
was therefore wrong—even in the dismal year for the British economy of
1972—to lament British *economic* "decline." He attributed the "decline" to
softness of mind and softness of will, arising especially from a new evangelical Christianity:

> The abolition of the slave trade in 1807 as a result of a campaign led by William
> Wilberforce and of slavery itself in the British Empire in 1833 were the earliest
> of the great social achievements of British evangelicalism. . . . To embrace one's
> fellow men in brotherly love rather than smite them with the sword of righteous-
> ness was the broad instruction of evangelicalism to the British people. . . . As
> a consequence of this spiritual revolution English policy ceased to be founded
> solely on the expedient and opportunistic pursuit of English interests. . . . As

Gladstone [one of the evangelical softies] put it in 1870: "The greatest triumph of our epoch will be the consecration of the idea of a public law as the fundamental law of European politics."[23]

Barnett's analysis sounds quite plausible, and it sounded even more so in the *realpolitik* days of 1972. Certainly British politics, at home and abroad, became in the nineteenth century more ethically driven, right down to coming to the aid of the French in 1914, against expediency, and then making a welfare state, expedient or not, and then its weak-willed shame when its masters embarked on one last exercise of hard-mindedness in Suez in 1956. But Britain, despite its lamentable descent into namby-pamby soft-heartedness, to be cured in the glorious war of conquest against the Argentinians, has remained one of the richest economies on earth, and has shared in the modern engine of innovation, which it started. No ceaseless struggle for survival, prosperity, and predominance backed by ships and men and money, by jingo, explains British economic success, now or in 1972 or in 1790. Innovation enabled by bourgeois dignity and liberty does.

25

AND EVEN THE DYNAMIC EFFECTS OF TRADE WERE SMALL

Nor does foreign trade rate very highly as an engine of growth when one descends from such heights of grand strategy down to the workaday world of supply and demand curves. Findlay and O'Rourke criticize static economic models about the issue because static models "cannot, by definition, say anything about the impact of trade on growth."[1] That's overstated. Static models have been *shown* to be inadequate to explain the greater part of modern economic growth, so large is the thing-to-be-explained. The showing has not been achieved by "definition." It has been achieved by finding that static gains are not of the right order of magnitude to do the scientific job. It is an empirical, scientific finding of the past fifty years of work on the subject, not a mere definition. (Definitions, though, are not to be scorned as historical tools—as for example in the definitions of national income or the share of foreign trade that permit the showing of the smallness of the static gain.) A few pages earlier in their book Findlay and O'Rourke themselves had used static models of demand and supply to make the correct point that Britain shared its gains from trade with its trading partners 1796 to 1860 by increasing the supply of its exports much more rapidly than the demand curves went outward, turning the terms of trade against itself. It is an old and good point (I made it myself in print a long time ago, so it must be right), and it is definitely "static" and definitely says a great deal about the impact of trade on growth.[2]

Considering that the static effects alleged so widely for trade as an engine of growth are small, the noneconomists, and some of the economists, are likely to claim that "dynamic" effects will rescue the engine. Possibly. The word "dynamic" has a magical quality—the economist Fritz Machlup once placed it on a list of "weaselwords."[3] Waving "dynamic" about, though, does not in itself suffice to prove one's economic and historical wisdom. As I noted about the argument from transportation improvements, one has to show that the proffered "dynamic" effect is quantitatively strong, and in the right direction. An existence theorem in a model without magnitudes—which is the routine in highbrow economics—will not do a scientific job.

For example, one might claim that the industries like cotton textiles encouraged by British trade were able to exploit economies of scale, in perhaps the making of textile machinery or in the training of master designers. There: a dynamic effect that makes trade have a larger effect than the mere static gain of efficiency. But the assertion is without quantitative oomph, and is not science, until it is actually measured. Until the measurement, a rejection of trade as the engine of growth might be imagined to work just as well, or better. One could imagine that economies of scale foregone in noncotton industries would have been larger. Imagination is cheap. To take another common "dynamic" argument, the profits from overseas trade were reinvested (I say again: were not the profits from house building and retail trade reinvested, too?), and so capital accumulation was increased. Yet is such a dynamic effect of reinvestment large? It seems not, as Guillaume Daudin has concluded for mercantilist France before the Revolution.[4]

Or again one could argue "dynamically" that a smaller cotton textile industry would have contributed less to the nation's betterment, considering that cotton was so progressive technologically. A smaller size would give its ingenious inventions less weight in pushing national income higher. One can confront the hypothesis that Cotton Did It by performing a thought experiment. The experiment requires that one know productivity change in various industries other than cotton textiles. Remember that the pattern of productivity in British industries can be calculated by looking at what G. T. Jones in 1933 called "real cost," that is, the price of, say, iron bars relative to, say, the prices of coal and labor that go into the iron. The pattern was something like table 2, using Harley's revision in 1993 of my table in 1981 (I am accepting for the sake of argument the dubious view of the Two Nicks that total growth was small in the 1700s, and therefore their implication drawn from my old calculation of residuals that productivity change outside the named sectors was vanishingly small).

Suppose the cotton textile industry were cut in half by an exclusion from

Table 2. Crude approximations of productivity change by sector UK, 1780–1860 (annual %)

Sector	Productivity growth	Value of output divided by national product	Contribution to the national growth of productivity
Cotton	1.90	.070	0.1330
Worsteds	1.30	.035	0.0455
Woolens	0.60	.035	0.0210
Iron	0.90	.020	0.0180
Canals & railways	1.30	.070	0.0910
Shipping	0.05	0.06	0.0300
Agriculture	0.70	.270	0.1900
All others implied as residual	[0.02]	.850	0.0200
TOTAL (from Crafts/Harley)		1.41	0.5485

Source: Harley 1993, table 3.6, p. 200, based on McCloskey 1981, p. 114, where the details of the original calculation and accounting are given. Harley leaves my estimates of income shares and my choice of sectors and my calculations of many of the sector's productivity changes unimproved. That the values of output divided by national product add up to more than 1.00, by the way, is not an error. It is implied by the taking of productivity measures from gross costs (as against merely value added, which would not give a correct measure of savings on material inputs from other sectors.

foreign markets. (It is a somewhat dubious counterfactual, because in the eighteenth century Manchester was anyway the best place in Europe to produce cotton cloth. It earned, to put it the way economists do, "rent," which is just another way of saying it was the low-cost location for the task. And so you have to assume that mercantilism would take the form not merely of taxing Manchester with French or Dutch tariffs but partially shutting down its activities, for no gain to anyone—though admittedly it would not be the first or last time that such an irrational policy had been implemented.) During 1780-1860 therefore the share of cotton in national income would have been 3.5 percent instead of its actual 7 percent. The 3.5 percent of resources would have had to find other employment. Suppose that the released resources now put to use in road mending and silk manufacturing and so forth would have experienced a productivity change of 0.5 percent per year (on the low end of the available possibilities) instead of the princely 1.9 percent they in fact experienced in cotton. The cotton industry in the *actual,*

1.9 percent world contributed a large amount—namely, (0.07) • (1.9 percent) = 0.133 percent per year—to the growth of national income. This one giant contributed some 24 percent of the conservatively measured total of about 0.55 percent-per-year growth of income per person nationally 1780-1860. (The argument is focusing on the classic period of the Industrial Revolution, another source of bias in favor of the hypothesis, because the order of magnitude to be explained down to the present is much larger, and trade-as-an-engine correspondingly less plausible.)

Now we can calculate the counterfact. With the hypothetical halfway cutoff of trade (though remember that a good deal of the textiles were consumed at home, and more would be if the output were forced to stay home) you can make so to speak a mechanical "static-dynamic" argument as follows. The Harley revision of my table implies that noncotton productivity change can be calculated from (1.41 − .07) • (the implied residual productivity change outside cotton) = (0.55 − 0.13). That is, the implied residual of productivity change outside cotton is 0.42/1.34, or 0.313 percent per year (I retain more than significant digits to avoid rounding errors). The resources in the hypothetical case would therefore contribute (0.035) • (1.9 percent) + (0.035) • (0.313 percent) = 0.077 percentage points a year. The fall in national productivity change can be inferred from the difference between the actual 0.133 percent per year attributable nationally to cotton and the hypothetical 0.077 percent per year attributable to a half-sized cotton industry and the industries its resources would go to. The difference is about a 0.056 percentage point per year fall in the national rate of productivity change, that is, a fall from 0.550 percent a year to 0.494 percent a year. In the eighty years 1780-1860 such a lag would cumulate at monthly interest, however, to merely 5 percent or so of national productivity change. Remember that we are speaking here of doublings of national income 1780 to 1860.

You could cut the productivity change in cotton to allow for alleged economies of scale in cotton and come to roughly the same result. No one has shown that such economies of scale were in fact important (though they are important in the imaginings of economists), or that economies or diseconomies of scale in other industries would not cancel the net gain. We are giving the protrade, "dynamic" argument all the advantages. Suppose the scale-effect productivity change were half of the princely 1.9 percent in cotton, or 0.945 percent per year. So now the calculation is (0.035) • (0.945 percent) + (.035) • (0.313 percent), or 0.0440 percentage points a year (as against 0.077 without the lost "economies of scale" inserted). National productivity change attributable to cotton falls from 0.133 percent per year all the way down to 0.0440 per year, a drop of 0.089 each year. So national productivity growth would decline on this account in the hypothetical world from 0.55 actual to 0.461 percent per year. The difference in final attainment in 1860 is again small, merely 8 percent of productivity change, and a smaller percentage of national income.

Note that the result is forced by widespread character of productivity change (even under the implausible Crafts-Harley calculation of zero productivity change outside the industries I chose in 1981 as the leading ones). Resources displaced from cotton do not simply disappear. They relocate. Their relocation does not result in a fall of national income equal to what they earned in cotton, as assumed by noneconomists. The resources of labor and capital go into other industries, albeit ones with lower productivity change than the amazing cotton textiles. Since cotton was *not* the only industry experiencing productivity change even in the classic period of the early Industrial Revolution—a point that the economic historians Peter Temin and John Clapham and I insist upon, and historians of technology such as Margaret Jacob and Joel Mokyr have affirmed in detail—the imagined shift is not deadly to progress.[5] The dynamic effect sounds promising. In quantitative terms, though, a cotton textiles industry counterfactually smaller (if foreign trade were shrunk) does not kill off growth. It's another popular explanation that doesn't work very well.

A "dynamic" argument, further, has a serious problem as an all-purpose intellectual strategy. If someone claims that foreign trade made possible, say, economies of scale in cotton textiles or shipping services, she owes it to her readers (as I have already said twice: I *wish* you would pay attention) to explain why the gains on the swings were not lost on the roundabouts. Why do not the industries made *smaller* by the large extension of British foreign trade end up on the negative side of the account? The domestic roads in Shropshire not constructed and the brass foundries unbuilt in Greater London because of Britain's increasing specialization in Lancashire cotton textiles may themselves have had economies of scale, untapped. (The argument applies later in British history to the worries over "excessive" British specialization in foreign investment, insurance, and shipping.)

And European trade with the rest of the world, as Patrick O'Brien showed long ago, was less than 4 percent of European domestic product—another reason for doubting its importance Continent-wide. Surprisingly, and rather against their training as economists, Findlay and O'Rourke attack the relevance of the low share of things in national income. They quote with approval a remark by the noneconomist Paul Mantoux (1877–1956), in his history of the Industrial Revolution—published in its last French edition in 1907.[6] Mantoux wrote thus: "If we may borrow an analogy from natural science, only a negligible quantity of ferment is needed to affect a radical change in a considerable volume of matter. The action of foreign trade upon the mechanism of production may be difficult to show, but it is not impossible to trace."[7] The notion that *natura facit salta*, nature makes jumps, has become popular after the realization that a flap of a butterfly's wing in China can cause in due course a hurricane in Cuba. It is sometimes true. If it were true in explaining the Industrial Revolution, though, *any* little part of the British economy could have been the engine of growth. Domestic service was larger than all the importation of tea and sugar and raw cotton and similarly exotic goods combined, or all the finished exports to pay for them, and so under such an instable model the hiring of more scullery maids could have set off the innovations. And if you really want "small," pick say the Birmingham brass industry with its continuous product innovation (as Maxine Berg has pointed out), or for that matter the vigorous silk industry in London around 1700. If the slave trade or the cotton industry or even foreign trade as a whole gives a satisfactory explanation of doublings and treblings of income, then we can turn also to a brass-and-silk industry explanation of why we are rich. Yet again we are led to wonder why similarly small industries in earlier times and other places did not tip the world into modernity.

∞

In establishing the growth-trade link, Findlay and O'Rourke use the static models to imagine a Britain without any trade at all ("if Britain had been closed to trade"; "absent trade").[8] An entire cutoff of trade, though, is not the relevant alternative. The question is whether the mercantilist policies that Britain employed, and above all its mercantile empire, helped or hindered industrialization, much. It's a matter of more or less trade, not yes or no.

People innocent of economics, to repeat, believe that trade just *is* growth. Export or die. That's not right, as Findlay and O'Rourke note when dismissing Keynesian models of trade as an engine of growth (of the sort in connection with the slave trade that William Darity boldly put forward in 1992). So they need a better model. The model they develop to answer the relevant question about imperialism, based on an earlier model by Darity (1982), puts a surprising emphasis on the slave trade. Findlay and O'Rourke argue that the New World and its cotton exports would have been impossible without slavery (note the similarity to the arguments of Inikori, who likewise cites Darity with enthusiasm; and Darity cites Inikori in the same terms [Darity 1992]). But on the contrary, cotton is easily grown without slaves, and it has been so grown early and late—early in India, late in postbellum Alabama. (Sugar is another matter. Sugar brought slavery with it from India to Syria to North Africa to the Azores, right down to the Jamaican and Mexican contract harvesters on H-2 visas working the cane sugar fields of Florida. Yet Findlay and O'Rourke are making the argument that an international taste for cotton dresses and bedsheets and underwear made the modern world, not that the international sweet tooth did.)

Cotton, they say, "depended" on slaves from Africa.[9] Likewise Marx: "Without slavery, no cotton; without cotton, no modern industry. Slavery has given the value to the colonies, the colonies have created world trade; world trade is the necessary condition of large-scale machine industry."[10] It does not seem so. Cotton seems to have been no more a necessarily slave crop than coffee was. Freedmen in the United States after 1865 picked cotton, just as freedmen in Brazil after 1887 picked coffee beans. Findlay and O'Rourke ask with a certain vexation in their tone whether "free white labor in the Americas . . . [would] have been able to fill the gap" in producing cotton.[11] Yet the formerly slaveholding American states did precisely that. As early as 1869, noted Stanley Lebergott, "the South had actually regained its pre-war production average [of cotton]. And by the period 1870–1879 [before the full imposition of Jim Crow and other pieces of "one kind of freedom"] was running 42 percent above its pre-war level."[12] Lebergott notes by way of contrast that in British *sugar* colonies the earlier emancipation had reduced production. Not in cotton.

The argument of Findlay and O'Rourke is that British imperialism helped British trade so much that the Industrial Revolution happened. The argument assumes that a counterfactually pacific and free trade Britain would not have benefited from *European* engagement with the rest of the world. It is an odd assumption, since European places like Denmark did benefit, with trivial overseas colonies. Sweden and Germany and Austria benefited, with few or none. Findlay and O'Rourke want to make a nationalist, militaristic, imperialist argument that British prosperity depended on British guns aimed abroad, especially at non-Europeans. It is an argument that David Landes has frequently made. The historian Paul Kennedy stated flatly in 1976 that "Britain's wealth would obviously have been lost had she herself surrendered command of the sea."[13] The assertion, though conventional in British strategic thinking for centuries, runs against the logic of "this sceptr'd isle . . . this fortress . . . set in the silver sea / Which serves it in the office . . . of a moat defensive to a house / Against the envy of less happier lands." A Britain with a little Tudor-style navy devoted to coastal defense would have remained independent for a long time—after all, a little Tudor-style navy, assisted by a divine wind, did defeat the mighty Armada. The wooden walls mattered up to the middle of the nineteenth century. In fighting Hitler it was not the expensive British fleet sitting in miserable inaction at Scapa Flow that chiefly prevented invasion but British ingenuity in inventing radar and breaking the German naval code (despite which, incidentally, its breaker, Alan Turing, was driven to suicide ten years later under the British anti-gay laws). The surplus violence of ships of the line and then dreadnoughts and then aircraft carriers in aid of dominion over palm and pine and the Falkland Islands was always dubious as an economic proposition. Britain's wealth was not at stake. Command of the seas supported national pride, certainly, and Margaret Thatcher's re-election. But it did not support the national income.

The economic models Findlay and O'Rourke use, whether formally or informally, are in fact about *European* trade with itself and with the rest of the world. A Quaker United Kingdom—however unlikely a counterfactual in 1801, with twenty thousand Quakers in an aggressively nationalistic population of 16.3 million—would have gotten the same prices and opportunities as the actual Britain, allowing for transshipment costs through Amsterdam or Le Havre. The scale of Manchester's cotton manufacturing would have been little affected, at any rate if in God's eyes Manchester had a comparative advantage in spinning cotton. Only the profits (those "rents" I mentioned, supernormal profits, which are profits in the economist's definition) in their British addressees would have been lower, because French transshippers of cotton would take a cut. As I said, if Manchester had been the right place to spin cotton before the invention of air conditioning, then European events would have put it there, regardless of whether Britain won at Plassey or Québec or Trafalgar or Waterloo. After all, the French side lost all those battles, and yet the making of cotton textiles flourished in Mulhouse and Lille—admittedly by importing British engineers and workers, as did the firm Motte et Bossuet in Lille in 1833.[14]

Europe as a whole opened itself to the world after Henry the Navigator. Even when nutmeg was a Dutch monopoly, nutmeg became cheaper. The European gains from trade were felt indirectly by everyone who bought tropical products. As an economist would put it, that's general equilibrium trade theory. Empires were not necessary. Thus Belgium, without an empire on its formation in 1830, industrialized smartly, as at the same time did the Rhineland, which was a part of a non-nautical and nonimperial (overseas) Prussia. Both of them saw the price of tobacco, sugar, spices, bananas, cotton, and other tropical and subtropical products fall greatly as imperialist and nonimperialist Europeans traded with the world. Overseas trade was not about Britain but about Europe.

Britain's overseas trade, in short, can't explain Britain's peculiarity. Lining up national conquest with national trade is an old claim, though Adam Smith and many economists since him have wisely contradicted it (without persuading many politicians or journalists). National conquest, though, doesn't explain early British industrialization, and certainly not the continuation on the way to the factor of sixteen.

∞

Yet denying that trade was the crucial engine of growth is not to say that the expansion of foreign trade was literally a nullity. Some goods—the banana for the Englishman's breakfast table was the popular instance late in the nineteenth century, raw cotton the most important instance throughout— simply cannot be had in England's clime, outside hothouses. The regional economist Gerald Silverberg has made the case to me for cotton as special because the technological unemployment caused by its expansion was felt not by politically connected guildsmen at home but by the bleached bones of Indians starving when their machineless industry was replaced by Manchester's mechanized one.[15] (The unemployment of British handloom weavers ["A trade that never yet can fail," in the words of a premechanization song] is being set aside in the argument.) The truth in Silverberg's argument is that trades like porcelain and cotton textiles in Britain could expand in country locations out of reach of the naysayers in established guild towns like Norwich or London. The trouble with the argument is that cotton did in fact have European substitutes, in wool and linen, as is shown by the fierce prohibitions on importing Indian calicoes into France and the rules in England that the dead were to be buried in shrouds made of good English wool. And the same trick could have been played in China or India, both having ample domestic sources of raw cotton, if the bourgeois rhetoric had triumphed there—as it spectacularly did in the expansion of Japanese and especially Indian mechanized cotton textile manufacturing before and during World War I. In those latter days the bleached bones, or at any rate the dole cheques, were of Mancunians and Glaswegians in Britain.

More important, trade insures against famine, as the British Raj knew in building the railways of India—though Amartya Sen has pointed out that trade has this good effect only under a government sensitive to its subjects. The Bengal famine of 1943 was caused exactly by a colonial and arrogant insensitivity to nonvoting subjects. The last widely and literally killing famine in England was in Shakespeare's hierarchical times. Good old trade.

And trade is surely a conduit of ideas and competitive pressures. In India recently the License Raj has been broken down by ideological change, and in consequence by the opening of the economy for trade. After 1994 you could for the first time buy Kellogg's Corn Flakes in New Delhi, praise be to Vishnu.[16] Such effects, however, have nothing to do with imperial conquest—as is again best shown by the opening of Japan after 1868. Japan opened to trade, and *then*, many decades later, under the influence of trade-follows-the-flag thinking at the height of Western imperialism, became itself a conqueror of Russia's eastern fleet, then Korea and then Germany's colonies in China and then Manchuria and then China itself and finally much of East and Southeast Asia. With most unsatisfactory economic consequences.

A literal closing of British trade, entirely foregoing bananas at breakfast, using vastly more cotton for underwear at home, not getting any wheat at all in a famine, is not what is contemplated. The question is: was trade a stimulus to growth in the simple, mercantilist way usually contemplated in the literature? Apparently not. Is it plausibly a secondary cause as a desirable context for invention? Perhaps, though India (to say it yet again) was the center of the largest trading network before the eighteenth century yet did not innovate. A Scots verdict seems wiser: not proven.

∞

Here is the economist's way of stating the problem with trade, reallocations, enclosure, investment, fuller employment, and all manner of shufflings. Think of the per capita output of Stuff (clothing, food, houses) and Services (financing, shipping, doctoring, teaching, soldiering) in 1780 in Britain as being measured along two axes (bring back that high-school algebra and geometry). The *possibilities* in 1780 are a curve along which the actual Britain of 1780 could have taken a nontrading point, which we'll call Self-Sufficiency (fig. 1). Inefficiency, misallocation, opportunities missed, distortions introduced *of the usual static sort* are about being inside or on that curve. Note the point Massive Unemployment. It would be a foolish place to be, since you could get out to the curve and have more of *both* Stuff and Services per capita. Indeed, you can get a little *outside* the curve by trading with foreigners. But only a little outside, to a point like Trade.

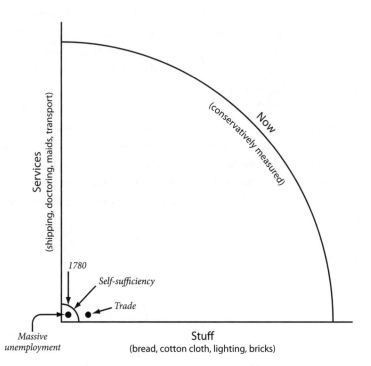

FIGURE 1. Mere reallocations such as foreign trade or better labor markets can't explain modern economic growth.

Good. Yet why have I drawn the so-called production possibility curve for 1780 as a miserable little scrunched-up curve in the very corner of the axes? Answer: it has to be a miserable little scrunched-up curve in order to represent Now on the same diagram. The amounts of Stuff and Services (averaged together) in the age of Now have to be *sixteen times per capita further out.* Of course: that's what the factor of sixteen means. And remember that in truth it's more like a factor of 100.

Look at the diagram. None of the static arguments, and few of the dynamic, have any chance of explaining what happened in modern economic growth. *No merely static improvement of conventional economic factors in 1780 or 1700 can come remotely close to the curve of Now.* That's why this greatest of secular historical events cannot be explained by static reallocation. And if it is to be explained by "dynamic" accumulation one has to explain, too, why earlier accumulation did not get the same explosive result. A dynamic explanation—for example, a foreign trade that induces innovation on the scale of 1780 to Now—is *so* dynamic that it makes no sense as history, at any rate within a language-and-discoveryless, conventionally Samuelsonian economics. The same problem infects models that depend on the Black Death, say, to explain European exceptionalism. Of course, one can always devise a model that "explains" anything. But that's a mathematical, not a scientific, truth. There are an infinity of models that "account for" any historical event. Most of them would apply to China in 213 BCE as much as to Britain in 1760 CE. Coal. Trade. Science. Rationality. To put it differently, such a modeling explanation is no explanation. It requires (but does not give) an answer to the question why *just then*, why the dynamism overtook the *British* economy in the eighteenth and nineteenth centuries. The correct explanation, I claim, requires scientific attention to bourgeois dignity and liberty.

26

THE EFFECTS ON EUROPE OF THE SLAVE
TRADE OR BRITISH IMPERIALISM
WERE SMALLER STILL

It follows from the unimportance of foreign trade that parts of foreign trade were unimportant, too—at any rate in explaining the doubling of per capita real income in the eighty years from 1780 to 1860 and especially in explaining the subsequent explosion on the way to the factor of sixteen. For example, the trade in slaves, which was quite a small part of Britain's or Europe's trade, could not have been the cause of British or European prosperity. As the economic historians Stanley Engerman and Patrick O'Brien showed, contrary to Inikori, the so-called profits were too small.[1] To attribute great importance to a tiny trade would make every small trade important—we are back to the brass industry as a cause of the modern world.

As another leading historian of the slave trade, David Richardson, puts it, "comparisons between earnings from slaving voyages [which Richardson himself has researched on a large scale] with general estimates of eighteenth-century British investment generally suggest, almost without exception, that slave-trading profits could have contributed at best only small amounts to financing early British industrial expansion."[2] The economic reasoning backing up Richardson's laboriously acquired facts on particular slaving voyages is that entry to the trade was free, and therefore marginal entrants could expect no more than the normal rate of return. Since the skills and equipment for slave trading were very widely available, furthermore, intra-marginal "rents" would also be low. Any merchant ship could turn to slaving, as earlier any armed ship could turn to piracy, or indeed as any ship whatever in view of the freedom of the seas could arbitrage between this labor market or that, or this capital market and that. By 1750 there would be few nonmarginal positions in the slave trade to be seized, and few rents or supernormal profits to be earned.

And indeed entry would have squeezed out *any* supernormal profits in the supply chain all the way from the interior of Sierra Leone to the slave markets of Charleston. (There was by the way a much older supply chain from Tanzania to Istanbul, and in volume as large or larger, not to speak of the massive trade from Slavic lands.[3] Yet the "profits" from the trans-Saharan or Indian Ocean slave trade, or of the Black Sea slave trade did not spark an industrial revolution in Arab or Ottoman lands.) A long time ago Robert Paul Thomas and Richard Bean argued persuasively that the only supernormal profits from the trade were likely to have been earned *by Africans*, namely, the specialists in violence in the interior who captured the slaves in the first place.[4] They were the ones with the bright and horrible and profitable idea of seizing their fellow Africans at low cost and selling them to Arabs or Europeans.

It is therefore no surprise to find that by the late eighteenth century the total profits of the trade constituted a minute portion even of total British investment generally, not to speak of total income. And in any case we have seen that "British investment generally" only accommodated innovation, and did not cause it. Capital fundamentalism works no better for eighteenth- and nineteenth-century Britain than it worked for late twentieth-century Ghana. As David Eltis and Stanley Engerman concluded in 2000, in a thorough review of the possible influences, "If the value added and strategic linkages of the sugar industry are compared to those of other British industries, it is apparent that sugar cultivation and the slave trade [note again the link of sugar with slavery] were not particularly large, nor did they have stronger growth-inducing ties with the rest of the British economy."[5]

The emotional problem in accepting the evidence that the slave trade didn't matter very much is that we properly regard it as terrible (though one should note that in 1700, before bourgeois clergymen in Europe got to it, practically nobody viewed it as anything but a God-given misfortune to the slave). We are rich. The populist, with his zero-sum and moralistic theory of the economy (as in Barnett 1972), wants to attribute our riches to the impoverishment or even the enslavement of someone else, just as he attributes every downturn in the economy to the "greed" of rich people on Wall Street. The noblest expression of the sentiment is Lincoln's Second Inaugural: "If God wills that [the War] continue until all the wealth piled by the bondsman's two hundred and fifty years of unrequited toil shall be sunk, and until every drop of blood drawn with the lash shall be paid by another drawn with the sword, as was said three thousand years ago, so still it must be said 'the judgments of the Lord are true and righteous altogether.'" Lincoln was wrong in his economics, if not in his ethics. Even in 1865 the wealth of the nation as a whole, if not the Black Belt, had little to do with slavery.

∞

Imperialism, too, was another part of trade, and again an obviously evil one, "obviously" at least to postimperial ethical ideas. Yet imperialism, it can be shown, did not much help the British, or the First World generally, to an industrial revolution and modern economic growth. True, the doctrine that imperialism made the West rich at the expense of the East and South is held passionately by the left in the West, and by nearly everyone elsewhere. But understand: the counterargument here does not praise imperialism, or excuse it. The counterargument claims that imperialism was economically stupid.

The simplest and historical argument is that the industrializing West did not really get going in its imperial adventure until *after* it had innovated in steam, steel ships, cartridge rifles, and machine guns—that is, after the Industrial Revolution, not before. As Goldstone puts it, "It was not colonialism and conquest that made possible the rise of the West, but the reverse—it was the rise of the West (in terms of technology) and the [comparative] decline of the rest that made possible the full extension of European power across the globe."[6] Lenin had that part right: imperialism, the last stage of capitalism. Not the first.

The modern corollary of the historical argument is that the prosperity of the West depends not at all, or at the worst very little, on exploiting the third world. Imperialism was bad. Badness, however, does not invariably bring profit to the bad man. Crime does not always pay. Admittedly such a corollary runs against the grain of much anti-imperialist thinking. A local fount of unreflective anti-imperialism in France was said to be the philosopher Maurice Merleau-Ponty. Raymond Aron complained in his *Memoirs* that when Merleau-Ponty wrote in 1947 "as though it were an obvious truth, that 'the moral and material civilization of England presupposes the exploitation of colonies,' he flippantly resolves a still open question."[7] Thus too in 1996 André Comte-Sponville, a teacher of philosophy at the Sorbonne, who doesn't claim to know much about economics, felt nonetheless confident in declaring without argument or evidence that "Western prosperity depends, directly or indirectly, on Third World poverty, which the West in some cases merely takes advantage of and in others actually causes."[8] On the other side politically, David Landes, as though admitting the truth of the left's loot theory of Western prosperity, dismisses "those who feel the West has gained its edge by domination and exploitation" by accepting their proposition as true but urging the whiners to grow up and get used it: "to this age-old anti-imperialist lament I can only say that this is world history as it has been played out, without any moral assessment of 'good' or 'bad,' 'just' or 'unjust.'"[9] As in *Realpolitik*, get real.

Yet we can do better than Merleau-Ponty, Comte-Sponville, or Landes. British imperialism was about protecting the sea routes to India. Yet India itself, one can show, yielded no economic benefit to the average person in Britain. Imperialism had therefore no national economic point. By the time Victoria became empress of India the thieving nabobs—Robert Clive of India (1725–1774, in 1757 the victor of Plassey) and Warren Hastings (1732–1818) and the like—were long gone. By 1877 there remained no additional straightforward opportunities for thievery by the British (Clive remarked that in the face of his opportunities for seizing loot "by God . . . I stand astonished at my own moderation"). William Cowper, a contemporary of Clive and Hastings, could complain like Edmund Burke about the scandal of the nabobs, that "thieves at home must hang; but he, that puts / Into his over-gorged and bloated purse / The wealth of Indian provinces, escapes."[10] But such thievery cannot account for British wealth. Rich as Clive had (briefly) been, the enrichment of him and his fellow nabobs was very small in national terms—Clive's *stock* of capital was under a million pounds, and was below 1 percent of the annual £115 million *flow* of U.K. national income. And to translate the stock into the comparable flow, the *income* from a million pounds invested in the funds would be, say, 5 percent of the million, or £50,000 a year, which would be only 1/2300 of annual national income.[11] Such a sum would be nice to have, an immense personal income in eighteenth-century society, on a princely level. The loot, however, was a trivial enrichment of the nation. In fact by 1877 the British East India Company had long gone, losing its police powers in 1857 after the First War of Indian Independence, and closing entirely in 1871. (The Dutch equivalent, the Vereenigde Oostindische Compagnie, had gone bankrupt and become state property much earlier, in 1798.) A private company is a more focused institution for looting than a responsible government. The directors of John Company would dearly have liked to have known of opportunities for supernormal profits to be gotten from India by 1857 or 1871. They themselves had not been able to discover the loot in time.

Britain in 1871, and in 1771 or for that matter in 1971, traded with India. Yet trade is trade, not looting—this contrary to Marxian notions of unequal trade. (Another Marx, Groucho, turning down with cruel wit a Marxist friend looking for work in the hungry 1930s, is reported to have said something like this: "George, I wouldn't want to violate your Marxist principles and 'exploit' you by . . . giving you a job.") Admittedly, when even an economist buys a house she is left with vague populist feelings that the seller robbed her. After all, he *could* have sold it to her, a very nice person, for thousands of dollars less. And certainly she feels instinctively that the realtor, a middleman, is a thief. The Soviet Union gave expression to the feeling (which can be found also in Adam Smith, in a rare misstep) by setting services at zero value in its accounting of national income. The house-buying economist, however, being an adult bourgeoise, corrects herself, and takes the wider, bourgeois view that made for modern economic growth, and nowadays is enriching India itself.

In 1871 Bombay sent jute to Dundee, and Manchester sent dhotis to Calcutta. Such trade could have been achieved on more or less the same terms if India had been independent. It would have likewise been achieved if India had become a French rather than a British colony—a more plausible counterfactual than entire independence, considering the disorders of the late Mughal Empire and the briefly superior military technology of all the European powers in the eighteenth century and the absence of national feeling in an India broken into scores of principalities (the sentiment and rhetoric of nationalism arose, as it commonly has, from the very imperialism it fought against). If it had been a French colony, India would have traded through Marseille, and in consequence Dundee probably would not have become a great center for the making of burlap bags out of imperial jute. Some Scottish millionaires in Dundee would have had to seek other opportunities, now taken up by French millionaires in, say, Dunkirk, and the ordinary Dundee worker would have gone to work elsewhere in the Scottish economy, or in England, or in Kentucky, at less loss to them in percentage terms than to the millionaires.

If imperialism was so very subordinating of Indian interests to British, furthermore, why were Indian cotton textile factories allowed to grow in the late nineteenth century? "Given the widespread impression that India's industrial development was impossible because of implacable British hostility to Indian competition," writes the economic historian Om Prakash, "India's cotton-mill history seems paradoxical: it flourished despite competing against the most important, the most internationally aggressive and politically most powerful industry in Britain. Its rapid expansion began only after 1870, but by 1910 the Indian industry had become one of the world's largest," presaging a deep depression for the British industry after the Great War.[12] (A somewhat similar point could be made about the Japanese cotton textile industry, which again belies the infant-industry notion, especially popular in Germany and the United States during the nineteenth century, that late industrializers had no chance against Manchester's might.)

And even if the trade with India contained some element of exploitation, which is unlikely, and certainly has never been proven, the trade was smaller than Britain's trade with rich countries like France or the German Empire or the United States. In 1899, Angus Maddison reckoned, the U.K. exported $153 million worth of goods (excluding, that is, services and bonds) to Imperial India, 9.5 percent of all British commodity exports. Exports to Europe and the United States at the time were $728 million, nearly five times the Indian total. Even confined to manufactures (and thus excluding steam coal from South Wales, for example), the India trade was well below half of British exports to the countries that were themselves big exporters of manufactures (the same Europe and United States), and was merely 14 percent of all British manufacturing exports.[13]

The way the issue is usually discussed speaks of the "drain" from India, said to be the excess of Indian exports over Indian imports, the trade surplus. (Notice that in strict mercantilist theory, such as that practiced by the Japanese over the century past, a trade surplus is supposed to be good, not bad. The drain theory is a little more sensible, considering that Japanese consumers are indeed made worse off, not better, if Japan exports in value terms more in Toyotas than it imports in soybeans. The Japanese nation is made worse off. The mercantilism would be especially damaging to the Japanese if the assets the Japanese bought in the United States to square the balance of payment were paid back in depreciated dollars [about a half in the event] or if like the Japanese purchase of Rockefeller Center the assets did not pay back at all. After the American antioriental hysteria during the 1970s over the Japanese Invasion, all these misfortunes for Japanese consumers and investors in fact came to pass. China, take note.) One might suppose in parallel, then, that the export of raw jute and cotton from India in, say, 1900, is to be viewed as a national loss to the degree it is greater than the imports of railway engines and steel. According to Angus Maddison's careful calculations, such a figure was on the order of 1 percent of Indian income, and likewise (at any rate before World War I) about 1 percent of British income (Britain was richer per head but of course smaller).[14]

Anyway there is something wacky about the concept of the drain. One version of the drain speaks of the burden on Indians of the costs of the Indian Army and the civil administration. But any polity would have required soldiers and administrators, so it is not clear why the *British* raj was especially objectionable. In any case there is no advantage to the British from such a "drain" unless one assumes what is to be proven, namely, that Britain did gain economically from its political domination of India. The other concept of the "drain" is the sheer balance of payments. The Indians got gold and silver and British bank accounts in pounds sterling for having a trade surplus—unless the exports were simply stolen from them, which after the age of the nabobs is nowhere alleged, and is not beyond reasonable doubt even for the nabobs, as the trial of Warren Hastings showed. Unlike the mercantilist Japanese in the 1970s seeking to have higher exports regardless of the internal damage to Japanese consumers, the Indian creditors of British firms demanded payment in full.

Now consider. The goods-and-services account, called also the trade balance, is exports minus imports—not merely goods but, say, Indian imports of British services, such as insurance. The *overall* balance of payments, which is the goods-and-services account together with the capital-and-monetary account, must always balance, to the last farthing. You pay for your groceries, if you can't simply steal them, either by paying from income you have earned by selling your labor or by borrowing from your bank and then paying. In either case your overall balance of payments—dollars of expenditure minus income, which is dollars of earned income plus borrowing—is exactly zero, always. That is a matter of accounting, not economics. It is always true, by definition of the accounts. (Unrequited payments—gifts or thefts—can even be accounted payments for "services" of benevolence or malevolence.) So: an Indian firm exports tea to England, for which someone in India is paid in sterling. The Indian owners of the firm, their suppliers, and their workers spend the money thus acquired in part to buy British goods, such as steel or boots. If such Indians (or other Indians having no connection with the tea exports) do not buy enough in Britain or elsewhere, they keep the pound notes or bank accounts or the IOUs or the gold that paid for the tea. The Indians are free to spend the money on British goods. They might choose not to. Their choice, however, does not transform the money balances they retain into a measure of a hurtful "drain."

Think again of your own balances of payments. You export more labor services to your employer than the labor services you *im*port from him (none, probably). You have a balance of trade surplus in labor with your employer. Do you feel "drained"? Of course you would prefer to get food and shelter for no expenditure of your labor at all, in the manner of a Mughal prince, or the minor princelings good at playing cricket whom the British kept "in power." But, no, in a world of trade you are not drained. You take the money paid by your employer and spend it at the grocery store (and the store, too, has a "drain," a surplus of exports over imports, relative to you: does that make you the exploiting Raj over the grocery store?). Or else, like the Indians, you keep your money in gold necklaces in Pushkar or bank balances in London. The world is composed of such "drains," between your house and the neighbors, between Ealing and Hampstead. All exchange, 100 percent of it, becomes on balance a shameful exploitation. That's what I mean by "wacky."

In short, the average person in Britain got little or nothing out of the British Empire. Yet in 1876 Queen Victoria loved becoming an empress and Disraeli loved making her one, and so imperial India was born (and in the same year five million Indians died of famine).

Acquiring Cape Town and its offshoots in 1814, to take another example, was an important part of protecting the sea routes to India, of course, as was messing about in Egypt from 1869 on, and various other imperial projects from Gibraltar to Afghanistan. Yet such ventures were no more "profitable" than India itself. True, some British investors, such as Cecil Rhodes, made a lot of money out of southern Africa—and Rhodes was by no means the most financially successful of the lot. But that does not mean that the great British public made a lot of money, too. "It is at least certain," wrote Rousseau in 1755, before Europe's proimperialism had hardened into convention, "that no peoples are so oppressed and wretched as conquering nations, and that their successes only increase their misery."[15] The cost of protecting the empire devolved almost entirely on the British people at home. (A century earlier the British people had likewise paid for the defense of the first British empire. Notoriously, the colonials in North America refused to pay even a little for imperial defense against the French and Indians.) British taxpayers at home 1877–1948 paid for the half of naval expenditure that was for imperial defense, a by-no-means negligible part of total British national income each year.[16] They paid for the First War against the Boer republics (1880–1881, lost but cheap) and the Second (1899–1902, won but expensive). They paid for the imperial portions of World War I and especially II. They paid for protection of Jamaican sugar during the eighteenth century and special deals for British engineering firms in India during the nineteenth. They paid in fatalities, 800,000 in the First World War and 380,000 in the Second, and lost all their foreign assets, too. For the great British Empire the great British public paid and paid and paid.

What were the vaunted benefits to the British people? Essentially nothing of material worth. They got bananas on their kitchen tables, as I said, that they would have got anyway by free trade—the Swedes did, via London or Amsterdam—or at a slightly higher cost if trade had not been entirely free. They got employment for unemployable twits from minor public schools. Above all—to go beyond the material realm—they got the great joy of seeing a quarter of the land area on world maps and globes shaded in British imperial red.

Economically, materially, it did not matter. Standards of literacy exceeding those of Southern Europe mattered a great deal more to later British economic growth, as did a tradition of industrial and financial innovation exceeding that of Germany, and a free society in which to innovate exceeding that of Russia, and above all an early shift to a rhetoric of bourgeois virtues exceeding most of the world except the seventeenth-century Dutch, and the British Americans north of Virginia. Look at the accounting and the magnitudes. Most of British national income was and is domestic. This is true of all countries much larger than Luxembourg or Singapore. And what income there was from abroad was largely a matter of mutually advantageous trade or lending having nothing to do with empire—Britain invested for example as much in places like the United States and Argentina as in comparable areas of the empire, and there is no evidence that returns to investment in the empire were especially high.[17]

The British worried in 1776–1783 and in 1899–1902 and in 1947 about the loss of their various bits of empire. Is the average British person, though, worse off now than when Britain ruled the waves? By no means. British income per head boomed after losing colonies in 1783 and again in 1947, and stagnated in 1902–1914 after expensively keeping the Boer Republics in the empire. Nowadays, after the tragic loss of world maps painted red over a quarter of their land area, British real national income per capita is higher than ever, and is among the very highest in the world—in 2007 a little bit above, adjusted to purchasing-power parity, that of France, Germany, Italy; though a good deal below its former and terribly exploited colonies of Hong Kong, Singapore, Ireland, Canada, and the United States. Did the acquisition of empire, then, cause spurts in British growth? By no means. Indeed, in the 1890s and 1900s, at the climax of imperial pretension, holding sway to the east and west of Suez, the growth of British real income per head notably slowed.

27

AND OTHER EXPLOITATIONS, EXTERNAL OR INTERNAL, WERE EQUALLY PROFITLESS TO ORDINARY EUROPEANS

The same accounting and magnitudes apply to other imperialisms. King Leopold II of the Belgians (reigned 1865–1909) was a ruthless thief in the Congo. Through his concessionaires and their native soldiers he starved and slaughtered and enslaved hundreds of thousands to gather rubber from the trees at nearly zero cost to himself, selling it high in Europe. Yet what benefit were his crimes to the ordinary Belgian? Did Belgian growth depend on Belgium's little and late-acquired empire—or to be exact, did it depend on the personal imperial income of the king, spent largely on castles in Belgium and southern France? Not at all. It depended on brain and brawn in coal mines and iron and steel mills at home from the early nineteenth century on, and the bourgeois society dating from the sixteenth century in the southern Lowlands supporting them.

The Germans in their Southwest Africa (now Namibia) fought two little wars 1904–1906 against their new African subjects. In October 1904, for example, General Lothar von Trotha issued a Vernichtungbefehl, an extermination order, an early German experiment in racial cleansing anticipating the greater experiment of the early 1940s: "Within German boundaries, every Herero [northern Namibian people], whether found armed or unarmed, . . . will be shot."[1] Yet there was no *economic* point to the Herero holocaust, three-quarters shot or starved in two years, because there was no economic gain to Germany in the first place from having German Southwest Africa, "whose assets comprised wealth of rock and sand, and whose liabilities [even before the war] cost the German taxpayers a subsidy of £425,000."[2]

So it proved for almost all the scrambles for Africa—or those for Asia or Polynesia or even the New World. The glorious Spanish and Portuguese empires, I note again, left Spain and Portugal at the last among the poorest countries in Europe. Even when the colonized people were reduced to a form of slavery, as in the concessionary system invented by King Leopold for his Congolese subjects and imitated by the French in their own Congo, only a few people gained from the severed hands and depopulated districts. When the clerk is murdered in the course of a convenience-store robbery, the gain to the robber of $45.56 is not the *same thing* as the loss of life of the clerk. His lost life is not a *gain* to the robber. Thus European imperialism.

Individual Dutch people got rich trading spices from the Dutch East Indies, as Multatuli explains in his strikingly early and influential anti-imperialist novel, *Max Havelaar* (1860)—compare *Uncle Tom's Cabin* (1852). From 1830 to 1870 the Dutch authorities compelled the Javanese to produce coffee, sugar, and indigo at derisory prices for the benefit of the Dutch treasury, a third of which at times was supported in this way.[3] Yet then down to 1913 the Dutch spent on navies and military conquest what they had gained by compulsion, and after the Great War, tortured now by guilt, "government expenditure on defense [well . . . 'defense' against the Japanese, perhaps, but also against the Indonesians themselves], education, and public health" in the colonies was greatly increased.[4] The Dutch damaged the Indonesians, probably, though in this as in other cases, short of Congo-ish horrors, it is not obvious that indigenous rulers, or an alternative European imperium, would have done much better for the common people. In the Dutch empire, writes Angus Maddison, "Control was exercised by the thick layer of European officials [and after 1870, entrepreneurs] who spent a good deal of time as watchdogs over a native administration whose ostensible dignity and regalia camouflaged their basic role as Dutch puppets."[5] Late in the game, in 1931, the Netherlands had a quite large Indonesian presence, 0.4 percent of the population there. It sounds small, but was eight times larger at the time than the British soldiers and administrators relative to the South Asian population they governed. The number of Dutch in Indonesia relative to their countrymen in Holland was much higher than the parallel figure for the British. After the fall of empire the ex-colonial administrators bulked larger in Dutch society and literature than the comparable class of old India hands did in Britain.

Most Dutch people back in the Netherlands, though, were not benefited by empire, and certainly not in the nineteenth century, by which time the "rich trades" in spices had been routinized, or competed away by such unhappy events as the reproducing of clove cultivation in far away and non-Dutch Zanzibar. Colonial pain in 1661 or 1861 or 1931 did not make for general European prosperity—merely for a few shocking fortunes, such as that of the Dutch royal family. The ordinary Dutch seaman or farmer earned what such work earned in Europe in 1661, or 1861, or 1931. The European supply and demand for labor determined the real wage. It did not depend on the profit from the imperial spice trade, constituting for all its glamour a tiny part of European expenditure.

Or again, would anyone claim that owning Greenland and Iceland and a few scattered islands elsewhere made the Danish farmers the butter merchants of Europe? No: what explains it were Danish liberties from the late seventeenth century on (though under attack from the imperial and divine-right pretensions of the Danish royals), and a bourgeois attitude among farmers. Did the French as a whole get great benefits from lording it over poor Muslims in Africa and poor Buddhists in Vietnam? One doubts it. French economic success depended on French law, French style, French labor, French banking, French education, French originality, French openness to ideas.

The temptation to attribute the Industrial Revolution to the overseas adventures of the Europeans from the 1490s to the 1950s comes from the confusion between conquest and enrichment that I have noted before in Landes, Kennedy, Diamond, Findlay, O'Rourke, Barnett (and many other such scholars otherwise admirable). And it comes from the crude correlation in time. Again it is a case of *post hoc*—or rather *dum hoc* (at the same time as this)—*ergo propter hoc*. It is true that the British for example prospered at the about same time that they acquired their empire—although, to repeat, the crucial industrializing decade of the 1780s, just to take one temporal problem with the argument, is precisely when Britain lost its first empire and had not established a firm grip over its second one. And Japan under the Tokugawa, one might argue, to make the case for empire by contraries, turned away from foreign trade and foreign conquests as growth-making just when the Europeans were getting started in the business. Had Japan opened themselves to foreign ideas in 1603 as they did in 1868, and especially had they adopted earlier the idea of bourgeois dignity, their lack of colonies such as they later acquired (*after* industrialization started) in Korea or Taiwan or Manchuria would not have mattered. One can point to specific factors in the non-European cases that made overseas imperialism less tempting to, say, Tokugawa Japan and Qing China—and therefore left them without the wonderful advantages of overseas empire for making the modern world. European colonization was easy in the Americas because the conquistadors and the fishermen brought measles and smallpox in their ships. It was not so easy, at least on account of the disease gradient, in, say, India, or Indonesia. China therefore lacked, Kenneth Pomeranz argues, easily colonized foreign lands to provide raw materials like cotton. But as Pomeranz also observes, in 1750 China had internally probably the largest source of cotton in the world. Why bother conquering India?

The point is that China and Japan could have industrialized without colonies, or indeed without world-girdling trade. Yet they didn't. Pomeranz argues that there was in China no political alliance in favor of foreign trade. That's no exaggeration. Yet the drawing back after the adventures of the great fleets in the early fifteenth century was in part a consequence of a much deeper obstacle to rapid industrialization in China, the disdainful attitude toward all merchants. (Goldstone would perhaps disagree, observing as he does that venturing beyond the Indian Ocean lacked point for China. The disdain for merchants and the ability to embody the disdain in arbitrary policy, though, was anyway palpable, as in the bizarre Ming policy of closing down entirely all economic activity on the coast in order to starve out the Japanese pirates.) Foreign merchants were confined for a while to the port of Guangzhou (or as the Westerners call it, Canton) in the south and Kyakhta in the northern inland, on the border with Russia, some 2,500 miles away. It would be as though the inlets for European trade were confined to Cadiz in the south and St. Petersburg in the north. Again the political unity of China figures. The Spaniards certainly *wanted* to make Seville and then Cadiz the sole entrepôt for the trade from the New World. But the pesky French and English would have none of it. They made Le Havre and Bristol into New World entrepôts, going so far in their presumption as to seize Cadiz from time to time and burn the Spanish ships.

Sic transit all manner of claims that Western wealth is founded on the despoilment of the East or the South. Rich countries are rich mainly because of what they do and did at home, not because of present or past foreign trade, foreign investment, foreign empire, or foreign anything except foreign ideas such as the inventions adopted from China and the crops adopted from the New World. Suppose the third world were transported tomorrow by magic to another planet, like the two-planet system in Ursula Le Guin's novel *The Dispossessed: An Ambiguous Utopia* (1974). In the long run the economies of the first world would scarcely notice it. In the short run they would face of course great disruption. Yet the economies of the West would adjust, rather as they adjusted to $150-a-barrel oil for a while in 2008, or to the abolition of slavery in the British Empire 1833–1840, or to the papal decision in 1537 that native Americans were to be treated as though they had souls. The one exception to the postwar *loss* of a literal empire supported by guns and tanks, that of Russia, was a failure. Formal or informal empires (take America's . . . please) have not on the whole enriched the home power. Russian income per head grew more slowly enchained to its Eastern European colonies than it would have if by some happy miracle it had adopted Western bourgeois dignity and liberty in 1945. Look at East Germany versus West, where the controlled experiment was in fact tried. Labor productivity in Ossi factories ended in 1991 at one-third what it was in Wessi factories, with no gain to East Germany's Russian overlords.[6]

That is, we cannot account for the riches of rich countries by reference to exploitation of poor people. This, to repeat, is not to say that there was no exploitation—that British or Belgian or French or Spanish or Portuguese or American or Russian imperialism was good news for the people imperialized. That is a separate question, and often has a rather obvious answer. For example, yes, Belgian imperialism in the Congo was an appalling event for the Congolese. Roger Casement recorded in 1903 what the people said about Leopold's concessionaires: "From our country each village had to take 20 loads of rubber. . . . We get no pay. We get nothing. . . . It used to take 10 days [per month] to get the 20 baskets of rubber—we were always in the forest to find the rubber vines, to go without food. . . . then we starved. Wild beasts—the leopards—killed some of us while we were working away in the forest and others got lost and died from exposure or starvation and we begged the white men to leave us alone. . . . but the white men and their [black] soldiers said: Go. You are beasts yourselves."[7]

Remember, though, the convenience-store robbery. That brutal imperialism or other forms of exploitation backed by the brief Western lead in the technology of guns and a peculiarly Western obsession with large-scale foreign adventuring was often bad for the non-European victims does not at all in logic—or as it happens in most facts 1492 to 1960—imply that the average citizen of the European perpetrator countries was enriched by it.

∞

Consider for example the sorry history of South African racism. Keeping the blacks uneducated and landless in the twentieth century, and the coloreds excluded from certain occupations, did *not* benefit white South Africans on the whole, no more than conservative Muslim men are made better off on the whole by keeping their women illiterate and refusing to allow them to drive. The novelist Alan Paton wrote in 1948 in the voice of progressive whites just as apartheid was about to come to a climax: "The earth has bounty enough for all, and . . . more for one does not mean less for another." The reply to such liberalism from the voice of conservatives is always about the political system as a whole, and the standing of the hegemonic group within it: "This is a danger, for better-paid labor will . . . read more, think more, ask more, and will not be content to be forever voiceless and inferior."[8] But we are discussing here the economics, not the pleasures or anxieties of a profitless hegemony.

From 1917, about the time the trammeling of blacks and coloreds in South Africa got seriously theorized, to 1994, when democracy was established, the real incomes per head of South African *whites* grew at about 2 percent per year.[9] Two percent per year is a respectable but not an unusually high rate of growth. At such a rate one's real income doubles every thirty-five years, a welcome event, and approximately what has been happening in the United States since the eighteenth century. Yet it is no Swedish or Japanese or Korean miracle, and certainly very far from the recent Chinese and Indian miracles of 7 to 10 percent annual real growth per capita. On its face the 2 percent does not justify a notion that the whites were greatly enriched by extracting loot or labor from people with non-European ancestors.

Look at closely comparable cases. The white growth rate of real income in South Africa 1917–1994 was somewhat higher than in Australia. The Australians lacked a large internal oppressed class. The tiny number of Aborigines who survived Eurasian diseases were still being hunted for sport in the 1930s, it is said, by drunken Western Australians of European descent. Yet no one would claim that such activities were the basis for the Australian economy. Everyone in Australia worked, pretty hard. Click go the shears, boys, click, click, click. Most European Australians were not up on horses ordering blacks about as *die base* ("the bosses," which until well into the twentieth century was the crippling career presumption of quite ordinary

Afrikaners). The growth rate of real incomes of South African whites was also a little higher than that of all people in New Zealand, where the Europeans did have a large class of Maori aboriginals to lord it over, though not anything like so large as white South Africa's endowment on this score. Yet in Canada or Ireland white incomes grew at about the same rate as in South Africa, with no such class of exploitables. And other countries entirely lacking a separate racial group to exploit at artificially low wages in mining or housework, such as Italy, Greece, Finland, and South Korea, had a higher rate of income growth than the privileged whites of South Africa achieved by their alleged profiting from privilege. Oppressing people is bad. Yet commonly, if not always, the oppression helps only a few rich and powerful people, while hurting or not benefiting the ordinary folk alleged in the racist rhetoric to do well.

Of course oppression can make *some* of the oppressors better off—to repeat, the rich and powerful and rare. That is the Prudence Only explanation of why they engage in the oppression, and often it explains something. Yet such beneficiaries in a zero- or negative-sum game are necessarily tiny minorities, the unusually well-connected or the unusually violent, such as a few Afrikaner trade unionists in South Africa, and the House of Saud in Saudi Arabia, and members of the Communist Party in China and Cuba. True, South African whites for a long time *believed* that their prosperity depended on oppressing non-Europeans. It is the rhetorical, nonprudent explanation for apartheid. A belief in fairies, however, does not strictly imply their existence. (Someone asked an Irish woman in the 1830s whether she believed in fairies: "She did not, she said. But they were there all the same.")[10] That people believe they are made better off by being associated with an empire or apartheid or slavery or segregation or discrimination or patriarchy does not mean they actually are. Because of improved varieties of cotton, American slavery was profitable right to its end for the Southerners who owned slaves (a small group—quite unlike the Cape Colony during the eighteenth century, in which nearly every white family owned a slave).[11] Yet slavery did nothing good for the poor whites of the Confederacy except to make them feel superior to at least somebody. Alas, like working-class imperialists in Britain, they *thought* the exploitation of blacks by rich people was good for them as poor whites, and therefore they flocked to the colors in 1861 under the command of plantation owners. So too in 1914 did the cockneys and agricultural workers flock to the British Empire's colors of the Pals

Brigades or the territorial regiments under the command of middle-class infantry officers (whose cousins were policemen in Burma).

In South Africa from 1936 to 1960 the racist policies devised mainly in the 1920s succeeded in raising Afrikaner unskilled workers and English trade unionists above migrant blacks and above coloreds (that is, people of Indian or mixed European-African origin). Incomes of lower-class Afrikaners did rise smartly, as they took jobs on the railways, and as their sons went to engineering school. Yet from 1975 until 1994, at the very height of a system supposed to enrich them, Afrikaner or English whites saw negligible growth in their real incomes (in such calculations one would need to correct the price deflators for the improvement in the quality of goods). And indeed South Africans as a whole, black and white and colored, saw their real incomes at the time stagnate or actually fall. More to the point, the rates of growth were below those even in many other African countries.[12] And, unsurprisingly, in no period since its founding did the system succeed strikingly for blacks *and* whites considered together. No wonder, a materialist would exclaim, that after 1986, rather quickly, like communism after 1989, the pass laws and the rest were given up. Yet then he would have to explain with the same materialist hypothesis why they were adopted in the first place.

What comes out of the economics, in other words, is that on the whole, and time and again, the attempt to live off poor people has not been very profitable. Even the rich in former times, who for millennia did in fact live off poor people, remained poor by the standard of ordinary people after modern economic growth. As Adam Smith memorably put it at the end of the first chapter of *The Wealth of Nations*, "The accommodation . . . of an industrious and frugal peasant . . . exceeds that of many an African king."[13] Smith was following Locke: in America, Locke wrote in 1690, for want of improvement of the land by labor, a native American "king of a large and fruitful territory there feeds, lodges, and is clad worse than a day laborer in England."[14] For 1690 or 1776 this may in fact be doubted, and was certainly not true of the pre-Columbian empires. And the *obas* of Benin 1170–1897, to speak of African kings, did seem to have lived pretty high off the hog, well above the standard of an English day laborer or an industrious and frugal peasant in the Lowlands of Scotland.[15] Yet by now, imagining the riches in health and wealth of a working person like you or me in Italy or New Zealand, and comparing these to the riches extracted in olden times from the poor, or still extracted today by the last absolute monarch in Africa, King

Mswati III of Swaziland, Smith's proposition cannot be doubted. As soon as the hierarchy relented, and positive-sum invention driven by monetary and nonmonetary profit became dignified and free, the rich *and* the poor became astonishingly better off. Even poor people in a modern economy have access to vaccination, air conditioning, automobiles, reliable birth control, the Internet, and flush toilets. The very Sun King himself had access instead to smallpox, open windows, bumpy carriages, leaky condoms, a small list of books, and relieving himself in the staircases of the Palace of Versailles.

If contrary to fact the exploited poor people were rich, not poor, and if the gain was all a matter of pass laws and violence, not mutually advantageous exchange, then some big parts of some societies, I repeat, could possibly benefit from violent imperialism abroad or violent apartheid at home. Yet that's not what the accounting and the magnitudes suggest about the British Empire, or about apartheid in South Africa or in the Southern United States (which South African commissions visited to learn how Jim Crow was done). Even enslaving *rich* people is not such a wonderfully enriching idea, as Hermann Göring's program of Continental enslavement showed. The formerly rich slaves didn't produce V-2 rockets or Messerschmitt Me 262 jet planes fast enough to tip the balance. And looting paintings from Paris and Amsterdam for the collections of the Führer and certain SS officers did not enrich ordinary Germans.

Voluntary trading with free, rich people, as against exploitation of enslaved, poor people, turns out to be the better plan. In fact the more the rich countries trade with each other (as they mainly do), the richer they become—though remember that the engine of growth is not trade such as this by itself, but innovation combined with trade. David Hume put it well: "The more the arts increase in any state the more will be its demands from its industrious neighbors. The inhabitants, having become opulent and skillful, desire to have every commodity in the utmost perfection."[16] As the financial historian Niall Ferguson has observed, Germany did better in "dominating" (which is mercantilist lingo for "trading with") Eastern Europe after 1945 and especially after 1989 than any of its imperial ambitions of the 1910s or its *lebensraumische* plans of the 1930s could achieve.[17] Ditto Japan. The Greater East Asia Co-Prosperity Sphere of Japanese militarism was economically speaking a dismal failure by comparison with Japan, Inc. And it is much nicer to be surrounded by Japanese trying to sell you TVs or automobiles than by Japanese armed with bayonets trying to stab your babies. We are made better off by having fellow citizens with whom we trade who are well educated and well trained and fully employed, even though we will then have to sacrifice having plentiful maids (the living rooms of middle-class people in Brazil and South Africa are strikingly clean, because they do have such maids). If exploiting *poor* people of color had been such a grand idea for rich white people, such as certain white Brazilians and white South Africans, then the white people in such countries would now be a lot better off than whites in Germany or Portugal or England or Holland, or the United States or Australia—places from which their ancestors came or to which their cousins went. They are not, and were not.

28

IT WAS NOT THE SHEER QUICKENING
OF COMMERCE

A perennial candidate for the Cause is "commercialization" and its dop-pelganger "monetization." The words dance with stage theories, such as Marx's, or with modernization theories like Weber's or Simmel's, or now with the neostage notions in the economists' growth theory. Like the middle class, the scope of commerce and money is always supposed to be rising, pretty much regardless of the period of prosperity considered. An economic historian, though, can tell you that the European economy, like the Greek or the Chinese or the Egyptian, has always been "monetized." The calcula-tive bent that is supposed to have arisen recently was in fact characteristic of all the mercantile or bureaucratic civilizations, that is, all cultures en-gaging in trade or taxation, at any rate among the traders, tax collectors, and temple priests themselves (admittedly, the extension of a quantitative rhetoric to ordinary people, not already merchants, was a characteristic part of the Bourgeois Revaluation). You can see utterly monetized thinking in Walter of Henley's treatise on estate management in the late thirteenth cen-tury as much as in courses on financial accounting at the Henley Business School in the early twenty-first century. The accounting is less sophisticated earlier, but among economic sophisticates early and late the counting in money ruled. In the European Middle Ages one could buy almost anything for cash—a husband, a marketplace, a kingdom, pardon for crimes, fewer years in purgatory. "But with these relics," says Chaucer about the Pardoner selling papal indulgences in the late fourteenth century, "when he found / A poor person dwelling on the land / Within a day he got out of him more money / Than the person got himself in two months."[1] In West African kingdoms in the seventeenth century, as in seventeenth-century Virginia, or seventeenth-century Istanbul, the very people, black or white, Africans or Russians, were for sale. Buyers and sellers in all ages thought in terms of money. And there have always been buyers and sellers, since we learned to talk. Offering money or a money equivalent like weighed coils of silver to get something is the only alternative to stealing it or begging for it or taking it by seigneurial right.

An economist will tell you, therefore, that (somewhat surprisingly viewed from outside economics) the history of money is not the same thing as the history of prosperity, and that money certainly did not cause industrialization. Historians who are not also economists suppose for example that a new industrial economy must have arisen from Spanish silver flowing into Europe and China in the so-called Price Revolution (whose rate of inflation, by the way, was a mere 1.4 percent a year: some "revolution"; the Ming inflation in China at the time, accommodated by paper money, was vastly higher; the worldwide inflation during the 1970s and 1980s, with by then an exclusively paper currency, was 8 percent per year, doubling the price level in less than one fifth of the time it took in the sixteenth century). After all, the noneconomists say, a commercial economy is about money, isn't it? And surely, they declare, the Price Revolution *caused* falling real wages, and therefore higher profits for protocapitalists, because "wages always lag behind prices." And indeed the Price Revolution itself must have been caused by rising population, which drove up food prices, yes?

The economist replies gently to all these indignant questions: no, dear. In her view—admitting its strangeness, though affirming its truth—the form and volume of money is largely irrelevant to deeper economic currents. Money, the economist says, is a veil. What matters for real enrichment, she continues (are you taking notes?), are the real, not monetary, magnitudes: real output, real wages, relative prices, real innovations in the way things are made. We eat pounds of meat, not dollars' worths. The money price of meat increased by a factor of four in the truly great inflation of the 1970s and 1980s (the fastest worldwide in history, putting ancient and early modern worldwide inflations in the shade, a quadrupling of the price level in fifteen years instead of the hundred years it took in the sixteenth century). We will therefore be perpetually startled if we keep remembering the money prices back in the good old days, when a Coke sold for a nickel. We get sticker shocked, like the protagonist's elderly dad in David Lodge's novel *Nice Work*.

Yet if meanwhile our money incomes have increased also by a factor of four, then in truth we are no worse off. And it has to be so. To the last sixpence the money spent by consumers and governments and builders has to be equal to the money earned by workers and stockholders and landlords. After the inflation, other things equal, we collectively get the same poundage of meat as we did earlier for the same sacrifice of hours of work or checks from our pensions. This or that person can be hurt. The average person cannot.

It is often alleged that the Price Revolution was caused by *increasing* population. "No, no, no," says the economist, now seriously vexed, "for Lord's sake, no!"[2] To be sure, population growth in Europe during the fifteenth and sixteenth centuries made labor less valuable relative to land, which is why real wages fell. The average worker in Shakespeare's time did in fact eat notably less bread and meat than his great-great-great-great-grandfather had in Sir Thomas Malory's time. You can visualize it as more agricultural workers than usual showing up at the farmer's gate on a Monday morning of April 1600 looking for work. The farmer says, "All right. I'll take more of you, but will set you to work doing less urgent tasks at lower wages relative to the price of the barley and wheat and wool that I sell. Ned, we'll do some additional harrowing for spring wheat on the Church Field. John, go chase the crows away from new-sown barley in the Nether Field." The technique of making things did not improve. On account of the falling price of labor relative to land the economy used a different but routinely available recipe. Labor substituted for land, as it did at the time in China. More labor on the acreage was the right recipe in 1600 for a newly labor-rich economy. Yet it was not itself an innovation in the book of recipes—not iron-tipped plows (China in 500 BCE), not clover in the fields (Holland and East Anglia in 1300), not mechanical harvesting (Illinois in the 1830s), not hybrid corn (Iowa in the 1950s).

Yet the amount of silver and gold money had nothing to do with the falling ratios of money wages to money prices, which is the falling *real* wage, pence to the worker per day divided by pence per loaf he eats. There were pence on both sides, which cancel out, leaving a number in units of loaves to be eaten per day of labor. Rising population did cause the *real* price of grain to rise, since a larger number of people pressed against the available land, while manufactured cloth, which used little land, was not so pressed. But a rising relative price of grain, one commodity among many, a land-intensive one, would not be the cause of the Price Revolution.[3] When the otherwise insightful Joyce Appleby casually mentions the sixteenth century's "inflation caused by high food prices" the economist grits her teeth.[4] Relative prices of food against cloth and iron, the economist argues, have nothing to do with absolute, money prices. One could equally well argue that if population had instead declined, and the price of labor-intensive goods like cloth had therefore risen relative to grain, then *that* would have caused an "inflation." So, in such a fractured logic, you see, *everything* causes inflation. Every change in relative prices, wheat against cloth, *up or down*, makes prices in general relative to silver go higher. Evidently something is wrong. The reductio shows that using relative prices to talk about general inflation is not sensible. (Admittedly, the talk is common. Even some misled economists think that a rise in, say, oil prices relative to bricks is especially inflationary. Talk of a "core" rate of inflation is of this character, embodied in the official if illogical declarations issuing monthly from the Bureau of Labor Statistics.)[5]

In fact rising population in the sixteenth century, supposing for a moment that it was all that happened (there was after all at the same time that notable rise in the amount of silver and gold from the New World, and, as the economic historian John Munro (2003) stresses, silver from Central European mines, and debasements of coinage by needy governments), would have forced an existing stock of silver and gold to do more work in transactions. The only way that could be accomplished is by *reducing* the amount of money needed to buy bread—a great deflation, as I said, not an inflation.[6] If population is supposed to be the driving force, it would have driven prices down, not up.

∞

And for some of the same reasons, the economist is suspicious of the story of "monetization." As in the stories of foreign trade or stories of environmental disaster or stories of institutions of property rights, the story gets part of its plausibility from imagining a world bereft. Suppose we had *no* trees at all? Suppose we had *no* trade? Suppose we had *no* private property? Suppose we had *no* monetary means of effecting a deal? In all cases, though, the relevant economic and historical question is what would happen with a little more or less trees, foreign trade, property rights, or monetary means of payment. The answer in the case of "monetization" is that it seems implausible on its face that *highly* advantageous trades were made impossible by an absence merely of a convenient and modern-looking means of payment, such as Spanish coins, or stably supported pounds-sterling paper money, or Visa cards. The economic logic is that when a very advantageous deal is to be made between a peasant offering wheat or rice and a town dweller offering pottery or cloth, both sides have a large incentive to make it happen, somehow. In historical fact they figure out some way to make the payment—in iron bars, say, or cowry shells, or cloth itself, or rice itself. The abundance, durability, portability, and therefore the convenience of a means of payment are secondary considerations. They matter, but usually not much. If copper or cowry shells are rare, their relative price goes up, which is to say that deflation occurs. So what? Money is a veil. The deals still get made. To put the point in economic jargon, the means of payment is endogenous, generated by economic forces internal to the deals made. "Monetization" is not some manna dropping from the skies to nourish baby capitalists. American silver did not "stimulate" European commerce, as is often claimed. Dropping more money on Europe merely caused all prices and wages and rents to rise, with no gain to commercial profits; and anyway the silver ended up in China and India—with no apparent "stimulus" there.

Contrary to what most educated people believe, Europe and certainly England was from the earliest times thoroughly "monetized" and was nothing like a "subsistence" or "barter" economy. It would be difficult otherwise to explain, to take an early sort of evidence, the English *danegelt* beginning in 991, assessed in silver and paid to the Vikings, or the hoards of precious metals found in England at every chronological level from the pre-Roman era on, or the ubiquity of money measures in the earliest records, such as the Domesday Book of 1086. Such facts have been known for a long time, and recently their meaning has become still clearer. As the leading scholar of trade in the "Dark Ages" (that is, before the eleventh century) wrote in 2001, "Economic historians are moving increasingly to the view that the advanced regions of the Frankish economy [that is, of Charlemagne and his son Louis the Pious, ruling over all of France, most of Germany, and the north of Italy 771–840] were more monetized than almost anyone dreamed three decades ago."[7]

True, commerce expanded. The quarrel here is with the common view that "commercialization" is some force outside the deal-making of individuals. The otherwise brilliant historian of China Peter Perdue, for example, speaks of "monetization" and "commercialization" of the Ming and then the Qing economy.[8] What such an expansion means, however, is that more deals were made. The desire to make deals did not change, as Perdue on reflection would certainly affirm: he would agree with Max Weber (and me) that greediness for deals is universal. As Weber put it, recall, "The impulse to acquisition, pursuit of gain, of money, of the greatest possible amount of money, . . . has been common to all sorts and conditions of men at all times and in all countries of the earth, wherever the objective possibility of it is or has been given." What changed was the ease of making the deals—and as I said, that is normally a secondary consideration. What changed were "transaction costs," in the phrase of the great economist Ronald Coase (1910–), that is, the costs of getting together to make a deal—transportation costs, the costs of robbers on the highway or in the market, the costs of trust, the costs of insurance, the costs of using credit, the costs of getting coins and bills, the costs of negotiation, the costs of taboo, the costs of sneering at the bourgeoisie. All these make deals more expensive, and many of them are directly measurable. When such costs fall, "commercialization" takes place. What the economist and economic historian Douglass North got right (amongst a good deal that he got wrong) is that we should focus on the history of the transaction costs—about which there is ample documentation—and cease believing that there is something separately measurable "spreading" to make people and their taxing governments rich, called "commercialization" or "monetization" (neither of which, by the way, are technical terms in economics, though they sound like they are). That's what's wrong with the way most historians think about the matter.

On the other hand, the economists have their own confusions in dealing with "commercialization." Economists want the modern world to come out of the expansion of what they understand, namely, commerce. Modern growth theorists in particular are entranced by endogenous theories in which growth leads to growth. Voilà! No need for rhetoric or history, about which most economists have succeeded in remaining ignorant. The economist Allyn Young, who inspired modern growth theory, wrote in 1928 that

> it is dangerous to assign to any single factor the leading role in that continuing economic revolution which has taken the modern world so far away from the world of a few hundred years ago. But is there any other factor which has a better claim to that role than the persisting search for markets? No other hypothesis so well unites economic history and economic theory. The Industrial Revolution of the eighteenth century has come to be generally regarded, not as a cataclysm brought about by certain inspired improvements in industrial technique, but as a

series of changes related in an orderly way to prior changes in industrial organization and to the enlargement of markets.

The conclusion was premature.

A recent example among scores of such hopeful arguments is provided by a clever paper by Klaus Desmet and Stephen Parente, "The Evolution of Markets and the Revolution of Industry: A Quantitative Model of England's Development, 1300–2000." They write:

> This paper argues that an economy's transition from Malthusian stagnation to modern growth requires markets to reach a critical size, and competition to reach a critical level of intensity. By allowing an economy to produce a greater variety of goods [see de Vries 2008b], a larger market makes goods more substitutable, raising the price elasticity of demand, and lowering mark-ups. Firms must then become larger to break even, which facilitates amortizing the fixed costs of innovation. We demonstrate our theory in a dynamic general equilibrium model calibrated to England's long-run development and explore how various factors affect the timing of takeoff.[9]

Interesting—though it depends on an assumed connection between the size of industries and the size of firms which I find dubious, at any rate as a Chicago School economist (though as one of the last students of Edward Chamberlain at Harvard I can see what they mean). The assumption is rejected by most of the evidence.

And another of the many troubles with such an argument from "markets reaching a critical size" is that the largest markets in the world 1300–1700 — which is the relevant era for the beginning of all this—having the greatest variety of goods and lowest markups and the highest amortization of the costs of innovation under the dubious assumption that the size of industries determines the size of firms—were in places a little east and west of the Indian Ocean. The smallest markets in the Eurasian oceans were European. And the expanding markets 1700–2000 were worldwide, not English. And the biggest markets in Europe were on the Continent. And yet England alone started it.

29

NOR THE STRUGGLE OVER THE SPOILS

Fernand Braudel's (1902–1985) astonishing product of his old age, Civilization and Capitalism, Fifteenth-Eighteenth Century (1979), and especially volume 2, *The Wheels of Commerce*, is the most full exposition of the idea by a historian that the modern world came naturally out the sheer expansion of commerce. Throughout *Wheels* Braudel admires markets, yet disdains people he calls "capitalists." "As a rule," he says, "[iron] foundries were capitalist, but iron-mining remained under free enterprise."[1] It gradually becomes clear that what he means by a "market" or "free enterprise" is something like the routine provisioning of a society. Capitalism "cannot . . . be confused with classic market transactions."[2] One goes to the Lindengracht market on Saturday in Amsterdam expecting to buy cheese or broccoli for a little less than what is charged by the two Albert Heijn supermarkets nearby. One does not expect enormous savings, and neither do the stall owners expect enormous profits. The provisioning is routine, and the profit, as Alfred Marshall's tradition puts it, following his *Principles of Economics* (1890), is "normal," not "super-normal."

Braudel argues that peddlers 1100–1789 slowly gave way to shopkeepers, and that the merchant fairs such as Champagne's slowly gave way to warehousing entrepôts like Genoa or Amsterdam. (In 1983 an American professor of history rather uncharitably compiled a collage of his undergraduates' exam-time versions of these events: "After a revival of infantile commerce slowly creeping into Europe, merchants appeared. Some were sitters and some were drifters. They roamed from town to town exposing themselves and organized big fairies in the countryside.")[3] Such developments, Braudel says, were routine matters of population density and the cost of transport. Before Germany's population boomed in the sixteenth century, the economical way to sell ribbons to Germans was by peddling, drifting from village to village or farm to farm in the style of *Oklahoma* or Chaucer's wandering merchant. Denser population of course makes it worthwhile for a peddler to settle in town, and become a sitter rather than roaming around exposing himself. The fairs of medieval times developed into the warehouses in Amsterdam of early modern times—which were able, Braudel reports, to hold nine years' worth of Dutch grain consumption, had that been their main use (it was not: it was to hold the consumption of grain, lumber, wine, cloth, salt, spices for the next few months of all the lands near the Rhine and the Meuse). In 1650 an English writer exclaimed about the mystery of Dutch success: "The abundance of corn grows in the East Kingdoms [Poland], but the great storehouses for grain to serve Christendom and the heathen countries (in time of dearth) is in the Low Countries. The mighty vineyards, and store of salt, is in France and Spain, but the great vintage [of casked or bottled wine] and [the] staple [marketplace] of salt is in the Low Countries."[4] The warehousers—the great merchants of Holland—were able to settle down on the Herengracht, and not dust their feet in twenty fairs a year, because the Dutch *fluyt*, broad of beam and light of crew, cut costs of shipping between the Baltic and the North Sea. Such economies were reversible. The Thirty Years' War cut the population of Germany by a third, and the peddlers once more hit the road. Over the longer run the little retail peddlers and the big wholesale merchants settled down, and no "capitalist" profit ensued.

By contrast to the honest cheese vendor along the Lindengracht, or by contrast for that matter to the honest if more fancy and more convenient and more expensive Albert Heijn grocery store on the Haarlemmerdijk, a "capitalist" in Braudel's scheme makes big profits. The profits are abnormal, supernormal, "quasi-rents" as Marshall called them, the short-run profits before entry brings back normality and routine. Braudel's capitalist makes his quasi-rents by Mafia techniques. He corrupts governments. He organizes government-sponsored monopolies. To defend his trading post in West Africa, his abnormally profitable turf, he is willing to engage in shocking violence, shocking at any rate to those who experienced European imperial commerce 1500–1960. He eagerly leaps into any new opportunity to buy *very* low in, say, Batavia in Indonesia or later in Kinshasa in Congo the better to sell *very* high, ten or twenty times higher, in Amsterdam or Antwerp. "It was along these trading-chains," for example from China to Europe, "with their ample opportunities for fraud that the real profits were to be made."[5] At "the pinnacle of the trading community" in early modern times, "this commanding height," one could hope for "legal or actual monopoly and the possibility of price manipulation."[6] Capital "takes up residence" in the places where a "hunt for maximization and profits," which were "already implicit rules of [early modern] capitalism," could succeed.[7] The capitalist sneers at the suckers who work 9:00 to 5:00 for merely normal profits. He is a crook, a player, a wise guy. No wonder Braudel doesn't love such a "capitalist." Who except Carmela could love Tony Soprano, really?

Braudel was very far from being an orthodox Marxist, at any rate by the high standard of, say, his contemporary the brilliant Stalinist Jean-Paul Sartre, or the next generation, such as the brilliant wife murderer Louis Althusser. Like all of us, however, he imbibed in his youth many Marxist ideas about how the economy functioned, ideas echoing through followers of Marx like Werner Sombart (who was Braudel's master) or Karl Polanyi or even revisionists of Marx such as Max Weber. You can't avoid Marxist ideas any more than you can avoid Darwinian or Freudian ideas. I can't, either. They're part of the rhetoric of the age, its commonplaces. (Yet awareness of rhetorical techniques, what Walter Lippmann called in the 1920s "the pictures in our heads," makes it possible to spot one's own commonplaces, at least sometimes, and to worry about their aptness. And one gets very good at spotting *other* people's commonplaces. By contrast, if you think of language as being merely a transparent system of signs to "convey" representations of pre-existing things you will often miss its persuasive slant.)

Braudel for example puts great emphasis on accumulate, accumulate. "Whether one likes it or not, there was, even in the pre-industrial era, a form of economic activity irresistibly evocative of this word [capitalist accumulation] and no other . . . identified as the realm of investment and of a high rate of capital formation."[8] He says it was "attached to the idea of money, of wealth for its own sake"—which is the ancient charge of "endless" accumulation.[9] And he adopts the Marxist supposition that exploitation is automatic in the employment relation, "the workers shorn of all but their labor power."[10] "The master boatmen, who lived in comfortable houses and married their daughters to each other, formed an elite, living off the painful labor of others."[11]

Braudel distinguished three levels of economic life, the material at home, the small market in the village, and the big market of capitalism worldwide. The line between the small market and the capitalists, he argues, is written in ethics. The "capitalists" cheat, and live off the painful labor of others, and because they are big-time cheaters and livers-off others, they get ennobled rather than hung. "Mr. Moneybags" (*Herr Geldsack*) was Marx's indignant characterization of such a character. "The triptych I have described," Braudel wrote in 1977, "—material life, the market economy, and the capitalist economy—is still an amazingly valid explanation, even though capitalism today has expanded in scope."[12] In quoting this claim the economist Alan Heston, who is less amazed, remarks that "it is a structure of thinking that is rather alien to trends in economic research that seek to explain the behavior of households, markets and business firms using similar [that is, similar to each other: maximization reigns] economic models."[13]

What Braudel gets wrong because of his *marxisant*, rise-of-classes rhetoric is his claim that there is a line between normal marketeers and big-time capitalists. A bourgeois economist does not think so. She does not mean simply that there's no *bright* line. She means that there's no line at all. Market participants *are* capitalists. You are, for example. True, you don't have Scrooge McDuck piles of moneybags to back your investment ideas—at any rate until you can with sweet words persuade Scrooge to invest. Yet when you bought your home, or invested in an education, or "invested" in a fur coat against the Chicago winter, you were engaging in the same activities as the masters of high finance. A worker is a capitalist of her skills. Every market, *haut* or *petit*, operates by buying low and selling high, expecting a capital gain on your condo to finance your retirement in south Texas, expecting your education to keep you employed, expecting the fur coat to yield "profits" in warmth over many winters to come. It's of course why people enter markets in the first place, to buy something for less than they can provide it by themselves. *Everyone* earns profit in trade, local or international. That is why we do it. If not achieved by force or fraud or bribery, profits are good, whether the steady return that compensates for investment in capital such as skill at hairdressing or the quasi-rent that draws investors into innovative fields like computers to the benefit of almost all of us.

Braudel's vision is of a routine world of normal profits for little people. Economists call it the "stationary state." It is not just normal and steady. It is stagnant. By contrast, Braudel claims that innovation—the modern

innovation that has made the average poor person rich by historical standards—depended on bribery, force, and fraud. No. Most it depended on
Kirzner's "alertness." That is, it depended on noticing opportunities for supernormal profit (and using them by the exercise of internal and external
persuasion, a necessary linguistic supplement to Kirzner's story). One can
notice that the booming South Loop of Chicago could really use a high-end
grocery store, such as Fox and Obel. The opportunity will make Fox and
Obel great profits in future years, worth as a capital sum now, say, $1 mil-
lion (I offer such persuasion gratis to Messrs. Fox and Obel—with the uneasy reflection that the advice is probably worth about what I am charging).
A million dollars is pocket change by the standard of a really big capitalist
like Donald Trump. Yet it is nonetheless innovation, and achieves, as the
Donald's first big real-estate project in Manhattan did, supernormal profit
from being the first to realize a new allocation of the Commodore-Hyatt
Hotel as the Grand. At least Fox and Obel will achieve such supernormal
profits until the competition wakes up and two or three more high-end grocery stores open in the South Loop.

The analogy extends even to the misbehavior that Braudel assigns to the
capitalist sphere. The *marxisant* vision attributes supernormal profit to *large*
capital accumulation and to *outrageous* behavior. Neither is correct. On the
whole you make a little or big fortune by alertness, not by theft, at any rate
in a well-ordered community of laws (on which North and I and all economists agree: without laws nothing can happen—although the case of the
routinely corrupt U.S.A. ["I seen my opportunities"] shows that the laws do
not need to be enforced in every jot and tittle for innovation to prosper).[14]
True, the oil executives who were granted numerous opportunities to chat
up vice president Dick Cheney when he ran the U.S. government are going
to earn more dollars than a local store owner complaining to her Chicago al-
derman that the opening of a WalMart will ruin her. Yet there's no difference
in principle—or, adjusting for scale, in practice—between the two cases of
lobbying. Alertness, not mainly corruption or monopoly (though unhappily
these, too, occur), drives a successful economy in which everyone, not just
the wise guys, get rich. Something broke into the rhetorical world of Europe
that made alertness explode—in Holland during the seventeenth century
and later in England and in Scotland and in British America; and then in the
very early nineteenth century in Belgium and France and the Rhineland. It
was dignity and liberty for the bourgeoisie, whether big capitalists or small.

On the other hand, Braudel had one important economic argument quite right, which some others—Weber, for example—did not. Namely: routine behavior yields routine, nonsupernormal profits. Braudel quoted Weber on sobriety and the like, what Weber called Protestant behavior (though even Weber admitted that such behavior was praised in numerous handbooks of proper business behavior by undoubted Catholics in Northern Italy, two centuries before the Calvinists, well after Calvin, got hold of the idea). Braudel knew, however, that sobriety and savings and the like do not yield supernormal profits. And the modern world is without doubt supernormal. Sobriety and savings are not novelties. They are not new ideas productive of unusual gain, private and social.

∞

Yet in another respect Braudel is an orthodox marxoid—a rhetoric, admittedly, that he shares with most economists and historians. He believes that the key to innovation is the *accumulation* of such profits. What the writer and economic historian Herbert Feis, speaking of Britain in the late nineteenth century, called a "free financial force," Braudel argues, stood ready in the West around 1800 to shift its Mafia-style attentions to manufacturing when that activity rather than long-distance trade in spices and china was the one in which to make supernormal profits—when "industry had become a [supernormal] profit-making sector."[15] It was, he claimed in effect, like the Mafia shifting from bootlegging to gambling to the trade in recreational drugs.

We've seen that the "original accumulation" part of Braudel's way of narrating the birth of the modern is unhelpful. But the other half is unhelpful, too, the emphasis on accumulation even if not "original. The surplus value stored up by Mr. Moneybags—*pace* Marx—is not what propels modern innovation. Such profit is merely a hope tempting to the imagination. Profit comes mostly from productivity, that is, from new ideas, creative destruction, not as the pessimists of the left and right insist mostly from monopoly. Paul Sweezy, Paul Baran, J. K. Galbraith, Stephen Marglin, William Lazonick, Bernard Elbaum, Edward Lorenz, Jon Cohen, Robert Allen, and other economic scholars on the left—an astonishing group presenting a scientific challenge largely ignored by the Samuelsonian/Friedmanian orthodoxy in modern economics—have been claiming for a long time that innovation was determined by the struggle over the spoils (in a phrase, by "monopoly capitalism"), for good [say Galbraith and Lazonick] or evil [say Baran and Sweezy]). It isn't—though as usual the economics and the politics shape the details, if not the tide.

The left-institutionalist argument was anticipated by Marx in 1846: "Since 1825, the invention and use of machinery resulted solely from the war between masters and workmen."[16] The left can claim that this or that change of technique—factories (Marglin) or mule spinning (Lazonick) or enclosure (Allen) was partly motivated by the share of the spoils, not by efficiency.[17] Lazonick summarized the program in his graceful presidential address to the Business History Conference in 1991: "For better or for worse, it has been the strategies of people entering into social relationships in attempts to control their lives that has shaped the markets for labor, capital, and products that have come to characterize the modern industrial world."[18] The idea is that the show was run not by invisible hands but by visible organizations—unions, corporations, conspiracies, politics. The wider literature of Marxist history, as in the writings on medieval and early modern Europe by Robert Brenner or Rodney Hilton or Immanuel Wallerstein, may be summarized therefore as "conflict theory."[19]

The left-wing (and the Schumpeterian and the institutionalist) critics of Samuelsonian economics often make their case persuasively. In the one example of such matters in which I too am a little knowledgeable, the English enclosures, the leftish Robert Allen agreed in 1992 with me that conflict over the share of spoils accruing to this or that actor (especially the powerful ones such as the lord and the church) mattered a good deal, and that the rise in productivity was anyway small (I did the scientific work arriving at the conclusion in the 1970s when I was still a happily orthodox Samuelsonian/ Friedmanite economist).[20] Indeed, Lazonick's theme in a book of 1991 is likewise close to mine: as the economist Richard Langlois elegantly summarized it, "If 'the market' really is what neoclassical economics says it is, and if the neoclassical model is merely about adaptation and not about innovation, then 'the market' is and can be only adaptive and never innovative. In this syllogism lies the essence of Lazonick's argument: it is a myth that 'the market' can produce economic growth and industrial competitiveness."[21] Aside from the phrase "industrial competitiveness," Lazonick's is my argument, too. Sheer allocation can't produce the greatest surprise in economic history. Langlois and I differ with Lazonick only in stressing that actual markets are in fact sites of innovation as much as adaptation.

Yet dividing up the spoils from efficiency gains—one version of the organizational struggle that economists on the left from Marx to Galbraith have emphasized—was not mainly what made the modern world. The struggle by unions for higher wages and better working conditions has inspired many good songs and many good people. Clearly, say the songs, we gotta' go down and join the union; we need to fight for Harry Bridges and build the CIO; and we need to be a union maid when she fought for higher pay. "She'd show her card / To the National Guard, / And this is what she'd say:/ 'Oh, you can't scare me: / I'm stickin' to the union.'" But the fight to get a higher share of the pie for union members leaves out nonunion members, who were always a high percentage of the workforce in the United States. If the size of the pie is pretty much fixed—the underlying assumption of classical economics and of union logic—then higher pay for auto workers implies lower pay for auto mechanics, not something to be celebrated in songs by Woody Guthrie and history books by progressive historians. The economist H. Gregg Lewis painstakingly estimated the effect of unions 1967–1979 on wages of their members relative to comparable nonmembers and found it to be, as an upper bound, rather small: some 14 percent.[22] My uncle, who was himself a union electrician in Michigan, paid union wages for his employees gladly, he said, because he passed the expense on to the companies and hospitals and school buildings that he wired. Oh, good. But who pays that? Other workers. There's no one else to pay it. As Pogo famously said, "We has met the enemy, and he is us."

And if, as was on the contrary the case, the pie was in fact exploding, then a shift in the size of the slice going to workers as a whole (setting aside that it would in fact go only to the minority of union members) would anyway play a small role in the betterment of even those workers. Workers in the United States and elsewhere grew radically better off from 1800 on, and 1900 on, and even from 1970 on because of the Bourgeois Deal, not because they went down and joined the union. How do I know? Answer: the nonunion people shared nearly equally in the gain, even though they were paying as consumers for the fancier wages for union electricians in Michigan. The maximum of 14 percent of "concessions" extracted by bargaining or strike doesn't come close to accounting for the great magnitude of rise in the real wage. There's not enough profit—usually 10 or 15 percent of national income—to raise the level of the rest of national income by a factor of even two, that is, 100 percent, much less the factor of eighteen it in fact rose after 1800.

Expropriating 15 percent of national income claimed by the wretched profi-
teers and transferring it to the 85 percent earned by us workers raises our
income only 18 percent. That's a long, long way from 1,700 percent.

Nor did government under the Progressives or the New Dealers or Lyn-
don Johnson make people rich. One can agree that it is desirable to prevent
flammable factories from having locked doors, or that mines should not
routinely collapse, or that workers should have leisure, or that the wages of
people of color and of women should not be subject to sheer discrimination. But a powerful case can be made that such improvements in wages
and working conditions came *after* capitalist markets had delivered much
of them anyway, voluntarily in competing for labor, not before. Child labor
was falling in England long before it was outlawed. And in any event what
mainly made people better off was the gigantically larger pie. People earning
$80,000 a year to work as police will not accept seventy-hour workweeks
and rotten working conditions, and in historical fact they did not, quite
independent of the will of legislatures or the bargaining of unions.

Nor was the modern world made by the "organizational capabilities" that
Lazonick and Robert Reich and Lester Thurow and others emphasize, at any
rate not in the competitive and nationalistic way they feature. The capability of the Americans to organize mass production or the capabilities of the
Japanese to organize worker-management cooperation are in the long run
imitable, and if they are very good ideas they are in fact imitated. It didn't
take Germans long to imitate British organizing of steam factories, or the
British long to imitate American capabilities of assembly lines for making
autos. And in the medium run the capabilities often become discapabili-
ties, handicaps, when the economic environment that made them profitable changes. Thus Henry Ford's capability in mass production of black tin
lizzies became a handicap in the 1920s when faced by the novel capability of
General Motors in annual model changes and in servicing a middle-class
market. The storied excellence of the Japanese of the 1970s dissolved into the
Lost Decade of the 1990s. The Soviet capability in exploiting economies of
industrial scale under central planning in the 1930s became the handicap of
the 1980s. The capability of British engineering in bespoke tailoring of railway locomotives in the 1890s became the handicap of the 1960s. The shun-
ning of defectors that enforced contracts among, for example, Jewish traders
of North Africa in the Middle Ages became the handicap in early modern
times of not sufficiently attending to courts.[23]

What chiefly made the modern world was the gigantic size of the entirely unprecedented spoils of innovation in product and process and organization and intellectual life, together with a roughly egalitarian distribution of the spoils in the long run driven by the invisible hand of entry and competition. The inventor Richard Roberts, true, was directly employed by English cotton-textile manufacturers to produce a device to break the bargaining power of the mule spinners. It was an instance of the *visible* hand of conflict and institutional capability, in this case a capability to organize in order to crush the working man. Shame on them. Yet most inventions achieved their profitability—as indeed the self-actor in the event also did—by making costs lower for a given output, not by exploiting the workers (whether or not along the way the workers *did* get exploited). Praise them. Exploiting the workers, to repeat, like overseas imperialism, does not yield enough loot to explain rises of 100 percent, not to speak of 1,500 percent, in the productivity of all—including paradoxically the exploited workers themselves.

Normal profits are ordinarily earned not by conflict or exploitation but by alertness to the right way of doing business—running a store as well or better than other people do, say—and *super*normal profits are earned by superior alertness, applying really new ideas, such as Sam Walton of WalMart exhibited. The piled-up alertnesses have made us rich. The Astors and the Carnegies and Waltons make the money in the first generation by alertness in the fur business or steel manufacturing or retail trade. (And they also employ an occasional but well-placed bribe, it must be admitted. But this is true of little capitalists, too, and is rampant in many socialist countries, or indeed in any little command economy, of the firm itself or of the household. And by the standards of the time, Carnegie and Rockefeller and Walton, contrary to journalism about them by the muckrakers, or muck-inventors, were in their dealings notably ethical.) Yet when everyone figures out how to get oil into tank cars, or cheap steel from Masabi ore, or close monitoring of retail inventories by computers, the profit goes back to normal, and we, poor exploited things, are left with cheaper kerosene and cheaper steel, and retail goods 30 percent cheaper than charged by our good neighbors the local hardware and clothing monopolists on Main Street.

30

EUGENIC MATERIALISM DOESN'T WORK

An extreme materialist hypothesis explaining the Industrial Revolution would be simply genetic. Its crudest form, as I have noted, would be sheer British racism. Scratch a modern member of the right-wing clerisy and you will often uncover such flatly racist ideas. "Having British genes is required for industrialization." "Africans will never develop, because, you know, they're inferior." Few social or historical scientists nowadays believe such notions straightforwardly (though it is well worth remembering that in 1910 a great many historical and biological scientists, and some of the best, most assuredly did). A pretty close approximation of crude British racism, however, has been asserted recently by the economic historian Gregory Clark, an old friend of mine, in his *A Farewell to Alms*, modestly subtitled *A Brief Economic History of the World* (2007). The book contains much that honors the energy and imagination of its author. The final scientific judgment, however, has been that the book serves as a cautionary tale about the excesses of dogmatic materialism.

The argument goes like this:

> For England. . . . 1250–1800. . . . the richest men had twice as many surviving children as the poorest. . . . The superabundant children of the rich had to . . . move down. . . . Craftsmen's sons became laborers, merchant's sons petty traders, large landholder's sons smallholders. . . . Patience, hard work, innovation, innovativeness, education . . . were thus spread biologically throughout the population. . . . The embedding of bourgeois values into the culture. . . . [in] China and Japan did not move as rapidly because . . . their upper social strata were only modestly more fecund. . . . Thus there was not the same cascade of children from the educated classes down the social scale. . . . England's advantage lay in the rapid cultural,

and potentially also genetic, diffusion of the values of the economically successful through society.[1]

The means of (re)production determine the superstructure. Social existence determines consciousness. Rich people proliferated, and by a social Darwinian struggle the poor and incompetent died out, leaving a master race of Englishmen with the consciousness to conquer the world.

Certainly it is a bold hypothesis, and was bold when first articulated by social Darwinists such as Charles Davenport and Francis Galton in the century before last. Clark defends it energetically, if narrowly. In fact, if the hypothesis were true it would fit smoothly with my own argument that a rhetorical change made the modern world. Clark says that "there must have been informal, self-reinforcing social norms in all preindustrial societies that discouraged innovation."[2] Precisely: the norms of antibourgeois aristocrats and clerics did discourage innovation, until the Venetians temporarily and on a local scale, the Dutch temporarily and on a wider scale, and at last the English and Scots permanently and on a world scale repealed the norms.

In one and a half pages toward the middle of his book Clark deals briskly with the numerous alternatives to his own materialist hypothesis: "Social historians may invoke the Protestant Reformation, . . . intellectual historians the Scientific Revolution . . . or the Enlightenment. . . . But a problem with these invocations of movers from outside the economic realm is that they merely push the problem back one step."[3] That's a good point, always a good point. Yet it is symmetrical—a material and economic proximate cause (a high birthrate among the rich, for example; or the invention of a steam engine with separate condenser) can have an ideal and rhetorical ultimate cause (an ideology of glorifying the family line, for example; or imagined experiments with heating and cooling the steam cylinder). Clark's own, and sole, case of pushing an ideal cause back into material causes is to ask why "after more than a thousand years of entrenched Catholic dogma" (set aside that such a characterization of medieval Christian theology might be a trifle lacking in nuance, and derivative in fact from crude anti-Catholic propaganda since Hume and Voltaire or indeed since Luther himself) "an obscure German preacher [was] able to effect such a profound change in the way ordinary people conceived religious beliefs?"

Clark, however, like doubting Pilate, does not stay for an answer. He readily admits in the same passage that "ideologies may transform the economic attitudes of societies." Yet he has no scientific interest in the causes of ideologies, unless they fit his notion of the material (that is, familial) inheritance of acquired characteristics ("and perhaps even the genes," says Clark). He has not reflected on the history of the Reformation, or on the Scientific Revolution, or on the Enlightenment, or on the Bourgeois Revaluation. To get rid of such pesky rhetorical factors he reaches at once for a materialist lemma: "But ideologies are themselves the expression of fundamental attitudes in part derived from the economic sphere."

Only the phrase "in part," a fleeting tribute to intellectual balance, keeps his sentence from being orthodox historical materialism. As it was put in 1848 by a pair of historical materialists: "Man's ideas, views and conceptions, in one word, man's consciousness, changes with every change in the conditions of his material existence, in his social relations and in his social life. What else does the history of ideas prove, than that intellectual production changes its character in proportion as material production is changed?"[4] Or as Marx by himself wrote eleven years later, "It is not the consciousness of men that determines their existence, but, on the contrary, their social existence determines their consciousness."[5] Or as Engels wrote another eighteen years later, "The final causes of all social changes and political revolutions are to be sought, not in men's brains, not in man's better insight into eternal truth and justice, but in changes in the modes of production and exchange. They are to be sought, not in the *philosophy*, but in the *economics* of each particular epoch."[6]

In this respect, Clark implies, we social scientists are all vulgar Marxists. Ideas are merely "the expression of fundamental attitudes in part derived from the economic sphere." He's right in his implied history of the social sciences: most social scientists 1890–1980 were indeed instinctive historical materialists. But the intellectually temperate beginning of the phrase "*in part* derived from the economic sphere" in Clark's sentence is not cashed. Rather, the check is written out but then absentmindedly torn up before our eyes. "There is, however," Clark declares in the next sentence, "no need to invoke such a *deus ex machina*" as a change in rhetoric. His own chapter 6 fully explains on materialist grounds (with its own unexplained *deus*—high breeding rates among the rich) "the forces leading to a more patient, less violent, harder-working, more literate, and more thoughtful society," namely, the bourgeois society that he and I join in admiring. In Clark's book, that's the end of ideology. A historian of the Dutch Republic, Anne McCants, similarly claims on slender evidence that a compassionate motivation for

transfers from the Dutch wealthy to the poor is "unlikely" and "can be neither modeled nor rationally explained." By "rationally explained" she means
"explained by Max-U, prudence-only, material interests." Anything else is a
mere screen for true, that is material, motives. Long before her, at the height
of the marxoid age 1890–1980, the historian Hugh Trevor Roper had advanced a similar axiom, that "in politics [Prudence Only political ambition]
is naturally by far the most potent" cause, as indeed Engels still earlier had
claimed that "interests, requirements, and demands of the various classes
were concealed behind a religious screen."[7]

Such evidence-poor side remarks are signs of the historical rhetoric prevalent 1890–1980—what Michael Novak calls "the materialist assumptions
and prejudices of the twentieth century"—that a human's consciousness
changes with every change in the conditions of her material existence, *and
only with such changes.*[8] Thus Durkheim in his great book *The Elementary
Forms of Religious Life* of 1912 argued that ritual, not doctrine, was the heart
of religion, because ritual performed the latent function of unifying a society. After all, what else does the history of ideas prove? It proves that ideas
don't matter, and that unifying a society must be the point of religion—not
all that nonsense about, say, a god who died. Look at the history of stoicism
or Protestantism or the abolition of slavery, or the history of Christianity
or mathematics or the liberations of the 1960s. All of them, obviously, were
motivated largely, probably exclusively, by material causes. Interests. Money.
Profit. The birthrate. Surely.

John Milton wrote to the contrary that books "are as lively, and as vigorously productive, as those fabulous dragon's teeth; and being sown up and
down, may chance to spring up armed men."[9] The Levellers of the 1640s,
writes their historian David Wootton, "did not envisage a commercial society of the sort that was actually dominant in early Stuart England, a society
of chartered companies and great capitalists; they hoped rather to establish a
nation of shopkeepers." All their other proposals took centuries to establish,
in what Wootton calls an "extraordinary paradigm shift, which marks the
birth of modern political theory"—manhood suffrage, a written constitution, non-self-incrimination (freedom from waterboarding, one might say),
right to counsel, liberty of religion, liberty of speech.[10] Yet remarkably in
England, a definite if small move toward liberty of internal trade (for poor
people as well as rich: in other words, the establishment of a nation of shopkeepers) came to pass, in the old age of the last surviving Leveller.

Clark, who admits that such rhetoric may transform economic attitudes, would nonetheless wisely urge us to push the problem back one more step: why the rhetorical change? A very good point, I repeat, always a good point. It would imply, *if we were committed to historical materialism,* that some cause for the rhetoric must be sought in the means of production or reproduction. Under the Materialist Postulate a rhetoric *never* changes independent of economics or demography—and certainly never as a result of causes within rhetoric itself such as the invention of the novel or the logic of Pascal-Nicole-Bayle in theology; not even as a result of such causes as the political settlement in England of 1689 or the obsession with Protestant egalitarianism of all believers in Holland and Scotland from the mid-sixteenth century or the ordinary man's unprecedented involvement in church governance and then in politics in Holland, England, and Scotland 1585 to 1660 or the chances of war, some of them mere effective words that left the New Model Army in possession of the English king and his country in 1645 ("I had rather have a plain russet-coated captain that knows what he fights for, and loves what he knows," wrote Cromwell in 1643, "than that which you call a gentleman and is nothing else"). Any noneconomic and merely rhetorical change (the materialists believe without thinking about it very much) is always to be derived from the economic/demographic sphere, where we have hard if dubious numbers and marxoid if erroneous theories. Intellectual production changes its character in proportion as material production is changed.

It has been a long time since even the Marxists depended on such a Materialist Postulate. The Italian communist theorist Antonio Gramsci, for example—whom Michael Walzer describes as "a rare bird in the twentieth century, an *innocent* communist"—spoke of such "economism" as an error.[11] While in prison in Fascist Italy during the 1930s Gramsci wrote that "the claim (presented as an essential postulate of historical materialism) that every fluctuation of politics and ideology can be presented and expounded as an immediate expression of the structure, must be contested in theory as primitive infantilism." Marxism, he contended, "is itself a superstructure, . . . the terrain on which determinate social groups [for example, the proletariat] become conscious of their own social being." The base and superstructure form a "historical bloc," quite different from the imaginings of bourgeois theorists of economism, in that the bloc is not *mere* theorizing but fulfills the dialectic of history. Gramsci claimed plausibly that in detailed political writings, such as *The Eighteenth Brumaire of Louis Bonaparte*, Marx himself was cautious in using the Materialist Postulate, and gave room for accident and "internal necessities of an organizational character" and the difficulty of identifying just what is at a particular moment the base or the structure that is supposed to be limiting thought.[12] Gramsci himself is chiefly important in the history of European socialism for denying that materialism does all the work. The bourgeoisie survived, he said, because its intellectuals had done their job and made capitalism seem natural. Gramsci's very career, and especially the career of his writings after his death—anticipating anti-Stalinist Euro-communism, as Walzer notes—illustrates the importance of mere nonmaterial ideas.[13]

And certainly Lenin, who established in 1902 the Bolshevik line against an "economism" such as that of Karl Kautsky, believed that ideas were necessary to inflame the working class to action. He asked, What Is to Be Done, and answered: do *not* wait for the material conditions of the workers to cause the workers to attain spontaneously the idea of revolution. On the contrary, "Class political consciousness can be brought to the workers *only from without*, that is only from outside the economic struggle. . . . The social democrats [by which he meant at the time the revolutionary socialists like himself] must *go among all classes of the population*; they must dispatch units of their army [of ideas, observe,] *in all directions*."[14] "A social-democrat must concern himself . . . with an organization of revolutionaries capable of guiding the *entire* proletarian struggle for emancipation."[15] Guide, not follow. Likewise Gramsci (says Walzer) was "a Leninist of the cultural struggle," urging the clerisy to teach the proletariat.[16] Ideas.

∞

Clark is a fine economic and historical scientist and in his book produces much numerical evidence about various assertions with which other economic and historical scientists agree. Yet it is crucial to distinguish the good arguments from the bad, in case some outsider to historical science should think that the good economic/quantitative arguments in the book do anything much to support the bad vulgar-Marxist/eugenic arguments. They don't. The linguist Geoffrey Sampson makes such a point in his devastating rebuttal of the psychologist Steven Pinker's equally eugenic theories of linguistic "nativism": "I should say to start with that I am far from wanting to contradict every point that Pinker [or in our case Clark] makes in his book. Quite a lot . . . has little or nothing to do with the nativism issue [or the eugenic theory of bourgeois virtues] and is not at all controversial, at least not among people versed in the findings. . . . It is possible to read *The Language Instinct* [or *A Farewell to Alms*] as a general survey."[17] Just so in Clark's case—it is a survey, at any rate, of what the numbers, if not the social and literary texts, might be viewed as saying. It is a historical survey, narrow in method but well done by its declared standards of Numbers Only, Please.

Much of Clark's book, in other words, is uncontroversially excellent, a review for outsiders of the quantitative side of what economic historians have learned since, say, Karl Polanyi in 1944. We all, we quantitative economic historians nowadays, agree that down to the seventeenth or eighteenth century England was trapped in a Malthusian logic, as the world has been trapped since the caves. (Some economic historians deny this, but in that case it is hard to see why the modern world did not emerge shortly after the caves.) There was no rapid innovation, though China for example had slowly acquired quite an impressive panoply. Lacking unlimited land or an ongoing explosion of innovations, if you get more mouths to feed then sooner rather than later you will get less bread per mouth. In consequence the life of man remained nasty, poor, brutish, and short.[18] All the economic historians whom Clark is summarizing agree that the escape from the Malthusian trap is the most important economic event in world history. And we agree on the magnitude of the escape: in the teeth of gigantic increases in population "the richest modern economies are now [conservatively measured, not taking account of better quality] ten to twenty times wealthier than the 1800 average."[19] We agree that the cause of the Great Fact was innovation, not capital accumulation—though we have to keep reminding our colleagues in economics of this. We agree that the Fact happened first in Holland and then in England and Scotland. We agree that in China and especially in Japan there were some signs around 1600 that it might happen there, and some of us think that it was short-circuited by Qing and Tokugawa tyranny and inegalitarianism and scorning of merchants. We agree that since 1848 the real rewards to labor have increased, and the rewards to capital and land have fallen as a share of total income, contrary to the predictions of the classical economists, whether bourgeois or Marxist. We agree that so sudden was the innovation that it permitted high income that led to a *fall* in birthrates, as for example in a once impoverished and once overpopulated Italy or Sweden. We agree that the poor of the world have been the largest beneficiaries of the escape from the Malthusian trap. We agree that trade unions and protectionism had nothing to do with the escape, and in fact slowed it down worldwide, as in Britain's unhealthy subservience to militant unions until the 1970s, or Latin America's disastrous love affair with dependency theory. We agree, in other words, on a great many historical findings from 1944 to the present that will strike the average enthusiast for Karl Polanyi or Louis Althusser or Immanuel Wallerstein or Naomi Klein, not to speak of Malthus and Marx, as bizarre and counterintuitive.

What other historical scientists do *not* agree with, however, is Clark's only distinctive argument, picked up by him recently from the writings of certain economic theorists. It revives in the style of Pinker a eugenic hypothesis— that English people became by virtue of the fast rate of breeding of their rich folk a race of *Übermenschen* living in an *Übergesellschaft*.

Clark attempts to distance himself from the cruder and still popular sorts of eugenics, most popular around 1920 and perennially popular among technically oriented antiliberals. The attempt, though, fails: his argument is eugenics all right, the sort that has haunted right-wing politics from Francis Galton in the late nineteenth century to the search for the gay gene in the early twenty-first. You can't "disassociate yourself from the whole social Darwinist enterprise" simply by saying you do, as Clark does indignantly in a reply to my strictures.[20] If you think that social pressures over a couple of centuries have resulted in people better for modern tasks, you are a social Darwinist. (We all agree that social pressures, such as shame evoked by language, do work over *millennia*; but that is an argument on a different scale of time, and at such scales we are all social Darwinists.) He quotes from his book a passage that I "seemingly missed" which said that "man was becoming biologically better adapted to the modern economic world." I did not miss it, and you can see that it is social Darwinism. In the passage quoted he speaks of "the long agrarian passage leading up to the Industrial Revolution," which again is a scale of millennia, not the mere centuries his explanation of England's success is about. The "modern economic world" sprang into being since 1700 or 1800, and the divergence of England from the pattern of the wider world is at the earliest the beheading of Charles on January 30, 1649. One of the few historical scientists with whom Clark agrees on the matter is David Landes, whom he commends briefly for being "correct in observing that the Europeans had a culture more conducive to economic growth"—though Landes thinks the superior culture had more ancient genetic sources than the breeding rates of late medieval families.[21] Both are cultural chauvinists, Clark of England and Landes of Western and especially northern Europe.

There are a lot of criticisms to be made of this distinctive part of Clark's book. The century-old eugenic hypothesis of Karl Pearson and Charles Davenport is that civic virtue is inherited, which is Clark's theme. The hypothesis has so many points against it—some made long ago against Pearson's and Davenport's views, some particular to Clark—that it is going to have to be abandoned.[22]

For one thing, non-European places have grown and exhibited civic virtue, after the example of Holland and England and Scotland. As the Nobel economist Robert Solow wrote in one of the flood of scathing reviews of Clark's book by economists and economic historians:

> Clark's pessimism about closing the gap between the successful and less successful economies may derive from the belief that nothing much can change unless until the mercantile and industrial virtues seep down into a large part of the population, as he thinks they did in preindustrial England. That could be a long wait. If that is his basic belief, it would seem to be roundly contradicted by the extraordinary sustained growth of China and, a bit more recently, India. Embarrassingly for Clark, both of those success stories seem to have been set off by institutional changes, in particular moves away from centralized control and toward an open-market economy.[23]

It is not the commercial virtues *inherited* by people but the virtues *praised* by people that are effective. China after 1978 began to repeal its laws against making money and a little afterward India started admiring entrepreneurs, and both were off to the races.[24] And of course similar races started in the rest of Europe very quickly after England led the way. How did economic growth come so rapidly to the Rhineland and Wallonia, a few decades after England, if economic success depended, as Clark claims, on an *englische Übergesellschaft* built up over centuries? The west of Germany and the south of the Lowlands were nothing like the tranquil lands that Clark thinks make for a bourgeois *Volk*. On the contrary, the strip from Flanders south to Lombardy was the cockpit of Europe for a millennium, the Western Front in the Great War, the "Habsburg Road," the tiny and continually warring states and substates of the "Lotharian axis" (as the military historian Geoffrey Parker calls it, after Charlemagne's grandson, who briefly governed it). Yet within a bare century of England's stirring, and despite the disturbances of the Napoleonic Wars, whose final battle was again fought in Wallonia, the Lotharian axis from Mons to Milan was an industrial hive.

For another, the *non*-Europeans, those non-English *Untermenschen* such as Bengalis or Jamaicans, became well-to-do when they decamped to places in which bourgeois values were accorded dignity and liberty. Their success seems to have had little to do with inherited values. It was similar to the way that the younger sons of English gentry in the eighteenth century prospered when apprenticed as merchants in Bristol and London. At any rate in the book Clark shows no interest in American economic history, which is the main instance of success by people with peasant genes in a bourgeois-honoring land. But his earlier work expressed in journal articles involved ingenious calculations about the gain from moving to bourgeois countries. The Italian Americans, whose ancestors with third-grade educations had followed the ox-driven plow in Calabria, became in a generation or two among the best-educated national subgroups of their adopted country.

Nor, to look at it from the other side, is Clark interested in his 2007 book in the numerous diasporas of Chinese or Armenians or whomever, who enriched themselves away from the imperial oppression or aristocratic chaos of their homelands. Cypriots move to London and in a generation become successful businesspeople. Parsees move from Pakistan, and in a generation become doctors and professors. In the book Clark shows no interest in the Scotland in which he was born (his parents, though, were Irish), which did have a very early Industrial Revolution. Yet, as recently as the century before, it had nothing like England's "extraordinary stability" from which bourgeois values are supposed to flow. (Partly of course the instability of Scotland resulted from centuries of invasions and other fishing in troubled waters by the supposedly stability-enjoying English.) Like the overseas Chinese or the immigrants to America, the Scots after 1707 journeyed south to become the economists and engineers and farm managers for England and its empire. Nor does Clark show an interest in his and my ancestors in Ireland, who, when they crossed the Irish Sea to staff the cotton and wool mills he has investigated in past decades with such empirical imagination, became rapidly the good workers (his father and mother, for example) who couldn't of course ever arise from such a turbulent and nonbourgeois and demographically unsound place as John Bull's troublesome Other Island—which in most parts did *not* have an industrial revolution.

And yet twenty years before his eugenic book Clark himself had given the relevant evidence:

> Evidence against the view that [textile] workers in low-wage countries were . . . incapable comes from the New England industry. . . . In 1911 . . . 27.8% of the workers . . . [were] Polish, Portuguese, Greek, or Italian, even though in Poland, Portugal, Greece, and Italy between three and six times as many workers were required. . . . Why did the Irish who happened to get on the boat to Lancashire exhibit lower efficiency . . . than those who . . . took the boat to New England?[25]

Good question. The answer isn't eugenic.

31

NEO-DARWINISM DOESN'T COMPUTE

Yet the main failure of Clark's eugenic hypothesis in his book—to apply rigorously Clark's own intellectual ideology—is its nonquantitative character. A book filled with ingenious calculations (hundreds upon hundreds of them, exhibiting Clark's historical imagination: the scientific virtue of asking questions and seeing your way to answering them) does not calculate enough. Clark insists dogmatically that the only valid evidence for a hypothesis is quantitative and materialist. Yet his book doesn't ask or answer the crucial *quantitative* historical questions.

The argument of the book can be diagrammed like this, as four states or events, 1, 2, 3, 4, linked by three causal and transforming causal arrows, A, B, C (fig. 2). Notice the bolded events at the ends. The two bolded events, 1 about breeding and especially 4 about enrichment, are the ones that get pretty satisfying amounts of empirical attention, if solely numerical. Still, even the arguments about event 1, Rich Breed More, have quite a few problems. For example, the bourgeois high-breeding rich whom Clark is talking about lived of course in cities, because that is what "bourgeois" means. Yet these were death traps until the late nineteenth century, and especially for the poor, casting doubt on his supposition that the heirs of rich burghers would survive to cascade down the social hierarchy. The heirs were mostly dead, and their places were made up with symbolic heirs adopted from whatever likely nephew or journeyman from the countryside presented himself. Such is the plot of a hundred European plays and novels and operas, as for example those about Dick Whittington (c. 1355–1423) of rural Gloucestershire, thrice lord mayor of London. As Goldstone noted in his comments in

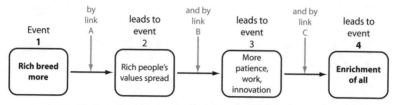

FIGURE 2. The Clark Hypothesis: Rich people are better, and drive out the poor.

a session about Clark's book at the November 2007 meetings of the Social Science History Association, "If the brightest merchants are drawn to London . . . [it is] fine [if] they have more kids. But if their kids drift down the social ladder, they die. So [Clark's genetic embourgeoisfication effect has] to peter out after a generation. There's no way it can accumulate once you take the urban death rate into account."[1] The economic historian Timothy Guinnane has declared apropos of Clark's comparisons that anyway the demographic rates in the European *countryside* in early times, to be compared with those in towns, are never going to be accurately calculable.[2] Still, in the early eighteenth century the calculated life expectancy at birth in England and Wales as a whole is said to have been 38.5 years. In London, grotesquely large as a share of British population even by the standard of Paris as a share of French population, it was a stunningly low 18.5 years. Life expectancy appears to have fallen steadily as one moved from the Wiltshire countryside to Bristol to the Great Wen of London.[3]

On event 4, the Enrichment of All, Clark's quantitative evidence is better, but entirely conventional. The numbers concerning the Enrichment of All, about which, to repeat, we post-Polanyi economic historians all agree, and on which all of us have worked, and of which it is most important that we persuade you noneconomic intellectuals, and especially the Polanyists among you, are nailed. Good for Clark.

Yet Clark insists throughout on hammering on exclusively quantitative nails. So he skimps event 3, More Patience, Work, Innovation, and especially event 2, Rich People's Values Spread. Clark, who believes that if you cannot measure, then your knowledge is meager and unsatisfactory, is not comfortable with literary and other "ego-document" sources, as German historians call them nowadays. He does not realize that written sources can themselves be counted, and that anyway part of the empirical evidence is what people say. Jesus is said to have said "Render unto Caesar," and in any case his followers claimed he did, which is therefore part of the empirical evidence about early Christianity's relationship to the state. That Luther did say "One prince, one faith" is similar evidence in the Reformation. The consequence of Clark's aversion to words is that he does not have much to say about how one would know that "informal, self-reinforcing social norms" of rich people had spread. Therefore about event 2, Rich People's Values Spread, his work is notably thin.

Event 3, More Patience, Work, Innovation, gets more attention, sometimes of a quantitative sort. Clark follows Mokyr and others, as I do, in emphasizing the applied innovation in cotton and iron and so forth, and uses the template of a statistical table which I devised a long time ago to show that the applied innovation in England 1780–1860, contrary to the Two Nicks, was extended in fact well beyond such heroic industries.[4] That's good.

The rest is not so good. What is most strikingly missing in Clark's argument are any calculations justifying the causal links A, B, C between the events 1, 2, 3, 4. It is a big, big problem. Consider link C, that between the event of having More Patience, Work, Innovation and the event of the Enrichment of All. Clark notes that in countries with ill-disciplined labor forces, such as India, the employer doesn't get as much output per worker as in England, because the nonbourgeois values of the Indian workers, and for that matter of the employers, do not inspire enough work. (One wonders, though, if Clark has seen Peter Sellars's portrayal of English antibourgeois values, as a shop steward in *I'm All Right, Jack* [1959]: "We do not and cannot accept the principle that incompetence justifies dismissal. That is victimization").

Yet the "as much" and "not enough" are nothing like the twenty to thirty times gap of real income per head between poor India and rich England nowadays that he claims to be explaining. True, Rodolfo Manuelli and Ananth Seshadri among others have argued somewhat plausibly, in line with dogma from the (usually empirically vacuous) claims of recent growth theory, that quite large gaps can be explained by a small difference in efficiency (strictly speaking, what economists call "total factor productivity"). In the received dogma the small difference is supposed to make for greater returns to education and training, and still greater accumulations of human capital in rich countries.[5] Maybe such an argument would work, if one were to overstate the effects of human capital on early growth. The trouble is that the model implies that a small change in the ethical evaluation of education at *any* time would have had the same strong effects—which it did not for instance in ancient Greece or in early Modern Europe. Shakespeare's and Molière's contemporaries benefited from a much improved system of education in England and France, as the historian George Huppert has shown, and the merchant academies in both countries were vigorous among the Protestants and many of the Catholics. Yet an industrial revolution did not occur—or, rather, it occurred with a mysterious two-hundred-year lag.

Be that as it may, the point here is that Clark doesn't make such an argument—he doesn't attend to the links. Mind the gap. Clark has not. Clark has failed for example to show *how much* Enrichment depends on Work, that is, event 4 on event 3 linked by C. "Magnitudes matter here," as Clark himself declared in a characteristically harsh review of Avner Greif's book in the year his own book came out, "and the proofs wielded by Greif are not geared to magnitudes."[6] Just so. Remember Montaigne on running oneself through with one's own weapons. Clark hasn't done a calculation on the size of link C. He hasn't asked about the oomph of the link. His proofs are not geared to magnitudes. And so he has no answer.

Clark has long noted, as I said, that employees in South Asia work less intensely than in Europe.[7] His argument is similar to that of the historian of Holland, Jan de Vries, who has beautifully documented an "industrious revolution" of more application to work in first the Dutch and then the English lands during the seventeenth and eighteenth centuries. Clark now claims that the greater industriousness in England came from distressed bourgeois pushed down into the working class, an implausible story on its face, for which indeed he offers little direct evidence. It would not explain, for example, the parallel rise of a work ethic in Holland. De Vries's more plausible story is that, as David Hume put it, "everything in the world is purchased with labor; and our passions are the only cause of labor." The greater variety of goods, for which de Vries offers a book full of evidence, passionately tempted early modern Dutch and English people to work 303 days per year in the eighteenth century as against only 255 days in the sixteenth century.[8] As the historian Anne Goldgar notes in her book deflating myths about the tulip mania in the 1630s, the Dutch at the time viewed the flower trade . . . "as a trade in a new product, one of many new products that had been flooding the country for the previous forty and more years."[9] The moderately well-off early-modern person said to himself: "I *must* have some of those tulips, that sugar, that tobacco, that porcelain, even one of those new paintings in oil," in the same way that nowadays you *must* have the latest cell phone or blue jeans or high-speed Internet hookup.[10] De Vries cites a finding from colonial Massachusetts that inventories at death in the 1640s had no chairs at all (merely stools and benches) but in the 1790s had on average sixteen chairs, and these often elegant items purchased from England or from skilled colonial craftsmen imitating English designs, such as that of the Windsor chair.[11] Wages were not leaping up in the seventeenth and eighteenth centuries as they did in the late nineteenth. Instead the people were laboring more at the same wages to satisfy their passion for flowers and tobacco, oil paintings and brass castings, china from China, and delicate and doubtfully inheritable Windsor chairs. Yet de Vries does not claim that a 19 percent increase of industriousness, 255 days of work each year rising to 303 days (with fewer holidays, whether holy or not), can explain a 2,100 percent difference between Indian and English incomes nowadays (or a 600 percent difference in 1800), or a 100 percent rise from 1700 to 1860 in British income per person, or a rise since the year 1800 of 1,500 percent. Clark does make such a claim.

Working harder is a fine thing, in other words, and is an important characteristic of the modern world. In 1998 Hans-Joachim Voth brilliantly used records of mentions of witnesses to alleged crimes to show that early in the eighteenth century on "Saint-Monday" people in London were standing around watching the human comedy rather than working.[12] He concludes nonetheless that the work week was similar to that in poor countries now, and "[E. P.] Thompson's image of a 'merry old England' where hours were short and work highly irregular is probably incorrect."[13] Harried young lawyers in Manhattan working seventy hours a week can reflect ruefully that their factory-hand great-great grandparents got along on sixty hours a week, their peasant forebears on forty, and their hunter-gatherer deep ancestors on a mere nineteen hours.[14] But in each case fewer hours was associated with less charming stuff to consume.

If Dutch and especially British workers had carried on with their preindustrial Saint-Mondays and drunk-at-work habits, their bourgeois employers would have had to hire more of them to do the same work, paying each one less. British and Dutch incomes per head 1700–1800 would probably have fallen some as population increased, rather than as they did staying level, against what were soon to be called Malthusian pressures. The bourgeois man would have faced a servant problem of the sort that dominated the domestic duties of his wife, who was perpetually in the business of hiring new servants to replace the ones recently dismissed for insolence or immorality or drunkenness.[15] A typical contract of apprenticeship which the husband filled in would routinely specify that the apprentice "will not commit fornication. . . . At card, dice, or any other unlawful thing he shall not play games. . . . Nor haunt ale-house, tavern, or playhouse."

The bourgeois passion for innovation, however, would not have been affected. A bleaching process was invented in the 1790s which substituted chlorine for sunshine and sharply decreased the real cost of pure white linens—once a product exclusively for the rich. Such a big innovation would still have been a fine and profitable thing to carry out, even if it had taken 19 percent more badly disciplined workers to run it than it in fact did. Some new ideas would be unprofitable if the workers were not sufficiently modern and bourgeois in their behavior. But many would have gone ahead, since so many of them yielded gigantic improvements, and wide fame for the inventor, resulting in the Great Fact.

Nor does Clark do a calculation on link B, to show that event 3, More Patience, Work, Innovation, depended mightily on event 2, Rich People's Values Spread. It's deucedly hard to do. I agree with Clark that the link was important (though notice that I think social attitudes *about* the bourgeoisie were much more important than the internal state of bourgeois psychology). Yet I can't think of ways to quantify it with the usual economic and demographic statistics. I have had to rely instead on the metaphysically unsatisfactory but enormously rich and ubiquitous *qualitative* evidence, which the other students of applied innovation such as Mokyr and Jacob and McLeod and Edgerton and Goldstone have exploited, and which Clark spurns. If one accepted his methodological rule of number, Clark could not be blamed that even his admirable if strictly quantitative historical imagination is stymied by the question of *how much* bourgeois values acted to increase applied innovation. Still, his methodological stridency about number— having myself been strident about such matters in my youth, I am familiar with the temptation—does make it a trifle embarrassing that he doesn't mention that for link B connecting ideas with innovation he has failed to provide any numbers at all. We old fools like Jack Goldstone or Deirdre McCloskey or George Grantham or Richard Easterlin or Claudia Goldin— who listen to what people at the time were saying about B or similar links between the qualitative and the quantitative—get a certain grumpy satisfaction that Clark is thus hoist by his own methodological petard.[16]

In light of Clark's methodological convictions, though, the most embarrassing broken link is A, between Rich Breed More and Rich People's Values Spread. As the economic historian Robert Margo wrote in another of the numerous vexed reviews by historical scientists, "Even if I believe the data to be trustworthy, how do I know I am observing a causal link between 'good' behaviors (for example, patience) that, in the best of circumstances (and these are far from the best) are barely, if at all, observable to the econometrician? What, precisely, are the mechanisms that allow good behaviors to be transmitted across generations? Don't institutions of one type or other play a role?"[17] Nowhere in a book that trumpets calculation as the Only Real Science does Clark *calculate* what higher breeding rates could have accomplished by way of rhetorical change, or talk about the new institutions, such as grammar schools or merchant academies or apprenticeships to London merchants. It could easily be done, at any rate under Clark's mechanical and materialist assumption about how the social construction of values works. And it is not even a matter as Margo assumes of econometric fit. It is a matter of the immensely more useful quantitative method in the social sciences, in which Clark and Jeffrey Williamson and Robert Fogel and I specialize: simulation.

Clark supposes that the children of rich people are by their richness the carriers of the sort of bourgeois values that made for an industrial revolution. (To be clear, and to repeat, I would say on the contrary that a rapid change around 1700 in attitudes *toward* the bourgeoisie mattered much more.) In any case Clark's argument depends on a peculiar characterization of the medieval or early modern relatively rich. A rich bourgeois of London in 1400 or 1600 depended in fact on special protection for his wool-trading monopoly. Dick Whittington was *appointed* to the first of his three terms as mayor of London by a troubled Richard II, because the king was in Whittington's financial debt. As late as 1601 one is not surprised to find the secretary of the Society of Merchant Adventurers, John Wheeler, writing against "dispersed, straggling, and promiscuous trades," that is, interlopers who threatened the state-sponsored monopoly of the Merchant Adventurers.[18] The younger sons of such a merchant might well take away the lesson, repeated by protectionists left and right down to the present, that it is a good idea for the state to control everything it can, and quite a bad thing to let people make the deals they wish to make without a state supervisor appointed by the country club, or by populist ideologues, or by corrupt politicians with large families. All the charters for trading companies in the

sixteenth and seventeenth centuries show the point: *haut bourgeois* and aristocratic adventurers corrupted politics in England, Sweden, France, and the
United Provinces precisely to create monopolies. And likewise a Brave Sir
Botany who had *stolen* his riches, say, or was a successful state bureaucrat
who had received his riches from Henry VIII's dissolving of the monasteries,
would not automatically, one would think, transmit sober, hardworking, innovative, market-respecting bourgeois values to younger sons. One wonders
if George Washington Plunkitt's children or grandchildren were notable for
their entrepreneurial vigor. It's quantitatively testable.

Around 1700, the historian Peter Earle has found, about a quarter of the
London middling sort he sampled at their deaths were sons of literal gentlemen, as one can judge from their adolescent contracts of indentures to
drapers and merchants and bankers.[19] Bourgeois values were not going to
be spread down the social order mechanically when the boys in fact started
out from the idle class of landowners and knights of the shire—yet such
boys became many of the successful merchants of London in the eighteenth
century. If the boys prospered in the upper reaches of bourgeois London
it was because they had learned their trades (getting into the trades with
apprenticeships costing many times the annual income of poor folk) and
were encouraged to practice as overseas merchants or domestic bankers in a
society according dignity and liberty to the middling sort, not because they
had inherited bourgeois values by being bourgeois sons.

Of course, the gentry and even the aristocracy of England, it is often
claimed, tended to bourgeois values and behaviors that would have disquali-
fied a Frenchman from the nobility. The same John Wheeler in 1601 praises
merchandising as "an honorable estate" (a claim, however, that in many circles of Elizabethan England would have raised a scornful laugh) "which may
be practiced by both commoners and nobles . . . without any derogation to
their nobilities."[20] It was not so, as I have noted, in France or Spain. Medievalists such as Marc Bloch and Alan Macfarlane and Ambrose Raftis remark
on "the distinctive pragmatic qualities of the English landed aristocracy, . . .
a striking contrast with the idealism of the French nobility."[21] Thus at Agin-
court the flower of French nobility charged gloriously on horseback against
the peasantly sharpened stakes that a practical-minded Henry V has insisted
his soldiers lug around the French countryside, and the yeomanly archers
most ingloriously mowed down the impractical French. Doubtless the rural
English middle class, the gentry, followed suit in practicality.

Yet bourgeois values prevalent among the gentry and aristocracy of England—making the social origin of merchants or workers irrelevant—would be the opposite of Clark's materialist argument, which depends on bourgeois fathers transmitting uniquely bourgeois values to their younger sons, who then decline into the working class. If everyone in England was pretty much bourgeois from the beginning (as many, such as Macfarlane, have indeed claimed), the argument fails as an explanation of social changes in the eighteenth century. And in the other direction a society that greatly admired aristocratic or Christian virtues, even if the society was objectively bourgeois, could corrupt even a Medici banker into thinking of himself as quite the lord and yet also a godly son of the church. Likewise nowadays an extravagant admiration for the neoaristocratic values of the clerisy—she learned them at the University of Iowa—corrupts a bourgeois daughter into scorning her father's selling of insurance or running of a furniture factory.

32

AND INHERITANCE FADES

Clark has recently fallen in love with neo-Darwinian theories applied to society. He now believes fervently that the bourgeois-behaving unit of meaning, a "meme" as some of the theorists call it, spreads strictly from parents to children, as does eye color, or which arm is on top when you cross your arms. But the biological metaphor here is inapt. From the sixteenth century on it gets inapter and inapter. As the economist Benjamin Friedman remarked in still another hostile review of Clark's book by economic and historical professionals, "If the traits to which Clark assigns primary importance in bringing about the Industrial Revolution are acquired traits, rather than inherited ones, there are many non-Darwinian mechanisms by which a society can impart them, ranging from schools and churches to legal institutions and informal social practices."[1] European publishing, for example, became cheap, if routinely censored. Readers grew radically in numbers, and down the social scale. The historian Lawrence Stone spoke of an "educational revolution" in England 1540 to 1640, during which for example in 1612–1614 nearly half of 204 men convicted of capital crimes in Middlesex escaped the hangman by showing their literacy—the "benefit of clergy," as the medieval liberty was called.[2] In citing Stone, the historical sociologist Jack Barbalet observes that "the most literate of social groups were merchants and businessmen."[3] It had always been so. After all, writing itself springs in the West from Sumerian and Phoenician and Cretan accounting. A businessman was known proverbially for ink-stained fingers, and was portrayed in the new oil paintings of Holland and England as writing, writing, writing (with the counting of money left to his wife). The middle-class women whom Jan

Vermeer painted in his small output are commonly portrayed while reading. The grammar schools spread (William Shakespeare in the sixteenth century, son of a glover). So did the universities (Immanuel Kant in the eighteenth century, son of a saddler). High schools for young merchants proliferated. If solidly bourgeois behavior makes people rich, you would think it would spread thus by imitation, *across* families, as from Defoe's *Essay upon Projects* (1697), which Benjamin Franklin cited as an influence, or from the hundreds of high-circulation handbooks for youths in business published in all major European languages from the sixteenth century on.

The research biologist and professor of theology Alistair McGrath notes that recent work on genome sequencing has shown that the very simplest forms of life do trade genes contemporaneously, and do not merely transmit them from mother cell to daughter cell. Or as Nicholas Wade puts it, "Organisms may acquire genes through borrowing as well as inheritance; bacteria, for instance."[4] And so of course, at the other end of complexity, human beings in their rhetorical cultures, such as those of seventeenth-century Europe, transmit values contemporaneously. "If Darwinism is about copying the instructions," writes McGrath, "Lamarckism is about copying the product. . . . It would seem that Lamarck, rather than Darwin, offers the better account of *cultural* evolution."[5] Or as Joel Mokyr noted in a comment on Clark's book, "We don't just learn from our parents . . . [but] horizontally from other people, from peers, from masters in apprentice or servant relationships."[6] In the printed contract of apprenticeship I quoted, the master undertook "to teach or cause to be taught or instructed the said apprentice in the trade and mystery of _____."

To put it another way, the metaphor of the *tree* of life which Clark unreflectively applies to human culture is not apt. It should give way in such cases to a *network* of life. Languages are sometimes like that. Among Australian Aborigines the mixing of peoples was such that "the family tree model of genetic relationship seems to be totally inappropriate. . . . There was much more diffusion from language to language . . . than is usually the case."[7] In southern Africa the ancient click languages of the Khoisan influenced the clickless Bantu languages spreading down from the northeast, to the extent that some of them (Nelson Mandela's Xhosa, for example) adopted many of the clicks (for example, in English the sound "tsk-tsk" of a scolding by your maiden aunt). Good habits such as wealth-producing behavior would spread in a greatly widened network of culture after the invention of printing, the Protestant Reformation, the fall of tyrants with nine-hundred-year old names. As some biologist recently put it in a survey of the experimental transfer of 246,045 genes to *E. coli*, "The phylogeny of [a primitive but extremely widespread form of] life seems better represented by a network than a tree."[8] If this is true of prokaryotes and eukaryotes, all the more is it true of Parisians and Bostonians. People themselves could move, steadily easier in the eighteenth and nineteenth centuries. And more importantly they could read, steadily better (silent reading is often said to be a modern accomplishment, though it has recently been argued that it was in fact commonplace among the few literates in ancient times).[9] Newspapers were invented in Europe and its offshoots in the late seventeenth century. Ben Franklin's older brother James started printing the cheeky *New England Courant* in Boston in 1721, which became at once an irritant to the British governors and the Puritan ayatollahs, and a model for more than his immediate family of printers. Newspapers became common. In reactionary countries after the fall of Napoleon the reading of (postrevolutionary) French newspapers was viewed as evidence of subversive, bourgeois liberalism.[10] And so the ideas of bourgeois dignity and liberty could move, through French and American newspapers, and through Dutch-printed books in a dozen languages. The memes moved more and more freely across families—and more and more and more—right down to our own worldwide echo chamber of ideas.

But set aside the actual, empirical stories of how values are made. Clark's lack of curiosity about the exact content of bourgeois values (values which he and I join in admiring) leaves him with a mechanical version of neo-Darwinism in explaining how values get transmitted. Suppose such a model is correct. Then a scientist of Clark's quantitative imagination, I repeat, would have found it trivial to calculate, mechanically, by simulation, what the higher rates of breeding would yield in bourgeois-minded but lower-class people in the next generation. He didn't.

∽

The underlying problem is that Clark wants to tell a very long-run story, because in the style of growth theory in recent economics he has ambitions for its endogeneity, which is to say its historical materialism. He wants bourgeois values and the modern world to arise with slow-chapped pow'r out of a thousand years of English history. No *dei ex machinis*, thank you very much—by which he means short-run and therefore contemptible events in the realm of mere ideas such as the birth of English political liberty or the Protestant Reformation or the Scientific Revolution or the Enlightenment or the Bourgeois Revaluation.

The problem is that his long-run ambition does not fit his eugenic machinery. His mechanical model of the transmission of values works too quickly, on a scale not of ten centuries or so but of a century or so. Then it dissipates. Regression to the mean alone would limit to a few decades the effect of bourgeois values' being pushed down the social scale in a family. After all, we say "clogs to clogs," or "shirt-sleeves to shirt-sleeves," in merely three generations. As Francis Galton put it in making a similar calculation— Galton in 1901 got a good deal further in the calculation than Clark did in 2007—high inherited height or intelligence or bourgeois virtue dissipates strongly in children and more in grandchildren, "owing to the combination of ancestral influences—which are generally mediocre—with the purely parental ones."[11] The fact accounts for the curious vocabulary in statistics of "regression" to describe the fitting of a curve to a scatter of points, because measuring the extent of regression to the mean was Galton's first application of the fitting. Galton himself was part of Darwin's family, first notable in Erasmus Darwin, who was Charles Darwin's and Francis Galton's joint grandfather. The family has continued to prosper down to the present, by careful selection of marriage partners. Yet how many such amazing families are there—one thinks of the Bachs and the Polanyis—as against hundreds of families that yield one genius and then regress promptly to the mean? The evolutionary logic puts paid to Clark's long-run story. As the economist Samuel Bowles put it in a hostile review in *Science*:

> If $h^2 = 0.26$ the correlation across 4 generations (great grandfather–great grandson) is 0.032. If we estimate h^2 from the observed intergenerational correlation of traits (r) as above, then the correlation of a genetically transmitted trait across n generations is just $r/2^{n-2}$. Thus the statistical association across generations becomes vanishingly small over the course of a single century, whether the trait is culturally or genetically transmitted.[12]

Clark rejects Bowles's argument by noting correctly that if we "eliminate the bottom 10 percent of the height distribution in one generation then we will for all time change the average height of the population. . . . We have changed the underlying average genotype of the population," citing the breeding of dogs and farm livestock.[13] But that is to suppose what Clark wishes to prove, that being poor is a simple matter of genetics like height. If being poor, or rich, is a temporary deviation from the mean, as Bowles is saying, then the heirs do regress.

Clark describes his central chapter 6 as identifying "strong selective processes."[14] But that's the problem: they are *too* strong for a slow story, as Bowles points out. So Clark's own argument, were it true, would turn out to be one of the despised *dei ex machinis* that work on a scale of decades or a few generations or a century at most. If he had followed his rule of number in the book and had tried to calculate according to his mechanical model the oomph of link A (Rich Breed More causing Rich People's Values Spread), he would have caught the scientific oversight before announcing an erroneous finding to the world. In his 2008 reply he does do the calculations, and does confirm that inheritance was quick and genetic, at least according to the researches of modern geneticists in search of IQ.[15] His slow story contradicts his long.

But anyway, a history of wealth, accumulated from activities having nothing to do with success in a modern industrial economy, seems a minor route to the modern world, if indeed it doesn't lead away from it. Consider for example one of the bourgeois values we can measure, and Clark does, again with his usual quantitative insight, literacy. Male literacy in England, Clark argues, was roughly in the Middle Ages the share of monks in the male population—thus the benefit in pleading as a clergyman against a felony. Illiterate monks were not unknown, but rare (though among the secular clergy illiteracy was perhaps more common). Then male literacy in England rose to perhaps 30 percent in 1580 and to 60 percent by the time national statistics start to be possible in the 1750s, comparable to the rate in Japan at the time.

Think about it, though. If you are the parent of four children, and can read, what is the transition probability that all four of your children will read? It is extremely high, especially if you are the mother of the brood, at any rate in a society which for some reason values literacy. It is the value placed on literacy by the society, not sheer inheritance, that determines its transmittal. Thus in families today "going to college" is extremely inheritable, but in one generation. When it happens, it happens quickly, and permanently. Michelle Obama's children and grandchildren and great grandchildren will all attend university. Yet in Clark's argument university attendance must begin at once the regression to the mean of values that would apply if genetics, not surrounding social values, were explaining it. The grandchildren of universitygoers would be illiterate. But it is clearly not so. My father was the first in his family to graduate from university (University of Wisconsin at Madison, '41, and intercollegiate straight-rail billiards champion 1942). All his three children did likewise (but with no intercollegiate honors), both of my two did, and doubtless my two grandchildren will, too. Every one of the five children of my father's brother (who left the University of Wisconsin in the late 1920s after two years) graduated from university, and their children so far overwhelmingly have. Social attitudes, not Mendelian inheritance, make it so.

Similarly looking back: unlike my Irish ancestors, many of my Norwegian ancestors on the Hardanger Fjord, according to records collected by the literate Norwegians (I can show them to you), were reading by the late sixteenth century, and never stopped. Why? Because of inheritance? No: clearly, they started and continued to read because of the surrounding social values attributable to the Protestant Reformation, a literal *Deus*, to which Clark in his book explaining modern Europe allots eight words. No religion, please: we're demographic historical materialists. The impoverished Norwegians of rural Dimelsvik (no bourgeois virtues inherited there) learned to read, quickly. The habit in the first place spread across families. And once in a family it stayed there, not reverting to the mean, unlike biological inheritance. The inheritance within families is too quick and the "inheritance" across families too strong and the lack of regression to the mean too obvious for Clark's intended story of a stately development over centuries of an English genetic *Überlegenheit*.

Clark becomes very cross when challenged on his materialism. Compare Marx in 1846 on Proudhon, whose writings Marx (trained as a Hegelian) describes as "Hegelian trash. . . . It is not history, it is not profane history—history of mankind, but sacred history—history of ideas."[16] Clark replied to my claim that he exhibits, as he put it, an "aversion to literary sources":

> Absolutely, because they are highly unreliable. What people say, what their explicit ideology is, often differs dramatically from how they behave. Doing economic history through analysis of written materials such as laws, political tracts, etc. is an invitation to error. Deirdre's invitation to us to come wallow in the cultural mud is the guarantee that we will continue to go round in circles in economic history forever. Better to say something and be wrong than to say things that are just not subject to empirical test.[17]

With many other economists, Clark thinks that "empirical" is a fancy word for "numbers." And so he ignores the evidence of experience that does not arrive in numerical form. "Empirical," recall, is from Greek "having to do with experience," in diaries and novels as much as censuses and probate inventories. Anyway, Clark has said something "subject to empirical test," and it is wrong. So much is clear.

He is wrong to dismiss "wallowing in the cultural mud," the lived life, the analyzed text, the salient image. Such a naïvely behaviorist and positivist and materialist ideology, dominant 1890 to 1980, throws away half the evidence, much of it more decisive than a questionable "sample" of birthrates from East Anglia. (Jan de Vries noted of Clark's book, "had this book been written by an historian its subtitle might have been: Some Findings from Suffolk Testators, 1620–1638.")[18] A historian cannot do his science well on numbers alone, confined to regional samples from 1620 to 1638. Indeed, as econometricians like Charles Manski point out, and as Stephen Ziliak and I have emphasized, the identification of what is salient in the numbers never inheres in the numbers themselves. "Identification problems cannot be solved," Manski writes, "by gathering more of the same kind of data." They "can be alleviated only by invoking stronger assumptions [based, say, on the lived life] or by initiating new sampling processes that yield different kinds of data [in, say, the analyzed text and the salient image]."[19] Clark is so hostile to the literary and philosophical side of his culture that he insists on hopping along, underidentified, on one leg.

So Clark's socio-neo-Darwinism picked up recently from articles on growth theory by some economic theorists has little to recommend it as history applicable to the past millennium.[20] The problem typifies modern growth theory in economics. It is mostly theory, with scant history; mostly mathematics, with scant measurement.[21] Yet the theorists who inspired Clark were more scientifically reasonable than he is in using their argument. The argument, they wrote, "suggests that the time period between the Neolithic Revolution and the Industrial Revolution [some 10,000 years] is sufficient for significant [biological] evolutionary changes."[22] That seems quite possible—lactose and alcohol tolerance, for example, do seem to have been evolved in such a range of years. After all, people whose ancestors did not milk their animals do now get sick from milk, and milking animals is a recent practice in the longer history of *Homo sapiens*.

Clark, though, proposes to apply the argument instead to the few centuries of what he characterizes as English peace (a "peace" covering the Wars of the Roses [1455–1485], the turbulent Tudors, the revolution-provoking

Stuarts, the long century of struggle with France after 1692)—and strangely not to the 265 years of domestic and foreign peace in Tokugawa Japan, interrupted by scattered peasant revolts, easily put down.[23] Consider the numerous very long episodes of peace in China away from the frontiers, which according to Clark's model should have resulted in a massive embourgeoisfication of the place, especially in view of low urban death rates in China. The average length of the thirteen "principal unified states" in the table of Chinese dynasties from the First Emperor in 221 BCE until the Last in 1911 is 168 years. The three longest of the thirteen were all in the last (potentially innovative) millennium: the Song at 319 years, the Ming at 276, and the (final and in fact ideologically reactionary) Qing at 266.[24] The long dynasties were not without Revolts of the Three Feudatories or extremely bloody Taiping Rebellions. On the whole, though, they make the allegedly long "peace" of England look notably disturbed, and they make the condition of Europe generally (a geographical area and population comparable at the time to China's) look positively chaotic.

The theorists, in the very footnote that inspired Clark ("the original hypothesis that sparked this study," Clark writes in a paper with Gillian Hamilton), claim that "The theory is perfectly applicable for either social or genetic transmission of traits. [A] cultural transmission is likely to be more rapid."[25] More rapid indeed. The theory of inheritance collapses, as I said, if "inheritance" happens across families, rapidly, as it did in a literate age, and as indeed it often did even among illiterate folk knapping arrowheads from a flint core. Humans talk to each other, and all primates imitate even if they don't talk. Monkey see, monkey do. As the Dutch do, so shall we. Neither Clark nor his theorists recognize that the sixteenth through nineteenth centuries in Europe saw changes in attitudes toward innovation that had little to do with returns to human capital—chiefly because most innovations were copied by precisely that cross-family inheritance, encouraged by the printing press and the new egalitarianism, and often yielded little pecuniary benefit to their inventors.

The change was not genetic (as Clark argues) or psychological (as Weber argued) or economic (as Marx argued) or legal (as North argues) but sociological and political. Literacy, printing, a free press, and free conversation make technology available. It became, as we now say, open source. Long ago the economic historian Robert Allen made the point.[26] More recently the economic historian Paul David has theorized the development by the early eighteenth century of open-source science.[27] Yet science was merely one of numerous cases: printed music was another open-source technology, journalism after the 1690s still another (one of its origins being the open printing of daily prices on exchanges, information formerly traded by letter among merchants as secret and proprietary). Open-source software is not inherited biologically from one's parents but socially from one's geeky and voluble friends.

An early version of Clark's hypothesis may be examined in Galton's Huxley Lecture to the Anthropological Institute in 1901, "The Possible Improvement of the Human Breed under Existing Conditions of Law and Sentiment":

> The number and variety of aptitudes, especially in dogs, is truly remarkable. . . . So it is with the various natural qualities that go towards the making of civic worth in man [p. 3]. . . . The brains of the nation lie in the higher of our classes [p. 11]. . . . Dr. Farr, the eminent statistician, endeavored to estimate the money worth of an average baby born to the wife of an Essex laborer. . . . Dr. Farr, with accomplished actuarial skill, capitalized the value at the child's birth. . . . [It] was found to be £5. On a similar principle the worth of an X-class baby would be reckoned in thousands of pounds. . . . They found great industries, establish vast undertakings, and amass large fortunes for themselves. Others, whether they be rich or poor, are the guides and light of the nation [pp. 11–12]. . . . Many who are familiar with the habits of [the lowest class] do not hesitate to say that it would be an economy and a great benefit if all habitual criminals were . . . peremptorily denied opportunities for producing offspring [p. 20]. . . . The possibility of improving the race of a nation depends on the power of increasing its best stock [p. 24].[28]

In 1901 eugenic reasoning such as Galton's was fresh and new and plausible. It was still influential after the Great War. It yielded then in places like Norway, Sweden, and the United States programs of compulsory sterilization which survived even their methodical application in Germany 1933–1945, coming to an end only during the 1970s—by then, perhaps, three generations of imbecilic if scientific social policy were deemed enough.

Yet recently the eugenic idea has revived, as in the works of Steven Pinker and others, now joined by Gregory Clark. Neo-eugenics has been greeted with enthusiasm by science journalists with short historical memories and weak understandings of social ethics. It introduces into the modern debate between status and contract a third possibility, genes. The eugenic reasoning declares that people are not what the society says they are (their status) or what they are able to arrange by persuading each other (their contract). People are what they were born to be, biologically speaking, like cocker spaniels. And then we can move to prenatal screening for among other things a gay gene, as I noted. Uncritical worshipers of a politically reactionary and just-so-story-admiring Science dote on such an argument. It is neat. It is formalizable. It puts people in their proper places, indulging an indignant disgust at, say, such undesirables as queers and Jews. It is calculable (though, to repeat, Clark has not done the calculations that Galton pioneered). But it is scientifically wrong even in its own terms, and epigenetics and evo-devo have undermined its assumption that genes are expressed simply and without regard to environment.

And for the historical question at hand it anyway doesn't make a lot of sense. Beyond the difficulties already mentioned, Clark's distinctive argument depends on measures of aptitudes that are, like height, influenced by more than inheritance and, unlike height, have no natural units invariant to social values. What made for riches in 1600 had little to do with what made for riches in 2000. A graceful way with sonnets and a good leg for bowing low to Gloriana are not genetically similar to a Harvard MBA and a knack for computers. During the English Revolution the Presbyterian Dr. John Bastwick told of instructing a young John Lilburne: he was "a mere country courtier and very rough hewn; so that he could neither make a leg with grace nor put off his hat seemly, till I had polished him and taught him all his postures of courtship, and now he is become a very gallant fellow. I have made him fit for all gentlemen's and noblemen's society."[29] Taught, not inherited. What mattered in modern economic growth was not a doubtfully measured change in the genetically or familially inherited abilities of English people. What mattered was a radical change 1600–1776, "measurable" in every play and pamphlet, in what English people honored, wanted, paid for, revalued.

33

INSTITUTIONS CANNOT BE VIEWED MERELY
AS INCENTIVE-PROVIDING CONSTRAINTS

Douglass North (b. 1920) is an astonishing economist and historian who has repeatedly reinvented himself. The heir to an insurance fortune, merchant seaman during the War, apprentice photographer to Dorothea Lange, deep-sea fishing buddy of the pop singer Perry Como, in his youth he was a Marxist—as were many of us of a certain age—but became from the study of economics an advocate of markets and their innovation. As a young professor at the University of Washington in the 1950s he was one of the chief entrepreneurs of the so-called "new" economic history, that is, the application of economic theory and statistics to historical questions, such as how regional growth happened in the United States before the Civil War. For this he was in 1993 awarded with Robert Fogel the Nobel Memorial Prize in Economic Science.[1]

North's pioneering study of ocean freight rates from the seventeenth to the eighteenth century (North 1968) led him in the 1970s to ponder the evolution of what had in an economics influenced by Ronald Coase come to be called "transaction costs," that is, the costs of doing business. Moving cotton from Savannah to Liverpool entails transportation costs, obviously. Less obviously—the point was made by Coase in all his work from the 1930s on—moving a piece of property from Mr. Jones to Ms. Brown entails *transaction* costs, such as the cost of arriving at a satisfactory contract to do so and the cost of insuring against its failure. By North's own account, in 1966 he had decided to switch from American to European economic history. With collaborators at Washington like Robert Paul Thomas, S. N. S. Cheung, Yoram Barzel, Barry Weingast, and John Wallis, North developed a story of the "rise of the West" focusing on the gradual fall in such transaction costs. Since the 1980s, now at Washington University of St. Louis (he favors places named after the first president of the United States), North has argued that Western Europe in the eighteenth and nineteenth centuries benefited uniquely from good institutions that held transaction costs in check, such as Britain's unwritten constitution of 1689 and the United States' written one of 1789.

North defines institutions as "the humanly devised constraints that structure political, economic and social interaction."[2] The economist Deepak Lal says in similar terms that the "institutional infrastructure . . . consists of informal constraints like cultural norms . . . and the more formal ones."[3] Steven Levitt and Stephen Dubner write in their second "freakonomics" book that "people are people, and they respond to incentives. They can nearly always be manipulated—for good or ill—if only you find the right levers."[4] That's how recent economists have come to think of laws, churches, manners, families, companies. Levers. Manipulations. The words "constraints" and "incentives" here matter a lot, because North and Lal and Levitt mean what all Samuelsonian economists mean by them. (North and Lal and Levitt are Samuelsonian economists right down to their wing-tipped shoes.) Consumers and producers, the economists say, maximize utility "subject to constraints," or "in view of the incentives," such as the laws against murder and theft, or the regulations of the Internal Revenue Service, or the customs of Bedouin hospitality, or the Ford Way of doing business. In other words, the main character in North's story, and the story of the other Samuelsonians, is always Max U, that unlovely maximizer of Utility, *Homo prudens*, the prudent human—never *Homo ludens* (the playful human, whom the economists Schumpeter and Knight emphasized) or *Homo faber* (the making human, Marx's man) and *Homo hierarchus* (the ranking human, irritating to Veblen and recently to the economists Hirsch and Frank) or, as I and most noneconomist social scientists would claim, *Homo loquens*, the speaking human.

"Max U," you see, is a man with the last name "U" who has peopled the arguments of economists since Paul Samuelson in the late 1930s elevated him to a leading role. The joke is that the only way that an economist knows how to think about life after Samuelson is to watch Mr. Max U coldly *Maximizing* a *Utility* function, $U(X,Y)$. Ha, ha. Max U is a pot-of-pleasure sort of fellow. He cares only for the virtue of prudence, and "prudence" defined in an especially narrow way, that is, knowing what your appetites are and knowing how to satisfy them. Never mind what the novelist Samuel Butler wrote truly around 1880: "There is no greater sign of a fool than the thinking that he can tell at once and easily what it is that pleases him."[5] In Yiddish such a fool would be a *goyisher kop*, a gentile jerk, by which is meant a man without learning or reflection or prayer. He just "chooses" to eat or drink or fight or whatever, intemperately, without consulting the impartial spectator of his conscience or of his education or of the Torah or the Mishnah or the Talmud. He has "tastes," as the economists put it in their Samuelsonian way, about which one should not dispute. (Note by the way the contradiction in having strong feelings about not disputing the hypothesis of not having strong feelings, and being passionately in favor of coldly calculating. The American economist J. N. Clark called it long ago the "irrational passion for dispassionate rationality." But rhetorical consistency is not a strong point of Samuelsonian economics.)

The "institutions" stop a person, or at any rate a *goyisher kop*, from doing certain things, such as shoplifting from the local grocery store or turning away hungry travelers. "As soon as we talk about constraining human behavior," Lal notes, "we are implicitly acknowledging that there is some basic 'human nature' to be constrained. . . . As a first cut we can accept the economists' model of 'Homo economicus' which assumes that people are self-interested and rational."[6] And as a second cut, and a third. The constraints are like money budgets. Then we can get on with prudent exchange. They are fences, good or bad, "limiting self-seeking behavior," as Lal puts it. From the individual's point of view the fences fall from the sky.

North and Lal and Levitt and other economists do not usually notice that other observers of society emphatically do not agree with the Samuelsonian metaphor of "constraint" or "incentive." The noneconomists think of cultural rhetoric, like language, as simultaneously constraint and creation, as an incentive and an impulse, as a negotiation and an art, as a community and a conversation. Institutions do not merely constrain human behavior, giving prices to which people have an incentive to respond. They express humanness, giving it meaning.

Levitt and Dubner—though on balance a force for good in stretching economics, and explaining the stretch to noneconomists—miss the point. They drag all human behavior under the lamppost of "incentives" simply by defining all of it as "rational." They declare that "human behavior is influenced by a dazzlingly complex set of *incentives*, social norms, framing references, and the lessons gleaned from past experience, in a word, context. We act as we do because, *from the choices and incentives at play* in a particular circumstance, *it seems most productive* to act that way. This is also known as rational behavior, which is what economics is all about."[7] Yes, it is what Samuelsonian economics is all about. And that's the problem, because it ain't so.

When we buy a car or go to a prostitute it is sometimes useful to frame it as rational, a case of "we act as we do because . . . it seems most productive." Fine. But wait a minute. The "framing references" are what sociology is all about, which leaves "incentives" aside. When the social values change fast—as they did in the early years of the Bourgeois Revaluation, for example, or in the 1960s—they become the relevant scientific explanations. When a stone is falling in quicksand rather than in air at sea level, the 32 feet per second squared is not the relevant figure for its acceleration. To assume that the quicksand behaves like air because the assumption is convenient, or because Lucas or Mas-Colell have taught it to us in our first-year graduate program, is not science. It is dogma. When the demand curve for investments is stable, then marching down the demand curve in response to incentives such as foreign trade is the correct scientific story. But if the demand curve is whizzing out for sociological or political reasons, leading to massive innovation, the story of incentives is for the most part scientifically irrelevant. If the ideology of labor force participation by women quickly changes, as it did in the 1960s, then the ideology should be emphasized, and not merely routine matters of supply and demand.[8]

Levitt and Dubner in the same chapter give a lucid description of the results from economic experiments, especially by John List. But they don't realize that their examples, and especially List's, point to the importance of how people talk to themselves or others about "context" or "a particular circumstance." The police in the notorious Kitty Genovese murder of 1964, Levitt and Dubner argue, lied in order to cover up their unhurried response to the emergency calls (calls from neighbors, reported in the *New York Times* story as not happening at all)—the police of course had an "incentive" to do so, and the journalists involved had "incentives" to lie about the police in order to draw attention to what they wished to see as the horrible decline of social ethics during the disturbing 1960s. But the very facts show that people are self-constructing beings—in this case the police constructing stories on the spot about "merely a domestic dispute" and later "our loyalties to one

another as members of the force," and two weeks later the journalists literally constructing the story within larger stories about the decline of social
cohesion, or a story of their journalistic professionalism, or lack of it.

Behavior is sometimes best described scientifically as being about incentives given to the social actors. But sometimes it is best described as Second-
City improvisational comedy, with or without suggestions from the audience. The joke is on the economist. Rakesh Khurana, for instance, gives a
typically sociological definition of institutions as "complex and interacting
system of norms, structures, and cultural understandings that shape individual and organizational behavior."[9] That's not a budget line facing someone who can tell at once and easily what it is that pleases him. Thus for
example the "distinction" that Pierre Bourdieu examined in his dissection
of the bourgeois and working classes in France is not merely an external
constraint.[10] You don't only get to a higher level of utility if you can name
(on a pop quiz set by the sociologist) the composer of *The Well-Tempered
Clavier*. By doing so you actively distinguish yourself from people with fewer
academic qualifications in a qualification-obsessed France. You are playing
a social game in which each move has meaning. "Johann Sebastian Bach."
"Ah, one of Us. Welcome."

The historian Margaret Jacob has characterized the economistic, "instrumental" view, by contrast, as imagining "de-cultured free and free-willed
agents [who] naturally pursue their self-interest." The economic notion of
"institution" understood as "constraints" was studied by the sociologist Erving Goffman. He spoke of "the social situation of mental patients and other
inmates," under constraints "imposed from above by a system of explicit
formal rulings and a body of officials."[11] Institutional budget lines, like rules
of the asylum in the movie *One Flew over the Cuckoo's Nest*, are not ne-
gotiable, not at least according to Nurse Ratched (Goffman: "Society is an
insane asylum run by the inmates"). North's asylum talk, and the talk of the
other Samuelsonian economists about "incentives" being the same as "institutions," puts one in mind of the American comedian Mae West: "I admire
the institution of marriage. But I'm not ready for an institution."

North speaks highly of the anthropologist the late Clifford Geertz. It is
hard not to. North reads Geertz and his coauthors, though, as supporting
the economistic notion that in caravan trade, such as in Morocco around
1900, in North's formulation, "informal constraints [on, say, robbing the
next caravan to pass by] . . . made trade possible in a world where protection was essential and no organized state existed." North misses the non-

instrumental, shame-and-honor, non-Max-U language in which Geertz in fact specialized, and misses therefore the dance between internal motives and external impediments to action, between the dignity of a self-shaping citizen-not-a-slave and the merely utilitarian "constraints." The toll for safe passage in the deserts of Morocco, Geertz and his coauthors actually wrote, in explicit rejection of Max U, was "rather more than a mere payment," that is, a mere monetary constraint, a budget line, a fence, an incentive, an "institution" in the reduced definition of Samuelsonian economics. "It was part of a whole complex," the anthropologists actually wrote, "of *moral rituals,* customs with the force of law and the weight of *sanctity.*"[12]

"Sanctity" doesn't mean anything to North the economist, who for example in a 2005 book treats religion with an unlettered contempt worthy of Richard Dawkins or Christopher Hitchens ("Ditchkins," says Stanley Fish out of Terry Eagleton).[13] Religion to North means just another "institution" in his utilitarian, subject-to-constraints sense, that is, rules for an asylum. He labels religion repeatedly "nonrational." Religion to him is not about sanctity or the transcendent, not about faithful identity, not about giving lives a meaning through moral rituals. It is certainly not an ongoing intellectual and rational conversation about God's love, not to speak of an ongoing conversation *with* God. Religion is just another set of constraints on doing business, whether the business is in the market or in the temple or in the desert. In this North agrees with the astonishing economist Laurence Iannaccone and his followers when they come to study religion—religion to them is a social club, with costs and benefits, not an identity or a conversation.[14] (Anyone who has actually belonged to a social club, of course, knows that it soon develops into "moral rituals, customs with the force of law and the weight of sanctity." I could instance as such a club the Chicago School of economics during its great days in the 1970s. One of our sanctified rituals was to repeat *De gustibus non est disputandum,* while passionately advocating a very particular intellectual *gustus.*)[15] North asserts, for example, that in a prelegal stage "religious precepts . . . imposed standards of conduct on the [business] players."[16] He spurns the worldview that goes with religious faith. (His own religion of Science, of course, is in fact nothing like a mere constraint. He construes it as his identity, his moral ritual, his sanctity—in short, the meaning of his life, negotiated continuously over its extraordinary course. But ethical consistency is not a strong point of Samuelsonian economics.)

The economic historian Avner Greif, North's ally in what is known as the

New Institutionalism, calls culture "informal institutions," and North tries to talk this way as well. The "informality," however, would make such "institutions" very different from asylum-type "rules of the game." One does not negotiate the rules of chess. But informality *is* continuously negotiated— that is what the word "informality" means, exactly the degree of setting aside rules that distinguishes a backyard barbecue from a state dinner. How to behave at the barbecue? (Hint: do not jump naked into the bushes.) Just how far can a man go in teasing his mates? Just how intimate can a woman be with her girlfriends? The rules are constructed and reconstructed on the spot, which in such cases makes the Samuelsonian metaphor of constraints inapt. One does not have to deny that an ethical persuasion is often influenced by incentives to believe that once it becomes part of a person's identity it has an effect independent of incentives. Once someone is corrupted by life in a communist country, for example, it is hard to reset her ethics. She goes on relying on the "bureau" model of human interaction as against the market. Once you are educated in Samuelsonian economics it is hard to reset your intellectual life. You go on thinking of every social situation in terms of Max U's mechanical reaction instead of a socially constructed dance. The Geertzian metaphor of negotiation and ritual often makes more sense.[17] "O body swayed to music, o brightening glance, / How can we know the dancer from the dance?"

Some economists grasp that institutions have to do with human meaning, not merely Northian "constraints." The Austrians and the old institutionalists managed to escape, Houdini-like, from the straightjacket that Douglass North, Gary Becker, Deepak Lal, Avner Greif, Steven Levitt, Max U, and their friends have so eagerly donned. The Austrian economist Ludwig Lachmann (1906–1990), for example, spoke of "certain superindividual schemes of thought, namely, *institutions*, to which schemes of thought of the first order [notice that to the Austrians the economy *is* thought, all the way down], the plans, must be oriented, and which serve therefore, to some extent, the coordination of individual plans."[18] Thus a language is a scheme of thought, backed by social approval and conversational implicatures. Thus too is a courtroom of the common law a scheme of thought, backed by bailiffs and law books.

North, like the numerous other economists such as Levitt who have settled into the straightjacket, talks a good deal about meaning-free "incentives," because that is what Samuelsonian economics can deal with. The constraints. The budget lines. The relative price. Yet one can agree that when the price of crime goes up (that is, the incentives change in the direction of, say, harsher punishment) less of it will be supplied, yet nonetheless affirm that crime is more than a passionless business proposition. (If you don't believe it, tune into one of the numerous prison reality shows and watch the inmates struggling with the guards, with mad purpose though prudent means; or listen to Ishmael on Captain Ahab: "In his heart, Ahab had some glimpse of this, namely: all my means are sane, my motive and my object mad.") The Broken Windows Effect is that major crime goes down if you punish immediately minor crimes like breaking windows or painting graffiti. The effect has little to do with price and a lot to do with shame and social imitation.[19] If crime is more than utterly passionless calculations by Max U, then changing the ethics of criminals and their acquaintances can affect it—ethics that do change, sometimes quickly (crime rates fall dramatically during a big war, for example, at any rate on the home front). The metaphors of crime as being "like" employment as a taxi driver, or of a marriage as being "like" a trade between husband and wife, or of children being "like" consumer durables such as refrigerators have been useful. Neat stuff. But they don't do the whole job.

Prudence is a virtue. It is a virtue characteristic of a human seeking purely monetary profit—but also of a rat seeking cheese and of a blade of grass seeking light. Consider that temperance and courage and love and justice and hope and faith are also virtues, and that they are the ones defining of humans. Unlike prudence, which characterizes every form of life and quasi-life down to bacteria and viruses, the nonprudence virtues are characteristic of humans uniquely, and of human languages and meanings. In no sense is a prudent blade of grass "courageous," or a prudent rat "faithful" (outside of the movie *Ratatouille*, whose humor turns on the irony of the rat hero being more faithful, and less motivated by Prudence Only, than many of the humans). As Hugo de Groot, Grotius, put it in 1625, "The saying that every creature is led by nature to seek its own private advantage, expressed thus universally, must not be granted. . . . [The human animal] has received from nature a peculiar instrument, that is, the use of speech; I say that he has besides that a faculty of knowing and acting according to some general principles; so that what relates to this faculty is not common to all animals, but properly and peculiarly agrees to mankind."[20] North, however, will have none of human speech and meanings and acting according to some general principle aside from one's own private interest. His positivistic talk about "constraints" and "rules of the game" misses what he could have learned from Geertz, Weber, Smith, Aquinas, Cicero, Confucius, Moses, or his mother (North's mother, or Moses's)—that social rules expressed in human languages have human meanings. They are instruments as well as constraints, as Lachmann says, playthings as well as fences, communities as much as ward rules.[21]

Take for example so trivial an institution for providing incentives as a traffic light.[22] When it turns red it surely does create incentives to stop. For one thing, the rule is self-enforcing, because the cross traffic has the green. (In the old joke a New York City taxi driver drives at high speed through every red light but screeches to a halt at every green. His terrified passenger demands to know why. "Today my brother is driving, too, and he *always* goes through red lights!") For another, the police may be watching, or the automatic camera may capture your license plate. The red light is a fence, a constraint, a rule of the game, or of the asylum. So far goes North, and with him most economists.

Yet the red light has meaning to humans, who are more than rats in a Prudence Only experiment facing food incentives. Among other things it means state dominance over drivers. It signals the presence of civilization, and the legitimacy granted to the state that a civilization entails. (Test: you are struggling through a pathless jungle and come upon . . . a traffic light: "Mr. Civilization, I presume.") It signals, too, the rise of mechanical means of regulation, in contrast to a human traffic officer on a raised stand with white gloves. The red light is in Lachmann's terms a system of thought. It is a system that some drivers find comforting and others find irritating, depending on their attitudes toward the state, toward mechanical inventions, toward traffic officers. For a responsible citizen, or an Iowan, or indeed for a fascist conformist, the red light means the keeping of rules. She will wait for the green even at 3:00 a.m. at an intersection obviously clear in all directions, an intersection lacking a license-plate camera or police person in attendance, or a reliably irresponsible brother on the road, even when she's in a bit of a hurry. Incentives be damned. But for a principled social rebel, or a Bostonian, or indeed for a sociopath, the red light is a challenge to his autonomy, a state-sponsored insult. Again, incentives be damned. If the Broken Window policy is applied *too* vigorously it could well evoke an angry reaction from potential criminals, and could result in more, not less, crime, or at any rate widespread resentment of the police.

Meaning matters. A cyclist in Chicago writing to the newspaper in 2008 about a fellow cyclist killed when he ran a red light declared that "when the traffic light changes color, the streets of our cities become an every-man-for-himself, anything-goes killing zone, where anyone who dares enter will be caught in a stream of intentionally more-deadly, high-mass projectiles, controlled by operators who are given a license to kill when the light turns green."[23] The motorist who unintentionally hit the cyclist probably gave a different meaning to the event. A good deal of life and politics and exchange takes place in the damning of incentives and the assertion of meaning—the mother's love or the politician's integrity or the teacher's enthusiasm, what Keynes (and after him George Akerlof and Robert Shiller) called "animal spirits" and what Sen calls "commitment" and what I call "virtues and corresponding vices other than Prudence Only."[24]

Or take the governance of the modern American corporation. Rakesh Khurana shows that the "agency theory" of the economists in business schools replaced after the 1970s the "managerialist ideology" that had provided the very reason for business schools in the first place:

> Agency theory dissolved the idea that executives should be held—on the basis of notions such as stewardship, stakeholder interests, or promotion of the common good—to any standard stricter than sheer self-interest. How could they if they were incapable of adhering to such a standard in the first place? Students were now taught that managers, as a matter of *economic principle*, could not be trusted: in the words of Oliver Williamson, they were "opportunistic with guile." . . . [Agency theory, Khurana continues,] represented, within the confines of a "professional school," a thorough repudiation of professionalism.[25]

Agency theory in the business-school form can be dated from an article by Milton Friedman, reprinted in the *New York Times* magazine in 1970, with a truncated title supplied by the editors: "The Social Responsibility of Business Is to Increase Its Profits." Khurana cites Michael Jensen, one of the chief proponents of the new and corrosive theory, as taking Friedman's article as the manifesto of the movement—though, by the way, Khurana and Jensen and most other people have read too hurriedly the crucial sentence, in which Friedman says that managers should increase the stock value of the firm *subject to the norms and laws of the society*—which is a rather different principle than "the public be damned." They might better have read Friedman—or Mill, or Smith—more widely.

Yet the tendency in the Chicago School of the 1970s cannot be doubted. The same notion that all actors are creatures of Prudence Only had animated the "public choice school" founded at the University of Virginia a decade earlier by James Buchanan (PhD Chicago) and Gordon Tullock (JD, and honorary doctorate in economics, Chicago). It animated, too, the "property-rights" economics inspired by Ronald Coase (who was a bridge between Virginia and the University of Chicago), and perfected by Armen Alchian of UCLA and Harold Demsetz of Chicago and then UCLA. Prudence Only lies behind the cynical interpretation of professionalism by Reuben Kessel at Chicago (left-wing sociologists such as Randall Collins and Magali Larson agreed: the left and the right joined in saying that doctors operate on one's wallet). The "law and economics" movement founded then by Coase, Aaron Director (Friedman's brother-in-law, and long at the Law School of the University of Chicago), and in extreme Max U form by Richard Posner (at Chicago and judge of the Seventh Circuit Court) takes Prudence Only as its motto, as does the "economic theory of regulation" founded again in the 1970s by George Stigler and Sam Peltzman at Chicago (with helpful supplements from the left by the historian Gabriel Kolko). My own school of "new economic history," invented by North at Washington (another Chicago School department at the time) and by Fogel, who was at Rochester (still another Chicago School department) and then at Chicago itself, tried to find out how far Prudence Only would go in history (Fogel at length concluded: only so far). The "quantitative finance" invented in the 1970s by Robert Merton at Pennsylvania and by Myron Scholes and Fischer Black at Chicago was another influential venture in agency theory and Prudence Only. The "new labor economics" was, too, invented in the 1970s by Jacob Mincer at Columbia and H. Gregg Lewis at Chicago and Gary Becker at Chicago and Columbia and then Chicago again. And the "rational expectations" approach to macroeconomics founded in the 1970s by Thomas Sargent at Minnesota and Robert Lucas at Carnegie and then Chicago brought Max U into the economics of business cycles and inflation. (You can see from the shower of "Chicago" and "the 1970s" in the list why the University of Chicago during the 1970s was the most exciting place for a young economist to work, comparable to Cambridge, England, during the 1930s in its effect on the science.) All the Chicago economists strode past meaning—love, temperance, courage, justice, faith, hope—and fixed on the individual agent's prudent self-interest, like a prudent blade of grass. In his study of marriage, for example, Becker elevated self-interested exchange between agents he called "M" and "F" to the whole purpose of the institution, and put the word "love" in scare quotes.

Yet meaning matters in business as much as love in a marriage or courage in an army or justice in a court of law. "The [agency] theory," Khurana notes, "has nothing to say about the stubborn, unavoidable fact that agents remain in touch with one another within an organization, and that this contact—like other sustained human contact—becomes layered with affect, content, and meaning."[26] Remember the club and its sacred rules. On the contrary, declared the economists teaching in business schools from the 1970s on: Align the incentives of managers with the interests of the stockholders. That is all ye know on earth, and all ye need to know. The Great Recession gave us all some perspective on how agency theory works.

Khurana does not mention, however, the deepest problem in agency theory in any of its forms (public choice, law and economics, finance, whatever). It declares that one has an "obligation" to make profit (and further that the economic analyst has an "obligation" to articulate such a theory, always, and has an "obligation" not to talk about the ethics of managerial or scientific obligation, since these are matters of value about which one has an obligation not to dispute). But where does the obligation come from? It comes in fact from the ethical responsibilities of a manager to her professionalism, her stewardship, her stakeholders' interests, or her promotion of the common good. The agent is not a pure Prudence Only, Max U creature after all. In the very theory that denies ethics to the agent she is imagined to be driven by an ethic, albeit a tacit and abbreviated one. Immanuel Kant fell into a similar self-contradiction when he claimed to base ethics on reason alone, yet gave no account of the reasons an agent would *want* to act on reason.[27] In truth, the agent wants to act because she attributes meaning to her life, as a manager or a civil servant or an economist or an ethical philosopher. She is a human with an identity, not a Max U calculating machine like grass or bacteria or rats. Ask any businessperson. I know personally a very successful one, a banker, who tells me that she has never been good at "saluting," that is, going along with whatever imprudent or unjust plan her boss proposes. She's not a yes-woman, and is valuable in some businesses precisely because of that ethical identity beyond Maxine U. It's not always good for her career, not always maximizing her personal prudence. But she can look at herself in the mirror in the morning.

Or take a still more elevated issue, that of liberty. The neo-Roman theory that the intellectual historian Quentin Skinner identifies can be thought of as turning on status, not contract. The neo-Roman theory is old-fashioned in one sense, dating in Continental legal theory back to Justinian. But in another sense, as the liberal theorists Montesquieu and Tocqueville insisted, gazing with envy at the common law of England, the neo-Roman theory was a novelty implied by the reception on the Continent (but not in England) from the twelfth century on of Roman law. Macfarlane notes that on the Continent down to the French Revolution "civilization moved away from a 'feudal' one based on the flexibility of 'contract,' to an *ancien régime* one based on [the rigidities of inherited] 'status.'"[28] "The Roman law," wrote Tocqueville bitterly, "was a slave law."[29] The *neo*-Roman theorists of liberty attacked the assignment of hierarchical status that has so long defaced the Roman legal tradition. That a person had the status of a slave in Roman law was itself an insult, no matter how cleverly he could manipulate his master to achieve maximum utility, in the style of Roman comedies down to *The Comedy of Errors*, *The Marriage of Figaro*, and *A Funny Thing Happened on the Way to the Forum*. Liberty in a sense that, say, John Milton would have understood is not about how much stuff you get, or where you are on your budget line, or how far out the "constraints" are. It is about whether you are under the orders of some other mortal, for example a husband or a wife in a marriage. By contrast, Becker's theory of marriage takes the benevolent husband as absorbing the welfare of his wife, and thinks it no slavery. After all, she gets all the diamonds she wants. A feminist would object, as did John Milton (though no feminist) in his first treatise on divorce.

North (like me a Chicago School economist) adopts unawares a liberal and consequentialist, as against what Skinner calls a neo-Roman, theory of constraints. The "liberal" notion of unfreedom, in this terminology, looks only at the actually exercised external impediments to action by solely self-interested agents, such as a prohibition on slave marriage or the demand by a landlord to vote for him for Parliament.[30] By contrast, the neo-Roman English theorists of liberty just before Locke, such as John Milton, James Harrington, and Algernon Sidney, with echoes and restorations later (Thomas Jefferson, for example, though a driver of slaves), noted that mere dependency itself was a scandal—even though a potential rather than an exercised impediment.

An actual impediment is a constraint, à la Max U. A potential impediment is a symbol and a shame, not captured by the meaning-less notion of a constraint or an alignment of incentives. It would often show itself, for example, through internalized self-contempt. It would show itself as self-censorship in a royal court, or as the dependency of a democratic mob on employers or advertisers. "Nothing denotes a slave," wrote Sidney in reply to the advocates of absolute monarchy, "but a dependency on the will of another." Dependency such as employment in a corporation, then, or an assistant professorship without tenure, would be slavery of a sort. What matters to a free person in the neo-Roman theory of liberty is the *potential* for damage (not the actual damages emphasized in liberal utilitarianism). It is a matter of meaning, of dignity, not budget constraints. Robert Burns sang, "The coward slave we pass him by: / We dare be poor for a' that." So likewise Sidney dared to refuse to plead when faced with charges of treason before Charles II's pet judges, and died for it. He died for meaning and morality, not for Prudence Only and incentives.

34

AND SO THE BETTER INSTITUTIONS, SUCH AS THOSE ALLEGED FOR 1689, DON'T EXPLAIN

In any event, with the Max U Only character in hand Douglass North believes he has equipped himself to explain the modern world. The axiom is that "economic actors have an incentive to invest their time, resources [in the economist's broad sense as 'means for achieving ends'], and [personal] energy in knowledge and skills that will improve their material status."[1] The question, North observes, is whether Max U's "investment" will be in sharp swords with which to steal money, or in efficient machines with which to spin cotton. Both investments improve Max U's material status.

Which path for our *goyisher kop* Max U? North puts his finger on a major problem facing political economy from the caves to the highest of civilizations, namely, the solidity of property rights. On the way to pointing out the problem, however, he and his school commit a logical error, begging the question. "Economic history," North declares, "is overwhelmingly a story of economies that failed to produce a set of economic rules of the game (with enforcement) that induce sustained economic growth."[2] The phrase "that induce sustained economic growth" makes the argument circular. An institution is not the institution he has in mind until it does cause the Industrial Revolution. He has assumed his conclusion, namely, that a change in property rights—his "institutions"—did make the Industrial Revolution. The argument is immune to refutation, because he is only concerned with changes in property rights that (he assumes without evidence) did in fact cause the Industrial Revolution.[3] North is *assuming* that sustained economic growth was caused by changes in rules/institutions, rather than by investment or by foreign trade or, more plausibly, by ideological development.

Making his statement into a meaningful hypothesis requires splitting it in two. Make part 1 into an empirical statement that "many economies failed to make rules," adding some factual standard for knowing when a rule has been sufficiently "made." (Which is going to be hard, because all societies have rules.) Then one could ask in part 2 whether "the change in rules in, say, seventeenth-century England was large enough to actually induce sustained economic growth." (Which is going to be harder.)

North's main example of growth-inducing institutions is the settlement of 1689 in England. That has seemed reasonable on its face to many economists, who don't know much about the Middle Ages, / Look at the pictures and turn the pages. They think, as I said, in terms of maximization *under constraints*, and therefore are fascinated by a claim that institutions just *are* constraints, which got relaxed in 1689. "Cute," they think. Some of the relaxing of constraints, too, North wants to make endogenous, caused by the very growth. "Cuter," say the economists in their charmingly innocent way. The Max U merchant's "investment in knowledge and skills would gradually and incrementally alter the basic institutional framework."[4] Cool.

North's endogenous story (he also has an exogenous one) resembles that of his friend Braudel. Braudel argued, as we have seen, that out of local markets there came, with the expansion of trade, the age of high commerce, and that out of the age of high commerce there came, with the expansion of trade, the Industrial Revolution. Likewise North writes, "Long distance trade in early modern Europe from the eleventh to the sixteenth centuries was a story of the sequentially more complex organization that eventually led to the rise of the western world."[5] Braudel was less celebratory than North has been about the progress from local to worldwide trade, and thence to industrial innovation, retaining the French intellectual's suspicion of *les bourgeois*.

But North and Braudel agree on the machinery involved. Expansion fueled it, they say, and so it awaited the late eighteenth century to come to fruition. Foreign trade is their engine of growth. "Increasing volume," writes North, "obviously made such institutional developments [as modern capital markets] possible."[6] "The size and scope of merchant empires" made arm's-length transactions possible. "The volume of international trade and therefore . . . economies of scale" made for standardization and information."[7] The result was a virtuous spiral of economic forces: "The increasing volume of long distance trade raised the rate of return to merchants of devising effective mechanisms for enforcing contracts. In turn, the development of such mechanisms lowered the costs of contracting and made trade more profitable, thereby increasing its volume."[8] The growth is endogenous because it is generated inside the economic sphere itself. Growth leads to growth, which leads to . . . growth. Neat.

But North's story tells of *routine* search for better institutions. The search is "routine" because it is a pretty much predictable result of investment. If you reorganize at great expense the docklands of London, and arrange to collect some of the gain for yourself, then you or your heirs will reap the accounting profit. The society-wide economic gains, from which you extract some accounting profit, are that traffic gets in and out of port with less delay. Ropes and sails and ship timbers are more readily available. Information about cargoes coming and going is cheaper. Loss in storage is lower. North's best and Nobel-winning scientific work, on ocean freight rates before the nineteenth century, gives evidence for such effects. Doubtless you as a dockland investor sometimes make a error, and over- or underinvest in the new docks, or fail to secure your claim to some of the profits. But the prospect of net profit, while not perfectly predictable, is what motivates you in such a routine investment. There is only a small element of discovery and glory. The improvement is like the draining 1848–1852 of the Haarlemmermeer (where Schiphol Airport now sits), one of the numerous great projects of Dutch water management. Cost: steam pumps. Benefit: farmland. *Goed idee.*

For such routine investment as an explanation of the modern world, however, there are two big problems. For one thing, as I've said, there's an economic problem. Routine, incremental investments, naturally, yield routine, incremental returns. North writes that his Max U merchant "would gain . . . from devising ways to bond fellow merchants, to establish merchant courts, to induce princes to protect goods from brigandage in return for revenue [note the quid pro quo: it is like hiring a policeman], to devise ways to discount bills of exchange."[9] The claim is that we grew as rich as we are by simply piling brick on brick, or in this case contract on contract. It was I have noted the usual way of thinking in economics from Smith in 1776 through Rostow in 1960. After all, that's how we as individuals save for old age, and it is what we urge on our children. But no one, to repeat, grows *very* rich by routine investment, and neither did Western society 1800 to the present. The new American economic history of the 1960s, which North helped invent, and the old British economic history of the 1950s, which explored the same issue with less rigorous economics, showed it. Routine investment was a good idea, just as the draining of the Haarlemmermeer was *een goed idee*, and just as saving for your old age is a good idea—provide, provide. But the astounding growth after 1800 needs an astounding explanation.

And that's the other, historical, problem, as I've also said. If routine investment explains the modern world, why didn't the modern world happen in ancient times? Routine is easy. That's why it is called "routine." Ancient China was peaceful and commercial for decades at a time, and often for centuries. Its foreign trade was enormous. In the Roman Empire, likewise, the disturbances were usually palace uprisings in the city of Rome or battles out on the Germanic or Parthian frontier, minor matters economically speaking—nothing like the economy-disturbing invasions and especially plagues that finally overcame the West. The ancient Egyptians, too, had command over resources and had famously stable regimes. The Muslim empires in the two centuries after Muhammad grew at gigantic rates, in extent and in economies of scale. The Aztecs and before them the Maya had great trading empires, as did earlier civilizations still to be explored in the New World. All these became brilliant in economy and culture—yet nothing like to the startling degree of northwestern and then all of Europe 1700–2000 CE. If growth produces growth, which produces growth, as the economists delight to hypothesize (the model is *so* beautiful), why did modern economic growth wait to happen in the eighteenth, nineteenth, and twentieth centuries, and then begin in a notably turbulent patch of the globe? If the causes of growth are endogenous, as against "exogenous" (the Greek means "outwardly born"), then why didn't the same institutional changes happen in Egypt under the pharaohs, or for that matter in Peru under the Incas?

∞

Endogeneity aside, North and numerous economists after him have focused, too, on the exogenous accident of the Glorious Revolution of 1688 and its settlement in 1689. North praises, as would many economists, including me, a "credible commitment to secure property rights."[10] But his seminal essay with Weingast in 1989 has been widely credited with claiming, as North and Weingast sometimes do and sometimes don't in their last few interesting but self-contradicting paragraphs, that the introduction of a Dutch-style national debt in the 1690s shows "how institutions played a necessary role in making possible economic growth and political freedom."[11]

It doesn't seem so. It shows rather how a state can become powerful by reliably paying its debts to citizens and to foreigners, as Venice, Genoa, Lübeck, Hamburg, and the Dutch Republic had long shown.[12] Continentals were stunned when well-financed British armies of conquest and occupation such as the Duke of Marlborough's *paid* for their supplies instead of simply stealing them. The novel and bourgeois practice gradually changed the image of Englishmen from barbarity to gentlemanliness.[13] But Robert Ekelund, in the style of North, claims that "the credible commitments . . . were required of new institutions [namely, the English and then British national debt] . . . [and led] to modern capitalism."[14] No they didn't. They allowed Dutch William to begin the 120-year war against France that characterized the long eighteenth century in Britain.

John Wells and Douglas Wills succeed in showing statistically that the Jacobite threat to the Protestant succession haunted early eighteenth-century politics in Britain (which event may have been weighed, perhaps with less trouble, by wallowing a bit in the cultural mud of novels and newspapers and street ballads. Concerning the Jacobites, for example, one of the ballads sang, "To England then they went, / And Carlisle they ta'en't [took it], / The Crown they fain would ha'en't [have it], / but behold"). In supporting North and Weingast, however, Wells and Wills too claim, offhandedly, that "the resulting institutional changes [of 1688] ushered in financial developments that laid the foundation for the Industrial Revolution and ultimately established Britain as a world power."[15] The second half of the claim, about power, is true. A parliamentary monarchy that could borrow reliably was one that could intervene in the balance of power on the Continent, and promptly did. But the first half is at best unproven by any of the analytic narratives offered in its favor. In the subtitle of their paper Wells and Wills summarize how they see the threats from the Old and New Pretender out of France connecting with the claims of North and Weingast: "The Jacobite Threat to England's Institutions [of financing the national debt] and [therefore] Economic Growth." But the national—that is, governmental—debt had no demonstrated connection to economic growth. In 1931 those founts of historical wisdom, Sellar and Yeatman, well anticipated the resulting mishmash: "It was Williamandmary who first discovered the National Debt and had the memorable idea of building the Bank of England to put it in. The National Debt is a very Good Thing and it would be dangerous to pay it off, for fear of Political Economy."[16]

That the British state did not then use the wealth acquired by such a Good Thing to obstruct economic growth and destroy political liberty—as so many states enriched by, say, drilling for oil have done—had nothing to do with the imitation under William III of the bourgeois and Dutch method of drilling for loans, and building the Bank of England to refine them in. A historian of the English Parliament noted of its new transcendent power that "despotic power was only available intermittently before 1688, but it was always available thereafter."[17] Despotic power can be misused, to kill economic growth and political liberty. That after all was what the ideologists of the Glorious Revolution from Locke to Macaulay were chiefly worried about. And as the economists Carmen Reinhart and Kenneth Rogoff put the point, "It is not clear how well the institutional innovations noted by North and Weingast would have fared had Britain been a bit less fortunate in the many wars it fought in subsequent years."[18] Britain got a military-financial complex up and running in the 1690s and had the good fortune of Churchills and Clives and Wolfes and Nelsons and Wellesleys in its operation. Good on them. But it is not the economy and it is not the modern world. As many histories do, the argument confuses economic enrichment with military victory.

What did matter was a change in political and economic rhetoric occurring about the same time that made the British state prudent in the financing of its wars of imperial adventure 1690 to 1815, as the Netherlands had earlier learned to be prudent in the financing of its wars of survival, 1568–1648 and (complements of the envious English) during the three Anglo-Dutch wars of 1652–1654, 1665–1667, 1672–1674 (no wonder the Dutch and the English finally gave up their quarrels and adopted William as their joint *stadhouder/king*). In 1787 the professor of civil law at Glasgow, John Millar, had it more right than North does: the "energy and vigor which political liberty [my claim], and the secure possession and enjoyment of property [North and Weingast's claim, and erroneous], are wont to inspire . . . was obtained by the memorable Revolution of 1688, which completed . . . a government of a more popular nature."[19] Secure possession of property is necessary. But it had little to do with the financial innovations that North and Weingast stress, or with the political liberty that Millar and other Whigs stress—because it had been established centuries before. A government of a more popular nature, and political liberty, and above all the energy and vigor that a new deal brought forth from England's bourgeoisie, were what mattered.

∞

But there is a deeper problem with North's glorification of the Glorious Revolution. It is: numerous societies—in fact, all of them, or else they are not societies but wars of all against all—have produced rules of property. The Code of Hammurabi early in the second millennium BCE did so. English kings, to leap over millennia of strict enforcement of property rights by Chinese and Romans, asserted in the Middle Ages the primacy of royal courts for free men over local and sometimes arbitrary authority. And the barons and the petty lords themselves were bound by traditional law, often bound hand and foot (as discovered for example in recent research by the historian and geographer of medieval agriculture, Bruce Campbell). Indeed, no society does well if it does not have such rules. As the prophet Micah (7: 2–3) said in the late eighth century BCE, "The good man is perished out of the earth: and there is none upright among men: they all lie in wait for blood; they hunt every man his brother with a net. That they may do evil with both hands earnestly, the prince asketh and the judge asketh for a reward." Every ordered community since Moses or Solon or Sargon the Great or the First Emperor of China has enforced property rights and prevented people from hunting their brothers with nets.

One is reminded of the anarchic and pre-Christian Norsemen, who when they approached a coast had to decide whether to kill the natives or to trade with them. They were, a Samuelsonian economist might suppose, Max U characters, largely indifferent when outside their own highly structured society in Norway—going with whatever maximized material utility on the coast of Ireland or the lands of the Rus. Thus A. A. Milne's "Bad Sir Brian Botany" "went among the villagers and blipped them on the head." Yet he received his comeuppance, and became "quite a different person now he hasn't got his spurs on, / And he goes about the village as B. Botany, Esquire," *not* blipping on the head. The move from bad to good Sir Botany is what North has in mind as the alleged cause of the Industrial Revolution.

The trouble is that it had already happened centuries before—that shift to good Sir Botany, with episodes of reversion to type. A lack of defined property perhaps characterizes some parts of Europe during the ninth century (though consider the ordered realms of Charlemagne or Alfred the Great) but certainly not England in the seventeenth century, as North to the contrary claims. Likewise the wild Norsemen of Bergen became Hansa merchants, or at any rate welcomed German and Frisian merchants into the wooden warehouses of the Hansa, ending blipping on the head. Violent rent-seeking in North's unhistorical account is supposed to have happened in the seventeenth century in, of all unlikely places, England. As late as the seventeenth century in England, North is claiming, Max U saw his best chance in violence, not in voluntary exchange. The claim is factually mistaken. Violence had been blocked by law and politics in England for centuries. Even the barons had at length been denied their independent armies, by the early Tudor kings. Ordinary violence and theft were pursued by the hue and cry: "Out! Out!" England (and every other civilized country) was drenched in laws, of property and tort and merchants and what you will, in manorial courts and the king's courts.

That is not to say that the law was perfectly just or prompt. It became especially unjust and unprompt in periods of quarrels over who would be king. A chronicler in 1457 early in the Wars of the Roses versified on the matter: "In every shire with Jacks and salets clean / Misrule doth rise, and maketh neighbors war; / The weaker goeth beneath, as oft is seen, / The mightiest his quarrel will prefer."[20] In 1459 the Commons had pled to the King that "in divers parts of this realm great and abominable murders, robberies, extortions . . . [are] done by such persons as either be of great might or else favored under persons of great power."[21] They viewed the situation as a descent from previous law-abiding. The gentry family of Pastons at the time, recently enriched, were under constant threat from the thuggish mighty, such as Lord Molynes and the Duke of Norfolk. In 1469 the Duke seized the Paston's Caister Castle with a force of 3,000 of his men. "England in the fifteenth century" wrote H. S. Bennett in 1921 describing the episode, "was too near the uncontrolled habits and customs of a more primitive civilization for men to have become peaceful or easily amenable to law. . . . The great lords themselves relied on the power of arms, rather than the pleas of their lawyers, and the rest of England took its lead from them."[22] And yet during all this, before Henry Tudor restored the rule of law in 1485, the law was at least honored in the breach. A commoner could bring suit against a great nobleman, and might win. If he had enough money and powerful friends he might even get a jury or judge corrupted to his side instead of the duke's. *Omnia pro pecunia facta sunt*, they said: All things are done for money. But the money paid for lawyers, witnesses, sheriffs, jailors—not only for thugs. The field of play for the abominable murders and extortions in England was the law.

England when at peace, which was the usual case throughout its history, was a nation of ordinary property laws, no more or less corrupt than Chicago in 1925 or the American South under segregation, places in which innovation flourished. It was so, for example, even when the Stuart kings were undermining the independence of the judiciary in order to extract the odd pound with which to have a foreign policy in a new age of standing armies and floating navies. And the amounts extracted, contrary to the Northian suggestion that the king owned everything, were by modern standards pathetically small. The figures offered by North and Weingast themselves imply that total central government *expenditure* under James I and Charles I was at most a mere 1.2 to 2.4 percent of national income. At the same time the Romanovs were spending nearly 15 percent of Russia's entire national income on war and domestic oppression, and shortly afterward the Hohenzollern learned how to spend comparable shares on the largest standing army in proportion to population in Europe.[23] We nowadays face central government expenditures among free countries ranging from the U.S.'s and South Korea's low of 21 percent to France's high of 46 percent.[24] The four forced "loans" from the rich of London 1604–1625 amounted to a trivial 1 percent of the national income earned over those years.[25]

Of course, as the American case in the 1770s showed, a tax on stamps taking a tiny portion of income can trip off a revolution, and so here. But even the Stuart kings, grasping though they were, and emboldened (as were many monarchs at the time) by the newly asserted divine right of kings, were nothing like as efficient in predation as modern governments—or indeed as were the Georgian kings of Great Britain and Ireland who eventually succeeded the Stuarts. Macaulay had in 1830 spoofed the alarm of "the patriots of 1640," who exclaimed, "A million a year will beggar us." By 1783, Macaulay noted, the alarm was instead over the 240 times more debt that the British state had by then issued.[26] By the end of the long century of struggle with the French, in 1815, the United Kingdom owed in its national debt a sum over twice its annual national income (which is over three times the ratio in the United States in 2009—though the American figure does not include the gigantic unfunded debt such as Social Security and, especially, Medicare; but these are modifiable promises, as government bonds are not so readily). Britain paid off the debt from the Napoleonic Wars by the 1840s, at the height of Political Economy.

North nonetheless stresses "the extent [to which] the state [after 1689] was bound by commitments that it would not confiscate assets."[27] North and Weingast imply that the Stuart kings of England were on the contrary masters at confiscating their subjects' wealth. But you can see from the figures that they weren't. It was a good thing, not a bad thing, that the Stuarts were in fact such tyros in expropriation, suffering the indignity of frequent breakdowns of their credit with bankers, and in 1672 actual bankruptcy. James I and II and Charles I and II were in fact stumbling amateurs by the standards of the modern bureaucratic state. Capitalists in the law-abiding, innovating United States were spooked in the 1930s, as the economic historian Robert Higgs has shown, by Roosevelt's reiterated rhetoric of expropriating the economic royalists—which gained force by being promised at a time in which communist and especially fascist states had just done so.[28] And in 1946–1951 England itself, the very home since the year of Our Lord 1272 and before of credible commitments to secure property rights, proceeded to nationalize in succession the Bank of England, coal, inland transport, gas, steel, health services, and much else. Even under the Conservatives, who reassumed power in 1951, the nationalization was only partly overturned, and the wartime (and anticapitalist) controls on prices persisted. After a failed attempt to lift controls on sweets in 1949, rationing of them was dropped at last on February 5, 1953, as every British child of that time well remembers. And yet afterward for a while in the land of original free enterprise the sugar itself continued to be rationed.

No quantitative case can be made, in short, that it was after 1689 that England moved from predation to security of property. Predation characterized periods of disorder, the Wars of the Roses above all, but shorter episodes like the Civil War, too—though even then, as I said, sheer violence paid at least lip service to the law. But England was on the whole and for many centuries a nation of laws, with busy courts at all levels, from the time of Quia Emptores (1290), or Edward I (ruled 1272–1307), or earlier, and remained so under the Stuarts. As North and Weingast themselves admit, "The fundamental strength of English property rights" could be dated from the Great Charter of 1215, and surely earlier.[29] And what then of secure Italian or for that matter Byzantine or Islamic or Chinese property rights? If property rights were the crucial novelty of 1689, why not industrialization before and elsewhere, in places in which property rights were also enforced?

In certain smallish matters the law of property was indeed improved by the Glorious Revolution—for example (not so small, actually), in 1689 and

1693 landlords were granted clear rights to tin, copper, iron, or lead under their properties, free of harassment for violating an old prerogative of the Crown which claimed the silver and gold thus extracted, even if incidental to the mining of the base metals. But there's not much in it. Certainly no economy can prosper, as North and Richard Pipes and Harold Demsetz and Richard Epstein and I warmly agree, in which a Bad Sir Botany can go around blipping people on the head and seizing whatever he wishes.[30] "Trade cannot live without mutual trust among private men," wrote Temple in 1672.[31] Otherwise we face a war of all against all. As Hobbes explained, "In such condition there is no place for industry, because the fruit thereof is uncertain: and consequently no culture of the earth; no navigation, nor use of the commodities that may be imported by sea; no commodious building; no instruments of moving and removing such things as require much force; no knowledge of the face of the earth; no account of time; no arts; no letters; no society."[32] North and Weingast correctly assert, with Millar, the importance of "the ability to engage in secure contracting across time and space."[33] Private property is not optional, and "market socialism" is a contradiction in terms. Even some Marxists nowadays, especially the economists among them, agree on the point. But the problem is, as I have said, that there was little news in British property rights around 1700 that can explain its subsequent economic success.

The Northian story has passed into conventional thinking, as for example in an alarming article titled "Growth and Institutions" for *The New Palgrave Dictionary of Economics* (2008) by the economist Daron Acemoglu:[34]

> Consider the development of property rights in Europe during the Middle Ages. Lack of property rights for landowners, merchants and proto-industrialists . . .

No, as has been known by historians of medieval Europe for a hundred years. Property was very fully developed, especially in land and in personal possessions. For Italy, of course, the fact is obvious, and the evidence there of fully developed rights in all sorts of property is overwhelming. But a market even in land even in remote England functioned in large and small parcels. Exchange on secure terms took place there in all commodities and factors of production at the latest from the Normans and their lawyers—or outside the king's court in leet courts registering peasant deals in the thirteenth century, and in most respects hundreds of years earlier, as has been a commonplace among English medievalists since the 1950s at the latest.[35]

was detrimental to economic growth during this epoch. . . .

No: lack of property rights had little to do with poor medieval productivity.[36]

> Consequently, economic institutions during the Middle Ages provided little incentive to invest in land, physical or human capital, or technology . . .

No: incentives of a strictly economic sort did not change between 1000 and 1800, not much.[37]

> and failed to foster economic growth.

Economic growth did not occur. But—outside of Russia—the absence was not because of a lack of property rights but because of a lack of massive innovation, and that in turn because of a lack of bourgeois dignity and liberty, and a lack of widespread education.

> These economic institutions also ensured that the monarchs controlled a large fraction of the economic resources in society, ...

No. Even in early modern times the percentage "controlled" by monarchs was small by modern or some ancient standards: think 5 percent of national income. Rents from royal estates, until sold off, would make the figure higher—but the estates are rental income, which is an affirmation rather than a violation of the rights of private property that any taxation represents. The *aristocracy* did "control" a large share of the land, though freeholders owned a great deal, too, and the serfs that Acemoglu thinks were part of the economic resources "controlled" by the "monarchs" were in fact largely independent—certainly from 1348 on, and in their ability to sell their labor and buy their long-leased land, earlier. But again it is ordinary property.

> solidifying their political power and ensuring the continuation of the political regime. The seventeenth century, however, witnessed major changes in the economic institutions . . .

No. The *economic* institutions, if by that one means property rights, or even taxation, did not change much then, by comparison with changes in other centuries.

> and political institutions . . .

Finally a partial truth, but only in England and Scotland and a few other places such as Poland: not in "Europe" as he claims.

that paved the way for the development of property rights . . .

No. Property rights, I repeat, were already developed, many centuries earlier.

and limits on monarchs' power.

A truth, but a Dutch and later a British and still later a Polish and Swedish truth, and having nothing to do with an allegedly novel security of property—for all the self-interested talk against the modest taxation by the gentry at the time, from John Hampden to Thomas Jefferson. The share of British government taxes in national income did not fall in the eighteenth century: it strikingly rose.[38]

Acemoglu in short has gotten the history embarrassingly wrong in every important detail, and his larger theme is wholly mistaken.

It is not his fault, however. The few economic historians he has consulted, especially North, have told the history to him mistakenly, since they, especially North, have not consulted the work of historians using primary sources and have not sufficiently doubted the tales told by nineteenth-century German Romantic historians about the Middle Ages and about the allegedly modern rise of rationality. The problem is, to say it yet again, that much of Europe—or for that matter much of China or India, not to speak of the Iroquois or the Khoisan, when it mattered—had credible commitments to secure property rights in the thirteenth century CE, and in some places in the thirteenth century BCE.[39] China, for example, has had secure property in land and in commercial goods for millennia. And in the centuries in which the economists claim that Europe surged ahead in legal guarantees for property, the evidence is overwhelming that China and Japan had secure property. True, early in the short century of their rule the Mongols (Yuan dynasty, 1279–1368) put in place such antieconomisms of bad property rights as prohibiting autumn planting—in order to give ample grazing for Mongol horses. But even the Mongols eventually realized that a prosperous and property-respecting China made a more profitable cash cow. And under the Ming and Qing (1368–1911), property and contract laws were enforced upon high and low, as they had been during most of Chinese history. Merchants appear to have been more, not less, secure on the roads of the Chinese Empire or the Tokugawa shogunate in recent centuries than they were in a Western Christendom plagued until the nineteenth century by pirates, or by highwaymen riding up to the old inn door. Chaucer's merchant in 1387 "wished the sea were kept [free of pirates] for anything / Betwixt Middleburg [in Zeeland] and Orwell [in Lincolnshire]," as the Chinese and the Japanese and the Ottomans had already long kept their seas, though with some difficulty.[40]

After all, the necessary condition for the creation of *any* economy is the ability to engage in secure contracting across time and space. No Mesopotamian merchant around 2000 BCE could buy copper from Anatolia without property rights, whether enforced by the state, or more powerfully by the customs of the merchants themselves. North and Weingast and their student Acemoglu are letting their chronology get radically and misleadingly compressed. Certainly the development of property rights away from the arbitrary rule of a war chief in, say, 588 CE in Wessex mattered for economic incentives. But by 1688 such a development in England had happened centuries before. (And war chiefs themselves get into trouble if they violate their followers' property rights: witness wide-ruling Agamemnon's troubles after he seized Briseis from godlike Achilles.) It was not true in England, as Sellar and Yeatman asserted in their loony way, that only in the eighteenth century did people "discover that Trespassers could be Prosecuted."[41]

North's is therefore a poor argument for explaining the Industrial Revolution or the modern world. The choice to escape from growth-killing investing in swords or in influence at court rather than investing in good textile machinery to make good woolen cloth, and in good organizations to administer the good machinery, has happened repeatedly in history—in China for whole centuries at a time, in Rome in the second century CE, in much of Europe after the eleventh century. Something was radically different about the case of eighteenth-century Britain. But the difference was not the rearrangement of incentives beloved of economists, those rules of the game. The incentives had already been rearranged, long before, and in many places.

Jan Luiten van Zanden has recently in a brilliant survey (*The European Economy in a Global Perspective, 1000–1800*) agreed in part with such a California School point, against the economists compressing institutional change into a few decades around 1700, and in England only. He argues that integration of markets and low interest rates betokened a good institutional context, and he pushes the drop in interest rate that Gregory Clark and I attributed to the fourteenth and fifteenth centuries back into the High Middle Ages.[42] One can agree that if people are not stealing from each other, and not absconding with loans, and not bribing judges to make seizures of property legal, the interest rate will be lower than in chaotic times and places. Consult the interest rate charged on loans today in poor neighborhoods. (Yet low interest rates characterized sober merchants in Florence without leading to an industrial revolution.) Zanden ingeniously argues that the premium for high-skilled over low-skilled workers represents the interest costs of apprenticeships and the like, and collects the facts to back up his argument. Though he bows politely to the economists Acemoglu and Johnson, who follow North in believing that improvements of institutions happened just in time to explain the Industrial Revolution, he does not believe it.[43] He joins Henry Adams and Deepak Lal and Eric Jones in finding a European exceptionalism in the twelfth and thirteenth centuries.

But turning back to the High Middle Ages is, I believe, another timing (and placing) mistake. One can agree that the Greatest of Centuries (the thirteenth) witnessed a "spectacular investment boom," such as in Winchester Cathedral. But Zanden contradicts his own imaginatively assembled evidence that by the eighteenth century China and Japan were ready for economic growth, too. And China was ready much earlier (Zanden's argument does not extend much back into the Song), as was the Arab world in the same centuries, inspiring many of the admirable intellectual developments in the High Middle Ages among the retarded Franks.[44] Zanden in the end relies on human-capital arguments borrowed from the economic theorists. The trouble is that human capital is just another form of capital, and like bricks and mortar has been widely accumulated at various different times and places. What explains the modern world is not investment but innovation. Zanden's learned book in the end does not pay sufficient attention to discovery, invention, creativity. He wants to interpret history exclusively with efficiencies succeeding inefficiencies. His is the model of scarcity since Ricardo and Malthus that I am criticizing. Scarcity and prudence and investments do a splendid job of accounting for the pattern of tidal intrusions on skill levels and interest rates—Zanden provides hundreds of pages of elegant examples. But they leave the tide itself, and the modern world, unexplained.

35

AND ANYWAY THE ENTIRE ABSENCE OF PROPERTY IS NOT RELEVANT TO THE PLACE OR PERIOD

In his persuasive and wide-ranging book of 1999, *Property and Freedom*, the historian of Russia Richard Pipes ventures at one point on an analysis of seventeenth-century English history with a promarket purpose similar to North's, whose guidance he acknowledges, à la Acemoglu. His venture is instructive. Like North (this time with the support of many other historians who know the history because they have done the primary research, such as Mark Kishlansky), Pipes correctly attributes the supremacy of the English Parliament to a long series of accidents in the provisioning of the monarchy. Fiscal crises, such as Charles I's crisis over "ship money" imposed on non-maritime English cities, certainly did raise up the Mother of Parliaments, for which we praise God. Political change in England was not "endogenous."

But Pipes, like North, then slips into the claim—it is not a major point in his book, and I admit to being picky in calling him on it—that the constitutional innovations of the very late seventeenth century somehow caused the economy of the modern world. It is a claim which we have seen is foggily seconded by a few other economic historians, so perhaps it's worth being picky. The Glorious Revolution surely had something to do with the Industrial Revolution indirectly, by way of the resulting freedom of discussion that made England into a land of conversation like Holland, even outside of aristocratic salons, and then a land of innovation, even outside of royal societies. "The Dutch invasion of 1688 by Prince William of Orange," writes the historian of the Netherlands Anne McCants, "remembered by the English as no invasion at all but as the 'Glorious Revolution,' was not the moment that Dutch culture ultimately swamped that of its close kin and rival. Instead, paradoxically, it was precisely the occasion on which the Dutch began to lose their own identity on the world stage, transferring their economic and political innovations to the very country whose throne they had usurped."[1] But it was not property rights that the Dutch transferred to the English. Both the Dutch and the English had them anciently. Yet North and in a careless moment Pipes (and Ekelund and Tollison, and Wells and Wills, and Acemoglu and others who keep springing up to offer reasoning beside the point), by contrast, want to claim that a perfection of property rights happened in the late seventeenth century and thereby improved incentives. Back to Max U and the constraints on his asylum/institution.

The reason Pipes falls into the error of overemphasizing the Glorious Revolution is not the Northian compression of chronology, but an irrelevant comparison. Quite understandably, since Russian history is his profession, he has always in mind the dismal Russian case. He argues persuasively that the development of private property was short-circuited in Russia by the Mongol invasion of 1237, which subordinated the rulers of Muscovy in the two centuries afterward to the Golden Horde, called in Russian "Tatars." When it first took direct control, the Horde governed from its camps on the lower Volga by absolute terror, as is the habit of conquering nomads, and brooked no countervailing powers or property rights. A Timur the Lame typifies nomad warfare, making pyramids of seventy thousand skulls in Isfahan. (On the way to his own conquests in 1395, by the way, he damagingly sideswiped the Golden Horde.) Such warfare was reintroduced in another key by the Germans and Japanese and the Russians themselves in the 1940s.

Pipes argues with ample documentation that the grand princes of Muscovy and their heirs after 1547, the tsars of all the Russias, were taught by the Mongols "patrimony" ("the father's law," the "patrimonial state" being a term from Weber).[2] Without the Mongols the commercial tradition of the powerful city state of Novgorod, founded by Swedish Vikings, would have triumphed, he says, as similarly bourgeois habits did elsewhere in Europe. But unhappily the bourgeois habits lost out, and instead in 1478 a warlike and now property-despising Muscovy annexed Novgorod, and a century later Ivan the Terrible methodically dispersed its bourgeoisie. As the leading historian of early modern Russia, the late Richard Hellie, put it, "By 1650 Moscow [that is, the Tsar personally] had nearly complete control over two of the major economic factors, land and labor, and had substantial control over the third, capital, as well."[3] In early modern times the Russian state enserfed the peasants just when serfdom was eroding in Western Europe. The Law Code of 1649 repealed a statute of limitations on recovering run-away serfs (compare the year-and-day custom in the West—city air makes one free: *Stadtluft macht frei*). The code "legally stratified the rest of society," Hellie noted, "thus giving the government control over nearly all of Russia's labor."[4]

"The rest of society" included its top. A mercantilist Peter the Great, and even an enlightened and physiocratic Catherine the Great, says Pipes, treated everyone in Russia from lowest to highest as in effect serfs. It amounted, one aristocrat put it, to "despotism tempered by assassination" (of Peter III, Paul I, Alexander II, Nicholas II). So long as the tsar survived the dagger or the pistol, everyone's property was at his disposal. Acemoglu's erroneous belief, acquired from North, that in *Western* Europe "economic institutions also ensured that the monarchs controlled a large fraction of the economic re-sources in society," is correct for Russia—but nowhere else in Europe, from Poland to Ireland. Once William the Conqueror divided up the land of Eng-land among his followers, they owned it, if in feudal theory "of" the king. The aristocrat paid knight service, as the serf paid six capons, but knight and peasant owned the land, and bought and sold it with enthusiasm from the earliest times. Even the arrogant Prussian dukes-margraves-kings were limited by property and customary law. But a great Russian lord, however arrogant and French-speaking, was still merely of the "service" class.

The Pipes history of Russia fits smoothly with that of "the Steppe and the Sown" (as the title of a famous book in 1928 expressed it).[5] Historians such as Peter Perdue (2005), William McNeill (1964), Owen Lattimore (1940), back to the Muslim historian Ibn-Khaldūn (1377)—with the example of Timur literally before him—have emphasized the role played again and again by conquerors from the steppe.[6] Perdue notes "that like good bank robbers, nomadic state builders went where the wealth was. As China centralized un-der a new dynasty [sometimes itself descended from the steppe], a nomadic state often rose along with it," by preying on it.[7] The stolid agriculturalists of Mesopotamia or Rome or the Ganges Plain or China or the Indus Valley were repeatedly subject to waves of barbarians on horses (or from dry areas, camels) riding out of central Asia, with a nautical variation on the theme around the edges, such as the barbarous Sea People in the Eastern Medi-terranean in the late second millennium BCE or the barbarous Vikings in Europe in the late first millennium of our era.

Hellie argued that Russia became in response a "garrison state," a modern version of Sparta, partly because the remnants of the Golden Horde "raided Russia ceaselessly in a search for slaves. . . . Had Moscow not taken effective countermeasures, all its population would have been sold through the Crimea into the slave markets of the Middle East and the Mediterranean."[8] In 1940 Owen Lattimore wrote that "the Manchu conquest of China in the seventeenth century was the last rush of the tide [he spoke in watery metaphors of a 'reservoir' of 'border nomads' sophisticated in the ways of both steppe and sown] whose ebb and flow along the Great Wall Frontier had been so important in working the mechanism of Chinese history."[9] Until the time of the disintegration of the Golden Horde and the decline of Mughal power in India and finally the conquest of the Mongolian lands and other central Asian reservoirs by the Qing Chinese—that is, until the coming of massed and disciplined gunpowder infantry—the wild horsemen ruled from time to time, and sometimes for quite a long time (Ibn-Khaldūn reckoned their time as forty years). If they did not become conquered in economic ideas by the city-dwelling proto-bourgeoisie they had conquered, which was what usually happened, they brought the propertyless rule of the steppe along with them. That is Pipes's grim claim for Russia. The Russian tsar (called today "the president," or sometimes the "prime minister"), he argues, owned everybody, all the way up to princes of the blood and arrogant oil millionaires. "Muscovy has tried to leave its despotism," wrote Montesquieu. "It cannot."[10] Property in Russia conferred no Jeffersonian and neo-Roman independence. In the lands of the sown by contrast it came gradually to do so, by immemorial custom.

Pipes rather struggles, though, when he extends the moral beyond Russia. He depends on surprisingly elderly historical opinion for his allegedly widespread examples outside Russia of "patrimony"—that is, in Pipes's usage, the literal ownership of the nation by the king, contrary for example to the history of China (except for the First Emperor or the early Mongol period or other and rare upheavals) or, for that matter, the history of the ancient Israelites. His references are centered on the 1920s, and likewise throughout his book for all manner of non-Russian facts.[11] (He justifies his dependence on histories quite early in the professionalization of history with a doctrine that historical knowledge does not advance.)[12]

The case of India's Mughal emperors, for example, ruling by their early adoption of gunpowder from 1526 until the British Raj, is sometimes said to be a good example of patrimony.[13] The emperors were literally descendents of Timur, and never lost the conviction, it is said, that having conquered northern and then all of India they owned it outright, lock, stock, and barrel. Mughal India was glorious in many ways. Yet innovation, except to serve the tastes of the emperor and his present selection of favorites, had a thin market. South Asia—though in 1526 in many parts much more sophisticated economically than the Western infidels—remained poor while Europe began to innovate. The conventional view of the Mughals is that like that of the Romanovs, in that every citizen from highest to lowest was subject to having all his wealth taken in a trice—in order, say, to construct the Taj Mahal to commemorate the emperor's favorite wife. True, recent work has . . . cast doubts on estimates that as much as half or more of national income flowed to the state, "thereby raising the issue of whether the Indo-Muslim state was, in fact, the crushing Leviathan that it has been made out to be. . . . There was . . . the growth of property rights in land."[14] And after all, Bengali textiles were the wonder of the eighteenth-century world. Yet *if* it was true, then it surely had Russian consequences, and would have spoiled the economy.

∞

But all this interesting historical assertion, whether true or false or merely memorable, is not relevant for explaining a change in Western Europe 1600–1800, or 1300–1900, or the lack of change in places comparable to Western Europe, such as Southern Europe, or China, or Japan, or the Ottoman Empire. The sad Russian and Mughal cases teach us that private property is essential for human flourishing beyond the patriarch's tent. They usefully warn against a socialism that analogizes to a whole nation an idealized patriarchal family (and in practice often an abusive family)—such as Papa Joe Stalin, the pipe-smoking father of the nation. But in places like Holland and Britain and France in 1600 the private property of people was solid, and secure, and sold, and neither the father nor the mother of the nation could seize it without due process of law.

Pipes himself points out that for all the talk of the divine right of kings in Western Europe in the seventeenth century (it spread even to the Swiss Confederation, in the form of an asserted divine right of the patriciate to rule over the mere "settlers") no monarch west of Russia believed he literally *owned* his subjects. On the contrary, Pipes's main theme is that in England the existence of private property—though guaranteed by the state—was a bulwark of liberty. He is certainly correct, as one can see through the exceptions in Russia and in parts of the rest of Europe; though one would like to know how slaves felt about the sanctity of their masters' property. In the Middle Ages there developed in various countries of Europe a doctrine of "the king's Jews." In 1091 the wife of the prince of neighboring Moravia argued to the Duke of Prague that he should stop attacking his neighbors in search of gold, since he had Jewish and other merchants of his own, whose gold was his to take. She thoughtfully provided him with their addresses in the village close to his castle.[15] But the doctrine was clearly an exception, and confirms the rule that most of a lord's subjects were *not* his to use. Thomas More in 1516 had one of his characters in *Utopia* complain that bad counselors tell the king "that all property is in him, not excepting the very persons of his subjects: and that no man has any other property, but that which the King out of his goodness thinks fit to leave him; . . . that . . . it were his advantage that his people should have neither riches nor liberty; since . . . necessity and poverty blunt them, make them patient, beat them down, and break that height of spirit." But, he continues, "I should rise up and assert, that such councils were both unbecoming a king, and mischievous to him: and that not only his honor but his safety consisted more in his people's wealth, than in his own; . . . I should show that they choose a king for their own sake."[16] He might have added that English kings were anyway subject to law, and that the bad counsel was therefore an irrelevant wish for a patrimony not in the English cards.

In 1649 King Charles defended himself against the Rump Parliament in the trial for his life by declaring, quite truly, that "pretend what you will [oh Parliamentarians], I stand more for their [that is, the people's] liberties. If power without law may alter the fundamental laws of the kingdom [for example, by executing an anointed king], I do not know what subject he is in England that can be sure of his life, *or anything he calls his own.*"[17] At his hour of execution he declared again that English law protected property against power, whether of king or of commons: "Liberty and freedom consists in having of government those laws by which their life and their goods may be most their own." Certainly in Stuart England, and even in the "absolutist" France of Richelieu and Louis, private property was itself absolute against the king—though taxed (incompetently) from time to time.

It is therefore misleading of Pipes to declare at one point, instructed by

North, and contrary to his own evidence just assembled (Homer nods), that "thus, *in the course of the seventeenth century*, it became widely accepted in Western Europe that there exists a Law of Nature . . . [and that] one facet of the Law of Nature is the inviolability of property."[18] It is true that more people *said* it in the seventeenth and especially in the eighteenth century, for which we are glad. It matters that people kept saying that "all men . . . have certain inherent natural rights . . . among which are . . . the means of acquiring and possessing property."[19] But Pipes himself shows that the idea and especially the practice was already many centuries old, in English law, in the writings of Aquinas, and, as he notes in the paragraph preceding his Northian and behavioral declaration, in those of Seneca of Rome. Pipes had just argued that even Jean Bodin, the influential French theorist of absolutism and of the divine right of kings, declared in 1576 that private property was a law of nature, secure against the grandest sovereign, citing Seneca to the same effect.[20] Bodin posits no serf or service class owned by a Timur or an Aurangzeb or an Ivan the Terrible. A Frenchman of the late sixteenth century was no item in the baggage of a propertyless nomad fondly remembering the wild life of the steppe.

As I said, in some ways modern economies—with their gigantic administrative states spending half of national income, and regulating still wider fields of economic activity—create less, not more, security of property than a feudal economy with diffuse centers of power, or than an early modern state such as Stuart England with a less-than-impressive ability to tax. The fact is a historical irony on which Pipes and North and Harold Demsetz and Richard Epstein and I would doubtless agree. An American government armed with the doctrine of eminent domain and the power to tax incomes at combined federal and state proportions of 35 percent, and with administrative agencies having broad powers over labor relations and air pollution, not to speak of unusual definitions of torture and the ability to tap telephones, and a passionate desire to limit people's consumption of recreational drugs, seems in this respect to be more, not less, like the Muscovy of old than did, say, France in 1576. The law professor Richard Epstein is pessimistic about the future of the administrative state, contrasting it with the liberties assured by common law.[21] The economist Milton Friedman was fond of quoting Will Rogers: "Thank God we don't get all the government we pay for." But we don't because of our libertarian ideology, and the judges influenced by it, not because the machinery of government automatically protects us. The machinery of modern government, even more than ancient government, can grind exceeding small.

To quote again the farsighted Macaulay in 1830, against Robert Southey's proto-socialism: Southey would suggest that "the calamities arising from the collection of wealth in the hands of a few capitalists are to be remedied by collecting it in the hands of one great capitalist, who has no conceivable motive to use it better than other capitalists, the all-devouring state."[22] But in Western Europe in 1200 or 1700 a right to property that protected in Lockean fashion against an all-devouring state was nothing new. Roman law had protected property very well, thank you, and the Roman state took little more than English Stuart's shares of national income for its purposes, 5 percent.[23] The Mughal state of popular fable, by contrast, erected on a principle of patrimony that would look reasonable to a tyrannical socialist state nowadays, is asserted (we have seen that the assertion might be wrong) to have taken 50 percent.

Ownership anyway is not a modern idea and not an exclusively bourgeois idea, though the town dwellers have worked most vigorously to extend the meaning of "property." Feelings of private property are hardwired into humans, or so anyone who has raised a two-year-old would attest. Little Daniel needs to be *taught* to play nice and to share in a sweetly socialist way—his instincts, like that of any two-year-old, are brutally selfish, the worst of capitalism, very much more interested in Mine than in Thine. The economist Herbert Gintis speaks of a "private property equilibrium," noting that "preinstitutional 'natural' private property has been observed in many species, in the form of the recognition of territorial possession."[24] A classic 1976 paper in evolutionary biology by John Maynard Smith and Geoffrey A. Parker spoke of an evolutionary stable strategy as "bourgeois" if existing property among animals was used to settle disputes (they were following the marxoid assumption widespread among the clerisy of the day that so far as humans are concerned private property is a new and novel stage of history). Two dogs recognize property rights by which the one who gets to the scrap first owns it, even against a larger dog capable of stealing it. A speckled wood butterfly, *Pararge aegeria*, intruding in a wood on a patch of sunlight on some ground already the "property" of another speckled wood butterfly would be inclined by evolution to yield. Gintis makes the Smith-Parker argument more precise and brings to bear other evidence that animals and two-year-old humans in fact have incentives to take a "bourgeois" attitude toward property, whether or not Leviathan enforces property rights.[25] And repeatedly it has been observed that when property comes to matter—that is, when the beaver or the acre of land or the right to take water from the Colorado River becomes valuable enough that its misallocation would cause substantial social loss—even a communalist or tyrannical government will often start enforcing its privateness.[26] It does so unless, indeed, it is under the influence of some antibourgeois rhetoric, such as the personal loyalty of the steppe horseman to his chief, or the collectivist, Romantic, post-Christian, and pseudo-familial dreams of nineteenth-century Europeans, bearing fruit in twentieth-century authoritarianism of *der Führer* or the general secretary.

As an example of the scientific missteps in this literature, consider the famous "tragedy of the commons" about which in 1968 Garrett Hardin wrote (in aid, it should be recalled, of an authoritarian proposition quite usual in his time—and persisting now among radical environmentalists—that freedom to have a family is intolerable and that population policy should be, as he put it, "mutual coercion mutually agreed upon").[27] True, as Hardin asserted, if villages in Europe allowed the common fields to be overstocked, there would be a loss of efficiency, because the sheep and cattle would tread down the grass, and eat up the early shoots renewing it. But Hardin didn't know that the European villagers in question, not surprisingly, understood the point as well as modern academics do, maybe even better, and to prevent the loss they introduced limitations ("stinting"). The loss from not stinting the commons would be gigantic at small numbers of grazers if, as Hardin assumes, each grazer acted in the way a "Cournot oligopolist" does, that is, if he mistakenly ignored the response of others when he put an extra cow on the commons.[28] As the historian Philip Hoffman concludes, "The moral here may well be that the group agricultural property rights one sees in small societies may be nearly optimal much of the time," on account of "repeated interactions."[29] As the great medievalist Ambrose Raftis puts it, against the obsolete notion of a three-field "system," "the current recognition" among agricultural historians is that "local decision-making" is "necessary to efficient productivity."[30]

Hardin admits that "in an approximate way, the logic of the commons has been understood for a long time, perhaps since the discovery of agriculture or the invention of private property in real estate." Perhaps. And perhaps it was understood even among hunter-gatherers irritated by the

overharvesting of deer by a competing tribe. Hardin's sole empirical argument for the relevance of his posited regime of non-property-even-
when-it-matters is that still "at this late date, cattlemen leasing national land
on the Western ranges demonstrate no more than an ambivalent understanding, in constantly pressuring federal authorities to increase the head count
to the point where overgrazing produces erosion and weed-dominance."
Of course they do: they farm the government, not merely the pastures, and
therefore the public lands have always been underpriced and overgrazed.
But in the medieval olden days of which Hardin speaks, such as the days of
open-field agriculture, the land was private or was regulated when it mattered. As Jan Luiten van Zanden points out, "Typically, new contributions
to this literature have suggested that institutions [in medieval Europe] previously considered 'conservative' and 'inefficient'—such as guilds and [in
Hardin's case] commons, manors, or sharecropping—were surprisingly efficient."[31] Certainly this is true of medieval field systems, though as Zanden
adds, citing Sheilagh Ogilvie's strictures on the late S. R. Epstein's pioneering
work on guilds and on North's views of manorial arrangements, "Some have
argued that this sounds too good to be true, and . . . ignores the 'dark side'
of institutions such as guilds."[32] Quite possibly.

In any case, the Nobel political scientist Elinor Ostrom has shown repeatedly, people cooperate, too: they do not always defect from the common
good, as assumed by Hardin.[33] It is one of the main findings of experimental
economics in the decades after Hardin that people cooperate much more
than the Prudence Only model Hardin was using would imply. Anyone who
troubles to examine local regulations or legal cases in the not-so-wild West,
or in English villages in the fourteenth century, will find stinting enforced
and cooperation common.[34] Hardin, although an impressive scholar in
some other ways, appears not to have looked into the evidence.

Likewise, if you look into the records in England of national and local
regulations and legal cases in the thirteenth century, you will find private
property enforced—even aside from the alternative of "preinstitutional
'natural' private property" enforced by shame and ostracism that Gintis talks
about. North, although an impressive scholar in some other ways, appears
not to have looked into the evidence. The legal historian Harold Berman,
whom North might have consulted, and on whom Pipes wisely depends, has
no doubts on the matter: "Modern English, German, French, Italian, Swedish, Dutch, Polish, and other national European legal systems were initially

formed in the twelfth and thirteenth centuries under the influence . . . of the new canon law . . . [and] of the discovery . . . [of] Justinian's Roman law and of the parallel . . . development of systems of [law] . . . not covered by canon law," such as the law merchant. The medieval foundations survived. "For example," Berman goes on to say, "the elaborate rules of contract law and of credit transactions . . . survived successive economic changes and were an essential foundation of the laissez-faire capitalist economy that emerged in the nineteenth century."[35] Already, and not merely after 1689.

36

AND THE CHRONOLOGY OF PROPERTY AND
INCENTIVES HAS BEEN MISMEASURED

That is to say, to return to the theme of North and Weingast's work, the political innovations alleged to lead to the financial revolution in late seventeenth- and early eighteenth-century Britain have no important connection to secure contracting—not even, as North and Weingast somewhat desperately put it, as indirect "evidence that such a necessary condition has been fulfilled."[1] Frederick Pollock and F. M. Maitland's great book of 1895 was *The History of English Law before the Time of Edward the First*. By the year 1272, they (principally Maitland) showed, English common law was firmly in place—though of course the endogenous elaborations, such as a wider law merchant, and statutes against perpetuities, and the extension of the king's common law to all free-born Englishmen, especially when all of them became in fact free-born, remained to be accomplished. Avner Greif begins his long-awaited book on the subject by reporting that "on March 28, 1210, Rubeus de Campo of Genoa agreed to pay a debt of 100 marks sterling in London on behalf of Vivianus Jordanus of Lucca. There was nothing unusual about this agreement. . . . Impersonal lending among traders from remote corners of Europe prevailed and property rights were sufficiently secure that merchants could travel."[2] Exactly, and so also in China and the Middle East and South Asia. The Glorious Revolution brought no unprecedented rule of property law. It was a constitutional, not a common-law or statute-law, revolution. The earlier James of England (the first Stuart and the grandfather of the James deposed in 1688 for his plans and misdeeds and papist allies), had reigned over one of the most law-depending countries in Europe—though violent in duels and other affrays (Ben Jonson killed an actor in a duel), and certainly not so peaceful as the Bourgeois Era would make it. English people went habitually to law, with all its delays, because it worked, and had done so for centuries.

North also praises patents. Many economists have been intrigued by the simple logic entailed. Make innovation into property and, voilà, innovation will be pursued as routinely as is plowing or building. It is another attempt by economists to bring one of the most unusual event in human history under a routine of marginal benefit and marginal cost. Joel Mokyr has written a devastating essay surveying the historical evidence on the matter. He asks, "What could be wrong with this picture [painted by North and, from North, by Acemoglu and other economists]? The answer is basically 'almost everything.'"[3] British patents for example were very expensive, a minimum of £100 (a respectable lower-middle-class annual income at the time: think of $80,000 a year nowadays) and requiring many months of attendance on law courts in London. Therefore they were taken out as only one of many alternative ways of establishing one's credibility as an ingenious person—as someone to be admired, and to be paid to do all sorts of engineering work, or to be given a governmental sinecure. Patents were considered undignified by many inventors, and were treated by judges with suspicion until the 1830s, as constituting monopolies (as of course they do). Getting a head start in producing one's idea, as usually also today, was a better assurance of fame and fortune. The economic theorists Aghion, Harris, Howitt, and Vickers have pointed out that weaker patent laws can make for fiercer competition to get there first—at least when the Grand Externality of according dignity and liberty to innovate has already taken place.[4] And it has long been realized that countries (or regions or firms or individuals) who can steal the spillover from knowledge can do very well indeed. Little countries like the Netherlands or Switzerland did well by free-riding on British patent, and did not bother to have their own domestic patents until the late nineteenth century. Indeed the United States did not offer copyright protection for foreign books fully in compliance with the Berne Convention of 1888 until the centenary of the convention. Patents and copyright sound neat, but they were not.

And North admires, too, "laws permitting a wide latitude of organizational structures," such as incorporation laws. But general incorporation laws were passed only in the middle of the nineteenth century (the first in 1844), and were taken up unevenly—many companies were mere shells, or dissolved quickly. Businesspeople, it appears, were not much constrained by the earlier lack of permission to incorporate. As late as 1893 Gilbert and Sullivan were spoofing general incorporation as a foolish flower of a false progress:

> Some seven men form an Association
> (If possible all Peers and Baronets),
> They start out with a public declaration
> To what extent they mean to pay their debts.
> That's called their Capital. . . .
> When it's left to you to say
> What amount you mean to pay,
> Why, the lower you can put it at, the better.[5]

The anglophile king of Utopia, eager to adopt all the elements that "have tended to make England the powerful, happy, and blameless country which the consensus of European civilization has declared it to be," inquires further: "And do I understand you that Great Britain / Upon this Joint Stock principle is governed?" To which Mr. Goldbury of the stock exchange replies: "We haven't come to that exactly—but / We're tending rapidly in that direction."

And so an embarrassing North Gap in the explanation of an economic revolution opens up, calculated from 1800, fully 528 years in length (1800 minus 1272). Or else it is 44 negative years, 1800 minus 1844. Legal developments in England that happened many centuries before or many decades after (not to speak of their prevalence in China and Japan) cannot explain the exceptional applied innovations of northwestern Europe beginning in the late eighteenth century. Security of property was a very old story in the England of 1689, as it was in the Chinese or Ottoman empires at the same time. The depredations by the Stuarts were minor, if infuriating to the wealthier Londoners of a non-Conformist disposition. The merely prudential incentives to innovate were just as great in the thirteenth century as in the eighteenth. Property rights, that is, were pretty full at both dates. Money was to be made. As Alan Macfarlane declared in 1978, "England was as 'capitalist' in 1250 as it was in 1550 or 1750."[6]

∞

One way of getting around the North Gap and the feeble economistic "incentives" in North's argument and the strange assertion that the financial revolution after 1689 was just the same as the introduction of secure property rights is to emphasize the modern state as a source of growth. North would then join with the political scientist Liah Greenfeld in elevating nationalism to a cause of modern economic growth.[7] The Greenfeld hypothesis has the merit of *not* depending entirely on monetary incentives. People can innovate for the honor of Britain. Some few probably did. Rule Britannia.

But it is a different proposition to say, as North does, that "the state was a major player in the whole process."[8] Thankfully, it was not. State-guided growth was for a while after the 1930s highly thought of by economists and economic historians, and it has always been understandably popular among statesmen. In 1975, for example, the eminent economic historian Marcello de Cecco wrote in praise of the "national economy" of Friedrich List (1789–1846), which sought a place in the sun for Germany beyond the shade of the then dominate British: "By adding dynamism and history to classical [that is, Ricardo's] analysis, List obtains a strategy for fast economic growth that is perfectly suitable to the socio-economic conditions of countries which want to undergo a process of modernization."[9] So thought many economists in 1975, or many statesmen in 1841 (*Das nationale System der politischen Öko-nomie*). But in the meantime Listian policies such as protection for "infant industries" (in 2009, for example, such wailing infants as General Motors Corporation) and "import substitution" (in Latin America under the influence of the Listian analysis of Raúl Prebisch [1959]) have had miserable results. De Cecco goes on: "We can clearly see . . . [List's realization] of the impossibility of founding a modernization on a bourgeois revolution, i.e. on the English model, and of the ensuing need to find a different 'national way,' based on collective action." I say on the contrary that without something like a Bourgeois Revaluation at least at the level of rhetoric, no lasting modernization can happen. You can lead the Russian people by "collective action" into gigantic auto factories, but you can't make them think. The Chinese and the Indians are now embourgeoisfying. That's the ticket.

The model is of technological causation, the technology being caused by the coming of bourgeois dignity and liberty. Many who advocate industrial policy and other economic planning by experts would disagree. But usually such intervention by the state reduces what could be achieved by bourgeois dignity and liberty. Of course, it doesn't have to in logic. The disabilities of intervention are a matter of fact, not pure theory. In some imaginable worlds a Listian or even a Maoist economic policy would succeed. On a blackboard one can prove, indeed, as A. C. Pigou and after him Paul Samuelson insisted, that state intervention to deal with externalities *will* improve the performance of an economy—if the intervention is performed by perfect and disinterested social engineers, probably Swedes.[10] But in the actual world, the actual interventions by actual states—American or Polish or South Asian—have usually not improved performance. Running an economy by the dictates of political pressure or the force of antibourgeois ideology has not normally led to decisions that were best for economic growth and for the incomes of the poor. Thus the Soviet Union kept its people antibourgeois, starving some six million petty-bourgeois peasants in Ukraine as a first step, and kept most Soviet citizens poor.

North and Weingast's article of 1989 praises the ability of the English and then British state to finance wars after 1689. They take it to be a good thing (except presumably from the French and Indian point of view). But financing wars is not the same thing—in fact, it is rather the opposite—of "the secure contracting over time and space" that North and Weingast anachronistically attach to the Financial Revolution.[11] Ask the British investors incommoded by the unanticipated starting and stopping of Britain's long eighteenth-century struggle with France, 1689 to 1815, whether they felt secure in contracting. Patrick O'Brien's estimates of the share of British national income going to warfare bounced up and down, from a low of 2 percent in the quinquennium centered on 1685 (under the wretched, expropriating Stuarts) to a high of an astonishing 17.6 percent during the last five years of the American Revolution (as against 3.6 when briefly at peace with the French in the five years centered on 1770; the American Revolution figure is higher even than the 14.1 percent over the last five years of the Napoleonic Wars).[12] Interest rates bounced up and down correspondingly, as did insurance rates for shipping, and demand for naval stores. Some security.

North and Weingast might argue (as have some people, reading their work generously) that the creation of a deep capital market by the issuing of government bonds brought down the interest rate, which indicates a rise in the confidence of investors in the institutions of the capital market. No, not likely: it indicates, I repeat, a rise in the confidence that the British Treasury would honor its obligations to pay interest.

The historian Jonathan Israel attributes the low interest rates in Holland to "to the efficiency and meticulousness of the Dutch federal state . . . for low interest rates are not just an expression of the abundance of money but also of absence of risk in lending."[13] But low interest rates in private commercial dealings are not produced by low interest rates on government debt. The "absence of risk" came from the credible commitment of the Dutch (and later the British) government to pay back its bonds issued for purposes of war, or at any rate to go on servicing them forever. If Europe supplied funds perfectly elastically with respect to interest rates at a given risk premium to any one portion of the European market, such as to private Dutch projects or to the the Estates General, then introducing less risk in lending to the Estates General would have no impact on the interest rate on the private projects. That's what "perfectly elastically supplied" means: the interest rate is given. The government would pay less than it once did because the quality of its promises have improved. The quality of the private promises would not have changed, and so the private borrowers would go on paying the same rate as before. But if at the other extreme Europe supplied the funds perfectly *in*elastically—that is, if there was a fixed fund to be invested in Dutch private projects or the Estates General's debt—then obviously the now better loans to the Estates General would drain *away* funds from the private projects, driving *up* the interest rate the private projects faced. So the range of possible effects of more honest, bourgeois behavior by the government on the other, *private* interest rates is from no effect to a negative effect. It is never positive. The lowering of Dutch and then British interest rates on the asset relevant to economic growth—private bonds—is to be explained by the abundance of loanable funds ("money"), not by fresh commitments by the government to pay its debts—which worked in the opposite direction, if they worked at all.

True, as I have repeatedly noted, contracting *with the British state* became more secure over time and space. But the state thus enabled can turn in a moment into a Frankenstein's monster, and often has. North well understands the point, when he is not trying to connect the Glorious Revolution to the Industrial Revolution. (Greenfeld sometimes appears not to emphasize it quite as much as a native Russian might.) The change in rhetoric that up-valued bourgeois virtues, fortunately, kept the British state from becoming an antibourgeois monster like the Russian state in 1649 or the French state in 1700 or the German state in 1871, or the Japanese state when it, too, in the late nineteenth century went on the gold standard and was suddenly able to finance wars of aggression. The Russian state after 1917, by contrast, was at least for a while confined by its inability to borrow abroad to merely domestic violence—until Hitler's imprudent invasion brought American credits for the Soviets, and the West's salvation, and Eastern Europe's woe.

∞

The long eighteenth century begins with the Glorious Revolution, and the Revolution was surely glorious. It created the "transcendent power of Parliament," as Maitland once called it, that could allow projects for canals, turnpikes, and enclosures to take from some and give to others, in the name of general efficiency. Economists call such trade or compulsion in aid of general efficiency the Hicks-Kaldor Criterion. But it didn't always work out in such a sweet way. Influence in Parliament replaced influence at court, most particularly after the death in 1714 of Queen Anne (who was the last British sovereign to veto a bill from Parliament, for example). After North's favored date of 1688, and after the formation of party politics in the 1680s, there is a case to be made that the opportunities for rent-seeking steadily increased rather than decreased, if not by violence (though tell that one to the citizens of York in 1745, or for that matter to the citizens of New York in 1776). In the early eighteenth century the cash value of influence at a court now able with the assent of Parliament to borrow from Dutchmen (look at the number of names beginning "van" in the subscribers to Bank of England stock), or the still larger gains from a transcendently powerful Parliament capable of stealing the goose from an enriching population, were greater than they had been under Charles I.

The pioneers of analytic studies of such matters, Robert Ekelund and Robert Tollison, have persuasively argued that when the power to protect domestic interests shifted from the king (and grants of monopoly) to Parliament (and protective tariffs), mercantilism became more expensive.[14] Yet the British king still had wide powers of appointment (Adam Smith himself was in his maturity appointed inspector of the very customs duties that he excoriated in *The Wealth of Nations*). The relative price of protection against foreign competition may have risen, but the total to be gained by corrupting king or Parliament taken together does not appear to have markedly fallen. Private bills, increasingly common in the eighteenth century, were ideally suited for extracting rents from one's fellow citizens directly—never mind the new abilities of Parliament to "protect" from foreigners like the French, in order to enrich West Indian landlords with a higher price for Jamaican sugar. In acts for agricultural enclosure the Parliamentary officials to be bribed with large sums were named in the very acts. Politics in eighteenth-century Britain was not called by the journalist of Napoleonic War times William Cobbett "the old corruption" for nothing. And rent-seeking from executive or legislature continued after industrialization, right down to Boeing's bid in 2008 to build tanker aircraft for the U.S. government, and the exemption of chicken and hog farms from responsibility for their animals' waste. Yet economic growth took place.

Dan Bogart has done some fine research claiming that 1689 made for more cumbersome but more fair Parliamentary procedures for instituting projects of transportation improvement. Parliament "reduced uncertainty about the security of improvement rights." By contrast, "for most of the seventeenth century, promoters turned to the Crown for patents or to Parliament for acts. Some undertakers lost their rights following major shifts in power like the Civil War and the Restoration."[15] Well, yes: revolutions do turn the world upside down. But the economics would require that people had anticipated the Revolutions, for otherwise the prospective uncertainty is not increased by the world turnings. If 1642, and especially its outcome, was a surprise, it cannot be counted as a source of ex ante uncertainty. That 1689 was a settlement, true, would make for a more tranquil environment for investment. But far into the eighteenth century, as Wells and Wills showed, the regime felt itself uncertain—if not as uncertain as, say, the English Commonwealth in September 1658. But in any case, as Bogart acknowledges and as I have argued above, canals, turnpikes, and enclosures were routine investments in capital with modest social savings, not epoch-making innovations like steam engines or electricity or organic chemistry. They changed locations, not amounts. They increased efficiency, but did not increase incomes by a factor or two or sixteen or a quality-corrected one hundred. The legal changes attendant on the Glorious Revolution and its aftermath had essentially nothing to do with the revolutionizing wave of gadgets.

As many economic historians before and after me have noted, the institutions relevant to the *economy* of Britain in fact did not change much in the very late seventeenth century, or even over the long eighteenth century 1688–1815. The eminent economic historian Nicholas Crafts notes that the various models of endogenous growth proposed by the economic theorists do a poor job of accounting for what happened in the eighteenth and nineteenth centuries. And as to the Northian version, he states flatly that "there was no obvious improvement in institutions at the time of the Industrial Revolution."[16]

Before and after North's favored long eighteenth century the sheer economic institutions-as-constraints and the budget-line incentives changed more sharply than during it. The ending of the Wars of the Roses in Henry Tudor's victory at Bosworth Field in 1485 really did end many decades of Brave-Sir-Botany disregard for the laws of property—but that was more than two centuries before the Glorious Revolution, and three centuries before the Industrial Revolution. The Tudor administrative revolutions of the sixteenth century were as important for the actual economy as any institutional change in the eighteenth century. The defeat of the armada in 1588 was as important for English economic liberties as the events of 1688. The English pattern of overseas settlement—England's decentralized and heavily populated empire—was set not in the decades after 1688 but in the few decades after the 1620s, a third of a million people leaving for Massachusetts, Virginia, and above all the West Indies, with consequences to follow. The big Revolution of 1642 as against the Glorious one of 1688 made ordinary people bold. They never forgot thereafter that they were free-born English people, free increasingly even to change jobs, even to invent machines—or free to behead their king. (The English kings didn't forget, either.) And anyway in England the rhetoric of freebornness was by 1688 hundreds of years old, whatever the actual incomes and privileges of a yeoman as against a duke.

And on the other side of the long eighteenth century the great Victorian codifications of commercial and property law did more to alter strictly economic incentives than anything that happened 1688–1815, as did the Victorian perfection of the common law of contract. Regulation of laissez-faire began with the Victorian Factory Acts. The democratization of the British electorate after 1867, slowly, had heavier consequences for economic performance, such as the welfare state and the later nationalizations, than any previous legal change since the Middle Ages, including even the triumph of Parliament in 1688. Most of the legal changes after 1815 occurred by way of statute, overcoming a common law romanticized in the Northian story, and had more economic effect than all the Georgian enclosure bills and other strictly economic results of 1688 combined.

And on a still wider view of what the professor of law Simon Deakin calls "the legal origin hypothesis" of North and his followers, one can see little evidence that the long history of English common law was causal for the Industrial Revolution. In the matters of employment contracts and joint stock companies, Deakin writes, "industrialization preceded legal change in Britain, whereas this relationship was reversed in France and Germany," merely because British law was imitated (he speaks of the "sharing of legal ideas," another example of lateral transfer of cultural memes). And then after a lag the results of Continental civil law were imitated in common-law regimes in the British Empire. Laws converged. Legal cultures did not matter for economic performance, at any rate in the England-admiring way that North's school wishes. Deakin concludes that "the picture is not one of a more market friendly common law contrasting with regulation in the civil law."[17] In a longer perspective, indeed, the point is obvious from the results—all rich countries have achieved essentially the same level of real national income per head, regardless of their supposedly inherited and varying cultures of law. North has the same problem that Gregory Clark has: memes move by imitation as much as or more than by inheritance. Countries such as France or Germany or Sweden or Japan or Taiwan, without the meme that he regards as an English uniqueness, caught on and commenced growing at modern rates.

In his 1991 essay North has a canny section describing the different fates of the lands "north and south of the Rio Grande.[18] "The gradual country-by-country reversion to centralized bureaucratic control characterized Latin America in the nineteenth century."[19] Yes, so it seems, and then in the twentieth century the Latin American centralized bureaucracies thus enabled carried out disastrously Listian policies. In other words, a national system of political economy has by no means always been good news for economic growth, and it is doubtful that Greenfeld is correct to credit even the Good Nation States (namely, Britain and the United States) with modern economic growth. Japan and Germany would have been much better off economically in 1945 without having gone through their defeated nationalisms. We all agree that abstaining from violating property rights through seizing or taxing all the gains from trade is a necessary condition for any economic growth. Witness Zimbabwean agriculture in recent times. But refraining from catastrophic intervention in the economy is not the same as being in an admirable sense "a major player in the whole process."

37

AND SO THE ROUTINE OF MAX U DOESN'T WORK

What actually changed between the thirteenth and the eighteenth centuries was, as Joel Mokyr puts it, "the mental world of the British economic and technological elite."[1] Indeed, the very idea that a mere inventor or merchant or manufacturer could be part of an "elite" was entirely novel in England in 1700, following the Dutch example of the Golden (and Gold-Earning) Age. What was new after 1688 in England was a new *honor* for trade. Hume knew this in 1741: "Commerce, therefore, in my opinion, is apt to decay in absolute governments, not because it is there less *secure*, but because it is less *honorable*. A subordination of ranks is absolutely necessary to the support of monarchy. Birth, titles, and place must be honored above industry and riches."[2] (France was his instance of "absolute" government. He should have visited Russia.)

And even then the so-called incentive to innovate was plainly not only the making of money. Robert Allen asserts that "technology was invented by people in order to make money," and therefore that "invention was an economic activity."[3] That doesn't seem to be the case. Technology was invented in the service of the virtue of prudence, yes, but also the virtues of courage, hope, temperance, justice, love, and faith. Allen adopts a reductionism that has lately become a standard rhetorical move in Samuelsonian and Beckerian economics. In 1725 Bishop Butler was already complaining about "the strange [and recent] affection of many people of explaining away all particular affections and representing the whole of life as nothing but one continued exercise of self-love."[4] "It is the great fallacy of Dr. Mandeville's book," wrote Adam Smith in 1759, "to represent every passion as wholly vicious [that is, a mere matter of profit-making prudence and self-interest] which is so in any degree and any direction."[5] Money mattered, but so did other motives. Joel Mokyr emphasizes the glory of the game: "The standard pecuniary incentive system [which does not in any case explain what it is meant to explain] was supplemented by a more complex one that included peer recognition and the sheer satisfaction of being able to do what one desires."[6] "When one loves science," the chemist Claude Louis Berthollet wrote to James Watt, "one has little need for fortune which would risk one's happiness," though as George Grantham observes, Berthollet was in fact paid well as a high-ranking civil servant.[7] Horace could not have put it better—or Adam Smith, the supposed prophet of profit, who declared the poor man sunning himself by the side of the road more happy than a prince.[8] Weak incentives that were fully present in the thirteenth century cannot explain frenetic innovation in the eighteenth and nineteenth centuries.

Allen himself admits that patents for invention, though available in England from 1624 on, were as I've noted little used, which would be odd if making money were all that was involved. And he argued long ago and persuasively, as also noted, that "collective invention" was often the ticket, because it "divided the costs and pooled the gains." In computerese it was an open-source technology.[9] Ben Franklin gave away his inventions, such as the lightning rod and the Franklin stove. So did Michael Faraday. Such examples argue against the reduction of innovation to monetary cost and benefit. Thomas Carlyle, the scourge of the classical economists, remarked in 1829 that people "have never been roused into deep, thorough, all-pervading efforts by any computable prospect of Profit and Loss, for any visible, finite object; but always for some invisible and infinite one."[10] Not "always": we should not abandon prudence, with temperance. But often faith and love and hope and justice and courage figure, too.

An economist who is thinking like an economist, instead of like a technician knowing only Max U's calculation of marginal balances, does not in fact find Carlyle's point so terribly antieconomic. Computable prospects would already have been discovered. Routine balances of profit and loss cannot have motivated the sudden, unique, and gigantic lurch forward 1700–1900. It is precisely the nonprudential part of human motivation that makes surprises possible, such as the greatest economic surprise since the domestications of wheat and rice and cattle and horses. Mokyr, citing John Nye's notion of "lucky fools," notes that "a large number of important inventors died in obscurity and poverty, indicating that the private returns to a socially useful invention were low [after the invention], but that the effort was carried out anyway because inventors overestimated the private payoff."[11] To do the science right in explaining the invention of invention you need to include more than prudence. You need to include hope and courage, too. Or so the economist would argue if he believed classical or neoclassical or even Samuelsonian economics *after* equilibrium. The margin of cultivation did not move out by just a little bit—it leapt forward. *Illa humanitatis fecerunt saltum.* Human affairs made a jump, a heroic and nonroutine event.

A recent calculation by the ever-useful economist William Nordhaus reveals that nowadays an inventor gets a mere 2.2 percent of the economic gain from an invention: "Only a miniscule fraction of the social returns from technological advances over the 1948–2001 period was captured by producers, indicating that most of the benefits of technological change are passed on to consumers rather than captured by producers."[12] The inventor had better get such a low share, or else economic growth would be a grim story of the Walt Disney Corporation getting richer and richer on its novelties, with no gain at all to those of us who don't own Walt Disney stock. The argument is another way of seeing that the Modern Jump cannot have been the result of the mere seizing of computable prospects of routine profit. Two percent of the entire social gain from the separate-condenser and then the high-pressure steam engine is of course immense. But most inventions were, Mokyr notes, "micro," that is, little improvements of existing inventions, the boy in 1713 inventing the self-acting device for the Newcomen atmospheric engine, not revolutions in the way of doing business.

What is true, however, is that during the decades up to 1700 the effective rulers of Britain became in theory and practice more and more mercantilist, and then by the end of the eighteenth century even a little bit free trading (thus Ekelund and Tollison). They became more and more after the late seventeenth century concerned with *national* profit and loss, instead of ensuring this man's monopoly profit and that woman's church attendance. No wonder that a worldly philosophy called "political economy" grew up pari passu, considering that it claims to take precisely the national, or international, view above the struggle of interests. The wise professor of English quoted earlier, Michael McKeon, put it this way: the mercantilist pretense of "state control of the economy becomes intelligible as one stage in a long process in which the power to modify the heavenly laws . . . and to reform the environment is vouchsafed to increasingly autonomous and individualized human agency."[13] That is, both a theorized mercantilism and then a theorized laissez-faire are distinguished from what came before by their focus on the new idea of the economy as a separate thing. What McKeon describes as the change from the "old system of knowledge [self-consciously rhetorical and Christian] that distinguishes between categories without countenancing their separability" to the new one organized in antirhetoric and the *Encylopédie* "according to separated and compartmentalized bodies of knowledge" is what T. S. Eliot called long ago the "dissociation of sensibilities" in the late seventeenth century.[14] The sensibility of a unified life was dissociated into privacy, polity, society, economy.

The wise philosopher quoted earlier, Charles Taylor, asserts a similar emergence of the economy as an explicit object of concern in the seventeenth century. The historian Joyce Appleby gave the story in detail of how by the time Hume and Smith took up their pens, "economic life had been successfully differentiated from the society it served."[15] In Thomas Mun's *England's Treasure by Foreign Trade* (1621), Appleby wrote, "for the first time economic factors were clearly differentiated from their social and political entanglements."[16] And the economist Albert Hirschman noted the semantic drift of the words "fortune," "corruption," and especially "interest(s)" toward those economic matters.[17]

Sir William Temple in 1672 noted of the great nations of Europe that until the end of the Thirty Years' War, "their trade was war." But "since the Peace of Munster, which restored the quiet of Christendom in 1648, not only Sweden and Denmark but France and England have more particularly than ever before busied the thoughts and counsels of their several governments . . . about the matters of trade."[18] He was premature in announcing Christendom's quiet. William's and then Anne's and then the Georges' eighteenth-century epic against the French was to begin in earnest after Dutch William III taught the undisciplined English to have a national debt and to store it in a Bank of England. Other countries at the time had still more of a trade of war, most notably Prussia. Voltaire is said to have quipped that most nations had an army, but in Prussia the army had a state. Yet Temple was right in emphasizing the spread of the Dutchlike subordination of politics to trade at least in Britain, and then gradually in other places. As Montesquieu put it in 1748, "Other nations have made the interests of commerce yield to those of politics; the English, on the contrary, have ever made their political interests give way to those of commerce."[19] Well . . . not "ever," but by 1748 often.

Such an ordering of ideas was second nature to the Dutch in 1600. It had to be learned by the English. The English and then the Scots, following the Dutch, came to be known in the world as unusually calculating—instead of as before unusually careless in calculating, and unusually brutal in carrying out their careless aggressions. No one in Europe in 1500 would have thought of the English as anything but arrogant and warlike, though they were minor players at the time outside their local sphere of influence. "See approach proud Edward's power," sang the nearby Scots, who experienced repeatedly such interventions in their business, "Chains and slavery." As late as 1650, when the English had just executed their king, writes the historian Paul Langford, they "had featured as Europe's mavericks, their history one of violence, turbulence, and instability. . . . They constituted a standing reminder of the spasmodic vigor of a people still close to barbarism."[20]

The actual alteration in individual behavior in the direction of bourgeois values by around 1700 was perhaps not great. Well into the twentieth century the rest of the world had occasion to be shocked by the aristocratic/peasant "vigor" of British soldiers, quite unlike what one would expect from a nation of shopkeepers (the phrase, by the way, is Adam Smith's invention, not Napoleon's). Consider General Kitchener ordering Boer and black women and children into his new invention of the concentration camps, in which a quarter died of hunger and disease during 1900–1901 (the incident makes the point that not all new ideas are good ones). Consider the massacre at Amritsar in British India in 1919, or the bold Black and Tans suppressing Irish rebellion in 1920. A little if rich island did not paint a quarter of the world red, or win two world wars (with a little help), by sweetly bourgeois persuasion alone. Aristocratic arrogance and ferocity among some of the British lasted long enough to staff the army with leaders, until in the First World War it became too large, requiring massive recruitment from the bourgeoisie (as Continental armies long had required). An early case was John Churchill (1650–1722), first Duke of Marlborough, a commoner by origin but notably aristocratic in bearing. Yet he carried over his bourgeois habits of punctiliousness in dealing with accounts and organizations for holding together an army of scattered allies, the better to beat the French aristocrats again and again and again.[21] The second sons of British aristocrats, such as Richard Howe, had long joined even the technically demanding and bourgeois navy. They stood on the quarterdecks facing enemy fire, as aristocrats should, but their fellow officers were the sons of lawyers or of clergymen (such as Sir Francis William Austen, Admiral of the Fleet in

1863 and Jane Austen's brother; and Sir Charles Austen, another brother and another admiral). But the change in rhetoric toward bourgeois cooperation, under the influence of an evangelical Christianity spread by the newly dignified bourgeoisie, was permanent and finally softening.[22]

∽

I want to initiate a discussion, to put the point another way, with my numerous friends in economics and even in economic history who have come to believe that all effects of ideas on the economy work mainly or exclusively or necessarily or obviously through incentive-summarizing "institutions." They want this to be true because the idea of the institution as a constraint fits easily with their training in Samuelsonian economics. Incentives are in the Samuelsonian view merely the prices—literally the slopes—built into budget lines. Identity, integrity, ethics, justice, temperance, professionalism, ideology, ideas, rhetoric, love, faith, hope have nothing to do with anything economic, my misled friends declare.

   I believe on the contrary, with Alexis de Tocqueville in 1853, that "institutions" such as laws are not fundamental: "I accord institutions," wrote Tocqueville in 1853, "only a secondary influence on the destiny of men. . . . Political societies are not what the laws make them, but what sentiments, beliefs, ideas, habits of the heart [in his famous phrase from *Democracy in America*], and the spirit of the men who form them prepare them in advance to be. . . . The sentiments, the ideas, the mores [*moeurs*] . . . alone can lead to public prosperity and liberty."[23] The Tocqueville/McCloskey hypothesis finds support, for example, in the magnificent tables of the *World Value Survey*, in which researchers such as Matteo Migheli have found evidence of great differences in attitudes toward state intervention in Western as against formerly Communist Europe.[24] The economic results differ. Habits of the heart and mind and lip matter to economies. The economic historian Philip Hoffman has shown that what mattered most for rural France from 1450 to 1815 were not institutions, such as allegedly communal property, which peasants had ample experience in working around. What mattered most were markets and, especially, political decisions motivated by heart and mind and lip—which they could not work around.[25]

   In 1973 North and Robert Paul Thomas boldly stated the hypothesis that has so charmed other economists: "Efficient economic organization is the key to growth; the development of an efficient economic organization in

Western Europe accounts for the rise of the West."[26] We have seen what is wrong with such a claim, even in the imaginative and thorough books by the economic historians Greif or Zanden, or the dazzling articles by the economists Acemoglu, Johnson, and Robinson: mere efficiency has little to do with massive innovation. It is the massive innovation, not a Harberger Triangle of gain from efficiency, that has transformed our lives. North and Thomas went on: "Efficient organization entails the establishment of institutional arrangements and property rights that create an incentive to channel individual economic effort into activities that bring the private rate of return close to the social rate of return." True. That's what efficiency means, though the definition offered does not give a scale on which to measure how close the returns need to be to be important. They conclude: "If a society does not grow it is because no incentives are provided for economic initiative." Again no scale is provided for judging how close to "no incentives" a social provision might be. And anyway the conclusion is true (in their terms) only if incentives for efficiency make for growth, which as I said is dubious. Interpreted in my terms, as saying that the habits of the mind and lip must offer another sort of "incentive for economic initiative," it is quite true—but irrelevant to matters of strict efficiency, and next door to a tautology: if there's no growth, then there's . . . no growth.

A few years before North and Thomas spoke out loud and bold, I myself, inspired by Steven N. S. Cheung (my office mate at the University of Chicago, and later an inspiring colleague of North's at the University of Washington), and by Ronald Coase across the way at the Law School, studied the legal history of England during the eighteenth century with the Samuelsonian prejudice about economic "incentives" and "efficiency." I wanted the story to be one of moving from bad allocation to good, from a point away from the intersection of supply-and-demand curves to that blessed intersection. The institutions simply let the intersection occur. The idea was delightful—and it was exactly what my Samuelsonian training and my Friedmanite employment told me. But I gradually realized that the timing of institutional change in England fits poorly with its economic change. The curves moved out violently, by a factor of two and then sixteen and more, far too much to be explained by routine changes in institutions, even educational institutions, which after all had come and gone many times before in human history. There was by contrast, I realized decades later, an obvious and historically unique improvement in the dignity and liberty of the bourgeoisie, apparent for example in the invention of the science of political economy itself. The surrounding *institutions* of the economy were old.

The economists want the big change to be a matter of Northian "institutions" because they want incentive to be the main story of the Industrial Revolution and the modern world. But suppose incentive (Prudence Only) is not the main story, and cannot be the main story without paradox: if it was Prudence Only, then the Industrial Revolution would have happened earlier, or elsewhere. Suppose that other virtues and vices matter a lot—not only prudence, beloved of the Samuelsonians; but temperance, courage, justice, faith, hope, and love, which changed radically in their disposition during the seventeenth and eighteenth centuries. Suppose that the ideology, the rhetoric, the public sphere mattered a great deal, and suppose that these (like legal and economic ideas) were often and quickly shared across countries. Voltaire and Montesquieu looked across the Channel, with the result that Anglophilia governed one strain in French opinion, and to some degree became an element in French public policy. Thomas Paine wandered the world looking for countries without liberty, and shared revolution. Suppose that the spread of institutions, such as dignity and liberty for the bourgeoisie, once revealed as efficacious, like reading, is as much horizontal across countries as vertical across time. Suppose that institutions viewed as incentives and constraints are not chiefly what mattered, but rather community and conversation.

That is what my economistic friends should consider. Insisting that every change in "institutions" is the same thing as a change in constraints, and insisting contrary to the evidence that the era of the Industrial Revolution witnessed a revolution in property rights, has a cleverly Samuelsonian air. But it is not good history and it is not a good explanation of the unprecedented economic event we are seeking to explain. I am not saying that an economy will do well with rotten institutions. Nor am I saying that there are no places in the world with rotten institutions—Zimbabwe, to repeat, jumps out of the headlines. Zim would do a lot better if its government stopped stealing private property and killing people who complain. What I am saying is that the rich countries in the actual historical event have pretty good economic institutions, whatever their history of similarity or difference on the scale of a law professor's detailed definition of *perfect* property rights. Countries as varied in institutions as France and Australia have pretty much the same income per head. France has Roman law, medium labor freedom, and high product market regulation. Australia has common law, the OECD's greatest labor freedom, and its lowest product market regulation. Yet the two countries differ in real GDP per capita adjusted for purchasing power by only $3,000 out of $30,000.[27] That sort of Harbergian differential precisely does *not* explain the modern world. Once both countries earned $8.22 per head per day, $3,000 a year in modern U.S. prices. Now they earn ten times as much, and have entered the modern world.

It does not seem, in short, that changes in "institutions" have much to do with the Industrial Revolution. Maybe you can believe that good institutions of property and contract divide us from hunter-gathers or herdsmen, especially if you do not look too closely into the economic lives of hunter-gatherers or herdsmen. But the institutions of property and contract do not happen to have changed much in the relevant period. Samuelsonian appeals to "institutional change," in other words, come down to still another attempt to reduce one of the greatest surprises in human history to a materialist routine, a routine which can't in its nature explain surprises. The attempt comes out of economics, the pure theory of prudent materialism. As Tocqueville wrote in 1834, "All the efforts in political economy seem today to be in the direction of materialism," and so they were from 1890 to 1980, even beyond political economy itself. "I would like," he continued, "to try to introduce ideas and moral feelings as elements of prosperity and happiness."[28] Just so.

38

THE CAUSE WAS NOT SCIENCE

We are back to what actually happened 1700–1848, and then on to 2010 and beyond, a rise of income per person by a factor by the end, let us say very conservatively, of sixteen. The happening was recognized slowly in the twentieth century. Among many economists and economic historians the recognition slowly killed the notion that thrifty saving was the way to massive and colossal productive forces. Early on, in 1960, Hayek questioned "our habit of regarding economic progress chiefly as an accumulation of ever greater quantities of goods and equipment."[1] In 2010 the economic historian Alexander Field reinforced the original insights of the 1960s from calculations of productivity change in the United States that technology was it, not capital accumulation; and in 2006 the economist Peter Howitt had arrived at a similar conclusion from cross-country studies.[2]

So: the Great Fact was not caused by capital accumulation, as desirable as was an interstate highway system valorized by the invention of the automobile and motor truck. Nor was it any such thing, such as the accumulation of educational capital. These are supplied if the innovation demands them. Nor was it the better allocation that comes with better institutions, or commercialization. Nice though efficiency is, it is not the main point. Innovation is. Even many good economists have not been able to grasp that static allocation is not the key to the success of market societies. It is not. The inefficiency of social democratic regimes such as that of France, therefore, is a pity, but it has not yet been a catastrophe either politically or economically. France is very rich and very free. A generous social provision has *not* led down the road to serfdom, which is why Western Europe's moderate version of socialism has proven viable, such as Sweden after 1960.[3] True, empirically, as a contingent fact about human nature, the dignities and liberties of the bourgeoisie do result in more innovation. But the "social market economies" of Finland and Holland continue to deliver pretty well, because they do not rigorously assault the dignities and liberties of the bourgeoisie.

It could be, conceptually, that the nature of man under the other, more rigorous socialism—central-planning, zero property, first-shoot-all-the-bourgeoisie socialism—would result in such a rise in public spirit, say, or such a reduction of alienation, that desirable innovation would flourish. Since nothing would stand in the way of the use of the Caspian Sea for irrigation, all would be well, and no destruction of the environment would result. The Public Good would be served by consulting the *Volonté General.* But the evidence is in, and it speaks unambiguously. Ant-farm socialism *is* a catastrophe and probably always will be. In 1917 one might reasonably have believed that a society without an admired and enabled bourgeoisie would in fact innovate more than one with the appalling bourgeoisie in power, and thereby socialism would pull the poor out of their poverty. By now, however, the belief that Stalinism Is Good For You is unreasonable. "Communist" China innovates, but does so precisely in its capitalist, bourgeois-admiring parts, only. Elsewhere it constructs by government fiat great armies to crush dissent and to exorcise the remote devils of European and Japanese imperialism, and constructs great dams that will silt up in twenty years.

All right. Again: what does then explain innovation?

New thoughts, new habits of mind and lip, what Mokyr calls the "industrial Enlightenment." "The rise of our standard of living," wrote Hayek, "is due at least as much to an increase in knowledge" as to accumulation of capital.[4] The great economist Simon Kuznets, notes his student Richard Easterlin, believed that "the 'givens' of economics—technology, tastes, and institutions—are the key actors in historical change, and hence most economic theory has, at best, only limited relevance to understanding long-term change."[5] Mokyr and Goldstone and Jacob and Tunzelmann and I and some others would go one step further, to ideas. It was ideas about steam engines and stock markets and light bulbs and grain storage that made northwestern Europe rich, and then much of the rest of the world, not buildings or BAs accumulated from savings—which were merely induced by the ideas. As Nicholas Crafts writes: "The hallmark of the Industrial Revolution was the emergence of a society that was capable of sustained technological progress and faster total factor productivity growth."[6] The new society was one of innovation.

∞

Many scholars with whom I agree on many other points, though, think that it was in particular the ideas of the Scientific Revolution that caused the innovation.[7] Lay people (not the scholars whom I refer to) speak loosely in a portmanteau phrase of "science-and-technology" making us better off. As it did. But the phrase makes it possible to ignore the political and social change—what I call the Bourgeois Revaluation—that put the science to work. There's some politics in it. With "science-and-technology" as the explanation of the modern world, you can sit comfortably on the left, for example. Contrary to the opinion of Marx and Engels, you will not need to admit that the bourgeoisie has created more massive and colossal productive forces than have all preceding generations. Or you can sit comfortably on the right, and admire the aristocratic genius of the great scientists—and disdain the alertness of the mere vulgar businesspeople who made the science economically relevant. Combining "science-and-technology" in one hurriedly pronounced phrase mistakes the past, and much of the present. It justifies for example a worshipful attitude toward expensive sciences such as astronomy and theoretical physics, which have no economic justification. The phrase needs to be broken in two. Science. Technology. To which, as Mokyr and Jacob have stressed, one must add *enlightenment.*

In one respect I am inclined to agree with the science-did-it scholars, and even the science-and-technology lay people, and certainly the enlightened, because the impulsive force is then ideas rather than matter alone. Mokyr declares that "engineers and mechanics such as Smeaton [breast waterwheel], Watt [separate condenser for steam engine], Trevithick [high pressure steam engine], and G. Stephenson [locomotive with high pressure engine] learned from scientists a rational faith in the orderliness of natural phenomena and physical processes; an appreciation of the importance of accuracy in measurement and controls in experiment; the logical difference between cause and correlation; and a respect for quantification and mathematics."[8] But these were rhetorical and ideal forces, as Mokyr would agree. Remember Richard McKeon's claim that "the [technical] power to modify the heavenly laws" was in the late seventeenth century increasingly vouchsafed to human agency—by human agents, for example, in the form of merchants and projectors. As Richard Easterlin put it, "The growth of scientific knowledge [he instances biological discoveries improving public and then private health] has been shaped much more by internal [that it, intellectual] factors than external factors such as market forces."[9]

But of course one problem that has to be faced by advocates of science as a cause, and to some degree even by the advocates of the Enlightenment as a cause, is that Chinese, and at one point Islamic, science and technology, separately and together, and their humanistic scholarship, were until very lately superior to Western science and enlightenment in most ways, and yet resulted in no industrial revolution. Koreans invented moveable type, yet had no great scientific conversation. Another problem is that the inspiriting discoveries of a Newtonian clockwork universe, and the great mathematization in Europe of earthly and celestial mechanics in the eighteenth century, had practically no direct industrial applications until the late nineteenth century at the very earliest. The historian of technology Nathan Rosenberg noted that "before the twentieth century there was no very close correspondence between scientific leadership and industrial leadership," instancing the United States, which had negligible scientific achievement by 1890 and yet industrial might, and Japan, ditto, by 1970.[10]

Agreeing with this last point, Mokyr concludes that "the full triumph of technology was only secured after 1870 with the arrival of cheap steel, electrical power, chemicals, and other advances associated with the second Industrial Revolution," and associated sometimes with science.[11] Sometimes. "Cheap steel," for example, is not a scientific case in point. True, as Mokyr points out, it was only fully realized that steel is intermediate between cast and wrought iron in its carbon content early in the nineteenth century, since (after all) the very idea of an "element" such as carbon was ill-formed until then. Mokyr claims that without such scientific knowledge, "the advances in steelmaking are hard to imagine."[12] I think not. Tunzelmann notes that even in the late nineteenth century "breakthroughs such as that by Bessemer in steel were published in scientific journals but were largely the result of practical tinkering."[13] My own early work on the iron and steel industry came to the same conclusion. Such an apparently straightforward matter as the chemistry of the blast furnace was not entirely understood until well into the twentieth century, and yet the costs of iron and steel had fallen and fallen for a century and a half.

The economic heft of the late-nineteenth-century innovations that did *not* depend at all on science (such as cheap steel) was great: mass-produced concrete, for example, then reinforced concrete (combined with that cheap steel); air brakes on trains, making mile-long trains possible (though the science-dependent telegraph was useful to keep them from running into each other); the improvements in engines to pull the trains; the military organization to maintain schedules (again so that the trains would not run into each other: it was a capital-saving organizational innovation, making doubletracking unnecessary); elevators to make possible the tall reinforced concrete buildings (although again science-based electric motors were better than having a steam engine in every building; but the "science" in electric motors was hardly more than noting the connection in 1820 between electricity and magnetism—one didn't require Maxwell's equations to make a dynamo); better "tin" cans (more electricity); asset markets in which risk could be assumed and shed; faster rolling mills; the linotype machine; cheap paper; and on and on and on.[14] Mokyr agrees: "It seems likely that in the past 150 years the majority of important inventions, from steel converters to cancer chemotherapy, from food canning to aspartame, have been used long before people understood *why* they worked. . . . The proportion of such inventions is declining, but it remains high today."[15] In 1900 the parts of the economy that used science to improve products and processes—electrical and chemical engineering, chiefly, and even these sometimes using science pretty crudely—were quite small, reckoned in value of output or numbers of employees. And yet in the technologically feverish U.K. in the eight decades (plus a year) from 1820 to 1900, real income per head grew by a factor of 2.63, and in the next eight "scientific" decades only a little faster, by a factor of 2.88.[16] The result was a rise from 1820 to 1980 of a factor of $(2.63) \cdot (2.88) = 7.57$. That is to say—since 2.63 is quite close to 2.88—nearly half of the world-making change down to 1980 was achieved before 1900, in effect before science. This is not to deny science its economic heft *after* science: the per capita factor of growth in the U.K. during the merely twenty years 1980 to 1999 was fully 1.53, which would correspond to an eighty-year factor of an astounding 5.5. The results are similar for the United States, though as one might expect at a still more feverish pace: a factor of 3.25 in per capita real income from 1820 to 1900, 4.54 from 1900 to 1980, and about the same frenzy of invention and innovation and clever business plans as Britain after 1980.[17]

Mokyr argues that what was crucial was the *belief* in science (in line with his conviction that the Enlightenment ideology was the crux) because it eventually paid off—perhaps a little even in the second half of the nineteenth century, the Age of the Dynamo as Henry Adams called it, but certainly in the twentieth century. "The belief that systematic useful knowledge and natural philosophy were the keys to economic development," Mokyr argues, "did not fade as a consequence of such disappointments" as the evident uselessness of most seventeenth-century science and the very slow progress during the eighteenth century of extending it in useful ways. "Yet the research continued, unshaken in its belief that at the end of the process there would be economic benefits, even if these were not yet known."[18] Physical and biological science, Mokyr argues, eventually prevented diminishing returns to mere engineering tinkering. "Without the work of natural philosophers, who would infuse it with new knowledge and connect different industries, an artisanal economy would eventually revert to a technologically stationary state." "On its own," Mokyr continues, "artisanal knowledge would be insufficient." Highbrow science, he is saying, prevented economic growth from running into diminishing return.

Mokyr persuades, but not entirely. The immediate objection would be that such an effect was important only in the late nineteenth century, and hardly at all in 1800. We would be enormously richer now than in 1700 even without science. But one can start to see Mokyr's point as the twentieth century proceeds. Had we lacked German organic chemistry, we would have no artificial fertilizer, and would have experienced diminishing returns in agriculture. Had we lacked American agronomy and genetics, we would have had no Green Revolution, with similar results. Yet without the first Industrial Revolution and its nineteenth-century denouement, which depended hardly at all on science, we would also have lacked the universities and the other riches to apply chemistry and physics and soil science and biology. Like imperialism and trade, science was more a result of economic growth than a cause.

All this remains to be shown, a tricky counterfactual. But understand the main point here: even today, as the calculations show, a great deal of economic growth in a country has little or nothing to do with science. The spread of economic growth to places like Brazil or Russia or India or China uses some science-based technologies, such as cell phones, but uses also a great many merely *technology*-based technologies ("artisanal" in Mokyr's vocabulary) free of much input from science—I offer again reinforced concrete and military organization of railway workforces. And the international spread of growth has intensively used the social "technology" of bourgeois dignity and liberty.

I do not deny that economic growth nowadays depends to some degree on scientists. We are all very thankful for the physical and biological scientists among us—though observing that most of them work on problems that will never bear technological fruit (an extreme case being modern pure mathematics, such as number theory; or astronomy, which is splendid, yet, for all the romantic talk about the High Frontier in aid of better funding for space telescopes, less useful per dollar even for the human spirit than poetry or Assyriology). But I do deny that modern enrichment by an unprecedented and Malthus-denying factor has been crucially dependent on the physical and biological sciences. It was certainly not so until 1900, and the asserted scientific contribution to economic growth in the twentieth century needs to be calculated, not merely indignantly asserted because one admires physical and biological science. Just as Britain in 1850 was far from exclusively a steam-driven cotton mill, so the world even now is very far from a computer-driven automatic lathe. Strictly speaking, a world without modern electrical, electronic, chemical, agronomical, aeronautical, or for that matter economic science, would be poorer, of course, but still it would be very much richer than the world of 1800—so long as the Bourgeois Revaluation had taken place. And there's the use of economic science.

Tunzelmann notes further that Britain was not "particularly conspicuous as a leader in science," which is to say that it was not conspicuously leading in propositional as against applied science, and especially as against applied technology. Scientific advance from Copernicus to Carnot was pan-European, and in the late nineteenth century became strikingly German. Yet the Industrial Revolution of the eighteenth and early nineteenth centuries was strikingly British. And despite the mistaken rhetoric of late Victorian "failure," the British continued into the late nineteenth and indeed into the twentieth century to be great innovators: the military tank, penicillin, jet planes, radar. It is conventional to observe that unlike the French or Germans the British were not significant theorists (with rare if glorious exceptions like Newton, Darwin, Maxwell, Kelvin, Hawking), but that they were nonetheless very significant tinkerers and muddlers through. Technologists. Bourgeois.

Goldstone defends the science-based argument this way:

The distinctive feature of Western economies since 1800 has not been growth per se, but growth based on a specific set of elements: engines to extract motive power from fossil fuels, to a degree hitherto rarely appreciated by historians; the application of empirical science to understanding both nature and practical problems of production; and the marriage of empirically oriented science to a national culture of educated craftsmen and entrepreneurs broadly educated in basic principles of mechanics and experimental approaches to knowledge. This combination developed from the seventeenth to nineteenth centuries only in Britain, and was unlikely to have developed anywhere else in world history.[19]

One can agree especially with the "since 1800" specification. The economic historian George Grantham has argued that the real economic payoff from Continental science—chemistry and plant science in particular—came as a result of the massive upscaling of science in the German universities during the 1840s, allowing the training of hundreds of careful experimenters and theorists, some of whom made breakthroughs such as the discovery of the carbon ring. Until then, science in Europe had been pursued mainly as a hobby, and on the Continent it was pursued as disproportionately an aristocratic hobby. "For science to develop on a wide base," Grantham argues, "it could not continue to rest on a small number of wealthy persons supporting themselves in a life of research. The growth of organized science thus implied an institutional structure in which researchers are salaried."[20] Like music, it came to be supported massively by the bourgeoisie. "From an intellectual standpoint," he concedes, "the Scientific Revolution takes its roots in the breakthroughs of the seventeenth century. But "from the institutional perspective, the Revolution belongs to the nineteenth," after (I would add) the Bourgeois Revaluation.[21] That's why the science important for our economic welfare started mattering much only after 1900.

The relative price of bourgeois standing changed long before 1900, and made for large and non-science-based innovation in total. In doubting with Tunzelmann and Grantham and me that theoretical science had much to do with the Industrial Revolution, Robert Allen quotes a fine passage from an author whom Adam Smith and I do not much admire, the Dutchman resident in England Bernard Mandeville, in 1714. The people who merely "inquire into the reason of things," declared Mandeville, are "idle and indolent," "fond of retirement," and "hate business."[22] Until 1871 the universities at Oxford and Cambridge excluded Jews and Catholics, of course, and Nonconformists (that is, non-Anglicans such as Quakers, Unitarians, Baptists, Congregationalists, and later in great numbers Methodists), which left the dissenting academies to give Nonconformist children an education that did not inspire the hatred of business, or favor retirement into studying the argument from design or the three forms of indirect speech in Attic Greek. From around 1700 the Scottish universities by contrast took a practical turn, notes Alastair Durie, and were "not merely concerned with the niceties of theology but endeavored to relate scientific enquiry to industrial application."[23] Theology itself in Britain joined enthusiastically with Newtonian science, whether inside or outside the universities. Scottish intellectuals invented a *social* "natural theology" in parallel with the physical one of their English neighbors, one step toward the Scottish discovery of economics.[24]

Celestial mechanics and anticlericalism, in other words, could not by themselves have revolutionized Europe, any more than China and the Muslim world were revolutionized by the great lead in science they had until 1600 or so. Mere curiosity and originality by a handful of Galileos and Newtons does not an industrial revolution make. Mandeville's dialogue again: "*Horatio*: It is commonly imagined that speculative men are best at invention of all sorts. *Cleomenes*: Yet it is a mistake." It is of course quite impossible to imagine our worldview without Galileo's *Dialogo* or Newton's *Principia* or Hutton's *Theory of the Earth* or Darwin's *Origin of Species*. But it is easy to imagine our industry up until about 1900 without them. The new dignity and liberty for the bourgeoisie were essential. Greece's invention of most of the arts and sciences (with borrowings from eastern sources), and its partial freedom to doubt the gods, had not revolutionized the Greek economy or enriched its poor. Ancient Greek society despised physical work as slavish and womanly, and devalued gadgets (with Archimedean and Antikytheran exceptions), and above all looked down on the bourgeoisie. French science in the eighteenth century depended notably on aristocrats such as Lavoisier and Laplace and Georges-Louis Leclerc (the Comte de Buffon), retaining a glorious and axiomatic impracticality imparted first by Descartes. As Jacob emphasizes, "The aristocratic character of French scientific institutions" was in sharp contrast to the workmanlike and practical tone in Britain.[25] Science in the Anglophone world depended much more on bourgeois, working, experimental figures like Newton or Priestley or Franklin or Hutton or Davy or Thomson.

And scientists are not always harbingers of progress. After all, a little after the stirrings of dignity for the bourgeoisie and its world-changing innovations, the most advanced scientists and the most enlightened thinkers commonly became the most virulent enemies of economic innovation, and often the most virulent enemies, too, of the freedom to have children or the freedom to speak one's mind or the freedom to live outside a concentration camp. Upper-class socialists like the great economist Joan Robinson, writes the economist and priest Anthony Waterman, who was her tutee at Cambridge, exhibited a "patrician disdain for capitalist acts between consenting adults."[26] Consider the much-admired geneticist and statistician R. A. Fisher (1890–1962), who passionately supported a racist eugenics; or the also-much-admired ecologist, as I have said, Garrett Hardin (1915–2003), who passionately supported compulsory sterilization. Though often very nice, the scientists and the atheists—the two are not the same—are not automatically the best friends of human dignity and liberty, and therefore not automatically the best friends of the modern world.

The crux around 1700 was not the new sciences about anatomy and astronomy (neither of which much affected industrial development), but the new rhetoric about bourgeois innovation. True, some little of the new science improved industry, as Jacob has argued for hydrology. Yet what mattered for the scale of innovation in total, Mandeville argued, is not to have scientists, but to have masses of "active, stirring, laborious men, such as will put their hand to the plow, try experiments [there's the scientific attitude], and give all their attention to what they are about."[27] And especially what matters is that the rest of the society honors and liberates such people.

Jacob and Mokyr would reply that such active people of whatever class merged increasingly with the scientists. Mokyr for example argues that "eighteenth-century Britain was what we may call a technologically competent society. It was teeming with engineers, mechanics, millwrights, and dexterous and imaginative tinkerers who spent their time and energy designing better pumps, pulleys, and pendulums."[28] In the English-speaking world, however, such practical savants attended to applications, not scientific theory, and that is the main point. Mokyr continues: "Even wealthy landowners and merchants [in Britain] displayed a fascination with technical matters." Yes. In 1752 an elaborate diagram of the "Yorkshire maiden" washing machine, which was in actual use, was displayed in the January 1752 edition of Gentleman's Magazine. Note: by then "gentlemen" had long been presumed in Britain to have an interest in mechanical devices other than machines of war. The very word "engine," which had once named hunting snares and then catapults and siege engines, comes by 1635 to name civilian machines, and gives rise by 1606 to "engineers" and their flourishing in England and Scotland and America and France toward 1800. It climaxes in the lives of the engineers, devoted to useable projects of industrial design, experimental madness, such as Isambard Kingdom Brunel's Thames Tunnel, the Great Western railway, and the Great Eastern steamship.

Robert Allen correctly observes that the connection between Mokyr's "industrial Enlightenment" of the fancier sort and many of the inventors was tenuous. Occasionally it was close, like Watt's friendship with Black. But the potter and member of the Lunar Society Wedgwood was not elected to the Royal Society until he was fifty-three.[29] The experimentalism that accompanied invention, Allen continues, was anyway necessary for any innovation, and "had precedents running back centuries."[30] Or millennia, in every part of the world. Doubtless some anonymous Romans "experimented" to invent the Roman arch, and food is an ancient and obvious case of experimentation—without "science" in the modern English sense of the word.

39

BUT BOURGEOIS DIGNITY AND LIBERTY ENTWINED WITH THE ENLIGHTENMENT

One can agree with Goldstone, who in defending the new-old view of Margaret Jacob and Joel Mokyr that Technological Ideas Supported by the Enlightenment Did It, writes that "what transformed [European] production was a generalized belief in the possibility . . . of progress. . . . The longstanding traditional barriers between upper-class philosophers, market-driven entrepreneurs, large-scale industrialists, and skilled craftspeople and technicians dissolved, so that all these groups came together to initiate a culture of innovation."[1] Social distance declined. But then it is not science but the "breakdown of traditional barriers"—precisely the coming of a business-respecting civilization—which is the crux. The widening belief that the physical and therefore the social world can be changed by human agency, and is not frozen in a great chain of being, might be attributed in part to science, though the Reformation and the Revolutions and above all the Revaluation surely figure, too. And one could just as well believe that a Newtonian universe would be worshiped instead for its clocklike stability, with conservative social and theological conclusions. Jacob has taught us that Newton himself drew such conclusions.[2] The success of business projectors, whether bourgeois or aristocratic, was surely more effective than science in showing people that they too, and not only God's grace and miracles, could change things. By the middle of the eighteenth century the literary man Samuel Johnson, though a Tory in politics, could write in favor of innovation thus:

> That the attempts of such men [projectors] will often miscarry, we may reasonably expect; yet from such men, and such only, are we to hope for the cultivation of those parts of nature which lie yet waste, and the invention of those arts which

are yet wanting to the felicity of life. If they are, therefore, universally discouraged, art and discovery can make no advances. Whatever is attempted without previous certainty of success, may be considered as a project, and amongst narrow minds may, therefore, expose its author to censure and contempt; and if the liberty of laughing be once indulged, every man will laugh at what he does not understand, every project will be considered as madness, and every great or new design will be censured as a project.[3]

There's a declaration for bourgeois dignity and liberty, against their enemies in church or manor house. It was an impossible sentiment in 1550 in England, or in China.

Easterlin draws a striking comparison between the Industrial Revolution and the Mortality Revolution. He describes the demographer Samuel H. Preston's decomposition of falling mortality into the outcome of mere enrichment with given technology as against the outcome of technology with given enrichment. Preston's decomposition, Easterlin notes, is analogous to the economist Robert Solow's decomposition of enrichment itself into mere capital accumulation as against technology. He concludes that "when the quest for the economic historian's Holy Grail, the causes of the Industrial Revolution, is couched in terms of commonalities in the Industrial and Mortality Revolutions, economic explanations of the Industrial Revolution become less persuasive."[4] So they do. "In seeking an explanation," he continues, " . . . one must ask what is new on the scene." For both revolutions, he says, with Jacob and Goldstone, that it was science, and with all of these and Mokyr that it was anyway a practical mentality.

But what was also "new on the scene," and tracks the beginnings of economic growth and mortality reduction more precisely is the attribution of bourgeois dignity and liberty, such as from Johnson. It is seen in an early form around 1720 as a new dignity and liberty for traders and innovators (consider *Robinson Crusoe*, and all Defoe's works). And a century before Defoe, the English were beginning to learn from the Dutch the improving spirit of active, stirring, laborious men, such as will put their hand to the plow, try experiments, and give all their attention to what they are about. Henry Robinson was very busy in the 1640s issuing pamphlets advocating improvements such as compulsory swimming lessons for the poor. Francis Bacon's proposals during the 1620s for improving science look like those of a bourgeois projector (though My Lord Bacon was as far as one can imagine from being bourgeois, or being an advocate for dignity and liberty). Let us do thus-and-such, organized in this way (declares the projector in Holland and then England) and—behold!—what great benefits will flow! It is a methodical and accounting rhetoric, tied to practical hope and courage, and foreign to the bold gestures in court and battlefield of an aristocratic society.

Much later the rhetoric appears in the public and bourgeois spirit of people of the 1840s and 1850s like Nassau Senior or Ignaz Semmelweis or John Snow calling for urban renewal and hospital handwashing and the redirection of water intakes. The germ theory of disease, Mokyr has emphasized, was of course a late nineteenth-century discovery, before which a cleanliness obsession, backed by no scientific ideas except the erroneous one that disease was spread by bad smells, had taken hold among bourgeois men and especially women, long anticipated in the Low Countries and finally spreading to France and England, and an occasional Hungarian doctor. Nobody took care of the water supply or public education in London in the eighteenth century. Benjamin Franklin stood out in Philadelphia for his bourgeois public spirit. A century later in both places a very great care indeed was being taken—again, proper theoretical science aside. The banker and writer Matt Ridley in 1996 looked back upon his hometown of Newcastle-upon-Tyne in 1800 as "a hive of local enterprise and pride" with "great traditions of trust, mutuality and reciprocity on which such cities were based."[5] Bourgeois dignity and liberty contains much more than isolated monads and an ethic of devil-take-the-hindmost. The market is not the monstrously disembedded monster that both left and right have imagined. "Market society" is not a contradiction in terms. *Gemeinschaft* intertwines with *Gesellschaft*.

Further, the political revolutions of the seventeenth century in England were surely more important to more people than the novelties of the Scientific Revolution—though the point can hardly be used against Margaret Jacob, because she herself made it. She writes in the preface to a new edition in 2006 of her book of 1981, which introduced the idea of a "radical Enlightenment," that "beginning in the 1680s northern and western Europe experienced a series of shock waves that in turn produced a new radicalism in thought both in matters political and religious. French bellicosity, the revocation of the Edict of Nantes in 1685, and the appearance on the English throne in the same year of a Catholic king threw Protestant Europe into turmoil."[6] It is her origin story, and a good one. But she and Jonathan Israel (who later carried on the argument with what Jacob characterizes with a hint of distaste "a very different and largely idealist methodology") see the results through political and intellectual life, with the political and intellectual life then affecting the society and the economy. A more direct chain of causation would be revolutions (1642 as much as 1688, as Jacob also emphasizes; or for that matter 1568 in the Netherlands and 1517 in Germany) causing a new self-respecting by the bourgeoisie, and other-respecting for it, too—and at length the Bourgeois Revaluation. The ideas directly in support of economic change, as Jacob's colleague Joyce Appleby showed in 1978, were fruits of social and intellectual change in England during the seventeenth century, coming to full ripeness much later in French physiocracy and Scottish political economy. Appleby argued, for example, using Barry Supple's early work on the economic crisis of the early seventeenth century, that the disorders of the 1620s forced English people to think hard about a thing increasingly conceived as a separate "economy."[7]

Goldstone defends the Jacobian chain of Boyle-Newcomen-Watt in which revolutionary consequences follow from the scientific discovery in England in the seventeenth century of the weight of the atmosphere (by the way, actually discovered in China centuries before, with no such practical result): "Great Britain had what no other nation on earth had, or would *for more than a generation*: a cheap and reliable means of converting heat energy (mainly from coal) into uniform rotary motion" (italics mine).[8] Note the phrase I have italicized, which Goldstone wrote with characteristic precision. That's right: for a mere generation or so the English coal miners and coal burners had an advantage. But a business-respecting civilization in, say, Japan would have adopted the steam engine pronto, with coal or not, as it did so with alacrity when business became Japan's business. Bourgeois dignity and liberty made for quick imitation as much as for ingenious invention.

Jacob noted that the very "backlash against the Enlightenment testifies to the enormous change in Western values witnessed in the eighteenth century."[9] Surely. But the change was not mere enlightenment. What finished the job, and carried the Enlightenment forward, was a society-wide shift toward the admiring of bourgeois virtues, taking the enlightened attitude among the elite toward the creative destruction from new knowledge and multiplying it among apprentice printers in Philadelphia and instrument makers in Edinburgh. Mokyr writes that "the Enlightenment affected the economy through two mechanisms. One of them is the attitude toward technology and the role it should play in human affairs. The other has to do with institutions and the degree to which rent-seeking and redistribution should be tolerated."[10] But such an answer to the question *Was ist Aufklärung?* comes very close to my supposed "dignity and liberty of the bourgeoisie." An instrumental (and bourgeois) attitude toward technology gives ordinary affairs a dignity they did not formerly have. And resistance to the rent-seeking and redistribution that characterize an ageless mercantilism and, later also Listian national economy, is precisely the liberty from interference that the bourgeoisie sought—once it had been compelled to surrender its medieval attitude toward preserving the home market for itself. There's not much in the difference. I readily admit that the issue is tangled. I only suggest that two strands, without which the rope of modernity would have broken, were bourgeois dignity and liberty. Jacob herself points out, for example, that the founding rhetoric of the new science emphasized the dignified *laboriousness* of scientific inquiry. Insight was to be achieved not by heroic gesture or God's grace but by thoroughly bourgeois works.[11] It is very Dutch, and then English and Scottish and American. And anyway bourgeois.

The Enlightenment, Jacob argues, was of Northern origin—"the beginning of the European Enlightenment can in many instances be traced to post-[Glorious] revolutionary England and the Dutch Republic," then shifted to France: "By 1750, the Enlightenment had left its northern roots and become remarkably Parisian."[12] But had it stayed remarkably Parisian it probably would not have stayed at all. The production of encyclopedias and the wit of salons, if it had not worked within an increasingly bourgeois civilization led by an astonishingly innovative Britain, would have resulted (as it did in France) in hot-air balloons and military signaling systems, not steam engines and railways. The heroic engineer/entrepreneur such as Brunel (British, but the son of an exile from France) would not have triumphed. Jacob notes that "the civil engineer [of docks and canals and roads] emerged in Britain by 1750; his French counterpart was a military man. . . . standing aloof from the entrepreneur."[13] From 1747 the Frenchman graduated from the state school, École nationale des ponts en chaussées. British engineers like Brunel by contrast graduated from the private school of commercial practice and public spirit.

Jacob writes that "the Enlightenment returned to England, the land of its [1680s] birth, largely as a result of the American Revolution."[14] She means a *political* enlightenment, since England and then Scotland never let go of the scientific and practical side. By 1750 in fact, the other, British enlightenment, of a much more practical nature, was being practiced in Edinburgh, and in 1765 in Birmingham, and even earlier in far Philadelphia. The coal mines of Northumberland were filled with Newcomen engines by the 1740s, pumping out the water and permitting the deepest coal mines in Europe, but it was well into the nineteenth century before such wonders affected much else in the economy. Jacob asks of the engineers and inventors, "Can we imagine an industrial revolution without Thomas Newcomen, Desaguliers, John Smeaton or James Watt?"[15] True, we can't. But the Bourgeois Revaluation, not high theory in science, made the engineers. Or rather, high theories in science—and innovations in literature, in Birmingham toys, in painting, in steam, in journalism, in theology, in music, in port design, in philosophy, in constitutions—were, as David Landes puts it, various "manifestations of a common approach. . . . The response to new knowledge . . . is of a piece, and the society that closes its eyes to novelty from one source has already been closing them to novelty from the other."[16] The economic historian Peter Mathias wrote that "both science and technology [in the British eighteenth century] give evidence of a society increasingly curious, increasingly questing, increasingly on the move, on the make, having a go, increasingly seeking to experiment, wanting to improve."[17] The originality of Japanese color prints in the eighteenth century representing the "floating world" of prostitutes and kabuki actors betokens an openness to novelty that one sees also in the Osaka merchant academies of the late seventeenth century.[18] But until 1868, alas, in the face of Tokugawa conservatism, these were swallows without a spring. It is not science that was the key to the door to modernity, but the wider agreement to permit and honor innovation, opening one's eyes to novelty, having a go.

Had the Ottoman or the Qing empires or the Japanese Shogunate admired trade and innovation sufficiently to overcome their worries about the maintenance of state power—encouraging innovation and having a go rather than crushing it—then they, not the Europeans, would have come first. But instead of taking advantage of their own highly developed cultures and sciences, the Eastern states of China, Japan, India, and the Middle East, and plenty of European regimes, too (one thinks of the Counterreformation in Poland and Spain), turned in the seventeenth and eighteenth centuries, as Goldstone argues persuasively, to an intellectual conformity quite foreign to their earlier openness to ideas. It was at the time the northwestern

Europeans, and a few in East Prussia, awakened from their dogmatic slumbers. Yet without a radical change in attitudes toward innovation for optimistically hoped-for glory in a society newly admiring the bourgeois virtues, with (for you) a little monetary profit on the side, the sheer intellectual awakening in Europe would not have enriched the world. The rediscovery of analytic geometry three centuries after an Arab had invented it, the rediscovery of chemical principles known for hundreds of years in China, the questioning of religion many centuries after sophisticated scholars in Baghdad and Delhi and Beijing, or for that matter Athens and Jerusalem, had been doing so would have yielded no industrial fruit.

Orthodox Christianity differed from Catholic Christianity in only a few minor doctrines (*filioque*; clerical celibacy), and yet a corner of the Catholic West initiated growth while the Orthodox world stagnated. The case (which is discussed by the historian of technology Lynn White) shows the drag from a rhetoric hostile to commercial values, and by contraries the importance of the Bourgeois Revaluation. The sociologist of comparative religion Michael Lessnoff summarizes with approval White's remarks on the matter: "In Greek Christianity, the influence of classical Greek culture was considerably greater [than in the West], including the philosophers' depreciation of technology, economic activity, and the active life generally. . . . Mechanical clocks, which proliferated in Western churches, were banned from Orthodox ones."[19] In the West, by contrast, Newtonian Anglicans took the clock as their central theological metaphor, and the pocket watch discovered in a field as their main argument for God's existence.

The new bourgeois society was pragmatic and nonutopian, but also a little mad—the madness that overcame European men and women once they came to believe that they were free and dignified and should have a go. Joel Mokyr cites the madness of the Montgolfier brothers and their floating of a sheep, a rooster, and a duck in a hot-air balloon in 1783 at Versailles. (Ben Franklin watched many such ascents, and at one powered by hydrogen replied to a skeptic about its usefulness: "Sir, of what use is a new born baby?"). The lurching progress of innovation has never been seriously in doubt since around 1800. For a time during the Great Depression many doubted (though the economic historian Alexander Field has shown that the 1930s in the United States was in fact an unusually progressive time in technology).[20] But the doubt was followed after the war by the greatest innovative boom since then, 1950 to 1973, and then continued to relieve poverty worldwide, if at a lower pace.

What was *not* routinely available in the eighteenth century was the great stock of inventions yet to be imagined, including the institutional inventions allowing cooperation among masses of people without the threat of knout and sword. It is why China and India, to repeat, can now grow at rates inconceivable in the eighteenth and early nineteenth centuries before the inventions were well launched. Goldstone observes that human innovation until the eighteenth and especially the nineteenth century was "sporadic and isolated."[21] The Chinese invented the blast furnace, yes, and the Europeans much later got hold of it. Then the technology of the furnace stagnated until in the eighteenth century the British started charging furnaces with coke and then in the late nineteenth century the Americans started hard driving with forced air and then in the twentieth the Austrians and the Japanese reformulated the charge with the new chemistry. It *is* a sort of madness, which now much of world outside the bottom billion has caught. Make your fortune with another invention. An Indian recently invented wide and light paddle-like shoes for walking about on the water in rice paddies. Bravo.

What did happen in the seventeenth and eighteenth centuries to prepare for all this, you might think, is an original accumulation of inventive people, such as Richard Arkwright and Benjamin Franklin. But such a Great Inventor account is not quite right, either. Notions of social or spiritual capital, alleged to give rise automatically to Arkwrights and Franklins, force the evidence to lie down on the economist's bed of accumulate, accumulate. The crucial change was rather about habits of the mind and lip. Accumulated physical, human, and spiritual capital help the talk and thought, surely. If you are illiterate you are probably superstitious and conservative. But talk and thought entail a creativity that mere piling up of capital of whatever sort does not.

One speaks of a "well-stocked mind," and the young economist obsesses on getting "good training in the tools" of the currently fashionable formalities of his trade. Yet both of these, likely as not, create a mind unable to think, mechanically marshaling her knowledge of the classical languages or his tool of an econometrics overaccumulated (yet well-stocked tools of Latin and Greek produced sometimes a Matthew Arnold, who certainly could think; or John Maynard Keynes, likewise; though we are still waiting for similar results for econometrics). But sheer accumulation of learning also produces Oxford dons who almost never have an original idea and don't publish on the rare occasions that they do. The poet and Latin scholar A. E. Housman wrote in 1921 a cruel essay against the nonthinkers in his field, "The Application of Thought to Textual Criticism." He recommended that his colleagues try thinking. Likewise in economics. Taking three of the standard graduate courses in econometrics (as I for example did) produces usually not an economist thinking but an idiot savant trained to follow erroneous rules of inference. A new dignity for innovators and a new liberty to try things out mattered more than such accumulations—although of course one needs minds minimally prepared, too. English literacy and technical apprenticeship did the job. Yet Japan at the time had similar levels of literacy, and technical apprenticeship, too, without yielding an industrial revolution.

The other problem with the Procrustean move of forcing creativity to lie down on models of accumulate, accumulate is that people, too, depreciate over time. What had to happen was a change in the social rhetoric making generation upon generation of people, educated in masses every year, *want* to innovate (or for that matter *want* to go on getting educated), and to innovate, and to innovate. There is the social or spiritual capital—but it's located in conversations and valuations, that is, in ideas and cultural mud. As suggested by the work of Christine MacLeod and Antonio Gramsci (an odd pairing, admittedly), the new rhetoric has to be renewed and strengthened with each new generation. Otherwise it returns to dust. The change of mind and lip was not once-for-all. MacLeod argues that the "commemorative statuary [for James Watt erected in 1834] and the fundraising efforts [1824–1834] surrounding it both raised awareness of new technology and helped shape attitudes more positively towards it."[22] What Gramsci called a "historical block" needed to be constantly renewed, as though it were a machine subject to rapid depreciation—the present book itself is an example of such rhetorical investment in renewal.

∞

I am not, however, making a loose argument for "culture" as the explanation of the North Sea success. Jack Goody, who knows a thing or two about culture, rails against "flaccid explanations of a 'cultural shift,' . . . which explains nothing as it omits any factor of human intentionality, of agency, and leaves causation in the hands of a blind, unthinking 'culture,' which alters patterns in accordance with other 'institutions' (functional analysis) or with an underlying formula (structural analysis)."[23] Landes, who favors culture, wisely remarks nonetheless that "culture does not stand alone. Economic analysis cherishes the illusion that one good reason should be enough, but the determinants of complex processes are invariably plural and interrelated."[24] The first big paper I wrote in college about economics was a callow attack on the social psychologist David McClelland's notion of "need for achievement." I was a sophomore, a very wise fool, and imagined I did not agree with McClelland. Landes does agree with McClelland, and I by now am much more respectful of McClelland's and Landes's argument than I was in 1962. (I wish I knew as much now as I did as that dogmatically materialist nineteen-year-old.) One can't just drop the Sacred and Sociology (the S variables) in favor of an exclusive focus on the Profane and Profit and Price (P variables). That's what economics has tried to do since Jeremy Bentham—with some successes and a lot of silliness. To do the science right you have to control for all the variables, not just pray that the S variables won't interfere in a way correlated with the error term.[25] (That said, however, Landes and I would now get back to our four-decade-long quarrel about numbers. He would say that S variables are not measurable. Fiddlesticks.)

The trouble is that culture, measurable or not, is startling, and ironically unpredictable, precisely because it is an instrument of human agency. "Culture can make all the difference," Landes says, frequently.[26] All right. Let's perform a mental experiment to test how culture can "make all the difference." No fair using hindsight. Suppose that in a very backward country—call it R—the established church decides to clean up the liturgy by eliminating some old corruptions in the holy texts. A group of believers, themselves stupidly conservative in every way, rejects the new liturgy: they are not interested in the application of thought to textual criticism. Which of the following does your social theory predict? (1) The establishment is hostile to these Old Believers. (2) The Old Believers retreat into self-imposed isolation. Outcome? Either (3), the Old Believers sink into poverty and obscurity, on account of (1) and (2). Or (4), the Old Believers go on to become the dominant force in the country's economy for the next two centuries, on account of (1) and (2).

The bizarre scenario played out in seventeenth-century Russia gives the correct answer to our quiz: (1) and (2); then *not* (3), but (4), as Alexander Gerschenkron explained in *Russia in the European Mirror* (1970). The example does not refute Landes's vague hypothesis of "culture." But it shows as difficult what he thinks is easy: to tell who will win. The Old Believers in Russia were the only successfully bourgeois portion of Russian society in the seventeenth through nineteenth centuries, except for an occasional

Jew and a good many of what Landes calls by the Greek name "metics" (*metoikoi*, "people beyond the household," noncitizen workers, in Russia mainly Germans).

There was nothing easy or inevitable about this. Some minorities do well when the establishment tries to crush them—witness the Old Believers, but also the overseas Chinese, and of course the European Jews, sometimes. But some badly treated minorities just do badly—witness Gypsies in Eastern Europe and American blacks under segregation, and European Jews, sometimes. It can go either way. One is reminded of Arnold Toynbee's charming and empty theory of "challenge and response." Too much challenge, as in Greenland, or too little, as in eighteenth-century China, and you get stagnation. It's difficult to predict the golden mean.

Landes takes a too-simple view of the inevitability of what happened, because his main intellectual tool is hindsight. It is the characteristic scientific vice of the historian (and of the evolutionary biologist), to suppose that since what happened did happen it must have been inevitable. Landes claims, for example, that "one could have foreseen the postwar economic success of Japan and Germany by taking account of culture. The same with South Korea vs. Turkey, Indonesia vs. Nigeria."[27] I don't think so. If events that happen are so easily foreseeable and therefore useful for policy or journalism or politics, why wasn't Germany's success foreseen? (And why aren't historians rich?) Most economists and historians in 1945 thought Germany would take fifty years to recover. It took fifteen. The very reason Germany's recovery after the war was called a "miracle" is because people very willing to take culture as "predictive" made wrong predictions. The error is well known in social psychology, the tendency to attribute to character what is in fact a result of conditions. Landes and I have been quarreling about character vs. conditions since 1966, historian vs. economist, S variables vs. P variables. You'd think that he and I would both grow up, and learn that it's both: the tide of dignity and liberty and spiritual culture interacting with the coastline of economics and science and material culture—and that predicting or postdicting how it turns out is never easy.

40

IT WAS NOT ALLOCATION

The main economic peculiarity of the explanations of the Age of Innovation examined so far is their premise that, until 1750 and the wave of gadgets sweeping over England, opportunities for profit were simply ignored. As I've said now repeatedly, that's not economically reasonable. If the spinning jenny was such a swell idea in 1764 CE, why was it not in 1264, or 264, or for that matter in 1264 BCE? If factories extracted surplus value in 1848, why not in 1148? Thus the economic puzzle of the Industrial Revolution.

The other, historical peculiarity, as I've also noted repeatedly, is that many of the so-called preconditions (high savings rates, lots of international trade, private property, education, science) happened long before, and in places other than northwestern Europe. Bragging, thrusting, crusading Christendom was notably backward compared to the great Asian empires even in 1700 and certainly in 1600, and quite embarrassingly so in 1500, which is why the Europeans were so eager to sail to Asia. Imagine as a mental experiment that preconditions of the European sort—material events such as investment and trade and empire with nonmaterial events such as education and science—do make for an industrial revolution and for the sustained enrichment of the poorest among us. In that case China or India should have had an industrial revolution in 1600, or centuries earlier, as should have Rome or Greece. The historical puzzle is the temporary oddness of the lands around the North Sea after, say, 1700 or 1800. One can offer plausible offsets in the case of Greece or Rome, especially the slavery and misogyny that supported a contempt for labor, and for active, stirring, laborious men of business. It might apply to China and India and the Ottoman Empire, too. In other words, I am claiming, the antibourgeois character of world society before 1700, and in Europe, too, explains the lag.

The economic and the historical puzzles are twins. If having lots of foreign trade in Britain in 1700 CE made for explosive opportunities for profitable innovation and an industrial revolution by 1800, and a sharp rise of living standards in northwestern Europe by 1900, then why did it not do so in China in 700 CE or Egypt in 1700 BCE? If security of property and other such legal institutions made the modern world, why did they not make it in Republican Rome or Muslim Spain? European people did not change around 1600 or 1700 in their greediness. It is a popular notion, reformulated nowadays as anticonsumerism, though hardly plausible. People are *always* saying that their neighbors are greedy ("Honey, don't you think those people in the next cave are vulgar, with their saber-toothed tiger skins and all?!"). And therefore it cannot be that heaps of 100-guilder or 100-pound-sterling notes or coins sat on the ground for hundreds of years un-picked up. Whatever the cause of the modern world, in other words, it has to be something that does not assume that earlier or non–North Sea people were so stupid as to ignore strikingly good deals. And it has to be unique to a very recent time and to a northwestern European place. It can't for example be the properly praised inheritance of Christianity and Greco-Roman culture, which after all characterized stagnant Russia—right down to its alphabet and its version of orthodoxy—and characterized Europe as a whole for millennia before it allegedly resulted in the explosion after 1700.

Why did the North Sea folk suddenly get so rich, get so much cargo? The answer can't be that the Dutch and English belatedly showed racial superiority. A sensible answer has to honor the Dutch and English around 1700, but not dishonor the rest of humanity in the same breath, including in the dishonoring the earlier Dutch and English. After all, the rest caught on to the North Sea routine pretty quickly by historical standards once it had been invented. If they happened to move to Holland or Britain or America, they did well, whatever their genes. And at home they often nourished their own if constrained traditions of bourgeois virtue. In the end people in Asia and Africa and all over, in Taiwan and Botswana and Chile, learned pretty quickly to perform the northwestern European trick. It follows that the trick could not have been an open opportunity lying around all over the place, unused even in England for centuries, such as the routine taking of opportunities for profit from digging a canal or from sending a ship to Africa. That would violate economics, just as its Eurocentrism violates history. The trick was the invention of a business-admiring civilization.

The trick was "merely" a way of speaking. But you know by now that I consider ways of speaking, the "conjective," to be as important as modes or relations of physical production. Marshall Sahlins puts it in a cultural anthropologist's way: a "cultural scheme is variously inflected by a dominant site of symbolic production, which supplies the major idiom of other relations and activities." Sahlins wants to show that modern, Western societies engage in "symbolic production" just as much as tribal societies such as the Moalans of Fiji. "The peculiarity of Western culture is the institutionalization of [symbolic production] . . . in and as the production of goods, by comparison with a 'primitive' world where the locus of symbolic differentiation remains . . . kinship relations. . . . Money to the West is what kinship is to the Rest."[1] I would say that at the threshold of the Age of Innovation the important contrast is between the markets of northwestern Europe and the kingships of the Rest, between *La pensée bourgeoise* (as Sahlins styles it, to contrast with *La pensée sauvage* of Lévi-Strauss) and the old *Pensée aristocratique* or *Pensée chrétienne*.

∞

I admit the danger in the argument here, the Fallacy of the Immeasurable Residue. It is not entirely cogent to keep measuring causes, finding the measurable ones to be small, and then concluding that the cause our author so persuasively proposes *must* be true, though a little hard to measure. The method of knocking off contrary hypotheses, I said, is what John Stuart Mill recommended in his *System of Logic*, and is the admired practice in physical and biological sciences. But it is biased toward the immeasurable—witness string theory in physics, or for that matter Newton's anti-Aristotelian but question-begging terminology of "gravity" as a force, measurable in result but not in cause. As Mill wrote, the Method of Residues works "provided we are certain that [in the present case, a rhetorical change] is the only antecedent to which [the Industrial Revolution] can be referred. But as we can never be quite certain of this, the evidence from [the method] is not complete."[2] What may be missing is an unnoticed but still material and measurable alternative. (There are immaterial *and* measurable causes, too, by the way. It is another of the numerous materialist prejudices floating in the minds of many historians and social scientists in the twentieth century that there aren't any. Opinion, for instance, is measurable—in many cases it can be better measured than, say, pot-of-pleasure "happiness" or technological change.)

Sophisticated believers in God have often made the tactical error of positing a God of Gaps, supposing on the eve of the discovery of evolution by natural selection, for example, that the complexity of the astonishing and delicate machinery of the eye implies an unexplained gap in materialist explanations, and therefore an eye- (and watch-) making God.[3] Like the unlucky theists, maybe I have overlooked some material cause that in contrast to all the dozens I have here examined, separately or in combination, actually explains the factor of two or sixteen or one hundred. I'm very willing to concede the scientific point—if some materialist can find a material cause that works, in the sense of explaining the most surprising event in economic history with material causes that do not also apply to China or Italy. I have little optimism that she will succeed, having myself tried repeatedly since 1962 to find one, and having discovered all of them in the end to be wanting. As Emerson noted, "An idealist can never go backward to be a materialist."[4] Or as I would prefer to say, once you have realized that a human science must be about the conjective, as I did around 1983, you can never go back to being a naïve positivist, demanding always that matter is caused by matter.

The piling up of rejected alternatives, all of the same reallocative character, does suggest by sober scientific criteria that we may be looking in the wrong place—perhaps under the lamppost of a static and materialist economics, or under a somewhat grander lamppost of a dynamics depending on statics, or under the grandest lamppost discovered so far, of a nonlinear dynamics of chaos theory. Perhaps we are looking in such places not because the evidence leads us to them, but on account of the Samuelsonian traditions of modern economics and the excellent mathematical light shining under all these impressively ornamented lampposts. Yet one after another of the proffered material explanations has failed. No believable case can be made that adding them all together would change much, or that other countries and other times did not have equally favorable material conjunctures—not if we are trying to explain the unprecedented factors of growing production per head.

The problem with all the economistic explanations lies deep within classical and most of subsequent economic thought: the conviction that shuffling stuff around makes us a little better off, which is true, and therefore that the shuffling makes us as rich as modern people are, which is false. Trade. Transportation. Reallocation. Information flow. Accumulation. Legal change. As Kirzner expressed it, "For [the British economist flourishing in the 1930s Lionel] Robbins [and the Samuelsonians], economizing simply means shuffling around available resources in order to secure the most efficient utilization of *known* inputs in terms of a *given* hierarchy of ends."[5] Yet the path to the modern was not through shuffling and reshuffling. It was not by the growth of foreign trade or of this or that industry, here or there, nor by shifting weights of one or another social class. Nor indeed was it by reshufflings of property rights. Nor, to speak of another sort of reshuffling, was it by rich people piling up more riches by shuffling income away from their worker-victims. They had always done that. Nor was it by bosses being nasty to workers, or through strong countries being nasty to weak countries, and forcibly shuffling stuff toward the nasty and strong. They had always done that, too. Piling up bricks and money and colonies had always been routine. "Foreigners shall rebuild your walls," says the Lord to Jerusalem though his prophet Isaiah, "and their kings shall be your servants. . . . Your gates shall be open continuously . . . that through them may be brought the wealth of nations and their kings under escort" (Is. 60:10, 11). The new path was not about anciently commonplace theft or accumulation or commercialization or reallocation or any other reshuffling.

It was instead about discovery, and a creativity supported by novel words. In terms of the seven principal virtues, the routine of efficiency that Samuelsonian economists love so passionately depends only on the virtue of Prudence.[6] What I am claiming here is that discovery and creativity depended also on other virtues, in particular on Courage and Hope. And I will claim in subsequent volumes that the conversational society honoring such a commercial Courage and Hope depended in turn on a new, bourgeois construal of the virtues of temperance, justice, love, and faith. As a result, previously unknown inputs were discovered (coal for steam engines; then coke for iron; then natural gas to replace the sickening coke burnt in French kitchens), fresh hierarchies of ends were articulated (in the new political economy, for example, which tended to the democratic end of general vs. privileged prosperity; in the new politics, which tended to the radical end of strict equality), new goods and services were created (black tulips, common stocks, reinforced concrete). All of it was very far from routine Prudence. The new path around 1700, on account of the change in rhetoric, led by around 1800 and especially by around 1900 to shocking innovations in factory machinery and in business practice. It was supported and extended by shocking innovations in politics, with the result that as early as 1832 a few countries protected your life, liberty, and pursuit of innovation from progressive or conservative assault. The result was a startling enrichment of our ancestors, poor though they began. We ourselves have now become better off than all but the richest of the ancestors were, riches measured by goods and by human flourishing.

In a deep sense, in other words, the economist's Prudence Only model of allocation does not come close to explaining the factor of sixteen. Macaulay said, in a Smithian way, "We know of no country which, at the end of fifty years of peace, and tolerably good government, has been less prosperous than at the beginning of that period."[7] Yes, agreed. Routine prudence is easy. But 100 percent better off, and most particularly on the way to 1,500 percent better off? There had been many times of such peace before, with no such result as the factor of sixteen. By 1860 "what had really changed" writes the wise Goldstone, "was that innovation became common and widespread, even expected, because a British culture of innovation gave people the outlook and the intellectual and material [and I say sociological] tools to search for their own new ways of working."[8]

To put it another way, economics in the style of Adam Smith, which is the mainstream of economic thinking, is about scarcity and saving and other Calvinistic notions.[9] In the sweat of thy face shalt thou eat bread, till thou return unto the ground. We cannot have more of everything. Grow up and face scarcity. We must abstain Calvinistically from consumption today if we are to eat adequately tomorrow. Or in the modern catchphrase: There Ain't No Such Thing as a Free Lunch (TANSTAAFL).

I have the greatest respect for such economics, which I acquired laboriously, Calvinistically, from 1961 to 1981 or so, and of which I am still learning new uses and new tricks. It is a great intellectual construct. I've written whole books in its praise. No joke.[10] But the chief fact of the quickening of industrial growth 1780-1860 and its amazing aftermath in the Age of Innovation is that scarcity was relaxed.

It was relaxed in the long view, not banished in the short view by an "affluent society." Whatever the size of income at any one time, more of it is scarce, and cannot be seized for admirable public purposes without some loss to be set against the gain, such as the great gain from invading Iraq in

2003. That is what economists mean by a "production possibility curve." It is the lesson of the virtue of Prudence. More housing has always an opportunity cost in all other goods and services. So far Samuelsonian economics goes, and is correct.

But over time, taking the long view, modern economic growth has been a massive free lunch. Discovery, not reshuffling, was the mechanism, and the springs were the nonprudential virtues. As Kirzner put it, entrepreneurship is not about optimal shuffling, since a hired manager can carry out such a routine. "The incentive is to try to get something for nothing, if only one can see what it is that can be done."[11] A new rhetorical environment in the eighteenth century encouraged (literally: gave courage to the hope of) entrepreneurs. As a result over the next two centuries the production possibility curve leapt out by a factor of sixteen. More.

∞

In 1871, a century after Smith, John Stuart Mill's last edition of *Principles of Political Economy* marks the perfection of classical economics. Listen to Mill: "Much as the collective industry of the earth is likely to be increased in efficiency by the extension of science and of the industrial arts, a still more active source of increased cheapness of production will be found, probably, for some time to come, in the gradual unfolding consequences of Free Trade, and in the increasing scale on which Emigration and Colonization will be carried on."[12] Mill (whom you know I admire) was here in error. The gains from trade, though commendable from a static point of view, and well worth having, were trivial beside the extension of the industrial arts. Elsewhere in the passage Mill exhibits his classical-economist obsession with the "principle of population," a leading theme in economics from 1798 to 1871. Mill, with many others, believed that the only way to prevent impoverishment of the working people was to restrict population growth, since he realized that the unfolding consequences of free trade were modest. His anxieties on this score find modern echo in the environmental and family limitation movements, such as China's one-child policy, which itself arose from pessimistic (and Orientalist) theorizing in the West. The prudence of such a policy seems doubtful today, and its lack of justice and liberty are plain. In any case the Malthusian idea told next to nothing about the century to follow 1871. The population of the United Kingdom increased by a factor of 1.8, yet real income per head more than tripled.[13] Nor did Mill's classical model, as we have seen, give an altogether reasonable account of the century before 1871.

Mill again: "It is only in the backward countries of the world that increased production is still an important object: in those most advanced, what is economically needed is a better distribution, of which one indispensable means is a stricter restraint on population"—still more wrong, in light of what in fact happened during the century before and the century after.[14] Mill did not anticipate the much larger pie to come, so strong was the grip of classical economic ideas on his mind—even in 1871, even after a lifetime watching the pie grow quite a lot larger. He says elsewhere, "Hitherto it is questionable if all the mechanical inventions yet made have lightened the day's toil of any human being," a strange assertion to carry into the 1871 edition, with child labor falling, education increasing, the harvest mechanizing, and even the work week shortening.[15]

Mill was too good a classical economist, in other words, to recognize a phenomenon inconsistent with classical economics. That the national income per head might triple in the century after 1871 in the teeth of rising population is not a classical possibility, and he would have seen the factor of sixteen in Britain from the eighteenth century down to the present as science fiction. And so the classicals from Smith to Mill put their faith in greater efficiency by way of Harberger Triangles and a more equitable distribution of income by way of improvements in the Poor Law. It should be noted that Mill anticipated social democracy in many of his later opinions, that is, the view that the pie is after all relatively fixed and that we must therefore attend especially to distribution. That the growth of the pie would dwarf the Harberger Triangles available from greater efficiency, or the Tawney Slices available from redistribution, did not fit a classical theory of political economy. Not Mill's pessimism but Macaulay's optimism of 1830 turned out to be the correct historical point: "We cannot absolutely prove that those are in error who tell us that society has reached a turning point, that we have seen our best days. But so said all who came before us, and with just as much apparent reason."[16] The pessimistic and Calvinistic and prudential classical economists, with the pessimistic and Calvinistic and Romantic opponents of industrialization at the time such as Goethe (in his grimmer moods) and Carlyle (who invented the very word "industrialization") and Ruskin, and the Calvinistic and Malthusian opponents of modern economic growth nowadays, too, have come up short, scientifically speaking.

41

IT WAS WORDS

The distinction is between a literally conservative view that reallocation of resources makes for a tiny improvement, maybe, if you're careful, and the radical/liberal view that the sky's the limit to the human imagination once it is made dignified and free. As my colleague the historian and literary critic Astrida Tantillo points out in her book *Goethe's Modernisms*, the unifying theme in Goethe's literary and scientific work is the "principle of compensation," or (as the physicist Hermann von Helmholtz saw in *Faust*) the physical law of the conservation of energy—what an economist would call "scarcity," "the production possibility curve," "trade-offs," "TANSTA-AFL," "opportunity cost." Look at Goethe's poem the "Metamorphosis of Animals" (Goethe, who was also a top civil servant at Weimar, fancied himself a scientist as well as a poet, novelist, and dramatist):[1]

> So, if you see that a creature possesses a certain advantage,
> Put the question at once: What is the fault that afflicts it
> Elsewhere?—and seek to discover the defect, always inquiring;
> Then at once you will find the key to the world of formation.

In the poem he applied the principle of scarcity to the social world, too, with an enthusiasm worthy of his contemporaries, the first generation of classical British economists: "May this beautiful concept of power and limit, of random / Venture and law, freedom and measure, of order in motion, / Defect and benefit, bring you high pleasure" (1:163). And in prose elsewhere:

> We will find that a limit is set to nature's structural range. . . . Nothing can be
> added to one part without subtracting from another, and vice versa. . . . Within

these bounds the formative force seems to act in the most wonderful, almost capricious way, but is never able to break out of the circle or leap over it. . . . If [nature] wants to let one have more, it may do so, but not without taking from another. Thus nature can never fall into debt, much less go bankrupt. (12:120–121)

But as Tantillo remarks on the passage, "The very principle demonstrates two contradictory elements at play. Depending upon the perspective, the world can either be seen as free (as when an animal changes its form through a creative impulse) or as determined (because of the costs and limits of those changes)."[2] Goethe puts Faust in a position to push Progress, as a means of criticizing it. Yet Goethe is not entirely conservative on the matter, because he recognizes that progress *is* progress, though he emphasizes, as many Romantics have, the opportunity cost—such as one's soul. What is clear (and Tantillo notes that Goethe says it) is that the principle of compensation alone would not allow for real progress. A truly progressive evolution (said Goethe) would require creativity, not tradeoffs. And that is what happened in the West.

In the beginning was the word. Free innovation led by the bourgeoisie became at long last respectable in people's words. For instance, the merchants and machine makers and manufacturers in northwestern Europe were elevated for the first time to the rank of "gentlemen" (and the ladies, once "women" or "wenches," were invited to participate as well). The middling sort of man came slowly to be called by the word previously reserved for the idle and well-born. For that matter some of the gentlemanly idle and well-born, in Holland and England and Scotland and the British colonies, and then a few decades later even in France, took to trade and innovation. The Leveller William Walwyn (1600–1681) was the second son of a landowner, and his grandfather had been a bishop, but he eschewed the name of "gentleman" that his elder brother assumed, in favor of plain "merchant," in London where he learned the trade. The Whig cloth merchant and politician Slingsby Bethel wrote in 1680 that "England has . . . the advantage of all other countries . . . as in . . . breeding the younger sons of gentlemen, and sometimes of the nobility, to the ministry, law, trade, and physic, without prejudice to their gentility."[3] In 1733 Voltaire, who himself made a fortune in speculation, wrote that in England "a peer's brother does not think traffic is beneath him. . . . At the time that the Earl of Orford [that is, Robert Walpole] governed Great Britain, his younger brother was no more than a factor in Aleppo."[4] A Swiss traveler wrote about the same time that "in England commerce is not looked down upon as being derogatory, as it is in France and Germany. Here men of good family and even of rank may become merchants without losing caste."[5] He meant it literally: in France and Spain a nobleman caught engaging in commerce could be stripped of his rank, "derogated," whereas in England, Bethel noted, the "heralds [are] not requiring so much as any restoration in such cases." The rule was ancient. "In Thebes," wrote Aristotle with evident approval, "there used to be a law that one who had not abstained from the market for ten years could not share in office."[6]

Surprisingly, such ancient attitudes changed. In its rhetoric the northwestern European elite began to deem a bourgeois career honorable. An English Whig pamphleteer wrote in 1695 that "trade was in all ages till within more than a hundred years past counted a contemptible thing, as it is still by some mighty and famous kingdoms, and is indeed but a modern [that is, very recent] system of politics, little descanted on by the great writers and professors of that science."[7] During the seventeenth and early eighteenth centuries at Rotterdam, Bristol, Glasgow, Boston, and then later at Rouen and Cologne and Stockholm (though the Swedish nobility, such as the Swedish Henry VIII, King Gustav Vasa, had long had an interest in trade), the younger sons of gentry and even of noblemen embarked at length on bourgeois careers. It was not a "bourgeois career" to take one's serfs and put them into factories making woolens, as Count Waldstein did in what is now the Czech Republic in 1715. The English upper classes got down into the factories themselves (though excusing themselves from duty at the machines). John Verney (1640–1717), a second son of the family of Verney gentry whose records we have in astonishing detail, spent eleven years 1662–1673 as, again, a lowly factor for another's gain in Aleppo, like Walpole's brother.[8] And indeed the honorable classes in Holland and England had long viewed the improving of their fortunes as a good idea—if not always going so far as to become a factor in Aleppo.

The historian Tim Blanning puts it so: "In the past it had been an axiom of English political theory that a virtuous polity depended on a tradition of civic humanism, sustained by a landed elite whose independence ensured their virtue"—thus Roman and neo-Roman theorizing down to Thomas Jefferson, and in the mid-twentieth century also certain British Tories and American Republicans. By the early eighteenth century in England, though, a century after its emergence in the Netherlands, "there emerged a greater willingness to view commercial society, not as a sink of corruption but as a wholly legitimate sphere of private sociability."[9] The debate in the middle of the eighteenth century, argues the political theorist John Danford, was "whether a free society is possible if commercial activities flourish."[10] The models on the anticommercial side of the debate, as Pocock and Skinner have shown, were Republican Rome and especially, of all nightmarish ideals, Sparta. Thus early in the debate Thomas More's *Utopia* sneered at commerce. Commerce such as the Athenian and now the British favored would introduce "luxury and voluptuousness," in the conventional phrase of the Scottish law lord Kames, as the debate reached its climax, which would "eradicate patriotism," and extinguish at any rate ancient freedom, the freedom to participate. As the Spartans vanquished Athens, so likewise some more vigorous nation would rise up and vanquish Britain, or at any rate stop the admirably Republican "progress so flourishing . . . when patriotism is the ruling passion of every member." And the poet William Cowper in 1785 felt otherwise: "Increase of power begets increase of wealth; / Wealth luxury, and luxury excess."[11]

Danford reads Hume as opposing such a civic humanist view, that is, the view that stressed "the primacy of the political." Commerce, said Hume, was good for us, and Georgian mercantilism in aid of political standing was bad for us. "In this denigration of political life," writes Danford, "Hume [is] thoroughly modern and [seems] to agree in important respects with [the individualism of] Hobbes and Locke."[12] Hobbes, Locke, and Hume constituted "the challenge posed by early modern thinkers to the understanding of human nature which had been regnant for nearly two thousand years," and regnant, too, in Confucian China and Muslim Iran and Hindu India.[13]

Danford does not claim that all we moderns now reject the nationalist, sacrificial, antiluxury, classical republican view. On the contrary, he says, no paradigm governs without challenge. We can see the Spartan ideal in politics left and right, Green and nationalist. Classical republicanism is alive and well and living in the pages of the *Nation* and the *National Review*. In Germany, for example, great social distance and a deference to various pseudo- and real aristocracies persisted into recent times, with unhappy results. The secularized Christianity known as socialism scorned the emerging bourgeoisie of Russia, with equally unhappy results. Today even in the strongholds of commercial prudence in America and Europe the old models of priest or knight continue to shine, alongside the new model of the entrepreneur. The academic expert is a new priest, the TV cop a new knight. The entrepreneur gets the blame—because after all she makes obscene amounts of money. Some of our fictional heroes are businesspeople (such as Jimmy Stewart in "It's a Wonderful Life"), but not many.

By the late nineteenth century in the democracy-honoring and bourgeois-admiring United States, which lacked real aristocrats, the word "gentleman"—so called in address, if less so behind his back—became almost completely democratic. It meant any adult, male, nonimmigrant citizen of European extraction. Outside the old Confederacy the aristocratic gesture was not admired, at any rate if practiced by men pretending to aristocratic status. If aristocratic gestures were practiced by proletarians or the bourgeoisie, on the other hand, as in the myth of the cowboys and their bosses, or in Herman Melville's elevation of "blubber boilers" hunting whales to heroic standing, it was using earlier cultural language to elevate the status of the democratic and sometimes bourgeois man. Walt Whitman of New York bid good riddance to Europe's "kings and castles proud, its priests and warlike lords and courtly dames / Pass'd to its charnel vault, coffin'd with crown and armor on, / Bronz'd with Shakespeare's purple page, / And dirged by Tennyson's sweet sad rhyme."[14] Outside of church, a peasant/Christian holiness was laughed at by the secular clerisy even in pious America. Twain spoofed Christian science in 1907 so harshly that those mild folk (it is said on admittedly dubious authority) were sworn to undertake to cut out any reprinting of the essay from public library books. Twain's Connecticut Yankee astounds the aristocratic and peasant rubes in King Arthur's court with industrial devices, not with gentlemanly heroism in violence, which on the contrary he thinks silly. By now over 90 percent of Americans identify themselves in surveys as part of a quasi-gentlemanly "middle class," and the phrase has stopped meaning much, except a general aspiration to a bourgeois life. It shows up in the terminology of American elections, in which "the middle class" means virtually everybody.[15] ("Don't tax him. Don't tax me. / Tax that duke behind the tree.") The words assume that dealing and marketing and innovating is what we Americans are supposed to do. Every gentleperson from truck driver to congresswoman in the United States thinks of herself as doing a little business, and dreams of innovation.

Less so in other countries. In a much more class-conscious Britain the percentage self-identifying as "middle class" in 2007 was only 37 percent, though well up from figures one would have gotten in 1907.[16] In France in 2004, 40 percent replied "middle" to the question, "To which class do you have the feeling of belonging?" About 23 percent in France replied "working"—high by American standards, if sharply down from what French (and British and even American) people would have said in 1904. That in the French survey only 4 percent called themselves *bourgeois* reflects the unpopularity of the B-word in modern European politics. It would be good to revive the word and its associations with liberty. But even so, note that 40 percent and more of people in rich countries call themselves middle class, if not the Marx-spoiled "bourgeois." Compare the much lower percentages one can imagine in the worlds of André Gide or of Stendhal, not to speak of Molière. The change in rhetoric has constituted a revolution in how people view themselves and how they view the middle class, the Bourgeois Revaluation. People have become tolerant of markets and innovation.

The argument applies to routine innovation as much as to great creative ideas, to Mokyr's microinvention as much to the macroinventions that stake out new worlds to conquer. The economist Alan Kirman has pointed out to me that much innovation is, as he puts it, "generated by demand," such as the improvement in the ballast-sweeping brooms on rail lines that an Australian friend of mine resident in Amsterdam has developed and sold to railways worldwide. This was the theme of the economist Jacob Schmookler, who in the 1960s pioneered the study of induced innovation. But such innovations depend *more* on respect for the bourgeoisie and the liberty to innovate than do the macroinventions. Great geniuses forcing the pace of innovation like Ford or Edison might have braved contempt and interference better than the modest genius improving ballast sweeping.

In his penetrating new book, *The Enlightened Economy*, with which I very largely agree, Joel Mokyr praises what he call the Baconian program, which he regards as the sustaining force in keeping science going long enough to matter economically. "The Baconian program," he writes, "was built on two unshakeable axioms: that the expansion of useful knowledge would solve social and economic problems, and that the dissemination of existing knowledge to more and more people would lead to substantial efficiency gains."[17] That may be so. Certainly the ideology launched by Francis Bacon in 1620 had a remarkably long shelf life, despite crushing evidence that it is a poor description of what scientists actually do and is exceptionally poor advice on how they should be organized. Darwin, for example, claimed on the first page of *The Origin of Species* in 1859 that he had used what are called

Baconian methods (that is, aimless induction) to arrive at the idea of natural selection. But as his autobiography and his private notes show, he was fibbing, and had gotten the theory (from the economist Malthus) before he got many of the observations. And, like Newton, Darwin worked alone, even secretively, though with massive correspondence of points of fact, not in a House of Intellect à la Bacon. He was at length forced to publish by Wallace's threatened scooping of his argument (fourteen years earlier he had written a summary essay, shown to his wife, with instructions to publish it in case of his death). And his theory had no payoff in efficiency gains until, at the earliest, fifty years later, when combined with (and explained by) the work of an obscure ethnic German monk in the Czech lands.

The gains in technology that Mokyr has done so much to bring to the attention of economists, in other words, did not depend on science, to repeat, until very, very late. Science, though proud, and persistently claiming to help humankind, usually followed technology, explaining in neat equations or rigorous experiments the results that tinkerers and engineers had already achieved in practice: the steam engine, the electric motor, anesthesia, hospital cleanliness, the end of water-borne diseases by proper drainage, the skyscraper, the internal combustion engine, the airplane, refrigeration, air conditioning. "The steam engine has given more to science," said Lord Kelvin, "than science has given to the steam engine." There did arise in the meantime an admiration for useful knowledge that might solve social and economic problems, disseminated to more and more people, and leading to substantial efficiency gains. (There also arose, less pleasingly, an attitude among the clerisy, well exemplified by Kelvin himself, that scientific knowledge in a narrow and late-nineteenth-century definition was of course the most useful and glorious. It sometimes had lamentable outcomes: eugenics, communism, the Vietnam War, the Great Recession of 2008.) The admiration for innovation, though, had little to do with My Lord Bacon and more to do, as Mokyr observes, with the wider Enlightenment—and as I would argue with the Bourgeois Revaluation.

The results of the Revaluation in the realm of useful ideas and their dissemination pop up all over the society of northwestern Europe and its offshoots, not merely in science. The conversation of humans sharply improved around the 1690s, in coffee houses and newspapers for the Dutch and British bourgeoisie, and in French salons for the clerisy and aristocracy. The background was of course the vigorous application in Europe of the Eastern innovation of moveable type. But the confidence to write what one thought, even if, say, the thought was Unitarian, came slowly, and with much chopping off of hands and fining of printers. The Third Earl of Shaftesbury retired repeatedly to his beloved Netherlands in the 1690s and 1700s in order to have free discussion dangerous even in England then. The breakdown of orthodoxy in New England about the same time (after Salem) was a typical piece of the new age of free discussion. Benjamin Franklin's Junto, a discussion group for journeymen in Philadelphia begun in 1727, predated even the Lunar Society of Birmingham (begun in 1765), itself inconceivable a couple of centuries before. Margaret Jacob speaks of the Freemasons and their newly free discussion. The new rhetorical environment had emerged fitfully in the Netherlands in the 1620s, despite the threat from Calvinist orthodoxy (in 1619 the Prince Maurits and the Anti-Remonstrants had Grotius jailed, and his political master Oldenbarnevelt executed). It was extended during the English Revolution to fundamental political issues in the Putney Debates of 1647, and came into its own, assisting at the birth of modern politics, in the 1690s in England. From all this imperfect but unique free speech came innovation and the modern world.

42

DIGNITY AND LIBERTY FOR ORDINARY PEOPLE, IN SHORT, WERE THE GREATEST EXTERNALITIES

I have argued that the Industrial Revolution and its sequel cannot be explained by opportunities open to routinely prudent people, such as trade or property rights lying about unused until taken up in the eighteenth century. They depended instead on a Bourgeois Revaluation that gave a commercial expression also to the six other principal virtues of temperance, justice, courage, love, faith, and hope. Prudence is a virtue, but as I argued in *The Bourgeois Virtues*, it's not the only one relevant to a commercial society. The usual economic theories, which depend on solely prudential routines such as accumulation or imperialism, can't explain the factor of sixteen. The innovation was fundamentally unpredictable, coming out of the hope and faith and so forth of a newly respectable class of traders and engineers. If it had not been so—if the modern world had sprung from routine and therefore from obviously prudential opportunities lying about—then it would have happened earlier or elsewhere. Prudence, I repeat, is reasonably easy, and has always been widespread.

But economists have a word for *closed* opportunities that *can* lie about unused, until stumbled into—"positive externalities." The more transparent word for the idea is "spillovers." In the jargon, a spillover or an "external effect" means some harm or benefit that is not paid for with money in a market. Therefore it spills over from one person to another without being subject to market discipline, or to the market signals for an opportunity. It stands external to the market's stage, so to speak, hidden in the wings, unpaid and unheeded. Yet it will from time to time loudly deliver its own lines, disrupting or advancing the play. It has real effects, in other words, though not accounted for in private financial prudence, and therefore not attended to.

Smoke from a power plant is called a "*negative* externality" (like all masters of mysteries, the economists love jargon). The harm caused by the smoke does not show up as a money cost to the power plant or to the users of its electricity. That's why the disruption is ignored, external, offstage, unpaid. "Luckily," says Charles Montgomery Burns, rubbing his hands with glee, "I don't have to pay money for the privilege of dumping the radioactivity from my power plant into the air you breathe. So what do I care?!" There's no market in which the victim can buy the radioactivity or smoke or aircraft noise to stop it, expressing her distaste in money bids.

But not all externalities or spillovers are bad, like power-plant smoke or aircraft noise or other dumping of by-products. Some are good, those *positive* externalities. Even some smoke—from leaf fires in autumn or from wood fires in winter—is not a harm but a benefit, at any rate to older folk remembering the sweet smells of 1959. Some of us even have a loony nostalgia for the smell of diesel exhaust from the old London buses. More seriously, having lots of educated people around is a spillover beneficial to you and to me and to many others, educated or not. We do not pay fully in a market for the benefit from an educated populace. (We do pay in part through wages to educated workers, and especially after the university movement of the 1960s.) The uncompensated part is an externality. I would pay a little if it could be arranged to get the sweet, nostalgic smell of autumn or winter, or of London in a late 1950s smog. You would pay a lot to deal with people who can read and can calculate and can see through the more obviously manipulative campaign advertisements. People routinely pay the big costs of migration to get from countries that don't have such positive externalities of education into those that do.

A pair of positive externalities, I have been arguing, had been untried on a large scale until stumbled into by the United Provinces in the seventeenth century, and then by the United Kingdom imitating the bourgeois Dutch in the eighteenth century. The external effects thus revealed were a new dignity for the bourgeoisie in its dealings and a new liberty for the bourgeoisie to innovate in economic affairs. Both were necessary for the modern world. The two, when linked, appear even to have been sufficient, if you supply a few routine background conditions enjoyed already in many places, as for example somewhat large cities and extensive trade and reasonable security of property and cheap if slow riverine or coastal transport in a biggish country. Such background conditions were widespread in the world of 1700, and cannot therefore be thought of as shocking Dutch and English novelties. China had them. So did Japan, the Mughal Empire, the Ottoman Empire, Northern Italy, the Hansa.

But without the two necessary, and large-scale, conditions of dignity and liberty for the innovating class, we would have no modern world. Both, I repeat, were necessary. Without the liberty to innovate, no amount of new social prestige for the previously scorned bourgeoisie would have done the trick. The unwritten English constitution of 1689, wrote Hume in the last volume of his *The History of England* (1754–1755), "gave such an ascendant to popular principles, as has put the nature of the English constitution beyond all controversy. And it may justly be affirmed, without any danger of exaggeration, that we, in this island, have ever since enjoyed . . . the most entire system of liberty that ever was known amongst mankind."[1] He perhaps overstates the case—Holland led the way, after all, and the Northern Italian and Swiss city states were free until bourgeois monopolies of power took control, to speak only of examples he could have known. And the poor in Britain, though vividly aware that they were freeborn English men and women (and very willing in the eighteenth century to riot in aid of such a notion), had not yet been emancipated in politics or in wealth. Yet Frenchmen like Voltaire and Montesquieu and later Tocqueville were right to emphasize the peculiarity of English liberties—habeas corpus, Parliamentary pre-eminence, and especially the dignity of traders and inventors. Tocqueville wrote in 1835 that "it is above all the spirit and habits of liberty which inspire the spirit and habits of trade."[2] Merchants and manufacturers could have been brought with full dignity into the British national elite of 1700, with ribands, stars, and a' that, but had they lacked the liberty to profit in money or prestige from innovation, either in machines or in ways of doing business, nothing would have happened. The French in the eighteenth century illustrate the problem in their state-sponsored prizes and industrial espionage, namely, that they did not give complete liberty to innovation. In France as in Japan and the Ottoman Empire one had to apply to *l'état* for permission to open a factory. With such lack of liberty the program of the French elite (especially if it had also lacked the irritating examples next door of the Dutch and then the British) would have stayed as it had for centuries, namely, the preservation of the old ways, the cake of custom. Or so at least an economist would claim.

Hayek put it this way: "Nowhere is freedom more important than where our ignorance is greatest—at the boundaries of knowledge, . . . where no one can predict." And the greater is "our" knowledge, the greater is the ignorance of any one of us, whether a central planner or a great scientist. "The more men know," Hayek continues, "the smaller the share of all that knowledge becomes that any one mind can absorb."[3] It is said that John Milton was the last man in Europe who had read *everything*—well, everything in Western European and certain dead languages. It has been a long time since Milton, and "we" now have a lot more knowledge. The more social knowledge there is, however, the more urgent it is for free arrangements to try out an idea in this or that way, since no one mind can predict where it will end. No one in 1990 could have guessed how the Internet would turn out. The spontaneous order that arises once a device or institution is invented commonly diverges from the inventor's purpose. Text messaging was used first by the telephone companies internally, by workers on the line, with no idea that it would become a madness of teenagers. The institution of intercollegiate athletics, uniquely American, has long been used by its customers for tribal identification, far from the original and declared purpose of giving young men (and an occasional heavily bearded ringer) some healthful exercise. Inventors themselves commonly do not know what use their invention will be. "Prediction is difficult," said Yogi Berra, "especially about the future." Nathan Rosenberg emphasized the unpredictable character of innovation, noting that Bell Labs didn't want to patent the laser, because the managers could see no possible use for such a silly toy; and that tricks used to make sewing machines in the nineteenth century came to have major uses for automobiles in the twentieth.[4] Thomas Edison believed his recording cylinders would be used mainly for office dictation. When someone asked Orville Wright what he thought the use of his airplane was going to be, he replied, "Sport, mainly."

But without the new dignity for merchants and inventors, no amount of the liberty to innovate would have broken the old cake, either. Or so at least a sociologist would claim. The foreigners were startled by the esteem in which trade was held in Britain, though also noting the continuing hauteur and practical power of the British aristocracy. Merchants in Japan and China were ranked for three millennia close to night-soil men. In Christian Europe they were considered for two millennia the enemies of God. Innovations were long viewed as threats to employment. And so the best minds went into war or politics or religion or bureaucracy or poetry. Some still do, often on antibourgeois grounds taught to them by the clerisy after 1848.

By adopting the respect for deal-making and innovation and the liberty to carry out the deals that Amsterdam and London pioneered around 1700, the modern world was born. Dignity and liberty were unpredictable in their effects, at least when viewed from the early eighteenth century. They were the chief modern example of what Brian Arthur and Paul David have taught us to call "path dependencies." Adopt dignity and liberty for the bourgeoisie, and prosper, to a surprisingly large degree. Resist such vulgar ideas, and predictably stagnate.[5] Dignity and liberty still work. By now maybe we should have ceased being shocked by their efficacy. The special development zone of Shenzhen in mainland China, a suburb of Hong Kong, went from being a small fishing village to an eight-million-soul metropolis in two decades. It didn't happen without some nasty rent-seeking by party officials and their friends, true. But out of such creative destruction are average incomes raised, to the benefit eventually of the poorest. Such a feat required a shift in rhetoric: stop jailing millionaires and start admiring them; stop resisting creative destruction and start speaking well of innovation; stop overregulating markets and start letting people make deals, corrupt or not.

In 1776 Adam Smith, who invented sociology as much as economics, called the new amalgam "the obvious and simple system of natural liberty."[6] But my point, and his, is that, astonishingly, the system was not considered "obvious and simple" until the eighteenth century. That's the point of theorizing it as an "externality." In many circles to this day it still is suspect. You can still hear people who do not pretend to have thought very deeply about the matter declaring confidently that the market of course needs to be closely regulated, or that trade needs to be fair, or that immigration must be restricted, or that jobs are to be created by governmental programs, or that businesspeople routinely cheat, or that markets are chaotic, or that the more complex an economy is, the more it needs government regulation, or that banking or financial speculation is robbery, or that governmental bureaucracies are always fair and efficient. And many still declare that it is ever-so-much more dignified to work as a professor or a civil servant or some other sort of nonprofit employee than as someone making deals in the financial services industry or in the wholesale meat trade. Such antibourgeois people (many of them my good friends) do not believe the bourgeois axiom that a deal between two free adults has a strong presumption in its favor, practically and ethically and aesthetically. They deny hotly that allowing such deals and honoring their makers has resulted in the modern enrichment of the poor. They think instead, quite against the historical evidence, that governments or trade unions did it.

But a sufficiently large number of Europeans were converted to a rhetoric of bourgeois-respecting in the late seventeenth and especially in the eighteenth century. Nowadays many people worldwide have come to believe in market-guided innovation, and have learned sometimes to speak kindly of it. The endlessly renewed schemes of protection, which seek to keep us doing what we have always done, have many more enemies than they did in 1600. The evidence has become overwhelming that letting innovation rip is the best plan for helping the poor—from the enrichment of poor Europeans around 1900 to the enrichment of poor Indians around 2000. It's not a matter of irrational faith. We've seen it happen. (One is reminded of the old joke: "Do I *believe* in infant baptism?! I've *seen* it!") As early as 1641 one Lewes Roberts in England praised "the judicious merchant, whose labor is to profit himself, yet in all his actions doth therewith benefit his king, country, and fellow subjects."[7] Adam Smith could not have put it better. In 1675 an anonymous English writer declared that "cupidity has taken the place of charity, and effects it after a manner which we cannot enough admire." Note the word "admire." He asked, "What charity will run to the Indies for medicines, stoop to the meanest employments, and not refuse the basest and most painful offices?" Note, too, the hierarchy in which many "employments" are reckoned mean and base, not honorable. A job of work in those hierarchical days was "service," as in "servant." And yet, the writer continued, "cupidity will perform all this without grudging," to our collective good.[8] John Stuart Mill could not have put it better. Dudley North, that man of aristocratic background enriched by a bourgeois career trading with the Ottomans, wrote in 1691 that "to force men to deal in any prescribed manner may profit some as happen to serve them; but the public gains not, because it is taking from one subject to give to another.[9] Milton Friedman could not have put it better. "I don't know which is the more useful to the state," wrote Voltaire in 1733 with heavy sarcasm, "a well-powdered lord who knows precisely when the king gets up in the morning . . . or a great merchant who enriches his country, sends orders from his office to Surat or to Cairo, and contributes to the well-being of the world."[10] The emphasis was soon to shift from merchants to manufacturers, though they also buy low and sell high. But the young Robert Nozick could not have put it better. Deals to buy spices or steam engines low and to sell them high were for the first time admired. The admiration overturned the various versions of antibourgeois hierarchy which had so long prevailed: that deals are dirty and unholy, that the dealers are dangerous and disreputable, and that men of honor, such as the gentry or the priests or the mandarins or the Securities Exchange Commission, should of course keep them in their place.

To put the historical point in the economist's jargon, then, the new bourgeois liberty and the new admiration for the bourgeois life constituted world-making externalities. They were not tried in earlier times or other places because they stood offstage, and the prevailing powers foolishly wanted to keep them there. The powers could not imagine how very rich allowing onstage the honoring and liberating of economic innovation would make the powers themselves—and incidentally their subjects. No economist, for one thing, had stated the argument persuasively. That economics itself is such a strangely modern invention lends plausibility to the case for a uniquely modern shift in rhetoric. The professors of Salamanca, the pamphleteers of Amsterdam and London, the political economists of Edinburgh were figures of the sixteenth, seventeenth, and eighteenth centuries, with startlingly modern defenses of free markets in eighteenth-century Spain and Italy. Nothing remotely like their thought can be found earlier in Europe, and only glimmers elsewhere. And in early times, for another, no stunning, whole-country examples of success from according dignity to the bourgeoisie and leaving it free to innovate had stood in mute testimony. People took the lesson from the Jewel of the Adriatic, for example, that the way to wealth was colonies, and keeping city gates open continually that through them may be brought the wealth of nations, such as the lions of St. Mark. They neglected to note the Venetian invention of double-entry bookkeeping and other arts of peace. But Holland in the seventeenth century, and now China in the twenty-first, show how it's really done.

Until the view suddenly changed in academic circles in Spain and in commercial and some political circles in Holland and then in Britain and then (in all circles) in the United States, dignity and liberty for the bourgeoisie was viewed as an outrageous absurdity. *Of course* the bourgeoisie was contemptible, in Confucianism the fourth and lowest of the social classes, or in Christianity the rich man of the gospels who can scarcely enter heaven. *Of course* the market needed to be regulated in the interest of the rich—or at least in the interest of the continued rule of the rich by way of giving a little to some selected and favored and relatively well-off poor people (unskilled

automobile workers earning $30 an hour, high-school-graduate adminis-
trators in Cook County (now "Stroger") Hospital earning $100,000 a year,
members of local 881 of the United Food and Commercial Workers International Union earning more than what Wal-Mart employees are eagerly
willing to work for). *Of course* people should be arrayed in a great chain of
being from God to slave, and kept in their place, except by special royal favor
or state examination or party membership.

My theme in short is the true liberal one of the de la Court brothers,
Richard Overton, John Lilburne, William Walwyn, Thomas Rainsborough,
Richard Rumbold, Spinoza, Dudley North, Algernon Sidney, Locke, Vol-
taire, Hume, Turgot, Montesquieu, Adam Ferguson, Smith, Thomas Paine,
Destutt de Tracy, Jefferson, Madame de Staël, Benjamin Constant, Wilhelm
von Humboldt, Charles [*not* Auguste] Comte, Charles Dunoyer, Malthus,
Ricardo, Harriet Martineau, Tocqueville, Giuseppe Mazzini, Frédéric Bas-
tiat, Mill, Henry Maine, Richard Cobden, Elizabeth Cady Stanton, Cavour,
Johan August Gripenstedt, Herbert Spencer, Lysander Spooner, Karl von
Rotteck, Johan Rudolf Thorbecke, Carl Menger, Lord Acton, Josephine
Butler, Knut Wicksell, Luigi Einaudi, H. L. Mencken, Johan Huizinga,
Frank Knight, Ludwig von Mises, Willa Cather, Rose Wilder Lane, Walter
Lippmann until the 1950s, Nora Zeale Hurston, Karl Popper, Isaiah Ber-
lin, Michael Polanyi, Friedrich Hayek, Raymond Aron, Henry Hazlitt, Ber-
trand de Jouvenel, Ronald Coase, Milton, Rose, and son David Friedman,
Murray Rothbard, James Buchanan, Ludwig Lachmann, Gordon Tullock,
Thomas Sowell, Joan Kennedy Taylor, Roy A. Childs, Julian Simon, Israel
Kirzner, Vernon Smith, Wendy McElroy, Norman Barry, Loren Lomasky,
Tibor Machan, Anthony de Jasay, Douglas Den Uyl, Douglas Rasmussen,
Deepak Lal, Chandran Kukathas, Ronald Hamowy, Tom Palmer, Don
Lavoie, David Boaz, Richard Epstein, Tyler Cowen, David Schmidtz, Donald
Boudreaux, Peter Boettke, and the young Robert Nozick. It is the obvious
and simple system of natural liberty. It contradicts the aristocratic sneering by conservatives at innovations and at the bourgeoisie, or the clerical
sneering by progressives at markets and at the bourgeoisie. The true-liberal
claim is that unusual bourgeois dignity and personal liberty in northwestern Europe, and especially in Holland and then in Britain, made for unusual national wealth, by way of a revaluation of ordinary, bourgeois life.
The modern libertarian thinker Tom Palmer defends the proposition by its
consequences:

If respect for individual rights were to be shown to lead not to order and prosperity, but to chaos, the destruction of civilization, and famine, few would uphold such alleged rights, and those who did would certainly be held the enemies of mankind. Those who can see order only when there is a conscious ordering mind—socialists, totalitarians, monarchical absolutists, and the like—fear just such consequences from individual rights. But if it can be shown that a multitude of individuals exercising [a liberty that extends just as far as my neighbor's nose] . . . generates not chaos, but order, cooperation, and the progressive advance of human well-being, then respect for the dignity and autonomy of the individual would be seen to be not only compatible with, but even a necessary precondition for, the achievement of social coordination, prosperity, and high civilization.[11]

The negative version of the new liberty was articulated in 1685 famously by the Leveller Richard Rumbold on the scaffold: "I am sure there was no man born marked of God above another; for none comes into the world with a saddle on his back, neither any booted and spurred to ride him."[12] The positive version was equally famously articulated in 1792 by Wilhelm von Humboldt: "The true end of Man [*Mensch*, and implied, *every* man and woman] is the highest and most harmonious development of his powers to a complete and consistent whole. Liberty is the grand and indispensable condition which the possibility of such a development presupposes."[13] Notice that a Kantian (and novel) respect for a dignified personhood is here combined with a political demand for liberty.

The conservative political theorist Tod Lindberg points out that neoconservatism was for a while animated by empirical studies of what did not work in the aspirations of postwar American liberalism—minimum wages that unfortunately damaged the poor, educational expenditure that unfortunately enriched middle-class teachers' unions and miseducated the poor, foreign aid that unfortunately enriched big men and was never seen by the poor, and so forth. We Chicago School economists in the 1970s simply *loved* making such arguments. But Lindberg concludes that "the proper response to a mugging by reality is not the abandonment of liberalism, broadly construed, in favor of a pre-liberal or antiliberal or 'conservative' alternative, neo- or otherwise, but rather the abandonment of those elements (rife in postwar liberalism) that reality would not accommodate in favor of those that reality would accommodate and, indeed, compel. This is our current and future politics."[14] I agree. The economic history of even "socialist" Sweden supports our opinion.

Dignity and liberty, to express the point in economic terms, were the

Greatest Externalities, and have poured out their benefits in modern economic successes like Britain and France and Australia and now India. As the historical anthropologist Alan Macfarlane writes in summarizing the liberal theme, "Political and religious freedom seem to have a close association with the generation of economic wealth."[15] That is to put it mildly. A notion of the liberty to try novelties that in its origins was "a liberty," in other words a special privilege, as in the phrase "a freeman of the City of London," came by various happy accidents to be asserted by wider and wider groups—the middle class, the working class, colonial peoples, women, blacks, queers— and to characterize northwestern Europe and its offshoots. Thus the Abbé Sieyès in 1789 in his revolutionary pamphlet *What Is the Third Estate?* wrote that "one is not free by privileges, but by rights that belong to all."[16] At the same time a life in trade and manufacturing came to be a little bit honored, at more than a local level. Liberty, I say again for the enlightenment of my libertarian colleagues, does not by itself suffice. The political theorist James Otteson asserts a theorem that many libertarians believe: "Those countries that respect private property and efficiently administer justice prosper, and those that do not do not. It is as simple as that."[17] Not quite, I would argue, unless the word "respect" has more meaning than "enforce the laws of property." Prudence is not enough. We need to assent to bourgeois virtues.

The older aristocratic and peasant/Christian rhetorics of the virtues, in which people did come into the world with a saddle on their backs, began to be questioned, if never entirely abandoned. When a bourgeois rhetoric born in Venice or Antwerp in the Middle Ages began to be elevated during the seventeenth century into an ideology, equipped with its own literature and its own history and its own symbolic life, no longer borrowing these entirely from court or church, and when public opinion therefore was able "to persuade, in the deepest sense of that word, their fellow inhabitants of the evils of the old order and the legitimacy of the new" (as the historian Leora Auslander recently put the rhetorical job of progressive politics in early modern Europe), and when the rhetoric acquired as it did first in Holland and then in the New Model Army the muskets and cannons and military drills to deal with challenge from reactionaries, the Bourgeois Era was fairly launched.[18] Richard Steele, with Joseph Addison, in the *Spectator* 1711–1712 later provided a weekly reflection on bourgeois vs. gentry-aristocratic virtues. (The *Spectator* was soon imitated in the Netherlands and in Sweden.) Ten years later, in his play of 1722, *The Conscious Lovers,* Steele has Mr. Sealand (thus the range of merchant, from sea to land) declare, "We merchants are a species of gentry [here meaning any dignified people just below the aristocracy, not as it came later to mean only rural landowners and their associates] that have grown into the world this last century, and are as honorable, and almost as useful, as you landed folks, that have always thought yourselves so much above us. For your trading, forsooth, is extended no farther than a load of hay, or a fat ox."[19] George Lillo's embarrassingly cloying play another ten years later, in 1731, *The London Merchant*, can stand as an emblem for the change—though a change always under challenge from the aristocracy and the clerisy and the peasantry/proletariat. The honest merchant of the title (absurdly named "Thoroughgood") declares in the first scene that "as the name of merchant never degrades the gentleman [think of the factor in Aleppo], so by no means does it exclude him."[20] The play was put on at least annually until 1818 for the edification of the apprentices of the City of London. And courtesy, once confined literally to the court, spread to the middle class. Later in the century at the Octagon Room in Bath the daughters of the better merchants ("a species of gentry") danced with the sons of the actual, rural gentry. A century later the heiresses of American manufacturers and of the kings of Wall Street, such as Churchill's mother, were refreshing the fortunes of British ducal families. And another century later the British House of Lords and the aristocracy of Sweden were stripped of their constitutional positions.

The initiating changes, I have emphasized, were sociological and rhetorical—that is to say, they were about habits of the lip, what people thought and said about each other. But the sociological change surely inspired psychological changes as well. Both the sociology and the psychology are from the economic point of view externalities. The honest automobile mechanic in Iowa City who wouldn't think of charging more than exactly what is just, or of violating his faithful self-esteem by not doing the work he undertook to do, is an actual, extant character in a properly bourgeois society. His brother mechanic in Chicago, though, is encouraged by the sociology of a large city to have a different psychology, one that views the next customer as the next sucker. One gets to be that way.

The dual ethical change of dignity and of liberty for ordinary bourgeois life led to a reign of sense and sensibility from which we are still benefiting. Its virtues are commercial prudence and family love, combined in the self-defined middle class with an almost insane inventive courage fueled by hope, protected in its politics by faith and temperance, and by a just if often unintended improvement in the condition of the other, working classes— the ancestors of all the rest of us, to say it again—who themselves at last by the competition among the innovative bourgeoisie and their purchased politicians came to partake of the citizenly, bourgeois dignity of a vote, a house, a car, an education, and became themselves "gentlemanly" middle class.

Thus Norwegian immigrants to the upper Midwest read a comic strip drawn by Peter Rosendahl from 1919 to 1935 in their community newspaper, *Decorah-Posten*, concerning the adventures of Han Ola and Han Per ("Han" means "Him" and also "Mister," with a hint perhaps of sarcasm, as in Irish English "himself" in reference to one's husband). One of the running jokes is Han Per's obsessive inventiveness, sometimes a crazy reuse of older technologies. During the life of the strip Per tries out with disastrous effect fully sixty new machines. As the editor of a collection of the cartoons notes, "Rosendahl presents him as the undying optimist, trying in every way possible to mechanize not only the outdoor work of the farmer but also the indoor work of his wife"[21] (fig. 3). It is all very American, as the characters keep saying. People in the Bourgeois Era were free to dream of innovation, and found the attempt dignified. Even fools were free to dream. They found their dignity, and their comeuppance, and the rising of all boats, in glorious or comical attempts at innovation. The rhetorical explanation for such a historically unique madness seems to cohere within itself and to correspond with the facts better than the materialist alternatives from left or right. It has the additional merit of being contingent, and being particular to northwest Europe. The Dutch historian Peter Rietbergen writes that "in a situation

1. "But what in the world kind of patent have you made now, Per?" "Oh, it's just an electric fan for driving the windmill. When you turn that pointer you can change the speed. There are three speeds: 'light wind,' 'strong wind,' and 'hurricane.'"

2. "I've set the pointer at 'light wind.'" "It won't run. Try 'strong wind.'"

3. "Does it turn around now, Per?" "Yes, now it runs lickety-split!"

4. "Now I've set the pointer on 'hurricane,' Per."

FIGURE 3. Peter J. Rosendahl, "Too Much and Too Little Are Equally Bad," cartoon 270 in the Decorah, IA, *Decorah-Posten*, May 6, 1927.

that was entirely contingent, many of [Europe's] otherwise unremarkable features came together remarkably."[22] It mattered remarkably that Newton thought as he thought, or that Voltaire wrote as he wrote. And it mattered remarkably how the Dutch and then the English talked as they came to talk in the late seventeenth and early eighteenth centuries about bourgeois dignity and liberty.

43

AND THE MODEL CAN BE FORMALIZED

The argument can be summarized in a diagram. Take it or leave it as your intellectual tastes dictate. The diagram restates some of the points in visual terms. (These could in turn be translated into a set of equations with time subscripts, differential terms, and so forth. I'll start toward such a formal economic model in a moment. But the arrow diagram is more widely accessible, and does not require us, as the usual functional mathematics does, to speak only of one sort of cause, Hume's billiard-ball causation.)[1]

In order to avoid a hopelessly confusing mass of causal spaghetti, one can as it were subtract out two sorts of alleged causal factors (strands of spaghetti) that did *not* contribute, or not much, to the Great Fact. Imagine the fullest imaginable spaghetti diagram, with all the major events of Europe 1500 to the present included, even if they contributed little or no oomph to explaining the Great Fact—foreign trade, for example, which flourished in the Indian Ocean centuries earlier, or European imperialism, mainly providing employment for twits and the painting of world maps in red. Omit therefore the sort of spaghetti that didn't matter as historical causes of the great economic growth.

One sort omitted did matter, but not differentially in Europe as against Asia. They are the background conditions, such as growth of cities or solid property rights. Many chapters above have been devoted to showing that such factors don't work very well in explaining the modern world, because they were present in China and India and in the Arab and then Ottoman lands, and even in some African and New World kingdoms, sometimes much earlier or in larger measure than in northwestern Europe (table 3). The other sort of spaghetti omitted are incidentals, that is, actual or supposed events

Table 3. Background conditions, good or bad, of all Eurasian civilizations before 1500, which merely intensified later

Literary, artistic, and scientific flowering

Respect for learning; universities

Education of elite

Printing and paper

Compass

Clocks (but especially in Europe)

Monotheism (especially in Europe including Orthodoxy, and the Muslim world)

Peace and bourgeois prosperity (less in Europe)

Urbanization (less so in northern Europe)

(–? or +?) High death rates in cities

Competent bureaucracy (especially in China)

High seed/yield ratios (not in Europe, which did not have much rice, or any maize)

Investment capability (less so in Europe: see yield/seed ratio)

Wide long-distance trade (less so in Europe)

Slavery and its trade (especially in the Middle East)

Wide and deep internal trade and markets

Good internal transportation, especially unimproved rivers, canals, and coastal ships

Temperate climate

(–) Onset of Little Ice Age (1300–1850) after climatic maximum before 1300

(–) Malaria

(–? or +?) The Plague

Desire for profit

Rule of law

Property rights

Money (in China even paper money)

Reasonably sophisticated financial institutions

High incomes in a few favored places

Coal widely used (China, India, Europe)

after 1500 in Europe that are sometimes alleged to have caused the modern world but have been shown to be mostly beside the point (table 4).

If an item raises your indignation ("*How* can she say that British imperialism was 'incidental'!"), you have not been persuaded by the arguments in the corresponding chapters (in this case chapters 26 and 27). You may be

Table 4. Incidental events 1500 to the present, not contributing much to the Great Fact

Protestant ethic

Thrift

Rise of rationality

Rise of greed

Spanish and Portuguese imperialism

The Price Revolution

Dutch, British, French trade (except as contributing to bourgeois dignity)

Dutch, British, French imperialism

Slave trade

Rises in the rate of saving

Original accumulation of capital

Surplus value, reinvestment

Routine investment

Education (until around 1900)

Exploitation of the working class

Science (until around 1900)

(–) Sustained high prestige of aristocracy and gentry

Routine transportation improvement (canals, harbors)

English genetics

English social inheritance

Stuart missteps and taxation

The Glorious Revolution

Institutional change

Economies of scale

right. But I'd ask you to show it scientifically, not merely to wax wroth. And "showing it," by the way (I remark to my historian colleagues) does not consist in marshaling scissors-and-paste evidence irrelevant to the economics involved. If you want to prove that, say, foreign trade was important—and not a mere "background condition" common to much of the world—you have to do the economic thinking framing what evidence you claim would be relevant. You can't just say, "The noneconomic historians who agree with me politically all believe that imperialism or trade were important." The

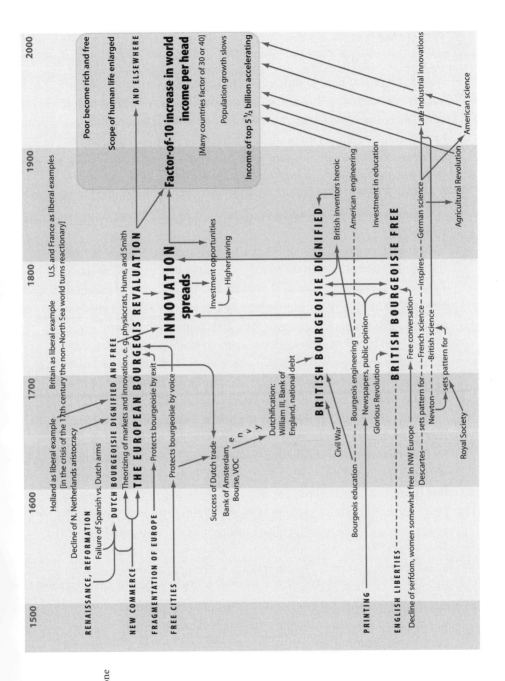

FIGURE 4.
The causes of the factor of sixteen, or of one hundred.

question is scientific, not political (though its answer surely has political implications). Nor beyond waxing wroth (I remark to my economist colleagues) does showing it consist in proposing a model of educational accumulation or the Black Death after some light historical reading that "calibrates" with the history. That's a six-inch hurdle, like statistical "significance." There are literally an infinite number of models that roughly "predict" (or more exactly postdict) the course of European history in this or that regard. The argument has to be able to stand up to confrontation with all the evidence, quantitative or qualitative. It has to make fully human, scientific sense.

My claim, in short, is that the model in figure 4, diagrammed here across the centuries, is better than the strictly materialist alternatives. The model, I repeat, could easily be expressed mathematically as differential equations, but the lines of influence organized here by centuries are I think a good way to summarize the book's argument for a diagrammatically-minded reader. A young and conventionally equipped economist will be a little puzzled by the model, because he will think that only a model with constrained maximization constitutes a "model." He is philosophically mistaken, and it is a disability of his education that he will not know that he is.

But the crux here (I repeat to my economist colleagues) is that a Max U model, as much as I have loved such a Samuelsonian-Beckerian idea, and have written numerous books and scores of articles in its praise, cannot work to explain real innovation. That, after all, is the central point here—that routine maximizations, such as by the extension of foreign trade or by investment in routine projects of swamp drainage or canal digging, do not explain the modern world. What explains it, as the Austrian economists would put it, is discovery. And, as they (such as Kirzner) argue correctly, a real discovery, Mokyr's "macro invention," is never an outcome of methodical investment, but always an accident in the prepared mind and in the open conversation. There is no U to max and no constraint to obey if real discovery is at issue, as against routine exploration for, say, oil. About oil, the startling macrodiscovery was that you could get it in bulk from the ground and then use it to make kerosene and then gasoline. By contrast, investing an optimal amount in drilling for additional oil, after the discovery of the idea, is a project of rational search. The difference (I speak again to economists) is the same as between Knightian risk (which is calculable, and therefore often insurable and therefore partially avoidable in a world of

Max U) and uncertainty (which is not). No one would have bet on Europe in 1500, or on England in 1600, or on the factor of sixteen in 1800. It was uncertain—as in "astounding."

∞

But I can satisfy a little the thirst of my economist colleagues for something closer to what they would consider "a model." The function for national product could be:

$$Q = I(D, B, R) \cdot F(K, sL)$$

in which I is the Innovation function, depending on D, the dignity accorded innovators, and on B, the liBerty of innovators (the letter L is need for labor), and on R, the rent or profit to innovation. The Innovation function multiplies a conventional neoclassical production function, F, depending on ordinary physical capital and land, K, and on raw labor, L, multiplied by an education-and-skill coefficient, s.

There is of course nothing profoundly mathematical about this way of saying what I am saying. The "mathematics" is merely a metaphorical language that economists understand, and which allows me to chat with them about the economic and social ideas involved without excessive confusion. The reason to separate out the I(.) function is to stress, as I have, that economic growth depends mainly on Schumpeterian/Austrian innovation, not, as some economists and historians still believe, on classical/Marxist/ Samuelsonian accumulation. Once upon a time the economists thought that growth depended on physical capital (here K) and now some think that it depends on various versions of human capital (sL). Aside from the evidence against such capital fundamentalism of the economists I have already offered from history, the economist Peter Howitt has reported on a recent literature of present-day cross-country comparisons which concludes that "more than 60 percent of the cross-country variation of per-worker GDP is attributable to productivity rather than to the accumulation of physical and human capital," and over 90 percent of its growth rate.[2] "Thus it seems," he argues, "that almost everything to be explained by the theory lies in the Solow residual," the A term in Solow's classic paper of 1957, here the I(.) function. "This is part of the evidence," Howitt continues, "that inclines me towards innovation-based growth theory." That seems a sensible conclusion. It was anticipated by Smith, whose *Theory of Moral Sentiments* (1759

[1790]) treats the D variable of dignity, and whose *Wealth of Nations* treats the B variable of liberty (amongst a great deal also about $F(.)$).Smith believed that the obvious and simple system of natural liberty (B, but linked with D) was necessary and sufficient for the (modest) growth he imagined.

Even with so vague a specification as the unspecified functional form, $Q = I(.) \cdot F(.)$ some qualitative points emerge—though without actual measurement, our knowledge is meager and unsatisfactory. In the innovation function, $I(.)$, the term R is what economists call rent, and the rest of us call profit. It represents in part the routine incentive to innovate, picking up the $100 bills. Whether routine or not, it has two aspects, depending on when you are looking at it—whether before or after innovation, "ex ante" or "ex post," as the economists after Gunnar Myrdal say, "from the before" or "from the after," that is, from the point of view of the outset or the point of view of the end. I say that R is sometimes "Routine" (a helpful mnemonic to remember the contrast with the noneconomic and nonroutine variables for *D*ignity and li*B*erty). But to the extent that it depends on alertness and the ability to form an image of the future, it is decidedly not routine. Ex ante it is precisely "the possible lives they imagine for themselves and their children" of Robert Lucas's formulation, expressed in money (that is, expressed in profane terms, and not mentioning the sacred matters, the animal spirits, such as the spiritual value of caring for one's children—which is a limitation on the economist's way of thinking). Such an R viewed ex ante is in part the routine gain hovering before the eyes of an entrepreneur in Madras imagining how very rich he could become if he could introduce air conditioning to the standard of Atlanta. But it is also the highly nonroutine gain of Israel Kirzner's formulation, such as what John Ericsson imagined would be gained from introducing screw propellers into ships. What innovations are imaginable depend on the new devices or institutions in the offing. The novelties floating in the offing are sometimes said to depend on relative factor prices, but we've seen the frailties of such an argument. On the other hand, when steam engines with separate condensers became common, it eventually occurred to many people that they might be made more compact for the same power at high pressures. It was something that Watt himself realized but was unwilling to implement, from the fear that such engines would be subject to terrible explosions. So they were, when applied for example to railways and steam vessels.

The private R of the entrepreneur's ex-ante imaginings, however, dissipates ex post by competition into a social R, imparting an actual, nonspeculative, ex-post height to the I(.) function. If R dissipates too soon—if it is too easily imitated, or is unpatentable knowledge—then the incentive to innovate is attenuated. But there's no blackboard formula for institutions or parameters that optimize R. Once laboriously discovered, the marginal cost of another person learning, say, the calculus is near zero: Newton and Leibnitz (they disagreed on which of them) should have gotten money credit, the economist says, in order to evoke the optimal amount of mathematical innovation (the example shows again, by the way, why macroinventions are perhaps not best analyzed as routine matters of money cost and benefit). But once the job of invention is done (the economist then says, switching sides), the optimal price for copying should be zero—and so the society should promptly stop the checks just issued to Newton and Leibnitz. It's a paradox, with no general resolution; it depends. The situation is that of a bridge. The Brooklyn Bridge was costly to build, and needed somehow to be financed, but the social opportunity cost of people going across it was, from May 24, 1884, zero, and so charging tolls to cross and to pay down the debt is from the economist's social point of view irrational. The Age of Innovation was an age of uncompensated intellectual bridge building on an immense scale.

The other arguments in I(.), D for dignity and B for liberty, are unpaid externalities. R is unpaid, too, after its private rewards have been dissipated. But before that time it is paid in supernormal profits earned in excess of the opportunity cost of the routine inputs K and sL. When being paid, the R disturbs the marginal-productivity rules for distribution, which depend solely on the routineness of the F(.) function. The manager knows how much to pay workers or investors if she knows what hiring them will produce; her expectation is disturbed if an R out-of-equilibrium is present. The disturbance provides one way to measure R, by seeing what financial return is *not* explained by routine marginal productivities of K and sL. The ex-post return of R sloshes around the social classes, in other words, unsettling the routine distribution by marginal product—early on it goes to Carnegie; later, by the competition of steel companies at home and abroad, it goes to hoi polloi. If there was no dissipation, and no ultimate gain to hoi polloi, innovation would not have a justification on egalitarian grounds—as in the historical event it surely did have. That is why ex-post rent from land has been since Ricardo under persistent ethical attack even from economists. The sociology is that large rents from mere possession of land, the half of national income in the Middle Ages that went to the dignified classes, tend to an aristocratic or priestly society. Large (and eventually dissipated) rents from innovation, by contrast, tend to a bourgeois society. Honor follows money, of course, and money honor.

The paid/unpaid distinction is why I(.) and F(.) are to be treated separately, and it justifies at least in mere logic my talk earlier of the Great Fact being a result of great externalities. The F(.) function is routine, and you can tell whether an economist acknowledges the role of the *non*routine in economic life by how she treats R. The Austrian economists treat R as unintended discovery; the Samuelsonians want to bring R back into a routine of marginal benefit and marginal cost, that is, to force it back into the economics of a routine F(.). (Both schools, incidentally, are "neoclassical," one out of Menger and the other out of Marshall, which shows why "neoclassical" is a poor title for the conventional Samuelsonians.) Howitt, referring to Mokyr's pioneering historical work on the matter, notes that "nations that experience the most rapid growth are not necessarily those in which people have the strongest incentives to develop new technologies [in my terms, high Samuelsonian Rs] but those which have developed the greatest tolerance for, and capacity to adjust to, the many negative side-effects of economic growth [namely, the high D and B that accompany a signing on to the Bourgeois Deal]. Those negative side-effects are almost always the result of . . . the destructive side of creative destruction."[3] The high D and B in the Netherlands (before the *regenten* in the eighteenth century became a virtual aristocracy and started to close off innovation) and Britain and the new United States made for less reaction, as in Continental anti-Semitism or on French dirigisme protecting this or that industry of concern to *l'état.*

The variables of dignity, D, and of liberty, B, have their own dynamics. When expressed as virtue, dignity draws on faith and justice, who you are and who you should respect. Liberty by contrast draws on hope and courage, the courage to be (as the theologian Paul Tillich put it) and the hope to venture. (Hope and courage do not suffice, I say once again to the libertarians). The rent in prospect or in achievement, R, draws on temperance (savings for investment) and prudence (rationality, picking up the $100 bills in plain sight). The seventh of the principal virtues, love of people or of the transcendent (science, God, the family), affects the other variables unacknowledged and certainly unpaid, but is not therefore unimportant. John

Ericsson's great love for the iron-shaper Cornelius H. DeLamater was important for the inventor's life and work.

Virtues unbalanced, though, are vices. Dignity, for example, tends to corruption—causing it then to become sometimes a negative rather than a positive influence on the height of I(.). The corruption happens if merchants develop into a proud aristocracy, as they did at Florence, for example, and as the left believes the power elite of the United States has. Liberty, too, including verbal action, can be dangerous. Liberty for example can be turned into a negative influence, a politically expressed envy, if it seems plausible to poor people now equipped with voices and votes that stealing from the rich is, after all, the most direct way to cure their poverty. (A *New Yorker* cartoon back in the 1960s showed a bank truck pulled up to the curb with the guards handing money out of bags to the people on the street, one of whom exclaims, "Well, at last the War on Poverty has gotten under way!")

Over time the I(.) variables of D, B, and R are entangled (just as K and L are entangled in the conventional F(.) function, as in substitutability, complementarity, specific human capital, diminishing returns). A society, like routine production, hangs together. For example, dignity for innovation in 1900 depended on earlier liberties and earlier rents from innovation. $Dt = g$ (B_{t-1}, R_{t-1}). Liberated people tend after a while to get accorded dignity, especially if their liberty results in high incomes for themselves or, as the acknowledged benefactors of the world, for the rest of us. The reverse causation can happen, too, from dignity to liberty after a while, or (less pleasantly) from dignity to high rents, as peers and baronets become the honorable chairmen of new corporations.

Likewise the variables in the innovation function, I(.), can have influences over time on the routine variables in the production function, F(.). One conventional way to think about it is to imagine the demand curves (the marginal revenue product curves) derived from the entire expression $Q = I(.) \cdot F(.)$. The I(.) function in such a derivation would be a multiplicative term raising the marginal product of capital and of more-or-less educated labor. The point made earlier about the noninitiating character of capital can be expressed here by saying that K and sL are elastically supplied in the long run. Accumulation, whether in physical or human capital, will therefore depend on the I(.)-altered valuation of its fruits. As I(.) rises in the Age of Innovation, savings will be found to make the appropriate investments, because the higher productivity makes R evident and routine. Likewise, education in technical subjects will respond elastically in the long run to the demand for them—though what is "technical" varies with the times, being fluency in Latin in the sixteenth century (the better to serve, say, as a diplomat), or fluency with differential equations in the twentieth century, or fluency with electronic simulation in the twenty-first century.

The international context in which innovation takes place matters. From the point of view of a stagnant economy such as Russia's in 1850, the imaginable R becomes larger and larger as the nineteenth century proceeds, finally overcoming in some countries their low values for D and B—this is the Gerschenkron-Pollard point. A place with low dignity for the bourgeoisie, such as prerevolutionary France, can compensate with high liberty for the despised class, a high level of B (though it in fact did not). And anyway it slowly gets dragged into the modern world if it is in the neighborhood of first a militarily and economically successful Holland and then a militarily and economically successful Britain, which makes obvious the great magnitude of ex-ante R. The embarrassment of the War of the Spanish Succession, 1701–1714, in which tiny Holland teamed up with emergent Britain (and aristocratic Austria on the southern front) to humble the great and mighty Louis XIV, taught France some of what it needed. Some.

The advantage of algebra, though, is that one can get beyond such existence-theorem, qualitative, merely philosophical claims and counterclaims, which after all can justify any pattern of alleged facts whatever. One can get a little scientific and focus on the relative importance of this or that effect. For example, suppose the I(.) and F(.) functions were Cobb-Douglas, that is, having constant exponents on each variable (you ask why: because it is mathematically convenient, and because starting with constants is a wise first step if you have no a priori knowledge of how they would vary, and have no particular reason to suppose that they vary endogenously). Then taking rates of change of each variable (using an asterisk, *, to mean "rate of change of the variable preceding the *") and using corresponding Greek letters to mean "elasticities—that is, exponential coefficients—of the variable following"), yields obviously:

$$Q^* = [\,\delta D^* + \beta B^* + \rho R^*\,] + [\kappa K^* + \lambda s^* + \lambda L^*]$$

If you like to think in logarithms, you can make the same expression into a log-linear one. In either case it holds without interaction terms only for small changes in the variables, but can be easily (if lengthily) rewritten with the interaction terms present. It should be so written if you have an interest in a particular interaction, for example between K^* and D^*, percentage changes in physical capital accumulation and the dignity of Mr. Moneybags.

The equation can be expressed in per-capita form by subtracting L^* from both sides:

$$(Q/L)^* = [\ \delta D^* + \beta B^* + \rho R^*] + [\kappa K^* + \lambda s^* + (\lambda - 1)L^*]$$

One can make all sorts of foxy points with such an equation. (I repeat: they are merely restatements of what has been argued earlier, not fascinating new insights.) If the skill variable is measured as years of education, for example, the slope of s relative to years of education would be quite small, relative to the massive change to be explained in the Great Fact, at any rate judging from cross-section studies of returns to education. A college graduate is not ten times better in contributions to Q than a high-school graduate (an insulting hypothesis anyway on its face, and silly if you have actually known any noncollege graduates). It might work out if college is accurately selecting for a tiny elite of geniuses. But such screening cannot in fact be done with accuracy, as the history of Britain's Eleven Plus examination showed, or as Einstein's inability at first to get an academic job showed. So the equation makes explicit why one might doubt the force of education.

On the other hand, the innovation variables D and B and even R might themselves be improved by education. You can see reasons for it, a higher skill level, s, resulting in higher dignity, D, because of admiration for a skilled bourgeois, or because of a better grasp of technical matters necessary for innovation; or indeed because instruction in economics (my own modest contribution to s) might lead people to admire liberty in economic matters, and achieve thereby higher B. I say again, however, that the s effect can be and often has been perverse, corrupting good bourgeois boys by educating them to believe that the bourgeoisie have no dignity at all, or corrupting good bourgeois girls to become state bureaucrats devoted to believing that bourgeois liberty is to be stamped out. Marx took a PhD degree in philosophy at Jena in 1841. The leader of the Shining Path Marxists in Peru was a professor of philosophy. A high percentage of the officers in Hitler's SS had advanced degrees in the humanities. German engineers built the gas chambers. Excellent computer engineers enforce the Chinese censorship of the Internet.

Likewise unless one has assumed, or (unlikely thought) in fact measured, economies of scale, which would make the elasticity κ large, even a large percentage change in K cannot explain what is to be explained in the rise of income per person. The economies of scale could explain the modern world if they actually were there in other times and places, too. But apparently they weren't present in other times and places, which makes one wonder why not, if they are supposed to arrive suddenly in England in 1700. And as actually measured (off the blackboard of existence theorems), economies of scale prove to be modest, raising the sum of coefficients in the F(.) variables from the 1.0 of Cobb-Douglas to perhaps 1.1. For reasons of competition and the marginal productivity theory of distribution, the share of capital in rewards to factors of production is the elasticity in question, here κ (strictly in the absence of economies of scale: and if the economies are small, approximately so). The elasticity is small in modern economies (on the order of 0.10 or 0.20), though larger when land bulked large.

Speaking of land bulking large: when it does *not*, and the share of L is therefore high, then the term $\lambda - 1$ (which is of course negative and captures simple diminishing returns to labor applied to fixed land) is small, because λ is then close to 1.0. (Indeed, economies of scale can tip $\lambda - 1$ into modestly positive territory, meaning that we are enriched a bit by having more of us, even without regard to economies of scale in the other, I(.) function). In a modern economy in which human-capital enhanced labor gets much of national income for itself, the impact of Malthusian diminishing returns is greatly weakened by the effect. To put it another way, when the rewards to labor get to be a higher percentage of national income, the other labor-related term, λs^*, which measures the effect of skills, gets higher. The mathematics reflects the point that human resources become more important than natural resources—land is buried here in K, but causes diminishing returns to the extent only that $\lambda - 1$ is large. The term was large in the Middle Ages, with only half of national income accruing to labor, and the rest to land. The move to modern times reduced $\lambda - 1$, and therefore the threat from diminishing returns, from 0.5 to 0.1. Listen up, environmentalists.

There is no reason in the facts for the coefficients in the other, I(.) function to add up to 1.0. On the contrary, a doubling of dignity might result in a far-more-than-doubling of output, by encouraging massive innovations. You will doubt that "dignity" can be measured, but wait (. . . until the next volume, in which I shall try!): it can be measured perhaps by public opinion polls such as the Values Survey, or from the prevalence of merchant-innovator heroes in lowbrow literature, or in the percentage in some textual sample of favorable mentions of innovation (such as the quotation from Samuel Johnson earlier). Liberty is easier to measure, and has been, in the surveys of days-to-open-a-business or ease-of-dismissing-workers now conventional. It, too, need not have a coefficient constrained by constant returns to scale: the β coefficient may by itself be well above 1.0, for example, which is to say that a 50 percent increase in liberty measured as book pages per capita in the vulgar languages sold uncensored, say, could easily result in well over 50 percent increases in national income per head.

Economists regard such sociological/political matters as those summarized in I(.) as relatively constant (or anyway exogenous to economic matters), and so they focus on F(.). But the larger lesson of the formalization is that F(.) is nice, and is what economists mainly talk about. But I(.) was the maker of the modern world. F(.) was the coastline; I(.) was the tide.

44

OPPOSING THE BOURGEOISIE HURTS
THE POOR

Some intellectuals, though, look with suspicion on the Bourgeois Era, calling it "globalization," which they think they detest, along with McDonald's
and the bourgeoisie and capitalism. The suspicion has been expressed since
1848 in repeated assaults by the clerisy on the bourgeoisie, commonly their
fathers, each new assault presented as a courageous speaking of truth to
power, a daring new insight, though expressed in identical form from Flau-
bert and G. B. Shaw to Sinclair Lewis and David Mamet. The antiglobalization clerisy focuses on globalization's losers, such as Jonson the Swedish
competitor of Svenson the Swedish Timber King, or Wrightman the English competitor of Swedish timber, and especially focus on the impoverished employees in the jobs on the Lose side instead of the Win-Win-Win-
Win-Win. Its conclusion is that economic growth has had unconscionable
costs. The Marxist literary critic Eagleton declared in 2006 that "global
capitalism . . . generates the hatred, anxiety, insecurity and sense of humili-
ation that breed fundamentalism."[1] The historical sociologist Immanuel
Wallerstein, an eminent man of the left, declared in 1983 that "it is simply
not true that capitalism as a historical system has represented progress over
the various previous historical systems that it destroyed or transformed."[2]

Such is the theme of the historians Kenneth Pomeranz and Steven Topik
in their brilliant economic-historical collage, *The World That Trade Created* (2006; a new edition of a 1999 book). They warmly commend, among
numerous other opponents of innovation, "village elders [in twentieth-
century China] who had banned a more efficient sickle on the grounds that
its benefits were not worth the new struggles it would touch off between

farmers, hired harvesters, and thieves."[3] That sounds nice, if rather old Russian and peasantly. Remember Owen Lattimore on Qing conservatism: "China changed in a way that created a centralized imperial bureaucracy, of which the personnel was recruited generation by generation from the landed gentry, whose combination of landed interest and administrative interest kept innovation well in check and prevented industrial development almost entirely."[4]

But it's *not* nice, though old Russian and peasantly, or old Chinese and mandarin. If local envy and protection and interest and keeping the peace between users of old and new technologies are allowed to call the shots, then innovation and the modern world is blocked. Jonson vetoes Svenson. The Inquisition silences Galileo. Joel Mokyr gives plentiful examples of such shooting-oneself-in-the-foot: In 1299 a law prevented bankers in Florence from adopting Arabic numerals. In the late fifteenth century the scribes of Paris delayed the adoption of the printing press (there) for twenty years. In 1397 the vested interests in Cologne outlawed the making of pins in presses rather than by hand. In 1561 the city council of Nuremburg passed an ordinance imprisoning anyone who would make and sell a new lathe that had been invented by a local man. In 1579 the city council of Danzig secretly ordered the inventor of the ribbon loom to be drowned.[5] And on and on into modern times—since the springs of such anti-innovative activities are prudent, self-interest, not some foolishness unique to primitive times. In the late 1770s the Strasbourg council prohibited a local cotton mill from actually selling its stuffs in town because the merchants who specialized in importing cloth would be disturbed: "It would upset all order in trade if the manufacturer were to become a merchant at the same time."[6] In 1865 the Wiggin's Ferry Company of St. Louis stopped the first attempt to build the Eads Bridge over the Mississippi. The white members of the City Council in Chicago, with the support of the intellectual left this time, stop WalMart from opening grocery stores in the food deserts of the South Side.

If bourgeois dignity and liberty are not on the whole embraced by public opinion, in the face of the sneers by the clerisy and the machinations of special interests, the enrichment of the poor doesn't happen, because innovation doesn't. You achieve merely through a doctrine of compelled charity in taxation and redistribution the "sanctification of envy," as the Christian economist the late Paul Heyne put it. The older suppliers win. Everyone else loses. You ask God to take out two of your neighbor's eyes, or to kill your neighbor's goat. You work at your grandfather's job in the field or factory instead of going to university. You stick with the old ideas, and the old ferry company. You remain contentedly, or not so contentedly, at $3 a day, using the old design of sickle. You continue having to buy food for your kids at the liquor store at the corner of Cottage Grove and 79th Street. And most of us remain unspeakably poor and ignorant.

Pomeranz and Topik are not wrong to note the exploitation when, say, increased demand for twine to bale American wheat straw led to Mayans and Yaqui Indians being forced in the Yucatán to harvest cactus to make the twine.[7] They are often wrong, though, in assigning the exploitation (usually without argument) to the innovation itself rather than to the precapitalist structures of power that allowed the tyrants to exploit in evil ways the opportunity to trade in twine or coffee or sugar or rubber. Such pre-existing evils (exploited in *other* ways before the evil market opportunity appeared) were often enough eroded in such countries by capitalism itself—if by nothing else than by the sheer rising tide of world real incomes per head, and the political power that it brought to ordinary people in its surge. And it was the British liberal bourgeoisie who supported early and uniquely the ending of slavery. It was the American bourgeoisie who supported the protections for free speech and religion, as in the First Amendment in 1789; and it was the French bourgeoisie who supported the various other liberties overturning the *ancien régime* in that dawn.

By 1800 in northwestern Europe, for the first time in economic history, an important part of public opinion, especially elite opinion, rejected local envy and How We've Always Done It, and came to accept creative accumulation and destruction in the economy, in the way it was doing in the parallel world of noneconomic ideas. The enlightened declared, "Out with the old ideas, in with the new," contrary to the interests of the purveyors of old ideas. The burst of school and then university foundings in the sixteenth and seventeenth centuries democratized learning to an extent not exceeded until the nineteenth century. Meanwhile the entrepreneurs of northwestern Europe were saying the same novelty-loving thing about inventions and market deals. Out with old machines, in with the new. Out with the old laws restricting innovation, in with the new laws allowing it. The historian Peter Rietbergen observes that the new culture of the printed instruction emanating from an elite and literate culture replaced a system of "orders that for centuries had been given orally by authorities who . . . retained some form of closeness" to those they were ordering. The "body of common rules" became official (from an *officio*, a literate gathering of clerks), standardized for all parts of France, in the official language of the chancery.[8] The resulting ethical change certainly did represent progress over the various previous historical systems that it destroyed or transformed, because it introduced a fresh utilitarianism of rules or a new constitutional political economy into the affairs of ordinary life. People were willing to change jobs and allow technology to progress, or at the least they believed that it was fruitless to resist. Machine breaking did not thrive. People stopped enviously attributing this man's riches or that woman's poverty to politics or witchcraft. They came to what the novelist Philip Roth calls "a civilized person's tolerant understanding of the puzzle of inequality and misfortune."[9] Or at least they shifted away from a belief in highly personal politics—such as had in the early seventeenth century provoked the burning of thousands of witches along the German borderlands with France—toward a disenchanted belief in the impersonal, the rule of Them or the Bureau or the Government or the Invisible Hand or That's Just How It Is. Said Alexander Pope in 1733–1734, by which time it was becoming a commonplace, "Thus God and Nature linked the general frame, / And bade self-love and social be the same."[10]

Accepting creative accumulation and destruction, it turned out, provided a near guarantee that almost all the boats would rise on the tide of innovation. You didn't even need a boat. People got new jobs like computer selling, and abandoned the old jobs like blacksmithing. The outcome was wholly unanticipated, a creative discovery in world history. I am saying that crucial to the creative discovery, and the creative destruction of old ideas and old ways of doing things it entailed, was accepting its results. Otherwise we get a reaction, as in part we did from left and right. From the left it is Karl Polanyi's "double movement," defining a wage as slavery. From the right it is a nostalgia for how we once were, with women in the kitchen and workers doffing their caps to the respectable classes. Both left and right, that is, declare new designs of sickles to be horrible. Both complain about profit for the sickle-supplying bourgeoisie. Both stop progress for the bourgeoisie, and soon after for the poor.

Consider the left's antibourgeois rhetoric. It is sweet and good to sympathize with the poor, as the left assuredly does. We all should, if only on the argument that all our ancestors once were poor, and it is faithless not to sympathize with people like your ancestors. If rightist ideologues prefer the rich to the poor, and claim that the poor are that way because they deserve it, they ought to be ashamed. Agreed. Yet even the sweet and self-satisfying ideas of the progressives have consequences. For the poor the consequences have not always been good. The left wing's fervent belief in the notion of "wage slavery," for example, grossly damages the poor, quite contrary to its generous intent. The left institutes minimum wages and legislates against sweatshops, and as a result the poor remain poor.

After all, to take up the left's dogma (the right's, I emphasize, is commonly no better), a choice to work for a wage at a terrible job—rather than, say, starve—is nothing like "slavery." Slavery, pogroms, state compulsion enforced by the police and army make people worse off, at any rate by the people's own standards. By contrast, the wages make people better off than the even more terrible alternatives, such as begging in the street. Workers line up to get jobs at the Nike shoe company in Cambodia. By contrast, no one *chooses* to be compelled by the army or police (Hobbesian fantasies of a freely chosen Leviathan aside). No one lines up voluntarily to be waterboarded by the CIA. But people do line up to work. Stopping people from taking terrible jobs—through prohibitions or protections or minimums, justified by the warm if mistaken feeling over one's second cappuccino that one is thereby being generous to the poor—takes away from the poor what the poor themselves regard as a bettering option. It's stealing deals from the poor. Sweatshops in the New York garment trade, for example, such as those in which the free-market economist Milton Friedman's parents briefly worked, lead on after a while to college-educated children and grandchildren. And in the short run the sweatshops of New York were better than the parents digging for food in the city dump, or sitting back in Russia waiting for the next pogrom. That's why people lined up to get the sweatshop jobs.

Both Marx from the left and Carlyle from the right, among many others suspicious of the modern world, called paid work by the name of slavery. It was part of Carlyle's argument, echoed in the American South, that slavery in the British Empire had been a good thing, darkies playing banjos in happy subservience, compared with the horrors of northern American and northern British wage labor. The usage echoes down to the present, as in *The Concise Oxford Dictionary* of 1999, in which a "wage slave" is defined coolly as "a person who is wholly dependent on income from employment," with the notation "informal"—but not "ironic" or "jocular."[11] Thus Judy Pearsall, the editor of the *Concise Oxford*, who lives it may be in a nice semidetached in NW6 and drives a new Volvo, is a "slave." You yourself are probably a slave. I certainly am a slave. We are all slaves. One finds Oscar Wilde in 1891 declaring that "socialism [about which he knew only the contents of a lecture by Shaw] would relieve us from that sordid necessity of living for others," by which he means charity, but also paid work: "An individual who has to make things for the use of others, and with reference to their wants and their wishes, does not work with interest, and consequently cannot put into his work what is best in him."[12] Even the owner of property is not exempt, for property "involves endless claims upon one, endless attention to business, endless bother." Worker or capitalist, both are slaves to making things for others. Only the artist is free. Such progressive or conservative terminology is like calling an exchange of harsh words "verbal rape." We need terms for the physical violence entailed in actual slavery and in actual rape, and should not cheapen them by applying them to our middle-class vexations in NW6 or Marin County.

And in the long run the acceptance of creative destruction relieved poverty. It has been in fact the only effective relief. Wage regulations and protection and other progressive legislation, contrary to their sweet (and self-gratifying) motives, have only preserved poverty, by preserving the old jobs. Innovation, not unions or regulations, permitted the new jobs, and financed the new college graduates, and raised the tide. The unions or regulations achieved their sweet purpose only if they worked for innovation (as often, say, in Sweden, or sometimes in the United States—the president of the United Mine Workers in the United States, John L. Lewis, declared that by raising union wages he planned to kill off the underground coal mining he properly despised. Good for him. He put workers on the side of progress in mining, in this case [hold your breath], strip mining).

That is, antiglobalization writers such as Pomeranz and Topik (among many of my left-wing friends) have less interest than they should in the gigantic gains from bourgeois dignity and liberty. They have cared passionately about the poor. So have Adam Smith and John Stuart Mill and Milton Friedman and I, all these years. My advice to the left (no extra charge) is therefore to stop attacking the only effective device for making the poor of the world better off—innovation. Naomi Klein's *The Shock Doctrine* attacks the economic liberalization of Milton Friedman's sort without realizing that it has enriched the poor of the world since it first became influential around 1973 (and in a longer perspective since 1776). A political poster current in

2009 read, "Milton Friedman, proud father of global misery."[13] Some misery: income per head in the world and the world's poor increased in real terms from 1973 (when Friedman was sixty-one, and three years from his Nobel prize) to 1998 (when Friedman was eighty-six years old) by 40 percent.[14] In the countries that followed his philosophy more exactly than the world-as-a-whole, the increase was much larger even than the world's average of 40 percent. In China, for example, much influenced by Friedman's ideas after 1978 (his book of 1962, *Capitalism and Freedom*, was widely read by Chinese reformers), it was a factor of 3.7, or 270 percent. In Ireland, which dramatically liberalized à la Friedman, it was a factor of 3.2, or 220 percent.[15] My poor Irish sixth cousins were saved by Friedmanian devotion to the market and innovation.

Nowhere in their book do Pomeranz and Topik, typically of the left in the matter, acknowledge the enriching results of free markets, such as the leap 1800 to the present of daily real income in Norway from $3 to $137, or the more widespread leap in the world's average from $3 to $30. The historians of the world that trade created do not acknowledge, in the middle of their story, the largest economic event in world history since the domestication of plants and animals. An elephant sits in the room, but Pomeranz and Topik speak only of the furniture.

To put it another way, the antiglobalization, antimodernization writers have less interest than they should in the misery of traditional, $3-a-day societies, in which village elders decide on the design of sickles, and of marriages, and of laws. Wallerstein claimed in 1983 that he did not "seek to paint [an] idyll of the worlds before historical capitalism," but went on to deny (in an argument he admitted was "audacious") the evident progress in the material and spiritual condition of ordinary people worldwide since 1800.[16] Pomeranz and Topik fail to note in their book, written when the progress was even more evident, that we were once all poor and that now very many of us (such as we professors) are already by historical and international standards rich—or that the top four to six billion are on the way to riches, or that there is even considerable hope now, on past and recent form, for the bottom billion. Those who imbibed world history about the past few centuries from Wallerstein and Pomeranz and Topik, or about the past few decades from Naomi Klein, would have no idea that such a shrinkage of world poverty had taken place.

Such denials of material progress articulated by the left (and denials of spiritual progress articulated by the right) are refuted by what is known in rhetorical theory as the "circumstantial ad hominem." Like a lawyer for the cigarette companies who falls down dead in court from a cigarette-caused cancer, the circumstances of the speaker against globalization and modern economic growth refute his own argument. The prosperity of Wallerstein and Klein, and Pomeranz and Topik—which compared with their impoverished ancestors has provided them with the computers and publishers and educations to claim indignantly and erroneously that the poor such as their ancestors in fact got poorer in goods and spirit—refutes the very claim. Pomeranz's and Topik's own ancestors were $3-a-day folk, like yours and mine. The detested capitalism permitted the descendents—Pomeranz and Topik and McCloskey, for example—to specialize in the arcania of Chinese or Latin American or British economic history, instead of cooking potatoes or mending clogs.

We all—my sweetly tender-minded left-wing friends and my harshly tough-minded right-wing friends and I—want the poor to do well. No one of sense cares very much how splendidly the good folk of Fisher Island, Florida, are doing in their mansions. True, the right wing is often foolishly impatient with the poor ("Get a job, you bum—preferably as a high-level financial advisor like me!"), and is reluctant to admit that the conservative institutions it admires with such affecting piety are sometimes instruments of class or racial or gender domination. Harvard College discriminated against Jews from the early 1920s on and until lately continued to, in a lesser degree.[17] The hospitals in the South were segregated, leaving the jazz singer Bessie Smith to die in 1937 on the way to a remote Negroes-only hospital; and racism still reigns, in a lesser degree. But the left wing in turn, ably represented here by Wallerstein and Pomeranz and Topik and Klein, is reluctant to admit that it was bourgeois innovation, not government protection or union organization, that made most poor people 1800 to the present so massively better off. As it has. If we get into the right jobs and innovate the right products, said the nineteenth-century liberals, it's win-lose-win-win-win-win. And so it was, and shockingly beyond what they expected.

We must not allow the threnody for the world we have lost to deafen us to the cheerful epithalamium for the world we have gained. Mill complained in 1848 about the right-wing version of the anti-industrial threnody then forming in the writings of Benjamin Disraeli and Mill's friend Thomas Carlyle (in this and many other respects the recent far left has revived the arguments of the old far right): in "the theory of dependence and protection . . . the lot of the poor . . . should be regulated *for* them, not *by* them. . . . This is the ideal of the future, in the minds of those whose dissatisfaction with the present assumes the form of affection and regret towards the past."[18] Let lords and experts rule. One sees it now in the nudging (and pushing) that even the sweet statists Thaler and Sunstein and Robert Frank favor.[19] Or as Bastiat put it about the same time as Mill, against the notion that "the government should know everything and foresee everything in order to manage the lives of the people, and the people need only let themselves be taken care of. . . . Nothing is more senseless than to base so many expectations on the state, that is, to assume the existence of collective wisdom and foresight after taking for granted the existence of individual imbecility and improvidence."[20] Conservatives and progressives alike suppose that village elders or members of the French Assembly or Cornell economists or University of Chicago law professors, or anyway our sort of people, are better suited to deciding about innovations than are mere peasants noting the advantage of a better sickle or mere railway men noting the advantage of a through route from Paris to Madrid. As the great liberal Lionel Trilling wrote in 1950, the danger is that "we who are liberal and progressive know that the poor are our equals in every sense except that of being equal to us." And in another essay, quoted by the professor of English James Seaton in his own far-reaching book in 1996, Trilling wrote that "we must be aware of the dangers that lie in our most generous wishes," because "when once we have made our fellow men the object of our enlightened interest [we] go on to make them the objects of our pity, then of our wisdom, ultimately of our coercion."[21] Every nurse or mother knows the danger, and when a lover for the beloved's own sake fends it off.

Seaton, who praises Trilling by criticizing the late Richard Rorty (a philosopher whose sophisticated epistemology I much admired, but whose naïve economics I could never persuade him to modify), notes that "Despite Rorty's celebration of irony, his definition of liberals [in the peculiar American use of the word] as the people who hate cruelty encourages the seductive (for liberals) notion that the [mere] expression of liberal opinions guarantees personal innocence in a cruel world."[22] You sit down with a cup of dark coffee and a nice croissant to read the *New York Times,* venting daily your hatred of the cruelties recorded there, and as a result are yourself saved, regardless of whether policies of "protection" advocated in its pages do the poor and tortured any actual good. You give personal witness to Christ risen and are saved, regardless of whether preaching hatred of the damned through a megaphone on the corner of State Street and Washington actually does any actual good for the people passing by. It is not incidental that American Progressivism had one large root in the children of ministers of the Word. The fact explains much about the contrast with the Marxist-based left of Europe, and the oddly moralistic character of the resulting American "liberal" politics (Rorty's, for example, as the grandson of the Baptist theologian and Social Gospel leader Walter Rauschenbusch).

45

AND THE BOURGEOIS ERA WARRANTS
THEREFORE NOT POLITICAL OR
ENVIRONMENTAL PESSIMISM

The economist Bryan Caplan has argued that the economist disagrees with the average citizen on four points.[1] The economist says that markets work well on their own because of profits, that foreigners deserve as much ethical weight as we do, that production for consumption (not "jobs") is the point, and that things are getting better and better. The average citizen believes on the contrary that the market in, say, food needs close regulation (which is to say that the discipline of profit for good bread and publicity for bad bread does not suffice), that protection of present job-holders against the "flood" of Chinese goods is ethically justified, that a new football stadium "generating jobs" must be a good idea, too, and that the sky is always falling.

I would add a fifth disagreement. The average citizen does not really believe that her paid work is beneficial to others. It's just a job, she thinks. I pretend to work and they pretend to pay me. She therefore believes that only charity or volunteer work "gives something back to the community." By contrast the economist, who looks at the economy from the eighth floor, sees markets and innovation as enormous engines of (often unintended) altruism. We do good by doing well. Profits, whether in our own jobs or in great industrial enterprises, have the function of drawing out our eager attempts to help customers by devising new ways of doing things. As Smith famously put it in 1776, "As every individual, therefore, endeavors as much as he can both to employ his capital . . . that its produce may be of the greatest value; every individual necessarily labors to render the annual revenue of the society as great as he can. He generally, indeed, neither intends to promote the public interest, nor knows how much he is promoting it

['I pretend to work']. . . . He intends only his own gain, and he is in this, as in many other cases, led by an invisible hand to promote an end which was no part of his intention. Nor is it always the worse for the society that it was no part of it. By pursuing his own interest he frequently promotes that of the society more effectually than when he really intends to promote it. I have never known much good done by those who affected to trade for the public good."[2]

Caplan argues that an economy governed on Citizen principles will impoverish the citizens. He worries, as many have since Buchanan and Hayek and Bastiat and Tocqueville and Mill, that a democratic politics can lead to disastrously protectionist and redistributive policies, as in Peron's Argentina. He's right. It is sadly true that democratic politics unprotected by a rhetoric of free trade and creative destruction and bourgeois virtues can ruin economies, if it kills innovation. (Democracy is thus the worst system—except for all those others that have been tried from time to time.) Every agricultural economy until Holland and Britain and British America was governed on a similarly self-destructive theory (though it took a long time for even the Dutch and British and Americans to look anything like *democratically* governed). The ruling theory for ages was the Aristocratic principle that poor people exist for the comfort of a small group of lords and priests and kings.

Bizarrely, the Aristocratic policy and the Citizen policy closely resemble each other in what they recommend. Against the positive-sum theory of the bourgeoisie, they recommend expropriation of bourgeois profit and the close regulation of markets,with xenophobia, irrational projects of glorious public works, comfort for a small group (in the Citizen case: public school teachers, public-service union workers, and state university professors), a protectionism amounting to staying forever in the same job, and a grim zero-sum belief that one person's or one country's gain must be another's loss—and that only charitable redistribution therefore can help the poor at home or abroad.

The point here is that the brief reign of the entirely new and more genial Bourgeois Economist's Principles led to the modern world and its Great Fact of astounding and scope-expanding economic growth. Yet in many countries, and in some groups in all countries, the civic religion recommended by the clerisy remains a version of the Citizen or the Aristocratic policy—protectionist, paternalistic, antitechnological, proudly anticapitalist from the left or the right, allied in Europe with anti-Americanism. French thinkers of the 1960s, for example, wrote elaborate books on the economy without reading any books on non-Marxist economics (and little enough of Marx). Gilles Deleuze, Jean Baudrillard, Georges Bataille, and other worthies talked about the economy without an acquaintance with the best that had been thought and written about it, excepting *The Communist Manifesto* and a few pages of the *Prison Notebooks*. The practice persists in university departments of the humanities worldwide, evolving into a routine corrosive of critical thought.

And therefore it persists in a good deal of teaching worldwide. The required texts for French secondary-school students of social sciences, for example, three volumes called *Histoire du XXe siècle* (2005), declares that "economic growth imposes a hectic form of life, producing overwork, stress, nervous depression, cardiovascular disease, and, according to some, even the development of cancer."[3] Such an assertion contradicts the experience of the hundreds of millions of bourgeois and working-class Westerners, and now Easterners, whose lives are spent in education up to their early twenties, and in retirement to a life of leisure (twenty years longer than the life expectancy of their grandparents) by their early sixties—or as early as age fifty if they are engine drivers on the French railways; and age fifty-five if they are railway managers—and a similar arrangement for public safety workers under union contract in the United States). In 1910 a job working sixty hours a week in a factory spinning cotton in Lille might just possibly have been more stressful than one nowadays working thirty-five hours a week as a computer salesperson in Paris, or even as a train driver. And before that, in 1810, a factory job in Lille just might have seemed less in the way of overwork and nervous depression than farmwork west of Puy-de-Dôme in the Auvergne, with no work at all in late winter and hectic harvests and endless threshing, and the children starving in April. At any rate people did move from the farm in the Auvergne to the textile factory in Lille, with alacrity, and later a smaller distance from the remaining farms to the Michelin tire factory. And then they did move, *avec plaisir*, from the factories to computer sales in Paris or to driving *le train à grande vitesse*.

Recent decades, the French school text admits, have witnessed "doubled wealth"—but also "doubled unemployment, poverty, and exclusion, whose ill effects constitute the background for a profound social malaise." Yet the unemployment in France, and the barring for example of French Muslims from wealth, might perhaps be caused not by "American" innovation but by exclusive elite education in France, devaluing university education outside of the *grandes écoles*, and by segregation of the Muslims in Le Corbusier–inspired high-rise concentration camps around Paris far from factories, and by heavy regulation of the terms of employment—for example, the near impossibility of firing someone in France once she has miraculously achieved a job. France ranked in 2006, according to the World Bank, 144 out of 178 countries in ease of employing workers. Germany, also then with a high unemployment rate, was 137, and South Africa, with an appalling unemployment rate (because of employment laws imitated from Germany), 91. This against low-unemployment countries such as the U.K. (21) and the U.S. (1).[4]

Capitalism, according to the French instructors of the young, is "brutal," "savage," and worst of all (wait for it) "American." Globalized capitalism is said to be much worse, for example, than those lovely examples of thoroughgoing socialism covering a quarter of the globe in 1970 from Cuba to North Vietnam. Many on the American left have agreed with their overseas comrades, and would advocate still, as the French schoolteachers put it, "the regulation of capitalism on a global scale"—retrying yet again the glorious experiment of central-planning-with-gulags during 1917–1989. Such opinions have deep roots among the clerisy. In 1966, at the height of Western optimism about the future of socialism, the United Nations issued an International Covenant on Economic, Social, and Cultural Rights which did not so much as mention the right to property. The true liberal heroes from Locke to Jefferson to Mill to Willa Cather spun furiously in their graves.

∞

The new alternative to central-planning socialism is environmentalism. It is taught now as a civic religion in the American schools (and with an even more fevered rhetoric in Germany and the Netherlands and especially in Sweden), the way anticommunism was in the American schools of the 1950s or nationalism in the French schools of 1890s or the great chain of being in the English schools of the 1590s. The physicist Freeman Dyson, no right-wing crank, wrote in the *New York Review of Books*, no right-wing rag, that "There is a worldwide secular religion which we may call environmentalism, holding that we are stewards of the earth, [that] the despoiling of the planet . . . is a sin, and that the path of righteousness is to live as frugally as possible. The ethics of environmentalism are being taught to children . . .

all over the world. Environmentalism has replaced socialism as the leading secular religion."[5] The economist and theologian Robert Nelson argues that the American civic religion was once in fact bourgeois economics, but has become progressive environmentalism.[6] The religion of the environment approaches closest to the old forms in Sweden. The worship starts at home and in the kindergartens, with stories of the beneficent troll Mulle, and is carried on in the rest of school, taking up substantial parts of the curriculum in the manner of religious instruction. By adulthood every Sweden is a passionate nature worshiper, and spends her Sundays picking berries in the woods. Humans need such contact with the transcendent (though the theologians observe that worshiping anything short of God has the problem of idolatry for things that will pass). Sweden nowadays is no more a secular country than it was in the time of the Norse gods, or of Lutheranism. The Swedes disdain Allah, yet worship passionately the transcendence of Mulle and Laxe and Fjällfina and Nova.

The environmental left has now worshipfully adopted Malthus, not on fresh scientific evidence but on the mathematical "logic" that "resources" "must" be limited. (Such evidence-free logic, requiring no wearisome study of the social sciences or of social facts, might explain why a mechanical environmentalism appeals to so many physical and especially biological scientists.) Forget about Marx, says the new left of 2010. Hurrah for Malthus.

Since 1798, however, the evidence has been no kinder to the clever priest-economist Malthus than to the clever philosopher-journalist-economist Marx. The economic historian Eric Jones notes that "economic history provides the antidote to the assumption that there is a static and readily exhaustible resource base." Yet the "fears of these kinds are hydra-headed and astonishingly resistant to contrary evidence."[7] The new environmental left has ignored the overwhelming evidence that incomes depend on human creativity, not on natural resources, that innovation has unleashed creativity in resource-poor places like Japan or Hong Kong, and that the resulting high incomes generate a supply of and a demand for a better environment. By what might be called an environmental Say's Law ("supply creates its own demand"), the creativity of innovation generates the supply of environmental improvement and the enrichment from innovation creates the demand for the improvement, by the newly embourgeoisfied citizens. It is starting to do so even in China, which now has a small but vigorous and necessarily courageous environmental movement. It has already done so in Europe and East Asia and the United States and other high-income places. The air quality of rich cities, for example, has improved radically since 1950.

But the hydra keeps growing new heads, against the evidence. A leading spokesman for the environmental left, Paul Ehrlich, wrote in *The Population Bomb* in 1968 that "The battle to feed all of humanity is over. In the 1970s and 1980s hundreds of millions of people will starve to death in spite of any crash programs embarked upon now. At this late date nothing can prevent a substantial increase in the world death rate."[8] After Ehrlich's firm scientific prediction of 1968, the world's death rate (and very soon the birthrate) fell sharply. The late economist Julian Simon, who articulated the economic findings from the 1950s to the 1990s against the population-bombers—and famously won a wager with Ehrlich against the notion that we were running out of mineral "resources"—wrote in 1996 that the bombers "are reduced to saying that all the evidence of history [that population growth in modern conditions is good for economic growth, not bad, and that economic growth results in lower, not higher, population growth] is merely 'temporary' and must reverse 'sometime,' which is the sort of statement that is outside the canon of ordinary science."[9]

The bombers, though, are hard to embarrass with scientific evidence, and carry on railing against motherhood. Many of them are fine scientists in their own fields. They become unsteady, though, when they venture into economics without troubling to read any. The paleontologist Niles Eldridge, for example, quoted in 1995 with approval a geologist at Columbia who had predicted in the 1960s on the basis of "simple measures of the volumes of the great sedimentary basins" that the world would run out of recoverable petroleum in the mid-1990s.[10] In fact after the 1960s the "proven oil reserves" grew worldwide (a miracle unless you realize that "proving" is itself an economic activity), which by 1995 Eldridge must have known, and the price of oil corrected for inflation had not risen. Yet he did not draw the appropriate lesson in economics from his error, or from Ehrlich's or the Club of Rome's similar errors during the 1960s, which he also quoted with approval. He did not see that in a world in which people respond to economic incentives, and to environmental worries, too, the mechanical extrapolation of economic or environmental variables is not going to work very well. For example, it didn't from the 1960s to the 1990s. Oil got temporarily expensive, and so the oil companies spent more money finding previously unknown reserves.

Infant mortality went down, birth control cheapened, women went into the paid workforce, and so mothers had fewer children. A path to a fuller life through education opened up, and so young people took it, and parents had fewer children, the better to invest heavily in each child's education when back work became less in demand relative to brain work.

In 1830 Macaulay had asked, "On what principle is it that, when we see nothing but improvement behind us, we are to expect nothing but deterioration before us?"[11] On what principle indeed? Ehrlich's 1968 book sold famously, and he continued well into the new millennium to defend the propositions that the Green Revolution and the fall in the world's birthrate and the rise of life expectancies and such triumphs of environmental reversals as the revivifying of Lake Erie, or the banning of soft coal dirtying the cities, or the banning of spray-can propellants eroding the ozone layer, are temporary and must reverse sometime, and that we have seen our best days and will see nothing but deterioration before us.

Despite its gross scientific failures, however, the environmental left has won the rhetoric. By now for instance, without evidence or much reasoning, the debate is closed about such a vague and questionably ethical idea as "sustainability" (which entails imposing burdens on present-day poor people in aid of a distant future generation likely to be very much richer). In the same way during the 1950s the discussion about such a vague and questionable idea as "progressive taxation" was closed without evidence or much reasoning, or during the 1910s the discussion about such a vague and questionable idea as "racial degeneration."[12]

∞

The economists have long tried to provide the reasoning and evidence— to the point where convinced environmentalists have in vexation stopped listening to them, so painful is the experience, and have stopped trying to show that the economists are wrong scientifically or ethically. Allyn Young, the economist responsible for inspiring the new generation of growth theorists in the late twentieth century, wrote thus in 1928 (he died prematurely, and his influence was tenuous until recently revived):

> No analysis of the forces making for economic equilibrium, forces which we might say are tangential at any moment of time, will serve to illumine this field, for movements away from equilibrium, departures from previous trends, are characteristic of it. Not much is to be gained by probing into it to see how in-

creasing returns show themselves in the costs of individual firms and in the prices at which they offer their products. . . . The counterforces which are continually defeating the forces which make for economic equilibrium are more pervasive and more deeply rooted in the constitution of the modern economic system than we commonly realize.[13]

One can only agree, and affirm that such agglomerating and upscaling models are plausible, at any rate to the point of offsetting diseconomies of scale. My economist colleagues (and especially my future-economist undergraduate students) are very, very smart. Their models properly deny, for example, the environmentalists' Malthusian notion that increasing population results in such strong diminishing returns to inputs of labor that people are going to be driven by a population bomb back to $3 a day. On the contrary, say the economists following Allyn Young (and I agree: otherwise I lose my union card), the natural resources on which the environmentalists obsess are unimportant constraints in the modern world. The "ultimate resource," as Julian Simon put it, is brain power.[14] If we are smart enough we can make cheap food, and can fix and store atmospheric carbon. And therefore when the world has become educated and free, and when the populist hostility to bourgeois innovation has faded, then success will breed more success. There develop, the economists put it, those "economies of scale." Virtuous spirals.

Getting more people and agglomerating them into cities becomes therefore a good thing, not bad, if the people have more going for them than strong backs and the ability to reproduce. Goldstone notes that "by the late twentieth century, in every 20 years [over any one generation, that is] the number of people being born was greater than the entire population of the world 200 years before."[15] But in the circumstances of the Age of Innovation this became good, not bad. In each generation we have more chances of a Socrates, an Ibn-Khaldūn, an Admiral Zheng He, an Isaac Newton, a James Watt than in all generations before 1800. Africa's genetic diversity—all the rest of us came from merely a thousand or so Africans, on account of the "founder effect," as the population geneticists call the falling away of lineages in small populations—implies that when over the next fifty years or so Africa acquires a European standard of living, it is going to dominate world culture, producing ten Mozarts and twenty Einsteins.[16]

But observe: without the dual ideas of the dignity and liberty for ordinary life and extraordinary innovation, no innovation is going to occur, no one is going to get properly educated, and we are back in the world of lives poor, nasty, brutish, and short (though by no means solitary)—a bomber's Malthusian world in which diseconomies to labor input overwhelm economies of scale. Changing social ideas, in short, explain the Industrial Revolution. Material and economic factors—such as trade or investment or exploitation or population growth or the inevitable rising of classes or the protections to private property—do not. They were unchanging backgrounds, or they had already happened long before, or they didn't actually happen at the time they are supposed to have happened, or they were weak, or they were beside the point, or they were consequences of the rhetorical change, or they required the dignity and liberty of ordinary people to have the right effect. And it seems that such material events were not in turn the main causes of the ethical and rhetorical change itself. On the contrary, for largely noneconomic reasons, the prestige of a bourgeois prudence rose around 1700, in the way northwest European people talked, within an economic conversation still honoring a balance of virtues. Economic prudence gradually came to be regarded as virtuous, though merely one among the virtues of a good townsperson.

46

BUT AN AMIABLE, IF GUARDED, OPTIMISM

If proinnovation ideas of the elite caused the Industrial Revolution, and if the artistic and intellectual elite turned against innovation after 1848, as it did, first in nationalism and then in socialism, and then in national socialism, and finally in radical environmentalism, why didn't such turns bring to a halt the Industrial Revolution?

One reply is that a split developed between the elite and public opinion, in a new world in which public opinion came to matter as much as or more than elite opinion. By now the clerical elite despises advertising, and advocates central planning, and believes we are doomed by population bombs and the destruction of the environment. Other people don't. Many artists after 1848, and at length professors, moved to the left, and developed a socialist and at length an environmentalist rhetoric. Others of them at the time moved to the right, and developed an elitist and at length a fascist rhetoric against free public opinion itself. But free public opinion outside the elite had meanwhile become favorable to innovation, and more and more it ran the political show, to the disgust of conservatives and progressives.

In economic scholarship an emblem of the elite's scorn for bourgeois virtues is the treatment of Friedrich Hayek, the great libertarian economist from Austria, a naturalized Briton. Mention of Hayek can to this day evoke ignorant sneers on the left and center even of economics. While he was still at the London School of Economics, an internationally famous economic scientist, the equal of J. M. Keynes in scientific reputation at the time, he wrote *The Road to Serfdom* (1944), an attack on socialism, then immensely fashionable. In Europe no one greatly minded such a popular book. But

when the book appeared in the United States it caused a furor, partly because a long précis of it appeared in the popular and steeply right-slanting
Reader's Digest. Because of *The Road*, Hayek, the equal of the great Keynes
in professional opinion up to 1944, was denied in 1950 an appointment in
economics at the University of Chicago, and spent his years at Chicago, 1950
to 1962, in the Committee on Social Thought—no hardship, that, certainly;
but the rejection from the fourth floor of the Social Science Building was
bizarre.

Lawyers and at length educated businesspeople, however, adhered to the
market values that Hayek admired, against both left and right. In the United
States the Eisenhower administration was another emblem of the split. Elite
opinion sneered at Ike and his economic policies—Eisenhower's cabinet
was called "eight millionaires and a plumber" (the secretary of labor, Martin
P. Durkin, had been the president of the plumbers' union). But the bourgeois policies stayed, and worked pretty well.

And certain institutions and countries stored the idea of bourgeois dignity and liberty, which could re-emerge after the pessimism on the left and
right about market societies in the decades following the 1930s had passed.
Hard political turns to the right could and did stop industrial revolutions.
Nationalist central planning in aid of a neo-Roman glory, war, *Lebensraum*,
and the corporate state was just as crippling as socialist central planning in
aid of war and steel and farm tractors. Yet, perhaps because fascism was in
such disrepute after World War II, the most obvious threat to liberalism
came to be seen as coming from the left. Economics itself went through a
flirtation with socialism, from 1933 to 1981, but then returned strongly to its
true liberal roots. Nonelite opinion in the United States (see the *Reader's
Digest*), and to a lesser degree even in welfare-state Britain, was always a
reservoir of antisocialist opinion. A world without a United States might
have permanently turned after 1945 against the Industrial Revolution, just as
a world without Britain and Holland would not have developed bourgeois
dignity and liberty in the first place.[1]

A deeper reply is that the turn to the left, and many of the turns to the
right, did in fact stop the Industrial Revolution and its follow-on, at any
rate in the places where anti-innovation was well and truly tried, such as
Communist China or Fascist Spain. To be sure, in 1945 it looked like market
societies were exhausted, and that even in the United States socialism was in
the cards. The best economists, such as Joseph Schumpeter, John Maynard

Keynes, Alvin Hansen, Oskar Lange, Paul Samuelson, and Abba Lerner, thought at the time—with greater or lesser pleasure at the thought—that the world was moving from capitalism to socialism, whether or not the embattled democracies survived. Many people were impressed in particular by the apparent Soviet economic success of the 1930s, whatever its precise dimension or its human cost (60 million souls, shall we say), and were very impressed indeed by Stalin's victory over Hitler.

They could not see that in the longer run, when opportunities for imitation had been used up, the admired central-planning socialism could not achieve real innovation. Among students of the Soviet experience only a few, such as G. Warren Nutter and Alexander Gerschenkron and Abram Bergson, stood in the 1950s and 1960s against the prevailing elite opinion that socialism in Eastern Europe had successfully forced fast growth superior to what capitalism would have achieved there.[2] It was later discovered that the Soviet rate of growth fell steadily after the heroic (and imitative) age of the 1930s, reaching such low levels in the 1980s that the growth of productivity relative to inputs was negative.[3] Indeed, in 1995 the World Bank economists William Easterly and Stanley Fischer reckoned that *only* in the 1950s was Soviet "total factor productivity" greater than zero.[4] In Soviet ideology the capital input was treated as a free good (*capital*-ism is evil—only labor produces value—and therefore capital should be valued at zero), and consequently capital in machines and buildings was overused, in "extensive growth." Build giant factories and full speed ahead.

It became apparent to some economists that central planning socialism such as that in the Soviet Union was an exceptionally bad idea in practice, and economists such as Hayek and Ludwig von Mises had already offered cogent reasons at a conceptual level why the Soviet Union must fail. Yet as late as 1984 the economist John Kenneth Galbraith was writing, "[That] the Soviet system has made great material progress in recent years is evident both from the statistics and from the general urban scene. . . . One sees it in the appearance of solid well-being of the people on the streets [Galbraith did not perhaps spend much time in the provinces] . . . and the general aspect of restaurants, theaters, and shops. . . . Partly, the Russian system succeeds because, in contrast with the Western industrial economies, it makes full use of its manpower." As late as 1985 the great economist Paul Samuelson wrote that "what counts is results, and there can be no doubt that the Soviet planning system has been a powerful engine for economic growth.

... The Soviet model has surely demonstrated that a command economy is capable of mobilizing resources for rapid growth." Even in 1989 Lester Thurow asked, "Can economic command [that is, the industrial policy that Thurow advocated] significantly . . . accelerate the growth process? The remarkable performance of the Soviet Union suggests that it can. . . . Today the Soviet Union is a country whose economic achievements bear comparison with those of the United States."[5] When the USSR collapsed and the Soviet statistics were at length opened—or indeed when in the early 1960s the crops had failed—Nutter and Gerschenkron and Bergson were proven correct. Output and consumption per head were a small fraction of that in the United States.

But the still deeper reply is that once the cat of dignity and liberty was out of the bag, she was hard to stuff back in. It was not impossible locally, as in Argentina or in Poland for a while, but the cat was on the prowl. If we work hard at it we can kill her again with war and tyranny and protectionism and anti-innovation. But it will be difficult.

∞

Still, if the new rhetoric of innovation is what caused the modern world, then it is possible—not logically inevitable, but possible—that losing the ideology can lose the modern world. In other words, the Age of Innovation might have led to anticapitalist ideologies that could destroy innovation. In fact on occasion, as I say, it has, in fascism and communism, and in a longer-running form in the clerisy's disdain for the bourgeoisie, and in the environmentalists' disdain for bourgeois economics. All such movements were annoyed reactions to the bourgeoisie and its innovations and its vulgarly prudent way of thinking

The problem is the old one of "the cultural contradictions of capitalism," as Daniel Bell put it in 1978, anticipated by Schumpeter's gloomy declaration in 1942—one of the darkest years of a dark decade—that the future lay with socialism, and Hayek's of 1944 that the clerisy were advocating a road to serfdom, or Aron's in 1955 that Marxism was the "opiate of the intellectuals." Expressed as hope rather than a problem, the reversion in rhetoric to central planning socialism is Karl Polanyi's "great transformation" of 1944, the hoped-for "double movement" in which society reacts against innovation and reestablishes a suitably embedded and conservative economy under central government control.

By now you will know that I would regard a loss of bourgeois and in-novative rhetoric as a deep worry, not a hope, and that the main purpose of my hopeful sestet on the Bourgeois Era is to argue against accepting such a disastrous loss. As the economic historian Stephen Davies puts it, "To rec-oncile the bourgeois and the artist [and intellectual] is one of the tasks of our time."[6] We need bourgeois virtues, the principal seven in various idio-syncratic combinations that frame our ethical lives—not merely the virtue of Prudence Only. We need the bourgeois rhetoric supporting such a rich and enriching palette of virtues. Bourgeois innovation supported by such a rhetoric has elevated the poor of the world. On the scale of actual relief of poverty from let-it-rip innovation practiced in England in the nineteenth century and nowadays in places like China and India, the policies and pro-grams directed at the poor have been often less than helpful. The dribbles of personal or religious charity, or government-to-government foreign aid, or helping hands from your good friends of the middle class, have often been negligible in size, and often enough have perversely damaged the poor, or have been stolen by the rich on their way to the poor. One cannot explain an increase of real income in a now rich country like the United States or Italy by a factor of, say, ten since 1900 by citing eight-hour-day laws or protec-tion for women's work (for example, the American protective legislation in the 1920s that forbad women from working more than eight hours, which made it impossible for them to become supervisors who come early and leave late). And if minimum-wage laws could explain a factor of ten, that would be wonderful—an explosion of real income caused by forbidding certain transactions, and moreover by sheer act of Parliament. Unhappily the activities of governments are no such miracle workers. Courts, public health, some police, some armies, civil rights laws, and, until seized by bu-reaucracies and unions bent on lifetime employment and large pensions, public schools have been excellent ideas. Yet the great bulk of modern en-richment has to be attributed to innovation. Only a tiny part—if indeed it is positive for the poor as a whole—can be put to the credit of government or union in markets.

And reverting to full-scale, central-planning socialism or fascism of the sort that many of the clerisy still pine for on old socialist grounds or on old nationalist grounds or on new environmental grounds would be a catas-trophe. Or so one would judge from the human results of actually existing socialism or fascism that prevailed over large swathes of the globe during the twentieth century. Surprisingly, the liberal capitalism that left and right scorned as wishy-washy in the 1920s and had little hope for in the 1930s and 1940s, and which is in the 1990s and 2000s in danger (as Francis Fukuyama put it) of boring people into not defending it, turned out to be the successful experiment. It would be scientifically strange to ignore the material and spiritual failures of full-blown socialism from 1917 to the present, from the Union of Soviet Socialist Republics to the Democratic People's Republic of North Korea, or of full-blown fascism from 1922 to 1945, with continuations after 1945 in Spain and Portugal, and in Iraq and Syria. Likewise it would be unscientific to ignore the present-day examples of market innovation in China and India, or to ignore the beginnings of innovation dating from the rhetorical change on the shores of the North Sea around 1700, and the factor of sixteen or one hundred.

On the other hand, for the same reasons I have adduced here for not believing that efficiency gains are the heart of past economic growth, I do not believe that in the immediate future the inefficiencies of a welfare state or of heavily unionized workforces are greatly to be worried over—so long as innovation supported by dignity and liberty for the bourgeoisie is not greatly damaged. Harberger Triangles are not the way to great wealth, and consequently the loss of a few of them from economically inefficient arrangements is not greatly to be lamented. That in fact was Harberger's finding, rather contrary to his (and my) ideological predispositions. Prudence is a virtue, and a good thing. But the other of the Seven Virtues—temperance, justice, courage, love, faith, and hope—support innovation, too, if embourgeoisfied.

The Swedish economy, for example, retains a good deal of bourgeois and innovative dynamism, for all its payments after the 1960s to able-bodied people who decide not to work (ordinary absenteeism by those who work, in this healthiest of modern countries, is fully fifty days a year, a new and clinical version of the old Saint Monday ["I am allergic to electricity," say the nonworking Swedes]).[7] Indeed, one might argue that the welfare state allows Swedes to take an entrepreneurial chance, rather like the higher average income in the United States and the nonstigma there attached to bankruptcy. In 1960 Sweden was a normal, rich, and capitalist economy, having moved from the 1850s on account of liberal reforms from being the poorest country in Europe (barring Russia only) to being the fourth richest in the world. For four decades centered on 1910 Sweden was the home of the largest number per capita in the world of first-rate true-liberal economists. Never has nationalization, for example, been popular in Sweden, and most companies are private: Saab's automotive division was private, and when owned by General Motors was calmly allowed in 2009 to go bankrupt. In 1938 at Saltsjöbaden, while Roosevelt in the United States was still ranting against economic royalists and terrifying the investing class, the unions and corporations in Sweden were agreeing to industrial peace, under a Social Democratic regime that gave wide latitude to the industrialists for investing in technology, and earning profits. The liberal economic spurt in the Sweden of the late nineteenth century found an echo in the welfare-state spurt of the mid-twentieth. True, the era of more dogmatic and union-driven extensions of the welfare state from 1960 to 1990 (Olof Palme said in the 1960s, "The political winds are to the left: let us set sail") drove Swedish income down to seventeenth in the world—though with the gain of the elimination of much poverty.[8] But welfare states such as Sweden's or Holland's, we know by now, have not in fact been the first step on the road to serfdom. They have not been yet, at any rate, despite such Swedish or Dutch assumptions, shocking to many of us Americans or Italians or Indians, that government officials almost always have the public good in mind,or that it is quite natural for high-culture institutions and risk-capital committees to be functions of the state.

As an empirical scientist I have to admit that social democracy has been a success, at least in countries with traditions of good administration (and after having achieved modern standards of living under thoroughly capitalist regimes; in fact such a sequence is orthodox Marxism: socialism is plucked like a fruit from the tree of mature capitalism). I have to admit so, if I am also going to fault the central-planning socialists or the radical environmentalists for not attending to the evidence. The evidence suggests that some countries can have social provision at a very generous level ("generous" with other peoples' money, a grumpy libertarian would add) without becoming communist dictatorships. (Others, like Venezuela, though, try to move straight to communist dictatorship.)

The danger of an all-devouring state is anyway as great nowadays from the right as from the left. Attacks on President Obama as a "socialist" neglected to mention that the Bush administration expanded the government in its military form to much the same extent as the Obama administration did in its nonmilitary form. Western European social democracy is surely democratic, at any rate by contrast with such cases as the German "Democratic" Republic, and has obviated what was in 1939 the very lively alternative of fascism (recent anti-immigrant movements aside).[9]

We need to strengthen the rhetoric of innovation. That does not mean celebrating "greed is good," which I argued at length in *The Bourgeois Virtues* is a childish and unethical rhetoric, however popular it has been on Wall Street and in the Department of Economics. Here I quite agree with my Marxist friends. David Harvey uses Paul Trainor's definition of neoliberalism: it "values market exchange as 'an ethic in itself, capable of acting as a guide to all human action.'"[10] That's Prudence Only. I say it's spinach, and say to hell with it. Strengthening the rhetoric of innovation does mean acknowledging *all* the virtues in our commercial societies, together with a sober weighing of their vices, such as a dangerous enthusiasm for Prudence Only. It means celebrating hopeful innovation and the respecting of market deals, if arranged with justice. It does not mean supporting big banks against small, or making American manufacturing "competitive" by picking winners to receive government subsidies. It means accepting creative destruction. We must not, of course, worship the bourgeois virtues. That would be in Abrahamic terms prideful idolatry. But we must not, either, cast them out thoughtlessly as Baal or Mammon. That tactic merely invites businesspeople to omit ethics (since they are anyway damned) and to recur to Prudence Only, the sin of greed.

The political scientist Richard Boyd summarizes the deep version of the "contradictions of capitalism" that people like Frank Knight or Robert Putnam or Francis Fukuyama have worried about: "The combination of tremendous wealth and extreme inequality, unscrupulous habits, disenchantment, individualism, the debasement of taste, and the conflicts bred by capital may conspire to undermine for once and for all the pre-modern social capital upon which liberal institutions depend."[11] I don't think so, on numerous grounds articulated here and in *The Bourgeois Virtues*.

But there is at the least a possibility of a fatal residuum of *ideological* corruption. Take for example the fraught issue of CEO compensation in the United States. Richard Nardelli was perhaps not worth every dime of the $50 million a year he earned for running Home Depot into the ground, or for the comparable amount he got during the descent of Chrysler into bankruptcy. On the other hand, few economists can be found who care very much. We economists have long pointed out, and correctly, that CEO pay even of the grotesque variety is a trivial percentage of the earnings of the companies involved. And yet in rhetorical terms the noneconomists are right. The danger, many people argue, is that the grotesque salaries and the ego-pleasing rides on corporate jets and the vacations for the whole family paid for by suppliers to the corporation undermine the American rhetoric that accepts creative destruction. *That* matters.

∞

A good deal hinges on whether the new understanding of our economic and ethical past that I have argued for here is true or false. If true, a finding that an ethical and rhetorical and ideological and conjective change made the modern world would be scientifically important. The Victorian travel writer and skeptic Alexander Kinglake suggested that every church should bear on its front door a large sign, "Important If True."[12] So here. Economic history faces no more important question than why industrialization and the reduction of mass poverty first started, and especially why it continued. The continuation made us richer and freer and more capable of human achievement than our ancestors. The latest continuation—located most spectacularly in China and India, of all surprising places—shows that the whole world can be so. It shows, in case you doubted it, that Europe was not special in genetics. It shows that in a world of innovation the curse of Malthus lacks force.

For instance, if ideas and ethics and "rhetoric" contributed largely to such a happy result, then perhaps we should point our social telescopes also toward ideas and ethics and rhetoric. Looking fixedly at trade or imperialism or demography or unions or property law—very interesting though all of them are—will not do the whole of the scientific job. Ideas are the dark matter of history, ignored for a century or so 1890–1980. In those days, I have noted, we were all historical materialists.

To be able to detect the dark matter we will need a new, more idea-oriented economics, which would admit for example that language shapes an economy. For such a humanistic science of economics—explored in this and related books, and on which a few others of us are working—the methods of the human sciences would become as scientifically relevant as the methods of mathematics and statistics now properly are.[13] Such a widened economic science would scrutinize literary texts *and* simulate on computers, analyze stories *and* model maxima, clarify with philosophy *and* measure with statistics, inquire into the meaning of the sacred *and* lay out the accounting of the profane. The practitioners of the humanities and the social sciences would stop sneering at each other, and would start reading each other's books and sitting in each other's courses. As their colleagues in the physical and biological sciences so naturally do, they would get down to cooperating for the scientific task. It is not very difficult, as one can see in the education of graduate students. A bright humanist can learn enough mathematics and statistics in a couple of years to follow their uses in economics. A bright economist, with rather more difficulty, can in a couple of years learn enough about rhetoric and close reading to follow their uses in the English Department. What prevents such scientific cooperation is sneering ignorance, not the difficulty of the task.

It will not have escaped you that there is of course a political moral, too. If the economy were understood as more than Prudence Only, then we could remoralize it. If innovation were an upshot of desirable ethical changes, then we could respect it. The rhetorical change, after all, was itself in part a feedback from dignity and liberty. Dignity and liberty were in turn the result in part (remember the diagram earlier) of the long perfected property rights of Europe, the medieval liberties of the towns, the competition among states smaller than the Asian giants, the decline of serfdom outsidesad Russia, the theory of individual dignity in Protestantism and more anciently in all Abrahamic religions, the partial liberation of women outside the Mediterranean, the mind-freeing shock of the Scientific Revolution to Europe's relatively primitive science, the uneven fall of religious and secular tyrants just when Asia was abandoning its own traditions of toleration, the emergence of at least a tiny public sphere, the careers of quite a few open to talents, the improvements in military technology that gave the West and the Chinese the weapons to defeat aristocratic warriors of horse-using steppe or elephant-using empire, the techniques of printing on paper imitated and improved from China and the Muslim world, making possible a periodical press and reasonably uncensored theaters and publishing houses. These all were imperfectly implemented 1600–1800, but startlingly novel, it seems, on the scale practiced in northwestern Europe, even allowing for recent findings that Orientalist notions of Asian backwardness are false.

If the technological change was in part a consequence of a new dignity and liberty, then we the respected and free heirs of the Bourgeois Revaluation could be modestly happy about it, without falling into the sin of pride. If our bourgeois building was not raised on foundations of imperialism or exploitation or unequal trade (excepting the brief reign of gunboats and rubber-tree slavery, and those in aid of tiny parts of the bourgeois economy), then we could admire it, though self-critically. If serious innovation were not immoral, then we could practice ethics more grown-up than a right-wing Greed is Good or a left-wing Down with the Bosses. We need to get beyond the understanding of the economic past that seemed plausible in 1848, and even to some in 1914, before the full development of professional history—sweet peasants, romantic Middle Ages, wicked mill owners, wretched machines, alienated workers, irritating consumerism on the part of social classes so obviously inferior to ours. The Marxist and the reactionary views of economic history—in many ways they are the same view—have poisoned our political lives for a century and a half. If we're going to have a future, it is desirable that we know what really happened, and listen to the lessons derived from the really-happened, and not go on and on getting inspiration for our politics from historical fairy tales of left or right.

Give a woman some rice, and you save her for a day. That's the simplest form of what Christians flatter themselves by calling "Christian charity." Give a man some seed and you save him for a year. That's the plan of investment in capital, tried for decades in foreign aid, without much success. But give a man and a woman the liberty to innovate, and persuade them to admire enterprise and to cultivate the bourgeois virtues, and you save them both for a long life of wide scope, and for successively wider lives for their children and their grandchildren, too. That's the Bourgeois Deal, which paid off in the Age of Innovation.

When bourgeois virtues do not thrive, and especially when they are not admired by other classes and by their governments and by the bourgeoisie itself, the results are sad. As the economists Virgil Storr and Peter Boettke note about the Bahamas, "Virtually all models of success to be found in the Bahamas' economic past have to be characterized as piratical," with the result that entrepreneurs there "pursue 'rents' rather than [productive] profits."[14] It hasn't worked very well to depend on a piratical greed, which is to say a self-interested prudence without the balance of other virtues such as justice (except, to speak of the actual history of piracy, democratic justice on shipboard among the pirates themselves). Contrary to a widespread opinion on left and right, such piratical Prudence Only is not characteristically bourgeois. Bernard Mandeville and Ivan Boesky got it wrong. Prudence is not the only virtue of an innovative society. People (not to speak of grass and bacteria and rats) have always been prudent, and there have always been greedy people among them unwilling to balance prudence with other virtues. What changed around 1700 was the valuation of economic and intellectual novelties within a system of all the virtues.

∞

Yet innovation, even in a proper system of the virtues, has continued to be scorned by many of our opinion makers now for a century and a half, from Thomas Carlyle to Naomi Klein. At the behest of such a clerisy we can if we wish repeat the nationalist and socialist horrors of the mid-twentieth century. If we imagine only the disruptions of a pastoral ideal, and reject the gains from innovation, we can stay poor shepherds and dirt farmers, with little scope for intellectual and spiritual growth. If we worship hierarchy and violence and the nation, we can hand our lives over to the military-industrial complex. If we abandon economic principles in our worrying about the environment, we can revert to $3 a day, and live in huts on a hillock in the woods by Walden Pond, depending on our friends in town to supply us with nails and books. Now in the early twenty-first century we can even if we wish add for good measure an antibourgeois religiosity, as new as airplanes crashing into the World Trade Center and as old as the socialist reading of the Sermon on the Mount.

But I suggest that we don't. I suggest instead that we recoup the bourgeois virtues, which have given us the scope, in von Humboldt's words, to develop the highest and most harmonious of our powers to a complete and consistent whole. We will need to abandon the materialist premise that reshuffling and efficiency, or an exploitation of the poor, made the modern world. And we will need to make a new science of history and the economy, a humanistic one that honors number and word, interest and rhetoric, behavior and meaning.

NOTES

PREFACE AND ACKNOWLEDGMENTS

1. Since the seventeenth century the word *rhetoric* has often been misunderstood as lies or bloviation. I use it in its ancient sense, "the means of [unforced] persuasion," which includes logic and metaphor, fact and story. Modern pragmatics, criticism, and social psychology have largely been a reinvention of ancient rhetoric, how words matter. If any of that strikes you as crazy or indefensible, you may wish to consult McCloskey 1985a (1998), 1990, 1994c.

2. Mueller 1999.

3. I will use the word *liberal* throughout not in its confused and twentieth-century American sense ("left-wing") but in its older and still European sense of "devoted to liberty, especially political and economic liberty." It is part of my argument that the American sense can be corrosive of true liberalism. (But so can neoconservatism.)

4. McCloskey 1990.

5. Mokyr 2010, p. 1.

6. Lanham 1993.

CHAPTER ONE: AN ECONOMIC TIDE WITHOUT ECONOMIC CAUSES

1. Strictly speaking, "1990 international Geary-Khamis dollars"—so I've inflated a bit (using the consumer price index in the USA since 1991) to bring the figures in a rough and ready way up to 2008 prices in the United States. That is, the $3 is to be understood as what you would live on in Chicago, say, in 2008 if you had the misfortune of the world's average real income in 1800. The figures were estimated by the late Angus Maddison in his amazing palace of numbers, *The World Economy* (2006), these particular numbers on p. 642. (It will become apparent how much I have relied on Angus's work, which would already have earned a Nobel Prize if economics were not so disdainful of "mere data collecting"; imagine how astronomy or biology would have done with such an attitude! Anyway, his work for me and for many others is *sine quo nullum*.) For "two centuries ago" I used the average of 'his world figures for 1700 and 1820. Economic historians agree on a factor of ten or so worldwide since the eighteenth century: for example, Easterlin 1995, p. 84.

2. In Maddison's calculation of the real per capita GDP of 12 West European countries, 1869 to 2001 (Maddison 2006, pp. 439–441; a reasonable aggregate since they were certainly tied by the business cycle, and were all developing), eight out of the twelve new highs were exceeded within only two or three years after the big crashes (1884, 1890, 1900, 1907, 1974, 1980, and 1992); after the two severe depressions (1875 and 1929) the peaks took as long as six or seven years to be exceeded; and the two world wars began in peak years not to be exceeded for sixteen (1913) and twelve years (1939).

3. World Bank 2008, pp. 161, 216, 112.

4. World Bank 2008, p. 58.

5. The "bumps on the handle" follow Walter Scheidel and Gregory Clark, reported in Zanden 2009, p. 274, fig. 35.

6. The "bottom billion" is Paul Collier's phrase (Collier 2007). The Norwegian ratio to average entire-world gross national income per capita in 2006 (at purchasing-power parity: adjusting for the cost of living) was 5.4 (according to World Bank 2008, pp. 8, 161). And relative to the average of low-income countries by World-Bank definitions the ratio was 27, that is, $137 a day compared with the low-income average of $5 a day (World Bank 2008, p. 10).

7. Maddison 2006, p. 615; U.S. Census Bureau, Population Division 2009, projecting that by 2050 the rate will be down to 0.5 percent per year, as against its historic peak of over 2.0 percent in the 1960s.

8. Sombart 1906.

9. Bureau of Labor Statistics, U.S. Department of Commerce, at http://www. bls.gov/oes / current/oes291123.htm.

10. Collier 2007, p. 3 (and for the next quotation, p. 4).

11. World population in 2009 was about 6.77 billion.

12. Again the figures are at (U.S.A.) purchasing-power parity, from World Bank 2008.

13. Abbing 2002.

14. Eva is a fiction—though in truth I have plenty of such cousins at Dimelsvik.

15. McCloskey and Klamer 1995.

16. A recent and comprehensive survey is Zanden 2009. On p. 289 and in many other places he admits that China and Japan were ready.

17. I am indebted to a conversation in August 2009 with Karl Wärneryd of the Stockholm School of Economics for this way of putting the point.

18. Lucas 2002, p. 17. Zanden (2009) uses Lucas's remark as the motto for his book, but the age of a million mutinies was after the date he ends his own researches, 1800.

CHAPTER TWO: LIBERAL IDEAS CAUSED THE INNOVATION

1. A full defense of this and the other categories of virtues is given in McCloskey 2006a, especially pp. 151–194.

2. As the economist Daniel Klein has argued to me.

3. Cather 1931 (1992), p. 675.

4. Lilburne, "The Just Defense of John Lilburne against Such as Charge Him with Turbulency of Spirit," 1653, at http://www.strecorsoc.org/docs/defence1.html. After quoting the formulation, H. N. Brailsford commends it as "one of the earliest and one of the boldest state-

ments of the liberal creed," and notes its strict libertarian implications—but then in the collectivist spirit of the British left in 1961, he rejects them (Brailsford 1961, p. 75).

5. De la Court 1669, part 3, chap. 7, "Conclusion." The wording here is from the 1743 English edition.

6. North 1691, preface, p. viii. I have modernized spelling and punctuation here and elsewhere, to avoid pointless distancing of the authors. The distinguished literary critic Stephen Greenblatt praises the Oxford edition's (1986) modernizing of Shakespeare's spelling for avoiding thereby "a certain cozy, Olde-English quaintness" (Greenblatt 1997, p. 73). The distance of the olde ffolke should be experienced by their strange thoughts, not by their premodern conventions of spelling and punctuation. For the same reason I have changed British spellings to American, "honour" to "honor" and the like, except in titles. Sometimes I cannot resist retaining "-eth" in sixteenth-century quotations. It's so cozy and quaint.

7. Tribe 1995; Rothschild 2001, p. 20.

8. Jacob 1981 (2006); Israel 2001. Israel wants to trace it all to Spinoza; and he spurns the Levellers and Freemasons (Israel 2010, p. 21, where he mentioned Jacob).

9. Heckscher 1931, vol. 1, p. 173.

10. Dean Stanley, 1834, quoted in MacLeod 1998, p. 96.

11. MacLeod 1998, p. 108.

12. MacLeod 1998, p. 108.

13. Goody 2010, p. 60.

14. Cohen 1992. An eloquent summary of the evidence for "capitalist" institutions in ancient Mesopotamia is Baechler 1971 (1975), pp. 37–38.

15. Grierson 1978, pp. 3, 5; Demetz 1997, p. 16.

16. Grantham 2003, p. 73.

17. Tönnies 1887 (1957), p. 34.

18. Kuhn, and others 2001: they speak of the emergence over a wide area rather suddenly of "redundant, standardized ornament forms" suggesting communicative purposes. The earlier art was rare, and unique, item by item, in design: it appears not to be a result of a talking culture. The evidence from genetic family trees and the (controversial) evidence from historical linguistics of the Joseph Greenberg–Merritt Ruhlen school point also to about the same time. The issue of when humans acquired language, though, is fraught, and recent findings suggest that some signs of it (voice box and brain ability; art; sacred burial) occurred much earlier in Southern Africa.

19. Sahlins 1974 (2004), esp. chap. 2, "The Domestic Mode of Production: The Structure of Underproduction."

20. Lebergott 1993, pp. 63–64.

21. The economics of hunters vs. farmers was lucidly outlined by Lebergott 1984, pp. 13–16.

22. Vargas Llosa 2008, p. 68.

CHAPTER THREE: AND A NEW RHETORIC PROTECTED THE IDEAS

1. For example, Kirzner 1976, p. 83, as elsewhere in his writings, and especially Kirzner 1973. I have criticized his very fruitful approach as not going quite far enough: as not recognizing

the importance of the social aspect of entrepreneurship, and especially the role of persuasion (McCloskey 2008d; compare Storr 2008).

2. W. L. Riordon, *Plunkitt of Tammany Hall* (1905), pp. 3–10, reproduced in Leland D. Baldwin, *The Flavor of The Past: Readings in American Social and Political Portrait Life*, vol. 2 (New York: Van Nostrand, 1968), pp. 57–60, and then at http://www.uhb. fr/faulkner/ ny/ plunkitt.htm. Plunkett's use of "honest," by the way, is a late use in the sense of "honorable."

3. Bastiat 1845, I.7.

4. In case you imagine that cases like Bastiat's are mere fictions, consider the officials nowadays of Hanchuan, China, anxious to create jobs for making the local liquor, *baijiu.* And so they required that state workers buy in total $300,000 worth of it in a year. Because such a figure worked out to three bottles per state worker per day of the "sinus-clearing" liquor, the requirement was canceled. Even in China people sometimes recognize a mercantilist absurdity when they see it (Sharon LaFraniere, "Chinese Mock Bewildering Rules," *International Herald Tribune*, Oct. 20, 2009, p. 2).

5. Cicero 44 BCE, I:42. Compare Finley 1973, pp. 60, 23.

6. More 1516, p. 132.

7. Israel 1995, p. 222. Yet by 1702 the Duke of Marlborough is addressing the states-general of cheesemen in the Hague as "your High and Mighty Lordships," with no irony.

8. Aquinas 1267–1273, Second Part of the Second Part, Q. 77, art. 4, "I answer that." And not all the Desert Fathers: "A brother said to Pistamon, 'I am anxious [for my soul] when I sell what I make.' Pistamon replied, 'There is no harm in this. . . . Set straight away the price [that is, don't bargain for advantage]. . . . However much you have, do not stop making things, do as much as you can, provided that your soul is at peace'" (Desert Fathers, p. 56).

9. MacLeod 2007, pp. 1, 13. MacLeod detects a decline in the prestige of inventors by the early twentieth century, but I would argue that by then the heroism had been routinized. In A. G. Macdonnell's comic novel *England, Their England* (1933) the engineer character, William Rhodes, a northerner, is still to be admired, though a trifle suspect from a southern English and upper-class point of view (Macdonnell was a Scot). MacLeod's argument, admittedly, is about inventors in the strict sense, not the users of inventions. Yet as Edgerton (1991, 1996, 2005) argues, Britain remains, for all the post-Victorian lament, one of the most inventive economies on earth.

10. For a discussion of the bourgeois tendency of the cowboy novel and film, and its tensions, see McCloskey 2006a, pp. 212–230. Hollywood soon became strangely hostile to commerce, as in *Giant* or *Wall Street.*

11. Cather 1913, p. 58.

12. Montaigne, *Essays*, book 3.2, "Of Repentance," quoted in Botton 2005, p. 46; alternatively translated in Montaigne, trans. D. Frame, *Essays*, p. 614.

13. Hexter 1961.

14. Cannadine 1994 (2005).

15. Appleby 1978, pp. 11–12.

16. Nye 2007.

17. Marx and Engels 1848 (1988), sec. 1, p. 59.

18. Quoted in Leo Marx 1964, p. 190.

19. Aquinas 1267–1273, Second Part of the Second Part, Q. 61, art. 2, "I answer that."

20. I owe these ideas to my friends Paul Turpin, as in Turpin (2005), and Samuel Fleischacker, as in Fleischacker (2004).

21. http://www.pemberley.com/janeinfo/novlsrch.html. *Sanditon*, eleven chapters in draft, contains two instances, both meaning "upright."

22. A fuller discussion of the illuminating vagaries of the word "honest" is given in McCloskey, forthcoming, *The Bourgeois Revaluation.*

23. On the great chain of being, see Tillyard 1943. Members of the school of literary critics known as the New Historicists, for whom (somewhat unreasonably) Tillyard is a whipping boy, point out that the great chain acquired its meaning from the challenges to it, Caliban challenging Ariel so to speak. Orthodoxy implies a heterodoxy to be worried about, and suppressed.

24. See Ethington 1997; an economist's use of such ideas is Akerlof 1997.

25. Quoted in Ethington 1997.

26. Stendhal 1839, p. 147, italics his.

27. Stendhal 1839, among many places expressing his contempt for the bourgeoisie (none of them is in *style indirect*, which would make them possibly contrary to Stendhal's own views): pp. 90 ("with his mind on nothing but money"), 103 ("Fabrizio . . . thought the middle class ridiculous"), 119 (in the France of Louis-Philippe "the sole passion that has outlived all the rest is lust for money"), 254 ("in the eyes of the middle class exaggeration passes for beauty"), 427 ("in a republic such as America, one is forced to bore oneself the whole day by paying serious court to the shopkeepers in the street, and become as dull and stupid as they are"). But I have not checked the French, and may be wrong.

28. Whitman 1855, p. 6.

29. The evidence for how much it stuck in the craw of English people in the seventeenth century is reviewed in Appleby 1978, chapter 4, "The Dutch as a Source of Evidence."

30. Otteson 2006, p. 178.

31. Sen 1985.

32. Mokyr 1990, p. 171.

33. Lal 2006, p. 2. Lal here perhaps falls in with Douglass North's ideas that literal "predation" was common as late as 1688 in England. Lal's own ideas about the High Medieval origins of property rights are better.

34. Appleby 2010, p. 7.

CHAPTER FOUR: MANY OTHER PLAUSIBLE STORIES DON'T WORK VERY WELL

1. In the field of history the fullest telling of the story of objectivism is Peter Novick's brilliant book, *That Noble Dream* (1988). My own book *The Rhetoric of Economics* (1985a; 1998) tells a similar tale about economics.

2. Bailyn 2003, especially chapter 1, "Politics and the Creative Imagination."

3. Israel 2010, pp. 37, 39; see also pp. 87, 91.

4. Sahlins 1976, pp. 206–207.

5. Khurana 2007, p. 11.

6. Stark 2003, p. 2: "Ideas about God have . . . consequences"; p. 11: "Monotheism has immense capacities to mobilize human action."

7. Mill 1843, p. 464.

8. "Samuelsonian" is an adjective describing modern, American-style economics, which was originated by the late, great, and amiable Paul A. Samuelson (1915–2009) and by his brother-in-law (also great and amiable) Kenneth Arrow (b. 1921), and announced in Samuelson's modestly entitled PhD dissertation of 1947, *The Foundations of Economic Analysis*. It insists that every economic issue must be treated as a problem of constrained maximization by utility-seeking individuals. To this, Arrow added the use of existence-theorem proof in the style of the department of mathematics (as against departments of physics or engineering, which care for derivation and approximations, and very little about the philosophical matter of existence). Samuelsonian economics, especially in its recent form melded with Milton Friedman's conclusions, is more commonly called "neoclassical." But the term perpetuates an anachronism, since neoclassical economics names the much earlier new economics during and after the 1870s (Menger, Walras, Jevons, Marshall, Clark, Wicksell), which was wider than Samuelsonian in method, and often not Friedmanite in conclusion

9. Hohenberg 2003, p. 179.

10. The word "divergence" and the idea that it happened after 1800 is from Pomeranz' (2000) and others of the "California School."

11. Goody 2010, p. 122.

12. Graff and Birkenstein (2005) and Graff (1992). Another of my friends, Jack Goldstone, has practiced the same method of teaching the conflicts and using the remainders in his elegant textbook *Why Europe? The Rise of the West in World History, 1500–1850* (2009), from which I have learned so much. I have not seen his forthcoming *A Peculiar Path*, but expect to learn from it even more.

13. Montaigne 1588, book 3.8, "Of the Art of Discussion," p. 709.

14. Asplund 2008, p. 51.

15. Snow 1855, p. 75.

16. Abramovitz 1956, Kendrick 1956 and 1961, and Solow 1957. Jones's *Increasing Returns* (1933) should be better known among economists. A student of Alfred Marshall, he anticipated the mathematics of what came later to be called the "price dual of the residual." He died young, and his work was forgotten except by economic historians. The notion that an input price (such as of coal, labor, lumber) divided by an output price (such as of iron, wheat, furniture) is a measure of productivity was a commonplace in the nineteenth century, rather obscured in the twentieth by fascination with the materialist "quantity primal."

17. For example, dialectic or not, Michael McKeon 1987 (2002).

18. Pope 1711, *Essay on Criticism*, lines 221–224, italics supplied.

19. You may persuade yourself of this by getting hold of a searchable text of any item by Mill and searching for "science," finding for example that he speaks of "a science of morals."

CHAPTER FIVE: THE CORRECT STORY PRAISES "CAPITALISM"

1. In modern literary criticism in the English-speaking world the term "humanist" is a fighting word, but the fight is sidestepped here. Here all it means is "a scholar in an academic department such as English, French, music, art, philosophy, theology, parts of history, that is, a person interested in *die Geisteswissenschaften* or *les sciences humaines*." It does not mean partisans of the approach to literary criticism following Matthew Arnold, T. S. Eliot, the Blooms (Harold or Allan), or my own teacher, Howard Mumford Jones.

2. Pearson 1900, pp. 26–28. Even on strictly genetic grounds, by the way, Pearson's remark is mistaken. Africa's genetic diversity ensures that it will eventually make contributions to the quota of human knowledge that will put the white and yellow and brown "races" in the shade.

3. Pearson and Moul 1925. Peart and Levy 2005 give a full and penetrating treatment of the Pearson and Moul paper (chap. 5, pp. 87–103) in the context of the new eugenic social sciences of the late nineteenth and early twentieth centuries.

4. Holmes 1895, p. 264.

5. Holmes, *Buck* v. *Bell*, 274 U.S. 200 (1927). See Alschuler's (2000) devastating critique of Holmes.

6. *Das Kapital* 1867, p. 168 (pt. 2, chap. 4, "The General Formula for Capital"). The usual English translation (though approved by Engels) errs in many important details. Thus the Moore and Aveling translation (in, say, the Modern Library edition): "this boundless greed after riches" (p. 171). But the word "greed" is not in the German (*Gier*, or *Geltgier*), and is in fact a word eschewed by Marx throughout the book, as moralistic and unscientific.

7. You may admire its beauty in McCloskey 1985b, available on line at deirdremccloskey .org.

8 . McCloskey 2008d.

9. McCloskey 1994c, pp. 201, 311, 347, 353, 378.

10. Sahlins 1976, pp. ix, viii. Sahlins views culture as a tertium quid, such as the conjective (p. x).

11. Sahlins 1976, p. 210.

12. Drafts of both volumes are available at deirdremccloskey.org.

13. Knight 1935, p. 97.

14. Plantinga 2000, p. xiv.

15. I won't call it a "hexology," the proper Greek corresponding to a tetralogy ("hex" in West Germanic languages means "witch"); and I certainly won't, despite the temptations of higher book sales, call it by the vulgar Latin-Greek mix "sexology."

16. Fielding 1749, vol. 2, p. 409 (book 18, chap. 1).

17. The point that left and right complain in much the same ways about the bourgeoisie is made also by Immanuel Wallerstein in 1983 (1995), p. 115.

18. Taylor 1992, p. 23.

CHAPTER SIX: MODERN GROWTH WAS A FACTOR OF AT LEAST SIXTEEN

1. For the international comparisons Maddison 2006, and in particular pp. 437, 443 for the factor of 16 from 1700 to 2001 in international Geary-Khamis dollars of 1990. When a figure such as this is not footnoted it will regularly be lifted from Maddison's amazing *oeuvre*, such as Maddison 2007. For Britain itself see Feinstein 1972, Feinstein in Feinstein and Pollard 1988.

2. Marglin 2008. Compare the great Marxist economist Joan Robinson (1966, p. ix): "In modern industrial countries . . . the real-wage level is normally rising as technical progress raises productivity."

3. Clark 2007a.

4. Maddison 2006, pp. 125–126.

5. More 1516, p. 65.

6. All these figure from Maddison 2006 (2001), appendix B, table 21, p. 264.

7. Payson 1994, pp. 113, 116–117.

8. Nordhaus 1997.

9. Officer 2009.

10. Boskin and others 1998. Gordon 2006 revises the figures up for one effect, down for another, implying a 1.0 percentage point per year upward bias in the conventional consumer price index. See the summary table on the earlier work in Moulton 1996.

11. To which should be added (as Fogel 2008 notes) health insurance supporting the Cadillac level of medical interventions that Americans insist upon, which the talk of stagnating wages also doesn't include—allowing for example immediate access to bypass surgery (not available widely until the 1970s), and organ transplants even for some poor people, with less of the queuing for ordinary procedures than most other national systems have.

12. Maddison 2006, p. 265.

13. Friedman 2005.

14. Payson 1994, p. 117.

15. Fogel 2002, pp. 1, 2, 4, 236.

16. Cox and Alm 1999, pp. 14–15.

17. Lebergott 1993, pp. 97, 101.

18. Cox and Alm 1999, p. 43.

19. Fogel 2002, p. 266.

20. Compare Fouquet 2008; Nordhaus 1997.

21. Quoted in Lebergott 1993, p. 119.

22. Temple 1986 (2007), p. 89.

23. Maddison 2007, p. 320.

24. The point about Carnegie is made by Otteson 2006, p. 165.

25. Payson points out, however, that truly useable light depends on the capacity of the human eye. In the bright light of modern houses our pupils contract: we could get along with less light perfectly well. Consider for example the wasted street lighting shining up into the night sky and blotting out the stars. In safety there's no gain from the light, since humans can't use it in the sky; and there's a spiritual loss from not seeing nightly the wonder of the heavens. In Sweden the standard wattages for light bulbs are 25 and 40, while they are 60 and 100 in blazing America. But Swedish houses seem little darker. Pupils adjust.

26. Berg 1998, p. 140.

27. Sokoloff 1988; Sokoloff and Khan 1990.

28. Berg 1998, pp. 146–148.

29. Berg 1998, p. 154.

30. Gordon 1990.

CHAPTER SEVEN: INCREASING SCOPE . . . IS WHAT MATTERED

1. Bresnahan and Gordon 1997, p. 19.

2. Easterlin 1973, 1974.

3. Easterlin 2003, p. 349.

4. Easterlin 2004, p. 52.

5. Frank 1985, who is rather more subtle than this characterization suggests; Frank and Cook 1995; Schor 1993, 1998, 2004; Scitovsky 1976; Veblen 1899.

6. Douglas and Isherwood 1979; Csikszentmihalyi and Rochberg-Halton 1981.

7. Lebergott 1993, pp. 6, 3.

8. Sahlins 1976, p. 168.

9. Easterlin 2004, p. 53.

10. Frey 2008, p. 13.

11. The point is made in full in Ziliak and McCloskey 2008.

12. Layard 2009.

13. Inglehart and other 2008, abstract. The next quotation is from the caption of figure 6, p. 277.

14. Nozick 1974, pp. 42–44; Schimdtz 1993, p. 170. I discuss these in McCloskey 2006a, pp. 123–125. Said Confucius of some goldfish, "See how happy they are!" His disciple said, "How do you know they are happy?" Confucius: "How do you know I do not know?"

15. Nussbaum and Sen 1993; Sen 1999; and Nussbaum 1999.

16. Jardine 1996, pp. 34, 33.

17. Stearns 2007, p. 296–297.

18. Sahlins 1976, p. 178, summarizing and extending Jean Baudrillard.

19. Vargas and Yoon 2006.

20. OECD 2009, p. 12.

21. Cowen 1998.

22. Menand 2009, p. 109.

23. Eagleton 2009, p. 40; the later quotation from Ferguson is on p. 19.

24. Hanawalt 1979, p. 271f.

25. Raftis 1964, chaps. 6–7.

26. Wrigley and Schofield 1981.

27. Dennison and Carus 2003. For the attachment to the figment, see Engels's first footnote to the 1888 English translation of *The Communist Manifesto*, in which Haxthausen's notions about the *mir* are praised. Tocqueville, exhibiting early the split in European ideologies about such matters, declared that Haxthausen had a "mind without breadth and without justice" (quoted in Epstein 2006, p. 17).

28. Coontz 1992.

29. Popkin 1979.

30. Folbre 2001, p. 20.

31. Bellah 1996, p. 284.

32. Bellah 1996, p. xlii.

33. Bellah 1996, p. 291.

CHAPTER EIGHT: AND THE POOR WON

1. Eagleton 2009, p. 326.

2. UN/World Bank common data base at http://globalis.gvu.unu.edu/ indicator.cfm? IndicatorID=19&country=BZ#rowBZ.

3. *Economist* Intelligence Unit 2005. The troubles of 2008–2009 did not much change

Ireland's rank. Sadly, by the way, the Unit's method has all the defects of pot-of-pleasure statistics, such as reliance on *t* tests of "significance." For instance, they drop equality of gender as "insignificant." Tell that to half the population limited in scope and unable therefore to feed its children.

4. Macfarlane 2000, p. 5.

5. Goldin and Katz 2008.

6. Zanden 2003, p. 57. The finding is not uncontroversial.

7. Harvey 2009.

8. Lebergott 1996, p. 36.

9. Fogel 2002, p. 37.

10. Eldridge 1995, p. 7.

11. Ó Gráda 2009, pp. 2, 1.

12. Milanovic 2009.

13. Maddison estimates per capita real income in Turkey as rising (rather slowly) 1950 to 2002, rising more slowly in Baathist Syria during the same period, and rising smartly in Iraq and Iran until the 1970s, and from then to 2002 actually falling (in Iraq's case to 20 percent of its peak per capita income, achieved in 1979). See Maddison 2006, pp. 564–565.

14. Rawls 1993; Buchanan 2003.

15. True, Marx himself didn't use *Kapitalismus*. In the German of *Das Kapital*, vol. 1, he used *Kapital* and *kapitalische* on nearly every page, but not *Kapitalismus*. The English translation used "capitalism" only twice. Carlyle 23 years before, in *Past and Present* (1843), uses "mammonism." Later, and especially in the twentieth century (that age of proliferating -isms) "capitalism" became common.

16. The reference to theology is not ornamental. See Nelson 1991, 2001, and 2009.

17. Marsalis and Ward 2008, p. 131.

18. Tunzelmann 2003, p. 85.

19. "Entrepreneurship" is from Schumpeter and his Austrian tradition (for example Schumpeter 1926 [1934] and "creative destruction" is from Schumpeter 1942 (1950), pp. 82–85 (borrowed from Werner Sombart's *Krieg und Kapitalismus* of 1913; some modern treatments are Baumol 2002 and Diamond, forthcoming); "continuously emergent novelty" from Usher 1960, p. 110; "invention of invention" from various hands, such as Nathan Rosenberg, David Landes, and Joel Mokyr, and ultimately from Whitehead 1925 (chap. 6), p. 96, "The greatest invention of the nineteenth century was the invention of the method of invention"; "creative accumulation" in Tunzelmann 2003, p. 88; and "consensual creativity" from Marsalis and Ward 2008, p. 167.

20. Young 1928.

21. Boswell 1791, for 1763, Aetat. 54 (vol. 1, p. 273).

CHAPTER NINE: CREATIVE DESTRUCTION CAN BE JUSTIFIED THEREFORE ON UTILITARIAN GROUNDS

1. Baumol 2002; Diamond, forthcoming.

2. Hollander 1994.

3. Nor that new ideas are always good, any more than are all new devices (mustard gas,

video pornography). The new scientific idea of race, prominent beginning around 1900 in Europe, crowded out better ideas for a long time, with disastrous results. The pathologizing of homosexuality (indeed, its naming) from the 1880s on by the newly (if irrationally) confident profession of psychiatrists was another disaster.

4. Mill 1843: "There are many virtuous actions, and even virtuous modes of action (though the cases are, I think, less frequent than is often supposed) by which happiness in the particular instance is sacrificed, more pain being produced than pleasure. But conduct of which this can be truly asserted, admits of justification only because it can be shown that on the whole more happiness will exist in the world, if feelings are cultivated which will make people, in certain cases, regardless of [that is, not caring about] happiness" (6.12.7). Twenty years later, in *Utilitarianism*, he had much more to say along the same lines.

5. Frank 1985.

6. Here's one: under act utilitarianism it is acceptable to slaughter Peter to feed Paul. You see what I mean by its "dramatic paradoxes" as a theory—a theory, however, embraced by most economists. Here is another: under act utilitarianism someone who is a better pleasure machine should get more to eat. "A Brahmin," noted a Hindu lawyer, "is entitled to exactly twenty-five times as much happiness as everyone else" (Lebergott 1993, p. 12).

7. Buchanan 1986.

8. Buchanan 2006, p. 991.

9. So I argue in McCloskey 2006b, observing that Kant had a parallel problem: "You must not," said he, base ethics on merely human facts, but gave no reason one would want to be in this sense ethical. Martha Nussbaum, I argue in 2006d, makes a similar mistake.

10. Bastiat 1845, 2.15.33.

11. For example McCloskey 1985b, sections 9.2, 10.2, 10.3, 24.1.

12. Mokyr 1990, p. 153.

13. Howitt 2005, p. 10, referring to Mokyr 1990.

CHAPTER TEN: BRITISH ECONOMISTS DID NOT RECOGNIZE THE TIDE

1. Schumpeter 1954, p. 571. "In the late 1940s" because he died early in 1950; the book was published posthumously, after herculean editing by his wife, the economic historian Elizabeth Boody Schumpeter.

2. Macaulay 1830.

3. It is customary, by the way, to use Carlyle's phrase "the dismal science" to encapsulate the pessimistic conclusions of the classical economists. But that was not its origin. Carlyle called his friend John Stuart Mill and Mill's colleagues "dismal" because they opposed slavery, which institution Carlyle found sweet and medieval and appropriate to the sadly deficient abilities of people of African origin (Persky 1990; Levy 2001; Levy and Peart 2001).

4. Mill 1843.

5. This was quoted to me many years ago by the late Rondo Cameron, from correspondence between Cameron and Wrigley.

6. Maddison 2006, pp. 125–126.

7. Moore 2006.

8. Hayek 1945.

9. As is argued at length in McCloskey 1990.

10. Gladwell 2006.

11. Letter to Thomas Bentley, quoted in Mokyr 2010, p. 86.

12. Boswell 1791, for 1783 (vol. 2, p. 447).

13. Price 1787.

14. Quoted in Mokyr 2010, p. 80.

15. Quoted in Mokyr 1999, p. 4.

16. Macaulay 1830: I, ii, p. 185.

17. Schumpeter 1954, p. 572n5.

18. Wex 2006, p. 95.

19. Schumpeter 1954, p. 572.

20. Macaulay 1830, p. 185.

CHAPTER ELEVEN: BUT THE FIGURES TELL

1. Berg 1985; McCloskey 1994b; Berg and Hudson 1994; Temin 1997, 2000.

2. Harley 1993; Crafts and Harley 1992, 2004. Their views are similar to the unpopular ones of Rondo Cameronon this score.

3. Mathias 1953 (1979), p. 209; and Mathias 1959.

4. For a contrary view, claiming in the Two Nicks style that "output growth before 1800 was largely driven by an 'Industrious Revolution'" (to use Jan de Vries's terminology), see Broadberry 2003, p. 253.

5. 1817 (1852), p. 235.

6. Carus-Wilson 1941, p. 41.

7. Adams 1907 (1918), p. 498.

8. Jones 1981, 1988; Maddison 2006, pp. 47–48; Lal 1998; Lal 2006, chap. 6.

9. Whitman 1888, p. 300n. In his recent history of the United States, Walter McDougall tells a similarly Elizabethan story (McDougall 2004, pp. 16, 22).

10. Mokyr 1985, p. 44.

11. McCloskey 1991a.

12. Boyd 2008, p. 16. The two-week limit is why below I use "three weeks" as the timing of the "butterfly effect."

13. Mitchell 1962, p. 60. Marx made a similar calculation, using the 1861 census to support his claim that machinery disemployed workers (Marx 1867 [1887], p. 488).

14. Clapham 1926, p. 67.

15. Clapham 1926, p. 74. Compare Pollard 1981, pp. 24–25.

16. Berg 1985; Hudson 1986, 1889, 1992.

17. Musson 1978, pp. 8, 61, 167-168. By the way, the usual identification of Blake's image with cotton mills, though I use it here, as many do, is doubtful. He probably meant "mills" in the sense of the monotonous and utilitarian grinding of grain.

18. Olmstead and Rhode 2008a, 2008b.

19. Compare Chapman and Butt 1988.

20. Davies and Pollard 1988.

21. McCloskey 1981, p. 114.

22. North 1968.

23. Hawke 1970.

24. Harley 1993, table 3.6, p. 200.

25. Olmstead and Rhode, 2008a and 2008b.

CHAPTER TWELVE: YET BRITAIN'S (AND EUROPE'S) LEAD WAS AN EPISODE

1. Macfarlane 1978.

2. Goldstone 2003, Pomeranz 2000.

3. Allen, Bassino, Ma, Moll-Murata, and Zanden 2009.

4. Goldstone 2002a, 2002b; he names R. Bin Wong, Kenneth Pomeranz, Richard von Glahn, Wang Feng, Cameron Campbell, Dennis Flynn, Arturo Giraldez, James Z. Lee, Robert Marks, and himself (all at the time residents of the Golden State); and Andre Gunder Frank, Jack Goody, James Blaut, and Janet Abu-Lughod. To which I would add Thomas Rawski, Robert Allen, and Francesca Bray. I myself was a spectator at some early conferences on the matter, and declare now that besides joining tardily the Cambridge/Johns Hopkins School of intellectual history I am an adjunct and amateur member of the California School of world history.

5. Goody 1996.

6. Goldstone 2009, p. 19; compare p. 47.

7. Amartya Sen has started, in Sen 2005.

8. Watson 1983.

9. Temple 1986 (2007).

10. Winchester 2008, pp. 267–277.

11. Temple 1986 (2007): paper, pp. 92–95, compass, pp. 162–166.

12. Needham himself makes the point about the blast furnace, in his introduction to Temple 1986 (2007), p. 10.

13. Perdue 2003, p. 491.

14. In Temple 1986 (2007), p. 10.

15. Jacob 2001, p. 23.

16. Goldstone 2009, p. 32.

17. Cosgel, Miceli, and Rubin 2009.

18. Lattimore 1940, p. 393.

19. Chao 1964, quoted in Goody 2010, p. 18, his translation from the French.

20. Needham in Temple 1986 (2007), p. 10.

21. Rawski 1995 and Rawski and Li 1992.

22. Balázs 1964.

23. Lessnoff 2003, p. 363.

24. Lessnoff 2003, p. 362.

25. It is sharply criticized by Goody 2006, chap. 8.

26. Appleby 1978, p. 73.

27. Ashton 1948, p. 59.

28. Mokyr 2002, p. 297.

29. A point made to me by the economist Pete Boettke of George Mason University.

30. O'Neill 2009, p. 46. On the history see for instance Baechler 1971; McNeill 1982; Berman 1983; Jones 1981, 1988; Macfarlane 2000, p. 274–275. The economic historian Stephen Davies is working on a book attributing the fragmentation to military technology.

31. Ringmar 2007, p. 289.

32. Goldstone 2009, p. 45.

33. Landes 1998, pp. 134, 135.

34. Landes 1998, p. 250.

35. Lehmann 1970, p. 4.

36. Rietbergen 1998, p. 230.

37. Milton writes in 1644, "No nation, or well-instituted state, if they valued books at all, did ever use this way of licensing; and it might be answered, that this is a piece of prudence [that is, state policy alleged by the advocates of licensed printing to be a good idea] lately discovered."

38. Clegg 1997, chap. 6.

CHAPTER THIRTEEN: AND FOLLOWERS COULD LEAP OVER STAGES

1. Readers of a certain age will pause at the name Rostow. Yes, he was the same man who advised President Johnson to carry on fighting in Vietnam. Largely because he did so, Rostow, who in the 1940s and 1950s had been a Nobel-worthy pioneer in applying economics to economic history, became after the 1960s a persona non grata in economic history.

2. Gerschenkron 1962; and Pollard 1981, pp. 184–190.

3. Sato 1963. Gapinski 1993 gives a more cheerful perspective on the calculation; but King and Rebelo 1993 show that sticking with the neoclassical model implies early in the transition insanely high returns to capital (e.g., 500 percent)—which suggests that taking innovations off the shelf, not routine accumulation, is the heart of the matter.

4. Schmoller 1884 (1897), italics supplied.

5. Davies and Ellis 2000, p. 25 of Internet version.

6. Landes 1998, p. 519.

7. Landes 1998, p. 522.

8. Thurow, p. 59.

9. Compare Krugman 1996 attacking Thurow and James Fallows on just these grounds, for what he calls "pop internationalism."

10. World Bank 2008, pp. 88, 112, 215.

11. Smith 1776, vol. 2, 4.8.49, p. 179. I will give citations to Smith in book-chapter-paragraph form because of the numerous editions with varying pagination, but page citations are to the Glasgow edition.

12. Landes 1969, p. 326, italics supplied.

13. Landes 1969, p. 336.

14. Broadberry and Irwin 2006, for example, show that Britain had a labor productivity "lead" (footrace talk again) in agriculture and services right through the 1880s.

15. This against the nostalgia for tough-minded assaults on the rest of the world that Correlli Barnett admires, in Barnett 1972 and elsewhere.

16. I refer to the question asked by Jared Diamond's New Guinean friend: "Why is it that

you white people developed so much cargo [goods] and brought it to New Guinea, but we black people had little cargo of our own?" (Diamond 1997, p. 14).

17. Diamond 1997, p. 6.

18. Tunzelmann 2003, p. 84.

19. Polanyi 1966.

20. Harris 1992, 1996, 2000.

21. Collins 1985.

22. Edgerton 2007.

23. In Temple 1986 (2007), p. 7.

24. Stephen Parente and Edward Prescott explore the obstacles to taking off the shelf (Parente and Prescott 2000).

25. Ringmar 2007, pp. 38–39 and throughout.

26. Goldstone 2002a, from electronic edition of 2001.

27. Easterlin 2003, p. 347.

28. Easterlin asked "why the whole world is not developed," and answered, building on work by the Chicago economist Mary Jean Bowman: inadequate education (Easterlin 1981).

29. Bértola 2010; the statistics mentioned are on p. 21.

30. Mokyr 2010, p. 90.

CHAPTER FOURTEEN: IT DIDN'T HAPPEN BECAUSE OF THRIFT

1. Tusser 1588, p. 13.

2. A full statistical analysis is given in McCloskey 2006a, pp. 446–450.

3. Introduction by A. L. Basham, p. 120, to the passage in Embree 1988, vol. 1. The passage below is *Dīgha Nikāya* 3.182ff., reprinted p. 123.

4. Walter, late thirteenth century, in Oschinsky 1971, p. 309.

5. *Seneschaucy*, late thirteenth century, in Oschinsky 1971, p. 269. Raftis speaks of the coming of "up-to-date double accounting by the end of the twelfth century" on big estates (1996, p. 120), which would be surprisingly early if he is speaking precisely, as he usually does.

6. Tusser 1588, p. 18.

7. Boswell 1791, April 14, 1778 (vol. 2, p. 203).

8. Marx 1867, chap. 24, sec. 3, p. 651.

9. Dickens, *David Copperfield*, 1849–1850, chap. 12.

10. Goldstone 2009, p. 11.

11. McCloskey 1976 and 1989 make such calculations of risk for medieval agriculture.

12. Braudel and Spooner 1967, fig. 23, p. 477.

13. McCloskey and Nash 1984. Compare Cipolla 1994, p. 89.

14. Innes 1988, p. 5.

15. Quoted in Leo Marx 1964, p. 148.

16. Marx 1867, chap. 24, sec. 3, p. 656.

17. Crafts, Leybourne, and Mills 1991, table 7.2, p. 113; and Feinstein 2003, p. 45.

18. Postan is thus quoted with approval by another great student of the times, Carlo Cipolla, in Cipolla 1994, p. 91.

CHAPTER FIFTEEN: CAPITAL FUNDAMENTALISM IS WRONG

1. Feinstein 2003, p. 47, from which subsequent quotations are also taken.

2. According to the "marginal productivity theory" developed by economists from the 1890s to the 1940s, the share in total costs of an input into production such as horses or land or labor is the farmer's opinion of the percentage change in final output that will come from 1 percent more of the input. The theory is exactly true if farmers face constant returns to scale and have no market power and are in the economist's sense rational; it is approximately true to the degree that the conditions are true; returns to scale and market power can be allowed for easily, if known.

3. Mill 1871, p. 111 (book 4, chap. 6).

4. Hansen 1939, 1941, out of Keynes 1937.

5. Fogel 2005.

6. Minksy 1992.

7. Coleridge 1817 (1852), p. 179; Hoppit 2002, p. 116.

8. Tunzelmann 2003, p. 89.

9. McCloskey 1995.

10. Feinstein 2003, p. 45. The table stands as a monument to the massive scholarly effort of numerous economic historians since Simon Kuznets invented the methods in the 1930s and 1940s.

11. Du Plessis 2008.

12. Feinstein 2003, p. 46.

13. Schumpeter 1939, vol. 1, p. 223. The next quotation is from p. 224.

14. Schumpeter 1954, p. 78.

15. Mathias 1973 (1979), p. 88.

16. Goody 2010, p. 62.

17. Rostow 1960; Easterly 2001.

CHAPTER SIXTEEN: NOT A RISE OF GREED OR OF A PROTESTANT ETHIC

1. Mauss 1925 (1990), p. 98.

2. Weber 1923, p. 355.

3. Weber 1904–1905, p. 17.

4. Quoted in Marx 1867 (Capital, vol. 1, p. 171n2). I can't find the phrase in any of the online editions of McCulloch's Principles. Note by the way the use of the word "capitalist," which occurs in McCulloch over 100 times (and "capitalism" never). The Oxford English Dictionary gives Arthur Young's Travels in France of 1792 as the first quotation for "capitalist." Ricardo used the word little. The first quotation in the OED for "capital" in the economic sense is 1709.

5. Hume 1777 (1987), p. 276.

6. For example, Marx 1867, chap. 24, sec. 1, p. 641; and chap. 26, p. 784.

7. Wallerstein 1983 (1995), p. 100. "Waste" such as decent housing for the Chinese.

8. Aristotle, Politics 1257a20, kai apeiros dè houtos ho ploutos.

9. Aquinas 1267–1273, Second Part of the Second Part, Q. 77, art. 4, "I answer that."

10. Danford 2006, pp. 328–329.

11. Hobsbawm, introduction to *Marx, Pre-Capitalist Economic Formations* (1964), cited by Pipes 1999, p. 52n.

12. Santhi Hejeebu and I have laid out the case in favor of Polanyi's understanding of second-best and against Polanyi's understanding of economic history in Hejeebu and McCloskey 2000 and 2003.

13. DeLong 1989, p. 12.

14. Marx 1867, chap. 24, p. 652.

15. Heilbroner 1953, p. 201. Compare p. 156, "an owner-entrepreneur engaged in an endless [*apeiros*] race," and so forth.

16. Weber 1904–1905, p. 53.

17. Appleby 2010, p. 17.

CHAPTER SEVENTEEN: "ENDLESS" ACCUMULATION DOES NOT TYPIFY THE MODERN WORLD

1. Weber 1922 (1947), p. 90.

2. Lawrence 1923, p. 23; compare for example Robert Louis Stevenson's sneer at the teachers of our average men, who "from Solomon down to Benjamin Franklin . . . have inculcated the same ideals of manners, caution, and respectability" (Stevenson 1881, p. 876). Even Alasdair MacIntyre, that perceptive Scot resident in America, mistakes Franklin.

3. Eduard Baumgarten, "Benjamin Franklin: Der Lehrmeister der amerikanischen Revolution," 1936, quoted in Roth 1987, p. 19. Lujo Brentano, the German economist, whose English (as Roth explains) was much better than Weber's, made the same point.

4. Lepore 2008, p. 78.

5. Lepore 2008, pp. 82, 81.

6. Seneca 62–65 CE, letter 47.17, p. 95, ending *nulla servitus turpior est quam voluntaria*.

7. Lepore 2008, p. 82.

8. Weber 1905, p. 51, italics supplied.

9. See the section "Retirement," pp.126–128 in Isaacson 2003.

10. Tronto 1993, p. 29.

11. Haskell's remark is quoted in Innes 1988, p. 39n61.

12. Macfarlane 1987, p. 226.

13. Cowley c. 1665, pp. 198, 197. The Horace is the First Satire (beginning "How comes it to pass, Maecenas, that no one lives content with his condition?"), but the alleged Ovid is actually Publilius Syrus, maxim 121, with *inopiae*, "to poverty," substituted for *luxuriae* (www.thelatinlibrary.com/syrus.html), and was quoted in Seneca.

14. From Owen 1996, pp. 501, 617–618.

15. Smith 1759 (1790), 3.6.6, p. 173.

16. Smith 1980, p. 262.

17. Lex Donaldson (1995, p. 75), following Alfred Chandler, argues that of the largest American corporations only 2 percent vanish every year, and few of these from closing down—they get merged instead. But they are the big boys, usually too big to fail. Siegel (2002, p. 638, fig. 14–1) reckons that all U.S. enterprises with any sort of payroll, not merely the big ones, have

death rates of about 17 percent in each of their first couple of years, decreasing to 7 percent per year if they survive to age fourteen.

CHAPTER EIGHTEEN: NOR WAS THE CAUSE ORIGINAL ACCUMULATION . . .

1. Crouzet 1985, p. 9.
2. Marx 1867, p. 784.
3. Gerschenkron 1957 (1962), p. 33.
4. Marx 1867, p. 785.
5. McCloskey 1975a, and works cited there.
6. Postan 1966, p. 622, that "in order to subsist an average smallholder [more than one half the population in a sample of 104 manors in southern England] had to supplement his income in other ways." Postan was not optimistic that all would get wage work, but from the hiring side he inferred that many did (p. 623).
7. Marx 1867, p. 833.
8. Wallerstein 1974.
9. Kritzler 2008.
10. Gerschenkron 1957 (1962), p. 34.
11. Augustine, *Confessions*, 398 AD, 4.10.
12. See Ogilvie's devastating empirical inquiry (2004) into such Panglossian hypotheses.
13. Schumpeter 1954, p. 572n2.
14. Schumpeter 1926 [1934], p. 72.
15. Pollard 1981, p. 175.
16. Marx 1867, p. 794.
17. Marx 1867, chap. 26, p. 784.
18. Dupré 2004, p. 178.
19. Sellar and Yeatman 1931, pp. 92–93.
20. Schama 1987.
21. Robinson 1966, p. ix.
22. The song is about mining lead in Teesdale in the Northeast, from the singing of Ewan MacColl.
23. Honeyman 2007.
24. Hayek 1954; Hartwell 1961; for the pessimistic case, see Hobsbawm 1957.

CHAPTER NINETEEN: NOR WAS IT ACCUMULATION OF HUMAN CAPITAL, UNTIL LATELY

1. Mitch 2003, p. 6; and Mitch 1992, 1999, 2003, 2004. Compare West 1978 and Allen 2009, pp. 260n.
2. Mitch 2004, p. 6.
3. Arrow 1969, quoted in Easterlin 2004, p. 61.
4. Mokyr 1990, p. 175.
5. Easterlin 2004, pp. 67–68.
6. Huppert 1977; 1999.

7. Huppert 1999, p. 100.

8. Mill 1845.

9. Sandberg 1979.

10. Schreiner 1883, p. 113.

11. Gilomee 2003, pp. 210–212, 319, 371, 405–406.

12. Maddison 2006, p. 525.

13. Nee and Swedberg 2007, p. 3.

14. Winthrop quoted in Innes 1994, p. 106.

15. Philip Benedict, "Faith, Fortune and Social Structure in Seventeenth-Century Montpellier," *Past and Present* 152 (1996): 46–78, discussed in Hoffman 2003b, pp. 366, 84.

16. Harry W. Pearson, p. 339, quoted in Hirschman 1958 (1988), p. 51.

17. Novak 2007, p. 227.

18. Earle 1989, p. 337.

19. Schultz 1964 and Bates 1981.

CHAPTER TWENTY: TRANSPORT OR OTHER DOMESTIC RESHUFFLINGS DIDN'T CAUSE IT

1. Gerschenkron 1957 (1962).

2. Harberger 1954, 1964; Hines 1999; McCloskey 1985b. A brilliant interview of Harberger by the professor of English Richard Lanham explores the significance of Harberger for modern economics (Lanham 2009).

3. For the protransport side in Britain, against my argument, see Szostak 1991 and 2003.

4. David 1969. Fogel's reply was his presidential address to the Economic History Association meeting that year in Toronto.

5. Fogel 1979.

6. The point was made as long ago as 1970 by Roger Ransom.

7. Krugman 1997, p. 52. The jibe apparently registered, since Krugman mentions it again in Krugman 2000, p. 55. Compare Luciani 2004, p. 4: "To say the clustering [of an industry in a city] is the result of localized external economies is too vague. It is a bit like saying agglomeration takes place because of agglomeration effects."

8. Sellar and Yeatman 1931, p. 94.

9. McCloskey 1972a and works cited there.

10. Federico 2005, p. 151.

11. McCloskey 1972a using the robust method of rent increases; compare McCloskey 1983; confirmed by Allen 1992, though using Arthur Young's dubious surveys, and processing them with dubious statistical methods (misusing statistical "significance," for example; see McCloskey 1995a).

12. McCloskey 1975a; Wordie 1983. Reconfirmed in later studies by Allen 1992.

13. Kussmaul 1981.

14. For example in Hudson 1989.

15. McCloskey 1981, 1994b; reprised in Harley 1993, p. 200.

16. I am indebted for this idea to a conversation with the lawyer-economist Robert Ashford of Syracuse University, who sharply disagrees with me. A technical way of putting it is that

the fixed-coefficient production functions once fashionable among Marxist economists do not seem to be correct. Howitt 2005, p. 15, makes a similar point: "At the macro level the system seems to maintain itself within five or ten percent of a full-employment growth path, except for a few dramatic exceptions such as the Great Depression," and even the exception, as I note, does not violate marginal productivity theory. Notice the similarity of the argument to that of Theodore Schultz (1964, p. 70) against the claim that Indian agriculture had in 1919 massive underemployment, violating marginal productivity theory. He noted that the deaths from the influenza epidemic of that year led to a fall in output in line with the (correct) theory.

17. Williamson 1990, p. 203.

18. Williamson 1990, p. 207.

19. Stigler 1967.

20. Williamson does not in fact ignore Stigler. In Williamson 1975, p. 317n16, he argues, just as he does here, that Stigler does not take account of dynamic effects.

21. Williamson 1990, p. 212.

22. Williamson 1990, p. 232.

CHAPTER TWENTY ONE: NOR GEOGRAPHY, NOR NATURAL RESOURCES

1. Diamond 1997, p. 14, italics supplied.

2. Diamond 1997, p. 80.

3. Diamond 1997, p. 81.

4. Mellinger, Sachs, and Gallup 2000, pp. 173, 186.

5. Reiter 2000.

6. Much of Robert Fogel's scientific work since the 1980s has been focused on such matters.

7. Landes 1998, p. 46.

8. Mellinger, Sachs, and Gallup 2000, p. 178.

9. Jones 2003, p. 60.

CHAPTER TWENTY TWO: NOT EVEN COAL

1. As Pollard does in complaining about "the influence of theoretical economists on economic historians" (Pollard 1981, p. 4).

2. Clark 2007, p. 137.

3. Clark and Jacks 2007.

4. Goldstone 2009, p. 13.

5. Allen 2006, p. 6.

6. Allen 2006, p. 10. See Temin 1966, 1971; and Mokyr 1990, p. 166.

7. Tunzelmann 2003, p. 87.

8. Jacob, personal correspondence, 2008. Compare MacLeod 1988, pp. 151–181 on the saving of capital vs. labor saving in patent applications.

9. Acemoglu 2002; but Boldrin and Levine (2009) have another model, with diminishing returns to inventive labor rather than fixed costs of inventing, with the opposite implication. It's that way with models independent of scientific test.

10. McCloskey 1973; Allen 1977.

11. Mokyr 1990, p. 160.

12. Fremdling 2000, referred to in Allen 2006, p. 18.

13. Temin 1964.

14. McCloskey 1973.

15. Allen 2006, p. 27.

16. Olmstead and Rhode 2008a, 2008b.

17. Harris 1992, p. 133.

18. Tocqueville 1835, p. 116.

19. Temple 1986 (2007), pp. 218, 197.

20. Maddison 2006 (2001), app. B, table 21, p. 264.

21. Smith 1776, vol. 1, 1.9.10, p. 108.

22. Smith 1776, vol. 1, 1.9.14, p. 111.

23. Smith 1776, vol. 1, 1.9.15, p. 112; compare 1.8.24, p. 89. Zanden 2009, p. 24, concludes that Smith was right, but Zanden's survey of the Chinese data is not entirely persuasive, and in any case he admits that in early modern times interest rates fell heavily in China, and more in Japan.

24. McCloskey 2008e.

25. Smith 1776, vol. 1, 1.1.8, p. 20.

CHAPTER TWENTY THREE: FOREIGN TRADE WAS NOT THE CAUSE . . .

1. Chartres 2003, p. 209.

2. Deane and Cole 1962, pp. 309, 312.

3. O'Brien and Engerman 1991 demur.

4. Allen 2006, p. 7.

5. Inikori 2002, p. 478; he discusses his trade model on pp. 10–14, which uses Hirschman 1958, Chenery 1960, and especially Balassa 1981.

6. Inikori 2002, p. 479.

7. Daudin 2008, abstract.

8. Goody 2010, p. 60.

9. Gilomee and Mbenga 2007, pp.3, 25, 32.

10. Goldstone 2009, p. 4.

11. Ringmar 2007, p. 14.

12. Frank 1998, p. xxv, quoted in Goldstone 2002a.

13. Goldstone 2009, p. 58.

14. Goldstone 2002a.

15. Williamson 1987; Neal 1990.

16. Pollard 1964; Richardson 1989.

17. Braudel and Spooner 1967, p. 470.

18. Studer 2007; Shiue and Keller 2007; and Zanden 2009, summarizing them and producing results for China, pp. 27 (fig. 3), 286 (fig. 37).

19. De Vries 2003; the deepest student of such matters is Dennis Flynn, as in Flynn 1996; and Flynn and Giráldez 1995a, 1995b, 2002, 2004; and Flynn, Giráldez, and Glahn 2003.

20. O'Rourke and Williamson 2002, esp. fig. 1.

21. McCloskey and Zecher 1976, 1984; Ziliak and McCloskey 2008.

22. And see too Hynes, Jacks, and O'Rourke 2009, which has very few uses of statistical

significance (pp. 9, 17), well below the average for such studies, and does not even mention "cointegration" in the text, which is practically unheard of.

23. For example, among dozens of such studies making the same mistake, Özmucur and Pamuk 2007.

24. Ippolito 1975.

25. Compare Mark Overton 1996, who stresses that 1750 to 1850 was still the classic period of the agricultural revolution—though he does reject the previous orthodoxy that saw the seventeenth century as crucial—and Michael Turner and others 2001, arguing on the contrary that the break was in what Michael Thompson called the "second" agricultural revolution in the first half of the nineteenth century. It is distressing to read in the late synthetic work of so fine a historian as Joyce Appleby the conventional story—conventional in 1848 and 1911—that "agricultural innovations . . . freed up workers and capital for other uses" (Appleby 2010, p. 12).

26. Van Vleck 1997, 1999.

27. Inikori 2002, p. 475.

28. Inikori 2002, p. 476; Pooley 1989, p. 66.

29. Pollard 1973, 1981a, 1981b; within Britain compare Hudson 1989.

30. Pollard 1973, p. 648.

31. Harley 1980. Pollard notes, with many others, that Germany had Eastern Europe as a hinterland rather the way the imperial powers had their colonies (Pollard 1891b, p. 174, quoting Otto Hintze).

32. Williamson 2010.

CHAPTER TWENTY FOUR: AND THE LOGIC OF TRADE-AS-AN-ENGINE IS DUBIOUS

1. Pollard 1981, p. 186, citing R. Zangheri. Pollard's "differential of contemporaneousness" is similar to Gerschenkron's notion of "comparative backwardness" (see Pollard, pp. vii, 187, and 364n179).

2. Pollard 1981, p. 184.

3. Mokyr, ed. 1985, pp. 22-23, and works cited there.

4. Mokyr 1977; and Mokyr 1990, pp. 151-153.

5. Hume 1777, p. 264 ("Of Commerce").

6. Unhappily, I have to class William Darity as "deeply misled." In 1992 he defended the importance of the slave trade during the industrial revolution (a tiny part of British trade) by positing a Keynesian model with multipliers. But if the slave trade had multiple effects, why not domestic service or the brass industry?

7. Fogel 1964.

8. Deane and Cole 1962; Mitchell and Deane 1962, p. 330. Imlah 1958.

9. Schultz 1964, p. 70; though see Sen's (not wholly persuasive) strictures in Sen 1967, and Dandekar 1966.

10. O'Rourke, Prados de la Escosura, and Daudin 2008, p. 11.

11. Prados de la Escosura 1993.

12. Inferred from Foreman Peck 2003, p. 375, who gives Maddison's figures. The scatter is a rectangular hyperbola, that is, a (negative) unit-elasticity curve.

13. On the opening of Japan see Bernhofen and Brown 2009 and works cited there.

14. Westphal and Kim 1977; Westphal 1990; Connolly and Yi 2009.

15. Findlay and O'Rourke 2007.

16. Findlay and O'Rourke 2007, p. 339.

17. Findlay and O'Rourke 2007, p. 351.

18. Findlay and O'Rourke 2007, p. 345.

19. *Krieg, Handel und Piraterie, / Dreieinig sind sie, nicht zu trennen* (*Faust* 11187–11188). That the phrase "Krieg, Handel, und Piraterie" is very well known to educated German speakers (111,000 hits on Google in the exact phrase in early 2010) shows the grip of the idea on the European imagination. I am indebted to my colleague Astrida Tantillo in the Department of History at UIC for the reference.

20. O'Rourke, Prados de la Escosura, and Daudin 2008, p. 2.

21. O'Rourke, Prados de la Escosura, and Daudin 2008, pp. 2–3.

22. Barnett 1972, p. 20.

23. Barnett 1972, p. 24.

CHAPTER TWENTY FIVE: AND EVEN THE DYNAMIC EFFECTS OF TRADE WERE SMALL

1. Findlay and O'Rourke 2007, p. 337; compare O'Rourke, Prados de la Escosura, and Daudin 2008, p. 11.

2. McCloskey 1980.

3. Machlup 1963 (1975).

4. Daudin 2004; compare my criticism ages ago of Jeffrey Williamson's calculation of the gain from reinvestment of the gain from the railways in the United States, in McCloskey 1975b.

5. McCloskey 1981 on widespread innovation; also Temin 1997, p. 80; Berg and Hudson 1994.

6. Findlay and O'Rourke always cite this very elderly book by a friend of Lloyd George, and the English translator for Clemenceau in the Versailles Conference, as "1962," fully fifty-four years after its last (and French) version of 1906, and thirty-three years after its only English translation. The impression unintentionally conveyed is that Mantoux was up-to-date in the scholarship of 1962, six years after his death. It is an outcome of the author-date system and the scholarly habits of careless whole-book citation encouraged by it. You can catch me doing it, too. Shame on us.

7. Findlay and O'Rourke 2007, p. 336 (p. 103 in Mantoux 1906).

8. Findlay and O'Rourke 2007, p. 344.

9. Findlay and O'Rourke 2007, p. 336.

10. Marx 1846.

11. Findlay and O'Rourke 2007, p. 339.

12. Lebergott 1985, p. 249.

13. Kennedy 1976 (2006), p. 87.

14. Margaret Jacob, personal correspondence.

15. Personal conversation, Dahlem Seminar, Berlin, Dec. 14, 2008.

16. Jordan 1998. Her lead is "The Indian cornflakes maker Mohan Meakin says it has something to thank Kellogg Co. for: a wake-up call that has helped it win more business."

CHAPTER TWENTY SIX: NOT THE SLAVE TRADE OR IMPERIALISM

1. Engerman 1972; O'Brien 1982.

2. Richardson 2003, p. 512.

3. Austen 1987.

4. Thomas and Bean 1974; and Bean 1975.

5. Eltis and Engerman 2000, abstract.

6. Goldstone 2009, p. 69.

7. Aron 1983 (1990), p. 216.

8. Comte-Sponville 1996 (2001), p. 89.

9. Landes 2006, pp. xvii–xviii. Compare Landes 1998 (p. 19), where he characteristically tweaks the nose of "a new 'multicultural' world history [which disgracefully] finds it hard to live with a Eurocentric story of achievement and transformation," and proudly calls his argument politically incorrect. On the other hand, he spends many eloquent pages showing how little Spain and Portugal got from their looting of the New World or the Indian Ocean.

10. Cowper 1785, *The Task*, book 1, "The Sofa."

11. National income in the mid-eighteenth century is crudely estimated as the midpoint of Maddison's real-dollar figures of per capita income in 1700 and 1820 (Maddison 2006, p. 264) and the midpoint of his population estimates in the same years (p. 241), and then the ratio of this notional midcentury figure to the 1700 figure is applied to Maddison's version of Gregory King's pound figure of £54 million in 1688 (p. 395) for England and Wales alone, providing something like a lower bound: £115 million. I openly confess that I rely on Wikipedia for Clive's fortune (capitalizing for example his £27,000 annual Indian quitrents at 5 percent, added to £300,000 plus £70,000 to be inferred from the article). An expert on these matters, Santhi Hejeebu of Cornell College, Iowa, assures me that the order of magnitude is anyway about right.

12. Prakash 2003, p. 32.

13. Maddison 1965, tables A1 and A3 (exports f.o.b. from/to at current prices), pp. 426 and 430.

14. Maddison 2007, p. 122.

15. Rousseau 1755, p. 20.

16. The locus classicus for these calculations is Davis and Huttenback 1988. The fuller case against all the empires is made in O'Brien and Prados de la Escosura 1999. A contrary case is made by Offer 1993, and a balanced case in Edelstein 1994b (see table 8.1, p. 205).

17. Edelstein 1994a.

CHAPTER TWENTY SEVEN: AND OTHER EXPLOITATIONS, EXTERNAL OR INTERNAL, WERE EQUALLY PROFITLESS

1. Pakenham 1991, p. 611.

2. Pakenham 1991, p. 602.

3. Emmer 2003, p. 391.

4. Emmer 2003, p. 392.

5. Maddison 2007, p. 137.

6. Ardagh 1991, p. 448.

7. Quoted in Pakenham 1991, pp. 598–599.

8. Paton 1948, p. 71.

9. Feinstein 2005, p. 11, fig. 1.3.

10. Eagleton 1996, p. 273n1.

11. Olmstead and Rhode 2008a, 2008b.

12. Feinstein 2005, p. 145, table 7.2, itself from Maddison 2006 (2001).

13. Smith 1776, vol. 1, 1.1.11, p. 24.

14. Locke 1690, book 2, para. 41.

15. Exhibit, Chicago Art Institute, 2008.

16. Hume 1777, p. 329. I thank Hector Luis Alamo, Jr., for bringing my attention to this remark.

17. Ferguson 1997.

CHAPTER TWENTY EIGHT: IT WAS NOT THE SHEER QUICKENING OF COMMERCE

1. Chaucer, General prologue to *The Canterbury Tales*, ll. 701–704.

2. John Munro (2003) gives the evidence, and I made the point in McCloskey 1972b.

3. I have not been able to persuade, over a few decades now of trying, the otherwise very canny Jack Goldstone, as in Goldstone 2002a: "The combination of sustained population growth since the fading of the plague circa 1450, plus a vast infusion of silver, have combined to raise prices in a dizzying spiral; taxes have not kept pace, weakening these regimes." The population growth would have lowered prices, not increased them. And the "dizzying spiral," I have noted, was a mere 2 percent per year, hardly fast enough to make it even mildly difficult for taxes or rents to "keep pace." Something growing at 1.4 percent takes five decades to double. It was not the speed of the price rise but the unequal struggle between landlord and traditional tenant—with the tenant having the upper hand in earlier centuries in setting the rules—that might make rents (for example) and the taxes collected out of them "not keep pace."

4. Appleby 1978, p. 27.

5. For the argument against "core" inflation see Ritholtz 2007, and for a defense of it by another usually canny thinker, DeLong 2007. DeLong argues that food and fuel prices typically have fluctuations that are "self-correcting," and therefore should not be the object of monetary policy. One wonders why other *relative* prices are not also self-correcting, if "correct" means "in the vicinity of supply-and-demand equilibrium."

6. McCloskey 1972b.

7. McCormick 2001, p. 681.

8. Perdue 2005, p. 560.

9. Desmet and Parente 2009, abstract.

CHAPTER TWENTY NINE: NOR THE STRUGGLE OVER THE SPOILS

1. Braudel 1979, p. 325.

2. Braudel 1979, p. 231.

3. Henriksson 1983.

4. John Keymer, quoted in Appleby 1978, pp. 75–76.

5. Braudel 1979, p. 327.

6. Braudel 1979, p. 373; compare p. 416: foreign trade allowed one to "evade the free market."

7. Braudel 1979, p. 248.

8. Braudel 1979, p. 231.

9. Braudel 1979, p. 237.

10. Braudel 1979, p. 325.

11. Braudel 1979, p. 317.

12. Afterthoughts on Material Civilization and Capitalism, p. 112, quoted in Heston 2000.

13. Heston 2000.

14. My father wrote in 1945 that until it introduced civil service in 1937 "Michigan had been, governmentally, a fairly representative American state, carrying the traditional burden of nepotism, jobbery and spoils" (McCloskey 1945, p. 121). In 2010 in Illinois and Chicago we're still working on it; and my father's hopes for Michigan under civil service may have been a little optimistic.

15. Braudel 1979, pp. 372–373.

16. Marx 1846. He continues, though, "but this is true only of England. As for the [Continental] European nations, they were compelled to use machinery by the competition they were encountering from the English," which implies that the machinery was more efficient—which is the bourgeois point.

17. Marglin 1974; Lazonick 1979, 1981; Elbaum and Lazonick 1986; Lorenz 1991; Allen 1992.

18. Lazonick 1991b, p. 2.

19. As it is for example by Raftis (1996, pp. 128–130).

20. McCloskey 1975a; Allen 1992.

21. Langlois 1994.

22. Lewis 1986.

23. See Greif 2006. But then also see Edwards and Ogilvie's critique (2008), and Greif's vexed reply (2008). I am indebted to Petr Barton of the University of Chicago and the University of Economics, Prague, for alerting me to the papers. Neither side in the debate entirely persuades, because neither, at any rate in these fusillades, does the necessary quantitative and comparative work, Magribi with Genoese.

CHAPTER THIRTY: EUGENIC MATERIALISM DOESN'T WORK

1. Clark 2007a, pp. 7–8, 11, 271.

2. Clark 2007a, p. 165.

3. Clark 2007a, p. 183–184, from which subsequent quotations come.

4. Marx and Engels 1848 (1988), sec. 2, p. 73.

5. Marx 1859, p. 43.

6. Engels 1877–1878, pt. 3, chap. 2, "Socialism: Theoretical."

7. Quoted in Stark 2003, p. 61.

8. Novak 2007, p. 232.

9. Milton 1644. H. N. Brailsford remarks justly that Milton "went a long way towards unwriting his masterpiece when he spent his genius supporting a dictator who destroyed the press" (Brailsford 1961, p. 82)

10. Wootton 1992, p. 83.

11. Walzer 1988, p. 81. I would add Eric Hobsbawm and the young Robert Fogel to the list in the twentieth century of innocent communists. Which then makes three.

12. Forgacs 2000, pp. 196–198 (Selections from the Prison Notebooks, 407–409; Selections from Cultural Writings, Q10, para. 2.41.xii).

13. Walzer 1988, p. 81.

14. Lenin 1902, pp. 143–144, his italics.

15. Lenin 1902, p. 179.

16. Walzer 1988, p. 83.

17. Sampson 2005, p. 110.

18. The agricultural historian George Grantham, however, has some telling criticisms of evidence for the simple Malthusian model on which Clark bets so much—see the discussion in Grantham 2007 (for example) of the problem with using wages in threshing, whose apparently straightforwardness conceals variation in other conditions of work.

19. Clark 2007a, p. 2.

20. Clark 2008, p. 182.

21. Clark 2007a, p. 11.

22. On Davenport, the American leader of the eugenics movement, see for example Witkowski and Inglis 2008.

23. Solow 2007.

24. See Adhia 2009.

25. Clark 1987, p. 166.

CHAPTER THIRTY ONE: NEO-DARWINISM DOESN'T COMPUTE

1. Goldstone 2007b.

2. Guinnane 2009.

3. Ó Gráda 2007, p. 350.

4. The table is Clark p. 233; and mine is in McCloskey 1981, reproduced in Harley 1993, and discussed above in chap. 25.

5. Manuelli and Seshadri 2005.

6. Clark 2007c, p. 731.

7. Clark 1987.

8. De Vries 2008a, p. 14; and de Vries 2008b for the full story. Compare Voth 1998, 2001, 2003. The Hume quotation, which de Vries gives, is from Hume's essay "On Commerce," first published in 1741.

9. Goldgar 2007, p. 224.

10. Hersh and Voth 2009 make a related point, that the Columbian Exchange gave Europeans a greater variety of products, which can be expressed (they argue) as about a 20 percent increase in real income for ordinary folk. They take this as contradicting the assertion by Clark and me and most economic historians that $3 a day characterized all humanity until 1800. But

plus or minus 20 percent does not an Age of Innovation make: 20 percent falls well within the $3 plus or minus $2 that was until recently the human condition.

11. De Vries 2008a, note 35.

12. Voth 1998.

13. Voth 2003, p. 256.

14. Hill and Hurtado 2003, p. 11.

15. Vickery 1998, pp. 135–146, as for example p. 135, "Hardly a week went by when a mistress might not be reeling from a servant's flight," as one can also see in realist novels that mention such matters, such as Fielding's *Tom Jones* or *Joseph Andrews*.

16. Compare Easterlin 2004, pp. 21–31.

17. Margo 2008.

18. Wheeler, *A Treatise on Commerce* (1601), p. 73, quoted in Barbalet 2008, p. 79.

19. Earle 1989, pp. 86–87. Earle handily defeats Lawrence Stone's counterclaim that the "gentlemen" fathers were themselves urban "men of limited means," as Stone wrote, who "did not dream of swaggering about with a sword at their sides." Oh yes they did.

20. Quoted in Barbalet 2008, p. 79.

21. Raftis 1996, p. 10.

CHAPTER THIRTY TWO: AND INHERITANCE FADES

1. Friedman 2007.

2. Stone 1964, pp. 42–43.

3. Barbalet 2008, p. 86.

4. Wade 2006, p. 215.

5. McGrath 2007, p. 127, his italics deleted and mine supplied; p. 41 on genome sequencing; compare Collins 2007, pp. 89–90.

6. Mokyr 2007b.

7. Lyovin 1997, p. 257.

8. McInerney and Pisani 2007, p. 1391; and Sorek et al. 2007, on which their article is based. Compare Wade 2006, p. 215: "Organisms may acquire genes through borrowing as well as inheritance; bacteria, for instance." Or the economist Herbert Gintis (2008, p. 5): "Similarly, alternative splicing, nuclear and messenger RNA editing, cellular protein modification and genomic imprinting, which are quite common, quite undermine the standard view of the insular gene producing a single protein, and support the notion of genes having variable boundaries and having strongly context-dependent effects." Dagan et al. in *Proceedings of the National Academy of Sciences* 105 (2008) found that fully 80 percent of 181 prokaryotes had had some borrowing. The reporter for *Science* remarked that "well-defined phylogenetic trees . . . become rather less clearly delineated when looked at over very long time periods" (*Science* 321 [August 8, 2008]: 747). And in humans in the modern world the "long" period would be a couple of generations.

9. Johnson 2000.

10. Thus Stendhal 1839, pp. 146–177 ("It is not for us to demolish the prestige of the powers that be, the French newspapers are demolishing it fast enough"), 475 ("convicted of having read a French newspaper"), and throughout.

11. Galton 1901, p. 15.

12. Bowles 2007.

13. Clark 2008, p. 183. He refers throughout the reply to "practical purposes of social policy" (p. 187, for example), as though his findings were to be applied to, say, encouraging fertility among the economically successful. I realize that such a rhetorical misstep comes from Clark's background as an economist, and because I know him personally I know it is innocent. But one can see why his book has evoked such distaste from its readers, and why they refer back indignantly to Galton and other eugenicists. What "social *policy*"? Shoot all the poor people?

14. Clark 2007, p. 183.

15. Clark 2008, pp. 184–190.

16. Marx 1846.

17. Clark 2007b, p.

18. De Vries 2008c, p. 1181.

19. Manski 2008, p. 4. Ziliak and McCloskey 2008.

20. Galor and Moav 2002.

21. Guinnane 2009 is devastating on these points.

22. Galor and Moav 2002, p. 1181.

23. Vlastos 1986.

24. Winchester 2008, pp. 279–280.

25. Clark and Hamilton 2006, p. 707; Galor and Moav 2002, p. 1180n4.

26. Allen 2006, p. 3, referring to Allen 1983.

27. David 2008.

28. Galton 1901.

29. Brailsford 1961, pp. 79–80. Lilburne was indignant in 1642 when his Royalist captors after the battle of Brentford indicted him for treason under the description of a mere "yeoman." He insisted they call him a gentleman (p. 87).

CHAPTER THRITY THREE: INSTITUTIONS CANNOT BE VIEWED . . . AS INCENTIVE-PROVIDING CONSTRAINTS

1. It is perhaps worth noting that the citation for the prize (which I partly wrote) does not praise the work I am criticizing here, but North's earlier and more strictly cliometric work.

2. North 1991, p. 97, and everywhere in his writings since the 1980s.

3. Lal 2006, p. 151.

4. Levitt and Dubner 2009, p. 125.

5. Butler 1912, p. 263.

6. Lal 2006, p. 151.

7. Levitt and Dubner 2009, p. 122, italics supplied.

8. On the influence of feminism on the labor force participation of British women, see for example McCloskey 2001.

9. Khurana 2007, p. 5.

10. Bourdieu 1979 (1984).

11. Goffman 1961, subtitle and p. 7.

12. Geertz, Geertz, and Rosen 1979, p. 137; quoted in North 1991, p. 104, italics supplied.

13. North 2005, for example, pp. 16 ("non-rational explanations embodied in witchcraft, magic, religions"), 18–19 ("non-rational beliefs . . . [of which] belief in religions is illustration"), 30, 40 ("superstitions, myths, dogmas, and religions"), 41 ("non-rational and supernatural beliefs"), 42, 44, 45, 72, 83, 102, 167, and elsewhere, always in repeated incantations. One is led to ask who is "irrational," the village atheist with incantations formulated at age fourteen and unamended by any later study on the one hand; or St. Thomas Aquinas, Richard Hooker, and Martin Buber on the other. Stanley Fish called Dawkins and Hitchens "Ditchkins" in a *New York Times* column in May 2009, commenting on Eagleton 2009.

14. Iannaccone, who is a good friend of mine, is more sophisticated than his theory: he does not carry the theory into his own church, and has worried deeply about the limits of the Beckerian model he employs.

15. Becker and Stigler 1977.

16. North 1991, p. 99.

17. Compare Hiser 2003.

18. Lachmann 1977, p. 62, quoted in Boettke and Storr 2002, p. 171.

19. Kelling and Wilson 1982; Keizer et al. 2008.

20. Grotius 1625, propositions vi and vii.

21. Lachmann 1977, p. 141; quoted in Boettke and Storr 2002, p. 171.

22. I learned after I wrote this that Erving Goffman in 1971 made the same point about traffic lights. Behavior is not just behavior. To the people involved, in the situation they believe they are in, it has meaning.

23. Aaron Keuhn, letter to the editor, *Chicago Tribune*, March 7, 2008, p. 20.

24. Keynes 1937, pp. 161–162; compare pp. 157, 170; Akerlof and Shiller 2009, p. 1; Sen 1985.

25. Khurana 2007, pp. 323–324. My thanks to Eduard Bonet of the Escuela Superior de Administración y Dirección de Empresas in Barcelona for drawing my attention to this fine book.

26. Khurana 2007, p. 325, a bow to the liberal discourse theory that I among many others would stress. Khurana adds that an organization also involves "power, coercion, and exploitation," which is a bow to Marxist conflict theory.

27. I discuss the point about Kant in McCloskey 2006a, pp. 179–280, 338.

28. Macfarlane 2000, p. 278.

29. Tocqueville 1856 (1955), p. 223.

30. Skinner 1998, p. 98, from where my learning below comes.

CHAPTER THIRTY FOUR: AND SO THE BETTER INSTITUTIONS . . . DON'T EXPLAIN

1. North 1991, p. 101.

2. North 1991, p. 98.

3. Gregory Clark makes a similar point in Clark 2007c (p. 7) about an argument in North and Thomas (1973, p. 6) that "new institutional arrangements will not be set up unless the private benefits of their creation promise to exceed the costs." Clark comments with stiletto precision: "This has an air of certainty that perhaps only truism can deliver."

4. North 1991, p. 109.

5. North 1991, p. 105.

6. North 1991, p. 106.

7. North 1991, p. 106.

8. North 1991, p. 107.

9. North 1991, p. 109

10. North 1991, p. 101.

11. North and Weingast 1989, p. 831.

12. Israel 1989, p. 412.

13. Langford 2000, pp. 140–141.

14. Ekelund 2003, p. 366.

15. Wells and Wills 2000, p. 418.

16. Sellar and Yeatman 1931, p. 77.

17. Hoppit 1996, p. 126.

18. Reinhart and Rogoff 2008, p. 53.

19. Millar 1787 (1803), chap. 3.

20. Bennett 1921/1932 (1970), p. 166.

21. Bennett 1921/1932 (1970), p. 183.

22. Bennett 1921/1932 (1970), pp. 172, 181.

23. Hellie 2003, p. 416.

24. World Bank 2005.

25. North and Weingast 1989, tables 2 and 3, with their guess at national income of £41 million in 1642.

26. Macaulay 1830, pp. 186–187.

27. North 1991, p. 107.

28. Higgs 1997, 2006.

29. North and Weingast 1989, once again on that pregnant p. 831. Peter Murrell (2009) has shown with seventeenth- and eighteenth-century data that there is no break in 1689.

30. Demsetz 1967 is a fount for the insight.

31. Temple 1672, chap. 6.

32. Hobbes 1651, p. 186.

33. North and Weingast 1989, p. 831.

34. Acemoglu 2008; compare Acemoglu, Johnson, and Robinson 2005, citing for example R. H. Tawney, unaware it appears that his Fabian views have largely been overturned.

35. Edward Miller wrote in 1951 that "there was a very flourishing land market amongst the [southern English] peasantry . . . in the early thirteenth century" (p. 131). One of the leading recent students of medieval English agriculture, Bruce Campbell, notes that "tenants of all sorts were active participants in the market, trading in commodities, buying and selling labor and land, and exchanging credit," citing some of the numerous medievalists who agree (2005, p. 8). That does not mean that everything worked smoothly. Campbell argues that the fourteenth century was characterized by "rural congestion engendered by the lax tenurial control exercised by most landlords" (p. 10). But anyway, his picture, based on the best scholarship over many decades, is the opposite of the exploitation and the absence of markets posited by

Acemoglu. The serfs owned the lords, not the other way around. Such a conclusion is found in most of the modern evidence-based literature on the peasantry in England, as for example in Raftis 1996, p. 4.

36. McCloskey 1975a. And Raftis 1996, p. 118: in the medieval historiography developing since the 1940s, "customary tenure [that is, serfdom] becomes no longer a block to [English] economic development but an instrument for such development. . . . Peasant progress occurred despite the limitations of the manorial system."

37. Berman 2003; and again Raftis 1996, pp. 9–10, 7: The major customary tenants [were] the most active economic agents" even in the "purest type of manor." A good, rough test of whether a student of the medieval economy actually knows the terrain is whether or not she is familiar with the work of Father Raftis (on this account see his own strictures on Robert Brenner [1996, p. 214n40]). Acemoglu and before him North, alas, fail the test.

38. O'Brien 1993, p. 126, table 6.1.

39. Clark 2007a is good on this, pp. 10, 212.

40. Chaucer, *Canterbury Tales*, "General Prologue," lines 276–277.

41. Sellar and Yeatman 1931, p. 94.

42. Zanden 2009, pp. 29–30.

43. Zanden 2009, pp. 29–31, where he summarizes his case.

44. Zanden gives a lucid review of the explanations for Arab decline in 2009, pp. 60–64, emphasizing the embourgeoisification of Europe. He admits on p. 293 that "late Ming and Qing China [and, one might ask, why not the Song?] and Tokugawa Japan had institutions, especially horizontal institutions [as against the 'vertical' institutions of state power] that were able to compete with those in Western Europe [one might ask, why not the north of Italy?]."

CHAPTER THIRTY FIVE: AND ANYWAY THE ENTIRE ABSENCE OF PROP-
ERTY IS NOT RELEVANT

1. McCants 2009.

2. Pipes 1999, pp. xi–xii, 101, 159–208 (esp. 162–166), 171, 180.

3. Hellie 2003, p. 415.

4. Hellie 2003, p. 416.

5. Peake and Fleure 1928.

6. Perdue argues persuasively that on China's western marches "one last nomadic state . . . held out against the military forces closing in on the steppe. . . . [The] true world historical transformation that tipped the balance against unfettered nomadism happened from 1680 to 1760," in the victories by the gunpowder armies of the Qing (Perdue 2005, p. 11).

7. Perdue 2003, p. 492.

8. Hellie 2003, p. 415.

9. Lattimore 1940, pp. 6–7.

10. Montesquieu (1748), 4.14.

11. For example, Pipes 1999, p. 103, on Alexander's successor states. One is startled to find the backing in footnotes 134–137 to consist of books published in 1934, 1906 (twice), 1941, as though we have learned nothing about the Hellenistic world for seventy years.

12. He defends such practices on p. 149, railing against such recent and execrable fashions

in historiography as "deconstructionism" (the scare quotes are his), about which he appears to know little. "It is for this reason," he asserts without evidence, "that the last word on any given historical subject is often the first."

13. For example, Braudel 1979, p. 596, says so.

14. Wink 2003, p. 27.

15. Demetz 1997, p. 41; compare p. 18.

16. More 1516, p. 11.

17. Quoted in Blanning 2007, p. 197; the next quotation is from p. 198.

18. Pipes 1999, p. 29, my italics.

19. As George Mason wrote in the Virginia Declaration of Rights the month before the Committee of Five drafted the Declaration of Independence.

20. Discussed in Pipes 1999, pp. 27–28.

21. Epstein 2009.

22. Macaulay 1830, p. 183.

23. Goldsmith 1984, p. 283.

24. Gintis 2006, p. 2.

25. Gintis 2006, p. 7. On the other hand, Alan Grafen argued plausibly (1987) that an intruder who will never get a place in the sun if he does not fight the bourgeois (who, if not fought, will be in possession for a long time) becomes a desperado (the Spanish means "hopeless one"), having every evolutionary (and revolutionary) incentive to expropriate the expropriators.

26. See for example, among a large literature, Carlos and Lewis 1999 and Anderson and Hill 2004.

27. Hardin 1968.

28. "Since, however, the effects of overgrazing are shared by all the herdsmen, the negative utility for any particular decision-making herdsman is only a fraction of 1." The mathematics works out to a rather large fraction of 1 if N is small.

29. Hoffman 2003a, p. 91.

30. Raftis 1996, p. 3.

31. Zanden 2009, p. 17.

32. On open fields, McCloskey 1976. On guilds, Epstein 1991, 1998; on guilds and North's panglossianism, Ogilvie 2004, 2007.

33. Ostrom 1990. The matter is to be discussed at length in Bowles and Gintis, *A Cooperative Species* (forthcoming).

34. Anderson and Hill 2004; McCloskey 1991b, esp. pp. 348–350.

35. Berman 2003, p. 377; compare p. ix; and Berman 1983. Berman is heavily relied on by Deepak Lal 1998 and 2006.

CHAPTER THIRTY SIX: THE CHRONOLOGY OF PROPERTY AND INCENTIVES HAS BEEN MISMEASURED

1. North and Weingast 1989, p. 831, a page which rewards rhetorical study as an example of how to claim in the conclusion of an essay propositions unconnected to the evidence offered.

2. Greif 2006, p. 3.

3. Mokyr 2008, p. 3.

4. Aghion, Harris, Howitt, and Vickers 2001.

5. Gilbert and Sullivan 1893, act 1, pp. 537–538, 532, 539.

6. Macfarlane 1978, p. 195.

7. Greenfeld 2001.

8. North 1991, p. 107.

9. De Cecco 1975, p. 11.

10. Swedish friends assure me that if the Swedish bureaucrats had been presented with the opportunities that Tammany Hall politicians faced they would have taken them, too. But my friends have not lived in the Upper Midwest in the United States, filled with startlingly honest Scandinavians, where the experiment has in fact been tried of giving Swedish immigrants American-scale opportunities for corruption.

11. North and Weingast 1989, p. 831.

12. O'Brien 1993, p. 126, table 6.1. O'Brien's figures are for half decades; only 11 out of 25 were peaceful.

13. Israel 1989, p. 413.

14. Ekelund and Tollison 1981, p. 223.

15. Bogart 2009, p. 28.

16. Crafts 2004 (2005), p. 10 of manuscript.

17. Deakin 2008, pp. 2, 26.

18. North 1991, p. 110.

19. North 1991, p. 111.

CHAPTER THIRTY SEVEN: AND SO THE ROUTINE OF MAX U DOESN'T WORK

1. Mokyr 2010, p. 85.

2. Hume 1777 (1987), p. 93 ("Of Civil Liberty"), his italics.

3. Allen 2006, pp. 2, 3.

4. Butler 1725, p. 349.

5. Smith 1749 (1790) 7.2.4–12, p. 312.

6. Mokyr 2010, p. 90.

7. All this is from Mokyr 2008, pp. 90–93. Grantham 2009, p. 4.

8. Smith 1749 (1790), 4.1.10, p. 185; Horace, *Odes*, 1.4.13, 2.18.32–34, 3.1 entire.

9. Allen 2006, p. 3, referring to Allen 1983. Nuvolari 2004 applies Allen's idea to Cornwall's pumping engines.

10. Carlyle 1829, quoted in Bronk 2009, p. viii.

11. Mokyr 1990, pp. 158–159; Nye 1991.

12. Nordhaus 2004. The quotation is from the abstract.

13. McKeon 1987 (2002), p. 201.

14. McKeon 1987 (2004), p. xxi; Eliot 1921.

15. Appleby 1978, p. 22.

16. Appleby 1978, p. 41.

17. Hirschman 1977, pp. 32–40.

18. Temple 1672, chap. 6.

19. Montesquieu 1748, book 20, sec. 7.

20. Langford 2000, p. 5.

21. Barnett 1974, p. 264: "He was able by tact, perseverance and sheer talent for management to create out of a ramshackle coalition an instrument of war formidable enough to bring
greatest monarchy in Europe to its knees." Barnett argues persuasively that Marlborough's
youthful experience of being poor and dependent on the great made him hesitant in politics,
"which contrasts so strangely with his behavior in the face of a French army" (p. 252), quite
different (see p. 60) from the character of an aristocrat by birth such as Wellington (or for that
matter Marlborough's descendant Winston Churchill).

22. As Correlli Barnett complains in Barnett 1972 and subsequent works.

23. Letter to Corcelle, Sept. 17, 1853, quoted in Swedberg 2009, p. 280. Of course, if you
define "institutions" broadly enough, as North sometimes does, then they explain everything,
because laws have been merged with *moeurs*, or with anything else outside their naked and
unsocialized will that leads people to do things.

24. Migheli 2009.

25. Hoffman 1997.

26. North and Thomas 1973, pp. 2–3.

27. The figures are taken from Munkhammar 2007, pp. 82, 107, 70. You are not to guess
which is higher: the point is that the difference is so small that no powerful force is at work.

28. Letter to Louis de Kergorlay, Sept. 28, 1834, quoted in Swedberg 2009, p. 3.

CHAPTER THIRTY EIGHT: THE CAUSE WAS NOT SCIENCE

1. Hayek 1960, p. 42.

2. Field 2010; Howitt 2005, p. 7, in the Brown University preprint.

3. Berman 2006.

4. Hayek 1960, pp. 42–43.

5. Easterlin 2004, p. 8.

6. Crafts 2004 (2005), p. 10 of manuscript.

7. The classic statement for science as the cause is Musson and Robinson 1969 and Musson
1972, but I refer here especially to later work by Jacob, Mokyr, and Goldstone.

8. Mokyr 1990, p. 168.

9. Easterlin 1995, p. 99.

10. Rosenberg 1978, pp. 282–283; compare Rosenberg 1982, p. 13.

11. Mokyr 2007a, p. 30.

12. Mokyr 1990, p. 169.

13. Tunzelmann 2003, p. 86.

14. See for example Prentice 2008,.

15. Mokyr 1990, pp. 169–170.

16. Maddison 2006, pp. 437, 439, 443, in 1990 international Geary-Khamis dollars, uncorrected for improved products à la Gordon/Nordhaus/Payson.

17. Maddison 2006, pp. 465, 466, 467.

18. Mokyr 2010, p. 61.

19. Goldstone 2002b, abstract.

20. Grantham 2009, p. 13.

21. Grantham 2009, p. 5.

22. Allen 2006, p. 14 of manuscript, quoting Mandeville 1705, 1714, vol. 2, p. 144 ("Third Dialogue"); also in Allen 2009, p. 251.

23. Durie 2003, p. 458.

24. The economist and theologian Paul Oslington has argued so to me.

25. Jacob 1997, p. 108.

26. Waterman 2003.

27. Mandeville 1705, 1714, vol. 2, p. 144 ("Third Dialogue").

28. Mokyr 2003, p. 50.

29. Allen 2009, p. 247.

30. Allen 2009, p. 257.

CHAPTER THIRTY NINE: BUT BOURGEOIS DIGNITY AND LIBERTY ENTWINED WITH THE ENLIGHTENMENT

1. Goldstone 2009, p. 134.

2. Jacob 1997, p. 65.

3. Johnson 1753.

4. Easterlin 1995, p. 99.

5. Ridley 1996, p. 263. Compare Prince Kropotkin 1901, giving a very similar view of an ideal town from what most people believe is very different political perspective.

6. Jacob 1981 (2006), p. vi.

7. Appleby 1978, chaps. 1 and 2. Supple 1959.

8. Goldstone 2002a.

9. Jacob 2001, p. 68.

10. Mokyr 2007a, p. 1.

11. Jacob 1997, p. 59.

12. Jacob 1981 (2006), p. x; Jacob 2001, p. 50.

13. Jacob 1997, p. 71.

14. Jacob 2001, p. 63.

15. Personal correspondence, 2008.

16. Landes 1998, p. 35.

17. Mathias 1972 (1979), p. 66.

18. Najita 1987.

19. Lessnoff 2003, p. 361.

20. Field 2003, 2006, 2010; confirmed from other sources by Alexopoulos and Cohen 2009.

21. Goldstone 2009, p. 29.

22. MacLeod 1998, p. 98.

23. Goody 2010, p. 77. This is not one of the occasions in which, as Montaigne says, I have run myself through with my own weapons. I do not omit human intentionality: agency emerges for example in my examples of literary propaganda for bourgeois dignity and liberty.

24. Landes 1998, p. 517.

25. For a full confession see McCloskey 2006a, chaps. 38–40.

26. Landes 1998, p. 522.

27. Landes 1998, p. 517.

CHAPTER FOURTY: IT WAS NOT ALLOCATION

1. Sahlins 1976, pp. 211, 216.

2. Mill 1843, p. 464.

3. Collins 2007, 93, 95, 193–195, 204.

4. *Essays*, "The Transcendentalist," p. 1.

5. Kirzner 1976, p. 79.

6. The analysis of the virtues derives from Aristotle, Aquinas, and Adam Smith—the three A's—and is detailed in McCloskey 2006a, *The Bourgeois Virtues*.

7. Macaulay 1830, p. 183.

8. Goldstone 2009, p. 120.

9. Again see Nelson 1991, 2001.

10. See all my writings before about 1983, and many afterward.

11. Kirzner 1976, p. 84, his italics.

12. Mill 1871, book 4, chap. 2, sec. 1.6. Note his usage of the word "science," in the older and wider sense of "systematic inquiry," as in all his writings.

13. Maddison 2006, pp. 415, 419, 439, 443.

14. Mill 1871, book 4, chap. 6, sec. 2.114.

15. Mill 1871, book 4, chap. 6, sec. 2.116.

16. Macaulay 1830, p. 186.

CHAPTER FOURTY ONE: IT WAS WORDS

1. My learning about Goethe's relevance to efficiency vs. growth, and the citations and translations, come from Astrida Tantillo's book (Tantillo, forthcoming). I thank her for allowing me to quote from it before its publication.

2. Tantillo, forthcoming, "Introduction."

3. Quoted in Pincus 2006, p. 120, and the same place for the next quotation from Bethel.

4. Voltaire 1733, p. 154. The remark is not strictly accurate, since Walpole, though the first and longest-serving prime minister in British history (1721–1742), became an earl only after his fall from power in 1742 (since a member of the aristocracy could not serve in the House of Commons, the honor of the [re-]created peerage was instead bestowed on Walpole's son, in 1723; Voltaire must have added the remark to a later edition than the first of 1733). But for my purposes it will do: Sir Robert Walpole when in power was made early a Knight of the Bath, and was in other ways, too, in effect a member of the aristocracy, or at least the very highest ranks of the gentry.

5. César de Saussure in 1727, quoted in Blanning 2007, p. 110.

6. Aristotle, *Politics* 1278a20–25.

7. *Considerations Requiring Greater Care for Trade in England*, anonymous, quoted in Pincus 2009, p. 382.

8. Tinniswood 2007, chap. 19, "The Levant Trader."

9. Blanning 2007, pp. 110–111.

10. Danford 2006, p. 319. The quotation from Lord Kames (1774) is Danford's.

11. Cowper 1785, book 4. The quotations from Kames are Danford's.

12. Danford 2006, p. 324.

13. Danford 2004, p. 325.

14. Whitman 1871, p. 264.

15. Pew Research Center 2008, p. 10. The authors of the report, for reasons they do not state, want to define people who call themselves "upper middle" (19 percent) as "upper" and people who call themselves "lower middle" (another 19 percent) as "lower," which is how they arrive at the assertion that only 53 percent identify as middle class (these being people who replied to the telephone survey by saying "middle" with no adjectives). That puts Americans in the same range as British and French respondents. But taking people at their self-defining word, all but the 2 percent pure "upper" and the 6 percent pure "lower" (and 1 percent not replying at all), use the middling word. The fact is at least rhetorically interesting.

16. National Centre for Social Research 2007, p. 2. Compare Marshall and others 1988, p. 144, 38.5 percent identifying as middle class.

17. Mokyr 2010, p. 61.

CHAPTER FORTY TWO: DIGNITY AND LIBERTY FOR ORDINARY PEOPLE

1. Hume 1754–1755, p. 531.

2. Tocqueville 1835, p. 116.

3. Hayek 1960, p. 26.

4. Rosenberg 1994, p. 223.

5. Arthur 1989, David 1990.

6. Smith 1776, vol. 2, 4.9.51, p. 687.

7. Quoted in McKeon 1987 (2002), p. 202.

8. Quoted in McKeon 1987 (2002), p. 197.

9. North 1691, preface, p. viii.

10. Voltaire 1733, letter 10, p. 154f.

11. Palmer 1997, p. 442.

12. Quoted in Brailsford 1961, p. 624. Compare John Lilburne's charge in 1646 that the upper house of Parliament was now acting as the king had: "All you intended . . . was merely to unhorse and dismount our old riders and tyrants, that so you might get up, and ride us in their stead" (Brailsford 1961, p. 93).

13. The first sentence of chapter 2 of *The Spheres and Duties of Government* (published only in 1851, after his death, because of its libertarian content, and swiftly translated into English.)

14. Lindberg 2004.

15. Macfarlane 2000, p. 207.

16. Sieyès 1789, chap. 2: "On n'est pas libre par des privilèges, mais par les droits qui appartiennent à tous."

17. Otteson 2006, p. 160.

18. Auslander 2009, p. 12. H. N. Brailsford puts it well when he remarks of the 1640s in Britain that "the arts of rousing public opinion and organizing men were new discoveries in that generation" (Brailsford 1961, p. 62). Such arts of liberty were born in the Netherlands in the

1620s and flourished later, with setbacks, in places like Amsterdam (where the Leveller Richard Overton [1620?-1680?] learned them; compare Locke in the 1680s).

19. Steele 1722, act 4, sc. 2 (p. 159 in Quintana 1952).

20. Lillo 1731, act 1, sc. 1 (p. 294 in Quintana 1952).

21. Rosendahl 1919-1935, p. xi. The cartoonist "Rosendahl," by the way, would appear to have come from the unique barony of that name (unlike Danes, and like the Swedes, the Norwegian peasants working their wretched soils were not on the whole serfs of any baron). It is three miles from the Dimelsvik of my Norwegian ancestors.

22. Rietbergen 1998, p. xxiv.

CHAPTER FOURTY THREE: AND THE MODEL CAN BE FORMALIZED

1. In her elegant recent book (Cartwright 2007) the philosopher of science Nancy Cartwright argues for a variety of causation beyond billiard balls—"assists," "encourages," "obviates obstacles to," and so forth. And we might profit also from reviving Aristotle's ruminations on material, formal, efficient, and final causes.

2. Howitt 2005, p. 7 in the Brown University preprint.

3. Howitt 2005, p. 10; and Mokyr 1990, p. 179.

CHAPTER FOURTY FOUR: OPPOSING THE BOURGEOISIE HURTS THE POOR

1. Eagleton 2006.

2. Wallerstein 1983 (1995), p. 98.

3. Pomeranz and Topik 2006, pp. 134-135.

4. Lattimore 1940, p. 393.

5. Mokyr 1990, p. 179.

6. Quoted by Pollard 1981, p. 60.

7. Pomeranz and Topik 2006, pp. 131-132.

8. Rietbergen 1998, pp. 234-235.

9. Roth 2006, p. 101.

10. *Essay on Man*, epistle 3, lines 17-18.

11. Oxford 1999, p. 1610.

12. Wilde 1891 (1930), pp. 257, 270. The next quotation is p. 259. The editor, Hesketh Pearson, remarks that Wilde had been inspired by a lecture of G. B. Shaw's, "without bothering himself much about economics" (p. xii). The astoundingly scholarly Wikipedia entry for "wage slavery" gives the arguments from people like Noam Chomsky against my views, and those by people like Robert Nozick in favor of them.

13. I realize you have settled opinions about Friedman because of your deep knowledge of his involvement with the Pinochet regime in Chile, acquired from numerous and irrefutable stories in the *Village Voice*. But let me try to unsettle your opinions. Friedman in fact, and on libertarian principle, never after his wartime service advised any governments or accepted money from them—including Chile under Pinochet, with which he had in fact slight contact. Friedman refused two honorary degrees from state universities in Chile precisely because he did not want to be associated with a government. I was present at a faculty meeting at the

University of Chicago at which Milton singlehandedly killed a proposal for the Department of Economics to get millions of dollars from the Shah of Iran to educate Iranian professors of economics. He stood up and scolded us: "We can't be associated with a dictator like the Shah." We were stunned, and ashamed at our impulse to accept, dazzled by dollar signs.

14. Maddison 2006, p. 264, and also for the Chinese figure below.

15. Maddison 2006, p. 273.

16. Wallerstein 1983 (1995), p. 100.

17. Karabel 2005, chap. 3.

18. Mill 1871, book 4, chap. 7, sec. 1. It is the same in the first, 1848 edition, and was much influenced then (Mill says in his *Autobiography*) by the thought of Harriet Taylor.

19. Thaler and Sunstein 2008; Hirsch 1976; Frank 1985; Frank and Cook 1995.

20. Bastiat 1845, 2.15.58–59.

21. Seaton 1996, p. 35, which alerted me to Trilling's worry. The references are to Trilling's essay on Henry James, "Princess Casamassima," and "Manners, Morals, and the Novel," both in Trilling 1950.

22. Seaton 1996, p. 34.

CHAPTER FOURTY FIVE: AND THE BOURGEOIS ERA WARRANTS THEREFORE NOT . . . PESSIMISM

1. Caplan 2007, chap. 2.

2. Smith 1776, vol. 2, 4.2.9, p. 456.

3. Theil 2008, from which subsequent quotations are also drawn.

4. World Bank 2006.

5. Dyson 2008, p. 45, examining sympathetically the arguments of that ever-useful economist, William Nordhaus, in his book *A Question of Balance: Weighing the Options on Global Warming Policies* (2008).

6. Nelson, 2009.

7. Jones 2003, p. 58.

8. Ehrlich 1968, p. xi.

9. Simon 1996.

10. Eldridge 1995, p. 9. Thus mistaken science comes from the English-language belief that the only "sciences" are physical and biological: Eldridge believed a geologist, and did not consult an economist or a historian.

11. Macaulay 1830, pp. 186, 187.

12. Blum and Kalven 1963; Pearson 1900.

13. Young 1928.

14. Simon 1981 (1996).

15. Goldstone 2009, p. 17.

16. Compare Tishkoff and others 2009 reporting on the genetic makeup of 2,400 people from 113 separate linguistic groups in Africa.

CHAPTER FOURTY SIX: BUT AN AMIABLE, IF GUARDED, OPTIMISM

1. I owe these hypotheses to a discussion with graduate students in economics at Northwestern University in March 2009.

2. Nutter 1962; Gerschenkron 1947 and a collection of his papers on Soviet growth in Gerschenkron 1962; Bergson 1961.

3. The summary table of Answers.com at http://www.answers.com/ topic/soviet-economic-growth tells the sad story, on the basis of research by Gur Ofer, Laurie Kurtzweg, James Noren, and Angus Maddison.

4. Easterly and Fischer 1995, p. 42, table 4.

5. The Galbraith, Samuelson, and Thurow quotations come from D'Souza 1997.

6. Davies 2005.

7. Schmitt 2007, table 1.

8. Lindbeck 2009.

7. As is argued persuasively by Berman 2006.

10. Harvey 2005, p. 3.

11. Boyd 1997, p. 529.

12. Tuckwell 1902, chap. 5.

13. Hirschman 1977; and recently Klamer 2003, 2007; Bronk 2009. Kenneth Boulding (1910–1993), a leading economist and a leading Quaker, would be an older case in point. The late Stanley Lebergott (1918–2009) of Wesleyan University was another example of someone who used all the evidence—of *King Lear* as much as of the Department of Commerce. (He was an example, too, of how economists at liberal arts colleges are well placed to discern a humanistic science of economics, if they will just stop checking for approval from the MITs of the world.) Down to the 1940s one could have cited many more economists, as I have earlier, from the sainted Adam Smith (1723–1790) to the blessed Frank Knight (1885–1972) and the insightful Joseph Schumpeter (1883–1950) and the paradoxical Maynard Keynes (1883–1946). The turn to specialized illiteracy among economists, fortified by a scornful ignorance of history, philosophy, theology, and literature, happened in the 1960s and 1970s, among the students of the first generation of Samuelsonians.

14. Boettke and Storr 2002, pp. 180–181. Compare Storr 2006.

I have regularly given the date of first publication of a work, since it is more informative about the intellectual history than a citation such as "Hobbes (1986)." Where a later edition than the first is used, it is indicated by the further publishing details.

∞

Abbing, Hans. 2002. *Why Artists Are Poor: The Exceptional Economy of the Arts*. Amsterdam: Amsterdam University Press; and Chicago: University of Chicago Press.

Abramovitz, Moses. 1956. "Resources and Output Trend in the United States since 1870." *American Economic Review* 46: 5–23.

Acemoglu, Daron. 2002. "Technical Change, Inequality and the Labor Market." *Journal of Economic Literature* 40: 7–72.

Acemoglu, Daron. 2008. "Growth and Institutions." In S. N. Durlauf and L. E. Blume, eds., *The New Palgrave Dictionary of Economics*, 2nd ed. London: Palgrave Macmillan.

Acemoglu, Daron, Simon Johnson, and James Robinson. 2005. "The Rise of Europe: Atlantic Trade, Institutional Change, and Economic Growth." *American Economic Review* 95: 546–579.

Adams, Henry. 1907 (published 1918). *The Autobiography of Henry Adams*. New York: Modern Library, 1931.

Adhia, Nimish. 2009. "Bourgeois Virtues in India: How Bollywood Heralded India's Economic Liberalization."Manuscript, Department of Economics, University of Illinois at Chicago. At http://www.allacademic.com/meta/p_mla_apa_research_citation/3/6/3/7/6/p363765_index.html.

Aghion, P., C. Harris, P. Howitt, and J. Vickers. 2001. "Competition, Imitation and Growth with Step-by-step Innovation." *Review of Economic Studies* 68: 467–492.

Akerlof, George A. 1997. "Social Distance and Social Decisions." *Econometrica* 65 (September): 1005–1027.

Akerlof, George A., and Robert J. Shiller. 2009. *Animal Spirits: How Human Psychology Drives the Economy, and Why It Matters for Global Capitalism.* Princeton: Princeton University Press.

Alexopoulos, Michelle, and Jon Cohen. 2009. "Measuring Our Ignorance, One Book at a Time: New Indicators of Technological Change, 1909–1949." Working paper 349. Department of Economics, University of Toronto.

Allen, Robert C. 1977. "The Peculiar Productivity History of American Blast Furnaces, 1840–1913." *Journal of Economic History* 37 (September): 605–633.

Allen, Robert C. 1983. "Collective Invention." *Journal of Economic Behavior and Organization* 4 (1) (January): 605–633.

Allen, Robert C. 1992. *Enclosure and the Yeoman: The Agricultural Development of the South Midlands, 1450–1850.* Oxford: Clarendon Press.

Allen, Robert C. 2006. "The British Industrial Revolution in Global Perspective: How Commerce Created the Industrial Revolution and Modern Economic Growth." Paper presented at Nuffield College, Oxford University. At http://www.nuffield.ox.ac.uk/users/allen/unpublished/econinvent–3.pdf.

Allen, Robert C. 2009. *The British Industrial Revolution in Global Perspective.* Cambridge: Cambridge University Press.

Allen, Robert C., Jean-Pascal Bassino, Debin Ma, Christine Moll-Murata, and Jan Luiten van Zanden. 2009. "Wages, Prices and Living Standards in China, 1738–1925: In Comparison with Europe, Japan, and India." London School of Economics Working Paper. At http://www.lse.ac.uk/collections/economicHistory/EconomicHistoryworking.

Alschuler, Albert W. 2000. *Law Without Values: The Life, Work, and Legacy of Justice Holmes.* Chicago: University of Chicago Press.

Anderson, Terry L., and Peter J. Hill. 2004. *The Not So Wild, Wild West: Property Rights on the Frontier.* Stanford: Stanford University Press.

Anthony, David W. 2007. *The Horse, the Wheel, and Language: How Bronze-Age Riders from the Eurasian Steppes Shaped the Modern World.* Princeton: Princeton University Press.

Appleby, Joyce Oldham. 1978. *Economic Thought and Ideology in Seventeenth-Century England.* Princeton: Princeton University Press.

Appleby, Joyce Oldham. 2010. *The Relentless Revolution: A History of Capitalism.* New York: Norton.

Aquinas, Thomas. 1267–1273. *Summa Theologica.* Translated by Fathers of the English Dominican Province.

Ardagh, John. 1991. *Germany and the Germans: After Unification.* New rev. ed. London: Penguin.

Aron, Raymond. 1983 (1990). *Memoirs.* Translated by George Holoch. Abridged ed. New York: Holmes and Meier.

Arthur, W. Brian. 1989. "Competing Technologies, Increasing Returns, and Lock-In by Historical Events." *Economic Journal* 99: 116–131.

Ashton, Thomas S. 1948. *The Industrial Revolution, 1760–1830.* Oxford: Oxford University Press.

Asplund, Martin. 2008. "The Shining Make-Up of Our Star." *Science* 322 (October 3): 51–52.

Augustine, St. 398 AD. *Confessions.* Translated by F. J. Sheed. New York: Sheed and Ward, 1943.

Auslander, Leora. 2009. *Cultural Revolutions: Everyday Life and Politics in Britain, North America, and France.* Berkeley: University of California Press.

Austen, Ralph. 1987. *African Economic History: Internal Development and External Dependency.* Portsmouth, N.H.: Heinemann; London: James Currey.

Baechler, Jean. 1971 (1975). *Les Origines du Capitalisme.* Paris: Gallimard. Translated as *The Origins of Capitalism.* Oxford: Basil Blackwell.

Baechler, Jean, John A. Hall, and Michael Mann, eds. 1988. *Europe and the Rise of Capitalism.* Oxford: Blackwell.

Bahtra, Ravi. 1987. *The Great Depression of 1990.* New York: Simon and Schuster.

Bailyn, Bernard. 2003. *To Begin the World Anew: The Genius and Ambiguities of the American Founders.* New York: Vintage Books (Random House).

Balassa, Bela. 1981. *The Process of Industrial Development and Alternative Development Strategies.* Princeton University, Department of Economics, International Finance Section.

Balázs, Étienne. 1964. *Chinese Civilization and Bureaucracy: Variations on a Theme.* New Haven: Yale University Press.

Baran, Paul A., and Paul M. Sweezy. 1966. *Monopoly Capital: An Essay on the American Economic and Social Order.* New York: Monthly Review Press.

Barbalet, Jack. 2008. *Weber, Passion and Profits: 'The Protestant Ethic and the Spirit of Capitalism' in Context.* Cambridge: Cambridge University Press.

Barnett, Correlli. 1972. *The Collapse of British Power.* London: Eyre Methuen.

Barnett, Correlli. 1974. *Marlborough.* London: Eyre Methuen. Ware, Hertfordshire: Wordsworth Editions, 1999.

Bastiat, Frédéric. 1845. *Economic Sophisms.* Translated by Arthur Goddard. Irvington-on-Hudson, N.Y.: Foundation for Economic Education, 1996.

Bates, Robert H. 1981. *States and Markets in Tropical Africa: The Political Basis of Agricultural Policy.* Berkeley: University of California Press.

Bauernschuster, Stefan, Oliver Falck, Robert Gold, and Stephan Heblich. 2009. "The Shadows of the Past: How Implicit Institutions Influence Entrepreneurship." Jena Economic Research Papers. At www.jenecon.de.

Baumol, William J. 2002. *The Free Market Innovation Machine: Analyzing the Growth Miracle of Capitalism.* Princeton: Princeton University Press.

Baumol, William J., Robert E. Litan, and Carl J. Schramm. 2007. *Good Capitalism, Bad Capitalism, and the Economics of Growth and Prosperity.* New Haven: Yale University Press.

Bayly, Christopher. 1989. *Imperial Meridian: The British Empire and the World, 1780–1830.* London: Longman.

Bean, Richard N. 1975. *The British Trans-Atlantic Slave Trade, 1650–1775.* New York: Arno Press.

Becker, Gary, and George Stigler. 1977. "De Gustibus Non Est Disputandum." *American Economic Review* 67: 76–90.

Becker, Sascha O., Erik Hornung, Ludger Woessmann. 2009. "Catch Me If You Can: Education and Catch-up in the Industrial Revolution." Stirling Economics Discussion Paper 2009–19. At https://dspace.stir.ac.uk/dspace/handle/1893/1613.

Bell, Daniel. 1978. *The Cultural Contradictions of Capitalism.* New York: Basic Books.

Bellah, Robert N., Richard Masden, William M. Sullivan, Ann Swidler, and Steven M. Tipton.

1985 (1996). *Habits of the Heart: Individualism and Commitment in American Life.* Updated ed. Berkeley: University of California Press.

Bennett, H. S. 1921/1932. *The Pastons and Their England.* Cambridge: Cambridge University Press, 1970.

Berg, Maxine. 1985. *The Age of Manufactures: Industry, Innovation and Work in Britain 1700–1820.* Oxford: Oxford University Press.

Berg, Maxine. 1998. "Product Innovation in Core Consumer Industries in Eighteenth Century Britain." Pp. 138–157 in Berg and Bruland.

Berg, Maxine, and Kristine Bruland, eds. 1998. *Technological Revolutions in Europe: Historical Perspectives.* Cheltenham: Elgar.

Berg, Maxine, and Patricia Hudson. 1994. "Growth and Change: A Comment on the Crafts-Harley View of the Industrial Revolution." *Economic History Review* 47: 147–149.

Bergson, Abram. 1961. *The Real National Income of Soviet Russia since 1937.* Cambridge, Mass.: Harvard University Press.

Berman, Harold J. 1983. *Law and Revolution: The Formation of the Western Legal Tradition* Cambridge, Mass.: Harvard University Press.

Berman, Harold J. 2003. *Law and Revolution, II: The Impact of the Protestant Reformations on the Western Legal Tradition.* Cambridge, Mass.: Harvard University Press.

Berman, Sheri. 2006. *The Primacy of Politics: Social Democracy and the Making of Europe's Twentieth Century.* Cambridge: Cambridge University Press.

Bernhofen, Daniel M., and John C. Brown. 2009. "Testing the General Validity of the Heckscher-Ohlin Theorem: The Natural Experiment of Japan." Paper, Hi-Stat, Institute of Economic Research, Hitotsubashi University, Tokyo. At http://d.repec.org/n?u=RePEc:hst:ghsdps:gd09–058&r=his.

Bértola, Luis. 2010. "Institutions and the Historical Roots of Latin American Divergence." Working paper, Economic and Social History Program, Universidad de la República, Urguguay.

Blanning, Tim. 2007. *The Pursuit of Glory: Europe 1648–1815.* New York: Viking and Penguin.

Blaut, James. 1993. *The Colonizer's Model of the World: Geographical Diffusionism and Eurocentric History.* New York: Guilford Press.

Blum, Walter J., and Harry Kalven, Jr. 1963. *The Uneasy Case for Progressive Taxation.* Chicago: University of Chicago Press.

Boettke, Peter J., and Virgil Henry Storr. 2002. "Post Classical Political Economy." *American Journal of Economics and Sociology* 61 (1): 161–191.

Bogart, Dan. 2009. "Did the Glorious Revolution Contribute to the Transport Revolution? Evidence from Investment in Roads and Rivers." Manuscript, Department of Economics, University of California, Irvine.

Boldrin, Michael, and David K. Levine. 2009. "A Model of Discovery." Department of Economics, Washington University of St. Louis. At http://levine.sscnet.ucla.edu/papers/aea_pp09.pdf.

Boskin, Michael J., Ellen R. Dulberger, Robert J. Gordon, Zvi Griliches, and Dale W. Jorgenson. 1998. "Consumer Prices, the Consumer Price Index, and the Cost of Living." *Journal of Economic Perspectives* 12 (1) (Winter): 3–26.

Boswell, James. 1791. *The Life of Samuel Johnson, LL. D.* 2 vols. London: J. M. Dent, 1949.

Botton, Alain de. 2005. *On Seeing and Noticing.* London: Penguin.

Bourdieu, Pierre. 1979 (1984). *Distinction: A Social Critique of the Judgment of Taste.* Translated by Richard Nice. London: Routledge and Kegan Paul.

Bowles, Samuel. 2007. "Genetically Capitalist? Review of *Farewell to Alms.*" *Science* 318, no. 5849 (October 19): 394–396.

Bowles, Samuel, and Herbert Gintis. 2006. "The Evolutionary Basis of Collective Action." Pp. 951–967 in Barry R. Weingast and Donald A. Wittman, eds., *The Oxford Handbook of Political Economy* (Oxford: Oxford University Press).

Bowles, Samuel, and Herbert Gintis. Forthcoming. *A Cooperative Species: Human Sociality and Its Evolution.*

Boyd, John. 2008. "Multiscale Numerical Algorithms for Weather Forecasting and Climate Modeling: Challenges and Controversies." *Sian News* (Newsjournal of the Society for Industrial and Applied Mathematics) 41 (9): 1, 16 only.

Boyd, Richard. 1997. "Frank H. Knight and Ethical Pluralism." *Critical Review* 11 (4): 519–536.

Brailsford, H. N. 1961. *The Levellers and the English Revolution.* Edited by Christopher Hill. Nottingham: Bertrand Russell Peace Foundation, Spokesman Books, 1976.

Braudel, Fernand. 1979. *Civilisation matérielle, economie, et capitalisme.* Translated by S. Reynolds. *Civilization and Capitalism, Fifteenth-Eighteenth Century.* Vol. 2, *Les jeux de l'échange* (*The Wheels of Commerce*). New York: Harper and Row, 1982.

Braudel, Fernand, and Frank Spooner. 1967. "Prices in Europe from 1450 to 1750." Pp. 378–486 in E. E. Rich and C. H. Wilson, eds., *The Cambridge Economic History of Europe,* vol. 4, *The Economy of Expanding Europe in the Sixteenth and Seventeenth Centuries* (Cambridge: Cambridge University Press).

Bray, Francesca. 2000. *Technology and Society in Ming China, 1368–1644.* American Historical Association Pamphlet.

Bresnahan, Timothy, and Robert J. Gordon. 1997. Introduction. Pp. 1–26 in Timothy Bresnahan and Robert J. Gordon, eds., *The Economics of New Goods* (Chicago: University of Chicago Press).

Broadberry, Stephen N. 2003. "Labor Productivity." In Mokyr 2003a.

Broadberry, Stephen N., and Gupta Bishnupriya. 2005. "The Early Modern Price Divergence: Wages, Prices and Economic Development in Europe and Asia, 1500–1800." CERP Discussion Paper "4947. London: Centre for Economic Policy Research.

Broadberry, Stephen N., and Douglas Irwin. 2006. "Labor Productivity in the United States and the United Kingdom during the Nineteenth Century." *Explorations in Economic History* 43: 257–279.

Bronk, Richard. 2009. *The Romantic Economist: Imagination in Economics.* Cambridge: Cambridge University Press.

Buchanan, James M. 1987. "The Constitution of Economic Policy." Nobel Lecture, Dec. 8. Reprinted in *American Economic Review* 77 (June): 243–250. At http://nobelprize.org/nobel_prizes/economics/laureates/1986/buchanan-lecture.html.

Buchanan, James M. 2003. "Justice among Natural Equals: Memorial Marker for John Rawls." *Public Choice* 114: iii–v.

Buchanan, James M. 2006. "Politics and Scientific Inquiry: Retrospective on a Half-Century." Pp. 980–995 in Barry R. Weingast and Donald A. Wittman, eds., *The Oxford Handbook of Political Economy* (Oxford: Oxford University Press).

Buchanan, James M., and Gordon Tullock. 1962. *The Calculus of Consent: Logical Foundations of Constitutional Democracy.* Ann Arbor: University of Michigan Press.

Butler, Joseph, Bishop. 1725. *Fifteen Sermons.* Pp. 335–528 in *The Analogy of Religion and Fifteen Sermons* (London: Religious Tract Society).

Butler, Samuel. 1912. *The Notebooks of Samuel Butler.* At Project Gutenberg http://www .gutenberg.org/etext/6173.

Campbell, Bruce M. S. 2005. "The Agrarian Problem of the Early Fourteenth Century." *Past and Present* 188: 3–70.

Campbell, Bruce M. S. 2009. "Factor Markets in England before the Black Death." Manuscript, School of Geography, Archaeology, and Palaeoecology, Queen's University, Belfast.

Campbell, Bruce M. S. 2000. *English Seigneurial Agriculture, 1250–1450.* Cambridge: Cambridge University Press.

Cannadine, David. 1994 (2005). *The Aristocratic Adventurer.* London: Penguin. Chapters from Cannadine, *Aspects of Aristocracy* (New Haven: Yale University Press).

Caplan, Bryan. 2007. *The Myth of the Rational Voter: Why Democracies Choose Bad Policies.* Princeton: Princeton University Press.

Carlos, Ann, and Frank Lewis. 1999. "Property Rights, Competition and Depletion in the Eighteenth-Century Fur Trade: The Role of the European Market." *Canadian Journal of Economics* 32: 705–728.

Carlyle, Thomas. 1829. "Signs of the Times." At http://www.victorianweb.org/authors/carlyle/signs1.html.

Cartwright, Nancy. 2007. *Hunting Causes and Using Them: Approaches in Philosophy and Economics.* Cambridge: Cambridge University Press.

Carus-Wilson, Eleanora M. 1941. "An Industrial Revolution of the Thirteenth Century." *Economic History Review* ser. 1, 11: 39–60.

Cather, Willa. 1913. *O Pioneers!* Harmondsworth: Penguin.

Cather, Willa. 1931 (1992). "Two Friends." Pp. 673–690 in Cather, *Stories, Poems, and Other Writings* (Library of America. New York: Viking Press).

Chapman, Stanley D. 1970. "Fixed Capital Formation in the British Cotton Industry 1770–1815." *Economic History Review* 23: 235–266.

Chapman, Stanley D., and J. Butt. 1988. "The Cotton Industry, 1775–1856." In Feinstein and Pollard 1988.

Chartres, John. 2003. "England: Early Modern Period." In Mokyr 2003a.

Chekola, Mark. 2007. "The Life Plan View of Happiness and the Paradoxes of Happiness." Pp. 221–236 in Luigino Bruni and Pier Luigi Porta, eds., *Handbook on the Economics of Happiness* (Cheltenham, U.K.: Edward Elgar).

Chenery, Hollis B. 1960. "Patterns of Industrial Growth." *American Economic Review* 50: 624–654.

Cicero, Marcus Tullius. 44 BC. *De officiis* [Concerning Duties]. Translated by by W. Miller. Loeb ed. Cambridge, Mass.: Harvard University Press, 1913.

Cipolla, Carlo M. 1994. *Before the Industrial Revolution: European Society and Economy, 1000–1700.* 3rd ed. New York: W. W. Norton.

Clapham, John H. 1926. *An Economic History of Modern Britain: The Early Railway Age.* Cambridge: Cambridge University Press.

Clark, Gregory. 1987. "Why Isn't the Whole World Developed? Lessons from the Cotton Mills." *Journal of Economic History* 47 (March): 141–173.

Clark, Gregory. 1988. "The Cost of Capital and Medieval Agricultural Technique." *Explorations in Economic History* 25: 265–294.

Clark, Gregory. 2007a. *A Farewell to Alms: A Brief Economic History of the World.* Princeton: Princeton University Press.

Clark, Gregory. 2007b. "Some Limited Responses to My Critics." PowerPoint presentation to the Social Science History Association, Chicago meeting, November 17.

Clark, Gregory. 2007c. "A Review of Avner Greif's Institutions and the Path to the Modern Economy: Lessons from Medieval Trade." *Journal of Economic Literature* 45 (September): 727–743.

Clark, Gregory. 2008. "In Defense of the Malthusian Interpretation of History." *European Review of Economic History* 12 (August): 175–199.

Clark, Gregory, and Gillian Hamilton. 2006. "Survival of the Richest: The Malthusian Mechanism in Pre-Industrial England." *Journal of Economic History* 66 (September): 707–736.

Clark, Gregory, and David Jacks. 2007. "Coal and the Industrial Revolution." *European Review of Economic History* 11 (April): 39–72.

Clark, Henry C., ed. 2003. *Commerce, Culture, and Liberty: Readings on Capitalism before Adam Smith.* Indianapolis: Liberty Fund.

Clegg, Cyndia Susan. 1997. *Press Censorship in Elizabethan England.* Cambridge: Cambridge University Press.

Clough, Arthur Hugh. "The Latest Decalogue." 1862. Reprinted p. 1034 in H. H. Abrams and others, *The Norton Anthology of English Literature,* vol. 2. New York: W. W. Norton, 1962.

Coatsworth, John H. 1979. "Indispensable Railroads in a Backward Economy: The Case of Mexico." *Journal of Economic History* 39 (December): 939–960.

Cohen, Edward E. 1992. *Athenian Economy and Society: A Banking Perspective.* Princeton: Princeton University Press.

Coleridge, Samuel Taylor. 1817 (1852). *A Lay Sermon.* In Coleridge, *Lay Sermons,* at Google Books.

Collier, Paul. 2007. *The Bottom Billion: Why the Poorest Countries Are Failing and What Can Be Done about It.* Oxford: Oxford University Press.

Collins, Francis. 2007. *The Language of God: A Scientist Presents Evidence for Belief.* New York: Simon and Schuster.

Collins, Harry. 1985. *Changing Order: Replication and Induction in Scientific Practice.* Chicago: University of Chicago Press.

Comte-Sponville, André. 1996 (2001). *A Small Treatise on the Great Virtues.* New York: Henry Holt, Metropolitan/Owl Books.

Connolly, Michelle, and Kei-Mu Yi. 2009. "How Much of South Korea's Growth Miracle Can

Be Explained by Trade Policy?" Working Paper 09-19, Federal Reserve Bank of Philadelphia. At http://d.repec.org/n?u=RePEc:fip:fedpwp:09-19&r=his.

Coontz, Stephanie. 1992. *The Way We Never Were: American Families and the Nostalgia Trap*. New York: Basic Books. Paperback ed., 2000.

Cosgel, Metin M., Thomas J. Miceli, and Jared Rubin. 2009. "Guns and Books: Legitimacy, Revolt and Technological Change in the Ottoman Empire." Department of Economics, University of Connecticut, Storrs. Working Paper 2009-12. March.

Cottrell, Philip L. 1980. *Industrial Finance, 1830–1914: The Finance and Organization of English Manufacturing Industry*. London: Methuen.

Cowen, Tyler. 1998. *In Praise of Commercial Culture*. Cambridge, Mass.: Harvard University Press.

Cowley, Abraham. c. 1665. "Of Avarice." Pp. 197–202 in Samuel Johnson and John Aikin, eds., *The Works of Abraham Cowley* (London). Republished 1806. Google books digitized November 13, 2006.

Cowper, William. 1785. *The Task*. At http://www.luminarium.org/eightlit/cowper/cowperbib.php.

Cox, Michael, and Richard Alm. 1999. *Myths of Rich and Poor*. New York: Basic Books.

Crafts, Nicholas F. R. 2004 (2005). "The First Industrial Revolution: Resolving the Slow Growth/Rapid Industrialization Paradox." *Journal of the European Economic Association* 3 (April/May): 525–534. Manuscript, London School of Economics. At http://www.lse.ac.uk/collections/economicHistory/pdf/First%20Industrial%20Revelution%20-%20NFRC.pdf.

Crafts, Nicholas F. R., and C. Knick Harley. 1992. "Output Growth and the British Industrial Revolution: A Restatement of the Crafts-Harley View." *Economic History Review* 45: 703–730.

Crafts, Nicholas F. R., and C. Knick Harley. 2004. "Precocious British Industrialization: A General Equilibrium Perspective." Pp. 86–110 in Leandro Prados de la Escosura, ed., *British Exceptionalism: A Unique Path to the Industrial Revolution* (Cambridge: Cambridge University Press).

Crafts, Nicholas F. R., S. J. Leybourne, and T. C. Mills. 1991. "Britain." Pp. 109–152 in Richard Sylla and Gianni Toniolo, eds., *Patterns of European Industrialization: The Nineteenth Century* (London: Routledge, and Fondazione Adriano Olivetti).

Crouzet, François. 1965. "La formation du capital en Grande-Bretagne pendant la Révolution Industrielle." Pp. 589–642 in *Deuxième conférence internationale d'histoire économique/Second International Conference of Economic History*, Aix-en-Provence 1962, École pratique des hautes études—Sorbonne, Sixième Section: Sciences économiques et sociales, Congrès et Colloques, tome VIII (Mouton and Co.: Paris-The Hague).

Crouzet, François. 1985. *The First Industrialists: The Problem of Origins*. Cambridge: Cambridge University Press.

Csikszentmihalyi, Mihaly, and Eugene Rochberg-Halton,. 1981. *The Meaning of Things: Domestic Symbols and the Self*. New York: Cambridge University Press.

D'Souza, Dinesh. 1997. "Justice to Ronald Reagan." *Washington Times*, November 6, 1997. Reprinted 2000 in American Enterprise Institute, *On the Issues*, http://www.aei.org/include/pub_print.asp?pubID=8269.

Dandekar V. M. 1966. "Transforming Traditional Agriculture: A Critique of Professor Schultz." *Economic and Political Weekly* 1 (1): 25–36.

Danford, John W. 2006. "'Riches Valuable at All Times and to All Men': Hume and the Eighteenth-Century Debate on Commerce and Liberty." Pp. 319–347 in David Womersley, ed., *Liberty and American Experience in the Eighteenth Century* (Indianapolis: Liberty Fund).

Darity, William A., Jr. 1982. "A General Equilibrium Model of the Eighteenth-Century Atlantic Slave Trade: A Least-Likely Test for the Caribbean School," *Research in Economic History* 7: 287–326.

Darity, William A., Jr. 1992. "A Model of 'Original Sin'": Rise of the West and Lag of the Rest." *American Economic Review* 82: 162–167.

Daudin, Guillaume. 2004. *Commerce et prospérité: La France au le XVIIIe siècle*. Paris: PUPS.

Daudin, Guillaume. 2008. "Domestic Trade and Market Size in Late Eighteenth-Century France." Oxford Economic and Social History Working Papers. http://www.economics.ox.ac.uk/index.php/papers/details/domestic_trade_and_market/.

David, Paul A. 1969. "Transport Innovations and Economic Growth: Professor Fogel On and Off the Rails." *Economic History Review* ser. 2, 22: 506–525.

David, Paul A. 1990. "The Dynamo and the Computer: A Historical Perspective on the Modern Productivity Paradox." *American Economic Review* 80: 355–361.

David, Paul A. 2008. "The Historical Origins of 'Open Science': An Essay on Patronage, Reputation and Common Agency Contracting in the Scientific Revolution." *Capitalism and Society* 3: 1–103. Berkeley Electronic Press.

Davies, Howard, and Paul D. Ellis. 2000. "Porter's 'Competitive Advantage of Nations': Time for a Final Judgment?" *Journal of Management Studies* 37 (8): 1189–1213.

Davies, R. S. W., and Sidney Pollard. 1988. "The Iron Industry, 1750–1850." In Feinstein and Pollard 1988.

Davies, Stephen. 2005. "Warriors and Merchants." *Freeman* (November): 38–39.

Davis, Lance E., and R. A. Huttenback. 1986. *Mammon and the Pursuit of Empire: The Economics of British Imperialism*. Cambridge: Cambridge University Press. And a shorter version in 1988 with Susan G. Davis as coauthor, to which reference is made.

De Cecco, Marcello. 1975. *Money and Empire: The International Gold Standard, 1890–1914*. Totowa, N.J.: Rowman and Littlefield.

de la Court, Pieter. 1662. *Interest van Holland*. English trans. At libertyfund.org.

de la Court, Pieter. 1669. Selections from *Political Maxims of the State of Holland*. Part of the 1669 edition of *Interest van Holland*, trans. J. Campbell, 1743. Pp. 10–36 in Clark 2003.

DeLong, J. Bradford. 1989. "The "Protestant Ethic" Revisited: A Twentieth-Century Look." *Fletcher Forum* 13 (Summer): 229–242, and in manuscript. At http://econ161.berkeley.edu/pdf_files/Protestant_Ethic.pdf.

DeLong, J. Bradford. 2007. "Barry Ritholtz Does Not Seem to Understand the Purpose of 'Core Inflation.'" At DeLong blog, Grasping Reality with Both Hands, http://delong.typepad.com/sdj/2007/09/barry-ritholtz-.html.

Dennison, Tracy K., and A. W. Carus. 2003. "The Invention of the Russian Rural Commune: Haxthausen and the Evidence." *Historical Journal* 46 (3): 561–582.

Desert Fathers. 300–500 CE (2003). *The Desert Fathers: Sayings of the Early Christian Monks.* Translated by Benedicta Ward. London: Penguin.

de Vries, Jan. 2003. "Long-Distance Trade between 1500 and 1750." In Mokyr 2003a.

de Vries, Jan. 2008a. "Did People in the Eighteenth Century Really Work Harder, and, If So, Why?" Paper presented to the Midwest Economics Association, Chicago, March.

de Vries, Jan. 2008b. *The Industrious Revolution: Consumer Behavior and the Household Economy, 1650 to the Present.* Cambridge: Cambridge University Press.

de Vries, Jan. 2008c. "Review of Clark, A Farewell to Alms." *Journal of Economic History* 68: 1180–1181.

Deakin, Simon. 2008. "Legal Origin, Juridical Form and Industrialization in Historical Perspective: The Case of the Employment Contract and the Joint-Stock Company." Centre for Business Research, University of Cambridge. Working Paper 369.

Deane, Phyllis., and W. A. Cole. 1962. *British Economic Growth, 1688–1959.* Cambridge: Cambridge University Press.

Demetz, Peter. 1997. *Prague in Black and Gold: The History of a City.* New York: Penguin.

Demsetz, Harold. 1967. "Toward a Theory of Property Rights." *American Economic Review* 57 (May): 347–359.

Desmet, Klaus, and Stephen Parente. 2009. "The Evolution of Markets and the Revolution of Industry: A Quantitative Model of England's Development, 1300–2000." Centre for Economic Policy Research Discussion Paper 7290. At http://d.repec.org/n?u=RePEc:cpr:ceprdp:7290&r=his.

Diamond, Jared. 1997. *Guns, Germs, and Steel: The Fates of Human Societies.* New York: Random House.

Donaldson, Lex. 1995. *American Anti-Management Theories of Organization: A Critique of Paradigm Proliferation.* Cambridge: Cambridge University Press.

Douglas, Mary, and Baron Isherwood. 1979. *The World of Goods.* New York: Basic Books.

Du Plessis, Stan. 2008. "Economic Growth in South Africa: A Story of Working Smarter, Not Harder." Presentation May 20 to a conference at the Faculty of Theology, University of Stellenbosch, on Religion and the Eradication of Poverty in the Context of Economic Globalization. Department of Economics, University of Stellenbosch.

Dupré, Louis. 2004. *The Enlightenment and the Intellectual Foundations of Modern Culture.* New Haven: Yale University Press.

Durie, Alastair J. 2003. "Scotland." In Mokyr 2003a.

Dyson, Freeman. 2008. "The Question of Global Warming." *New York Review of Books* 55 (20) (June 12). At http://www.nybooks.com/articles/21494.

Eagleton, Terry. 1996. *Heathcliff and the Great Hunger: Studies in Irish Culture.* London: Blackwell Verso.

Eagleton, Terry. 2006. "Lunging, Flailing, Mispunching: Review of Dawkins, *The God Delusion.*" *London Review of Books,* October 19, 32–34. At http://www.lrb.co.uk/v28/n20/terry-eagleton/lunging-flailing-mispunching.

Eagleton, Terry. 2009. *Reason, Faith, and Revolution: Reflections on the God Debate.* New Haven: Yale University Press.

Eagleton, Terry. 2009. *Trouble with Strangers: A Study of Ethics.* Malden, Mass.: Wiley-Blackwell.

Earle, Peter. 1989. *The Making of the English Middle Class: Business, Society and Family Life in London, 1660–1730*. London: Methuen.

Easterlin, Richard A. 1973. "Does Money Buy Happiness?" *Public Interest* 30: 3–10.

Easterlin, Richard A. 1974. "Does Economic Growth Improve the Human Lot? Some Empirical Evidence." Pp. 89–125 in Paul David and Melvin Reder, eds., *Nations and Households in Economic Growth: Essays in Honor of Moses Abramowitz* (New York: Academic Press).

Easterlin, Richard A. 1981. "Why Isn't the Whole World Developed?" *Journal of Economic History* 41 (1): 1–19.

Easterlin, Richard A. 1995. "Industrial Revolution and Mortality Revolution: Two of a Kind?" *Journal of Evolutionary Economics* 5: 393–408, reprinted in Easterlin 2004.

Easterlin, Richard A., ed. 2002. *Happiness in Economics*. An Elgar Reference Collection. Cheltenham, U.K.: Edward Elgar.

Easterlin, Richard A. 2003. "Living Standards." In Mokyr 2003a.

Easterlin, Richard A. 2004. *The Reluctant Economist: Perspectives on Economics, Economic History, and Demography*. Cambridge: Cambridge University Press.

Easterly, William. 2001. *The Elusive Quest for Growth: Economists' Adventures and Misadventures in the Tropics*. Cambridge, Mass.: MIT Press.

Easterly, William, and Fischer, Stanley. 1995. "The Soviet Economic Decline: Historical and Republican Data." *World Bank Economic Review* 9 (3): 341–371.

Economist Intelligence Unit. 2005. "Quality of Life Index." At http://www.economist.com/media/pdf/QUALITY_OF_LIFE.pdfy.

Edelstein, Michael. 1994a. "Foreign Investment and Accumulation, 1860–1914." Pp. 173–196 in Floud and McCloskey 1981.

Edelstein, Michael. 1994b. "Imperialism: Cost and Benefit." Pp. 197/–216 in Floud and McCloskey 1981.

Edgerton, David. 1991. *England and the Aeroplane: An Essay on a Militant and Technological Nation*. London: Macmillan. Full pdf at http://www3.imperial.ac.uk/pls/portallive/docs/1/7292625.PDF.

Edgerton, David. 1996. *Science, Technology and the British Industrial "Decline," 1870–1970*. Cambridge: Cambridge University Press, for the Economic History Society.

Edgerton, David. 2005. *Warfare State: Britain, 1920–1970*. Cambridge: Cambridge University Press.

Edgerton, David. 2007. *The Shock of the Old: Technology and Global History since 1900*. Oxford: Oxford University Press.

Edwards, Jeremy, and Sheilagh Ogilvie. 2008. "Contract Enforcement, Institutions and Social Capital: The Magribi Traders Reappraised. CESifo Working Paper 2254. At CESifo-group .org/wp.

Ehrlich, Paul R. 1968. *The Population Bomb*. New York: Ballantine.

Ekelund, Robert B., Jr., and Robert D. Tollison. 1981. *Mercantilism as a Rent-Seeking Society: Economic Regulation in Historical Perspective*. College Station: Texas A&M University Press.

Elbaum, Bernard L., and William Lazonick, eds. 1986. *The Decline of the British Economy*. New York: Oxford University Press.

Eldridge, Niles. 1995. *Dominion*. New York: Henry Holt.

Eliot, T. S. 1921. "The Metaphysical Poets." Pp. 241–250 in Eliot, *Selected Essays, 1917–1932* (London: Faber).

Eltis, David, and Stanley L. Engerman. 2000. "The Importance of Slavery and the Slave Trade to Industrializing Britain." *Journal of Economic History* 60: 123–144.

Embree, Ainslee, ed. 1988. *Sources of Indian Tradition*. Vol. 1, *From the Beginning to 1800*. 2nd ed. New York: Columbia University Press.

Emmer, P. C. 2003. "Low Countries: Dutch Empire." In Mokyr 2003a.

Engels, Friedrich. 1877–1878. *Anti-Dühring*. At http://www.marxists.org/archive/marx/works/1877/anti-duhring/index.htm.

Engerman, Stanley L. 1972. "The Slave Trade and British Capital Formation in the Eighteenth Century: A Comment on the Williams Thesis." *Business History Review* 46: 430–443.

Epstein, Joseph. 2006. *Alexis de Tocqueville: Democracy's Guide*. New York: Harper-Collins.

Epstein, Richard. 2009. "Property Rights and the Rule of Law: Classical Liberalism Confronts the Modern Administrative State." Speech to the Mont Pelerin Society, Stockholm, August 17.

Epstein, S. R. 1991. *Wage Labor and Guilds in Medieval Europe*. Chapel Hill: University of North Carolina Press.

Epstein, S. R. 1998. "Craft Guilds, Apprenticeship, and Technological Change in Preindustrial Europe." *Journal of Economic History* 58: 684–714.

Ethington, Philip J. 1997. "The Intellectual Construction of 'Social Distance': Toward a Recovery of Georg Simmel's Social Geometry." In *Cybergeo*, refereed electronic edition of *European Journal of Geography* 30 (September 16), http://www.cybergeo.presse.fr/essoct/texte/socdis.htm.

Federico, Giovanni. 2005. *Feeding the World: An Economic History of Agriculture, 1800–2000*. Princeton: Princeton University Press.

Feinstein, Charles H. 1972. *National Income, Expenditure and Output of the United Kingdom, 1855–1965*. Cambridge: Cambridge University Press.

Feinstein, Charles H. 2003. "National Income Accounts: Investment and Savings." In Mokyr 2003a.

Feinstein, Charles H. 2005. *An Economic History of South Africa: Conquest, Discrimination and Development*. Cambridge: Cambridge University Press.

Feinstein, Charles H., and Sidney Pollard, eds. 1988. *Studies in Capital Formation in the United Kingdom, 1750–1920*. Oxford: Clarendon Press.

Fenoaltea, Stefano. 1971–1972. "Railroads and Italian Industrial Growth, 1861–1913." *Explorations in Economic History* 9 (1): 325–351.

Ferguson, Niall. 1997. "What If Britain Had 'Stood Aside' in August 1914?" Pp. 228–280 in Ferguson, ed., *Virtual History* (London: Picador. New York: Basic Books, 1999).

Field, Alexander J. 2003. "The Most Technologically Progressive Decade of the Century." *American Economic Review* 93: 1399–1413.

Field, Alexander J. 2006. "Technological Change and U.S. Productivity Growth in the Interwar Years." *Journal of Economic History* 66: 203–236.

Fielding, Henry. 1749. *The History of Tom Jones, a Foundling*. 2 vols. Bohn's Popular Library. London: Bell and Sons, 1913.

Findlay, Ronald, and Kevin H. O'Rourke. 2007. *Power and Plenty: Trade, War, and the World Economy in the Second Millennium.* Princeton: Princeton University Press.

Finley, Moses. 1973. *The Ancient Economy.* Sather Classical Lectures 43. Berkeley: University of California Press.

Fleischacker, Samuel. 2004. *A Short History of Distributive Justice.* Cambridge, Mass.: Harvard University Press.

Floud, Roderick C., and Deirdre N. McCloskey, eds. 1981. *The Economic History of Britain since 1700.* Vol. l, *1700–1860.* 1st ed. Cambridge: Cambridge University Press.

Floud, Roderick C., and Deirdre N. McCloskey, eds. 1994. *The Economic History of Britain since 1700.* Vol. l, *1700–1860.* 2nd ed. Cambridge: Cambridge University Press.

Flynn, Dennis O. 1996. *World Silver and Monetary History in the Sixteenth and Seventeenth Centuries.* Collected Studies Series. Aldershot: Ashgate/Variorum Press.

Flynn, Dennis O., and Arturo Giráldez. 1995a. "Born with a Silver Spoon: The Origin of World Trade in 1571." *Journal of World History* 6: 201–221.

Flynn, Dennis O., and Arturo Giráldez. 1995b. "Arbitrage, China, and World Trade in the Early Modern Period." *Journal of the Social and Economic History of the Orient* 38: 429–448.

Flynn, Dennis O., and Arturo Giráldez. 2002. "Cycles of Silver: Global Economic Unity through the Mid-eighteenth Century." *Journal of World History* 13 (2): 391–427.

Flynn, Dennis O., and Arturo Giráldez. 2004. "Path Dependence, Time Lags and the Birth of Globalisation: A Critique of O'Rourke and Williamson." *European Review of Economic History* 8: 81–108.

Flynn, Dennis O., Arturo Giráldez, and R. von Glahn, eds. 2003. *Monetary History in Global Perspective, 1500–1808.* Aldershot: Variorum.

Fogel, Robert W. 1964. *Railroads and American Economic Growth: Essays in Econometric History.* Baltimore: Johns Hopkins University Press.

Fogel, Robert W. 1979. "Notes on the Social Saving Controversy." *Journal of Economic History* 39: 1–54.

Fogel, Robert W. 2002. *The Fourth Great Awakening and the Future of Egalitarianism.* Chicago: University of Chicago Press.

Fogel, Robert W. 2004. *The Escape from Hunger and Premature Death, 1700–2100: Europe, America, and the Third World.* New York: Cambridge University Press.

Fogel, Robert W. 2005. "Reconsidering Expectations of Economic Growth after World War II from the Perspective of 2004." NBER Working Paper W11125.

Fogel, Robert W. 2008. "Forecasting the Cost of U.S. Health Care in 2040." NBER Working Paper 14361.

Folbre, Nancy. 2001. *The Invisible Heart: Economics and Family Values.* New York: New Press.

Foreman-Peck, James. 2003. "Long Distance Trade: Long-Distance Trade since 1914." In Mokyr 2003a.

Forgacs, David, ed. 2000. *The Antonio Gramsci Reader: Selected Writings 1916–1935.* New York: New York University Press.

Fouquet, Roger. 2008. *Heat, Power and Light: Revolutions in Energy Services.* Cheltenham: Edward Elgar.

Frank, Andre Gunder. 1998. *Reorient: Global Economy in the Asian Age.* Berkeley: University of California Press.

Frank, Robert H. 1985. *Choosing the Right Pond: Human Behavior and the Quest for Status.* New York: Oxford University Press.

Frank, Robert H. 1999. *Luxury Fever: Money and Happiness in an Era of Excess.* New York: Free Press.

Frank, Robert H., and Philip J. Cook. 1995. *The Winner-Take-All Society: Why the Few at the Top Get So Much More Than the Rest of Us.* New York: Free Press.

Fremdling, Rainer. 2000. "Transfer Patterns of British Technology to the Continent: The Case of the Iron Industry." *European Review of Economic History* 4: 197–220.

Frey, Bruno. *Happiness: A Revolution in Economics.* Cambridge, Mass.: MIT Press.

Friedman, Benjamin M. 2005. *The Moral Consequences of Economic Growth.* New York: Knopf.

Friedman, Benjamin M. 2007. "Industrial Evolution [review of *Farewell to Alms*]." *New York Times Sunday Review of Books,* December 9.

Galor, Oded, and Omer Moav. 2002. "Natural Selection and the Origins of Economic Growth." *Quarterly Journal of Economics* 117 (November): 1133–1191.

Galton, Francis. 1901. "The Possible Improvement of the Human Breed under Existing Conditions of Law and Sentiment." Huxley Lecture to the Anthropological Institute, printed as pp. 1–34 in Galton, *Essays in Eugenics* (London: Eugenics Education Society).

Gapinski, James H. 1993. *The Economics of Saving.* Boston: Kluwer Academic.

Geertz, Clifford, Hildred Geertz, and Lawrence Rosen. 1979. *Meaning and Order in Moroccan Society.* New York: Cambridge University Press.

Gerschenkron, Alexander. 1947. "The Soviet Indices of Industrial Production." *Review of Economics and Statistics* 29: 217–226.

Gerschenkron, Alexander. 1957 (1962). "Reflections on the Concept of 'Prerequisites' of Modern Industrialization." *L'industria* 2. Reprinted as pp. 31–51 in Gerschenkron, *Economic Backwardness in Historical Perspective: A Book of Essays* (Cambridge, Mass.: Harvard University Press).

Gerschenkron, Alexander. 1962. *Economic Backwardness in Historical Perspective: A Book of Essays.* Cambridge, Mass.: Harvard University Press.

Gerschenkron, Alexander. 1970. *Europe in the Russian Mirror: Four Lectures in Economic History.* Cambridge University Press.

Gilbert, W. S., and A. S. Sullivan. 1893. "Utopia, Limited." In *The Complete Plays of Gilbert and Sullivan.* New York: W. W. Norton, 1976.

Gilomee, Hermann. 2003. *The Afrikaners: Biography of a People.* Cape Town: Tafelberg; Charlottesville: University of Virginia Press.

Gilomee, Hermann, and Bernard Mbenga, eds. 2007. *New History of South Africa.* Cape Town: Tafelberg.

Gintis, Herbert. 2007. "The Evolution of Private Property." *Journal of Economic Behavior and Organization* 64: 1–16. At http://www-unix.oit.umass.edu/~gintis/.

Gintis, Herbert. 2008. "Five Principles for the Unification of the Behavioral Sciences." Manuscript, Sante Fe Institute and Central European University. May 13, 2008. At http://www.umass.edu/preferen/gintis/NewUnity.pdf.

Gladwell, Malcolm. 2006. "The Formula: What If You Built a Machine to Predict Hit Movies?" *New Yorker* (October 16): 138–149.

Goffman, Erving. 1961. *Asylums: Essays on the Social Situation of Mental Patients and Other Inmates.* New York: Doubleday.

Goldgar, Anne. 2007. *Tulipmania: Money, Honor, and Knowledge in the Dutch Golden Age.* Chicago: University of Chicago Press.

Goldin, Claudia, and Lawrence F. Katz. 2008. *The Race between Education and Technology.* Cambridge, Mass.: Harvard University Press.

Goldsmith, Raymond W. 1984. "An Estimate of the Size and Structure of the National Product of the Early Roman Empire." *Review of Income and Wealth* (September): 263–288.

Goldstone, Jack A. 2002a. "The Rise of the West—or Not? A Revision to Socio-economic History." *Sociological Theory* 18 (2): 175–194. Manuscript available at http://www.hartford-hwp.com/archives/10/114.html.

Goldstone, Jack A. 2002b. "Efflorescences and Economic Growth in World History: Rethinking the 'Rise of the West' and the Industrial Revolution." *Journal of World History* 13: 323–389.

Goldstone, Jack A. 2003. "Feeding the People, Starving the State: China's Agricultural Revolution of the Seventeenth-/Eighteenth Centuries." Paper presented to the Global Economic History Network. Irvine, California.

Goldstone, Jack A. 2007a. "Discussion of Clark's *Farewell to Alms.*" Meet-the-author session at the Social Science History Convention, Chicago, November. http://eh.net/bookreviews/ssha_farewell_to_alms.pdf.

Goldstone, Jack A. 2007b. "Review of Clark's *Farewell to Alms.*" *World Economics* 8 (3): 207–225.

Goldstone, Jack A. 2009. *Why Europe? The Rise of the West in World History, 1500–1850.* New York: McGraw-Hill.

Goldstone, Jack A. Forthcoming. *A Peculiar Path: The Rise of the West in World History, 1500–1850.* Cambridge, Mass.: Harvard University Press.

Goody, Jack. 1996. *The East in the West.* Cambridge: Cambridge University Press.

Goody, Jack. 2006. *The Theft of History.* Cambridge: Cambridge University Press.

Goody, Jack. 2010. *The Eurasian Miracle.* London and Malden, Mass.: Polity.

Gordon, Robert J. 1990. *The Measurement of Durable Goods Prices.* Chicago: University of Chicago Press.

Gordon, Robert J. 2006. "The Boskin Commission Report: A Retrospective One Decade Later." NBER Working Paper 12311.

Grafen, Alan. 1987. "The Logic of Divisively Asymmetric Contests: Respect for Ownership and the Desperado Effect." *Animal Behaviour* 35: 462–467.

Graff, Gerald. 1992. *Beyond the Culture Wars: How Teaching the Conflicts Can Revitalize American Education.* New York: W. W. Norton.

Graff, Gerald, and Cathy Birkenstein. 2005. *They Say/I Say: The Moves That Matter in Academic Writing.* New York: W. W. Norton.

Grantham, George. 2003. "Agriculture: Historical Overview." In Mokyr 2003a.

Grantham, George. 2007. "Discussion of Clark's *Farewell to Alms.*" Meet-the-author session at the Social Science History Convention, Chicago, November. http://eh.net/bookreviews/ssha_farewell_to_alms.pdf.

Grantham, George. 2009. "Science and Its Transactions Cost: The Emergence of Institutionalized Science."Manuscript, McGill University and Paris School of Economics. At http://d.repec.org/n?u=RePEc:mcl:mclwop:2009-05&r=his.

Greenblatt, Stephen. 1997. "General Introduction." Pp. 1–76 in *The Norton Shakespeare* (New York: Norton).

Greenfeld, Liah. 2001. *The Spirit of Capitalism. Nationalism and Economic Growth.* Cambridge, Mass.: Harvard University Press.

Greif, Avner. 2006. *Institutions and the Path to the Modern Economy: Lessons from Medieval Trade.* Cambridge: Cambridge University Press.

Grief, Avner. 2008. "Contract Enforcement and Institutions among the Magribi Traders: Refuting Edwards and Ogilvie." Department of Economics, Stanford University. At mpra.ub.uni-meunchen.de/9610/.

Grierson, Philip. 1978. "The Origins of Money." *Research in Economic Anthropology* 1: 1–35.

Grotius (Hugo de Groot). 1625. "Preliminary Discourse concerning the Certainty of Rights in General," in *De iure belli ac pacis.* English trans. of 1738, from the French of Jean Barbeyrac, 1720. At Online Library of Liberty, http://oll.libertyfund.org.

Guinnane, Timothy. 2009. Speech to the Chicago Friends of Economic History, May 8. Department of Economics, Yale University.

Habakkuk, H. J. 1962. *American and British Technology in the Nineteenth Century: The Search for Labour-Saving Inventions.* New York: Cambridge University Press.

Hanawalt, Barbara. 1979. *Crime and Conflict in English Communities, 1300–1348.* Cambridge: Harvard University Press.

Hansen, Alvin H. 1939. "Economic Progress and Declining Population Growth." *American Economic Review* 29 (March): 1–7.

Hansen, Alvin H. 1941. *Fiscal Policy and Business Cycles.* New York: W. W. Norton.

Harberger, Arnold C. 1954. "Monopoly and Resource Allocation." *American Economic Review* 44 (May): 77–87.

Harberger, Arnold C. 1964. "The Measurement of Waste." *American Economic Review* 54 (May): 58–76.

Hardin, Garrett. 1968. "The Tragedy of the Commons." *Science* 162: 1243–1248.

Harley, C. K. 1980. "Transportation, the World Wheat Trade and the Kuznets Cycle." *Explorations in Economic History* 17: 218–250.

Harley, C. K. 1993. "Reassessing the Industrial Revolution: A Macro View." Pp. 171–226 in Mokyr 1999.

Harris, John R. 1992. *Essays in Industry and Technology in the Eighteenth Century: England and France.* Aldershot, England: Ashgate Variorum.

Harris, John R. 1996. "Law, Espionage and Transfer of Technology from Eighteenth-Century Britain." Pp. 123–136 in Robert Fox, ed., *Technological Change: Methods and Themes in the History of Technology* (Amsterdam: Harwood Academic Publishers).

Harris, John R. 2000. *Industrial Espionage and Technology Transfer: Britain and France in the Eighteenth Century.* Aldershot, England: Ashgate.

Hartwell, R. M. 1961. "The Rising Standard of Living in England, 1800–1850." *Economic History Review*, ser. 2, 13: 397–416.

Hartwell, R. M. 1965. "The Causes of the Industrial Revolution: An Essay in Methodology." *Economic History Review* 18: 164–182. Reprinted as pp. 53–80 in Hartwell, ed., *The Causes of the Industrial Revolution in England* (London: Methuen, 1967).

Harvey, David. 2007. *A Brief History of Neoliberalism.* New York: Oxford University Press.

Harvey, David. 2009. "The Crisis and the Consolidation of Class Power: Is This *Really* the End of Neoliberalism?" *Counterpunch* (March 13/15). At http://www.counterpunch.org/harvey03132009.html.

Hawke, G. R. 1970. *Railways and Economic Growth in England and Wales 1840–1870.* Oxford: Oxford University Press.

Hayek, Friedrich A. 1945. "The Use of Knowledge in Society." *American Economic Review* 35 (4): 519–530.

Hayek, Friedrich A., ed. 1954. *Capitalism and the Historians: Essays by Hayek, T. S. Ashton, L. M. Hacker, W. H. Hutt, and B. de Jouvenel.* Chicago: University of Chicago Press.

Hayek, Friedrich A. 1960. *The Constitution of Liberty.* Chicago: University of Chicago Press.

Heckscher, Eli. F. 1931. *Mercantilism.* Translated by Mendel Shapiro. London: Allen and Unwin, 1934.

Heilbroner, Robert. 1953. *The Worldly Philosophers: The Lives, Times, and Ideas of the Great Economic Thinkers.* 7th ed. New York: Simon and Schuster, 1996.

Hejeebu, Santhi, and Deirdre McCloskey. 2000. "The Reproving of Karl Polanyi," *Critical Review* 13 (Summer/Fall): 285–314.

Hejeebu, Santhi, and Deirdre McCloskey. 2003. "Polanyi and the History of Capitalism: Rejoinder to Blyth." *Critical Review* 16 (1): 135–142.

Hellie, Richard. 2003. "Russia: Early Modern Period." In Mokyr 2003a.

Henriksson, Anders. 1983. "Life Reeked with Joy." *Wilson Quarterly* (Spring): 169–171.

Hersh, Jonathan, and Hans-Joachim Voth. 2009. "Sweet Diversity: Colonial Goods and the Rise of European Living Standards after 1492." Manuscript at http://d.repec.org/n?u=RePEc:upf:upfgen:1163&r=his.

Heston, Alan. 2002. "Review of Fernand Braudel, *Civilization and Capitalism, Fifteenth-Eighteenth Century.*" EH.Net Economic History Services, Aug 1. http://eh.net/bookreviews/library/heston.

Hexter, Jack. H. 1961. "The Myth of the Middle Class in Tudor England." In *Reappraisals in History.* London: Longmans, Green.

Higgs, Robert. 1997. "Regime Uncertainty: Why the Great Depression Lasted So Long and Why Prosperity Resumed after the War." *Independent Review* 1 (Spring): 561–590.

Higgs, Robert. 2006. *Depression, War, and Cold War: Challenging the Myths of Conflict and Prosperity.* New York: Oxford University Press.

Hill, Kim R., and A. Magdalena Hurtado. 2003. "Hunting." In Mokyr 2003a.

Hines, James R., Jr. 1999. "Three Sides of Harberger Triangles." *Journal of Economic Perspectives* 13 (2): 167–188.

Hirsch, Fred. 1976. *The Social Limits to Growth.* London: Routledge and Kegan Paul.

Hirschman, Albert. O. 1958 (1988). *The Strategy of Economic Development.* New Haven: Yale University Press.

Hirschman, Albert O. 1977. *The Passions and the Interests: Political Arguments for Capitalism before Its Triumph.* Princeton: Princeton University Press.

Hiser, Rodney F. 2003. "Moral Consequences of Institutional Structure." *Planning and Markets* 6 (1). At http://www-pam.usc.edu/.

Hobbes, Thomas. 1651. *Leviathan.* Edited by C. B. Macpherson. Harmondsworth: Penguin, 1986.

Hobsbawm, Eric J. 1957. "The British Standard of Living, 1790–1850." *Economic History Review,* ser. 2, 10: 46–68.

Hoffman, Philip T. 1997. *Growth in a Traditional Society: The French Countryside, 1450–1815.* Princeton: Princeton University Press.

Hoffman, Philip T. 2003a. "Agriculture: Property Rights and Tenure Systems." In Mokyr 2003a.

Hoffman, Philip T. 2003b. "France: Early Modern Period." In Mokyr 2003a.

Hoffman, Philip T. 2006. "The Church in Economy and Society." Pp. 72–86 in Stewart J. Brown and Timothy Tackett, eds., *Enlightenment, Reawakening and Revolution, 1660–1815* (Cambridge History of Christianity, vol. 7. Cambridge: Cambridge University Press).

Hohenberg, Paul. 2003. "Urbanization." In Mokyr 2003a.

Hollander, Anne. 1994. *Sex and Suits: The Evolution of Modern Dress.* New York: Knopf.

Holmes, Oliver Wendell, Jr. 1895. "An Address Delivered on Memorial Day, May 30." Pp. 263–270 in Joseph T. Cox, ed., *The Written Wars: American Prose through the Civil War* (North Haven, Conn.: Archon).

Honeyman, Katrina. 2007. *Child Workers in England, 1780–1820.* Aldershot: Ashgate.

Hoppit, Julian. 1996. "Patterns of Parliamentary Legislation, 1660–1800." *History Journal* 39: 109–131.

Hoppit, Julian. 2002. *Risk and Failure in English Business, 1700–1800.* Cambridge: Cambridge University Press.

Housman, A. E. 1921. "The Application of Thought to Textual Criticism." *Proceedings of the Classical Association* 18: 67–84.

Howitt, Peter. 2005. "Coordination Issues in Long-Run Growth." In K. Judd and L. Tesfatsion, eds., *Handbook of Computational Economics,* vol. 2, *Agent-Based Computational Economics.* Preprint at Department of Economics, Brown University.

Hudson, Patricia. 1986. *The Genesis of Industrial Capital: A Study of the West Riding Wool Textile Industry c. 1750–1850.* Cambridge.

Hudson, Patricia, ed. 1989. *Regions and Industries: A Perspective on Britain's Industrial Revolution.* Cambridge: Cambridge University Press.

Hudson, Patricia. 1992. *The Industrial Revolution.* Sevenoaks, Kent: Edward Arnold.

Hume, David. 1754–1755. *The History of England.* Vol. 6. 1778 ed. Indianapolis: Liberty Fund, 1983.

Hume, David. 1777 (1987). *Essays Moral, Political and Literary.* Edited by E. F. Miller. Rev. ed. Indianapolis: Liberty Fund.

Huppert, George. 1977. *Les Bourgeois Gentilhommes: An Essay on the Definition of Elites in Renaissance France.* Chicago: University of Chicago Press.

Huppert, George. 1999. *The Style of Paris: Renaissance Origins of the French Enlightenment.* Bloomington: Indiana University Press.

Hynes, William, David S. Jacks, Kevin H. O'Rourke. 2009. "Commodity Market Disintegration in the Interwar Period." Institute for International Integration Studies. Discussion paper 285. Trinity College, Dublin. At http://www.tcd.ie/iiis/documents/discussion/pdfs/iiisdp285.pdf.

Iannaccone, Lawrence. 1998. "Introduction to the Economics of Religion." *Journal of Economic Literature* 36 (3): 1465–1495.

Imlah, J. A. H. 1958. *Economic Elements in the Pax Britannica: Studies in British Foreign Trade in the Nineteenth Century.* Cambridge, Mass.: Harvard University Press.

Inglehart, Ronald H., R. Foa, C. Peterson, and C. Welzel. 2008. "Development, Freedom, and Rising Happiness: A Global Perspective (1981–2007)." *Perspectives on Psychological Science* 3: 264–285.

Inikori, Joseph E. 2002. *Africans and the Industrial Revolution in England: A Study in International Trade and Development.* Cambridge: Cambridge University Press.

Innes, Stephen. 1988. Introduction. In Innes, ed., *Work and Labor in Early America.* Institute of Early American History and Culture, Williamsburg. Chapel Hill: University of North Carolina Press.

Innes, Stephen. 1994. "Puritanism and Capitalism in Early Massachusetts." Pp. 83–113 in J. A. James and M. Thomas, eds., *Capitalism in Context: Essays on Economic Development and Cultural Change in Honor of R. M. Hartwell* (Chicago: University of Chicago Press).

Ippolito, R. A. 1975. "The Effect of the Agricultural Depression on Industrial Demand in England: 1730–1750." *Economica* 42: 298–312.

Isaacson, Walter. 2003. *Benjamin Franklin: An American Life.* New York: Simon and Schuster.

Israel, Jonathan. 1989. *Dutch Primacy in World Trade, 1585–1740.* Oxford: Oxford University Press.

Israel, Jonathan. 1995. *The Dutch Republic: Its Rise, Greatness, and Fall, 1477–1806.* Oxford: Clarendon Press. .

Israel, Jonathan. 2001. *Radical Enlightenment: Philosophy and the Making of Modernity, 1650–1750.* Oxford: Oxford University Press.

Jacob, Margaret C. 1981 (2006). *The Radical Enlightenment—Pantheists, Freemasons and Republicans.* London: Allen and Unwin. 2nd rev. ed. Lafayette, Louisiana: Cornerstone. New preface and introduction at http://www.cornerstonepublishers.com/radical.pdf.

Jacob, Margaret C. 1997. *Scientific Culture and the Making of the Industrial West.* New York: Oxford University Press.

Jacob, Margaret C. 2001. *The Enlightenment: A Brief History.* Boston: Bedford/St.Martin's.

Jardine, Lisa. 1996. *Worldly Goods: A New History of the Renaissance.* London: Macmillan.

Johnson, Samuel. 1753. *Adventurer* 99 (October 16).

Johnson, William A. 2000. "Towards a Sociology of Reading in Classical Antiquity." *American Journal of Philology* 121: 593–627.

Jones, Eric L. 1981. *The European Miracle: Environments, Economies, and Geopolitics in the History of Europe and Asia.* Cambridge: Cambridge University Press.

Jones, Eric L. 1988. *Growth Recurring: Economic Change in World History*. Oxford: Clarendon Press.

Jones, Eric L. 2003. "Natural Resources: Historical Overview." In Mokyr 2003a.

Jones, G. T. 1933. *Increasing Returns*. Cambridge: Cambridge University Press.

Jordan, Miriam. 1998. "Foreign Rivals Spur India's Homegrown Firms." *International Herald Tribune*, February 5.

Karabel, Jerome. 2005. *The Chosen: The Hidden History of Admission and Exclusion at Harvard, Yale, and Princeton*. Boston: Houghton Mifflin.

Keizer, Kees, Siegwart Lindenberg, and Linda Steg. 2008. "The Spread of Disorder." *Science* 322: 1681–1685.

Kelling, George L., and James Q. Wilson. "Broken Windows." *Atlantic* (March 1982).

Kendrick, John W. 1956. "Productivity Trends: Capital and Labor." Occasional papers of the National Bureau of Economic Research, New York.

Kendrick, John W. 1961. *Productivity Trends in the United States*. Princeton: Princeton University Press.

Kennedy, Paul. 1976 (2006). *The Rise and Fall of British Naval Mastery*. Amherst, N.Y.: Humanity Books.

Kennedy, Paul. 1987. *The Rise and Fall of the Great Powers: Economic Change and Military Conflict from 1500 to 2000*. New York: Random House.

Keynes, John Maynard. 1937. "Some Economic Consequences of a Declining Population." Galton Lecture to the Eugenics Society. February.

Khurana, Rakesh. 2007. *From Higher Aims to Hired Hands: The Social Transformation of American Business Schools and the Unfulfilled Promise of Management as a Profession*. Princeton: Princeton University Press.

King, Robert G., and Sergio T. Rebelo. 1993. "Transitional Dynamics and Economic Growth in the Neo-classical Model." *American Economic Review* 83: 908–931.

Kirzner, Israel M. 1973. *Competition and Entrepreneurship*. Chicago: University of Chicago Press.

Kirzner, Israel M. 1976. "Equilibrium vs. Market Processes." In Edwin Dolan, ed., *The Foundations of Modern Austrian Economics*. Kansas City: Sheed and Ward..

Klamer, Arjo. 2003. "A Pragmatic View on Values in Economics." *Journal of Economic Methodology* 10 (2): 191–212.

Klamer, Arjo. 2007. *Speaking of Economics: How to Get Into the Conversation*. London: Routledge.

Knight, Frank. 1923. "The Ethics of Competition." *Quarterly Journal of Economics*, reprinted as pp. 33–67 in Knight 1935.

Knight, Frank. 1935. *The Ethics of Competition*. New York: Harper and Bros. Reprinted New Brunswick, N.J.: Transaction Publishers, 1997.

Kritzler, Edward. 2008. *Jewish Pirates of the Caribbean*. New York: Random House.

Kropotkin, P. A., Prince. 1901. "Modern Science and Anarchism." Trans. 1903, reprinted pp. 57–93 in E. Capouya and K. Tompkins, eds., *The Essential Kropotkin* (New York: Liveright, 1975).

Krugman, Paul. 1996. *Pop Internationalism*. Cambridge, Mass.: MIT Press.

Krugman, Paul. 1997. *Development, Geography, and Economic Theory.* Cambridge, Mass.: MIT Press.

Krugman, Paul. 2000. "Where in the World Is the 'New Economic Geography'?" Pp. 49–60 in G. L. Clark, Maryann P. Feldman, and M. S. Gertler, eds., *The Oxford Handbook of Economic Geography* (Oxford: Oxford University Press).

Kuhn, Steven L., Mary C. Stiner, David S. Reese, and Erksin Güleç. 2001. "Ornaments of the Earliest Upper Paleolithic: New Insights from the Levant." *Proceedings of the National Academy of Science* 98: 7641–7646.

Kussmaul, Anne. 1981. *Servants in Husbandry in Early Modern England.* Cambridge: Cambridge University Press.

Lachmann, Ludwig. 1977. *Capital, Expectations and the Market Process.* Kansas City: Sheed Andrews and McMeel.

Lal, Deepak. 1998. *Unintended Consequences: The Impact of Factor Endowments, Culture, and Politics on Long-Run Economic Performance.* Cambridge, Mass.: MIT Press.

Lal, Deepak. 2006. *Reviving the Invisible Hand: The Case for Classical Liberalism in the Twenty-First Century.* Princeton: Princeton University Press.

Landes, David S. 1965. "Technological Change and Industrial Development in Western Europe, 1750–1914." In H. J. Habakkuk and M. M. Postan, eds. *Cambridge Economic History of Europe,* vol. 6. Cambridge: Cambridge University Press.

Landes, David S. 1969. *The Unbound Prometheus: Technological Change and Industrial Development in Western Europe from 1750 to the Present.* Cambridge: Cambridge University Press.

Landes, David S. 1998. "East Is East and West Is West." Pp. 19–38 in Berg and Bruland.

Landes, David S. 1998. *The Wealth and Poverty of Nations: Why Some Are So Rich and Some So Poor.* New York: W. W. Norton.

Landes, David S. 2006. *Dynasties: Fortune and Misfortune in the World's Great Family Businesses.* New York: Penguin.

Langford, Paul. 2000. *Englishness Identified: Manners and Character 1650–1850.* Oxford: Oxford University Press.

Langlois, Richard. 1994. "Review of Lazonick, *Business Organization. Journal of Economic Behavior and Organization* 23: 244–250. At http://www.ucc.uconn.edu/~langlois/lazonick .html.

Lanham, Richard A. 1993. *The Electronic Word: Democracy, Technology, and the Arts.* Chicago: University of Chicago Press.

Lanham, Richard A. 2009. *A. C. Harberger: A Conversation.* DVD and transcript. Indianapolis: Liberty Fund.

Lattimore, Owen. 1940. *Inner Asian Frontiers of China.* New York: American Geographical Society.

Lawrence, D. H. 1923. *Studies in Classic American Literature.* London: Penguin, 1991.

Layard, Richard. 2009. "Now Is the Time for a Less Selfish Capitalism." *Financial Times.* March 12, p. 17 only.

Lazonick, William. 1979. "Industrial Relations and Technical Change: The Case of the Self Actor Mule." *Cambridge Journal of Economics* 3 (September): 231–262.

Lazonick, William. 1981. "Production Relations, Labor Productivity and Choice of Technique: British and US Cotton Spinning." *Journal of Economic History* 41: 491–516.

Lazonick, William. 1991a. *Business Organization and the Myth of the Market Economy.* New York: Cambridge University Press.

Lazonick, William. 1991b. "Business History and Economics." *Business and Economic History* ser. 2, 20. At http://www.h-net.org/~business/bhcweb/publications/BEHprint/v020/p0001-p0013.pdf.

Lebergott, Stanley. 1984. *The Americans: An Economic Record.* New York: W. W. Norton.

Lebergott, Stanley. 1993. *Pursuing Happiness: American Consumers in the Twentieth Century.* Princeton: Princeton University Press.

Lebergott, Stanley. 1996. *Consumer Expenditures: New Measures and Old Motives.* Princeton: Princeton University Press.

Lee, James, and Cameron Campbell. 1997. *Fate and Fortune in Rural China.* New York: Cambridge University Press.

Lee, James, and Wang Feng. 1999. *One Quarter of Humanity: Malthusian Mythology and Chinese Realities.* Cambridge, MA: Harvard University Press.

Lehmann, Helmut T. 1970. Introduction. [*Martin Luther's*] *Three Treatises.* 2nd ed. Philadelphia: Fortress Press.

Lenin, V. I. 1902. *What Is to Be Done?* Translated by J. Fineberg, G. Hanna, and R. Service. London: Penguin, 1988.

Lepore, Jill. 2008. "The Creed: What Poor Richard Cost Benjamin Franklin." *New Yorker* January 28: 78–82.

Lessnoff, Michael. 2003. "Religion." In Mokyr 2003a.

Levitt, Steven B., and Stephen J. Dubner. 2009. *Super Freakonomics.* New York: William Morrow.

Levy, David M. 2001. *How the Dismal Science Got Its Name: Classical Economics & the Ur-Text of Racial Politics.* Ann Arbor: University of Michigan Press.

Levy, David M., and Sandra J. Peart. 2001. "The Secret History of the Dismal Science, Part I: Economics, Religion and Race in the Nineteenth Century." January 22. Library of Economics and Liberty. At http://www.econlib.org/library/Columns/LevyPeartdismal.html.

Lewis, H. Gregg. 1986. *Union Relative Wage Effects: A Survey.* Chicago: University of Chicago Press.

Lewis, Sinclair. 1922. *Babbitt.* Modern Library. New York: Harcourt, Brace.

Lillo, George. 1731. *The London Merchant.* Pp. 287–343 in Quintana 1952.

Lindbeck, Assar. 2009. "Three Swedish Models." Speech to the Mont Pelerin Society, Stockholm, August 17.

Lindberg, Tod. 2004. "Neoconservatism's Liberal Legacy." *Hoover Institution Policy Review* October/November. At http://www.hoover.org/publications/policyreview/3436416.html.

Lorenz, Edward. 1991. *Economic Decline in Britain: The Shipbuilding Industry.* Oxford: Oxford University Press.

Lucas, Robert E., Jr. 2002. *Lectures on Economic Growth.* Cambridge, Mass.: Harvard University Press.

Luciani, Patrick. 2004. "Do Cities Create Wealth? A Critique of New Urban Thinking and the

Role of Public Policy for Cities." AIMS Urban Futures Series 2. Atlantic Institute for Market Studies Halifax, Nova Scotia. June. At http://www.aims.ca/library/Luciani.pdf.

Lyovin, Anatole V. 1997. *An Introduction to the Languages of the World*. Oxford: Oxford University Press.

Macaulay, Thomas Babbington. 1830. "Southey's Colloquies on Society." *Edinburgh Review*, Jan. Reprinted in *Critical, Historical, and Miscellaneous Essays by Lord Macaulay* (Boston, 1860 [1881]), 2: 132–187.

Macdonnell, A. G. 1933. *England, Their England*. London: Macmillan.

Macfarlane, Alan. 1978. *The Origins of English Individualism: The Family, Property, and Social Transition*. Oxford: Basil Blackwell.

Macfarlane, Alan. 1987. *The Culture of Capitalism*. Oxford: Basil Blackwell.

Macfarlane, Alan. 2000. *The Riddle of the Modern World: Of Liberty, Wealth, and Equality*. Basingstoke: Palgrave.

Machlup, Fritz. 1963 (1975). *Essays in Economic Semantics*. New York: New York University Press, 1975.

MacLeod, Christine. 1988. *Inventing the Industrial Revolution*. Cambridge: Cambridge University Press.

MacLeod, Christine. 1998. "James Watt: Heroic Invention and the Idea of the Industrial Revolution." Pp. 96–115 in Berg and Bruland.

MacLeod, Christine. 2007. *Heroes of Invention: Technology, Liberalism and British Identity, 1750–1914*. Cambridge: Cambridge: Cambridge University Press.

Maddison, Angus. 1965. *Industrial Growth and World Trade*. National Institute of Economic and Social Research. Cambridge: Cambridge University Press.

Maddison, Angus. 2006. *The World Economy*. Comprising *The World Economy: A Millennial Perspective* (2001) and *The World Economy: Historical Statistic* (2003) bound as one. Paris: Organization for Economic Cooperation and Development.

Maddison, Angus. 2007. *Contours of the World Economy, 1–2030 AD*. Oxford: Oxford University Press.

Malthus, Robert Thomas. 1798. *An Essay on the Principle of Population*. 2nd ed. 1803.

Mandeville, Bernard. 1705, 1714. *The Fable of the Bees, or Private Vices, Publick Benefits*. 2 vols. (enl. eds. 1723, 1728; from poem of 1705, "The Grumbling Hive"). With a Commentary Critical, Historical, and Explanatory by F. B. Kaye. Indianapolis: Liberty Fund, 1988.

Manski, Charles F. 2008. *Identification for Prediction and Decision*. Cambridge, Mass.: Harvard University Press.

Mantoux, Paul. 1906. *La révolution industrielle au XVIIIe siècle*. Translated by Marjorie Vernon as *The Industrial Revolution in the Eighteenth Century* (London: Jonathan Cape, 1929).

Manuelli, Rodolfo, and Ananth Seshadri. 2005. "Human Capital and the Wealth of Nations." Manuscript, Department of Economics, University of Wisconsin–Madison. At http://www.ssc.wisc.edu~manuelli/research/humcapwealthnation5_05.pdf.

Marglin, Stephen A. 1974. "What Do Bosses Do? The Origins and Functions of Hierarchy in Capitalist Production." Part 1, *Review of Radical Political Economics* 6 (Summer): 33–60; and Part 2, 60–112. Reprinted in A. Gorz, ed., *The Division of Labour: The Labour Process and Class Struggle in Modern Capitalism* (Brighton, 1976) and as pp. 25–68 in Warwick Organizational Behaviour Staff, eds., *Organizational Studies* (London: Routledge, 2001).

Marglin, Stephen A. 2008. *The Dismal Science: How Thinking Like an Economist Undermines Community*. Cambridge, Mass.: Harvard University Press.

Margo, Robert. 2008. "Review of Clark's *Farewell to Alms*." EH-Net. March. http://eh.net/mailman/listinfo/eh.net-review.

Marsalis, Wynton, and Geoffrey C. Ward. 2008. *Moving to Higher Ground: How Jazz Can Change Your Life*. New York: Random House.

Marshall, Alfred. 1890. *Principles of Economics*. London: Macmillan.

Marshall, Gordon, D. Rose, H. Newby, and C. Volger. 1988. *Social Class in Modern Britain*. London: Unwin Hyman.

Marx, Karl. 1846. "Letter [on Proudhon, in French] to Pavel Vasilyevich Annenkov." Translated by Peter and Betty Ross, *Marx Engels Collected Works*, vol. 38, p. 95, December 28. Reproduced at http://www.marxists.org/archive/marx/works/1846/letters/46_12_28.htm.

Marx, Karl. 1859. "Selections from the Preface to *A Contribution to the Criticism of Political Economy*." Translated by N. I. Stone, 1904. Pp. 42–46 in Lewis S. Feuer, ed., *Basic Writings on Politics and Philosophy, Karl Marx and Friedrich Engels* (New York: Anchor Books, 1959).

Marx, Karl. 1867. *Capital: A Critique of Political Economy*. Vol. 1. Edited by F. Engels. Translated from the 3rd German ed. by S. Moore and E. Aveling, 1887. New York: Modern Library, n.d.

Marx, Karl. 1867 (1962). *Das Kapital*. German ed., Zurück zum Gesamtverzeichnis Karl Marx/Friedrich Engels—Werke. Seitenzahlen verweisen auf: Karl Marx—Friedrich Engels—Werke, Band 23, S. 11–802, Dietz Verlag, Berlin/DDR, at http://www.mlwerke.de/me/me23/me23_000.htm.

Marx, Karl, and Friedrich Engels. 1848 (1988). *The Communist Manifesto*. 1888 English translation, with additional notes and introduction by F. L. Bender. Norton Critical Edition. New York: W. W. Norton.

Marx, Leo. 1964. *The Machine in the Garden: Technology and the Pastoral Ideal in America*. London: Oxford University Press.

Mathias, Peter. 1953 (1979). "An Industrial Revolution in Brewing, 1700–1830." *Explorations in Entrepreneurial History* 5: 208–224. Reprinted pp. 209–230 in Mathias, *The Transformation of England: Essays in the Economic and Social History of England in the Eighteenth Century* (New York: Columbia University Press, 1979).

Mathias, Peter. 1959. *The Brewing Industry in England*. Cambridge: Cambridge University Press.

Mathias, Peter. 1972 (1979). "Who Unbound Prometheus? Science and Technical Change, 1600–1800." In Mathias, ed., *Science and Society, 1600–1800*. Cambridge: Cambridge University Press. Reprinted pp. 45–87 in Mathias, *The Transformation of England: Essays in the Economic and Social History of England in the Eighteenth Century* (New York: Columbia University Press, 1979).

Mathias, Peter. 1973 (1979). "Credit, Capital and Enterprise in the Industrial Revolution." *Journal of European Economic History* 2: 121–143. Reprinted as pp. 88–115 in Mathias, *The Transformation of England: Essays in the Economic and Social History of England in the Eighteenth Century* (New York: Columbia University Press, 1979).

Mauss, Marcel. 1925. *Essai sur le don*. Translated as *The Gift*. Oxford: Routledge, 1990. Routledge Classics 2002.

Maxwell, Lee M. 2003. *Save Women's Lives: History of Washing Machines*. Eaton, Colo.: Oldewash.

McCants, Anne. 1997. *Civic Charity in a Golden Age: Orphan Care in Early Modern Amsterdam*. Champaign: University of Illinois Press.

McCants, Anne. 2009. "Review of Lisa Jardine's *Going Dutch: How England Plundered Holland's Glory*." EH-NET. At eh.net-review@eh.net.

McCloskey, Deirdre N. 1970. "Did Victorian Britain Fail?" *Economic History Review* 23: 446–459.

McCloskey, Deirdre N. 1972a. "The Enclosure of Open Fields: Preface to a Study of Its Impact on the Efficiency of English Agriculture in the Eighteenth Century." *Journal of Economic History* 32: 15–35.

McCloskey, Deirdre N. 1972b. "Review of Ramsey's *The Price Revolution in Sixteenth Century England*," *Journal of Political Economy* 80 (November/December): 1332–1335.

McCloskey, Deirdre N. 1973. *Economic Maturity and Entrepreneurial Decline: British Iron and Steel, 1870–1913*. Cambridge, Mass.: Harvard University Press.

McCloskey, Deirdre N. 1975a. "The Economics of Enclosure: A Market Analysis." Pp. 123–160 in E. L. Jones and William Parker, eds., *European Peasants and Their Markets: Essays in Agrarian Economic History* (Princeton: Princeton University Press).

McCloskey, Deirdre N. 1975b. "Review of Williamson's *Late Nineteenth-Century American Development*." *Times Literary Supplement* (December 12).

McCloskey, Deirdre N. 1976. "English Open Fields as Behavior Towards Risk." *Research in Economic History* 1 (Fall): 124–170

McCloskey, Deirdre N. 1980. "Magnanimous Albion: Free Trade and British National Income, 1841–1881." *Explorations in Economic History* 17 (July): 303–320. Reprinted in Forrest Capie, ed., *Protectionism in the World Economy* (Cheltenham: Edward Elgar, 1992).

McCloskey, Deirdre N. 1981. "The Industrial Revolution, 1780–1860: A Survey." Chapter 6 in Floud and McCloskey 1981, pp. 103–127, reprinted inMokyr 1985.

McCloskey, Deirdre N. 1983. "Theses on Enclosure." Pp. 56–72 in Papers Presented to the Economic History Society Conference at Canterbury, simultaneous meetings of the Agricultural History Society.

McCloskey, Deirdre N. 1985a. *The Rhetoric of Economics*. Madison: University of Wisconsin Press. 2nd rev. ed., 1998.

McCloskey, Deirdre N. 1985b. *The Applied Theory of Price*. 2nd ed. New York: Macmillan.

McCloskey, Deirdre N. 1989. "The Open Fields of England: Rent, Risk, and the Rate of Interest, 1300–1815." Pp. 5–51 in David W. Galenson, ed., *Markets in History: Economic Studies of the Past* (Cambridge: Cambridge University Press).

McCloskey, Deirdre N. 1990. *If You're So Smart: The Narrative of Economic Expertise*. Chicago: University of Chicago Press.

McCloskey, Deirdre N. 1991a. "History, Nonlinear Differential Equations, and the Problem of Narration." *History and Theory* 30: 21–36.

McCloskey, Deirdre N. 1991b. "The Prudent Peasant: New Findings on Open Fields." *Journal of Economic History* 51: 343–350.

McCloskey, Deirdre N. 1994a. "Bourgeois Virtue," *American Scholar* 63 (2) (Spring): 177–191.

McCloskey, Deirdre N. 1994b. "The Industrial Revolution: A Survey," a new essay, in Floud and McCloskey, eds., *The Economic History of Britain, 1700-Present*, 2nd ed. Cambridge: Cambridge University Press.

McCloskey, Deirdre N. 1994c. *Knowledge and Persuasion in Economics.* Cambridge: Cambridge University Press.

McCloskey, Deirdre N. 1995a. "Allen's *Enclosure and the Yeoman*: The View from Tory Fundamentalism." Manuscript, available at deirdremccloskey.org.

McCloskey, Deirdre N. 1995b. "Once Upon a Time There Was a Theory." *Scientific American* (February): 25 only.

McCloskey, Deirdre N. 1998. "Bourgeois Virtue and the History of *P* and *S*," *Journal of Economic History* 58 (2) (June): 297–317.

McCloskey, Deirdre N. 2001. "Women's Work in the Market, 1900–2000." In Ina Zweiniger-Bargielowska, ed., *Women in Twentieth Century Britain: Economic, Social and Cultural Change.* London: Longman/Pearson Education.

McCloskey, Deirdre N. 2006a. *The Bourgeois Virtues: Ethics for an Age of Commerce.* Chicago: University of Chicago Press.

McCloskey, Deirdre N. 2006b. "*Keukentafel* Economics and the History of the British Empire." *South African Journal of Economic History* 21 (September): 171–176.

McCloskey, Deirdre N. 2006c. "The Hobbes Problem from Hobbes to Buchanan," First Annual Buchanan Lecture, George Mason University, April 7, 2006. Reproduced at http://www.gmu.edu/centers/publicchoice/pdf%20links/dpaper4706.pdf and at deirdremccloskey.org.

McCloskey, Deirdre N. 2007. "Thrift as a Virtue, Historically Criticized." *Revue de Philosophie Économique* 8 (December): 3–31.

McCloskey, Deirdre N. 2008a. "The Prehistory of American Thrift." Forthcoming in Josh Yates, ed., *Thrift and American Culture.* New York: Columbia University Press.

McCloskey, Deirdre N. 2008b. "'You Know, Ernest, the Rich are Different from You and Me': A Comment on Clark's *A Farewell to Alms. European Review of Economic History* 12 (2) (August): 138–148.

McCloskey, Deirdre N. 2008c. Comments on Clark's *Farewell to Arms*, Social Science History Association, November, 2007, *Newsletter of the Cliometrics Society*, 2008.

McCloskey, Deirdre N. 2008d. "How to Buy, Sell, Make, Manage, Produce, Transact, Consume with Words." Introductory essay in Edward M. Clift, ed., *How Language Is Used to Do Business: Essays on the Rhetoric of Economics.* Lewiston, N.Y.: Mellen Press.

McCloskey, Deirdre N. 2008e. "Adam Smith, the Last of the Former Virtue Ethicists." *History of Political Economy* 40 (1): 43–71.

McCloskey, Deirdre, and Arjo Klamer. 1995. "One Quarter of GDP is Persuasion." *American Economic Review* 85 (2) (May): 191–195.

McCloskey, Deirdre N., and John Nash. 1984. "Corn at Interest: The Extent and Cost of Grain Storage in Medieval England." *American Economic Review* 74 (March): 174–187.

McCloskey, Deirdre N., and J. Richard Zecher. 1976. "How the Gold Standard Worked, 1880–1913." Pp. 357–385 in J. A. Frenkel and H. G. Johnson, eds., *The Monetary Approach to the Bal-*

ance of Payments. London: Allen and Unwin. Reprinted as pp. 63–80 in B. Eichengreen, ed., *The Gold Standard in Theory and History* (London: Methuen).

McCloskey, Deirdre N., and J. Richard Zecher. 1984. "The Success of Purchasing Power Parity: Historical Evidence and Its Implications for Macroeconomics." Pp. 121–150 in Michael Bordo and Anna J. Schwartz, eds., *A Retrospective on the Classical Gold Standard 1821–1931.* National Bureau of Economic Research (Chicago: University of Chicago Press).

McCloskey, Robert G. 1945. "The Case for 'Foot in the Door.'" *National Municipal Review* 34 (March): 121–124, 128.

McCormick, Michael. 2001. *Origins of the European Economy: Communications and Commerce A.D. 300–900.* Cambridge: Cambridge University Press.

McDougall, Walter A. 2004. *Freedom Just Around the Corner: A New American History, 1585–1828.* New York: HarperCollins.

McGrath, Alistair. 2007. *Dawkins' God: Genes, Memes, and the Meaning of Life.* London: Blackwell.

McInerney, James O., and Davide Pisani. 2007. "Paradigm for Life." *Science* 318 (November 20): 1390–1391.

McKeon, Michael. 1987 (2002). *The Origins of the English Novel, 1600–1740.* 2nd ed. Baltimore: Johns Hopkins University Press.

McNeill, William H. 1964. *Europe's Steppe Frontier, 1500–1800: A Study of Eastward Movement in Europe.* Chicago: University of Chicago Press.

McNeill, William. H 1982. *The Pursuit of Power: Technology, Armed Force, and Society since A.D. 1000.* Chicago: University of Chicago Press.

Mellinger, Andrew D., Jeffrey D. Sachs, and John L. Gallup. 2002. "Climate, Coastal Proximity, and Development." Pp. 169–194 in G. L. Clark, Maryann P. Feldman, and M. S. Gertler, eds., *The Oxford Handbook of Economic Geography* (Oxford: Oxford University Press).

Menand, Louis. 2009. "Show or Tell? Should Creative Writing Be Taught?" *New Yorker* June8 & 15: 106–112.

Migheli, Matteo. 2009. "The Two Sides of a Ghost: Twenty Years without the Wall." Manuscript, University of Eastern Piedmont, Department of Public Policy and Collective Choice, Alessandria, Italy. At http://d.repec.org/n?u=RePEc:uca:ucapdv:125&r=his.

Milanovic, Branko. 2009. "Global Inequality and Global Inequality Extraction Ratio: The Story of the Last Two Centuries." At http://mpra.ub.uni-muenchen.de/16535/.

Mill, John Stuart. 1843. *A System of Logic, Ratiocinative and Inductive.* London: John W. Parker.

Mill, John Stuart. 1845. "The Claims of Labour." *Edinburgh Review.* Reprinted in *The Collected Works of John Stuart Mill,* vol. 4, *Essays on Economics and Society, Part I,* ed. John M. Robson (Toronto: University of Toronto Press; London: Routledge and Kegan Paul, 1967). At Liberty Fund, Online Library of Liberty.

Mill, John Stuart. 1871. *Principles of Political Economy and Taxation.* Books 4 and 5. Donald Winch, ed. London: Penguin, 1970.

Millar, John. 1787 (1803). *An Historical View of the English Government.* 1803 posthumous reprint of 2nd ed. available at Liberty Fund: On-Line Library of Liberty. At http://oll.libertyfund.org/.

Miller, Edward. 1951. *The Abbey and Bishopric of Ely*. Cambridge:' Cambridge University Press.

Milton, John. 1644. "Areopagitica: A Speech for the Liberty of Unlicensed Printing to the Parliament of England." Renascence [*sic*] Editions. At http://www.uoregon.edu/~rbear/areopagitica.html.

Minsky, Hyman P. 1992. "The Financial Instability Hypothesis." Paper. Jerome Levy Economics Institute, Bard College, New York.

Mitch, David. 1992. *Education and Economic Development in England*. Princeton, N.J.: Princeton University Press.

Mitch, David. 1999. "The Role of Education and Skill in the Industrial Revolution." Pp. 241–279 in Mokyr 1999.

Mitch, David. 2003. "Human Capital." In Mokyr 2003a.

Mitch, David. 2004. "Education and Skill of the British Labour Force." Chap. 12 in Floud and Johnson, eds., *The Cambridge Economic History of Modern Britain*, vol. 1, *Industrialisation, 1700–1860*. Cambridge: Cambridge University Press.

Mitchell, Brian, with the assistance of Phyllis Deane. 1962. *Abstract of British Historical Statistics*. Cambridge: Cambridge University Press.

Mokyr, Joel, ed. 1985. *Economic History and the Industrial Revolution*. Totawa, N.J.: Rowman and Littlefield.

Mokyr, Joel. 1977. "Demand vs. Supply in the Industrial Revolution." *Journal of Economic History* 37: 981–1008.

Mokyr, Joel, ed. 1985. *The Economics of the Industrial Revolution*. Totawa, NJ: Rowman and Allanheld.

Mokyr, Joel. 1990. *The Lever of Riches: Technological Creativity and Economic Progress*. New York: Oxford University Press.

Mokyr, J., ed. 1999. *The British Industrial Revolution: An Economic Perspective*. Boulder: Westview.

Mokyr, Joel. 2002. *The Gifts of Athena: Historical Origins of the Knowledge Economy*. Princeton: Princeton University Press.

Mokyr, Joel, ed. 2003a. *The Oxford Encyclopedia of Economic History*. 6 vols. Oxford: Oxford University Press.

Mokyr, Joel. 2003b. "Industrial Revolution." In Mokyr 2003a.

Mokyr, Joel. 2007a. "The European Enlightenment, the Industrial Revolution, and Modern Economic Growth." Max Weber Lecture, European University Institute, Bellagio, March 27. At http://facultywcas.northwestern.edu/~jmokyr/Florence-Weber.PDF.

Mokyr, Joel. 2007b. "Discussion of Clark's *Farewell to Alms*." Meet-the-author session at the Social Science History Convention, Chicago, November. http://eh.net/bookreviews/ssha_farewell_to_alms.pdf.

Mokyr, Joel. 2008. "Intellectual Property Rights, the Industrial Revolution, and the Beginnings of Modern Economic Growth." Research Symposium on Property Rights Economics and Innovation. Searle Center on Law, Regulation, and Economic Growth. Northwestern University School of Law. Nov. 13. At http://www.law.northwestern.edu/searlecenter/papers/Mokyr_industrial.pdf. Published in *American Economic Review* 99 (May 2009): 349–355.

Mokyr, Joel. 2010. *The Enlightened Economy: An Economic History of Britain 1700–1850*. London: Penguin Press; New Haven: Yale University Press.

Montaigne, Michel de. 1588. *The Complete Essays of Montaigne.* Edited and translated by Donald Frame. Stanford: Stanford University Press, 1958.

Montesquieu, Charles-Louis de Secondat, baron de La Brède et de. 1748. *De l'esprit des lois (The Spirit of the Laws).* Numerous editions.

Moore, Basil J. 2006. *Shaking the Invisible Hand: Complexity, Endogenous Money and Exogenous Interest Rates.* Basingstoke: Palgrave Macmillan.

More, Thomas. 1516. *Utopia.* Translated by C. H. Miller. New Haven: Yale University Press, 2001.

Moulton, Brent R. 1996. "Bias in the Consumer Price Index: What Is the Evidence?" *Journal of Economic Perspectives* 10 (4) (Fall): 159–177.

Mueller, John. 1999. *Capitalism, Democracy, and Ralph's Pretty Good Grocery.* Princeton: Princeton University Press.

Munkhammar, Johnny. 2007. *The Guide to Reform.* Stockholm: Timbro Publishers.

Murrell, Peter. 2009. "Design and Evolution in Institutional Development: The Insignificance of the English Bill of Rights." At SSRN: http://ssrn.com/abstract=1522864.

Musson, A. E. 1972. *Science, Technology and Economic Growth in the Eighteenth Century.* London: Methuen.

Musson, A. E. 1978. *The Growth of British Industry.* New York: Holmes and Meier.

Musson, A. E., and Eric Robinson. 1969. *Science and Technology in the Industrial Revolution.* Manchester: Manchester University Press.

Najita, Tetsuo. 1987. *Visions of Virtue in Tokugawa Japan: The Kaitokudō Merchant Academy of Osaka.* Honolulu: University of Hawaii Press.

National Centre for Social Research. 2007. Press release. *Perspectives on a Changing Society.* British Social Attitudes, 23rd Annual Report. January 24. At http://www.natcen.ac.uk/natcen/pages/news_and_media_docs/BSA_%20press_release_jan07.pdf.

Neal, Larry. 1990. *The Rise of Financial Capitalism: International Capital Markets in the Age of Reason.* Cambridge: Cambridge University Press.

Nee, Victor, and Richard Swedberg. 2007. Introduction. Pp. 1–18 in Nee and Swedberg, eds., *On Capitalism* (Stanford: Stanford University Press).

Nelson, Robert H. 1991. *Reaching for Heaven on Earth: The Theological Meaning of Economics.* Lanham, Md.: Rowman & Littlefield.

Nelson, Robert H. 2001. *Economics as Religion: From Samuelson to Chicago and Beyond.* University Park: Pennsylvania State University Press.

Nelson, Robert H. 2009. *The New Holy Wars: Economic Religion Versus Environmental Religion in Contemporary America.* University Park: Pennsylvania State University Press.

Nordhaus, William D. 1997. "Do Real Output and Real Wage Measures Capture Reality? The History of Lighting Suggests Not." Pp. 29–70 in Timothy Bresnahan and Robert J. Gordon, eds., *The Economics of New Goods* (Chicago: University of Chicago Press).

Nordhaus, William D. 2004. "Schumpeterian Profits in the American Economy: Theory and Measurement." National Bureau of Economic Research Working Paper W10433.

Nordhaus, William D. 2008. *A Question of Balance: Weighing the Options on Global Warming Policies.* New Haven: Yale University Press.

North, Douglass C. 1968. "Sources of Productivity Change in Ocean Shipping, 1600–1850." *Journal of Political Economy* 76: 953–970.

North, Douglass C. 1990. *Institutions, Institutional Change and Economic Performance.* Cambridge: Cambridge University Press.

North, Douglass C. 1991. "Institutions." *Journal of Economic Perspectives* 5 (1) (Winter): 97–112. At http://www.compilerpress.atfreeweb.com/Anno%20North%20Institutions.htmt.

North, Douglass C. 1993. "Nobel Prize Autobiography." From *Les Prix Nobel. The Nobel Prizes 1993*, Editor Tore Frängsmyr [Nobel Foundation], Stockholm, 1994. At http://nobelprize.org/nobel_prizes/economics/laureates/1993/north-autobio.html.

North, Douglass C. 2005. *Understanding the Process of Economic Change.* Princeton Economic History of the Western World. Princeton: Princeton University Press.

North, Douglass C., and Robert Paul Thomas. 1973. *The Rise of the Western World: A New Economic History.* Cambridge: Cambridge University Press.

North, Douglass C., and Barry R. Weingast. 1989. "Constitutions and Commitment: The Evolution of Institutions Governing Public Choice in Seventeenth-Century England." *Journal of Economic History* 49 (December): 803–832.

North, Dudley. 1691. *Discourses upon Trade.* Edited by Jacob H. Hollander. Baltimore: Johns Hopkins University Press, 1907. Indianapolis: Liberty Fund, Library of Liberty.

Novak, Michael. 2007. "Beyond Weber." Pp. 220–238 in Nee and Swedberg 2007.

Novick, Peter. 1988. *That Noble Dream: The "Objectivity Question" and the American Historical Profession.* Cambridge: Cambridge University Press.

Nozick, Robert. 1974. *Anarchy, State, and Utopia.* New York: Basic Books.

Nussbaum, Martha. 1999. *Sex and Social Justice.* Oxford: Oxford University Press.

Nussbaum, Martha, and Amartya Sen. 1993. *The Quality of Life.* Oxford: Clarendon Press.

Nutter, G. Warren. 1962. *The Growth of Industrial Production in the Soviet Union.* NBER. Princeton: Princeton University Press.

Nuvolari, Alessandro. 2004. "Collective Invention during the British Industrial Revolution: The Case of the Cornish Pumping Engine." *Cambridge Journal of Economics* 28: 347–363.

Nye, John V. C. 1991. "Lucky Fools and Cautious Businessmen: on Entrepreneurship and the Measurement of Entrepreneurial Failure." Pp. 131–152 in Joel Mokyr, ed., *The Vital One: Essays in Honor of Jonathan R. T. Hughes.* Research in Economic History 6.

Nye, John V. C. 2007. *War, Wine, and Taxes: The Political Economy of Anglo-French Trade, 1689–1900.* Princeton: Princeton University Press.

Ó Gráda, Cormac. 2009. *Famine: A Short History.* Princeton: Princeton University Press.

O'Brien, Patrick K. 1982. "European Economic Development: The Contribution of the Periphery." *Economic History Review* 35 (2): 1–18.

O'Brien, Patrick K., and Stanley Engerman. 1991. "Exports and the Growth of the British Economy from the Glorious Revolution to the Peace of Amiens." Pp. 177–209 in Barbara L. Solow, ed. *Slavery and the Rise of the Atlantic System* (Cambridge: Cambridge University Press).

O'Brien, Patrick K. 1993. "Political Preconditions for the Industrial Revolution." Pp. 124–155 in O'Brien and Ronald Quinault, eds., *The Industrial Revolution and British Society* (Cambridge: Cambridge University Press).

O'Brien, Patrick K., and Leandro Prados de la Escosura. 1999. "Balance Sheets for the Acquisition, Retention and Loss of European Empires Overseas." *Itinerario* 23: 25–52.

OECD. 2009. *Highlights from Education at a Glance.* Paris: Organization for Economic Cooperation and Development. At http://browse.oecdbookshop.org/oecd/pdfs/browseit/9609011E.PDF.

Ofer, Gur. 1987. "Soviet Economic Growth, 1928–1985." *Journal of Economic Literature* 25 (4): 1767–1833.

Offer, Avner. 1992. "The British Empire, 1870–1914: A Waste of Money?" *Economic History Review* 46: 215–238.

Officer, Lawrence H. 2009. *Two Centuries of Compensation for US Production Workers in Manufacturing.* New York: Palgrave-Macmillan.

Ogilvie, Sheilagh. 2004. "Guilds, Efficiency, and Social Capital: Evidence from German Proto-industry." *Economic History Review* 57 (May): 286–333.

Ogilvie, Sheilagh. 2007. "'Whatever Is, Is Right?' Economic Institutions in Pre-Industrial Europe." *Economic History Review* 60 (4): 649–684.

Ohlin, Bertil. 1933. *International and Interregional Trade.* Cambridge, Mass.: Harvard University Press.

Olmstead, Alan L., and Paul W. Rhode. 2008a. "Biological Innovation and Productivity Change in the Antebellum Cotton Economy." *Journal of Economic History* 68: 1123–1171.

Olmstead, Alan L., and Paul W. Rhode. 2008b. *Creating Abundance: Biological Innovation and American Agricultural Development.* New York: Cambridge University Press.

O'Neill, Joseph. 2008. *Netherland.* New York: Pantheon.

O'Rourke, Kevin H., Leandro Prados de la Escosura, and Guillaume Daudin. 2008. "Trade and Empire, 1700–1870." Paper, Institute for International Integration Studies. Available at http://www.tcd.ie/iiis/documents/discussion/pdfs/iiisdp249.pdf.

O'Rourke, Kevin, and Jeffrey G. Williamson. 2002. "After Columbus: Explaining Europe's Overseas Trade Boom, 1550–1800." *Journal of Economic History* 62: 417–455.

Oschinsky, Dorothea. 1971. *Walter of Henley and Other Treatises on Estate Management and Accounting.* Oxford: Clarendon Press.

Ostrom, Elinor. 1990. *Governing the Commons: The Evolution of Institutions for Collective Action.* New York: Cambridge University Press.

Otteson, James. 2006. *Actual Ethics.* Cambridge: Cambridge University Press.

Overton, Mark. 1996. *Agricultural Revolution in England: The Transformation of the Agrarian Economy 1500–1850.* Cambridge: Cambridge University Press.

Owen, Stephen. 1996. *An Anthology of Chinese Literature, Beginnings to 1911.* New York: W. W. Norton.

Oxford University Press. 1999. *The Concise Oxford Dictionary.* 10th ed. Edited by Judy Pearsall Oxford: Oxford University Press.

Özmucur, Süleyman, and Şevket Pamuk. 2007. "Did European Commodity Prices Converge during 1500–1800?" Pp. 59–85 in T. J. Hatton, K. O'Rourke, and A. M. Taylor, eds., *The New Comparative Economic History: Essays in Honor of Jeffrey G. Williamson* (Cambridge, Mass.: MIT Press).

Pakenham, Thomas. 1991. *The Scramble for Africa: White Man's Conquest of the Dark Continent, 1876–1912.* New York: Random House.

Palmer, Tom G. 1997. "The Literature of Liberty." In David Boaz, ed., *The Libertarian Reader*

(New York: Free Press, 1998), reprinted as pp. 425–475 in Palmer, *Realizing Freedom* (Washington, D.C.: Cato Institute, 2009).

Parente, Stephen L., and Edward C. Prescott. 2000. *Barriers to Riches*. Cambridge, Mass.: MIT Press.

Paton, Alan. 1948. *Cry, the Beloved Country*. London: Jonathan Cape. Reprinted London: Vintage, Random House, 1987.

Payson, Steven. 1994. *Quality Measurement in Economics: New Perspectives on the Evolution of Goods and Services*. Aldershot: Edward Elgar.

Peake, Harold, and Herbert Fleure. 1928. *The Steppe and the Sown*. New Haven: Yale University Press.

Pearson, Karl. 1900. *The Grammar of Science*. 2nd ed. London: Adam and Charles Black.

Pearson, Karl, and Margaret Moul. 1925. "The Problem of Alien Immigration into Great Britain, Illustrated by an Examination of Russian and Polish Jewish Children." *Annals of Eugenics* 1: 1–125.

Peart, Sandra, and David Levy. 2005. *The "Vanity of the Philosopher": From Equality to Hierarchy in Post-Classical Economics*. Ann Arbor: University of Michigan Press.

Perdue, Peter. 2003. "Silk Road." In Mokyr 2003a.

Perdue, Peter. 2005. *China Marches West: The Qing Conquest of Central Eurasia*. Cambridge, Mass.: Harvard University Press.

Persky, Joseph. 1990. "A Dismal Romantic." *Journal of Economic Perspectives* 4 (Autumn): 165–172.

Pew Research Center. 2008. "Overview." In *Inside the Middle Class: Bad Times Hit the Good Life*. At http://pewsocialtrends.org/assets/pdf/MC-Executive-Summary-and-Overview.pdf.

Pincus, Steven C. A. 2006. *England's Glorious Revolution, 1688–1689: A Brief History with Documents*. Boston: Bedford/St.Martin's.

Pincus, Steven C. A. 2009. *1688:The First Modern Revolution*. New Haven: Yale University Press.

Pipes, Richard. 1999. *Property and Freedom*. New York: Knopf.

Plantinga, Alvin. 2000. *Warranted Christian Belief*. New York: Oxford University Press.

Plattner, Marc F. 1999. "From Liberalism to Democracy." *Journal of Democracy* 10: 121–134.

Polanyi, Karl. 1944. *The Great Transformation*. Boston: Beacon Press.

Polanyi, Michael. 1958. *Personal Knowledge: Towards a Post-Critical Philosophy*. Chicago: University of Chicago Press.

Polanyi, Michael. 1966. *The Tacit Dimension*. Garden City, N.Y.: Doubleday.

Pollard, Sidney. 1964. "Fixed Capital in the Industrial Revolution." *Journal of Economic History* 24: 299–314.

Pollard, Sidney. 1973. "Industrialisation and the European Economy." *Economic History Review* 26 (2): 634–648.

Pollard, Sidney. 1981a. *The Integration of the European Economy since 1815*. London: Allen and Unwin.

Pollard, Sidney. 1981b. *Peaceful Conquest: The Industrialization of Europe, 1760–1970*. Oxford: Oxford University Press.

Pollock, Fredrick, and F. M. Maitland. 1895. *The History of English Law before the Time of Edward the First*. Cambridge: Cambridge University Press.

Pomeranz, Kenneth. 1993. *The Making of a Hinterland: State, Society, and Economy in Inland North China, 1853–1937*. Berkeley: University of California Press.

Pomeranz, Kenneth. 2000. *The Great Divergence: China, Europe, and the Making of the Modern World Economy*. Princeton: Princeton University Press.

Pomeranz, Kenneth, and Steven Topik. 2006. *The World That Trade Created: Society, Culture, and the World Economy 1400 to the Present*. London, and Armonk, New York: M. E. Sharpe.

Pooley, Colin G. 1989. "Segregation or Integration? The Residential Experience of the Irish in Mid-Victorian Britain." Pp. 60–83 in R. Swift and S. Gilley, eds., *The Irish in Britain, 1815–1939* (London: Rowman and Littlefield).

Popkin, Samuel L. 1979. *The Rational Peasant: The Political Economy of Rural Society in Vietnam*. Berkeley: University of California Press.

Porter, Michael E. 1990. *The Competitive Advantage of Nations*. New York: Free Press.

Postan, M. M. 1966. "England." Pp. 549–632 in Postan, ed., *The Cambridge Economic History of Europe*, vol. 1, *The Agrarian Life of the Middle Ages*, 2nd ed. (Cambridge: Cambridge University Press).

Prados de la Escosura, Leandro. 1993. "La pérdida del imperio y sus consecuencias económicas." In Prados de la Escosura and S. Amaral, eds. *La independencia America: Consecuencias económicas*. Madrid: Alianza.

Prakash, Om. 2003. "India: Colonial Period." In Mokyr 2003a.

Prebisch, Raúl. 1959. "Commercial Policy in the Underdeveloped Countries." *American Economic Review* 49 (May): 251–273.

Prentice, David. 2008. "The Origins of American Industrial Success: Evidence from the US Portland Cement Industry." Manuscript, La Trobe University. At http://mpra.ub.uni-muenchen.de/13409/.

Price, Richard. 1787. "The Evidence for a Future Period of Improvement in the State of Mankind." At http://www.constitution.org/price/price_7.htm.

Quintana, Ricardo, ed. 1952. *Eighteenth-Century Plays*. New York: Random House.

Raftis, J. Ambrose. 1964. *Tenure and Mobility: Studies in the Social History of the Medieval English Village*. Toronto: Pontifical Institute of Medieval Studies.

Raftis, J. Ambrose. 1996. *Peasant Economic Development within the English Manorial System*. Montreal: McGill-Queens University Press.

Ransom, Roger L. 1970. "Social Returns from Public Transport Investment: A Case Study of the Ohio Canal." *Journal of Political Economy* 78 (September/October): 1041–1060.

Rawski, Thomas G., ed. *Economics and the Historian*. Berkeley: University of California Press.

Rawksi, Thomas G., and Lillian M. Li., eds. *Chinese History in Economic Perspective*. Berkeley: University of California Press.

Rawls, John. 1971. *A Theory of Justice*. Cambridge, Mass.: Harvard University Press.

Rawls, John. 1993. *Political Liberalism*. New York: Columbia University Press.

Reinhart, Carmen M., and Kenneth Rogoff. 2008. "This Time Is Different: A Panoramic View of Eight Centuries of Financial Crises." At http://www.publicpolicy.umd.edu/news/This_Time_Is_Different_04_16_2008%20REISSUE.pdf.

Reiter, Paul. 2000. "From Shakespeare to Defoe: Malaria in England in the Little Ice Age." *Merging Infectious Diseases* 6 (January/February). Coordinating Center for Infectious

Diseases, Centers for Disease Control and Prevention, Atlanta, GA. http://www.cdc.gov/ncidod/EID/vol6no1/reiter.htm.

Richards, John F. *The Mughal Empire*. New Cambridge History of India, Vol. 1, pt. 5. Cambridge: Cambridge University Press.

Richardson, David. 2003. "Slave Trade." In Mokyr 2003a.

Richardson, Philip. 1989. "The Structure of Capital during the Industrial Revolution Revisited: Two Case Studies from the Cotton Textile Industry." *Economic History Review* 42: 484–503.

Ridley, Matt. 1996. *The Origins of Virtue: Human Instincts and the Evolution of Cooperation*. New York: Penguin.

Rietbergen, Peter. 1998. *Europe: A Cultural History*. 2nd ed. London: Routledge.

Ringmar, Erik. 2007. *Why Europe Was First: Social Change and Economic Growth in Europe and East Asia, 1500–2050*. London: Anthem Press.

Ritholtz, Barry. 2007. "Inflation: CPI, Core Rate, Inflation ex-Inflation." At Rotholtz blog Seeking Alpha, http://seekingalpha.com/article/48927-inflation-cpi-core-rate-inflation-ex-inflation.

Robinson, Joan. 1966. *An Essay on Marxian Economics*. 2nd ed. London: Macmillan (first ed. 1942).

Rosenberg, Nathan. 1978. *Perspectives on Technology*. Cambridge: Cambridge University Press.

Rosenberg, Nathan. 1982. *Inside the Black Box: Technology and Economics*. Cambridge: Cambridge University Press.

Rosenberg, Nathan. 1994. *Exploring the Black Box: Technology, Economics, and History*. Cambridge: Cambridge University Press.

Rosenberg, Nathan, and L. E. Birdzell. 1986. *How the West Grew Rich*. New York: Basic Books.

Rosendahl, Peter J. 1919–1935. *More Han Ola og Han Per*. Bilingual Edition. Edited by Einar Haugen and Joan N. Buckley. Iowa City: University of Iowa Press, 1988.

Rostow, W. W. 1960. *The Stages of Economic Growth: A Non-Communist Manifesto*. Cambridge: Cambridge University Press.

Roth, Guenther. 1987. Introduction. Pp. 1–24 in H. Lehmann and G. Roth, eds., *Weber's Protestant Ethic: Origins, Evidence, Contexts* (Cambridge: Cambridge University Press).

Roth, Philip. 2006. *Everyman*. London: Vintage.

Rothschild, Emma. 2001. *Economic Sentiments: Adam Smith, Condorcet, and the Enlightenment*. Cambridge: Harvard University Press.

Rousseau, Jean-Jacques. 1755. *A Discourse upon Political Economy*. Liberty Fund ed. Online Library of Liberty.

Sabel, Charles, and Jonathan Zeitlin. 1985. "Historical Alternatives to Mass Production: Politics, Markets and Technology in Nineteenth-Century Industrialization." *Past and Present* 108: 133–176.

Sahlins, Marshall. 1974 (2004). *Stone Age Economics*. New York: Aldine de Gruyter. 2nd ed., London: Routledge.

ShalinsSahlins, Marshall. 1976. *Culture and Practical Reason*. Chicago: University of Chicago Press.

Sampson, Geoffrey. 2005. *The "Language Instinct" Debate*. Rev. ed. London: Continuum.

Samuelson, Paul A. 1947. *The Foundations of Economic Analysis*. Cambridge, Mass.: Harvard University Press.

Sandberg, Lars G. 1979. "The Case of the Impoverished Sophisticate: Human Capital and Swedish Economic Growth before World War I." *Journal of Economic History* 39: 225–242.

Sato, R. 1963. "Fiscal Policy in a Neo-classical Growth Model: An Analysis of Time "Required for Equilibrating Adjustment." *Review of Economic Studies* 30 (1): 16–23.

Schama, Simon. 1987. *The Embarrassment of Riches: An Interpretation of Dutch Culture in the Golden Age*. Berkeley: University of California Press.

Scheidel, W. 2008. "Real Wages in Early Economies: Evidence for Living Standards from 2000 B.C.E. to 1300 C.E." SSRN working paper. At papers.ssrn.com/sol3/papers.

Schmidtz, David. 1993. "Reasons for Altruism." Pp. 52–68 in Ellen Frankel Paul, Fred D. Miller, and Jeffrey Paul, eds., *Altruism* (Cambridge: Cambridge University Press). Reprinted as pp. 164–175 in Aafke E. Komter, ed., *The Gift: An Interdisciplinary Perspective* (Amsterdam: University of Amsterdam Press, 1996).

Schmitt, John. 2007. "Is the Unemployment Rate in Sweden Really 17 Percent?" *Issue Brief*. Washington, DC: Center for Economic and Policy Research. http://static.scribd.com/docs/b6wb0alv0m8m9.swf.

Schmoller, Gustav. 1884 (1897). "The Mercantile System and Its Historical Significance." A chapter from the English edition of 1897 of *Studien uber die wirtschaftliche Politik*. At http://socserv2.socsci.mcmaster.ca/~econ/ugcm/3ll3/schmoller/mercant.

Schmookler, Jacob. 1966. *Inventions and Economic Growth*. Cambridge, Mass.: Harvard University Press.

Schmookler, Jacob. 1972. *Patents, Invention and Economic Change*. Cambridge, Mass.: Harvard University Press.

Schor, Juliet B. 1993. *The Overworked American: The Unexpected Decline of Leisure*. New York: Basic Books.

Schor, Juliet B. 1998. *The Overspent American: Upscaling, Downshifting, and the New Consumer*. New York: Basic Books.

Schor, Juliet B. 2004. *Born to Buy: The Commercialized Child and the New Consumer Culture*. New York: Scribner.

Schreiner, Olive. 1883. *The Story of an African Farm*. Harmondsworth: Penguin, 1939.

Schultz, Theodore W. 1964. *Transforming Traditional Agriculture*. New Haven: Yale University Press.

Schumpeter, Joseph A. 1926 (1st ed. 1912; trans. 1934). *The Theory of Economic Development*. Cambridge, Mass.: Harvard University Press.

Schumpeter, Joseph A. 1939. *Business Cycles: A Theoretical, Historical and Statistical Analysis of the Capitalist Process*. New York: McGraw-Hill.

Schumpeter, Joseph A. 1942 (1950). *Capitalism, Socialism and Democracy*. 3rd. ed. New York: Harper and Row. Harper Torchbook ed. 1962.

Schumpeter, Joseph A. 1954. *History of Economic Analysis*. Edited by Elizabeth B. Schumpeter. New York: Oxford University Press.

Scitovsky, Tibor. 1976. *The Joyless Economy: An Inquiry into Human Satisfaction and Consumer Dissatisfaction*. New York: Oxford University Press.

Seaton, James. 1996. *Cultural Conservatism, Political Liberalism: From Criticism to Cultural Studies*. Ann Arbor: University of Michigan Press.

Sellar, Walter C., and R. J. Yeatman. 1931. *1066 and All That: A Memorable History of England*. (Bound with *And Now All This.*) New York: Blue Ribbon Books, 1932.

Sellers, Charles. 1991. *The Market Revolution: Jacksonian America, 1815–1846*. Oxford: Oxford University Press.

Sen, Amartya. 1967. "Surplus Labor in India: A Critique of Schultz's Statistical Test." *Economic Journal* 77: 154–161.

Sen, Amartya. 1985. "Goals, Commitment, and Identity." *Journal of Law, Economic, and Organization* 1: 341–355.

Sen, Amartya. 1999. *Development as Freedom*. Oxford: Oxford University Press.

Sen, Amartya. 2005. *The Argumentative Indian: Writings on Indian History, Culture and Identity*. London: Allen Lane.

Seneca, Lucius Annaeus. 62–65 CE. *Letters from a Stoic* (*Epistulae Morales ad Lucilium*). Selected and trans. R. Campbell. London: Penguin, 1969.

Shiue, C. H. 1999. "Market Arbitrage and Transport Routes: Evidence from Eighteenth-Century China. Cliometric Society sessions at the ASSA.

Shiue, C. H., and W. Keller. 2007. "Markets in China and Europe on the Eve of the Industrial Revolution." *American Economic Review* 97: 1189–1216.

Siegel, Jacob S. 2002. *Applied Demography: Applications to Business, Government, Law and Public Policy*. San Diego: Academic Press.

Simmel, Georg. 1908. "The Stranger." In Simmel, *On Individuality and Social Forms: Selected Writings*, ed. Donald N. Levine (Chicago: University of Chicago Press, 1971).

Simon, Julian L. 1981 (1996). *The Ultimate Resource*. 2nd ed. Princeton: Princeton University Press.

Simon, Julian L. 1996. "A Reply to My Critics." In Simon 1981 (1996). At http://www.juliansimon.com/reply-critics.html.

Skinner, Quentin. 1998. *Liberty before Liberalism*. Cambridge: Cambridge University Press.

Smith, Adam. 1759 (1790). *The Theory of Moral Sentiments*. Glasgow ed. Edited by D. D. Raphael and A. L. Macfie. Oxford University Press. Reprinted Indianapolis: Liberty Classics, 1976, 1982.

Smith, Adam. 1776. *An Inquiry into the Nature and Causes of the Wealth of Nations*. Vol. 1. Glasgow ed. Edited by Campbell, Skinner, and Todd. Indianapolis: Liberty Classics, 1976. Vol. 2, 1981.

Smith, Adam. 1980. *Essays on Philosophical Subjects*. Edited by W. P. D. Wightman and J. J. Bryce Glasgow ed. Oxford: Oxford University Press.

Snow, John. 1855. *On the Mode of Communication of Cholera*. 2nd ed. (1st ed. 1849). London. At http://www.ph.ucla.edu/EPI/snow/snowbook3.html.

Sokoloff, Kenneth L. 1988. "Inventive Activity in Early Industrial America: Evidence from Patent Records, 1790–1846." *Journal of Economic History* 48: 813–850.

Sokoloff, Kenneth L., and B. Z. Khan. 1990. "The Democratization of Invention during Early Industrialization: Evidence from the United States, 1790–1846." *Journal of Economic History* 50: 363–378.

Solow, Robert. 1957. "Technical Change and the Aggregate Production Function." *Review of Economics and Statistics* 39: 312–320.

Solow, Robert. 2007. "Survival of the Richest? (Review of Clark's *Farewell to Alms*)." *New York Review of Books* 54 (18) (November 22).

Sombart, Werner. 1906. *Warum gibt es in den Vereinigten Staaten keinen Sozialismus?* [Why is there no socialism in the United States?]. Tübingen: J. C. B. Mohr. Trans. New York: Sharpe, 1976.

Sorek, Rotem, and others. 2007. "Genome-Wide Experimental Determination of Barriers to Horizontal Gene Transfer." *Science* 318 (November 30): 1449–1452.

Stark, Rodney. 2003. *For the Glory of God: How Monotheism Led to Reformations, Science, Witch-Hunts, and the End of Slavery.* Princeton: Princeton University Press.

Stearns, Peter N. 2007. *The Industrial Revolution in World History.* 3rd ed. Boulder: Westview.

Steele, Richard. 1722. *The Conscious Lovers.* Pp. 109–178 in Quintana 1952.

Stendhal. 1839. *The Charterhouse of Parma.* Translated by Margaret Shaw. Harmondsworth: Penguin, 1958.

Stevenson, Robert Louis. 1881. "Crabbed Age and Youth." Pp. 875–883 in *Virginibus Puerisque and Other Papers;* pp. 898–903 in *The Works of Robert Louis Stevenson* (New York: Walter J. Black, n.d.).

Stigler, George. 1967. "Imperfections in the Capital Market." *Journal of Political Economy* 75 (June): 287–292.

Stone, Lawrence, and Jeanne C. Fawtier Stone. 1984. *An Open Elite? England 1540–1880.* Oxford: Oxford University Press.

Stone, Lawrence. 1964. "The Educational Revolution in England, 1560–1640." *Past and Present* 28: 41–80.

Storr, Virgil. 2006. "Weber's Spirit of Capitalism and the Bahamas' Junkanoo Ethic." *Review of Austrian Economics* 19 (4): 289–309.

Storr, Virgil Henry. 2008. "The Market as a Social Space: On the Meaningful Extraeconomic Conversations That Can Occur in Markets." *Review of Austrian Economics* 21: 135–150.

Studer, R. 2007. "India and the Great Divergence: Assessing the Efficiency of Grain Markets in Eighteenth- and Nineteenth-Century India." University of Oxford Discussion Papers in Economic History and Social History 68.

Sullivan, Richard J. 1989. "England's 'Age of Invention': the Acceleration of Patents and Patentable Invention during the Industrial Revolution." *Explorations in Economic History* 26: 424–452.

Supple, Barry. 1959. *Commercial Crisis and Change in England 1600–1642: A Study in the Instability of a Mercantile Economy.* Cambridge: Cambridge University Press.

Swedberg, Richard. 2009. *Tocqueville's Political Economy.* Princeton: Princeton University Press.

Szostak, Rick. 1991. *The Role of Transportation in the Industrial Revolution.* Montreal: McGill-Queen's University Press.

Szostak, Rick. 2003. "Road Transport: Historical Overview." In Mokyr 2003a.

Tantillo, Astrida Orle. 2010. *Goethe's Modernisms.* New York: Continuum.

Taylor, Charles. 1989. *Sources of the Self: The Making of Modern Identity.* Cambridge, Mass.: Harvard University Press.

Taylor, Charles. 1992. *The Ethics of Authenticity.* (Massey Lectures, *The Malaise of Modernity,* 1991). Cambridge, Mass.: Harvard University Press.

Temin, Peter. 1964. *Iron and Steel in Nineteenth Century America: An Economic Inquiry.* Cambridge, Mass.: MIT Press.

Temin, Peter. 1966, "Labor Scarcity and the Problem of American Industrial Efficiency in the 1850s." *Journal of Economic History* 26: 277–298.

Temin, Peter. 1971. "Notes on Labor Scarcity in America." *Journal of Interdisciplinary History* 1: 251–264.

Temin, Peter. 1997. "Two Views of the British Industrial Revolution." *Journal of Economic History* 57: 63–82.

Temin, Peter. 2000. "A Response to Harley and Crafts." *Journal of Economic History* 60: 842–846.

Temple, Robert. 1986 (2007). *The Genius of China.* Forward by Joseph Needham. 3rd ed. London: Andre Deutsch.

Temple, William. 1672. *Observations upon the United Provinces of the Netherlands.* Edited with an introduction by G. N. Clark. At http://en.wikisource.org/wiki/Observations_upon_ the_United_Provinces_of_the_Netherlands.

Thaler, Richard H., and Cass R. Sunstein. 2008. *Nudge: Improving Decisions about Health, Wealth, and Happiness.* New Haven: Yale University Press.

Theil, Stefan. 2008. "Europe's Philosophy of Failure." *Foreign Policy* (January/February). At www.foreignpolicy.com.

Thomas, Robert Paul, and Richard N. Bean. 1974. "Fishers of Men: The Profits of the Slave Trade." *Journal of Economic History* 34: 885–914.

Thurow, Lester C. 1985. *The Zero-Sum Solution: Building a World-Class American Economy.* New York: Simon and Schuster.

Tillyard, E. M. W. 1943. *The Elizabethan World Picture: A Study of the Idea of Order in the Age of Shakespeare, Donne & Milton.* London: Chatto and Windus.

Tinniswood, Adrian. 2007. *The Verneys.* New York: Riverhead Books (Penguin).

Tishkoff, Sarah, and [24] others. 2009. "The Genetic Structure and History of Africans and African Americans." *Science* 324: 1035–1044. At http://www.sciencemag.org/cgi/data/ 1172257/DC1/1.

Tocqueville, Alexis de. 1835. *Journeys to England and Ireland.* Edited by Jacob Peter Mayer. Translated from the French by G. Lawrence and K. P. Mayer. New Haven: Yale University Press, 1958. New Brunswick: Transaction Books, 1988.

Tocqueville, Alexis de. 1856 (1955). *The Old Régime and the French Revolution.* Translated by S. Gilbert. Garden City, New York: Anchor Doubleday.

Tönnies, Ferdinand. 1887. *Community and Society:* Gemeinschaft and Gesellschaft. Translated and edited by Charles P. Loomis. New York: Dover, 2002.

Tribe, Keith. 1995. "Natural Liberty and *Laissez Faire*: How Adam Smith Became a Free Trade Ideologue." Pp. 23–44 in S. Copley and K. Sutherlands, eds. *Adam Smith's Wealth of Nations: New Interdisciplinary Essays* (Machester: Manchester University Press).

Trilling, Lionel. 1950. *The Liberal Imagination: Essays on Literature and Society.* New York: Viking Press.

Tronto, Joan C. 1993. *Moral Boundaries: A Political Argument for an Ethics of Care.* New York: Routledge.

Tuckwell, W. 1902. *A. W. Kinglake: A Biographical and Literary Study.* Project Gutenberg EBook at http://www.gutenberg.org/dirs/etext96/awkbi10h.htm.

Tunzelmann, Nick von. 1995. *Technology and Industrial Progress: The Foundations of Economic Growth.* Aldershot: Edward Elgar.

Tunzelmann, Nick von. 2003. "Technology." In Mokyr 2003a.

Turner, Michael E., J. V. Beckett and B. Afton. 2001. *Farm Production in England 1700–1914.* Oxford: Oxford University Press.

Turpin, Paul. 2005. *Liberal Political Economy and Justice: Character and Decorum in the Economic Arguments of Adam Smith and Milton Friedman.* PhD diss., Annenberg School for Communication, University of Southern California.

Tusser, Thomas. 1588. *Five Hundred Points of Good Husbandry.* Edited by Geoffrey Grigson. Oxford: Oxford University Press, 1984.

U.S. Census Bureau, Population Division. 2009. International Data Base. At http://www.census.gov/ipc/www/idb/worldgrgraph.php.

Usher, Abbott Payson. 1960. "The Industrialization of Modern Britain." *Technology and Culture* 1 (2) (Spring): 109–127.

Van Vleck, Va Nee. 1997. "Delivering Coal by Road and Rail in Britain: The Efficiency of the 'Silly Little Bobtailed' Coal Wagons." *Journal of Economic History* 57: 139–160.

Van Vleck, Va Nee. 1999. "In Defense (Again) of '*Silly Little* Bobtailed' Coal Wagons: Reply to Peter Scott." *Journal of Economic History* 59 (4): 1081–1084.

Vargas, Patrick T., and Sukki Yoon. 2006. "On the Psychology of Materialism: Wanting Things, Having Things, and Being Happy." *Advertising and Society Review* 7 (1). At http://muse.jhu.edu/journals/asr/v007/7.1vargas.html#NOTE68.

Vargas Llosa, Mario. 2008. *Wllsprings.* Cambridge: Harvard University Press.

Veblen, Thorstein. 1899. *The Theory of the Leisure Class.* New York: Macmillan.

Vickery, Amanda. 1998. *The Gentleman's Daughter: Women's Lives in Georgian England.* New Haven: Yale University Press.

Vlastos, Stephen. 1986. *Peasant Protests and Uprisings in Tokugawa Japan.* Berkeley: University of California Press.

Voth, Hans-Joachim. 1998. "Time and Work in Eighteenth-Century London." *Journal of Economic History* 58 (1): 29–58.

Voth, Hans-Joachim. 2001. *Time and Work in England, 1760–1839.* Oxford: Oxford University Press.

Voth, Hans-Joachim. 2003. "Labor Time." In Mokyr 2003a.

Voth, Hans-Joachim, and Nico Voigtländer. 2008. "The Three Horsemen of Growth: Plague, War and Urbanization in Early Modern Europe." Manuscript. At http://www.econ.upf.edu/docs/papers/downloads/1115.pdf.

Wade, Nicholas. 2006. *Before the Dawn: Recovering the Lost History of Our Ancestors.* New York: Penguin.

Wallerstein, Immanuel. 1974. *The Modern World System.* Vol. 1, *Capitalist Agriculture and the Origins of the European World-Economy in the Sixteenth Century.* New York: Academic Press.

Wallerstein, Immanuel. 1983 (1995). *Historical Capitalism* (1983). Bound with *Capitalist Civilization* (1995). London: Verso.

Walzer, Michael. 1988. *The Company of Critics.* New York: Basic Books.

Waterman, Anthony. 2003. "Joan Robinson as a Teacher." *Review of Political Economy* 15: 489–596.

Watson, Andrew M. 1983. *Agricultural Innovation in the Early Islamic World: The Diffusion of Crops and Farming Techniques, 700–1100.* Cambridge: Cambridge University Press. Weber, Max. 1904–1905. *Die protestantische Ethik und der Geist des Kapitalismus (The Protestant Ethic and the Spirit of Capitalism).* Translated by T. Parsons 1930 from the 1920 German edition. New York: Scribner's, 1958.

Weber, Max. 1922 (1947). *Wirtschaft und Gesellschaft: Grundriß der Verstehenden Soziologie (The Theory of Social and Economic Organization).* Translated by A. M. Henderson and Talcott Parsons. New York: Free Press.

Weber, Max. 1923 (1927). *Wirtschaftsgeschichte (General Economic History).* Translated by Frank Knight. Glencoe, Ill.: Free Press. New Brunswick, N.J.: Transaction Books, 1981.

Wells, John, and Douglas Wills. 2000. "Revolution, Restoration, and Debt Repudiation: The Jacobite Threat to England's Institutions and Economic Growth." *Journal of Economic History* 60 (June): 418–441.

West, E. G. 1978. "Literacy and the Industrial Revolution." *Economic History Review* 31: 369–383. Reprinted in Mokyr 1985.

Westphal, Larry E. 1990. "Industrial Policy in an Export Propelled Economy: Lessons from South Korea's Experience." *Journal of Economic Perspectives* 4 (Summer): 41–59.

Westphal, Larry E., and Kim, Kwang Suk. 1977. "Industrial Policy and Development in Korea." World Bank Staff Working Paper 263.

Wex, Michael. 2006. *Born to Kvetch: Yiddish Language and Culture in All of Its Moods.* New York: Harper Perennial.

White, Lynn, Jr. 1962. *Medieval Technology and Social Change.* New York: Oxford University Press.

Whitehead, Alfred North. 1925. *Science and the Modern World.* New York: Simon and Schuster, 1997.

Whitman, Walt. 1855. "Preface to the [First Edition of] *The Leaves of Grass."* Pp. 5–27 in Whitman 1945.

Whitman, Walt. 1871. "Song of the Exposition" (from *Drum Taps*). Pp. 262–272 in Whitman 1945.

Whitman, Walt. 1888. "A Backward Glance." Pp. 296–312 in Whitman 1945.

Whitman, Walt. 1945. *The Portable Whitman.* Ed. Mark Van Doren. Rev. Malcolm Cowley. New York: Viking Press.

Wilde, Oscar. 1891 (1930). "The Soul of Man under Socialism." Pp. 257–288 in Wilde, *Plays, Prose Writings, and Poems,* ed. H. Pearson (London: J. M. Dent).

Williamson, Jeffrey G. 1975. *Late Nineteenth-Century American Development: A General Equilibrium History.* Cambridge: Cambridge University Press.

Williamson, Jeffrey G. 1987. "Did English Factor Markets Fail During the Industrial Revolution?" *Oxford Economic Papers* 39: 641–678.

Williamson, Jeffrey G. 1990. *Coping with City Growth during the British Industrial Revolution.* Cambridge: Cambridge University Press.

Williamson, Jeffrey G. 2010. *Trade and Poverty: When the Third World Fell Behind.* Cambridge, Mass.: MIT Press.

Winchester, Simon. 2008. *The Man Who Loved China.* New York: HarperCollins.

Wink, André. 2003. "India: Muslim Period and Mughal Empire." In Mokyr 2003a.

Witkowski, Jan A., and John R. Inglis, eds. 2008. *Davenport's Dream: 21st Century Reflections on Heredity and Eugenics.* Cold Spring Harbor, NY: Cold Spring Harbor Laboratory Press.

Wolcott, Susan, ed. 2007. "Discussion of Clark's *Farewell to Alms.*" Meet-the-author session at the Social Science History Convention, Chicago, November. http://eh.net/bookreviews/ssha_farewell_to_alms.pdf.

Wootton, David. 1992. "The Levellers." Pp. 71–89 in John Dunn, ed., *Democracy: The Unfinished Journey, 508 BC to AD 1993* (Oxford: Oxford University Press).

Wordie, Ross. 1983. "The Chronology of English Enclosure, 1500–1914." *Economic History Review* 2, 36: 483–505.

World Bank. 2005. *Central Government Finances.* At http://siteresources.worldbank.org/DATASTATISTICS/Resources/table4_10.pdf.

World Bank. 2006. *Doing Business.* At http://www.doingbusiness.org/economyrankings/?direction=Asc&sort=0.

World Bank. 2008. *The Little Data Book, 2008.* Washington, D.C.: International Bank for Reconstruction and Development.

Wrigley, E. A. 1962. "The Supply of Raw Materials in the Industrial Revolution." *Economic History Review*, ser. 2, 15 (1): 1–16.

Wrigley, E. A. 1988. *Continuity, Chance, and Change: The Character of the Industrial Revolution in England.* Cambridge: Cambridge University Press.

Wrigley, E. A., and Roger Schofield. 1981. *The Population History of England, 1540–1871.* Cambridge: Cambridge University Press.

Young, Allyn A. 1928. "Increasing Returns and Economic Progress." *Economic Journal* 38: 527–542.

Zanden, Jan Luiten van. 2003. "Inequality of Wealth of Income Distribution." In Mokyr 2003a.

Zanden, Jan Luiten van. 2004. "The Skill Premium and the 'Great Divergence.'" At http://www.iisg.nl/hpw/papers/vanzanden.pdf.

Zanden, Jan Luiten van. 2009. *The Long Road to the Industrial Revolution: The European Economy in a Global Perspective, 1000–1800.* Leiden: Brill.

Ziliak, Stephen, and Deirdre McCloskey. 2008. *The Cult of Statistical Significance: How the Standard Error Costs Us Jobs, Justice, and Lives.* Ann Arbor: University of Michigan Press.

INDEX